SAMUEL JOHNSON:
NEW CONTEXTS FOR A NEW CENTURY

SAMUEL JOHNSON:
NEW CONTEXTS FOR A NEW CENTURY

Edited by Howard D. Weinbrot

Huntington Library
San Marino, California

1151 Oxford Road, San Marino, California 91108
www.huntington.org

Jacket design by Doug Davis
Interior design by Janine Vigus
Copyediting and indexing by Jean Patterson
Proofreading by Sara K. Austin
Printed by Sheridan Books in the United States of America

The publication of this volume was significantly aided by the generous support of the William Freeman Vilas Trust, University of Wisconsin, Madison, and the Hyder E. Rollins Fund of Harvard University. The editor and the Huntington Library express their gratitude for such generosity.

Library of Congress Cataloging-in-Publication Data

Samuel Johnson : new contexts for a new century / edited by Howard D. Weinbrot.
pages cm
Includes index.
ISBN 978-0-87328-259-8 (alk. paper)
1. Johnson, Samuel, 1709-1784—Criticism and interpretation. I. Weinbrot, Howard D., editor of compilation.
PR3534.S29 2013
828'.609—dc23
2013013510

Contents

continued overleaf

Part VI: Johnson after Johnson

Acknowledgments

Samuel Johnson: New Contexts for a New Century was conceived in 2009, as a contribution to the 300th anniversary of Samuel Johnson's birthday on September 18, 1709. As such, it joins Harvard University Press's *Johnson after Three Centuries* and Oxford University Press's *Samuel Johnson: The Arc of the Pendulum* as published versions of major scholarly conferences held at the Houghton Library and Pembroke College, respectively.[1] The Huntington Library conference itself took place on September 9 and 10, 2011, with twelve speakers from the United States, Canada, and the United Kingdom. It was authorized some two years earlier by Roy Ritchie, then Director of Research at the Huntington, and generously supported by the William French Smith Endowment. Dr. Ritchie's assistant, Carolyn Powell, was wonderfully helpful on various important details, as were Susi Krasnoo and her successor, Juan Gomez, for the conference itself. In September 2011 Steve Hindle replaced Roy Ritchie as Director of Research and presided over the conference, his first. The conference program featured three illustrations: Joshua Reynolds's *The Infant Johnson,* from the Hyde Collection at the Houghton Library, Harvard; Reynolds's *Blinking Sam*, from a Frances and Loren Rothschild gift to the Huntington Library; and John Bacon's 1796 statue of Johnson, from St. Paul's Cathedral, London. We thank all for permission to reproduce these images.

Susan Green, Huntington Library Press director, has encouraged us to add contributions so that we could more fully cover areas of Johnsonian interest. These are David Fairer, "The Agile Johnson"; Robert Folkenflik, "*Blinking Sam*, 'Surly Sam,' and 'Johnson's Grimly Ghost'"; Stephen Fix, "'The Dreams of a Poet': Vocational Self-Definition in Johnson's *Dictionary* Preface"; David Nunnery, "'Hoot him back again into the common road': The Problem of Singularity and the Human Comedy of the *Lives of the Poets*"; Lynda Mugglestone, "Writing the *Dictionary of the English Language:* Johnson's Journey into Words"; and Howard D. Weinbrot, "''Tis well an old age is out': Johnson, Swift, and His Generation." Publication of this ample volume also was made possible in part by generous subventions. The editor, contributors, and Huntington Library Press thank the Department of English, University of Wisconsin,

1. For these, see *Johnson after Three Centuries: New Light on Texts and Contexts*, ed. Thomas A. Horrocks and Howard D. Weinbrot (Cambridge, Mass., 2011), reprint of special issue, *Harvard Library Bulletin* 20, nos. 3–4 (2009), based on papers presented at the 2009 Houghton Library symposium "Johnson at 300"; and *Samuel Johnson: The Arc of the Pendulum*, ed. Freya Johnston and Lynda Mugglestone (Oxford, 2012), based on papers presented at the 2009 Pembroke College conference "Johnson at 300."

Madison, Theresa Kelley, then Chair; Steve J. Stern, Vice Provost for Faculty and Staff Programs, University of Wisconsin, Madison; and James Engell and the Hyder E. Rollins Fund of Harvard University. These subventions help to keep the book more affordable for Johnsonians, students of the eighteenth century in general, and, we hope, the large number of international general readers so keen on Samuel Johnson and his manifold achievements.

The contributors add a special note of thanks to Gordon Turnbull, General Editor of the Yale Editions of the Private Papers of James Boswell. His close reading of the many essays discovered several small errors that we corrected before going to press. Of course, any lingering such blunders remain our own.

The editor and contributors also gratefully thank Susan Green, Huntington Library Press director, Jean Patterson, managing editor, and Sara Austin, editor, for their encouragement, patience, and meticulous editorial guidance. They have helped to make this a book that, we hope, is worthy of its subject.

We dedicate this book to the Huntington Library and to the William French Smith Endowment, which generously subsidized the initial conference.

Contributors

Howard D. Weinbrot was a 2011 nominee for a Balzan Prize in Enlightenment Studies. He is Ricardo Quintana Professor of English Emeritus and William Freeman Vilas Research Professor Emeritus in the College of Letters and Science at the University of Wisconsin, Madison. He has written on several eighteenth-century British authors, on Anglo–classical and Anglo–French relations, on satire, and on intellectual, political, and religious history. His most recent books are *Menippean Satire Reconsidered: From Antiquity to the Eighteenth Century* (2005), *Aspects of Samuel Johnson: Essays on His Arts, Mind, Afterlife, and Politics* (2005), and *Literature, Religion, and the Evolution of Culture, 1660–1780* (2013).

Robert DeMaria Jr. is the Henry Noble MacCracken Professor of English at Vassar College. He is the author of *Johnson's Dictionary and the Language of Learning* (1986), *The Life of Samuel Johnson: A Critical Biography* (1993), and *Samuel Johnson and the Life of Reading* (1997). He is the editor of the *Johnsonian News Letter*, and, with Gwin J. Kolb, the co-editor of *Johnson on the English Language* (2005) for the *Yale Edition of the Works of Samuel Johnson*, of which DeMaria became the general editor in 2007.

James Engell is Gurney Professor of English and Professor of Comparative Literature, Harvard University. He has published numerous articles and book chapters on Samuel Johnson. His books include *The Creative Imagination: Enlightenment to Romanticism* (1981), *Forming the Critical Mind: Dryden to Coleridge* (1989), and *The Committed Word: Literature and Public Values* (1999). He is co-author, with Anthony Dangerfield, of *Saving Higher Education in the Age of Money* (2005), and he has co-edited, with W. Jackson Bate, Coleridge's *Biographia Literaria* (1983). He has edited *Johnson and His Age* (1984) and *Coleridge: The Early Family Letters* (1994), and is co-editor of *Environment: An Interdisciplinary Anthology* (2008). He currently is at work on a study of Coleridge as well as an illustrated and annotated edition of Wordsworth's *Prelude*.

David Fairer is Professor of Eighteenth-Century English Literature at the University of Leeds. His most recent book, *Organising Poetry: The Coleridge Circle, 1790–1798* (2009), traces the development of English poetry during the 1790s, building on the concerns of his previous comprehensive study, *English Poetry of the Eighteenth Century, 1700–1789* (2003). With Christine Gerrard he co-edits *Eighteenth-Century Poetry: An Annotated Anthology* (2nd ed., 2003).

Stephen Fix is Robert G. Scott Professor of English at Williams College, where he teaches courses on eighteenth-century literature, history of the novel, and history of poetry. He is a member of the editorial committee of the *Yale Edition of the Works of Samuel Johnson*, and he edited the life of Milton for the *Lives of the Poets* volumes (2010) in that edition. With Robert DeMaria Jr. and Howard D. Weinbrot, he is co-editing a teaching anthology of Johnson's works, forthcoming from Yale.

Robert Folkenflik is Edward A. Dickson Professor Emeritus of English at the University of California, Irvine. He writes on several kinds of eighteenth-century narratives, on book history, and on the relations between literature and art. His publications include *Samuel Johnson, Biographer* (1978), *Samuel Johnson: Pictures and Words* (1984; with Paul Alkon), and an edition of *Tristram Shandy* (2004).

William Gibson is professor of ecclesiastical history at Oxford Brookes University. He has published widely on the church in Britain in the seventeenth and eighteenth centuries, and his most recent works are *James II and the Trial of the Seven Bishops* (2009), *A Brief History of Britain*, vol. 3, *The Making of the Nation, 1660–1851* (2011), and, as co-editor, *The Oxford Handbook of the British Sermon, 1689–1901* (2012). He is a fellow of the Royal Historical Society and of the Royal Society of Arts.

Nicholas J. Hudson is professor of English at the University of British Columbia. His books include *Samuel Johnson and Eighteenth-Century Thought* (1988), *Samuel Johnson and the Making of Modern England* (2003), and *A Political Biography of Samuel Johnson* (2013).

Freya Johnston is a university lecturer and tutorial fellow at St. Anne's College, Oxford. She is the author of *Samuel Johnson and the Art of Sinking, 1709–1791* (2005), and the co-editor, with Lynda Mugglestone, of *Samuel Johnson: The Arc of the Pendulum* (2012). She is the general editor of the forthcoming *Cambridge Edition of the Novels of Thomas Love Peacock*.

Thomas Kaminski is professor of English at Loyola University in Chicago. He is the author of *The Early Career of Samuel Johnson* (1987) and the co-editor of Johnson's *Debates in Parliament* for the *Yale Edition of the Works of Samuel Johnson* (2012).

Thomas Keymer is Chancellor Jackman Professor of English at the University of Toronto and general editor of the *Review of English Studies*. His work on Johnson includes the Oxford World's Classics edition of *Rasselas* (2009) and chapters in *The Cambridge Companion to Samuel Johnson* (1997), edited by Greg Clingham, and in *Christopher Smart and the Enlightenment* (1999), edited by Clement Hawes.

F. P. Lock is professor of English at Queen's University at Kingston, Ontario, Canada, and a Fellow of the Royal Society of Canada. His several books include *The Politics of "Gulliver's Travels"* (1980), *Swift's Tory Politics* (1983), *Burke's "Reflections on the Revolution in France"* (1985), the two-volume *Edmund Burke* (1998–2006), and *The Rhetoric of Numbers in Gibbon's "History"* (2012). He currently is at work on a new "Life" of Samuel Johnson.

Jack Lynch is professor of English at Rutgers–Newark. He is the author of *The Age of Elizabeth in the Age of Johnson* (2003) and *Deception and Detection in Eighteenth-Century Britain* (2008) and the editor of *Samuel Johnson in Context* (2012). With J. T. Scanlan, he edits *The Age of Johnson*.

Lynda Mugglestone is professor of the history of English at the University of Oxford and a fellow of Pembroke College, Oxford. She has published widely on the history of English and on the social, cultural, and ideological issues that dictionary-making can reveal. Recent books include *Lost for Words: The Hidden History of the "Oxford English Dictionary"* (2005), *Talking Proper: The Rise of Accent as Social Symbol* (rev. ed., 2007), and *Dictionaries: A Very Short Introduction* (2011). She is the editor of *The Oxford History of English* (rev. ed., 2012) and the co-editor, with Freya Johnston, of *Samuel Johnson: The Arc of the Pendulum* (2012). She is currently writing a book on eighteenth-century language and Samuel Johnson.

David Nunnery teaches English for the Stanford University Online High School, a division of Stanford Pre-Collegiate Studies, and formerly was an assistant professor at the University of Louisiana-Monroe. He is Field Editor for Historical, Social, and Economic Studies for *The Eighteenth Century Current Bibliography* and has published essays on Johnson's *Lives of the Poets*, on which he is writing a monograph.

Stuart Sherman is an associate professor of English at Fordham University and the author of *Telling Time: Clocks, Diaries, and English Diurnal Form, 1660–1785* (1996). His current project is "News and Plays: Evanescences of Page and Stage, 1620–1779."

Marcus Walsh is Kenneth Allott Professor of English Literature at the University of Liverpool and has written extensively on the theory, practice, and history of literary editing in the seventeenth and eighteenth centuries. He has edited two volumes of Oxford's *Poetical Works of Christopher Smart* (1983, 1987), and, most recently, *A Tale of a Tub* for *The Cambridge Edition of the Works of Jonathan Swift* (2010). He is an associate editor of the *Oxford Companion to the Book* (2010). His monograph *Shakespeare, Milton, and Eighteenth-Century Literary Editing* was published in 1997.

Notes toward New Johnsonian Contexts

Howard D. Weinbrot

MUCH HAS BEEN WRITTEN about the achievements of Samuel Johnson. These studies include discussions of his works as a lexicographer, moralist, poet, political commentator, psychologist, sermon writer, periodical essayist, stylist, biographer, literary critic and theorist, canon formulator, editor, dramatist, conversationalist, and biographical character, among other roles. Commentators tend to combine such areas of inquiry, often with interests appropriate for their own generation. The breadth of this partial list suggests one of the reasons Johnson's arts of mind and letters remain so justly celebrated among native English speakers and those from many other linguistic cultures. I will look at a few instances of the relationship of old texts to newly enlarged contexts in both less familiar and more familiar areas of Johnsonian inquiry.

Making the New: Less-Familiar Johnsonian Contexts

A prominent French Anglicist has expressed the dominant view of Johnson as apparently perceived in France: "Johnson's intellectual stature has never assumed the size described by Anglo-Saxon literary historians."[1] Such a never-land is indeed an assumption rather than a historical truth. France was of course the dominant intellectual force in eighteenth-century Europe. It thus is instructive to read some French elites' responses to a few of Johnson's major texts. In 1756, the *Journal étranger* called Johnson's *Dictionary of the English Language* (1755) one of the most important works on the English language and one of the greatest ever produced by a single writer. The preface itself should be a model for "ceux d'entre nous qui seroient tentés de rendre le même service à la Langue Françoise."[2] Johnson's edition of Shakespeare (1765) was

1. Michel Baridon, "On the Relation of Ideology to Form in Johnson's Style," in *Fresh Reflections on Samuel Johnson: Essays in Criticism*, ed. Prem Nath (Troy, N.Y., 1987), 85–105 at 85. See also Miriam Bridenne, who thinks that Johnson would not have been known, if not for Boswell: Bridenne, "Notice," in Samuel Johnson, *Le paresseux: Traduit de l'anglais par M. Varney* (Paris, 2000), [119]. This was Johnson's *Idler*, translated by Jean Baptiste Varney (Paris, 1790).

2. "Angleterre," *Journal étranger* (December 1756): 111, 112, with a full translation of Johnson's preface to the *Dictionary*. Boswell thought that Diderot was the translator but offered no evidence. See his letter to William Johnson Temple, November 6, 1775, in *The Correspondence of James Boswell and William Johnson Temple, 1756–1795*, vol. 1, *1756–1777*, ed. Thomas Crawford, vol. 6 of the *Yale Editions*

published while Voltaire's harsh judgments were dominant on the French side of la Manche. Johnson's *Shakespeare*, its Preface and notes, however, were instrumental in putting Voltaire on the defensive and then-modern French theorists on the offensive. Pierre Le Tourneur's preface to his own version of *Shakespeare* (1776–83) regularly challenges the unnamed Voltaire and, Le Tourneur says, "plus communément nous suivons" Johnson's text and notes.[3]

Such importance extended well into the later eighteenth and nineteenth centuries. By 1823 Stendhal had deployed Johnson's "célèbre préface" as an argument against the authority of the classical unities. Earlier, in 1798, the comte de Fouchecour had acknowledged "la célébrité de l'immortel auteur de *Rasselas*," whose beauties establish it "à la tête des romans anglois."[4] Jean-Baptiste-Hugues-Nelson Cottreau probably agreed. In 1808 he freely adapted the seventy-year-old *London* (1738) as *Satire contre le vice, ou Tableaux satiriques et épisodiques de moeurs, au commencement du XIXe siècle; suivie de Londres, poëme traduit de l'anglais, du docteur Samuel Johnson; par Hugué-Nelson C****. Albin-Joseph-Ulpien Hennet knew Johnson as poet and especially as biographer and critic. Hennet's three-volume *La poétique anglaise* (1806) regarded Johnson as "l'oracle littéraire de son pays";[5] it also borrowed from Johnson for comments on virtually all of the authors Johnson discussed in his *Lives of the Poets* (1779–81). For Hennet, regular remarks like "observe Johnson" (1:128) and "dit Johnson" (1:156) indicate borrowings from oracular wisdom. Perhaps such clear admiration and advocacy helped to encourage a French translation of several of those lives. It is prefaced by a "Vie de Johnson" based on a heavily cleansed version of Sir John

of the Private Papers of James Boswell (Edinburgh and New Haven, Conn., 1997), 403, 404n5. Boswell's guess is at least plausible. By 1755 Diderot had translated Temple Stanyan's *Grecian History* (1707–39) as *Histoire de Grèce* (1743), and he had joined with two colleagues to translate Robert James's *Medicinal Dictionary* (1743–45) as *Dictionnaire universel de médecine* (1746–48), among other ventures. The *Encyclopédie* (1751–72) began as an attempt to translate Ephraim Chambers's *Cyclopaedia* (1728) and of course outgrew that original intention.

3. Pierre Le Tourneur, *Shakespeare traduit de l'anglois, dédié au Roi*, 20 vols. (Paris, 1776–83), 1:4n1. Voltaire was outraged by the translation and by the cover which the dedication to Louis XVI seemed to give it. The energetic barbarian Shakespeare, like the generally insane English people, were dangers to French letters and civilization. See "Lettre de M. de Voltaire à l'Académie française," August 25, 1776, in *Oeuvres complètes de Voltaire*, vol. 9 of *Mélanges* (Paris, 1880), 352, 358, among other places. For fuller discussion of Johnson in France, see Howard D. Weinbrot, "Johnson before Boswell in Eighteenth-Century France: Notes toward Reclaiming a Man of Letters," in Weinbrot, *Aspects of Samuel Johnson: Essays on His Arts, Mind, Afterlife, and Politics* (Newark, Del., 2005), 270–98.

4. Stendhal (Marie-Henri Beyle), *Oeuvres complètes*, vol. 37, *Racine et Shakespeare*, new ed., ed. Pierre Martino with an afterword and notes by Victor Del Litto (Geneva and Paris, 1970), 59, 61, and 337n, with Stendhal's name for Johnson as "le père du romantisme"; Jean-François-Louis-Marie-Marguerite de Salivet de Courtenay, Comte de Fouchecour, *Rasselas, prince d'Abissinie: Roman, traduit de l'anglais de Dr. Johnson, par le comte de Fouchecour, enrichie de taille douces* (London [?], 1798), [iii]. Fouchecour was an aristocrat who no doubt saved his own life by immigrating to England, where he also was married, on December 26, 1793.

5. Albin-Joseph-Ulpien Hennet, *La poétique anglaise*, 3 vols. (Paris, 1806), 2:438, hereafter cited in text.

Hawkins's life of Johnson (1787), and it appeared in 1823 and again in 1843: *Vies des poètes anglais les plus célèbres, avec des observations critiques sur leurs ouvrages, par le docteur Samuel Jonhson* [*sic*]: *Traduites de l'anglais par E. Didot et E. Mahon.*[6] Many Gauls apparently were as perceptive regarding Johnson's stature as were Angles, Saxons, and others with hybrid ancestry. As I will show, many such Gauls indeed learned English with Johnson as *enseignant.*

These observations support a major point of this essay collection in particular and of Johnsonian scholarship in general: however much we know about Johnson and his "age," there is a great deal more to know and from which we can profit. Both *Vies des poètes anglais* and *Satire contre le vice*, for example, remain undiscussed among students of Johnson and of Anglo-French cultural relations.

Johnson's sermons are somewhat better known but are inadequately appreciated for their Christian and moral artistry, and for reader and auditor response. James Gray's *Johnson's Sermons: A Study* appeared in 1972, and the Yale edition of the *Sermons* appeared in 1978.[7] Further studies of Johnson's religion have remained thin on the ground and in several cases have been dragooned into polemical and political studies. The excitement with which Johnson's posthumous volume of sermons was greeted, however, has not been replicated by modern students.

Specifically, Thomas Bellamy was a minor but valued later eighteenth-century man of letters who knew and admired Johnson. As editor of the *General Magazine and Impartial Review* (1787–92), he printed Shakespeare's plays, featured contemporary actors and actresses, and reviewed recent books. In the process, he discussed Johnson and the several competing biographies of a man about whom, Bellamy said, all information should be gratefully received: "nothing true can be known tending to disgrace him."[8] Bellamy understood that part of Johnson's distinction was embedded in "certain *Sermons* [by Johnson] said to be in [John Taylor's] possession." Johnson's sermon

6. *Vies des poètes anglais* is both scarce and puzzling. So far as I can tell, there are only three copies in the United States: at the University of Washington, Seattle; the Beinecke Library at Yale; and most recently the Hyde Collection at Harvard's Houghton Library. The British Library does not own a copy. Google Books includes a digitized version of the 1843 edition with the stamp of the Bibliothèque de la Ville de Lyon and one other that I cannot decipher. The Bibliothèque nationale's one-volume copy is dated 1823 in its catalogue, but with an 1842 cover and 1850 printed in red and with the stamp of the Bibliothèque royale. The 1823 publisher J. Didot aîné apparently sold the copyright to Lebailly, who printed the later edition, with a nominal two volumes in one. I am indebted to Professor Isabelle Bour for this information. The 1823 volume includes the same thirteen lives as the 1843 volume, which ends on p. 448 with FIN DU PREMIER VOLUME. Its putative second volume begins new pagination but lacks a title page and consists only of the first portion of the life of Dryden; it ends on p. 159 with Johnson's discussion of Dryden's digression to the original and progress of navigation and how the Royal Society can foster that useful art. These puzzles require further research. The Didot family was a prominent printing firm, one of the translators was Édouard Didot, and they must have sensed a commercial market for Johnson's *Vies.*

7. James Gray, *Johnson's Sermons: A Study* (Oxford, 1972); Johnson, *Sermons*, vol. 14 of *The Yale Edition of the Works of Samuel Johnson* (hereafter cited as *YE*), ed. Jean Hagstrum and James Gray (New Haven, Conn., 1978).

8. *General Magazine* 2 (January 1788): 143.

"for the Funeral of His Wife" would appear in April 1788. This only whetted Bellamy's appetite for others that Taylor still held and from which he had preached. Bellamy often "heard Dr. Taylor in the pulpit; but four-fifths of the discourses he delivered were certainly written by Dr. Johnson."[9]

Bellamy thus was pleased in June 1788 when he reviewed *Sermons on Different Subjects, Left for Publication by John Taylor, LL.D.*, which included only thirteen of the forty that Johnson said he wrote and for which Taylor seemed to take credit. Bellamy insists that Johnson's authorship be acknowledged both because it is right and because Johnson's name will attract the otherwise indifferent: many "would read his Discourses, and might thereby reap great advantages, who cannot be tempted to peruse those of an ecclesiastic, especially an ecclesiastic of so little celebrity as Dr. Taylor."[10]

About a year later Bellamy celebrated the publication of twelve more of Johnson's ghostwritten sermons together with the memorial sermon for his wife Tetty's funeral. "Rejoice!" Bellamy says regarding the sermons' religious purity, handsome style, and moral sentiments. He then adds a remark that forces us to reconsider the received wisdom regarding Johnson's sermon for Tetty: it "was never preached" because Taylor found it too luxurious in its praise (*YE*, 14:261n1). Taylor would not read it in March 1752, but it must have had its uses for those dearly departed Taylor thought, or pretended to think, worthy of the praise Johnson bestowed on his beloved wife. Bellamy "well recollects, Dr. Taylor preaching or rather reading [that sermon] at Ashborne, in Derbyshire before what is called a 'Benefit Society' about the year 1777."[11] Bellamy and his *General Magazine and Impartial Review* make several matters plain regarding a significant portion of the late eighteenth-century literate classes: Johnson's sermons were anxiously awaited, warmly received, heard from pulpits, and known to be Johnson's. They now supply a new context for audience response and urge reconsideration of the utility of Johnson's sermon for Tetty's or for other sadly lost wives' funerals.

Johnson was powerful in other unacknowledged ways. We are familiar with his conversational brilliance, but his written discourse also was famous for its value as a guide to learners of English. Pedagogues on both sides of the Channel regularly used his prose and poetry as literary and moral models for beginners learning to write and to think as rational adults. *Rasselas* was printed in 1787 with facing French and English pages as an aid for French students of English. Thereafter it again became an agent for English pedagogy in *Nouveau cours de langue anglaise* (1818): "Johnson est reconnu pour l'auteur le plus classique de l'Angleterre." *Rasselas* is written "avec autant de force que de correction et d'élégance."[12] Several of Johnson's periodical essays, we shall see, and poems were reproduced in educational tracts printed at the least in London, Warrington, Dublin, Edinburgh, Aberdeen, and New York. William Enfield's *The Speaker: or, Miscellaneous Pieces, Selected from the Best English Writers* (London, 1780), hopes to

9. *General Magazine* 2 (April 1788): 199.
10. *General Magazine* 2 (June 1788): 311.
11. *General Magazine* 3 (August 1789): 354.
12. *Nouveau cours de langue anglaise* (Paris, 1818), vii.

teach its charges both how to pronounce words and how to read well. In so doing, it offers students parts of Johnson's *Rambler* 72 (November 24, 1750). William Scott's *Lessons of Elocution* (Edinburgh, 1779) is comparably keen on "the Improvement of Youth in Reading and Speaking" and gives them much of *Rambler* 201 (February 18, 1752) to help that effort. We know a great deal about Johnson as conversationalist and a little about Johnson as schoolteacher in Edial. It is time for us to know about what may be called his distance-learning pedagogy.

Making the New: More-Familiar Johnsonian Contexts

Samuel Johnson: New Contexts for a New Century cannot possibly map all of the Johnsonian territories that remain unexplored—or even those that appear well settled but nonetheless need new immigrants. In such cases we can at least move into the fringes of those areas in hopes of fertilizing lands once thought plowed over, or so hitherto productive that they now lie fallow. I cite just two examples of how familiar texts can be illumined by new contexts that further help us to understand Johnson's work and its relationship to our personal and general worlds.

Rasselas (1759) was promptly translated into French, Dutch, German, Russian, and Italian and even crossed the ocean to the American colonies. As Gwin J. Kolb has observed, "Between 1759 and 1800 *Rasselas* was available to readers in six foreign languages and some fifty editions, English and non-English." *Rasselas* later enjoyed multiple translations, both into those languages and into Amharic, Arabic, Armenian, Bengali, Danish, Greek, Hindustani, Hungarian, Japanese, Latin, Marathi, Polish, and Spanish.[13] Johnson's intense concerns with the ordinary, however much expressed in extraordinary terms within an extraordinarily privileged group, have made him accessible far beyond the academy.

We recall one of *Rasselas*'s more moving passages. The benevolent but self-isolated astronomer thinks that he can control the weather. He hopes to induce rain in specific places, the better to nourish crops for a parched world. The astronomer is relieved to have met Imlac, an equally wise and benevolent man whom the astronomer fancies will continue his good work but first must be warned about an insoluble problem. He "found it impossible to make a disposition by which the world may be advantaged; what one region gains, another loses by any imaginable alteration." He tells Imlac, "Never rob other countries of rain to pour it on thine own" (*YE*, 16:148).

Johnson here seems to have adapted a concept from what William Lowth called the prophetic books' "Treasure of Heavenly Wisdom."[14] Amos was one of the twelve

13. Johnson, *Rasselas and Other Tales*, vol. 16 of *YE*, ed. Gwin J. Kolb (1990), 258; see 253–58 for further discussion of *Rasselas*'s European diffusion. For the fuller list of *Rasselas* translations, see *A Bibliography of the Works of Samuel Johnson: Treating His Published Works from the Beginnings to 1984*, comp. J. D. Fleeman, prepared for the press by James McLaverty, 2 vols. (Oxford, 2000), 1:954–89. A translation of *Rasselas* into Mandarin Chinese is under way.

14. William Lowth, *A Commentary upon the Larger and Lesser Prophets; Being a Continuation of Bishop Patrick* (London, 1728), i.

lesser Old Testament prophets who regularly appeared in sermons and, for William Warburton, in defensive polemic.[15] Amos is harsh toward the ten tribes and their repeated disobedience of Yahweh, who chose them to help civilize a primitive world. The prophet speaks on behalf of that angry God, impatient with the often-warned Israelites: "And also I have with-holden the Rain from you when there were yet three Months to the Harvest.... And I caused it to rain upon one City, and caused it not to rain upon another City.... So two or three Cities wandered to one City to drink Water, but they were not satisfied."[16] Samuel Stennett later glossed the passage as a cautionary aspect of sublime omnipotence: "the more deeply to impress their minds with the idea of the influence of Divine Providence in their calamities, the prophet particularly recalls their attention to one remarkable fact"—God's power to choose which cities he will bless with rain prior to harvest, the better to punish vice and reward virtue.[17] That choice, though, is a function of omnipotence and omniscience, traits clearly beyond our strengths.

The episode thus suggests the danger of the astronomer's misdirected vision. He looks to the heavens for secular adjustments of climate; that weak human perspective cannot resolve the logistics of moral vision in conflict with human reality. The sublime act of controlling the weather belongs to God's monitory function. The astronomer cannot know which parts of the world deserve reward and which deserve punishment. If he could so know, he nonetheless should not usurp God's role. Johnson stresses the unbridgeable gap between the human and the divine by allowing the well-intentioned astronomer a human, not a spiritual, cure—especially through the company of the poet-intellectual Imlac and the attractive Pekuah. She uses astral knowledge she learned from her Arab abductor, and womanly knowledge she learned on her own, to flatter her new instructor and to instruct him in the delights of sublunary conversation. Johnson indeed invites us to contrast that abductor and the benign meteorologist as teachers. This modest but psychologically powerful transformation engages the entire surrogate family of Imlac the guide, Rasselas the prince, Nekayah the princess, and Pekuah the clever, luxuriously dressed maid—all unified in a curative process for their valued new friend. The foursome break the book's normal pattern of introducing individuals who exemplify failed choices of life and then disappear into a fictive ether. Only the astronomer joins them, and only the astronomer is worthy of them as they are worthy of him, but on the human level, not the divine one vastly beyond our reach. The choice of eternity comes at the end of the fable and at the end of life, rather than now. The parallel with Amos is a small key to a large plot-and-character development.

15. For some relevant sermons, see Thomas Prince, *The Natural and Moral Government and Agency of God, in Causing Droughts and Rains* (on Amos 4:7), 2nd ed. (Boston and London, 1751), 30; and Henry Lee, *God's Summons after Despised Forbearance, Enforced in a Sermon on Amos iv. 12* (London, 1756), 4, which quotes germane portions from Amos, above. For the polemic and another quotation regarding God's withholding of water, see William Warburton's defense against attacks on his *Divine Legation of Moses* (London, 1742) in *Remarks on Several Occasional Reflections: In Answer to the Reverend Doctors Stebbing and Sykes* (London, 1745), 197–98.

16. As quoted in Lowth, *Commentary*, 434.

So far as I know, this biblical intervention remains unexplored in discussions of *Rasselas*, whose mode of proceeding it complicates. It requires that we acknowledge an Old Testament allusion in Johnson's paradoxically New Testament Christian work, set in a loosely Middle Eastern Muslim world.

David Fleeman's *Bibliography of the Works of Samuel Johnson* (2000) has handsomely illustrated the wide physical and chronological dissemination of Johnson's many books. Those re-publications, often in domestic and familial contexts, also remain at the least insufficiently known, as with several *Rambler*s reprinted in *The Matrimonial Preceptor* (1755). The book's contents claim to have been published with the consent of the "Proprietors."[18] Whether that was a benign fiction, or the editor contacted one or all of the triumvirs John Payne, Joseph Bouquet, and Edward Cave, or even Johnson himself, is not clear. Johnson's letters do not mention such a request in 1755–56. *The Matrimonial Preceptor* nonetheless makes plain that, even before the *Dictionary*, Johnson's *Rambler* had established him among Britain's most celebrated writers and its most celebrated marriage counselors. This *Preceptor* reprints three germane *Rambler*s, each of which of course concerns marriage. Each also relates to and may help to date Johnson's first sermon, on Genesis 2:24, "Therefore shall a man leave his father, and his mother, and shall cleave unto his wife" (*YE*, 14:3). *Rambler*s 18 (May 19, 1750), 45 (August 21, 1750), and 167 (October 22, 1751) all include striking conceptual and verbal similarities to that first, still-undated sermon.

These *Rambler*s repeat a social term that Johnson regularly emphasizes in his letters in the mid-1750s.[19] In *Rambler* 45, reprinted in the *Matrimonial Preceptor,* we read that those who fail in marriage did not consider "that marriage is the strictest tie of perpetual friendship, that there can be no friendship without confidence, and no confidence without integrity" (*Matrimonial*, 30). In *Rambler* 167, we also read that "We considered marriage as the most solemn league of perpetual friendship, a state from which artifice and concealment are to be banished for ever" (*Matrimonial*, 186). Johnson begins his first sermon's analysis of "the nature and end of marriage" by insisting

17. Samuel Stennett, *National Calamities the Effect of Divine Displeasure: A Sermon, Preached in Little Wild-Street . . . On Occasion of the General Fast, February 21, 1781* (London [1781]), 3.

18. *The Matrimonial Preceptor: A Collection of Examples and Precepts Relating to the Married State, from the Most Celebrated Writers Ancient and Modern* (London, 1755), sig. A4v, hereafter cited in the text. *The Matrimonial Preceptor* enjoyed a second edition in 1759 and a third in 1765. There are other *Rambler* reprints in *The Moral Miscellany: Or, A Collection of Selected Pieces, in Prose and Verse, for the Instruction and Entertainment of Youth* (Leipzig and Züllichau, 1764). There was an American version in *The American Spectator, or Matrimonial Preceptor: A Collection of Essays, Epistles, Precepts, and Examples, Relating to the Married State* (Boston, 1797). This is the only such reprint not listed in Fleeman's *Bibliography*. Nor does Fleeman list the reprinted life of Dr. Herman Boerhaave in *The Christian's Magazine; Or, A Treasury of Divine Knowledge* 4 (1764): 51–64. The life originally appeared in *The Gentleman's Magazine* 9 (1739): 72–73, 114–16, 172–76. According to Fleeman, a "short extract" appeared in *Memorials and Characters, Together with Lives of Divers Eminent and Worthy Persons* (London, 1741), and a "modified version" in the *Universal Chronicle* 38 (1758): 9–16. See *Bibliography*, 1:48.

19. For one of many such examples, see Samuel Johnson to Edmund Hector, October 7, 1756, in *The Letters of Samuel Johnson*, ed. Bruce Redford, 5 vols. (Princeton, N.J., 1992–94), 1:142: "Friendship is indeed one of those few states of which it is reasonable to wish the continuance through life."

that the marriage vow confirmed by civilized nations and the Christian church "may be properly considered as a vow of perpetual and indissoluble friendship" (*YE*, 14:9). In *Rambler* 45, we read that, in spite of all the grumbling about marriage, it remains the normal course of events. Johnson thus "cannot but conclude, that society has something in itself eminently agreeable to human nature," and that "its pleasures [are] so great that even the ill choice of a companion can hardly over-balance them" (*Matrimonial*, 34). Johnson's first sermon begins with this affirmation: "That society is necessary to the happiness of human nature, that the gloom of solitude and the stillness of retirement . . . neither extinguish the passions, nor enlighten the understanding . . . every one may be easily convinced, either by his own experience or that of others" (*YE*, 14:3). These overlapping words and concepts suggest that, early in the 1750s, Johnson indeed was considering the nature of marriage. His wife Tetty, Elizabeth Jarvis Porter, died on March 17, 1752, but had been ill for some months before that. Her drinking and use of opiates had long concerned Johnson. Presumably the sermon was written to help John Taylor join a young couple who needed such biblical and Johnsonian wisdom. It seems reasonable to hypothesize that Taylor's request mobilized Johnson's thoughts regarding marriage in general and his own in particular, especially as Tetty's death might end it. Reading Johnson's *Ramblers* as reprinted in the *Matrimonial Preceptor* allows us to offer a reasonable range of dates for Johnson's own sermon on marriage, which I suggest was written between the late summer of 1750 and the autumn of 1751.

As so often in Johnsonian studies, our expanded knowledge of contexts is likely to evoke our expanded understanding of texts. That is one of the volume's prime goals—both with less-familiar and more-familiar aspects of Johnson's canon, his varied achievements, modes of proceeding, and afterlife, a small part of which we hope to illumine.

Samuel Johnson: New Contexts for a New Century—The Essays

This volume is divided into six necessarily overlapping parts. Part I discusses Johnson's arts of thought. Stuart Sherman's "'The *future* in the instant'" examines one of Johnson's consistent moral and psychological concerns—prolepsis, how our role as agents in space and time, and how the theater specifically, encourages us to believe that the thought is the deed. Sherman focuses on Johnson's remark that time is obsequious to the imagination—for the playwright, player, and playgoer—like David Garrick and James Boswell, for whom theatrical time was very different from Johnson's time. David Fairer's "The Agile Johnson" observes that Johnson's intellectual agility is a function of his mental preparedness, of his well-stocked mind always "ready for use." His *Dictionary* definition acknowledges the etymology of *agile*, originating in action, in the quick response to an impulse that differs from mere flexibility. Johnson often was suspicious of sudden sparks of wit that led nowhere. He was committed, instead, to mental exercise rather than mere sweep of thought. Johnson when apparently most unwieldy can be most learnedly agile, just waiting to pounce on an idea, focus on it, and make it his own. Howard D. Weinbrot discusses Johnson's often-disturbing appraisal of Jonathan

Swift as man and as author. Weinbrot shows that Johnson's criticisms are similar to his criticisms of other authors in the *Lives of the Poets* and similar to his discomfort with earlier poets' personal and literary brutality, beyond which, Johnson believed, his own age had progressed. He generally disliked Swift's role in his own disagreeable generation—its political and religious rage, its licentious sexual morality and hostile treatment of women. Johnson was especially troubled by what he regarded as Swift's harsh treatment of his presumed wife Stella: "''Tis well an old age is out.'"

Part II focuses more intensely on aspects of Johnson's life of writing. Tom Keymer's "Johnson's Poetry of Repetition" combines formal and historical criticism to suggest how Johnson cleverly takes poetic clichés and turns them into new images, insights, and perspectives. We now know more about Johnson's relationship to the poetic idioms and developments within his own moment. He disparaged several innovative contemporaries, but his verse was colored by the new expressive resources they developed. He gives dead poetic language new life. Jack Lynch tackles Johnson's ample correspondence and his attitude toward his correspondents. He both needed them as surrogate company and resented them when called on to respond if he had little to say. The letters also show us a man very different from Boswell's hero or Mrs. Piozzi's burden. We see him coping with physical and psychological pain as well as the normal chores of quotidian life. David Nunnery considers the complicated uses of humor in Johnson's *Lives of the Poets*. Nunnery argues that such humor comes in two sometimes-overlapping forms. One is deflationary humor that "hoot[s] back" those who disregard the common duties and comforts of sociability, either by familiar self-puffery or by the more dangerous self-regard Johnson calls "singularity." The other is the deliberately ambiguous humor by which Johnson challenges his reader to decide whether and how to laugh, and why, in the service of Johnson's larger project in the *Lives*: preparing his reader to confront the uncertainties and contingencies of real life, which much previous biography had elided.

A striking feature of the *Lives* is Johnson's regular awareness of his biographical subjects' status in their publishing worlds, as with the popularity of *Gulliver's Travels,* the number of books printed and sold, and authorial revision. Part III thus deals with Johnson the working man of letters. He lived in the vibrant world of books like the *Dictionary* and *Shakespeare* that required commerce rather than patronage. Given recent productive work on the *Dictionary* itself, this section instead includes two complementary essays on Johnson's earlier *Plan* (1747) and the later Preface to the *Dictionary.* Lynda Mugglestone shows how Johnson adapts earlier lexicographers' images of language as the sea they were to navigate. The dictionary could be a ship, a compass, or an anchor, for example. Johnson also navigates "this vast sea of words" but changes direction as his knowledge grows. The early "Scheme" and *Plan* sailed him toward language as a fixed construct. Experience of the *Dictionary*'s voyage sailed him toward a different destination—language as a necessarily ongoing and unfinished human construct. Stephen Fix explores the question of why Johnson himself is so intensely and persistently present in the Preface to his *Dictionary*. Through close readings of the imagery and diction Johnson uses to present himself and describe his work, Fix argues that writing the *Dictionary* constitutes an act of "vocational self-definition" in which Johnson anxiously acknowledges that he has chosen or perhaps slid into the life of the scholar and critic rather than the life of the poet. Nevertheless, Johnson seeks to assert the creative dimension of his project, and in complex ways his language associates the work of a lexicographer with the work of a poet. Marcus Walsh argues that Johnson's 1765 *Shakespeare* was the first variorum edition of Shakespeare. It was influenced both by knowledge gained in preparing for the *Dictionary* and by engagement with Shakespeare's earlier editors. Johnson, though, did not fully employ available textual arts, like scholarly documentation and parallel passages, which he found less useful for explanatory purposes. There, as indeed consistent with Johnson's other practices, he preferred general "disquisition" to the fragmented commentary practiced by predecessors like Pierre Bayle and William Oldys.

Students of Johnson recall the last decades' squabbles regarding Johnson's politics: liberal or conservative, Jacobite or loyal, royalist Tory or Old Whig acknowledging the people's right to rebel. Part IV considers some of those issues but tactfully avoids what Johnson in the Preface to *Shakespeare* laments as paper "wasted in confutation."[20] F. P. Lock argues that Johnson's considered opinions regarding politics should not be drawn from his earlier works of 1738–39 but from the key period of 1770 to 1775. Johnson then published a series of pamphlets on behalf of Lord North's ministry, describing his aim: "to preserve order and support Monarchy." For Lock, Johnson's most settled political convictions are to be found in that later group. To support this interpretation, he adduces parallels from Johnson's less polemical writings, his sermons, and the law lectures with which he assisted Robert Chambers. Thus viewed, Johnson's defense of Lord North's policies, as in *Taxation No Tyranny* (1775), accorded with his belief in the value of social hierarchy and subordination.

Thomas Kaminski's edition of Johnson's *Parliamentary Debates* (1741–44) recently appeared in Yale's edition of Johnson's works. Kaminski now presents some of his findings here with three contexts for reading those *Debates*. He considers their accuracy as historical documents, compares Johnson's efforts with the rival series published in the *London Magazine*, and attempts to place them in a broader historical and political context. In the process, Kaminski overturns several common misconceptions. For instance, Johnson always worked from notes that provided specific information about what had been said on the floor of the House. The notes were often insufficient, and he was forced to embellish and expand on that material, but no debate merely springs from his own imagination. In addition, the rival series in the *London Magazine* was compiled in much the same manner as Johnson's debates and should not be thought to contain a more accurate record of parliamentary events. Finally, since Johnson's speeches were a primary means by which the oratory of men like Chesterfield and Pitt came to public notice, Johnson helped to establish the public reputations of these important political figures.

20. Preface to *Shakespeare*, in *Johnson on Shakespeare*, vol. 7 of *YE*, ed. Arthur Sherbo (1968), 99.

Johnson was a deeply religious Anglican whose many sermons, we have seen, were heard from the pulpit and anxiously awaited from the publisher. Part V considers his religion and the philosophy that so often supported it. William Gibson examines some of the influences on Johnson's religious ideas as well as the recent debates regarding his churchmanship. Gibson concludes that, given Johnson's long life and tendency toward irony and opposition, finding a definitive Johnson on religion would be difficult. His inconsistency after all was consistent with that of other public religious figures like John Wesley and Benjamin Hoadly. Nicholas Hudson's Johnson also is "inconsistent," here in the changing philosophy in his periodical essays of the 1750s. The *Rambler* and the *Adventurer* explain human conduct by reference to our dual nature. We perpetually seek something better that we perpetually cannot find in this world, because it exists only in a benign afterlife if we are worthy of it. The *Idler*, however, was written during the height of the Seven Years' War, about which Johnson was deeply troubled. The *Idler* reflects that pessimism and characterizes human beings as, in a term drawn from Newtonian physics, subject to the *vis inertiae*, an inert force by which we are moved only to seek ease in this life. During his later career, Johnson seems torn between the nobler vision of human nature in the *Rambler* and the darker vision in the *Idler*.

Part VI concludes the book with something that is never concluded—namely, Johnson's extensive afterlife. He lived for some seventy-five years, but he celebrated his three-hundredth birthday in 2009. Three contributors examine Johnson as perceived in art and in the Romantic and early Victorian periods. Robert Folkenflik studies the vexed history, identification, provenance, and reception of Sir Joshua Reynolds's portrait, now at the Huntington, that Johnson denigrated as "blinking Sam." Folkenflik establishes that this indeed is the painting Mrs. Piozzi described and to which Johnson objected. He also discusses early copies of the portrait, including those almost certainly misattributed either to Sir Joshua's sister Frances or to Gilbert Stuart. *Blinking Sam* and Reynolds's *Self-Portrait as a Deaf Man* probably allude to the European visual tradition of the representation of the senses. Freya Johnston shows how useful Johnson was for Byron's defense of Pope's reputation in the 1820s and how Johnson reinforced Byron's view that literature should be continuous with real life. That continuity included a shared resistance to rigid definitions, a willingness to engage in the literary marketplace's combative games, and a comparable willingness to follow his own instincts in the face of stern opposition. Byron generally adapted these views from Johnson's own writings rather than from Boswell's biographical representation of Johnson. James Engell, however, focuses on that biography as a parallel to John Gibson Lockhart's biography of Sir Walter Scott. Engell analyzes a previously unexplored analogy within Anglo-Scottish literary relations. Johnson came to represent England and English culture as Scott in somewhat different ways came to embody Scotland and Scottish culture. The essay explores how Boswell and Lockhart shaped their biographical subjects as national representatives and how Lockhart employed Johnson's presence to highlight his portrait of Scott. Engell's essay also traces Johnson's presence in Scott's letters and autobiographical writing, the fate of Scott's extensive notes to Boswell's *Tour*, and Lockhart's suggestion, accepted by John Wilson Croker, to include the *Tour* in Boswell's *Life of Johnson*.

This section and the volume end with Robert DeMaria Jr.'s "A History of the Collected Works of Samuel Johnson: The First Two Hundred Years." There is some evidence that Johnson planned to collect his own works, but he made little if any progress on that project. Within weeks of his death, the London publishers thus engaged Sir John Hawkins to do that job. His eleven-volume edition (1787) later was supplemented by other editors' four further volumes (1787–89) and became the basis for all future texts, including the so-called Oxford edition of 1825. As David Fleeman has made plain, all such versions, and especially that in 1825, were poorly edited. DeMaria assesses the history of these editions, including Yale's, which began in 1955 and is nearing completion.

Intellectual anorexia is scarcely a problem for Johnsonian studies. As the synopses and the essays themselves suggest, there is a great deal of remaining Johnsonian nourishment available both for full and for empty plates, if we know where to look. To extend the culinary metaphor, those asking, "Please sir, I want some more," will find their bowls gladly filled.

PART I:
JOHNSON AND THE ARTS OF THOUGHT

"The *future* in the instant": Johnson, Garrick, Boswell, and the Perils of Theatrical Prolepsis

Stuart Sherman

FROM JOHNSON'S *Dictionary of the English Language*:

> FU'TURE. *n. ſ.* . . . Time to come; somewhat to happen hereafter.
>
> Thy letters have transported me beyond
> This ign'rant present time; and I feel now
> The *future* in the instant. *Shakespeare's Macbeth*[1]

As Robert DeMaria Jr. has taught us, the *Dictionary* deals not only in definitions but in precepts, too.[2] For the problems of time that preoccupied Johnson throughout his writing life, he could not have chosen a quotation more illustrative than the one he offers here for *future*. Lady Macbeth, greeting her husband with an exultant vision of their prospects, is making a mistake recapitulated again and again in Johnson's writings: by the "young enthusiast" in *The Vanity of Human Wishes* (1749), who feels "Bacon's mansion" trembling auspiciously "o'er his head";[3] by the weather watcher in *Rambler* 5 (1750), who "refer[s] the removal of all his uneasiness to the coming of the next spring";[4] by the restless folk in *Idler* 31 (1758), who "are always in a state of preparation, occupied in previous measures, forming plans, accumulating materials, and providing for the main affair";[5] and by the self-delusionist Imlac describes in *Rasselas* (1759),

1. Samuel Johnson, *A Dictionary of the English Language*, 2 vols. (London, 1755), s.v. "Future"; italics in original.

2. Robert DeMaria Jr., *Johnson's "Dictionary" and the Language of Learning* (Chapel Hill, N.C., 1986), 11–25.

3. Johnson, *Poems*, vol. 6 of *The Yale Edition of the Works of Samuel Johnson* (hereafter cited as *YE*), ed. E. L. McAdam Jr. with George Milne (New Haven, Conn., 1964), 97–98, lines 136, 140. Text references are to this edition.

4. Johnson, *The Rambler*, vols. 3–5 of *YE*, ed. W. J. Bate and Albrecht B. Strauss (1969), 3:26 (*Rambler* 5, April 3, 1750).

5. Johnson, *The Idler and The Adventurer*, vol. 2 of *YE*, ed. W. J. Bate, John M. Bullitt, and L. F. Powell (1963), 96 (*Idler* 31, November 18, 1758).

who, left to "his own thoughts" and prey to the dangerous prevalence of imagination, "expatiates in boundless futurity, and culls from all imaginable conditions that which for the present moment he should most desire."[6]

For all such Johnsonian exemplars, the mistake consists not so much in the anticipation itself, in the imaginative leap from the present to the future, as in the selectivity and self-deception that make the leap seductive. The self-projector unfailingly factors out the darker components of the future that will actually ensue, and Johnson makes it his job as moralist to reinstate them into the reckoning. He did this of course in real life, too, most succinctly on his pocket watch, whose dial, Boswell reports, bore the Greek inscription "Νυξ γαρ ερχεται"—the first words of Christ's pronouncement in John 9:4, "the night cometh, when no man can work."[7] Here is the future in the instant rendered palpable, visible, audible: the ancient phrase abides amid the watch hands' movements and the clockwork's ticking—but as admonition, not exultation. It invokes the reality of the night's coming in order to regulate the wearer's imagination, which might otherwise entertain the option of deferring the day's proper labors indefinitely. For Johnson, the future poses for the "ignorant present" a doubled threat: it is scary because it is dangerous (that night is really coming), but also dangerous because it is pliable—too easily cherry-picked and tailor-made. Like Touchstone, scrutinizing the sundial in *As You Like It*, Johnson makes it his business at every turn to "moral on the time." Touchstone specializes in mutability ("from hour to hour we ripe and ripe, / . . . from hour to hour we rot and rot"), Johnson in the perils of hyperactive prolepsis—of eagerly, delusionally inviting the future to overwhelm the instant.[8]

Johnson's pervasive preoccupation with this phenomenon has been well documented and extensively explored. But one possible payoff has not yet been collected, and it has to do with the contexts in which Lady Macbeth speaks her lines. I'll argue here that her words, the play text that proffers them, the venues (page and stage) in which she delivers them, and the temporalities operating in each of these may offer us a way in to an oddly under-lit chamber of Johnson's thought and experience: his relations, deeply inflected by his sense of real and moral time, to playgoing as a source of pleasure, and to performance as a mode of art. "The future in the instant" turns out, in ways undreamed of by Lady Macbeth but profoundly understood and deployed by Shakespeare, to epitomize a feature of playhouse life on which Johnson in his theatrical writings predictably focuses: the theater's fascination with the psychological pliabilities of time. From the *Shakespeare* (1765), the *Lives of the Poets* (1779–81), and much else, we know plenty about what Johnson thought on the question of how plays work as texts. Apart from some dazzling passages in the *Shakespeare* Preface, his handful of

6. Johnson, *Rasselas and Other Tales*, vol. 16 of *YE*, ed. Gwin J. Kolb (1990), 151–52.

7. *Boswell's Life of Johnson, Together with Boswell's Journal of a Tour to the Hebrides and Johnson's Diary of a Journey into North Wales*, ed. George Birkbeck Hill, rev. L. F. Powell, 6 vols. (Oxford, 1934–50), 2:57 (hereafter cited as *Life*).

8. William Shakespeare, *As You Like It*, in *The Norton Shakespeare*, ed. Stephen Greenblatt et al. (New York, 1997), 2.7.29, 26–27. Unless otherwise noted, text references to Shakespeare are to act, scene, and line of this edition.

playhouse prologues, and a few offhand utterances in Boswell's *Life*, we know much less about how he thought they worked as shows, unfolding at a specific place in a time at once real and imaginary. Contemporary accounts offer scant testimony. Even Boswell, himself hopelessly hooked on theater since some moment shortly after infancy, tends to accentuate the negative in Johnson's encounters with the art; he misconstrues the long ordeal of *Irene* (1749), for example, as mere disappointment and near disaster. But even the evidence Boswell summons suggests a more nuanced reading of Johnson's theatrical experience than the one he offers; and of course there is much more, in both the life and work, that he does not touch on. Time—and in particular, the pleasures and perils of prolepsis to which *Macbeth* devotes sustained, even obsessive attention—may help us make sense of Johnson's own lifelong, shifting encounters with the theater. And because Johnson kept close company with Garrick, the theater's most prodigious practitioner, and Boswell, among its most addicted attendees, the three men's ongoing if sometimes subliminal dialogue about theatrical time may be worth tracking, too. Each was differently beguiled, and differently troubled, by the many ways, at the theater, in which the future might impinge upon the instant.

For all three, *Macbeth* served as a sort of litmus test, but for Johnson it seems to have been much more. In his *Shakespeare*, in his *Dictionary*, and in many places elsewhere, he construes *Macbeth* almost as a morality play on the perils of prolepsis. What makes Lady Macbeth's utterance worth dwelling on in the *Dictionary*, for example, is the compressed precision of its language about time, the patterns of diction that feed into it from Shakespeare's play, and out from it to shape even the wording of Johnson's definition. One curious feature of the quotation is the inverse relation between its speaker's stated preoccupation and her actual word choice: only one word names the *future*, amid three for the present—"beyond the ign'rant *present*"; "I feel *now* . . . "; "in the *instant*" (italics added). Quantitatively, Lady Macbeth is talking more about the present than the future, partly out of disdain (it's "ign'rant") and partly out of astonishment that such a time shift can take place. By grounding the future so firmly in the *now*, at a ratio of three to one, she is quite literally channeling the form, and indeed the key term, of the peculiar temporality that suffuses the play she inhabits, in which the future *always* overtakes the instant. Johnson's quotation omits the extraordinary opening lines of Lady Macbeth's first speech to her spouse:

> Great Glamis, worthy Cawdor,
> Greater than both by the all-hail hereafter,
> Thy letters have transported me . . .
>
> (1.5.52–54)

What subliminally enthralls audiences, and has sometimes stymied critics, is that Lady Macbeth here echoes very closely words that we have heard but she has not: the core phrases of the witches' prophecy, culminating in their "All hail, Macbeth, that shalt be king hereafter!" (1.3.48). The tantalizing implication is that she has somehow become one of them. *Hereafter*, the most memorable channeled term, encapsulates in a single word the strange temporal relation that her ensuing lines will unpack, and that for Johnson became a moral preoccupation: fusing *here* with *after*, it grafts future onto present.

The word recurs throughout the play, and its import proves even more pervasive: the future overtakes the present almost everywhere, as in Macbeth's extraordinarily compressed soliloquy moments after he has heard the prophecy:

> My thought, whose murder yet is but fantastical,
> Shakes so my single state of man that function
> Is smothered in surmise, and nothing is
> But what is not.
>
> (1.3.138–41)

Which Johnson, in his *Shakespeare*, paraphrases thus: "nothing is present to me, but that which is really future."[9] He is in effect pre-echoing Lady Macbeth, in what may be another instance of her suasive power: her lines, still two scenes into the future, partly dictate his present commentary. And perhaps his *Dictionary* definition, too, which culminates in her key word even before it quotes her: "Time to come; somewhat to happen hereafter." On Johnson, then, *Macbeth* operates as both force field and vortex. It draws him in, it cues his echoes, precisely because it deals so thickly with what was for him a core problem of human time, the dangerous prevalence of temporal imagination.

It is all the more striking, then, that in the Preface to *Shakespeare* the theater should figure as a solution to the problem, and a dissolution of the danger. "Time," Johnson avers in his most famous pronouncement on that topic, "is, of all modes of existence, most obsequious to the imagination" (*YE*, 7:78). The proposition has proven endlessly quotable, partly because of the way in which it combines the magisterial and the elusive (what exactly can it mean to call time a *mode* of existence?), but mostly because in the context of Johnson's oeuvre it operates as both echo chamber and pivot point. In Johnson's writings, it is time's obsequiousness—its lability, its ductility, its availability to manipulation by the human imagination—that fosters the dangerous, perhaps ineluctable fusion of *here* and *after*, *now* and *next*, that will get the Macbeths into so much trouble, and that Johnson explores so assiduously throughout his works. But in the Preface to *Shakespeare* the whole problem of *hereafter* becomes strikingly disinfected, transmuted from moral crux into a fundamental, fundamentally liberating component of theatrical experience.

9. *Johnson on Shakespeare*, vols. 7–8 of *YE*, ed. Arthur Sherbo (1968), 8:760. Text references to Johnson's commentary, and to the Shakespearean passages he comments on, are to this edition.

In fact, the word itself, by its cross-dimensional synesthesia—the way it starts from space (*here*), then shifts to time (*after*)—can serve as shorthand for the quick, hypnotic argument by which Johnson in the Preface debunks the neoclassical strictures on the unities. He, too, starts with space, in his almost hilariously commonsensical assertion that playgoers at the playhouse, wherever the play itself may take them (Alexandria, Rome, Pharsalia, Actium, Sicily, Athens), are firmly and knowingly *here*: "the spectators are always in their senses, and know, from the first act to the last, that the stage is only a stage, and that the players are only players"; they know their actual location to be "neither Sicily nor Athens, but a modern theatre" (*YE*, 7:77). The argument promptly modulates from the spatial to the temporal—"By supposition, as place is introduced, time may be extended"—and culminates in the pronouncement on time's obsequiousness, explicated in sentences that distill decades of Johnson's moral thought on the ways in which minds move in time: "a lapse of years is as easily conceived as a passage of hours. In contemplation we easily contract the time of real actions, and therefore willingly permit it to be contracted when we only see their imitation" (*YE*, 7:78).

Within this proposition, though, Johnson engineers an unexpected, curiously comfortable conflation of real life with theatrical effects. In *The Vanity of Human Wishes*, the *Rambler*, *Rasselas*, the *Lives*, and at many other loci in Johnson's writing, the imagination's real-life capacity to "contract the time of real actions," and so to promise delusively their ease and success, generates innumerable, familiar footholds for human folly, stepping-off points for disappointment, disaster, even tragedy. But in the Preface to *Shakespeare*, that same capacity to contract real time turns out instead to be the source of something close to iconoclastic exultation. It unknots the constrictions of the unities, and it refutes Lady Macbeth's scornful accounting of the "ign'rant present." For patrons of the drama, the present—their physical presence at the playhouse, the temporal present tense of their viewing and auditing during the two and more hours' traffic of the stage—turns out to be not ignorant but knowing and remarkably supple. (At a play as familiar as *Macbeth* they even know, far better than the fretful protagonists, how the hereafter will turn out, within the established framework of plot and play text; they can survey with extensive view a temporality that the characters experience only as tormenting prolepsis.) The theater becomes a safe haven in which the imagination can be properly exercised, precisely because it is exercised within palpable, self-insistent limits. "The use of travelling," Johnson would later write to Hester Thrale, "is to regulate imagination by reality."[10] In the Preface, by contrast, the purpose of the playhouse is to regulate imagination by *un*reality. In ordinary life, the imagination is dangerously free to bend "the time of real actions" to its own distortive purposes; at the playhouse it is safely governed by the known unreality of theatrical "imitation." The spectators, "always in their senses," "willingly permit" illusions that

10. Samuel Johnson to Hester Thrale, September 21, 1773, *The Letters of Samuel Johnson*, ed. Bruce Redford, 5 vols. (Princeton, N.J., 1992–94), 2:78.

they also capably delimit. In Johnson's theory, the temporal imagination, operating within such wholesome restraints, cannot dangerously prevail.

In messy theatrical practice, though, it can. At real playhouses, as Johnson had learned years earlier when his sole play was produced, real actions—by actual actors, by active audience members—might wreak havoc with tidy temporal expectations. *Irene* was Johnson's only attempt at sculpting an entire evening at the theater; at every phase of its creation and production, it moved through ineluctable modalities of the proleptic. What first propelled Johnson to London, with Garrick at his side and drafts of *Irene* in his pocket, was the keen ambition to put his play on stage. As Thomas Kaminski reminds us, he in effect recapitulated this inaugural trip two times in the span of six months, leaving London once for Greenwich, and once again for Lichfield; at each destination he worked further on his tragedy, returning to the capital with new hopes for its success. At each arrival and rearrival, *Irene* itself was the present endeavor through which Johnson focused most fiercely on his own chosen future, the means by which *now* was to give way to *next*.[11] But even before his first departure from Lichfield, Johnson had received, from his mentor Gilbert Walmsley, a critique of the play, the earliest criticism we have on record, centered on its impetuous error of timing: "When [Johnson] had finished some part of it," Boswell reports, "he read what he had done to Mr. Walmsley, who objected to his having already brought his heroine into great distress, and asked him, 'how can you possibly contrive to plunge her into deeper calamity?'" (*Life*, 1:101). The aspiring playwright, another recorder of the encounter writes, "had left no possibility of heightening the catastrophe in the concluding part of the play."[12] Johnson here recapitulates as author Lady Macbeth's mistake as character: he has moved the dramatic future too fast into the present instant.

The papers that rustled in his pockets en route to London ran temporality another way. They may well be the most stupefyingly atemporal manuscripts in the whole history of playwriting. The early drafts consist "[f]or the most part," as Bertrand Bronson declares in his searching, sprightly lecture-essay on the subject, "of setting down completely unconnected passages, one after another, without any identification of speakers, and . . . without any regard to the order of scenes intended."[13] On the one hand, this seeming chaos bears witness to the same powers of memory and faculties of organization that would later be associated with Johnson's composition, half-line by half-line, at a rate as high as a hundred lines in a day, of *The Vanity of Human Wishes*; in both cases Johnson is able to write down only parts of the text while remembering the rest, and to hold in the mind an overall structure not evident on the page (*YE*, 6:90). On the other hand, Bronson suggests, "the fragmentary eruption of Johnson's ideas," made manifest in the manuscript, disrupts the potential for effective drama: "out of such materials no living dialogue could rise. The draft is more a commonplace-book

11. Thomas Kaminski, *The Early Career of Samuel Johnson* (New York, 1987), 5–11.

12. *Gentleman's Magazine and Historical Chronicle* 55, pt. 1 (1785): 288n.

13. Bertrand Bronson, "Johnson's *Irene*: Variations on a Tragic Theme," in *Johnson Agonistes, & Other Essays* (Berkeley, Calif., 1965), 100–135 at 120.

than a dramatic sketch," and so provides evidence as to "the radically untheatrical quality of Johnson's imagination."[14]

Perhaps. But there may be a genre distinction worth noting here. What is remarkable about the *Vanity* manuscript is its testimony to an astonishing fore-ordering, grounded partly in the Juvenalian original that Johnson was closely imitating: the poem's 368 lines were fully shaped and sequenced before pen hit paper; in the words of the Yale editors, "all of the poem was composed before any of it was set down" (*YE*, 6:91). In the "dramatic sketch" for *Irene*, the temporality is immeasurably looser and far more dependent for its future ordering, long after pen hit paper, on Johnson's memory and creative imagination. In the raw original the future mingles with the present instant so pervasively that there is barely any distinguishing between the two. But this sense of time's ductility, even its incipient chaos, which in the *Irene* manuscripts makes Johnson seem to Bronson a foredoomedly "untheatrical" playwright, will render him, in the Preface to *Shakespeare*, a radically "theatrical" critic—a revolutionarily perceptive reader of the way in which time actually works in the minds of playgoers. Messy practice and lucid theory derive in tandem from the same pervasively moralized perception: that "in contemplation we easily contract," for better (at the playhouse) or worse (in delusion-driven real life), "the time of real actions."

Of course the playhouse is a place of real actions, too—of all those things, whether planned or spontaneous, that spectators and performers actually did during the exceedingly interactive four or five hours of an eighteenth-century evening at the theater; *action* was in fact the common term for what we now call *acting*. When *Irene* at last made its way to the stage, Johnson saw the real actions at the playhouse impinge with extraordinary force upon the carefully programmed temporality of his finished script; the elegance of moralized time converged with the messiness of theatrical time to unanticipated effect. On the opening night of *Mahomet and Irene*, as its star Garrick had now retitled the play a dozen years after his and Johnson's London arrival, the playgoers expressed their minds most vehemently at two key moments: they applauded a speech in the middle of the play, and they mocked at play's end the moment intended as its tragic climax. The applause had everything to do with time moralized, the mockery with time theatricalized. Here's the speech, delivered by the hero Demetrius in response to the reassurance, by one of his fellow conspirators, that today's plan will become "To-morrow's action":

To-morrow's action? Can that hoary wisdom
Born down with years, still doat upon to-morrow?
That fatal mistress of the young, the lazy,
The coward, and the fool, condemn'd to lose
An useless life in waiting for to-morrow,
To gaze with longing eyes upon to-morrow,

14. Bronson, "Johnson's *Irene*," 119, 123.

Till interposing death destroys the prospect!
Strange! that this gen'ral fraud from day to day
Should fill the world with wretches undetected.
The soldier lab'ring through a winter's march,
Still sees to-morrow drest in robes of triumph;
Still to the lover's long-expecting arms,
To-morrow brings the visionary bride.
But thou, too old to bear another cheat,
Learn, that the present hour alone is man's.
(*YE*, 6:154–55; 3.2.19–33)

To Johnsonians such sentiments will be familiar. For that first-night audience, they were apparently sensational, and the sensation clearly derived in part from the speech's structure. The incantatory, syncopated anaphora (six *tomorrows* in thirteen lines) memorably sustains the hero's scorn: "the speech on *to-morrow*," Charles Burney called it, looking back decades later to this signal moment on the opening night.[15] But the lines probably acquired much of their impact from a resonant ripple effect, from the way they echoed back across minutes, months, decades, and centuries to retrieve textual tags already lodged in the auditors' memories. Like the aria midopera or the big number in the middle of a musical, which brings to full fruition small motifs hitherto scattered imperceptibly through the score, the speech builds on lines and phrases, which Johnson has threaded through the previous scenes, on the dangerous delusions of prolepsis—for example, the vizier Cali Bassa's earlier warning against "wand'ring in the wilds of future being" (*YE*, 6:119). For many in that first-night audience, the speech may have triggered memories of one of Dryden's most celebrated set pieces: "When I consider Life, 'tis all a cheat; . . . To morrow's falser than the former day," from *Aureng-Zebe* (1676).[16] For still more, of course, it would have recalled Macbeth's own "speech on tomorrow"—and "tomorrow and tomorrow, / Creep[ing] in this petty pace from day to day" (5.5.18–19), which Johnson here emphatically echoes and expands, doubling the *tomorrows* while mirroring the *days*. But the most powerful echo may well have been more recent. On January 9, 1749, exactly four weeks before opening night,

15. *Memoirs of Dr. Charles Burney, 1726–1769*, ed. Slava Klima, Garry Bowers, and Kerry S. Grant (Lincoln, Neb., 1988), 81–82 (February 6, 1749); quoted in Steven William Bouler, "'Thunder o'er the Drowsy Pit': The Performance Historiography of Samuel Johnson's *Mahomet and Irene* at Drury Lane" (PhD diss., University of California at Santa Barbara, 2002), 360. Emphasis in the original. *Irene* has in recent decades come in for considerable reconsideration; in addition to Bouler's usefully thorough dissertation, see Katherine H. Adams, "A Critic Formed: Samuel Johnson's Apprenticeship with *Irene*," in *Fresh Reflections on Samuel Johnson: Essays in Criticism*, ed. Prem Nath (Troy, N.Y., 1987), 183–200; Joel J. Gold, "The Failure of Johnson's *Irene*: Death by Antithesis," in *Fresh Reflections*, ed. Nath, 201–14; Chella C. Livingston, "Johnson and the Independent Woman: A Reading of *Irene*," *The Age of Johnson* 2 (1989): 219–34; Nailini Jain, "Johnson's *Irene*: The First Draft," *British Journal for Eighteenth-Century Studies* 13 (1990): 163–67; and Wendy Laura Belcher, *Abyssinia's Samuel Johnson: Ethiopian Thought in the Making of an English Author* (New York, 2012).

16. John Dryden, *Aureng-Zebe*, in *The Works of John Dryden*, vol. 12, ed. Vinton A. Dearing (Berkeley, Calif., 1994), 4.1.33–44.

there had appeared in print a poem for which Demetrius's speech might serve as précis: *The Vanity of Human Wishes*, the first work—and in his fortieth year—to bear Johnson's name as author on the title page. A few days later, the *Gentleman's Magazine* published copious extracts of the poem, coupled with a blazon for the imminent play: "We hope to be able soon to give our readers a specimen of a tragedy, entitled *Irene*, by the same ingenious author, Mr Garrick having it now in rehearsal."[17] The delusive powers of tomorrow, the moral perils of prolepsis, had become, over the course of a few weeks, Johnson's signature theme, his stock in trade.

And by evening's end at Drury Lane, they had become, too, a kind of source code for theatrical miscalculation. The tragedy of *Irene*, and of its eponymous heroine, turns on an act of fatal prolepsis. At the play's conclusion, the tyrannic sultan Mahomet learns that, at his command, his cherished albeit complicatedly corrupt queen has been peremptorily executed for a treason of which he now thinks she was innocent. His henchmen have performed in an instant what should have been deferred to a more malleable future: "Could not her prayers," Mahomet pleads in anguished retrospect, "her innocence, her tears, / Suspend the dreadful sentence for an hour? / One hour had freed me from the fatal error, / One hour had sav'd me from despair and madness." She should, in short, have died hereafter. But on opening night, not only the Sultan of Turkey but also the manager of Drury Lane got his timing wrong. Garrick had insisted, over Johnson's objections, that Irene's execution should take place not offstage, but on: Hannah Pritchard, Boswell records, "was to be strangled upon the stage, and was to speak two lines with the bow-string round her neck. The audience cried out '*Murder! Murder!*' She several times attempted to speak; but in vain. At last she was obliged to go off the stage alive" (*Life*, 1:197). Garrick had chosen to transmute into real action what Johnson had chosen to leave to the imagination. Both performer and playwright evidently deplored the effect: Johnson's original intentions were reinstated for the ensuing eight nights of the play's run.

Garrick's decision to stage the killing, in the teeth of classical tradition and authorial intention, was characteristic, and characteristically controversial. Five years earlier, he had mounted a famous production of *Macbeth* in which he promised to restore Shakespeare's text, which had not been heard on stage for seven decades. To a remarkable extent he fulfilled the promise—with one much-noted exception. The First Folio's stage directions about the closing combat are notoriously murky and scarcely stageable. Macbeth and Macduff exit fighting, then reenter fighting for what is in effect a separate and silent scene: Macduff kills Macbeth and presumably drags off his corpse without a word being said on either side. Garrick of course had something else in mind: "He composed," recalls his assiduous but at times acerbic biographer Thomas Davies, "a pretty long speech for Macbeth, when dying, which, though suitable perhaps to the character, was unlike Shakespeare's manner, who was not prodigal of bestowing abundance of matter on characters in that situation. But Garrick excelled in the expression of convulsive throes and dying agonies, and would not lose any opportunity that offered to shew

17. Quoted in *The Monthly Review* 77 (1787): 135.

his skill in that part of his profession."[18] The Garrick who chose to stage Irene's execution in 1749 was the here-and-now theatrical literalist and hyperbolist whose highly articulate agonies had finished off *Macbeth* in 1744; the Johnson who chose to sequester it was at least *in potentia* the theatrical theorist whose faith in the power of spatial and temporal imagination would find fullest expression in the Preface to *Shakespeare*.

In one sense, Johnson's *Shakespeare* was already underway four years before Garrick produced *Irene* at Drury Lane. In 1745 Johnson, pursuing literary work that might provide him with a steady and substantial income, had published his *Miscellaneous Observations on the Tragedy of Macbeth: with . . . Proposals for a New Edition of Shakespeare*. The choice of *Macbeth* for such purposes was arbitrary to an extent—any of the great plays might have served—and so perhaps all the more significant. It may have been prompted in part by the success of Garrick's production the year before; Johnson had consulted with his former pupil on the restoration of Shakespeare's text (though not on the insertion of that dying speech), and there is something of the relay race about the way in which the writer and the actor handed the Scottish play back and forth over the course of their first shared London decade. But for reasons I've already tried to sketch, I think that *Macbeth* had long attracted Johnson by virtue of temporal affinity. The problem of imaginative prolepsis, the question of how the future can, does, and should impinge upon the present instant that is central to Johnson—and implicit to some extent in perhaps every play ever written—becomes in the web of *Macbeth* both thematic warp and imagistic woof.

But as editor of *Macbeth*, Johnson, perhaps by virtue of his long and deep engagement with the play, manifests in both his *Observations* and his *Shakespeare* an odd temporal schism. As general commentator, in the long first note on witches and prophecy that operates as introduction, and in his closing comments on the dangers of ambition, he inveighs against the perils of prolepsis in a fashion thoroughly familiar: "The danger of ambition is well described," he remarks in the edition's closing summation; and "in Shakespeare's time, it was necessary to warn credulity against vain and illusive predictions" (*YE*, 8:795). In Johnson's time as well, perhaps: he is here describing, and indeed enacting, something close to his own moral mission. But as line editor and textual critic, he strangely packs his commentary with misreadings that actually impose prolepsis at points where Shakespeare's text resists or postpones it; he commits as close reader the kinds of future-driven error that as moral writer he deplored. When Macbeth, for example, early in the play, is thrust by the witches' prophecies into that deep disorientation where "nothing is / But what is not"—where, in Johnson's gloss, "nothing is present to me but that which is really future"—he attempts, in his very next lines, to wrangle himself back into ordinary time: "Come what come may, / Time and the hour runs through the roughest day" (1.3.145–46). "I suppose," Johnson writes in his commensurately disorienting commentary, that "every reader is disgusted at the tautology in this passage, 'Time and the hour,' and will therefore willingly believe that Shakespeare wrote it thus: 'Come what come may, / *Time*! *on*!—the hour runs thro' the

18. Thomas Davies, *Dramatic Miscellanies*, 3 vols. (London, 1783–84), 2:118.

roughest day.' Macbeth is deliberating upon the events which are to befal him, but finding no satisfaction from his own thoughts . . . [and] to shorten the pain of suspense, he calls upon time in the usual stile of ardent desire, to quicken his motion, Time! on!——" (*YE*, 8:760). Here, Johnson's Macbeth, urging the present to rush toward the future, and the future to invade the instant, is doing exactly what Shakespeare's Macbeth is trying to resist, by coupling time not tautologically but urgently with the ordinary "hour," and freeing it from the convulsions of prophecy. Johnson's reading confesses its willfulness by its diction: "I suppose every reader . . . will therefore willingly"; this is *will* in overplus. The note may confess its auspices as well: "This conjecture," Johnson writes at comment's end, "is supported by the passage in [Macbeth's] letter to his lady in which he says, 'They referred me to the *coming on of time,* with Hail, King that shall be'" (*YE*, 8:760). But let me make bold to suggest that Johnson reads the echo wrong; the *coming on of time* (he italicizes the phrase), like "Come what come may," admits duration, and registers Macbeth's comparative, precarious temporal lucidity. It is the Lady herself who, while reading the letter aloud, will willingly goad Time on, and will feel, under the letter's spell, the future in the instant. As in his *Dictionary* definition of *future*, Johnson here seems to be writing under her spell, too.

Something comparable happens in Johnson's commentary on Shakespeare's darkest time piece, "the speech on tomorrow" (to echo Burney's description of the matching moment in *Irene*) that Macbeth delivers on hearing news of his wife's death:

She should have died hereafter.
There would have been a time for such a word.
Tomorrow, and tomorrow, and tomorrow . . .
(5.5.16–18)

"This passage," Johnson notes in his early *Observations*, "has very justly been suspected of being corrupt," primarily because the phrase "such a word" has no clear referent: which word is Macbeth talking about? And why at this moment of crisis, is he talking about any *word* at all? In truth, Johnson explains in his early *Observations*, this "is a broken speech in which only part of the thought is expressed" before it catapults the speaker into a more global lamentation:

She should have died hereafter.
There would have been a time for—such a *world*!—
To-morrow *&c.*
(*YE*, 7:41)

Again with the aposiopesis! As in the previous passage, Johnson cracks open Shakespeare's smooth syntax—"Time and the hour"; "time for such a word"—to interpellate an exclamatory self-interruption: "Time! on!"; "such a *world*!" But if these speeches are broken, it is Johnson who has broken them, and in this second instance the import of the breakage needs assessing. In the original text, "such a word" points to several possible referents, as Johnson partly conceded twenty years after the *Observations*, when in the *Shakespeare* edition proper he declared himself "less confident" in his previous reading; "such a word," he now suggested, may simply refer to the news Macbeth has just received, the "word" he has just heard about his wife's death (*YE*, 8:793).

"Such a word," though, may in fact refer to something else. The most immediate available antecedent for the phrase is the last word of the previous line. "She should have died *hereafter*": that word now makes its last appearance in the play but its first in Macbeth's own mouth. In other mouths—the witches', his Lady's—it has become the play's catchword for the fusion of the future with the instant. But if *hereafter* is the word Macbeth here means, then it is working differently this time round. An Empsonian reading might go something like this: "There should have been a time to say 'hereafter' —and it would have been, simply, after here; that is, not now, later. Now is the time to think only of ordinary time, and of the burdens it brings with it." Macbeth, in short, is severing the future from the instant. He here accomplishes in full tragic spate what he fleetingly attempted once before, in the line about "Time and the hour": he is at last supplanting the delusive fusions of *hereafter* with an unbearably sober reckoning of real, present human time. He will spend the rest of the speech calling *tomorrow*'s bluff: "Tomorrow, and tomorrow, and tomorrow / Creeps in this petty pace from day to day / . . . / And all our yesterdays have lighted fools / The way to dusty death" (5.5.18–22). This, of course, is what Johnson's Demetrius, channeling Macbeth, will do in his own "speech on tomorrow" in *Irene*. That Johnson should here disrupt rather than endorse Macbeth's proto-Johnsonian method of moralizing time is striking, and may have something to do with where the lines go next:

> Life's but a walking shadow, a poor player
> That struts and frets his hour upon the stage,
> And then is heard no more. It is a tale
> Told by an idiot, full of sound and fury,
> Signifying nothing.
>
> (5.5.23–27)

Signifying nothing: the vacuity that Johnson struggles against throughout his writing Macbeth here deems inescapable; and the futility of all human time is here imaged—famously, harrowingly—in the evanescence of theatrical life.

And evanescence—that empty prolepsis in which the nothing of the future impinges oppressively upon the real actions of the present—may help account for Johnson's intermittent unease not only with this passage in *Macbeth*, but with the theater itself, and it may even help explain his withdrawal from the stage after his sole play's substantially successful and (for him) strikingly lucrative nine-night run. Macbeth's "poor player" partly confirms Johnson's long-cherished convictions about time's proper deployment but emphatically confounds them, too. In Johnson's reckoning, the deliberate, attentive distribution of real actions in real time should lead to fulfillment—the happiness proffered at the end of the *Vanity*—and even salvation: think of the inscription on that watch. The poor player's single "hour upon the stage" is real enough—and is ensconced in a speech that, like so many of Macbeth's and so few of his Lady's, strives to regulate rather than accelerate the temporal imagination. But the player's time ends, *contra* Johnson, in "no more" and "nothing": no fulfillment, no salvation, only evanescence.

Johnson was, to put it mildly, terrified of evanescence; in the first decades of his career, he did all he could to shift his work as writer from the realm of the underpaid ephemeral to that of the profitably monumental. The *Observations on Macbeth* constituted his most significant down payment to date on the prospect of a project that would take time, last long, make money. He would of course complete the modulation in the ensuing decades, when not only the *Dictionary*, the *Shakespeare*, and the *Lives*, but also those potentially more fragile ephemerides the *Rambler* and the *Idler* attained a permanence made palpable in bound volumes accessible almost everywhere. Theater, notoriously, proffered no such prospect; it was for Johnson and his epoch a reigning emblem of evanescence. For Johnson the emblem may have been particularly unsettling, because theater could seem at key moments a way out of what he perceived as the besetting problems of human time. In his moral writings, the mind's capacity to contract the time of real actions necessitates admonition. In his Preface to *Shakespeare*, it prompts celebration: it is the power that makes plays work, and helps them please. But the actual playhouse could also serve as site for all those components of temporality and problems of prolepsis that troubled Johnson most. On real stages, as in Macbeth's speech, poor players, in the midst of their delusive strut, have everything to fret about: the inevitable imminence of their own vanishing; the advent of the night, when they can work no more. The theater, though it figures in the Preface as a rare locus of temporal clarity, can also be a place of temporal damage and temporal delusion. "To-morrow's Action," to echo the caustic opening of Demetrius's celebrated speech, proves doubly fraudulent, not only because it is deferred until tomorrow but also because action itself—whether the real actions of real life or the stage action in which the performer playing Demetrius is now engaged—can come, as Johnson fears, as his watch plate warns, and as Macbeth insists, to nothing.

For all of this, Macbeth's poor player served Johnson as epitome. But for the prosperous player Garrick, and the passionate playgoer Boswell, Shakespeare's dark lines on theatrical evanescence amounted to a kind of mandate, a call to remedial action via stage and page. When, in 1769, Boswell audaciously suggested that Garrick had deserved a mention in Johnson's monumental *Shakespeare*, Johnson scornfully demurred:

> I complained that he had not mentioned Garrick in his Preface to Shakspeare; and asked him if he did not admire him. JOHNSON. "Yes, as 'a poor player, who frets and struts his hour upon the stage;'—as a shadow." BOSWELL. "But has he not brought Shakspeare into notice?" JOHNSON. "Sir, to allow that, would be to lampoon the age. Many of Shakspeare's plays are the worse for being acted: *Macbeth*, for instance." BOSWELL. "What, Sir, is nothing gained by decoration and action? Indeed, I do wish that you had mentioned Garrick." (*Life*, 2:92, italics added)

Here an old argument about page vs. stage meshes with one about actors, time, and permanence, to which Garrick's greatness had begun to impart new urgency. In Johnson's dictum, Macbeth's own printed testimony about strutting, fretting, and shadows, in a text that Johnson singles out as better read than staged, gives grounds sufficient for dismissing those poor players who make bold to impersonate him. And even Boswell, though enraptured with the playhouse and already deeply engaged in the ways print might render the ephemeral permanent, confirms by his rueful anxiety ("Indeed, I do wish that you had mentioned Garrick") the common wisdom that actors, left to the stage alone, unprotected and unpreserved by other media, possessed no prospect of immortality.

Garrick knew Johnson's reckoning well; it chimed with his own misgivings as to the durability of theatrical fame. "He was," Boswell reports, "always jealous that Johnson spoke lightly of him. I recollect his exhibiting [that is, mimicking] him to me one day, as if [Johnson were] saying, 'Davy has some convivial pleasantry about him, but 'tis a futile fellow'" (*Life*, 2:326). Like teacher, like pupil. Garrick, too, feared the futility implicit in his profession, but he learned to work the fear for all it was worth, by means of a carefully calculated, deeply theatrical prolepsis. He was perhaps the first celebrity to harp adroitly on the matter of his own mortality, deploying the inevitability of his evanescence as a means of ramping up his postmortem staying power. In the prologue he wrote for his best play, *The Clandestine Marriage* (1766), Garrick contrasted his own position as artist with that of his friend the late William Hogarth, on whose series *Marriage A-la-mode* the plot of this new comedy was based:

> The painter dead, yet still he charms the eye;
> While England lives, his fame can never die.
> But he who struts his hour upon the stage
> Can scarce protract his fame for half an age;
> Nor pen nor pencil can the actor save,
> The art and artist share one common grave.[19]

"But he who struts his hour upon the stage": Garrick here reworks Macbeth's words to address a specific hour in his own and his audience's lives. He had recently returned,

19. David Garrick, prologue, *The Clandestine Marriage*, in *The Plays of David Garrick*, ed. Harry William Pedicord and Fredrick Louis Bergmann, 7 vols. (Carbondale, Ill., 1980–82), 1:256, lines 17–22.

with his energies much depleted, from a twenty-month tour of Europe, during which he had survived an illness that he had at first feared was terminal. His tempo of performance had attenuated accordingly; till now, during his years at Drury Lane, he had performed on an average of ninety evenings a season; in this, his first season back, he would do only thirty. For the premiere of *The Clandestine Marriage* he had even given to someone else the juicy comic role he had originally written for himself; and the very words of this prologue were delivered on opening night not by Garrick but by Charles Holland, the actor who had stood in for him as surrogate during his time abroad. The occasion is haunted by all these layered absences, and via the verse, by one more, too: into the present instant of the prologue's performance, Garrick folds that future moment, imaginable and inevitable, of his permanent disappearance into the art's and artist's common grave. But the theater's propensity toward prolepsis and evanescence, which prove so troubling for Johnson, here become for Garrick a kind of inverse opportunity. He is practicing, with a conjurer's power, the arts of anticipatory nostalgia: love me now; you'll miss me soon.

He found in later years that the proleptic trope might work more powerfully as joke, not lamentation. In his little rehearsal play *The Meeting of the Company* (1774), Garrick's comic doppelganger, the actor-manager Mr. Patent, blithely sums up the intermittently brutal treatment he has recently received from the newspapers: "Ay, ay," he says, "they killed me one day and revived me the next. Newspaper life, like real life, is chequered. . . . What they took away yesterday they'll give again tomorrow, sometimes dead, sometimes alive. . . . If the fools of our profession would have more sensibility upon the stage and less off it, they might strut their hour without fretting."[20] That last loud echo of *Macbeth* caps off a subtler sequence of tragic allusion and comic reversal. Patent effectually translates Macbeth's doomy incantation—"Tomorrow and tomorrow and tomorrow"—into something sprightlier: "What they took away yesterday they'll give again tomorrow, sometimes dead, sometimes alive"—with "alive" cheerily ensuing *after* "dead." The sequence indexes the actor's peculiar powers of resilience and neutralizes, at least within the confines of the joke, the danger of his total destruction, his utter disappearance into the common grave.

Garrick's tactic, of tangled prolepsis as the comic antidote to evanescence, reached its apogee in a prologue so successful that its performance became a hot-ticket annual event. The purpose of the piece (which in some years he delivered as epilogue instead) was to raise money for the Theatrical Fund Garrick had created for the benefit of aging actors; its method was to invoke all the deaths those actors had undergone on stage:

> Sha'n't I, who oft have drench'd my hands in gore,
> Stabb'd many, poison'd some, beheaded more:
> Who numbers slew in battle on this plain,
> Sha'n't I, the slayer, try to feed the slain?

20. Garrick, *The Meeting of the Company*, in *The Plays of David Garrick*., 2:240, lines 70–79.

Brother to all, with equal love I view
The men who slew me, and the men I slew.
I must, I will, this happy project seize,
That those, too old to die, may live with ease.
Suppose the babes I smothered in the Tower
By chance or sickness lose their acting power.
Shall they, once princes, worse than all be served,
In childhood murdered, and in manhood starved?[21]

Dead every evening, alive the next night, and with so many years still ahead that it will take a Theatrical Fund to sustain them: Garrick's verse confers on actors an extraordinary staying power; it scrambles the future with the present to produce a temporal leapfrog so comically chaotic as to forestall, at least while the laughter lasts, the prospect of these artists' annihilation. Still, in the poem's last lines, the aging Garrick traded wit for sentiment. A letter from Hannah More to a friend shows how the move hit home: "He spoke a charming Epilogue of his own; in which He displayd an infinite Variety of Powers. . . . Yet *my Heart ach'd* [her italics] for the Depredations Time is beginning to make in his Face . . . of which He affectingly reminded us in these Words[:] 'I was *young* Hamlet once.'" Here, at epilogue's end, Garrick reverses Lady Macbeth, investing the present instant with not the future but the past. (Nostalgia is but prolepsis flipped.) Yet even More's response registers how deftly Garrick had managed, late in his career, to complicate the question of the actor's evanescence: "Surely," she exclaims mid-epistle, "He is above Mortality."[22]

"I was young Hamlet once": Boswell, at a signal moment in the *Life of Johnson*, lodges a comparable claim, and it is with a quick look at his time tricks that I'll conclude. The *Life* purveys its brand of retrospective prolepsis on practically every page. Take, as one among innumerable examples, its recounting of Johnson's and Garrick's life-changing trip to London in 1737. The biographical fact gets a single sentence; its residue over the long span since fills both a short paragraph, about an allegorical poem on the subject

21. Garrick, "An Occasional Prologue, spoken by Mr. Garrick," in *The Poetical Works of David Garrick*, ed. George Kearsley, 2 vols. (London, 1785), 2:326.

22. Dr. James Stonhouse to David Garrick, May 21, 1774, in *The Letters of David Garrick*, ed. David M. Little and George M. Kahrl, 3 vols. (Cambridge, Mass., 1963), 3:1358. Stonhouse's letter includes his transcription of More's. For studies of Garrick's intricate engagement with the question of immortality, see Michael S. Wilson, "Garrick, Iconic Acting, and the Ideologies of Theatrical Portraiture," *Word and Image* 6 (1990): 368–94; Shearer West, *The Image of the Actor: Verbal and Visual Representation in the Age of Garrick and Kemble* (London, 1991); Heather McPherson, "Garrickomania: Art, Celebrity, and the Imaging of Garrick," essay for the 2005 Folger Shakespeare Library exhibition *David Garrick (1717–1779), A Theatrical Life*, Folger Shakespeare Library website, http://www.folger.edu/template.cfm?cid=1465; and Stuart Sherman, "Garrick among Media: The '*Now* Performer' Navigates the News," *PMLA* 126 (2011): 966–82.

written decades afterward, and a long footnote, recounting Johnson's and Garrick's teasing back-and-forth recollections of the trip (*Life*, 1:101n1). This mode of prolepsis—retroactively stuffing the future via footnote into the long-ago datelined instant—is of course a privilege of prose narrative by and large unavailable to the theater; imagine trying to stage Fielding's *Tragedy of Tragedies* complete with commentary. But Boswell evinced throughout his writings, in the journals as well as the *Life*, a deep desire to claim for prose some of the privileges of theatrical time, by his methods for representing conversation as play text (speaker's name, speaker's utterance, stage directions), and by his habit of casting autobiographical anecdote into the prefabricated molds provided by well-known plays. That aspiration produces its most piquant effects in the famous account of Boswell's first meeting with Johnson, May 16, 1763, in the back of Thomas Davies's bookshop:

> Johnson unexpectedly came into the shop; and Mr. Davies having perceived him through the glass-door in the room in which we were sitting, advancing towards us,—he announced his aweful approach to me, somewhat in the manner of an actor in the part of Horatio, when he addresses Hamlet on the appearance of his father's ghost, "Look, my Lord, it comes." (*Life*, 1:391–92)

In this intricate game of time, the trump cards come from central casting, assigning multiple roles in layered time frames: Boswell, young Hamlet here, will in his future (our present) work as Shakespeare, too, staging this moment before his readers' eyes; Davies, playing Horatio, was himself once an actor, is in the text's present a bookseller, and in his future (our past) will become biographer, too (and of David Garrick, to boot); Johnson, then living, now dead, figures as proper, potent ghost and fresh-claimed father; and even the glass door gets a walk-through role as stand-in for Boswell's book, the glass through which we see—and feel—all these palimpsestic futures in this present instant of radically theatricalized narration.

For ordinary mortals, Johnson had argued throughout his work, prolepsis poses real dangers; it can do so, as he learned from *Irene* and from *Macbeth*, at the playhouse, too. But at the playhouse the human tendency to contract the time of real actions, to import the future into the present instant, can also entail both powers and privileges, variously distributed. Johnson awards them to the audience; Garrick to the actor; Boswell to the author.

The Agile Johnson

David Fairer

ONE OF THE MORE REMARKABLE but less familiar incidents during Johnson's Highland Tour of 1773 occurred at the inn at Inverness on the evening of August 29. The following morning Johnson and Boswell set off on horseback, beginning what Boswell terms their *equitation*, and he was struck by the transformation of the "laborious" Johnson of London into the figure he saw "for the first time on horseback, jaunting about at his ease in quest of pleasure and novelty." Boswell remarks that "To see Dr. Johnson in any new situation is always an interesting object to me . . . and the contrast made a strong impression on my imagination."[1]

But Boswell remains entirely silent on the "strong impression" Johnson must have given his imagination the previous night at the inn, and it is to the Reverend Alexander Grant, who supped with them, that we owe its preservation:

> Mr. Grant used to relate that on this occasion Johnson was in high spirits. In the course of conversation he mentioned that Mr. Banks (afterwards Sir Joseph) had, in his travels in New South Wales, discovered an extraordinary animal called the kangaroo. The appearance, conformation, and habits of this quadruped were of the most singular kind; and in order to render his description more vivid and graphic, Johnson rose from his chair and volunteered an imitation of the animal. The company stared; and Mr. Grant said nothing could be more ludicrous than the appearance of a tall, heavy, grave-looking man, like Dr. Johnson, standing up to mimic the shape and motions of a kangaroo. He stood erect, put out his hands like feelers, and, gathering up the tails of his huge brown coat so as to resemble the pouch of the animal, made two or three vigorous bounds across the room![2]

1. *Boswell's Life of Johnson, Together with Boswell's Journal of a Tour to the Hebrides and Johnson's Diary of a Journey into North Wales*, ed. George Birkbeck Hill, rev. L. F. Powell, 6 vols. (Oxford, 1934–50), 5:132 (hereafter cited as *Life*).

2. Boswell, *The Journal of a Tour to the Hebrides*, ed. Robert Carruthers (London, [1852]), 96. Carruthers records the anecdote in a footnote.

This memorable demonstration of Johnsonian agility was not a picture Boswell wanted to preserve, probably because of its element of the ludicrous, which the Reverend Grant no doubt highlighted in numerous retellings over the years. But it is helpful to reach beyond the vivid image and note the purpose of Johnson's performance. After offering the company a verbal account of the creature's "appearance, conformation, and habits," Johnson was prompted into physical action—"in order to render his description more vivid and graphic." He was not merely "doing an impression," as we might say, but using his body further to clarify and define the character of this new animal.[3]

The incident is offered, however, as a picture of incongruity and potential clumsiness, one of those occasions when Johnson's physical activity is seen as something indecorous, even embarrassing, an odd performance of a body not fully under control. Frances Reynolds recollected his "gigantick straddles," as she called them, "as if trying to make the floor to shake":

> On entering Sir Joshua's house with poor Mrs. Williams, a blind lady who lived with him, he would quit her hand, or else whirl her about on the steps as he whirled and twisted about to perform his gesticulations; and as soon as he had finish'd, he would give a sudden spring, and make such an extensive stride over the threshold, as if he was trying for a wager.[4]

As we read the various accounts of Johnson's stretchings, treadings, touchings, and other odd maneuvers, it is easy to overemphasize the pathological element and lose sight of the sheer physical playfulness. This came to the fore on a visit to Bennet Langton in Lincolnshire, when Johnson insisted on rolling down a steep hill, much to the concern of his friends: "we endeavoured to dissuade him," Langton recalled, "but he was resolute, saying, 'he had not had a roll for a long time.'"[5] Mrs. Thrale's account of one spontaneous expression of Johnsonian agility combines the grotesque and sublime:

> because he saw Mr. Thrale one day leap over a cabriolet stool, to shew that he was not tired after a chace of fifty miles or more, *he* suddenly jumped

3. The "Kanguroo" is described (from Banks's account) in John Hawkesworth, *An Account of the Voyages Undertaken by the Order of His Present Majesty for Making Discoveries in the Southern Hemisphere*, 3 vols. (London, 1773), 3:577–78. Hawkesworth remarks that "an idea of it will best be conceived by the cut, plate XX [facing p. 569], without which, the most accurate verbal description would answer very little purpose, as it has not similitude enough to any animal already known, to admit of illustration by reference." Hawkesworth's *Voyages*, with its illustration, had been published on June 9; see John Lawrence Abbott, *John Hawkesworth: Eighteenth-Century Man of Letters* (Madison, Wis., 1982), 151.

4. Frances Reynolds, "Recollections of Dr. Johnson," in *Johnsonian Miscellanies*, ed. George Birkbeck Hill (Oxford, 1897; reprint, New York, 1966), 2:275, 273. See also *Life*, 1:484–86.

5. Henry Digby Beste, *Personal and Literary Memorials* (London, 1829), 65 (see *Life*, 1:477n1). Beste refers to it as "this extraordinary freak of the great lexicographer," adding: "He must have been more than half a century old at the time of this *lark*. When old men, being also wise men, play fool's tricks, it ought to be considered as a good-natured condescension on their part" (65–66).

> over it too; but in a way so strange and so unwieldy, that our terror lest he should break his bones, took from us even the power of laughing.[6]

Again the clumsy and incongruous are stressed. Poor Johnson's love of movement, of twistings and turnings, reachings and rollings, is never far from caricature, as if it were merely quirky at one extreme, and pathological at the other, rather than something he might have enjoyed. This was, after all, the man who remarked in *Rambler* 85 (1751) on "how much happiness is gained, and how much misery escaped by frequent and violent agitation of the body."[7]

In what follows it is not Johnson's bodily agility that is my chief concern, but rather his agile mind. Nevertheless, this sense of unwieldy physicality will not be entirely absent; and it will be useful to preserve some sense of it, and of how close on occasion Johnson's agility is to what might be thought a degree of clumsiness. Boswell's observing him for the first time on horseback "jaunting about at his ease" can be glossed by Johnson himself: To JAUNT. *Verb*: "To wander here and there; to bustle about. It is now always used in contempt or levity." JAUNT. *Noun*: "[from the verb] . . . commonly used ludicrously."[8]

But the incident of the kangaroo, offered as a ludicrous picture, is a useful reminder that the agile Johnson is also a mind in focus. What might seem ungainly can evince concentration and precision. In describing the new creature, when his words reached their limit, Johnson happily put his body to use. The first substantial point to be made, therefore, has to be that Johnson's agility risks unwieldiness, but is in the service of precision. It is no mere flexibility, but rather the opposite: an aim for sharpness and more definition. This is especially important when considering his mental agility. It can often be present at moments of seeming clumsiness: indeed this can be a marker that Johnson's agile mind is at work.

A well-known example of Dictionary Johnson at his most unwieldy and incongruous is his definition of the word NETWORK: "Any thing reticulated or decussated, at equal distances, with interstices between the intersections." We seem momentarily to be at the wrong end of a telescope, with the word needed to define the definition rather than vice versa. But the adventure is only just beginning. In response, we look up RETICULATED. *Adjective*: "Made of network; formed with interstitial vacuities," and here we encounter *Woodward on Fossils*, noting their "pretty kind of *reticulated* work."[9] Now more curious, we turn to DECUSSATE. *Verb*: "to intersect at acute angles," a definition supported by two quotations from John Ray about the formation of the

6. Hester Lynch Thrale Piozzi, *Anecdotes of the Late Samuel Johnson LL.D*, in *Johnsonian Miscellanies*, 1:149–50, italics in original.

7. *The Rambler*, vols. 3–5 of *The Yale Edition of the Works of Samuel Johnson* (hereafter cited as *YE*), ed. W. J. Bate and Albrecht B. Strauss (New Haven, Conn., 1969), 4:83 (*Rambler* 85, January 8, 1751).

8. Samuel Johnson, *A Dictionary of the English Language: in Which the Words are Deduced from Their Originals and Illustrated in Their Different Significations by Examples from the Best Writers*, 2 vols. (London, 1755). All quotations from the *Dictionary* are from this edition.

9. John Woodward, *An Attempt Towards a Natural History of the Fossils of England*, 2 vols. (London, 1729), 1:49.

retinal image, the "*decussation* of the rays in the pupil of the eye" through which an inverted image allows itself to be viewed the right way up.[10] Having picked up this information we move to INTERSTICE: "Space between one thing and another," where we find Newton performing one of his optical experiments, shining a sunbeam through a comb placed behind a prism, in which "seven teeth together with their *interstices* took up an inch in breadth."[11] Returning to the original entry for NETWORK, we read the accompanying quotation, which is from Spenser's description of the spider's web in "Muiopotmos" (1591):

Nor any skill'd in workmanship emboss'd;
Nor any skill'd in loops of fing'ring fine;
Might in their diverse cunning ever dare,
With this so curious *network* to compare.[12]

We close, then, with the fineness and delicacy of a spider's web. The key word here is "skill'd." Johnson's little definitional *jaunt*, which we have followed, bespeaks the agility of a curious mind. What seemed a clumsy, overloaded definition has turned into an invitation to think more precisely, and with a wider understanding and delight, about various networks and how they function, whether those of nature, science, or the "curious network" of Johnson's own brilliant verbal web.

Johnson's definitions in the *Dictionary* can often have this discursive potential: To DEFINE. *Verb*: "To give the definition; to explain a thing by its qualities and circumstances." The move into *qualities and circumstances* can be particularly useful. The agility of Johnson's definitions lies in the way in which his words come across as ready for use. As well as synonyms we find precise placings—signs that become signals: SIGNAL. *Noun*: "A sign that gives notice." Johnson's definitions can often "give notice" in that pointed way, so that we sense their direction, what might lead from them. And this is true of his definition of *agile*.

What is immediately striking about this definition, which does not distinguish mental from physical agility, is the emphasis he places on the quality of readiness: AGILE. *Adjective*: "Nimble; ready; having the quality of being speedily put in motion; active." As often with Johnson's definitions, he attends to the etymology, here from the Latin *ago-agere*, literally to set in motion physically or morally, to drive, urge, impel, act. Nathan Bailey, for his definition of *agile*, had been content simply with "quick, nimble, swift."[13] Johnson shifts the emphasis to the *readiness to act* ("having the quality of being speedily put in motion"), moving in other words from mere nimbleness and

10. John Ray, *The Wisdom of God Manifested in the Works of the Creation*, 6th ed. (London, 1714), sig. B3r.

11. Sir Isaac Newton, *Opticks*, 4th ed. (London, 1730), 125.

12. Edmund Spenser, "Muiopotmos, or The Fate of the Butterflie," first printed in *Complaints. Containing Sundrie Small Poemes of the Worlds Vanitie* (London, 1591), 365–68.

13. Nathan Bailey, *An Universal Etymological English Dictionary* (London, 1721).

speed to the idea of responding to an impulse. Johnson draws *agile* into the context of responsive action, with all that might imply for the nature of one's character.

The idea is repeated in the definitions of both AGILENESS ("readiness for motion") and AGILITY ("readiness to move"). For Johnson, *agile* implies a kind of preparedness. This is clear from the second of the three supporting quotations, a reference in Matthew Hale's *Origin of Mankind*, to "the immediate and *agile* subservience of the spirits to the empire of the mind or soul."[14] *Agile subservience* seems a strange notion, until we realize that Johnson's leading idea is readiness and responsiveness, a potential for reactive activity.

Here lies a concept at the core of Johnsonian agility: his mind's "readiness for use." The phrase is Sir Joshua Reynolds's, in a note that singles out this feature of his friend:

> the most distinguished [quality] was his possessing a mind which was, as I may say, always ready for use. . . . In this respect few men ever came better prepared into whatever company chance might throw him, and the love which he had to society gave him a facility in the practice of applying his knowledge of the matter in hand in which I believe he was never exceeded by any man.[15]

Boswell makes the same point on many occasions, when he notes Johnson's *readiness*: "by reading and meditation, and a very close inspection of life, he had accumulated a great fund of miscellaneous knowledge, which, by a peculiar promptitude of mind, was ever ready at his call"; Boswell elsewhere records that "Dr. Johnson was in very good humour, lively, and ready to talk upon all subjects"; or simply "Johnson was . . . ready."[16] We can sense at these moments Boswell himself sharpening his mental pencil, readying himself for whatever this Johnsonian *promptitude* might bring.

Mrs. Thrale expresses the same idea more vividly:

> Promptitude of thought . . . and quickness of expression, were among the peculiar felicities of Johnson: his notions rose up like the dragon's teeth sowed by Cadmus all ready clothed, and in bright armour too, fit for immediate battle.[17]

One scene of many in Boswell's *Life* where this "promptitude of thought" is acted out occurs when Johnson and Boswell, along with Reynolds, visit Richard Owen Cambridge at his Twickenham villa, and meet their host in the library:

14. Sir Matthew Hale, *The Primitive Origination of Mankind, Considered and Examined According to the Light of Nature* (London, 1677), 21.

15. C. R. Leslie and Tom Taylor, *Life and Times of Sir Joshua Reynolds*, 2 vols. (London, 1865), 2:454–55 (*Life*, 2:365n1).

16. *Life*, 1:203–4; 2:99; 3:51; 1:467.

17. Piozzi, *Anecdotes*, reprinted in *Johnsonian Miscellanies*, 1:285.

> No sooner had we made our bow to Mr. Cambridge, in his library, than Johnson ran eagerly to one side of the room, intent on poring over the backs of the books. Sir Joshua observed, (aside,) "He runs to the books, as I do to the pictures: but I have the advantage. I can see much more of the pictures than he can of the books." Mr. Cambridge, upon this, politely said, "Dr. Johnson, I am going, with your pardon, to accuse myself, for I have the same custom which I perceive you have. But it seems odd that one should have such a desire to look at the backs of books." Johnson, ever ready for contest, instantly started from his reverie, wheeled about, and answered, "Sir, the reason is very plain. Knowledge is of two kinds. We know a subject ourselves, or we know where we can find information upon it. When we enquire into any subject, the first thing we have to do is to know what books have treated of it. This leads us to look at catalogues, and at the backs of books in libraries." Sir Joshua observed to me the extraordinary promptitude with which Johnson flew upon an argument. "Yes, (said I,) he has no formal preparation, no flourishing with his sword; he is through your body in an instant."[18]

What we might think of as Boswell's choreography of the scene, brings out Johnson's agility, from the moment he runs to the side of the room, to his sudden starting, and his wheeling about, to deliver what amounts to a disquisition to his courteous host. At first unsociably concentrated on the backs of the books, closed off and intent, he instantly swings round, opening up like a book himself, the pages turning briskly. Even at a moment when he seems inert and obtuse, he is agile, *ever ready*, waiting only for a prompt. And when the response comes it causes surprise: it is no mere reply but an articulate, reasoned discourse ("Knowledge is of two kinds . . ."), as if his mind has turned a page and alighted on the relevant passage.

Johnson's *agility* does not occur as a flash, or a spark of wit, but is offered as a more precise and considered response. It grows into something. In the Dedication of the *Life* Boswell speaks of "the wonderful fertility and readiness of Johnson's wit";[19] but although the term *wit* may catch the liveliness, it can miss the more substantial way in which an idea registers. On occasion the wit expands into that less often noted phenomenon, the Johnsonian *joke*, whose character extends beyond a moment of delighted recognition to something of richer effect. Mrs. Thrale records a delightful example:

> A young fellow, less confident of his own abilities, lamenting one day that he had lost all his Greek—"I believe it happened at the same time, Sir (said Johnson), that I lost all my large estate in Yorkshire."[20]

18. *Life*, 2:364–65.
19. *Life*, 1:3.
20. Piozzi, *Anecdotes*, in *Johnsonian Miscellanies*, 1:286.

It is delicately done, yet with a conclusiveness that allows not the smallest room for reply. The remark is couched as sympathy and fellow feeling—until that devastating dropping of the penny in the final silence. Tone is everything. Somehow the term *wit* does not quite fit this alert human responsiveness, which is less a remark than an engagement with an idea: here, a reflection on the self-comforting power of the might-have-been. Johnson makes it clear that the young man never lost what he did not own. Johnson's agility is not a sudden spark but an immediate readiness to catch the thought and open it up. At such moments, the prompt may be generated in an instant; but unlike the sparkish metaphysical wit that Johnson found so inimical,[21] the *agility* is capable of being sustained, of impressing itself on the mind, as in this piece of dialogue from the *Life*:

> BOSWELL. "Pray, Sir, is not Foote an infidel?" JOHNSON. "I do not know, Sir, that the fellow is an infidel; but if he be an infidel, he is an infidel as a dog is an infidel; that is to say, he has never thought upon the subject." BOSWELL. "I suppose, Sir, he has thought superficially, and seized the first notions which occurred to his mind." JOHNSON. "Why then, Sir, still he is like a dog, that snatches the piece next him. Did you never observe that dogs have not the power of comparing? A dog will take a small bit of meat as readily as a large, when both are before him."[22]

The sharpness of this is not a matter of wit but of observation and mental agility, Johnson's readiness of response. Boswell's question about Samuel Foote's irreligion brings not a witty image but an analogy with a theological point. When Boswell suggests it is a case of Foote's human failings, his superficial "first notions," Johnson is not distracted and makes no concession: he stays with the dog and draws on his store of observation, his ready knowledge of the canine mind, pursuing his analogy further. Although the human infidel fades from the picture, the issue of human choice and animal choice is uncomfortably driven home. It seems a natural maneuver, but the point has been sharpened in the process. Unlike the dog, Johnson does not seize on the nearest morsel but keeps his eye on the important matter.

Johnsonian agility is not just making a witty *turn* but finding a direction in the process. To use Johnson's distinction, it is "strength of thought" rather than "happiness of language."[23] It is more than a witty comparison at which we smile and move on. Once again the key element is being ready, having a thought in store that can branch and develop. This is where Johnson's moral landscape plays its part, his familiar terrain of principles, judgments, and distinctions. An appeal to this home ground can on

21. "Cowley," *The Lives of the Most Eminent Poets: With Critical Observations on Their Works*, ed. Roger Lonsdale, 4 vols. (Oxford, 2006), 1:199–200.

22. *Life*, 2:95–96.

23. *Lives of the Poets*, 1:200.

occasion become mechanical; but when his mind is agile, the result is forceful, even incontrovertible, as in the following exchange with Dr. William Adams of Pembroke College, on the thorny topic of the Earl of Chesterfield. Johnson's famous letter has been causing a stir (the italics are Boswell's):

> Dr. Adams . . . insisted on Lord Chesterfield's general affability and easiness of access, especially to literary men. "Sir, (said Johnson) that is not Lord Chesterfield; he is the proudest man this day existing." "No, (said Dr. Adams) there is one person, at least, as proud; I think, by your own account, you are the prouder man of the two." "But mine (replied Johnson, instantly) was *defensive* pride." This, as Dr Adams well observed, was one of those happy turns for which he was so remarkably ready.[24]

It is an agile move; but such a "happy turn" could not have been made without a reserve of deep thought about himself and his lost patron. Again, "wit" does not seem the *mot juste* here for an idea finding such resolved deliverance. Johnson's is more than a neat reply, it is a resolute response. One of the *Dictionary*'s definitions for *Resolution* is "settled thought," and this is the demand Johnson makes of true wit, which, though sharp and fresh, should have the virtue of being a settled thought rather than a light fancy. He could of course enjoy the airy playfulness of wit, but to be anything more it should tap into the natural and just: it never flies free of human experience. In his life of Cowley, after his assault on the superficialities of "metaphysical" wit, we find him immediately praising Cowley himself for his poetic *agility*. Johnson uses the term to underline his crucial distinction between the agile and the merely flexible:

> [Cowley's] *Chronicle* is a composition unrivalled and alone: such gaiety of fancy, such facility of expression, such varied similitude, such a succession of images, and such a dance of words, it is vain to expect except from Cowley. His strength always appears in his agility; his volatility is not the flutter of a light, but the bound of an elastic mind. His levity never leaves his learning behind it; the moralist, the politician, and the critic, mingle their influence even in this airy frolick of genius.[25]

Johnson is determined to dissociate agility from mere lightness or levity. It does not flutter, but has a responsive energy within a field of force: it is "the bound of an elastic mind." Elastick. *Adjective*: "Having the power of returning to the form from which it is distorted or withheld." *Agility* is again marked out by its responsive strength, and part of its strength is its combination of restlessness and tenacity: it feels the pull of that experiential home ground.

24. *Life*, 1:265–66, italics in original.
25. *Lives of the Poets*, 1:215.

It is no surprise, therefore, to find that the opposite pull from Johnsonian agility is toward *ease*. Here there is no dancing but something much more sedentary, a relaxing into what is comfortable and conformable. In *Rambler* 85 he makes just this contrast:

> Ease is the utmost that can be hoped from a sedentary and unactive habit; ease, a neutral state between pain and pleasure. The dance of spirits, the bound of vigour, readiness of enterprize, and defiance of fatigue, are reserved for him that braces his nerves, and hardens his fibres, that keeps his limbs pliant with motion.[26]

It is the agile quality that Johnson admires here, signaled by that phrase "readiness of enterprize." There is no neutrality; instead we are in a force field, braced, expectant, defiant, even. "The bound of vigour" again suggests as much a quality of the spirit as of the body. Like Cowley's "dance of words," this "dance of spirits" has an elastic energy, whereas an unchallenging life of ease and acquiescence is in danger of sapping the mental energies, too.

This scenario is developed in the story of Vivaculus in *Rambler* 177 (1751). Here is someone blessed with the possibility of evermore pleasing himself. Finding himself in possession of an independent estate and sufficient wealth, the lively young man determines to exploit his situation of being able to shape his world to his tastes and wishes. Self-congratulation and complacence guide Vivaculus's days of intellectual pleasure and indulgence, where every choice becomes a selection. Nothing is there to check or thwart him, and at first he lives "with complete acquiescence in my own plan of conduct." But the very ease begins its inevitable process of sapping his energies. With nothing to block or deny him, and nothing to challenge or impel him, either, his life begins to atrophy, and his mind loses its *agility*. The process of relaxation is insidious: "[I]n time, I began to find my mind contracted and stiffened by solitude. My ease and elegance were sensibly impaired; I was no longer able to accommodate myself with readiness to the accidental current of conversation, my notions grew particular and paradoxical, and my phraseology formal and unfashionable. I spoke, on common occasions, the language of books. My quickness of apprehension, and celerity of reply, had entirely deserted me."[27]

Vivaculus has lost that mental readiness. Becoming set in his ways, he has gradually ceased to be part of debate, response, and alert mental activity. The "accidental current of conversation" (just what Johnson himself thrived on) leaves him behind: he can no longer steer through it, and so he takes refuge in set ideas, a fixed kind of wit no longer part of a round of lively promptings and replies.

One of the professed aims of *The Rambler* is to stir the mind into activity, not by novelty and amusement, but by setting it in deliberative motion. This is easily mistaken for ponderousness, and for many readers, "agile" would be the last word to come

26. *YE*, 4:83.
27. *YE*, 5:169 (*Rambler* 177; November 26, 1751).

to mind.[28] From the beginning, pomp, dignity, and solemnity were stylistic attributes singled out for praise.[29] But, to speak personally, when I enter that mind, I sense how it is keeping my own in motion, not drawing it along a single path but creating a mental space through which thoughts can move. The consciousness of *The Rambler* is a circumspect one, in the literal sense: it looks around, turns to face complications, considers qualifications, measures up to objections, and in all finds a direction and purpose.

A notable example is *Rambler* 52 (1750), Johnson's consideration of how far grief and loss can be assuaged by thoughts of the greater miseries of others. As he moves through a series of scenarios, we begin to understand that Johnson's aim is not to bring ease but to locate ways in which the grieving mind can exercise itself, how it can begin to engage with a situation, and what resources might be employed. His answer seems to be to find within our thoughts a kind of systolic rhythm, the pulse of life itself, expanding and contracting by turns, moving out from the self to the miseries of the world, and back to the confines of our own heart:

> Thus when we look abroad, and behold the multitudes that are groaning under evils heavier than those which we have experienced, we shrink back to our own state, and instead of repining that so much must be felt, learn to rejoice that we have not more to feel.

In that agile move from *repine* to *rejoice*, a retrenchment into our own limited situation is followed by an elastic springing back of the spirit. There is an appropriate moment to "shrink," but from that shrinking we can "learn to rejoice" and expand our minds again:

> By this observation of the miseries of others, fortitude is strengthened, and the mind brought to a more extensive knowledge of her own powers. As the heroes of action catch the flame from one another, so they to whom providence has allotted the harder task of suffering with calmness and dignity, may animate themselves by the remembrance of those evils which have been laid on others, perhaps naturally as weak as themselves, and bear up with vigour and resolution against their own oppressions, when they see it possible that more severe afflictions may be born.[30]

Again, we repeatedly move between self and others, from a core of feeling to a wider sympathy, and back again, and in the process Johnson draws energy and animation out of seemingly passive suffering. The phrase "heroes of action" assumes there is another kind of heroism, too: not mere stoical acceptance, but an engagement with the "harder

28. Discussing Topham Beauclerk's "keenness of mind," Johnson remarked to Boswell: "every thing comes from him so easily. It appears to me that I labour, when I say a good thing." Boswell replied: "You are loud, sir; but it is not an effort of mind" (*Life*, 5:76–77).

29. See some of the early criticism of the *Rambler* essays extracted in *Johnson: The Critical Heritage*, ed. James T. Boulton (London, 1972), 68–89.

30. *YE*, 3:283 (*Rambler* 52; September 15, 1750).

task of suffering," and he finds there an expansion of the mind, "a more extensive knowledge of her own powers."

It is vital for Johnson that this mental agility be differentiated from the unimpeded projections that often pass for strength of thought—what Johnson refers to in *Rasselas* as "visionary bustle."[31] Johnson knows how readily the mind delights in flexing itself among the deceptive phantoms of hope and pride, and a good deal of Johnsonian comedy is to be had from such false expansiveness. In the experience of the sublime, for example, he finds only limitation. Addison may have remarked that "Our Imagination loves to be filled with an Object,"[32] but for Johnson this is constraining, a suspension of the mental energies. He says in *Rambler* 137:

> Wonder is a pause of reason, a sudden cessation of the mental progress, which lasts only while the understanding is fixed upon some single idea, and is at an end when it recovers force enough to divide the object into its parts, or mark the intermediate gradations from the first agent to the last consequence.[33]

The mind only "recovers force" when it grapples with an idea, makes distinctions, and marks discursive gradations. This is where the agility lies: not in the sweep of thought but in its strenuous exercise. Johnson values elasticity of mind not for its reach but for its ability to return home.

This difficult agility of Johnson's mind is evident in the *Rambler* essays and also characterizes some of his best poetry. The effect can sometimes be awkward, but it is so in a powerful, uncompromising way. In writing elsewhere about "the awkward Johnson," I have suggested that he is always alert to false notes of fluency and ease, to the allurements of polished elegance, and in his poetry he works to halt the flow and introduce resistant elements: "Others with softer Smiles, and subtler Art, / Can sap the Principles, or taint the Heart."[34] As I have been attempting to show, Johnson's concept of agility is not incompatible with these elements of awkwardness; on the contrary, his mental energies are sharpened by resistance, by the untoward, and whatever might check and impede. He works his way through contingency and difficulty. The awkward and uncomfortable elements are integral to the intelligent movements of his thought.

When we read the memorable passage about the fallen patron in *The Vanity of Human Wishes*, we realize that it is premised on the loss of that graceful ease that had once oiled the wheels of patronage and sustained a whole world of ingratiating politeness and ambitious insinuation. The show has come to an end, and so, instead of a

31. *Rasselas and Other Tales*, vol. 16 of *YE*, ed. Gwin J. Kolb (1990), 18.

32. *Spectator* 412 (June 23, 1712), in *The Spectator*, ed. Donald F. Bond, 5 vols. (Oxford, 1965), 3:540.

33. *YE*, 4:360 (*Rambler* 137; July 9, 1751).

34. Johnson, *London: A Poem, in Imitation of the Third Satire of Juvenal* (London, 1738), 75–76, in *The Complete English Poems*, ed. J. D. Fleeman (Harmondsworth, UK, 1971), 63. See David Fairer, "The Awkward Johnson," in *Johnson After 300 Years*, ed. Greg Clingham and Philip Smallwood (Cambridge, 2009), 145–63.

composed scene, we are presented with a pageant in which various forces begin to work against each other. The flow of patronage, pleasure, and advancement has been diverted elsewhere, and the place is closing down. The agile way in which Johnson negotiates this disintegration puts pressure on his language, and in doing so brings home the embarrassment and indignity of the scene:

Unnumber'd Suppliants croud Preferment's Gate,
Athirst for Wealth, and burning to be great;
Delusive Fortune hears th'incessant Call,
They mount, they shine, evaporate, and fall.
On ev'ry Stage the Foes of Peace attend,
Hate dogs their Flight, and Insult mocks their End.
Love ends with Hope, the sinking Statesman's Door
Pours in the Morning Worshiper no more;
For growing Names the weekly Scribbler lies,
To growing Wealth the Dedicator flies,
From every Room descends the painted Face,
That hung the bright *Palladium* of the Place,
And smoak'd in Kitchens, or in Auctions sold,
To better Features yields the Frame of Gold;
For now no more we trace in ev'ry Line
Heroic Worth, Benevolence Divine:
The Form distorted justifies the Fall,
And Detestation rids th'indignant Wall.[35]

In manuscript, the crowd of suppliants were originally "*panting* to be great";[36] but with the subtle shift to *burning*, Johnson sets the elements in tension: "Athirst for Wealth, and burning to be great" now hints at a dual self-torture in which the burning ambition is mocked rather than assuaged by the thirst for riches. The various movements, too, are checked or reversed, as things mount and sink, grow and descend, shine and smoke. The "growing Names" and "growing Wealth" seem positive, until we realize that in this scene of loss and diminution, the men of *growing* reputation and wealth are now elsewhere. The lively picture changes, and Johnson's agility is to convey a restless, crowded scene in course of thinning out: fullness emptying. The momentum is retained, but subtly the activity shifts from the busy secretaries to the busy bailiffs. What began by pouring in, now drains out. What drew the "Worshiper," the iconic *Palladium* of the place, ends up as scrap metal. It is a frenetic passage, itself a passage rather than a structured description, given the insidious way the details slip, merge, turn round, and melt away. The description is at all points in process; it is not framed so much as taken out of its frame, like the generic family portraits, and rolled up as we

35. Johnson, *The Vanity of Human Wishes. The Tenth Satire of Juvenal, Imitated* (London, 1749), 73–90, in *Complete English Poems*, 84–85.

36. See *Complete English Poems*, 169.

read. The terms shift. That dignified and potentially triumphant pentameter, "Heroic Worth, Benevolence Divine," stands in glorious graceful isolation, a self-contained line that is less a description than a superseded *in*scription ("For now no more we trace in ev'ry Line / Heroic Worth, Benevolence Divine"). "The Form distorted . . . ," the passage continues, toying with the ambiguous implications of that faded and now untraceable *Line*—the lineaments of a once handsome face? The noble line of ancestors? Or Johnson's own lines, through which we watch the nobility and easy command inexorably slip away? "The Form distorted justifies the Fall, / And Detestation rids th'indignant Wall"—that word "indignant" perhaps reflecting the last glimmer of the building's lost dignity.

This, I would contend, is agile writing. It is a compressed poetic style, not easy or fluent, but negotiating a difficult dreamlike terrain on the edge of nightmare. Once again, it is all too easy to think of it as *ponderous*, but if it is so, it is in Johnson's own three senses of that adjective: 1. Heavy; weighty. 2. Important; momentous. 3. Forcible; strongly impulsive. How interesting that in Johnson's *Dictionary* there is no mention of *clumsy, unwieldy, slow, tedious, laboured, dull, verbose, pompous*—all of which terms feature under "Ponderous" in the modern *OED*. And it is equally intriguing to note that Johnson's final dynamic sense of "forcible; strongly impulsive" is entirely missing from that standard modern dictionary.

This essay opened with Johnson as a kangaroo. But in the end, it is perhaps another animal, seemingly incongruous and unwieldy, that best represents those agile aspects of his mind that I have been exploring—and it is an analogy that evidently had the sanction of the man himself. Mrs. Thrale recalled an occasion when Johnson's friends attempted to characterize his mind:

> He was not at all offended, when comparing all our acquaintance to some animal or other, we pitched upon the elephant for his resemblance, adding that the proboscis of that creature was like his mind most exactly, strong to buffet even the tyger, and pliable to pick up even the pin.[37]

This delightful picture of Johnson's mind as an elephant's trunk catches perfectly the way in which his potential clumsiness and his mental agility are part of the same phenomenon. We may recall how in Milton's Paradise, Adam and Eve are entertained by "th'unwieldy Elephant," who "to make them mirth us'd all his might, and wreath'd / His Lithe Proboscis."[38] It is a picture of strength as well as agility, and Johnson was not embarrassed by the implied similitude. His friends understood their man, and knew that although he was not always light on his feet, his mental agility was an extension of a commanding strength.

37. Piozzi, *Anecdotes*, in *Johnsonian Miscellanies*, 1:287.

38. Milton, *Paradise Lost*, 2nd ed. (1674), 4.345–47. William Hazlitt (mis)quotes these lines to characterize what he calls Johnson's "efforts at playfulness"; see "On the Periodical Essayists," *Lectures on the English Comic Writers*, in *The Complete Works of William Hazlitt*, ed. P. P. Howe, 21 vols. (London and Toronto, 1930–34), 6:101.

In March 1781 a notice appeared in *The Morning Post* that the great Dr. Johnson was taking dancing lessons from the famous Signor Vestris, and it reported:

> our correspondent assures us, that the Doctor has improved so rapidly in the *minuet de la cour*, that it is thought he will be done out of hand in less than a fortnight. The Doctor's first appearance in public, it is said, will be before their Majesties at St James's, and that he is to be honoured with the fair hand of Her Grace of Devonshire: such is the rumour of the day.

At the next meeting of The Club, Johnson's friends wondered what to do. As Boswell records:

> I ventured to mention a ludicrous paragraph in the newspapers, that Dr. Johnson was learning to dance of Vestris. Lord Charlemont, wishing to excite him to talk, proposed, in a whisper, that he should be asked, whether it was true. "Shall I ask him?" said his Lordship. We were, by a great majority, clear for the experiment. Upon which his Lordship very gravely, and with a courteous air said, "Pray, Sir, is it true that you are taking lessons of Vestris?" This was risking a good deal, and required the boldness of a General of Irish Volunteers to make the attempt. Johnson was at first startled, and in some heat answered, "How can your Lordship ask so simple a question?" But immediately recovering himself, whether from unwillingness to be deceived, or to appear deceived, or whether from real good humour, he kept up the joke: "Nay, but if any body were to answer the paragraph, and contradict it, I'd have a reply, and would say, that he who contradicted it was no friend either to Vestris or to me. For why should not Dr. Johnson add to his other powers a little corporeal agility? . . . Then it might proceed to say, that this Johnson, not content with dancing on the ground, might dance on the rope; and they might introduce the elephant dancing on the rope."[39]

With an impressively agile turn of foot, Johnson not only swings the joke around but develops it into a playful fantasy. Consciously performing for his friends, and for us, he leaves us all with a final delightful image of Johnsonian agility, unabashedly embracing the potentially clumsy but turning it into a dance of triumph.

39. *Life*, 4:79.

“’Tis well an old age is out”: Johnson, Swift, and His Generation

Howard D. Weinbrot

JOHNSON’S *LIVES OF THE POETS* (1779–81) immediately became transcendent assets for the arts of biography, literary criticism, and human assessment. The *Annual Register* (1784) insisted that no age or country had “ever produced a species of criticism more perfect in its kind.” Boswell later said that the collection was as if “by some modern Aristotle or Longinus . . . such as no other nation can shew.”[1] The *Lives* soon also were scolded for their apparent evaluative heresy. In that more sentimental and whiggish age, Johnson seemed guilty of denigrating Gray’s nationalist odes and Milton’s republicanism. Thomas Sheridan made the prosecution’s case in his own life of Swift. Johnson’s strictures on great geniuses evoked “indignation” from their admirers and “great regret” from Johnson’s friends. Johnson’s “Swift,” Sheridan says among other graceful subtletics, was “miserably executed,” a “disgrace,” “contemptible,” “shameful,” and “invidious.”[2] As the less testosterone-poisoned John Courtenay notes, Johnson

1. The essay’s title is from the second-to-last line of Dryden’s “Secular Masque” (1700), reflecting his discontent with the loves, wars, and general disruptions of his lifetime. For the references in the text, see *The Annual Register, or a View of the History, Politics, and Literature, for the Year 1782* (London, 1784), 203; *Boswell’s Life of Johnson, Together with Boswell’s Journal of a Tour to the Hebrides and Johnson’s Diary of a Journey into North Wales*, ed. George Birkbeck Hill, rev. L. F. Powell, 6 vols. (Oxford, 1934–50), 4:35–36 (hereafter cited as *Life*). Johnson expected and welcomed criticism as a form of publicity (*Life*, 3:375) and as intellectual contest: he was “entrusted with a certain portion of truth. I have given my opinion sincerely; let them shew where they think me wrong” (4:65). See also 63–65 for some of the detractions that Boswell called “feeble, though shrill” (65).

2. Thomas Sheridan, *The Life of the Rev. Dr. Jonathan Swift, Dean of St. Patrick’s, Dublin* (1784), 2nd ed. (London, 1787), sig. A7v (indignation and great regret), 447–55 (the insults). Sheridan no doubt included Johnson’s “Swift” as part of the “foulmouthed calumny” inflicted on the author (sig. A8v). Percival Stockdale was among those so outraged by Johnson’s lapses that he often labeled the *Lives* “a disgrace to English literature.” Stockdale hoped to cleanse that stain with his own *Lectures on the Truly Eminent English Poets* (London, 1807), which, perhaps sadly, few chose to hear or to read. For an example of Johnson as a disgrace, see *The Seasons, by James Thomson; with His Life, an Index, and Glossary . . . and Notes to The Seasons, by Percival Stockdale* (London, 1793), [246]. Stockdale used that term in letters to friends as well as in his *Lectures*; see, for instance, Stockdale to Edward Jerningham, March 30, 1793, Huntington Library, MS JE 832, transcribed in Howard D. Weinbrot, “Samuel Johnson, Percival Stockdale, and Brick-bats from Grubstreet: Some Later Response to the *Lives of the Poets*,”

"By subtle doubts would Swift's fair fame invade, / And round his brows the ray of glory shade."[3] Fellow Swiftians today also seem puzzled by Johnson's insufficient veneration for the Dean as man and as preeminent man of letters.[4]

Some of these responses are as perplexing as they are perplexed.[5] After all, the "excremental vision" to which Johnson objected has been discussed by twentieth-century critics from both psychoanalytic and historical perspectives.[6] Certain con-

Huntington Library Quarterly 56 (1993): 105–34 at 127–29, reprinted in Weinbrot, *Aspects of Samuel Johnson: Essays on His Arts, Mind, Afterlife, and Politics* (Newark, Del., 2005), 241–69.

3. John Courtenay, *A Poetical Review of the Literary and Moral Character of the Late Samuel Johnson, L.L.D. with Notes*, 3rd ed. (London, 1786), 3. In a gloss on this passage, Courtenay complains that Johnson unfairly quoted Sir Richard Blackmore's attack on *A Tale of a Tub* (1704) as sarcastic and spiteful toward the state religion. For Courtenay, this is the "malevolent dullness of bigotry": the *Tale* "is a continual panegyrick on the Church of England, and a bitter satire on Popery, Calvinism, and every sect of dissenters" (3n3). Courtenay nevertheless is both fair and admiring, saying of Johnson: "In judgment keen, he acts the critick's part, / By reason proves the feelings of the heart; / In thought profound, in nature's study wise, / Shews from what source our fine sensations rise; / With truth, precision, fancy's claims defines, / And throws new splendour o'er the poet's lines" (16). The note to the last line reads "See his admirable *Lives of the Poets*, and particularly his Disquisition on metaphysical and religious poetry" (16n31). For Johnson, see *The Lives of the Poets*, vols. 21–23 of *The Yale Edition of the Works of Samuel Johnson* (hereafter cited as *YE*), ed. John H. Middendorf (New Haven, Conn., 2010), 22:767–68. Blackmore's hostility to *A Tale* was part of a larger and continuing eighteenth-century response to it. See, among other examples, the Unitarian Richard Moseley's *A Letter to the Right Reverend the Lord Bishop of Clogher, in Ireland, Occasioned by His Lordship's Essay on Spirit: To which is Added, a Letter to the Right Honourable John Earl of Orrery: Occasioned by the Character Which His Lordship Gives of Dean Swift's Sermon On the Trinity, in His Remarks on the Life and Writings of the Dean* (London, 1752). According to Moseley, Swift does not understand the Trinity, and he always was quite mad: "I do not intend by this to accuse the *Dean* of having ridiculed the Doctrine of the Trinity in his Sermon, though he has done so in his *TALE OF A TUB*; but . . . he was a very unfit Person to write upon that Subject; who, it is plain from his numerous other Writings . . . had never made Christianity, or indeed any Thing that was *serious*, his study" (42).

4. John T. Scanlan summarizes much of the consternation in "'He Hates Much Trouble': Johnson's *Life of Swift* and the Contours of Biographical Inheritance in Late Eighteenth-Century England," in *Representations of Swift*, ed. Brian A. Connery (Newark, Del., 2002), 99–116. There is a common denominator among those who have studied Johnson on Swift: something must have gone terribly wrong for Johnson to have blundered so badly. That also is the common denominator for Miltonists and students of the Metaphysical poets, among others. Johnson was not willing to beatify, much less to sanctify, literary or other human works. Perhaps the life of Watts comes closest to being an exception. Here is the probable reason: in his work, "philosophy is subservient to evangelical instruction; it is difficult to read a page without learning, or at least wishing, to be better. The attention is caught by indirect instruction, and he that sat down only to reason is on a sudden compelled to pray." See "Watts," *YE*, 23:1305. Johnson was unable to find much positive instruction in Swift that helped the reader "to be better."

5. The need to think well of Swift's private life is based in part on Thomas Sheridan's assumption: "it is of moment to the general cause of religion and morality, to make it appear, that the greatest Genius of the age, was, at the same time, a man of the truest piety, and most exalted virtue"; Sheridan, *Life of Swift*, sig. A8v. Most readers today are comfortable with a different assumption, one that Johnson regularly urged but, as in the case of Swift, did not always practice: a writer's art may be inferior to his life; unless the life is monstrous, it is the art that matters.

6. Johnson devotes a paragraph to his perception that "the greatest difficulty that occurs in analysing [Swift's] character is to discover by what depravity of intellect he took delight in revolving

temporaries were troubled by Johnson's life of Swift, but many also thought it familiar, accurate, or both. One critic wrote that Lord Orrery's *Remarks on the Life and Writings of Dr. Jonathan Swift* (1751) allows us to see Swift's "real Character," admire his wit, but "tremble at the Lengths it often carried him." The *Annual Register* later said that the life was "well executed, [but] little new was to be expected." W. H. abstracted it for his *Beauties of Swift* (1782) and praised Johnson's effort for being "as just as it is elegant."[7] Objectors then and now nonetheless rightly sensed that Johnson was dismayed by aspects of Swift's life and art. Such misgivings should not surprise us. Swift and Johnson were radically different men in radically different ages in radically different countries. I cite a few of these differences.

ideas, from which almost every other mind shrinks with disgust" (*YE*, 22:2010). Perhaps the best-known and most often reprinted psychoanalytic statement of Swift's apparently murky "ideas" is in Norman O. Brown's chapter "The Excremental Vision," in *Life Against Death: The Psychoanalytical Meaning of History* (Middletown, Conn., 1959), 179–201. For one of several respectful modifications of Brown's point of view, see Donald T. Siebert, "Swift's *Fiat Odor*: The Excremental Re-Vision," *Eighteenth-Century Studies* 19 (1985–86): 21–38. Siebert's notes, especially 21n1, list several other discussions of Swift's "scatological" poems, together with general studies of his poetry. The quotation marks frequently put around *scatological* in modern criticism connote the change of attitude toward such "depravity of intellect." In one respect, Siebert nonetheless seconds Johnson. He observes of "Strephon and Chloe": "one could scarcely think of a work more bent on destroying . . . illusions by the coarsest, most indelicate means available" (30). For a historical approach to Swift's presumed depravity, see particularly Carole Fabricant's discussion "Excremental Vision vs. Excremental Reality," in *Swift's Landscape* (Baltimore, 1982), 24–42. She briefly summarizes the psychological vs. the "landscape" explanations for Swift's frequent use of the ideas Johnson found unfortunate (24). Hermann J. Real and Heinz J. Vienken offer a generally critical assessment of psychoanalytic approaches to Swift. See their "Psychoanalytic Criticism and Swift: The History of a Failure," *Eighteenth-Century Ireland* 1 (1986): 127–41.

7. ["Sir" John Hill?], *Some Observations on the Writers of the Present Age, and Their Manner of Treating Each Other; More Particularly Relative to the Treatment of Lord O–y* (London, 1752), 24. The annoyed Thomas Sheridan observes "that as the sale of the first Essay on this subject [of Swift's life], written by Lord Orrery, was infinitely superior to that of all the others put together, the prepossessions in favour of the accounts delivered by him, have . . . made too deep an impression on the bulk of mankind, to be easily erased." Sheridan does his limited best to correct Orrery's putative misrepresentations. See Sheridan's *Life of Swift*, sig. A8r. For the other references, see the *Annual Register* for 1782, 208; W. H., *The Beauties of Swift: or, The Favorite Offspring of Wit & Genius* (London, 1782), sig. A1r. There was a second edition of *Beauties* in the same year and another in Dublin in 1783. Robert Shiells, *Lives of the Poets of Great Britain and Ireland*, with additions and revisions by Theophilus Cibber, 5 vols. (London, 1753), also states that, thanks to Orrery, we see the real and brilliant Swift, who, like the rest of us, is "distant from perfection" (5:73). The Stella episode, for which see below, also sullied Swift's reputation across the ocean. For instance, see the first American edition of John Bennett, *Letters to a Young Lady, on a Variety of Useful and Interesing* [*sic*] *Subjects*, 2 vols. (New York, 1796), letter 53: Sheridan is too flattering; Swift's relationship with Stella is "an *eternal* stigma on his memory and his virtue" (1:92). Orrery's *Remarks* of course often were reprinted in literary magazines and had significant readership. Johnson's own remarks were indeed "little new," though expressed with formidable strength of mind and style. I quote below from John Boyle, Fifth Earl of Cork and Orrery, *Remarks on the Life and Writings of Dr. Jonathan Swift*, ed. João Fróes (Newark, Del., 2000). I quote Patrick Delany's response from *Observations upon Lord Orrery's Remarks on the Life and Writings of Dr. Jonathan Swift* (London, 1754).

Swift feared and denigrated the Royal Society; Johnson honored it as an emblem of British commitment to the scientific arts that improve human life. Swift regularly saw the Church in danger; Johnson felt that it was not properly respected but knew that in spite of much turmoil, change, and the absorption of the Methodist revolution, the Church of England was reasonably secure. Swift regarded the Moderns as upstart threats to stability and order in a declining world. Johnson regarded them as variously distinguished or undistinguished, but as part of the expanded world of literacy and national achievement that he celebrated in his edition of Shakespeare (1765) and in the *Lives of the Poets*.

Several other important differences between the two men make psychological distance rather than natural sympathy more likely.[8] Swift complained that he was "the poorest gentleman in Ireland that eat upon plate" (*YE*, 22:994). He thus oriented himself toward the class to which he aspired and among or above which he spent much time during his English political phase. Johnson regarded himself as part of the rabble, complained that "SLOW RISES WORTH BY POVERTY DEPRESSED," and was arrested for debt.[9] Swift essentially was a government employee whom the Church of Ireland materially supported and for whom it supplied necessary social order and duties, which he performed admirably. Johnson was an independent man of letters who made his way in London's difficult commercial publishing world. Swift generously gave away the copyrights for his printed texts. Johnson used his publishing proceeds for food, rent, compassion, and, when compiling the *Dictionary*, the support of six sometimes-sober amanuenses at his side. Swift mistrusted the book trade and the book as a physical, cultural, and moral object. Johnson was a bookseller's son for whom books were

8. There are better reasons for Johnson's apparent dislike of Swift than the hypothesis that Johnson saw in Swift the horrible darkness and madness within himself, and from which he needed to hide. See W. B. C. Watkins, *Perilous Balance: The Tragic Genius of Swift, Johnson, & Sterne* (Princeton, N.J., 1939; reprint, Cambridge, Mass., 1960), in which Johnson is more "rational" than Swift but is linked with him and with Sterne as fellow "Tragic" melancholics; Walter Jackson Bate, *Samuel Johnson* (New York, 1977), 275, 490–93, 537–38; and Irvin Ehrenpreis, *Swift: The Man, His Works, and the Age*, 3 vols. (Cambridge, Mass., 1962–83), 3:451. See also Claude Rawson, "Intimacies of Antipathy: Johnson and Swift," *Review of English Studies* 63 (2012): 265–92.

9. *London* (1738), in *Poems*, vol. 6 of *YE*, ed. E. L. McAdam Jr. with George Milne (1964), 56, line 177. Johnson was arrested for debt on March 16, 1756, and released with Samuel Richardson's help. Jacob Tonson saved Johnson from another threat of debtors' prison in February 1758. Johnson kept Oliver Goldsmith from debtors' prison by reading and then selling his manuscript of *The Vicar of Wakefield* as the bailiff stood ready; see *Life*, 1:415–16. Johnson discusses and laments the practice of imprisonment for debt in *Idler* 22 (September 9, 1758) and *Idler* 38 (January 6, 1759). Orrery observed that Swift was casual toward his "humble followers" but used "a real dignity, and a most delicate kind of wit in all his poems" to lords Oxford, Peterborough, and Carteret, the Countess of Winchilsea, and William Pulteney and Biddy Floyd: "These names abetted him in his pursuit of fame" (*Remarks*, 167). See also Johnson's observations regarding Swift's "affectation of familiarity with the great, an ambition of momentary equality sought and enjoyed by the neglect of those ceremonies which custom has established as the barriers between one order of society and another" (*YE*, 22:1019). Such remarks suggest that Johnson was troubled by Swift's version of Pride, of course a deadly sin that implied lack of subordination to God.

fallible but necessary tools for intellectual growth. In the *Lives of the Poets*, he regularly discusses copyright, sales, the number of books printed, and authorial revisions. He thus notes that *Gulliver's Travels* (1726) was "received with such avidity, that the price of the first edition was raised before the second could be made" (*YE*, 22:1001).[10] One of Swift's characteristic tropes is dismay at the collapse of norms. One of Johnson's characteristic tropes is the necessary search for uncertain but functioning norms—norms often perceived in Johnson himself and in his works.

Swift refused to believe in the real if slow progress toward improvement that Johnson saw around him every day. As Johnson says in *Rambler* 14 (May 5, 1750), an author must propose the "idea of perfection . . . [so] that we may have some object to which our endeavours are to be directed." His *Adventurer* 137 (February 26, 1754) adds a larger perspective: "The progress of reformation is gradual and silent." We nonetheless "know of every civil nation that it was once savage, and how was it reclaimed but by precept and admonition?"[11] The difference in perspective regarding progress evoked different perspectives regarding the reader, to whom Swift often is hostile "and dictates rather than persuades" (*YE*, 22:1018).[12] On April 2, 1727, angry Gulliver, with perhaps joking Swift behind him, complains that mankind has not improved six months after he displayed Houyhnhnm wisdom: "I wrote for their Amendment, and not their Approbation." Johnson sought to ingratiate himself with his readers in hopes of amending them. As he says in the first *Rambler* (March 20, 1750), unless readers are inclined to favor him, "they will hardly be persuaded to hear the cause" (*YE*, 3:5). The causes included politics. Swift had little good to say about legislators anywhere, and in the *Legion Club* (1736), he regards them as brainless lunatic devils.[13] He well earns his putative cookmaid's remark that, as for exalted senators, "the Dean would sooner h–g them up with cords."[14] For Johnson, "the wisdom of the nation is very reasonably supposed to reside in the parliament" ("Butler," *YE*, 22:323). I cite two further specific alien modes of proceeding that suggest radically different personalities.

10. For an excellent discussion of Swift and books, see Stephen E. Karian, *Jonathan Swift in Print and Manuscript* (Cambridge, 2010).

11. *The Rambler*, vols. 3–5 of *YE*, ed. W. J. Bate and Albrecht B. Strauss (1969), 3:76; *The Idler and The Adventurer*, vol. 2 of *YE*, ed. W. J. Bate, John M. Bullitt, and L. F. Powell (1963), 489.

12. Johnson uses similar language regarding William Warburton, whose learning he admired, but whose haughty arrogance "made his readers his enemies" and alienated "some who favoured his cause." Warburton "used no allurements of gentle language, but wished to compel rather than persuade" ("Pope," *YE*, 22:1130). These remarks are further evidence that Johnson shares criticisms of Swift with many other literary figures.

13. *Gulliver's Travels* (1726), vol. 11 of *The Prose Works of Jonathan Swift*, ed. Herbert Davis, introduction by Harold Williams (Oxford, 1965), 8 (hereafter cited as *PW*). The typically Swiftian passage mingles outrage, despair, and paradox: Yahoos are incapable of reformation; yet I have tried to reform them; they do not listen; I am outraged because they have proven what I already said I knew. For Swift on legislators, see Joseph McMinn, "The Prosecution of Power: Swift's Defence of Ireland," in *Reading Swift: Papers from the Fifth Münster Symposium on Jonathan Swift*, ed. Hermann J. Real (Munich, 2008), 365–73.

14. Mary the Cookmaid, *Dean Swift for Ever: Or, Mary the Cook-Maid to the Earl of Orrery: To Which Are Added, Thoughts on Various Subjects, from the Dean's Manuscripts in Mrs. Mary's Possession* (London, [1752]), 9.

Johnson's "Swift" praises *An Argument against Abolishing Christianity* (1708), including one of Swift's many attacks upon abolition of the Test Act. Johnson quotes a passage in which Swift ironically and characteristically darkens what he thinks the only option. If Anglican Christianity as supported by the Test Act is abolished, religion and its necessary constraints upon human action will also be abolished. Johnson responds with an amalgam of agreement and his characteristic "but" clause that opens alternatives: the "reasonableness of a Test is not hard to be proved; but perhaps it must be allowed that the proper test has not been chosen" (*YE*, 22:982).

We see a comparable contrast in personalities when Swift and Johnson consider the use of triplets and alexandrines, which Johnson discusses in his life of Dryden (*YE*, 21:493). In a letter on April 12, 1735, Swift ridicules these verse forms, which he proudly mocked at the end of his "City Shower."[15] He is pleased that Pope, Gay, and Arbuthnot then eliminated such devices from their works. Johnson again finds an alternative based on shared human experience and poetic utility rather than on annihilation and imposed power. Yes, poetics should be a science of regularity; yes, triplets and alexandrines admitted capriciously violate expected order; but no, poetics are not in fact rigidly scientific and until they are, these verse forms may be cautiously admitted: "I wish them still to be retained in their present state. They are sometimes grateful to the reader, and sometimes convenient to the poet. [Elijah] Fenton was of opinion that Dryden was too liberal and Pope too sparing of their use" (*YE*, 21:493).

Given such differences, it is surely time to reconsider the familiar and, at best, partial view that Johnson disliked Swift because he saw in him a frightening version of himself that he needed to exorcise. It also is time to place "Swift" within the *Lives of the Poets*' larger framework. When so viewed, many of Johnson's less favorable remarks regarding Swift are consistent with his objections to other poets rather than unique attacks upon Swift. Johnson indeed often is less severe than, say, Orrery and even the more sympathetic Patrick Delany.

Johnson's mingled admiration and denigration of Swift in the *Lives of the Poets* is part of his larger sense of how human beings do and should relate to one another in moral and in literary ways. One such way is through civil public discourse, toward which Swift often was indifferent.

Johnson represented a large community offended by Swift's scatological incursions. Johnson was troubled that Swift so often delighted in images of "disease, deformity, and filth" (*YE*, 22:1020). He also extended this criticism to Pope's *Dunciad* and to Gay's *Trivia*, in which the "appearance of Cloacina is nauseous and superfluous" (803). Johnson was comparably troubled by *A Tale of a Tub*, which he can think "with-

15. For Swift's letter to Thomas Beach, see *The Correspondence of Jonathan Swift, D.D.*, ed. David Woolley, 4 vols. (Frankfurt am Main, 1999–2007), 4:88. Swift was so angry at Dryden's corrupt use of alexandrines "that above 25 years ago I banished them all by one Triplet with the Alexandrian, upon a very ridiculous Subject." Swift "absolutely" prevailed with Pope, Gay, Young, and others.

out ill intention" only by an exercise of charity (979). That perhaps-malign intention refers to the *Tale*'s widely perceived attacks upon religion and the clergy. Johnson again had a similar objection, here to Dryden: "Malevolence to the clergy is seldom at a great distance from irreverence of religion, and Dryden affords no exception to this observation," for he often is disturbingly impious (*YE*, 21:430). Johnson's remark also concerns the *Tale*'s wild and dangerous allegory of the father and his three wayward sons, who represent the propagation of the Bible in the Roman, English, and Dissenting churches. For Johnson, sacred history in prose or poetry always fails—whether practiced by Abraham Cowley, John Denham, Edmund Waller, or Swift: "The ideas of Christian theology are too simple for eloquence, too sacred for fiction, and too majestick for ornament" and are only distorted by "tropes and figures" ("Waller," 315–16). Dictionary Johnson is comparably harsh on Swift's unrealistic desire to fix the English language (*YE* 22:984). He also scolds the Earl of Roscommon, who like Swift hoped for a Continental-style English academy to do that job. Even if such schemes were practicable rather than oblivious of human nature, he says, bloody-minded Britons would not tolerate that restraint upon their liberty. They would read the academy's edicts "only that they might be sure to disobey them." Britons agreed with Johnson: Roscommon's scheme, like Swift's thereafter, "has never since been publickly mentioned" (*YE* 21:245, 244).

Nor is Johnson's sometimes-harsh judgment of Swift's works unusual in the *Lives of the Poets*. Such remarks indeed are commonplace regarding others. Swift's Houyhnhnms may have given disgust, but Dryden's critical judgments often were "precipitate, and his opinions immature" ("Butler," *YE*, 21:225). Pope's *Elegy to the Memory of an Unfortunate Lady* (1717) celebrates her suicide: "Poetry has not often been worse employed than in dignifying the amorous fury of a raving girl" (*YE*, 23:1056). Pope's concept of the ruling passion in the *Essay on Man* is "in itself pernicious as well as false" (1140). James Hammond produced "nothing but frigid pedantry" (*YE*, 22:841). Johnson admires Joseph Addison, who nonetheless "thinks faintly" (841) and in *Cato* embodies "unaffecting elegance and chill philosophy" (657). Alicia in Nicholas Rowe's *Jane Shore* "is a character of empty noise" (593). "Nothing favourable can be said" of Mark Akenside's odes (*YE*, 23:1450). My own favorite dismissal is Johnson on Matthew Prior's *Carmen Saecularae*: "I cannot but suspect that I might praise or censure it by caprice, without danger of detection; for who can be supposed to have laboured through it?" (*YE*, 22:724).

Who also can be supposed not to be offended by the conclusion of *Gulliver's Travels* and its defamation of man, whom Anglican church father Richard Hooker had called the "perfection of Nature" and "the noblest creature in the world"?[16] Johnson argues that after the first flush of excitement, the public regarded the Houyhnhnms as

16. *Of the Laws of Ecclesiastical Polity* (1593), vol. 1 of *The Folger Library Edition of the Works of Richard Hooker*, ed. Georges Edelen, gen. ed. W. Speed Hill (Cambridge, Mass., 1977), 77 (1:7), 93 (1:9). For the vexed matter of Hooker on original sin, see Nigel Voak, *Richard Hooker and Reformed Theology: A Study of Reason, Will, and Grace* (Oxford, 2003); and Ranall Ingalls, "Sin and Grace," in *A Companion to Richard Hooker*, ed. W. J. Torrance Kirby, foreword by Rowan Williams (Leiden and Boston, 2008), 151–83. Hooker regularly emphasizes that reason is God's defining gift to man.

giving the most disgust, a comment that also alludes to the Yahoos (*YE*, 22:1001). That disgust was a regular response, one based on violation of the human nobility that Hooker and others attributed to human nature.

The contrasting satire against man was familiar; it was practiced in Nicholas Boileau's eighth satire, adapted and darkly enhanced by Lord Rochester, and widely regarded as the product of a mind alienated from Christian belief. An anonymous author in 1699 responded to Rochester's *Satyr against Reason and Mankind* (1674?; 1679) with arguments that later were applied to apparently comparable texts. God "In Vain" made us in His image if we prefer beast to man. "In Vain" He gave us reason and knowledge if other creatures are better than we are. By implication, satires against mankind are heretical if they remove us from "what Resembles his Omnipotence. / And how, . . . I can't conceive i'th least, / A Man of Sence cou'd wish Himselfe a Beast."[17]

This orthodoxy gained yet more force in the eighteenth century and localized itself around the term "the dignity of human nature." The concept was foreign to Hobbes, Mandeville, Rochester, and Swift but consistent with much post-Restoration moral thought. Addison's *Spectator* 209 (October 30, 1711) berated Boileau's eighth satire as useless, superficial, and misguided: "What Vice or Frailty can a Discourse correct, which censures the whole Species alike, and endeavours to shew . . . that Brutes are the more excellent Creatures?" John Hughes, whose Christianity Johnson praised, promptly added a compelling psychological framework for the relationship of such dignity to human behavior—namely, we live up to our self-image. As Hughes puts it in *Spectator* 210 (October 31, 1711), one who "has a mean Opinion of the Dignity of his Nature, will act in no higher a Rank than he has allotted himself in his own Estimation." Like-minded commentators included Thomas, Lord Paget; Aaron Hill; Joseph Warton; and Edward Young—all of whom knew that such presumed dignity was one of Swift's chief targets. As Gulliver says when acknowledging his literal and social insignificance in the Brobdingnagian court, he is "upon such a Foot as ill became the Dignity of Human Kind."[18]

17. "An Answer to the Satyr, Against Man," in *Corinna; or, Humane Frailty: A Poem, With an Answer to the E of R——'s Satyr against Man* (London, 1699), 19–20, lines 53–55, quoted in Nicholas Fisher, "The Contemporary Reception of Rochester's *A Satyr against Mankind*," *Review of English Studies* 57 (2006): 185–220 at 205.

18. *The Spectator*, ed. Donald F. Bond, 5 vols. (Oxford, 1965), 2:321. For Gulliver, see *PW*, 11:123 (2:v). For discussion of the "undignified" quality of *Gulliver's Travels*, see Merrel D. Clubb, "The Criticism of Gulliver's 'Voyage to the Houyhnhnms,' 1726–1914," in *Stanford Studies in Language and Literature*, ed. Hardin Craig (Stanford, Calif., 1941), 203–19. Of course Swift deservedly had defenders, as in [John Arbuthnot], *Critical Remarks on Capt. Gulliver's Travels; Particularly his Voyage to the Houyhnhnms Country. Part I. By Doctor Bantley* (London and Dublin, 1735). Arbuthnot acknowledges broad criticism of part 4 and has "Bantley" show that the Houyhnhnms were real and were known to antiquity: "this will clear *Gulliver* from another severe Imputation which he lay under, for debasing human Nature by making *Men* inferior to *Horses*." If mankind thinks itself "disgraced by the Comparison, it is to their own *Vices* . . . we ought to impute it" (24). For the larger intellectual context, see Bertrand A. Goldgar, "Satires on Man and 'The Dignity of Human Nature,'" *PMLA* 80 (1965): 535–41. Goldgar concludes: "*Gulliver's Travels* was published in an age when the genre of which it is the leading example was under fire, and . . . was something less than fashionable, especially if the object of . . .

The list of readers troubled by satires upon man included Lord Orrery, who complained that Swift placed "human nature . . . in the worst light" (*Remarks,* 175). Perhaps more surprising, however, is that Swift's nominal defender Patrick Delany was at least as severe as Orrery, whom he hoped to correct. In *Gulliver's Travels,* we read, Swift "turns up those dregs and foulnesses which were before suppressed" (*Observations,* 142); the Houyhnhnms are "a piece more deform [*sic*], erroneous, and (of consequence) less instructive, and agreeable, than any of his productions" (161); the Yahoos are "too offensive to be copied, even in the slightest sketch," for Swift debases "the human form to the lowest degree of a defiled imagination" (162). *Gulliver* indeed was "among the follies of his life" and, with a definitive thump, Delany says, "I am sick of this subject" (172). This remark differs only in a small degree from Orrery's insistence not only that part 4 is "a real insult upon mankind" but that "I am heartily tired" of it (*Remarks,* 217). Johnson is among the more temperate commentators regarding *Gulliver's Travels.* It seems reasonable to say that Johnson thinks of *Gulliver's Travels* as he thinks of *A Tale of a Tub.* Each is a product of what Delany calls "a defiled imagination" that Johnson's own generation sought to correct, return to a version of normalcy, and make relevant to ordinary life.

Johnson's "Swift," thus, is resolutely not idiosyncratic in its judgments of Swift and is in the approximate evaluative mode of the *Lives.* The operative term, though, indeed is "approximate." Generations of readers have sensed Johnson's significant reservations regarding Swift's character and achievement. Those reservations are the clearer when set against what Johnson admired in Swift's personal and religious life.

Johnson is keen on Swift's churchmanship throughout his career. At Laracor, Swift "increased the parochial duty by reading prayers on Wednesdays and Fridays, and performed all the offices of his profession with great decency and exactness" (*YE,* 22:979). Johnson also acknowledges Swift's relative temperance in political theology: *The Sentiments of a Church of England Man* "is written with great coolness, moderation, ease, and perspicuity" (981). As Dean of St. Patrick's, Swift "was seldom in the wrong" (993). He indeed was "a churchman rationally zealous" who honored his clergy and respected Dissenters' rights, if not their expansion of rights. He managed revenues, repaired the Church, improved the choir, restored weekly communion, performed it "in the most solemn and devout manner with his own hand," and preached far better than he claimed (1013–14).

Johnson is comparably impressed with Swift's commitment to Irish rights and especially with his compassion toward the Irish people—the vast majority of Catholic subjects. Such defense satisfied Swift's ambition, willingness to speak truth to power, and love of his version of liberty. *The Drapier's Letters* brought him deserved honor "as the champion, patron, and instructer" of a rescued nation (999).[19] Johnson's metaphors

laughter was the 'dignity' of the human species" (541). It is a pleasure to acknowledge the excellence of this essay by a late friend.

19. I cite two unsigned warmly approving responses to Swift's role in the opposition to William Wood's coinage. In the broadside *Poem to Dr. Jo——n S——t* (Dublin, 1725), Swift is the patriot who

are bluntly pro-Irish and anti-English as he praises Swift for having saved "Ireland from a very oppressive and predatory invasion." Swift was "zealous on every occasion where the publick interest" was concerned (1000). The Irish had a "natural right" to use and promote the products of their own labor rather than England's (995).

Swift's varied roles as a young man, as an English political agent, and as a friend often were equally fortuitous. He compensated for a second-rate Trinity College degree by studying for eight hours a day during the next seven years (973). His *Conduct of the Allies* (1711) successfully urged peace through the Treaty of Utrecht and characterized Marlborough as a war profiteer. In other places, Johnson praises Swift for helping the worthy Thomas Parnell to Irish preferment ("Parnell," 22:562) and enlarges on the concept of friendship by quoting Delany's remarks to Orrery. Swift not only embodied "fidelity in friendship" to individuals but also, at his own risk, was "a steady, persevering, inflexible friend, a wise, a watchful, and a faithful counsellor" to the Irish nation; "he lived a blessing, he died a benefactor, and his name will ever live an honour to Ireland" (1021–22).

Johnson, then, warmly praises Swift when he attaches himself to familiar institutions or benevolent actions—to the established church, to the Irish nation and the prosperity and dignity of an oppressed people, to the cause of peace, and to acts of friendship. Such handsome public and private sociability improves the human condition and conduct. It is not the often-destructive individualism that Johnson sees in much of Swift's life and art and that Johnson studiously avoids in the *Lives of the Poets*. His life of Swift, after all, is virtually framed by sociability. It begins with Johnson's praise of his friend John Hawkesworth's biography of Swift, and it nearly ends with Delany's praise of Swift as both personal and Irish national friend.

Johnson's social *Lives* help to teach us how to negotiate a difficult world. He warns us about the vanity of human wishes, exemplifies the disappointments of those who aspire to greatness, and urges the need to adapt to the restraints upon human nature. Johnson the professional writer in a commercial world also stresses the author's role, problems, and successes in practical publishing contexts. Much of Johnson's complex agenda in the *Lives of the Poets*, however, concerns moral and literary progress. They locate the genesis of principled British literary criticism in Dryden. They trace the movement of British poetry from the Metaphysicals' excesses to the increasing polish of Denham, Waller, and Dryden and to the couplet's perfection in Pope. They relate the literary to the moral and praise the improvements in culture, as in the *Tatler* and *Spectator*. Addison and Steele were almost unprecedented "masters of common life" who elegantly reformed their readers and induced civility. Until then, "an arbiter eligantiarum was yet wanting" to advance art and life. Johnson surely knew that Taci-

"sav'd a sinking State, / And snatch'd it from the Precipice of Fate." Only heaven can "pay the Tribute for so great a Deed." Another young poet issued his broadside *Poem to D—— S——* (Dublin, 1724–25) and called Swift "The Justest Patriot, and the truest Friend." Many were involved in the crusade; Swift was the vocal and focal point. See Sabine Baltes, *The Pamphlet Controversy about Wood's Halfpence (1722–25) and the Tradition of Irish Constitutional Nationalism* (Frankfurt am Main, 2003).

tus had used the Latin term "elegantiae arbiter" to describe the salacious Petronius, whom Nero chose as his judge of taste.[20] Addison and Steele mark a modern British advance from both classical and earlier British life.

One useful word to describe Johnson's global intention in the *Lives* is *piety*, which he hopes they will induce. The religious term overlaps with classical *pietas* and its veneration for nation, parent, relations, and community. Johnson thus regularly blames irreverent uses of pagan mythology in a British Christian world and regularly praises social relations, friendship, and familial bonds.[21] Cowley, for example, acknowledged his mother's "care, and justly paid the dues of filial gratitude" (*YE*, 21:6). Johnson laments Pope's malignity but admires his affection for frail parents, with whom he abandoned his irritability: "to them he was gentle. Life has, among its soothing and quiet comforts, few things better to give than such a son" (*YE*, 23:1117–18). Johnson is at once impressed with the depth of friendship between Addison and Steele and saddened by its politically induced collapse: "Every reader surely must regret that these two illustrious friends, after so many years passed in confidence and endearment, in unity of interest, conformity of opinion, and fellowship of study, should finally part in acrimonious opposition" (*YE*, 22:636).

Johnson illustrates domestic piety by contrasting two playwrights. The technically brilliant but immoral William Congreve ignored his family's needs by leaving £10,000 to the already rich Henrietta, Duchess of Marlborough. The money "to her was superfluous and useless" but "might have given great assistance to the ancient family from which he descended, at that time by the imprudence of his relation reduced to difficulty and distress" (746–47).[22] The morally different and fatally ill John Hughes sacrificed artistic integrity for his family's integrity. He allowed the

20. "Addison," *YE*, 22:612–13. Tacitus, in *Annals* 16.18–19, uses that term regarding Petronius. There were three sets of Tacitus in Johnson's library. See Donald Greene, *Samuel Johnson's Library: An Annotated Guide* (Victoria, Canada, 1975), 108. Petronius as "arbiter elegantiarum" was a commonplace. See Pope's *Dunciad, in Four Books* (London, 1743), 71n290. Johnson's view of the *Spectator* project was of course benignly un-Petronian. It sought to do far more than bring philosophy to the tea table. It hoped also "to banish Vice and Ignorance out of the Territories of *Great Britain*," we read in *Spectator* 59 (May 8, 1711). The contrast with Gulliver's rage for a comparable, if failed, attempt is clear; see *The Spectator*, 1:245.

21. James D. Garrison has offered a valuable relevant study: *Pietas from Vergil to Dryden* (University Park, Pa., 1992). On Good Friday, April 2, 1779, Johnson wrote: "Last week I published the lives of the poets written I hope in such a manner, as may tend to the promotion of Piety": *Diaries, Prayers, and Annals*, vol. 1 of *YE*, ed. E. L. McAdam Jr. with Donald and Mary Hyde (1958), 294.

22. Johnson erred in thinking that Congreve had ignored his family. He left this approximate amount to Mary, Lady Godolphin, the child of his affair with the second Duchess of Marlborough. See John C. Hodges, *William Congreve, the Man: A Biography from New Sources* (New York, 1941), 117–23; and Brian Corman, "Johnson and Profane Authors: The *Lives* of Otway and Congreve," in *Johnson after Two Hundred Years*, ed. Paul J. Korshin (Philadelphia, 1986), 233. The error also is noted by John Middendorf in *YE*, 22:747n1, and in Roger Lonsdale's edition of *The Lives of the Most Eminent English Poets: With Critical Observations on Their Works*, 4 vols. (Oxford, 2006), 3:320 (hereafter cited as *Lives*). Here, as elsewhere, Johnson's hostility to certain authors, like Swift, was based on accepted but wrong information. See also Frederick W. Hilles, "Dr. Johnson on Swift's Last Years: Some Misconceptions and Distortions," *Philological Quarterly* 54 (1975): 370–79.

actors to dictate the conclusion of his *Siege of Damascus* (1720) so that his heirs would not "lose the benefit of his work" (685). These consanguine domestic virtues enhance life. Johnson's praise of Swift's positive traits generally relates to values and actions that Johnson praises elsewhere in the *Lives of the Poets.*[23] Swift at his best encouraged both piety and *pietas*.

Such responses are unlike the often-destructive idiosyncrasy that Johnson and others saw in much of Swift's and his early contemporaries' behavior. I suggest that Johnson's attitude toward Swift was conditioned by his attitude toward the two generations that preceded his own and toward the tendencies he often found within Swift's life and art—disordered religion, inordinate severity in political involvement, and especially sexual aggression and denials of family obligation so grave that they amounted to a violation of God's design for the universe. This unlovely and excessive picture was at the least thought plausible well into the later eighteenth century. I will deal briefly with the first two objections and extensively with the third.

The life of Swift was one of the last three lives that Johnson wrote.[24] By then he had established an overview of his repeated themes, likes and dislikes, and the varied moral and literary places in which he could situate his authors. Johnson disapproved of the mingled political and religious Interregnum, which characterized in the life of Butler and its contrast of then and now. *Hudibras* seems strange to those unfamiliar with the sour, solemn, and superstitious old Puritans: "It is scarcely possible, in the regularity and composure of the present time, to image the tumult of absurdity, and clamour of contradiction, which perplexed doctrine, disordered practice, and disturbed both publick and private quiet, in that age" (*YE*, 21:222).

23. As Isobel Grundy has shown, Johnson also admired Swift's prose, which he handsomely mined for illustrative quotations in the *Dictionary*; see Grundy, "Swift and Johnson," *The Age of Johnson* 2 (1989): 154–80. Grundy and Paul J. Korshin agree that Swift was most congenial for Johnson in his earlier and middle years, up to his work on the *Dictionary* (1755). He reformulated his judgment when Orrery's *Remarks* appeared in 1751. See Korshin, "Johnson and Swift: A Study in the Genesis of Literary Opinion," *Philological Quarterly* 58 (1969): 464–78. John T. Scanlan, in "'He Hates Much Trouble,'" has studied Johnson's adaptations of Orrery, Delany, and Hawkesworth. See also Wayne Warncke, "Samuel Johnson on Swift: The *Life of Swift* and Johnson's Predecessors in Swiftian Biography," *Journal of British Studies* 7 (1968): 56–64. Others have looked more closely at Hawkesworth, whom Johnson compliments at the beginning of "Swift." See John Lawrence Abbott, *John Hawkesworth: Eighteenth-Century Man of Letters* (Madison, Wis., 1982), 52–56; and Martin Maner, "Johnson's Redaction of Hawkesworth's *Swift*," *The Age of Johnson* 2 (1989): 311–34.

24. For other recent discussions of the life of Swift, its sources, and some controversies, see *Lives*, 3:426–30, and John Middendorf's commentary in *YE*, 22:969–72. I gratefully acknowledge my debt to each of these handsome editions and their editors. James Engell well considers the life of Blackmore and its relationship between the good man and the less good poet. See "Johnson on Blackmore, Pope, Shakespeare—and Johnson," in "Johnson after Three Centuries: New Light on Texts and Contexts," ed. Thomas A. Horrocks and Howard D. Weinbrot, special issue, *Harvard Library Bulletin* 20 (2011): 51–61.

The post-Interregnum generation paid the price as well in James II's brief and potentially violent reign, again disturbed by religious quarrels. "All know how soon that reign began to gather clouds," Johnson says. The economics of "government was yet unsettled" in Dryden's age, thanks in part to the "turbulence of King James's reign." His "enormities grew every day less supportable" until he was "frighted away, and a new government was to be settled," which, alas, was temporary and evoked yet further distress.[25]

Johnson thus was troubled by the malaise and fierce political climate of Anne's reign. The "rage of party," the "storm of faction," and the "inflamed nation," on "fire with faction," induced "anxiety, discord . . . confusion and . . . turbulence."[26] His norm is Addison, whose party zeal "did not extinguish his kindness for the merit of his opponents; when he was secretary in Ireland, he refused to intermit his acquaintance with Swift" (*YE*, 22:640)—in spite of Swift's denigration of Addison and frequent stoking of partisan fires.

For example, Johnson notes Swift's refusal to respect political or personal disagreement, sometimes masked behind literary judgment. Both Swift and Pope mock the distinguished George Montagu, Earl of Halifax, whom Johnson describes as an "artful . . . statesman, employed in balancing parties, contriving expedients, and combating [that is, ameliorating] opposition" (553). Swift spoke of him with "slight censure, and Pope in the character of Bufo with acrimonious contempt" (557). The Hanoverian succession "filled the nation with anxiety . . . and confusion" when Addison's *Whig Examiner* appeared and his "vigorously exerted" genius sought to calm the nation. When the paper ended, "Swift remarks, with exultation that 'it is now down among the dead men'" ("Addison," 627–28). Swift dislikes Bishop Burnet's *History of the Reformation* "with something more than political aversion, [and] treats him like one whom he is glad of an opportunity to insult" (987). Insults and paper death are modest in comparison to the hostility and projection of power that Swift expressed to the Whig Justice and then Archbishop Hugh Boulter during the Wood's controversy. Boulter recommended moderation rather than "exasperating the people." Swift "exculpated himself by saying, 'If I had lifted up my finger, they would have torn you to pieces'" (1000). Swift preferred the match when "the nation was . . . combustible, and a spark could set it on fire"—as he nearly did in the 1711 *Conduct of the Allies* (986–87).

Schismatic seventeenth-century religion and incandescent early eighteenth-century politics finally yield to modern "regularity and composure" (21:222). That decency was equally required for sexual conduct in art and life.

One drumbeat in the *Lives of the Poets* is condemnation of Restoration sexual and moral ethics toward women. Johnson embodies his awareness of improvement in the *Lives*' sense of the pastness of Restoration values. The germane *Lives* include theories of causation for why such depraved art disappeared—self-destruction of the

25. "Sheffield" (all know), *YE*, 22:692; "Dryden" (unsettled), 21:434; "Roscommon" (turbulence), 21:245; "Dorset" (enormities), 21:331; "Sprat" (frighted), 22:549.

26. "Hughes," *YE*, 22:685 (rage); "Addison," 642, (storm), 627 (inflamed), 620 (fire), 628 (anxiety).

dramatists and their culture, the progress of human decency, and the onslaught by Jeremy Collier. His *Short View of the Immorality and Profaneness of the English Stage* (1698), Johnson says, had "no other motive than religious zeal and honest indignation." The "wise and pious" theatergoers soon refused to suffer "irreligion and licentiousness to be openly taught at the public charge" (742–43). Dryden thus retracted his comedies' abuses of morality (*YE*, 21:428), Congreve's harsh reply to Collier was dismissed, and his unimproving plays were condemned as relaxing "those obligations by which life ought to be regulated" (*YE*, 22:473).[27] Thomas Otway's "want of morals, or of decency" ingratiated him with "the dissolute wits" who probably enjoyed "the despicable scenes of the vile" comic portions of *Venice Preserv'd*. Solipsistic Otway consulted "nature in his own breast" (*YE*, 21:255, 258).[28] So malign a nature helped to destroy Lord Rochester, who "addicted himself to dissolute and vitious company" and so corrupted him that he lived "worthless and useless" until his early death (*YE*, 21:228, 229). His later colleague John Sheffield, Earl of Mulgrave, took his religion from Hobbes and his sentiments regarding women from the licentious and exploitive "Court of Charles" (*YE*, 22:695).

Such critiques are part of Johnson's larger dislike of the Restoration period's vulgarity, as in an aristocrat's violent drunken disorder during Dryden's funeral. Given the "gradual change of manners," the brute at a funeral today would be removed "and compelled to be quiet." This is "to the honour of the present time" (*YE*, 21:421), as it was to the dishonor of Dryden's that he remained poor: "it is impossible not to detest the age" (431). Thereafter, Otway's comedy *Friendship in Fashion*, "whatever might be its first reception, was, upon its revival at Drury-lane in 1749, hissed off the stage for immorality and obscenity" (255).[29]

We recall that Johnson praised Swift when he piously supported church or state and contributed to friendship, patriotism, and peace. At other times Swift's conduct seemed too like that of the era into which he was born, a detested moral "then" rather than a superior moral "now" that hisses obscenity into obscurity and refuses to "trade

27. For fuller discussion of Collier's presumed effect on eighteenth-century drama, see Robert D. Hume, "Jeremy Collier and the Future of the London Theater in 1698," *Studies in Philology* 96 (1999): 480–511. Collier mattered to individual actors and playwrights "in the period from 1698 to 1705, but very little to the history of the drama and theater" (481).

28. Johnson either recalls or consciously alludes to his own "Prologue Spoken at the Opening of the Theatre in Drury Lane, 1747," a progress poem that also denigrates Restoration comedy as morally illicit. As for the "wits of Charles": "Themselves they studied, as they felt they writ, / Intrigue was plot, obscenity was wit, / Vice always found a sympathetick friend; / They pleas'd their age, and did not aim to mend" (*YE*, 6:88, lines 17, 19–22).

29. The many eulogies upon Dryden's death included [Tom Brown], *A Description of Mr. D—n's Funeral* (London, 1700). The raucous, confused event included "Mob with Mob in great Disorder." Brown asks: "Was e'er Immortal Poet thus buffon'd?" Dryden was accompanied to the grave by "A Crowd so nauseous, so profusely lewd, / With all the Vices of Times endu'd" (8). Robert D. Hume observes that Otway's comedies fell out of production from about 1700 to 1750: "The wonder is that they lasted as long as they did after the time of Jeremy Collier. *Friendship in Fashion*, tried after a lapse of at least thirty years, provoked a near riot at Drury Lane (22 January 1750), after which the managers stuck to safer fare"; see "Otway and the Comic Muse," *Studies in Philology* 73 (1976): 87–116 at 88. See also Corman, "Johnson and Profane Authors," 225–44.

in corruption."[30] Of course Swift was hardly a Restoration rake in decanal clothing, Harry Horner in a tiewig; but belief can be more powerful than fact. Several biographers and adversaries feasted upon sordid meals of defamation for which Swift himself sadly was the chef. One such hearty meal was his relationship with Esther Vanhomrigh and the poem *Cadenus and Vanessa* (1713; 1726). Delany rejected Orrery's dark vision of that couple, but Orrery's view was long anticipated and widely known. In 1726 a sexually anorexic Irish woman implored Swift to leave England and satisfy her Vanessa-like appetite. In 1730 Leonard Welsted evoked unbuttoned Cadenus cuddling in Vanessa's arms. Vanessa herself, it seemed, was willing to be thought Swift's concubine, but she finally demanded marriage, which the already-married Swift angrily rejected. Orrery echoes Jonathan Smedley's earlier attack and quotation of several mischievously coquettish lines from the poem. These dishonor Swift by dishonoring Vanessa, whose "agonies of despair" contributed to her death.[31]

Swift as Cadenus writes that Vanessa's conduct with the Dean remains a secret, whether she pleased him with romantic talk, whether he was "less seraphic," whether

30. The full context is in "Dryden": "Of the mind that can trade in corruption, and can deliberately pollute itself with ideal wickedness for the sake of spreading the contagion in society, I wish not to conceal or excuse the depravity" (*YE*, 21:426).

31. Delany discusses the episode in *Observations*, 57–58, 111–24. See Orrery, *Remarks*, 154–59, for the entire passage; 159 (agonies). Leonard Welsted writes in *One Epistle to Mr. A. Pope, Occasion'd By Two Epistles Lately Published* (London, 1730), 20: "So when *Vanessa* yielded up her Charms, / The blest *Cadenus* languish'd in her Arms." He is there with "His Vest unbutton'd, and his God unsung." A second edition appeared in the same year. See *A Young Lady's Complaint for the Stay of Dean Swift in England* (Dublin, 1726) for the erotically lush broadside. The Vanessa episode remained controversial and morally compromising throughout the century. For negative or at least slanted response, see Jonathan Smedley, *Gulliveriana: Or, A Fourth Volume of Miscellanies. Being a Sequel of the Three Volumes, Published by Pope and Swift* (London, 1728), xxix–xxx; *The Humours of the Court: Or, Modern Gallantry. A New Ballad Opera*, 2nd ed. (London, 1732), in which Vanessa is "a gay young Lady, with Child by *Adonis*," who is "an amorous young Prince" [viii]. The subtitle of *The Fair Concubine: Or, The Secret History of the Beautiful Vanella* (London, 1732) promises *An Account of several curious Incidents . . . in the Course of her Rivalship with Miss Mordantia* (title page). There were at least four editions. Mordantia hopes that Vanella will die in childbirth so that she can replace Vanella in "Prince *Alexis*'s Favour" (45). See also *A Candid Appeal from the Late Dean Swift to the Right Hon. the Earl of O—y* (London, 1752), 5–6; *Emendations on an Appeal from the late Dean Swift. Or Right Hon. Earl of Orrery Vindicated* (London, 1752), 5–7; Thomas Hudson, "The Dean to Lord Orrery," in *Poems on Several Occasions. In Two Parts* (Newcastle upon Tyne, 1752), [205]; John Brett, *Conjugal Love and Duty: A Discourse Upon Hebrews xiii 4* (Dublin, 1757), xviii–xix; and *The Beauties of English Poesy*, ed. Oliver Goldsmith, 2 vols. (London, 1767), 2:175. For some defense, see Delany, *Observations*; *Letter II. From a Gentleman in the Country, to his Son in the College of Dublin. Relating to the Memoirs of the Life and Writings of . . . Swift Ascribed to the Right Honourable the Earl of Orrery* (Dublin, 1752), 27–43; and parts of *A Candid Appeal* in the lines cited above. Nathalie Zimpfer has discussed Orrery's influence on Swift's reputation in France; see Zimpfer, "From 'Rabelais in his Senses' to 'The Father of Black Humour': Notes on Jonathan Swift's Critical Reception in France," *Swift Studies* 23 (2008): 80–93, esp. 83–84. For other useful discussions of Swift and Orrery, see Paul J. Korshin, "The Earl of Orrery and Swift's Early Reputation," *Harvard Library Bulletin* 16 (1968): 167–77; Korshin, "Johnson and the Earl of Orrery," *Eighteenth-Century Studies in Honor of Donald F. Hyde*, ed. W. H. Bond (New York, 1970), 29–43; A. C. Elias Jr., "The First Printing of Orrery's *Remarks on Swift*," *Harvard Library Bulletin* 25 (1977): 310–21; and Elias, "Lord Orrery's Copy of *Memoirs of the Life and Writings of Swift* (1751)," *Eighteenth-Century Ireland* 1 (1986): 111–25. See also João Fróes's valuable introduction to his edition of Orrery, *Remarks*, 13–50.

"they temper[ed] love and books together." All this "Must never to mankind be told / Nor shall the conscious muse unfold." Orrery is severe: "It is impossible to read this cruel hint without great indignation against the *conscious muse*, especially as it is the finishing stroke of a picture, which was already drawn in too loose a garment, and too unguarded a posture." The "Dean must remain inexcusable."[32]

Whatever the scandal regarding Vanessa, commentators generally agreed that Swift's presumed marriage to Stella was oddly chaste because of his oddly distant attitude toward women, whom he considered marble busts. As Orrery says, Swift's poems to Stella are "fuller of affection than desire." *Gulliver's Travels*' sexual amusements, though, projected enough desire to produce scabrous responses. The perpetrator of *A Letter from a Clergyman* (1726) regarding *Gulliver* berates Swift as "profane and impious," the "Scandal of his Cloth [and] a Reproach to Religion." His behavior for the last thirty years would "disclose such Scenes that all Mankind" must think "very defective." *Some Memoirs of the Amours and Intrigues of a Certain Irish Dean* (1728) adds that Swift seldom had "less than two or three Intrigues at a time." Thomas Newcomb may have shared that view. He leagues Swift with Pope, who enjoyed vicious railing for its own sake: his muse would have been sorely disappointed "Had all been like Your *D——on* so chaste and white." Swift's indelicate *Lady's Dressing Room* (1732) allowed Lady Mary Wortley Montagu to respond with her own crudely comic scenes of Swift's limp lust. The Dean visits a prostitute, pays her four pounds, engages in furtive foreplay but cannot rise to the occasion. Her close stool, dirty smock, and smelly toes render him a tame Hercules. When the nymph refuses to return his money, he threatens to write the *Lady's Dressing Room*, to which she replies: "Perhaps you have no better Luck in / The Knack of Rhyming than of ——."[33]

32. *The Poems of Jonathan Swift*, ed. Harold Williams, 2nd ed., 3 vols. (Oxford, 1958), 2:683–714, lines 821, 823, 825–27; Orrery, *Remarks*, 158. *Cadenus and Vanessa* has been much studied in valuable books on Swift's poetry; see Maurice Johnson, *The Sin of Wit: Jonathan Swift as a Poet* (Syracuse, N.Y., 1950); Nora Crow Jaffe, *The Poet Swift* (Hanover, N.H., 1977); Peter J. Schakel, *The Poetry of Jonathan Swift: Allusion and the Development of a Poetic Style* (Madison, Wis., 1978); John Irwin Fischer, *On Swift's Poetry* (Gainesville, Fla., 1978); A. B. England, *Energy and Order in the Poetry of Swift* (Lewisburg, Pa., 1980); Louise K. Barnett, *Swift's Poetic Worlds* (Newark, Del., 1981); and Arno Löffler, *"The Rebel Muse": Studien zu Swifts kritischer Dichtung* (Tübingen, 1982). Among other useful articles, see Peter J. Schakel, "'What Success it Met': The Reception of *Cadenus and Vanessa*," in *Reading Swift: Papers from the Third Münster Symposium on Jonathan Swift*, ed. Hermann J. Real and Helgard Stöver-Leidig (Munich, 1998), 215–24; and Igor Djordjevic, "*Cadenus and Vanessa*: A Rhetoric of Courtship," *Swift Studies* 18 (2003): 104–18.

33. Orrery, *Remarks*, 165. This is a perceptive passage regarding Swift's attitude toward women. Since he thought of women "rather as busts, than as whole figures, . . . he has seldom descended lower than the center of their hearts." Swift's relationship to women has been much discussed. Aside from several studies of specific poems, see, for example, Ellen Pollak, *The Poetics of Sexual Myth: Gender and Ideology in the Verse of Swift and Pope* (Chicago, 1985); Margaret Anne Doody, "Swift and Women," in *The Cambridge Companion to Jonathan Swift*, ed. Christopher Fox (Cambridge, 2003), 87–111; Claude Rawson, "Rage and Raillery and Swift: The Case of *Cadenus and Vanessa*," in *Pope, Swift, and Women Writers*, ed. Donald C. Mell (Newark, Del., 1996), 154–91, esp. 188, where Rawson

The recently well-married and decorous Pamela also commented on Swift's bedside manner. His *Letter to a Young Lady upon Her Marriage* (1723) seems written by a woman's enemy rather than friend. Yet Swift deserves leeway: "we know not what Ladies the ingenious Gentleman may have fallen among in his younger Days." Swift's nonce cook Mary later tried to rescue his sexual reputation from Lord Orrery's inference that Swift "never knew what is what." Fiddlesticks. The Dean was no kiss-and-tell lover; not boasting of a son scarcely makes him "chaste and dainty"; he never names his parents but certainly had them; and most of all, he was Irish, and so "the Case is plain." As it was to Horace Walpole. On June 20, 1766, he writes to George Montagu regarding a newly read letter from Swift to Vanessa. He concludes that it is "plain he lay with her, notwithstanding his supposed incapacity." However malign, this view of Swift circulated broadly and was epitomized in *A Rap at the Rapsody* (1734): "A Wit! A Libertine! A Priest!"[34] Both libertinism and wit were concepts Johnson excoriated in the *Lives of the Poets*' rejection of loose garments.

discusses and is troubled by the same passage that Orrery quotes; and Louise Barnett, *Jonathan Swift in the Company of Women* (Oxford, 2007), esp. "The Question of Misogyny," 124–53, and "Swift and Women Critics," 154–70. For the other texts quoted, see *A Letter from a Clergyman to His Friend, with an Account of the Travels of Captain Lemuel Gulliver* (London, 1726), 19, 22; and *Some Memoirs of the Amours and Intrigues of a Certain Irish Dean* (London, 1728), sig. A3v, 2. The author of the latter adds that the Dean "was a Man of Gallantry" of whom the women should beware. If you want to guess at his identity, "*think of* V—— in a celebrated Poem" (sig. A3v). See also [Thomas Newcomb], *A Supplement to One Thousand Seven Hundred Thirty-Eight. Not Written by Mr. Pope* (Dublin, 1738), 28; and [Lady Mary Wortley Montagu], *The Dean's Provocation for Writing the Lady's Dressing-Room. A Poem* (London, [1734]), 7. For a fuller discussion of the poem and of Lady Mary's hostility to Swift, see Robert Halsband, "'The Lady's Dressing Room' Explicated by a Contemporary," in *The Augustan Milieu: Essays Presented to Louis A. Landa*, ed. Henry Knight Miller, Eric Rothstein, and G. S. Rousseau (Oxford, 1970), 225–31. Helen Deutsch has placed Swift's relationship with Stella in the context of friendship; see Deutsch, "Swift's Poetics of Friendship," in *Politics and Literature in the Age of Swift*, ed. Claude Rawson (Cambridge, 2010), 140–61. Of course, all this hostility toward Swift is numerically and conceptually inferior to the many eulogies to him, living and dead, some for the *Drapier's Letters* and some in general gratitude. See the unsigned *Essay on Preferment: By the Author of the Rapsody on the Army* (Dublin, 1736), 15–16. Swift's was a "Life of Virtue, and of action too" (16).

34. Samuel Richardson, *Pamela: Or, Virtue Rewarded*, 4 vols. (London, 1742), 4:347; see also *The History of Sir Charles Grandison*, 2nd ed., 6 vols. (London, 1754), 1:324. The manuscript for the *Letter* is at the Huntington Library, MS HM 1599, and is reproduced in George P. Mayhew, *Rage or Raillery: The Swift Manuscripts at the Huntington Library* (San Marino, Calif., 1967), 57–68. It is hard to believe that the lady, Deborah Staunton, who would become Mrs. John Rochfort, was not at least as offended as Pamela. For the other references, see Mary the Cook Maid, *Dean Swift for ever*, 7–8; *Horace Walpole's Correspondence with George Montagu*, vols. 9–10 of *The Yale Edition of Horace Walpole's Correspondence*, ed. W. S. Lewis and Ralph S. Brown Jr. (New Haven, Conn., 1941), 10:218–19. Walpole was reading from *Letters Written by the late Jonathan Swift . . . and Several of His Friends* (London, 1766). Walpole admired Swift perhaps even less than he admired Johnson, for which, see Stephen Clarke, "'Prejudice, Bigotry, and Arrogance': Horace Walpole's Abuse of Samuel Johnson," *The Age of Johnson* 14 (2003): 239–57. Swift, in turn, was "that brute, who hated everybody that he hoped would get him a mitre and did not"; *Correspondence*, 10:218. See also *A Rap at the Rapsody* (London, 1734), 7. The Rapper is among the many disturbed by *Gulliver's Travels*' vision of humanity. Swift is a traitor to church, state, and humankind. "For shame!" (7).

❦

Johnson was both more tactful and perhaps more damning than Orrery. Johnson knew that Esther Vanhomrigh was "fond of [Swift's] person"—loved him, courted him, was passionate about him. Swift was proud of her passion, encouraged her advances, and, "no other honest plea can be found," did not tell her that he was married because he waited for the right moment and feared an emotional outburst. Swift so neglected Vanessa that she "died of disappointment." Johnson neither implies the couple's carnal relations nor explores the alternative meaning of a "dishonest plea." He nonetheless thinks Swift wrong and complains that Esther was "ignominiously distinguished by the name of Vanessa" (*YE*, 22:997–98). There is no ignominy in combining Van and a diminutive of Esther. Johnson may think the insult a play on *vannus*, a winnowing basket into which corn is dropped and shaken and the husk separated from the grain—Esther as receptacle. He may have thought of *vanus*, something that is vacant, vain. He may have known the slang term *van-neck*, "a woman with large breasts, a bushel-bubby."[35] Whether one, some, or all of these, Johnson heard the name Vanessa and heard Swift insulting a woman who died loving him.

There is a greater sense of ignominy implicit in the relationship, however. She was "a woman made unhappy by her admiration of wit" (*YE*, 22:995). Johnson often denigrates poets by means of this word, which he associates with Restoration-era verbal brilliance at virtue's expense. Otway was attractive to "dissolute wits" (*YE*, 21:255). Richard Duke's "wit . . . seems to have shared the dissoluteness of the times" (*YE*, 22:537). Swift's attacks on Richard Bentley and William Wotton were ignorant, but "Wit can stand its ground against Truth only a little while" (*YE*, 22:980). Vanessa's wit also could stand its ground only a little while. Orrery stresses that Vanessa was "ambitious" to be thought a wit and hoped "to keep company with wits" like Swift.[36]

Lord Rochester exemplified the wit whose "contempt of all decency and order" destroyed him (*YE*, 21:229) if not his poems, which Johnson included for the anthologized portions of the *Lives*.[37] One such poem was *A Letter from Artemisia in the Town to Chloe in the Country* (1674?; 1679), which chronicles Corinna's hitherto fortunate sexual adventures. She was courted, admired, loved, and fed with presents. She had

35. Francis Grose, *A Classical Dictionary of the Vulgar Tongue,* 2nd ed. (London, [1788]), sig. Gg1v. This slang word does not appear in the first edition (1785). Grose also gives a cross-reference from "Van" to Madam; but that reference points to Madam Ran, not Van, as a cant term for whore.

36. Orrery, *Remarks*, 155. *Cadenus and Vanessa* includes sixteen instances of the word *wit*, often in different senses. Contrast Otway's *wit* with Johnson adapting Thomas Tickell on Addison, wit, and the change of generations: "he employed wit on the side of virtue and religion. He not only made the proper use of wit himself, but taught it to others; and from his time it has been generally subservient to the cause of reason and of truth. He has dissipated the prejudice that had long connected gaiety with vice, and easiness of manners with laxity of principles" (*YE*, 22:648).

37. John Middendorf notes that, early in September 1777, Johnson gave George Steevens Rochester's poetry "to castrate for the edition of the poets" (*YE*, 21:227; as drawn from *Life*, 3:191). Roger Lonsdale so notes as well and adds that it is "just conceivable" that Johnson wrote the life early in November 1777. Lonsdale also suggests that Johnson himself may have done some of the "castration" of Rochester's poetry. If so, this, too, would have been late in 1777; see *Lives*, 2:240–41.

youth in her looks "and pleasure in her bed; / Till fate or her ill angel thought it fit / To make her doat upon a man of wit." He found it tiresome to love longer than a day, "Made his ill-natured jest, and went away." Corinna is bereft and abandoned. "Now scorn'd of all, forsaken and opprest, / She's a *memento mori* to the rest."[38] Corinna doted "upon a man of wit." Vanessa was "made unhappy by her admiration of wit." I doubt that Johnson consciously alludes to *Artemisia*, but we note misfortune whether the woman dotes or admires. Corinna is a *memento mori.* Vanessa is dead.

Swift's relationship with Stella is fatality writ large. It lacks the slightly softened blame that Johnson allows with Swift and Vanessa, who, after all, aggressively courted the wit and paid the terrible price. So far as Johnson could tell, the woman he calls "poor Stella" and "unfortunate Stella" was the victim of conjugal oppression (*YE*, 22:1003–5).

Johnson of course believed that Swift and Stella were married.[39] Johnson also believed that God ordained the social demands of marriage as the "order of Providence," that Swift violated "the laws of nature," and that he was more tyrant than husband. We know what Johnson means by these terms: his first sermon elaborates upon God's design for human happiness within Christian marriage, which makes "the constitution of the world."[40] Marriage is communal, mutually respectful, and reinforces the *Lives of the Poets'* emphasis on piety and *pietas*. Swift's treatment of Stella nearly reverses such spiritual design.

The sermon's text is Genesis 2:24: "a man shall leave his father and mother, and shall cleave unto his wife." Johnson's first sentence makes clear that "society is necessary to the happiness of human nature." We thereby remove ourselves from "the gloom of solitude, and the stillness of retirement." The fantasy of delights in isolation yields to the reality that gloomy and melancholic solitude is subject only to accidental pleasures. Even these "are but imperfectly enjoyed" without amiable companionship (*YE*, 14:3). God derives "all his happiness from himself" (4), but humans depend upon one another for solace: "the bosom is disburthened by a communication of its cares" (3).

38. Samuel Johnson, *The Works of the English Poets. With Prefaces, Biographical and Critical... Volume the Tenth* (London, 1779), 312. Swift may have it right when, in "The Author upon Himself" (1714), he said that he "had the Sin of Wit, no venial Crime." He also claimed to have "reconciled Divinity and Wit." Johnson and others thought not. See Swift, "The Author upon Himself," *Poems of Jonathan Swift*, ed. Williams, 1:193, 194, lines 9, 12.

39. Most late twentieth-century critics have denied that Swift and Stella were married. Irvin Ehrenpreis found no evidence and ignored it except for a footnote: *Swift*, 3:405n1. J. A. Downie agreed and supplied a careful overview of the evidence in *Jonathan Swift, Political Writer* (London and Boston, 1984), 341–43. David Nokes briefly argued the case for marriage in *Jonathan Swift, A Hypocrite Reversed* (Oxford, 1985), 217–18n. There have been several other discussions of the putative marriage and of Stella, about whom we know very little: Maxwell B. Gold, *Swift's Marriage to Stella: Together with Unprinted and Misprinted Letters* (Cambridge, Mass., 1937); Herbert Davis, *Stella: A Gentlewoman of the Eighteenth Century* (New York, 1942); Ehrenpreis, *Swift*, 2:353–55; 3:405–25, 544–50; Richard F. MacD. Byrn, "Jonathan Swift's Locket for Stella Swift: A Sacramental Marriage Certificate," *Swift Studies* 3 (1988): 2–8; Hermann J. Real, "Stella's Books," *Swift Studies* 11 (1996): 70–83; Stephen Karian, "Swift's Epitaph for Stella? A Recently Discovered Document," *Swift Studies* 16 (2001): 109–13; and Joâo Fróes, "Swift's Prayers for Stella: The Other Side of the Satirist," *Swift Studies* 18 (2003): 56–62. Fróes well chronicles Swift's grief regarding the loss of his beloved friend.

40. *Sermons*, vol. 14 of *YE*, ed. Jean Hagstrum and James Gray (1978), 7.

Only those "with the rage of licentiousness and impatience of restraint" (7–8) oppose marriage and indeed suffer the consequences of human void: "In solitude perplexity swells into distraction, and grief settles into melancholy" (3).

Marriage is a "sacred obligation" with important duties, denial of which denotes loss of the moral senses. Men are not blind; they willfully "abandon themselves to their passions with their eyes open; and lose the direction of truth, because they do not attend to her voice." Offenses against society are punished by law, but "cruelty and pride, oppression and partiality, may tyrannize in private families without controul; meekness may be trampled upon, and piety insulted, without any appeal but to conscience and to Heaven" (4–6).

Johnson mentions "tyranny" three times to stress the political implications of an abusive marriage, and he offers socially pious antidotes to spousal oppression. The first is "a vow of perpetual and indissoluble friendship." United and shared interests are immune to change of fortune and competition from others. Friendship denotes dedication to that person, with whom one is equal, an equality that in part extends to marriage: "No disadvantage of birth or fortune ought to impede the exaltation of virtue and of wisdom; for with marriage begins union, and union obliterates all distinctions" (12). Johnson may well have remembered this sentiment when he read Orrery's lament: Swift refused to acknowledge the "diamond" and the "jewel" Stella because he hoped to keep "free from a low alliance."[41]

The duties of marriage are even more exalted than those of friendship: they include love and confidence, fidelity and tenderness, patience and forgiveness of errors. The yet more major difference again concerns spousal politics: friends are equal; husband and wife are not. One side has more authority than the other, who has the "unpleasing duty" of obedience. Johnson's distinction is clear: "to govern and to tyrannize are very different, and . . . oppression will naturally provoke rebellion." This conjugal wisdom "is the law of God," which must not be broken. Those who nonetheless violate it destroy "the great source of mutual happiness," as Johnson saw in the relationship between Stella and Swift (13–15).

For Johnson, Stella entered Swift's life shortly after he arrived at Laracor, where she and Rebecca Dingley established a proper social and personal world. With them, but surely with Stella, "he opened his bosom," though in separate houses and in others' company (*YE*, 22:979). Swift then experienced the emotional comfort of speaking with a trusted friend. Nothing changed after they moved to Dublin, when, during public days at the Deanery, "she regulated the table, but appeared" to be a guest like other women (994). Nothing changed when she became his wife in 1716. They again had separate homes, except when Swift was ill, and even then only with a third person present—something so important to Swift that he includes such adult chaperoning in *Gulliver's Travels*.[42] Stella was failing when he returned from England in 1727, and on January 28,

41. Orrery, *Remarks*, 82–83.

42. *Gulliver's Travels*, part 1, chap. 6, which Swift calls "*His Vindication of a great Lady*" (*PW*, 11:xxxix). Gulliver insists that he did not have a sexual liaison with Lady Flimnap: "I own she came

1728, he lamented "the death of her whom he loved most, aggravated by the consciousness that himself had hastened it" (1003).

Johnson discusses several of Swift's works as wild, singular, or dangerous. He joins Delany in extending that irregular trait to Swift's personal life and his relationship with Stella. Swift was "fond of singularity and desirous to make a mode of happiness for himself, different from the general course of things and order of Providence." He denied Stella another good match and married her himself only "to appropriate her." He thereby expected "all the pleasures of perfect friendship, without the uneasiness of conjugal restraint." The consequence for "poor Stella" was to appear to the world as "a mistress" and not as a wife. She "lived sullenly on, in hope" that he would change, as he did when he was mentally disabled and she found it too late. She surrendered to "sorrowful resentment, and died under the tyranny of him by whom she was in the highest degree loved and honoured" (1004).

Johnson understood why Swift's singularity and alienation from humanity were dangerous, antiquated, insulting to providential order, and personally tragic. They substituted withdrawal for a benevolent "intercourse of sentiments, and an exchange of observations" (*YE*, 14:3). Both Swift and Stella thus suffered from Swift's inadequate *pietas,* what Johnson calls "excentrick tenderness." Swift's refusal to acknowledge her as his wife was "fatal to the unfortunate Stella." Before her death she "gave up herself to sorrowful resentment." After her death Swift contracted his benevolence, increased his severity, "drove his acquaintance from his table, and wondered why he was deserted." His increasing bitterness "condemned him to solitude; and his resentment of solitude sharpened his asperity" (*YE*, 22:1004–7). He again chose singularity, refused to wear spectacles, eliminated the community of books and ideas, and "left his mind vacant to the vexations of the hour" and finally to madness, upon rejecting God's design for companionate happiness (1009). That rejection evoked what might seem a sexual ethic drawn from morally defective, defaming, and fatally oppressive Restoration-era values.

The overlap of themes, words, and consequences between sermon and biography provides causation for Johnson's dislike of Swift the man, which carried into his dislike of Swift the author. In the sermon, Johnson praises the community between man and woman, through which "the bosom is disburthened, by a communication of its cares" (*YE*, 14:3). In the life, Swift "passed his hours of relaxation [with Stella and Rebecca Dingley], and to them he opened his bosom." In the sermon, only those "with the rage of licentiousness and impatience of restraint" (7–8) oppose marriage. In the life, Swift expected "all the pleasures of perfect friendship, without the uneasiness of conjugal restraint."[43] In the sermon, Johnson insists that one person in the marriage must govern, but "to govern and to tyrannize are very different." In the life, Stella "died under the tyranny of him by whom she was in the highest degree loved and honoured."

often to my House, but always publickly, nor ever without three more in the Coach" (49). Even Swift's *Journal to Stella* had reading company in Rebecca Dingley.

43. Johnson makes plain that healthy Stella was Swift's great solace: "Mrs. Johnson, whose conversation was to him the great softener of the ills of life, began in the year of the Drapier's triumph to

In the sermon, "In solitude perplexity swells into distraction, and grief settles into melancholy" or a version of madness. In the life, Swift dies alone, with "madness . . . compounded of rage and fatuity."

Let us reprise Johnson's sense of how his own age has improved over at least the two previous generations, much of which Swift's life straddled. His world progressed beyond Interregnum religious chaos, when superstition and schism destroyed order. It progressed beyond Restoration social, moral, sexual, and cultural vulgarity. It progressed beyond political hostility that burns, inflames, and destroys. It progressed beyond Swift's apparently singular self-absorption, which contributed to the pain and death of two women who loved him, and to his own grief and isolation.

The dramatic change in culture starts at about the time that Swift's Whig enemies Addison and Steele began their *Tatler* and then *Spectator* papers, "undertaken to reform either the savageness of neglect or the impertinence of civility."[44] By the mid- to late eighteenth century, a version of politeness had been absorbed into British culture. Johnson did not always exemplify such change, but he knew what no longer was acceptable and should be so labeled, even if that meant demonstrating how the learned and brilliant Dean of St. Patrick's violated "the order of Providence." Under such circumstances, well might Johnson have said what Dryden had eighty-one years earlier: "'Tis well an old age is out / And time to begin a new."

An earlier version of this essay appeared in *Reading Swift: Papers from the Sixth Münster Symposium on Jonathan Swift*, ed. Kirsten Juhas, Hermann J. Real, and Sandra Simon (Munich, 2013), 595–620. I thank Professor Doctor Hermann Real for permission to republish and for the excellent symposium at which the paper was presented.

decline" (*YE*, 22:1000). See also Delany, *Observations*: Stella's "cordial friendship, sweet-temper, and lenient advice, poured balm and healing into his blood"—which "boiled, fretted, and fermented" after her death (144). This is one of several examples of Johnson's adaptation of received wisdom regarding Swift.

44. Lawrence Klein has studied this phenomenon; see "The Third Earl of Shaftesbury and the Progress of Politeness," *Eighteenth-Century Studies* 18 (1984–85): 186–214; and *Shaftesbury and the Culture of Politeness: Moral Discourse and Cultural Politics in Early Eighteenth-Century England* (Cambridge, 1994). My own view is that Addison's and Steele's periodical essays are the more important motivators of civility and verbal politeness and of course lack Shaftesbury's Deism. Johnson praises the proper moral design in "Addison"; his essays had a "perceptible influence upon the conversation of that time, and taught the frolicks and the gay to write merriment with decency" (*YE*, 22:614).

PART II:

JOHNSON THE WRITER

Johnson's Poetry of Repetition

Thomas Keymer

SINCE THE CLASSIC 1941 STUDY by W. K. Wimsatt Jr.[1]—indeed, since the eighteenth century itself—we have heard more about the prose style of Samuel Johnson than about his poetic style. That is not to say that Johnson's poems, or at least his two great imitations of Juvenal, *London* (1738) and *The Vanity of Human Wishes* (1749),[2] have not been keenly debated in modern criticism. But it is the overt or covert politics of these poems that has dominated the debate, and it is probably the case that more commentary has been devoted to topical innuendoes concerning the figure of Swedish Charles in *The Vanity of Human Wishes* than to the specifically literary qualities that make the poem worth reading in the first place. If our approach to poetry has been marked over the past few years by the emergence of a "new formalism"—a formalism no longer hostile, that is, to historical context or political reading—Johnson has not been a conspicuous beneficiary.[3]

Yet of course there have been interesting exceptions, and the proliferation of recent essay collections about Johnson—companions, handbooks, and anniversary volumes, all with obligations of coverage—has guaranteed a fresh overview of the poems every few years. Outstanding among these is Howard D. Weinbrot's essay "The Poetry of Samuel Johnson," originally written for the first volume in the Cambridge Companions to Literature and Classics series to be devoted to an eighteenth-century author, and then reprinted in a monograph version. Here Weinbrot's goal is to make the case for Johnson's verse as a body of work that matches, or at least approaches, "the extraordinary intellectual and moral achievements within his prose," and in consequence Weinbrot gives primary attention to philosophic theme and method in the poems. The following essay seeks to complement this analysis with more direct and

1. W. K. Wimsatt Jr., *The Prose Style of Samuel Johnson* (New Haven, Conn., 1941).

2. Parenthetical line references are to *The Poems of Samuel Johnson*, ed. David Nichol Smith and Edward L. McAdam, 2nd ed. (Oxford, 1974).

3. On this development in general, see Marjorie Levinson, "What Is New Formalism?," *PMLA* 122, no. 2 (2007): 558–69. On its potential for eighteenth-century studies, see J. Paul Hunter, "Formalism and History: Binarism and the Anglophone Couplet," *Modern Language Quarterly* 61, no. 1 (2000): 109–29; John Richetti, "Formalism and Eighteenth-Century English Fiction: An Introduction," *Eighteenth-Century Fiction* 24, no. 2 (2012): 157–60; and James Noggle, "Epilogue: Taste in the New Formalism," *The Temporality of Taste in Eighteenth-Century British Writing* (Oxford, 2012), 204–11.

concentrated attention to features of style, and in so doing to develop Weinbrot's initial suggestion that "Johnson is a great prose writer in part because he is a great poet," or again that the poems "include many devices that make his prose memorable, for his prose is memorable in part because it is so poetic."[4]

This sense of the poems and the prose as two sides of the same rhetorical coin leads back in turn to Wimsatt's suggestion—somewhat buried in the penultimate chapter of his dense study—that the measured and emphatic eloquence one associates with the *Rambler* (1750–52) or the *Lives of the Poets* (1779–81) flows not so much from earlier prose traditions as from the verse couplet form of Dryden or Pope. With its concentrated rhetoric of parallel, antithesis, and chiasmus, and the impression of truth-telling authority and epigrammatic closure that results, Augustan poetry could inform the language of periodical journalism or critical discussion. In this respect, the style that so interested Wimsatt "seems to proceed by a very short step, across the line from verse to prose." It could be seen in its native generic state in Johnson's own verse output, even if this output sometimes appears to strike Wimsatt as little more than an incubator, of limited importance in its own right. "[I]n his couplet satires," Wimsatt concludes, Johnson "was employing a rhetoric which needed only to be taken out of verse and inflated to solemnity by philosophical diction to become the rhetoric of his *Ramblers*."[5]

Silver Floods and Other Clichés

Perhaps it is because of the looming, sidelining enormity of Johnson's prose rhetoric that some of the keenest insights into his verse have come not from paid-up Johnsonians but from specialists in poetic practice such as Christopher Ricks, a virtuoso close reader whose dexterity with verbal nuance led W. H. Auden to call him "exactly the kind of critic every poet dreams of finding."[6] Unfortunately, when Johnson finds Ricks it is

4. Howard D. Weinbrot, *Aspects of Samuel Johnson: Essays on His Arts, Mind, Afterlife, and Politics* (Newark, Del., 2005), 72–91 at 72; previously published in *The Cambridge Companion to Samuel Johnson*, ed. Greg Clingham (Cambridge, 1997), 34–50. Notable twentieth-century accounts include David Nichol Smith, "The Heroic Couplet—Johnson," in *Some Observations on Eighteenth Century Poetry* (Toronto, 1937), 31–55; T. S. Eliot, "Johnson as Critic and Poet" (1944), in *On Poetry and Poets* (London, 1957), 162–92; Frederick W. Hilles, "Johnson's Poetic Fire," in *From Sensibility to Romanticism: Essays Presented to Frederick A. Pottle*, ed. Frederick W. Hilles and Harold Bloom (London, 1965), 67–77; D. V. Boyd, "Vanity and Vacuity: A Reading of Johnson's Verse Satires," *ELH* 39, no. 3 (1972): 390–96; Lawrence Lipking, "Learning to Read Johnson: *The Vision of Theodore* and *The Vanity of Human Wishes*," *ELH* 43, no. 4 (1976): 527–35; Howard D. Weinbrot, "Johnson's *London* and Juvenal's Third Satire: The Country as 'Ironic' Norm" (1976) and "No 'Mock Debate': Questions and Answers in *The Vanity of Human Wishes*" (1980), both in *Aspects of Samuel Johnson*, 92–124; William Edinger, *Samuel Johnson and Poetic Style* (Chicago, 1977); John E. Sitter, "To *The Vanity of Human Wishes* through the 1740's," *Studies in Philology* 74, no. 4 (1977): 445–64; David R. Anderson, "Johnson and the Problem of Religious Verse," *The Age of Johnson* 4 (1991): 41–57; Howard Erskine-Hill, "Johnson: Poems on Affairs of State," in *Poetry of Opposition and Revolution: Dryden to Wordsworth* (Oxford, 1996), 109–66 (see also Weinbrot's responses in *Aspects of Samuel Johnson*, 340–400); and David F. Venturo, *Johnson the Poet: The Poetic Career of Samuel Johnson* (Newark, N.J., 1999).

5. Wimsatt, *Prose Style*, 125, 128.

6. "The Poet of No More—W. H. Auden Offers Some Personal Reflections on Tennyson," *The Listener* 88 (August 10, 1972): 181.

usually in passing, and the insights take the form of brilliant but localized observations in such wide-ranging surveys as *Allusion to the Poets* (2002) and Ricks's earlier *The Force of Poetry* (1984)—a title that points, of course, to Johnson's *Rambler* account of *Macbeth*, 1.5.48–52, as lines that exert "all the force of poetry, that force which calls new powers into being, which embodies sentiment, and animates matter."[7] In these and other studies, a favorite theme for Ricks is the reanimation of dead metaphor and the creative deployment of cliché, a phenomenon he finds tellingly exploited in works that range from Samuel Beckett's *Murphy* (1938: a year, it so happens, when Beckett's fascination with Johnson was still at its height) to Johnson's *London* two centuries earlier. In Ricks's hands the teasing opening of *Murphy*, in which "The sun shone, having no alternative, on the nothing new," briskly defamiliarizes a hoary proverb—nothing new under the sun—and at the same time presents the reader "not just with a cliché but with a meta-cliché, a cliché about the clichéness of everything."[8] No less deft and calculating is line 22 of *London*, "Where GREENWICH smiles upon the silver Flood," a line Ricks pinpoints to demonstrate "that the metaphorical life in the poems of Johnson is often a matter of invigorating dead or flat metaphor, of using clichés so that their pristine force is recreated or so that they are seen in a new perspective."[9] Here, what otherwise might seem an egregious cliché is in context subtly barbed, artfully contaminated by the poem's insistence on corruption and peculation as attributes of the city watered by this silver flood. London is a place, the satire goes on to reveal, "devote to Vice and Gain" (line 37) or motivated again by "Thirst of Pow'r and Gold" (line 62): *thirst*, as though insatiable Londoners might in the end not merely smile at but actually swallow this "silver Flood," the river of cash that defines their city in pecuniary, not pastoral, terms.

A few clicks of the mouse can now confirm, in ways Ricks could not have specified at the time of writing, just how grating a cliché "silver flood" must have seemed in 1738. Witness some of Johnson's favorite targets of mockery or condescension elsewhere, such as the lousy Samuel Boyse ("SWEET *Solitude*, where with delightful Sound / The fair *Dordonna* rolls its Silver Flood") or the wearisome Gilbert West ("And Thou, where *Thames* impels his silver Flood, / Quitting the Care of thy own rising Wood").[10] Again, a few years earlier, witness the *Piscatory Eclogues* (1729) of Johnson's sometime *Gentleman's Magazine* acquaintance Moses Browne ("I sit, and sing, to th'echoing Wood / . . . by fair *Thames* or *Medway's* silver flood") or the *Miscellany Poems* (1722) of Elizabeth Thomas, a Curll author who gets an inglorious walk-on part in the life of Pope:

7. Johnson, *The Rambler*, vols. 3–5 of *The Yale Edition of The Works of Samuel Johnson* (hereafter cited as *YE*), ed. W. J. Bate and Albrecht B. Strauss (New Haven, Conn., 1969), 5:127 (*Rambler* 168, October 26, 1751).

8. Christopher Ricks, *Beckett's Dying Words* (Oxford, 1993), 62–63.

9. Christopher Ricks, *The Force of Poetry* (Oxford, 1984), 81; the chapter titled "Samuel Johnson: Dead Metaphors and Impending Death" previously appeared as "Johnson's 'Battle of the Pygmies and Cranes,'" *Essays in Criticism* 16, no. 3 (1966): 281–89.

10. Samuel Boyse, *Translations and Poems Written on Several Subjects* (Edinburgh, 1731), 51 ("Ode de Monsieur Fenelon . . . Translated"), italics in original; Gilbert West, *Stowe* (London, 1732), 3, italics in original.

"Close by the Margin of a silver Flood, / There stands a lofty venerable Wood."[11] It says something about just how threadbare the diction is across these examples that all four of them rhyme "silver flood" with the same pastoral-sylvan standby, the inevitable "wood."[12] It would be no exaggeration to say, in fact, that in the decade or two prior to Johnson's *London* the unusual thing to find in poems about rivers is a flood that *isn't* silver—but in his own already expert poetic hands the cliché springs meaningfully to life. In the greed-is-good London of this particular poem, there really is a silver flood, a flood of silver, and the act of smiling on this silver flood gains further irony from a later passage in which "all are Slaves to Gold . . . and Smiles are sold" (lines 178–79). It is surely relevant to this masterly line that a colossal statue of George II was erected facing the river at Greenwich in 1735, perhaps indeed smiling, though the facial expression is now eroded from John Michael Rysbrack's sculpture.[13] Johnson's poem evokes a world, as finally becomes inescapable, in which Londoners and their rulers not only bestow their smiles on the current but also cynically trade these smiles for currency.

Johnson was not the only poet of the day to observe and exploit the absurdity of "silver flood." But the memorably grotesque derision of Pope's *Dunciad* (1728, 1743), which at one point hails the polluted Fleet Ditch as "King of dykes! than whom no sluice of mud / With deeper sable blots the silver flood," entirely lacks the finesse of *London*'s line about Greenwich, and at this point, at least, the political bite.[14] Pope's substitution of "mud" for the default "wood" rhyme is superb, as is his juxtaposition of hackneyed "silver" with euphemistic "sable." But Johnson's mischievous play on the cliché outdoes Pope in its sly inauguration of the poem's oppositional theme, and in the resonances this sets up for later lines; the meanings gather as the treasures rise.

To read *London* in this way is not only to embellish Ricks's point but also to historicize it, and to connect the line, in new-formalist vein, with political readings of the poem as anti-Walpole or even—for the seditious poses of *Marmor Norfolciense* (1739) are now just a year away—as anti-Hanoverian satire. Yet it is also to remain very much within the spirit of Ricks's one sustained analysis of a Johnson poem, which is based—one might almost suspect fulfillment of a donnish bet—on the apparently unpromising case of "The Battle of the Pygmies and Cranes," a translation Johnson undertook in his youth from the neo-Latin verse of Joseph Addison. Ricks's point here is not to make grand claims for this otherwise forgotten piece of juvenilia, which "is not a work of great intrinsic merit, though it does include some remarkable felicities."

11. Moses Browne, *Piscatory Eclogues* (London, 1729), 26 ("An Essay in Defence of Piscatory Eclogue," quoting a seventeenth-century precursor, Phineas Fletcher, italics in original); Elizabeth Thomas, *Miscellany Poems on Several Subjects* (London, 1722), 154 ("On the Death of John Tanner, Esq."); Johnson, *The Lives of the Most Eminent English Poets: With Critical Observations on Their Works*, ed. Roger Lonsdale, 4 vols. (Oxford, 2006), 4:5, 32.

12. As Boyse continues, "Two lovely Isles its Waves encompass round, / Whose gently rising Banks are crown'd with Wood."

13. Clive Aslet, *The Story of Greenwich* (Cambridge, Mass., 1999), 147. Johnson lived in Greenwich for some months in 1737.

14. Alexander Pope, *The Dunciad: in Four Books*, ed. Valerie Rumbold, 2nd ed. (Harlow, U.K., 1999), 190 (2.273–74).

It is rather to argue that the technique he finds characteristic of Johnson—the "revivification of dead metaphors into a disconcertingly relevant prominence"—is observable even in Johnson's earliest verse.[15]

It is not hard to find similar techniques operating elsewhere in the juvenilia, even in Johnson's schoolboy translations from Horace as they survive in the Yale Boswell papers (some having first been printed in Boswell's *Life*). Something of the same reinvigoration of dead metaphors, so that their latent potential is released, can be seen in Johnson's characteristically deliberate rendering of Horace's *Odes* 2.9, as posthumously published by Boswell in 1791. Here the poet consoles his addressee, Valgius, on the loss of a favorite slave boy—or, in the more decorous explanation that prevailed in the eighteenth century, the death of his son. In Johnson's hands, the second stanza of the poem contrasts the obsessive, relentless grief of the mourning Valgius with the more mixed, changeable condition of the wider world, in which clouds sometimes part, storms abate, and winter alternates with summer:

> Nor, Valgius, on th' Armenian Shores
> Do the chain'd waters always freeze;
> Not always furious Boreas roars,
> Or bends with violent force the Trees.

At this point (lines 5–8), Johnson's determination to eschew received poetic diction, or to reproduce it only, as in *London*, with some ironic or other creative twist, is clearly not yet realized. It is no great surprise, for example, to find Boreas furious or roaring, while the later, more vigilant Johnson might well have asked himself what kind of force could bend trees *without* being violent. In the previous lines, however, the chaining of waters, and then the freezing of these chains, involve richly paradoxical suggestions that have no exact counterpart in the Latin source. They refuse the easy route of literalism while looking forward to one of the most celebrated, plangent moments in *The Vanity of Human Wishes*, when Xerxes lashes the waves "and enchains the Wind" (line 232).

More interesting still are the lines that follow in the third quatrain—"But you are ever drown'd in tears, / For Mystes dead you ever mourn" (lines 9–10)—in which the seemingly hackneyed "drown'd in tears" turns out on inspection to be something more, a moment of imaginative surplus that connects Valgius's futile weeping for his boy with a world that weeps, from the clouds, showers, and storm-tossed sea of the opening to the "humbler wave" of Niphates near the close of the poem (line 21).[16] Like *London*, this is at key points an emphatically liquid poem, and the drowning of its addressee in debilitating, self-indulgent grief compresses into one eloquent phrase the odd mixture of sympathy and rebuke that marks the ode as a whole.[17]

15. Ricks, *Force of Poetry*, 88.

16. Like other translators of the day, Johnson takes the mountain Niphates to be a river.

17. For a subtle account of the Horatian original, see Michael C. J. Putnam, "Horace Carm. 2. 9: Augustus and the Ambiguities of Encomium," in *Between Republic and Empire: Interpretations of Augustus and His Principate*, ed. Kurt A. Raaflaub and Mark Toher (Berkeley, Calif., 1990), 212–38.

Horace was noted in the eighteenth century, of course, for his surprising lexical combinations—for that "*curiosa felicitas*" that Christopher Smart was to gloss, with all the appreciation of a kindred spirit, as "the lucky risk of the Horatian boldness . . . that unrivalled peculiarity of expression . . . the curiosity of choice diction."[18] Yet in this case the little poetic shocks delivered by the text are Johnson's own. Horace's original, and for that matter Smart's verse translation of 1767, are without the same intensity of focus on the flow of water—clouds, showers, storms, waves—that makes Valgius's hapless condition in Johnson, ever drowning, ever mourning, so poetically apt. The submersion is Johnson's elaboration, and it brings new thematic concentration to a poem in which originally, to quote Smart's literal prose version of 1756, Valgius merely "pursue[s] Mystes, who is taken from you, with mournful measures." Or as Smart puts it again in his verse translation: "But you, in one continual dirge, / Th'untimely death of Mystes urge."[19]

Another and the Same

An alternative way of making this point about the silver flood and thirst for gold in Johnson's *London*, or about the poetic water world in which Valgius weeps and drowns in the Horace translation, is to say that here and elsewhere the distinctive force of Johnson's poetry arises from repetition—repetition, in these cases, of lexical patterns that gather mutually reinforcing significance, and typically irony, as they accumulate in each work. In the Horatian case, which in itself is a poem about repetition, specifically an unending cycle of grief, verbal repetition—"ever drown'd . . . ever mourn"—precisely enacts the entrapment of its addressee. At the same time, that most fundamental figure of repetition, inherited poetic cliché, is creatively reworked to give further point to Valgius's predicament.

We see this technique at its simplest with the emphatic repetition in Johnson's poems not just of cognate groups but also of single key words, creating an effect not unlike the incremental repetition associated with traditional ballads (though ballads were a form, as they grew in prestige, that Johnson would disparage with gusto). The extreme example is his quizzical early poem "On a Lady's Presenting a Sprig of Myrtle to a Gentleman," first published in a magazine version of 1747 but apparently composed in 1731, with its relentless focus on the myrtle—a tree that enigmatically connotes both love and death—as "Ambiguous Emblem of uncertain Fate" (line 2). As the poem unpacks the associations of this emblem in lines 7–10:

In Myrtle Groves oft sings the happy Swain,
In Myrtle Shades despairing Ghosts complain;
The Myrtle crowns the happy Lovers Heads,
Th'unhappy Lovers Graves the Myrtle spreads[.]

18. Christopher Smart, *The Works of Horace, Translated into Verse*, vol. 5 of *The Poetical Works of Christopher Smart*, ed. Karina Williamson (Oxford, 1996), 4–5.

19. Christopher Smart, *The Works of Horace, Translated Literally into English Prose*, 2 vols. (London, 1756), 1:101; Smart, *Works of Horace, Translated into Verse*, 67. In the second version, Smart's heading—"TO VALGIUS, That he would at length desist from bewailing the death of Mystes"—nicely catches the ode's testiness of condolence.

Cliché is in a sense the subject of this poem, and Johnson is absolutely right that in myrtle groves, oft sings the happy swain. There are myrtle groves on every side in Restoration and early eighteenth-century verse, and many of them shelter singing swains: no fewer than five turn up, for example, in the work of Henry Baker, one each in Jane Barker and Aphra Behn, and five more in Sir Richard Blackmore, before one even starts on Colley Cibber and the rest of the alphabet. Even the most distinguished poets of the period were not immune. In Dryden's Virgil translation of 1697, the souls of lovers "In secret Solitude, and Myrtle Shades, / Make endless Moans," while John Gay turns out a lazy couplet about "blest *Elysium*; where in myrtle groves / Enamour'd ghosts bemoan their former loves."[20] It was becoming a cliché, indeed, to note that myrtle groves were becoming a cliché. "So much is said and sung of Plains, / Of Fields, of Groves, of Nymphs and Swains, / Of purling Streams, and Myrtle Shades, / Of list-ning Ecchoes and deaf Maids," Mary Monck protests in a posthumously published poem of 1716.[21] In John Philips's *The Splendid Shilling* (1705), the poet deplores his own weakness for melancholy night poetry, in which "Darkling I sigh, and feed with dis-mal Thoughts / My anxious Mind; or sometimes mournful Verse / Indite, and sing of Groves and Myrtle Shades."[22] It is as though Johnson is seeking out a challenge here, writing a poem not only about one of the most glaring clichés in the repertoire of pas-toral and pastoral elegy, but also about a cliché the mockery of which was a cliché of verse satire.

How, then, to tackle this self-imposed problem? Boldly and head on, first, by placing the word "myrtle" and its meaning—or lack of meaning—right at the center of the poem; second, by repeating the word more frequently and insistently than in any previous poem; and third, by turning the poem as a whole into a self-conscious medi-tation on poetry itself, and specifically on the fluctuating valence or outright indeter-minacy of poetic emblems. What carries the trick technically is the syntactic and rhythmic variation that leavens the verbal repetition, with devices best expressed in rhetorical terms: not only the obvious anaphora of lines 7–8 ("In Myrtle . . . / In Myr-tle") but also chiasmus, in which grammatical structures are reversed in successive clauses ("sings the . . . Swain / . . . Ghosts complain"); polyptoton, in which the same word recurs in different parts of speech, so that the adjectival "myrtles" of lines 7–8 give way to nouns in lines 9–10; antithesis, in the structured alternation between pas-toral groves and funereal shades, happy heads and unhappy graves; the roughly anti-metabolic patterning of lines 9–10, in which the bracketing of the couplet from an initial "Myrtle crowns" to a terminal "Myrtle spreads" encloses a matching arrange-ment of parallel phrases in reversed line position: "happy Lovers Heads / . . . unhappy Lovers Graves."

20. John Dryden, *Poems: The Works of Virgil in English*, vols. 5–6 of *The Works of John Dryden*, ed. William Frost and Vinton A. Dearing (Berkeley, Calif., 1987), 5:547 (*Aeneis*, 6.599–600); John Gay, *Dramatic Works*, ed. John Fuller, 2 vols. (Oxford, 1983), 1:294 (*Dione: A Pastoral Tragedy*, 2.1.11–12), italics in original.

21. Mary Monck, *Marinda: Poems and Translations upon Several Occasions* (London, 1716), 19 ("Answer to the Foregoing Eclogue").

22. John Philips, *The Splendid Shilling* (London, 1705), 6.

None of this does more than exploit the ready-to-hand potential of heroic couplets, and the poem remains a fairly trifling piece of magazine verse by which Johnson set no evident store. It heralds, nonetheless, the rhetorically and thematically more ambitious patterns of verbal emphasis, such as the incremental repetition of "gold" in both the Juvenal imitations, that concentrate and structure his major poems. It also demonstrates the inseparability in Johnson's poetic style of both verbal and syntactical repetition, used to throw varying kinds of emphasis on a recurrent keyword. Here again is the "rhetoric of parallel, of antithesis, of chiasmus" that Wimsatt reads as Johnson's inheritance from Pope, though we should not forget Johnson's immersion in Latin sources.[23] To talk of repetition in the poems, at moments like this, is to talk as much about syntactical arrangement as about lexical choice.

As a critic, of course, Johnson was wary of repetition in poetry or indeed in any writing. His ridicule of monotony in Thomas Percy's *Reliques* (1765) was well-enough aimed for Wordsworth to need to refute it in *Lyrical Ballads* (the preface of 1800), and the pseudo-orality of the Ossian poems—an effect James Macpherson achieved by endlessly echoing a very limited range of tropes and figures—led Johnson to disparage *Fingal* as "a mere unconnected rhapsody, a tiresome repetition of the same images."[24] In the Preface to *Shakespeare*, it is a sign of Shakespeare's disregard for posterity, and his interest only in immediate success, that he "made no scruple to repeat the same jests in many dialogues, or to entangle different plots by the same knot of perplexity."[25] And in the *Lives of the Poets* Johnson singles out several verse subgenres—funerary epitaphs, devotional poems, martial panegyrics—as doomed by their very nature to tedious repetition. Notable offenders include Matthew Prior's poem on the Battle of Ramillies, in which "an uniform mass of ten lines, thirty-five times repeated, inconsequential and slightly connected, must weary both the ear and the understanding." Then there is the prolific hymnology of Isaac Watts: "The paucity of its topicks enforces perpetual repetition, and the sanctity of the matter rejects the ornaments of figurative diction."[26] Criticism extends even to the fourteen epitaphs of Alexander Pope, which "comprise about an hundred and forty lines, in which there are more repetitions than will easily be found in all the rest of his works."[27] Within an oeuvre such as this, and certainly in the literary tradition as a whole, repetitions of both style and substance are regrettable. "He who writes much, will not easily escape a manner, such a recurrence of particular modes as may be easily noted," as Johnson puts it in his life of Dryden.[28]

23. Wimsatt, *Prose Style*, 126. See also the emphasis placed by Weinbrot on parallelism in Old Testament poetry, in light of which "'Latinate' Johnson can sound very biblical indeed" (Weinbrot, *Aspects of Samuel Johnson*, 162).

24. *Boswell's Life of Johnson, Together with Boswell's Journal of a Tour to the Hebrides and Johnson's Diary of a Journey into North Wales*, ed. George Birkbeck Hill, rev. L. F. Powell, 6 vols. (Oxford, 1934–50), 2:126 (hereafter cited as *Life*).

25. *Johnson on Shakespeare*, vols. 7–8 of *YE*, ed. Arthur Sherbo (1968), 7:92.

26. Johnson, *Lives of the Poets*, 3:59; 4:110.

27. Johnson, *Lives of the Poets*, 4:88.

28. Johnson, *Lives of the Poets*, 2:123.

Idler 85 expresses helpless frustration in the face of what we might now call the infinity of intertextuality: "Yet surely there ought to be some bounds to repetition; libraries ought no more to be heaped for ever with the same thoughts differently expressed, than with the same books differently decorated."[29]

Similar opinions recur elsewhere, which in itself supports the implication of *Idler* 85 that repetition is the inevitable condition of human discourse. Yet Johnson's animus in these cases is always against *artless* repetition, whether in a primitive ballad, a mock-primitive pseudo-epic, a thematically restricted poetic subgenre, or an incompetently fashioned stanzaic form. There remain other, more admirable, kinds of repetition to which he is clearly drawn. Though Dryden has in Johnson's view his "recurrence of particular modes," he avoids crass and direct repetition in a way that makes him "always *another and the same*" or again "always equable and always varied,"[30] the repetition lying in a recognizable cast of mind and language beyond the reach of simple definition. Again, whereas Prior's panegyric stanzas are crass and grating, those of Gray's odes are intricate and compelling, and not repeated often enough: "the ode is finished before the ear has learned its measures," Johnson regrets, "and consequently before it can receive pleasure from their consonance and recurrence."[31] There is good and there is bad repetition, to put it bluntly, and to see Johnson recoil as a critic from repetition in poetry is to be reminded not that he thought about it as illegitimate as such, but rather that he thought about it repeatedly, and valued its artful exploitation. There was a need, indeed, to embrace repetition and practice it to maximum expressive effect, for the concentration deriving from recurrence could be dissipated by its opposite, gratuitous variation. In *Idler* 36, Johnson stresses that a successful author cannot become "[t]he man of exuberance and copiousness, who diffuses every thought thro' so many diversities of expression, that it is lost like water in a mist." The syndrome identified here is a recurrent point of criticism in the *Lives of the Poets*. One target is the undisciplined copia of Mark Akenside's *Pleasures of Imagination* (1744), where "luxuriance of expression" clouds meaning and fragments attention, and "[t]he words are multiplied till the sense is hardly perceived."[32]

And then perhaps repetition was not only a condition of discourse, to be exploited rather than merely resisted, but also a condition of life itself: a limiting fact of our mundane existence that was central to Johnson's view of the human predicament, and one that—style and meaning being inseparable—could find appropriate expression in repetitive language. Hill Boothby astutely judged the views of her addressee when she asked Johnson in a letter of July 4, 1755: "What is common life, but a repetition of the same things over and over? And is it made up of such things, as a thinking, reflecting being can bear the repetition of, over and over, long, without weariness?

29. Johnson, *The Idler and The Adventurer*, vol. 2 of *YE*, ed. W. J. Bate, John M. Bullitt, and L. F. Powell (1963), 266 (*Idler* 85, December 1, 1759).

30. Johnson, *Lives of the Poets*, 2:123, italics in original; see also Lonsdale's note on "*another and the same*" at 2:350n215.

31. Johnson, *Lives of the Poets*, 4:183.

32. *YE*, 2:113 (*Idler* 36, December 23, 1758); *Lives of the Poets*, 4:173.

I have found not."[33] Johnson found not, too, and had already said as much in *Rambler* papers such as No. 108, in which "[m]any of our hours are lost in a rotation of petty cares, in a constant recurrence of the same employments."[34] He continued to say it in his *Idler* columns some years later, notably *Idler* 103, on our "secret horrour of the last": here all marks of variation and change must be rigorously sought out because "he that lives to-day as he lived yesterday, and expects that, as the present day is, such will be the morrow, easily conceives time as running in a circle and returning to itself."[35]

The poems find more eloquently compressed ways of putting the same point, enlisting linguistic repetition to define our entrapment within a state of practical repetition—within a human condition in which, in the famous chiastic equation of *The Vanity of Human Wishes*, "Life protracted is protracted Woe" (line 258). Here is a poem that, in its very structure of Janus-faced allusion back to the Rome of its classical source and forward to the present of writing and reading, represents humanity as doomed to futile repetition not only within the individual life but also across the arc of history. Wolsey is fated to be a second Sejanus, his Juvenalian prototype, locked in the same empty and finally disastrous pursuit of power; Walpole, Wolsey's modern shadow in the poem, is fated to be a third Sejanus, and there will be more. However exceptional we might strive to be, we end the same way as mere repetitions—a point Johnson brilliantly makes by reconciling one of the most notorious political antagonisms in living memory in a shared fate of helpless, diminished senility: "From *Marlb'rough*'s Eyes the Streams of Dotage flow, / And *Swift* expires a Driv'ler and a Show" (lines 317–18).

Fail Again, Fail Better

By the time of Johnson's last poems, an inclusive first-person plural registers our shared entrapment. "Condemn'd to hope's delusive mine, / As on we toil from day to day," open his verses of the 1782 "On the Death of Dr. Robert Levet," in which repetitive syntactical, lexical, and rhythmic patterns are only brought to their close by death in the poem's conclusion: "Death broke at once the vital chain, / And free'd his soul the nearest way" (lines 35–36). Here death is a matter of blessed release, yet the abrupt, almost offhand nature of this final couplet also repeats the effect of arbitrary curtailment that Dryden had achieved when mourning young John Rogers of Gloucestershire, who, "knowing heaven his home, to shun delay / . . . leaped o'er age, and took the shortest way."[36] This was not Kierkegaard's repetition, an optimistic, forward-moving process of recommencement and advancement, opposed to regressive recollection, in which "the person who chose repetition—he lives."[37] It is more like a dreadful effect of

33. *An Account of the Life of Dr. Samuel Johnson . . . To Which Are Added, Original Letters to Dr. Samuel Johnson, by Miss Hill Boothby*, ed. Richard Wright (London, 1805), 93–94.

34. *YE*, 4:211 (*Rambler* 108, March 30, 1751).

35. *YE*, 2:315 (*Idler* 103, April 5, 1760).

36. *The Poems of John Dryden*, ed. Paul Hammond and David Hopkins, 5 vols. (London, 1995–2005), 5:621 ("Upon Young Mr Rogers of Gloucestershire," lines 7–8).

37. Søren Kierkegaard, *Fear and Trembling / Repetition*, ed. Howard V. Hong and Edna H. Hong, Kierkegaard's Writings 6 (Princeton, N.J., 1983), 132; quoted in Catherine Neal Parke, *Samuel Johnson and Biographical Thinking* (Columbia, Mo., 1991), 163.

Beckettian stasis, a condition of being irremediably stuck in a world of the nothing new—the very effect, one might speculate, that drew Beckett so powerfully to Johnson's work and led him to spend a year in the 1930s working on a play about Johnson, "Human Wishes," which turned out to be impossible to write. The Johnson I have in mind at this point is very much Beckett's Johnson, the Johnson for whom life is a matter of endless and typically failing recurrence, a grim treadmill the nature of which finds expression not in eloquent variation of language but instead through forceful, unrelenting reiteration, or perhaps at certain points even by silence. As Beckett wrote in a letter of 1937: "It isn't Boswell's wit and wisdom machine that means anything to me, but the miseries that he [Johnson] never talked of, because unwilling or unable to do so. The horror of annihilation, the horror of madness, the horrified love of Mrs. Thrale."[38]

If horror is kept at bay in Johnson's last poems, and does not quite slide into silence, it is because of the reassuring sense of discipline and measure that can arise from calibrated celebration of a well-lived life. It is revealing here to compare the terse, pared-down stanzas of the poem on Levet (stanzas 2–3 and 5–7 are quoted below) with an earlier attempt to celebrate the same kind of mundane, unostentatious virtue, as exemplified in the same unflagging diurnal performance of routine duties:

Well tried through many a varying year,
 See LEVET to the grave descend;
Officious, innocent, sincere,
 Of ev'ry friendless name the friend.

Yet still he fills affection's eye,
 Obscurely wise, and coarsely kind;
Nor, letter'd arrogance, deny
 Thy praise to merit unrefin'd.

. . . .

No summons mock'd by chill delay,
 No petty gain disdain'd by pride,
The modest wants of ev'ry day
 The toil of ev'ry day supplied.

His virtues walk'd their narrow round,
 Nor made a pause, nor left a void;
And sure th' Eternal Master found
 The single talent well employ'd.

38. Samuel Beckett to Mary Manning, [July?] 11, 1937; quoted in Frederik N. Smith, *Beckett's Eighteenth Century* (New York, 2002), 115. On the relationship between linguistic and experiential repetition in Beckett, and between repetition, identity, and death, see Steven Connor, *Samuel Beckett: Repetition, Theory, and Text* (Oxford, 1988).

The busy day, the peaceful night,
  Unfelt, uncounted, glided by;
His frame was firm, his powers were bright,
  Tho' now his eightieth year was nigh.

The kind of celebration attempted here had numerous precedents, and in one of these, Samuel Wesley the Younger's *The Parish Priest* of 1731, the poem's exemplar is one who, "fix'd and faithful to the Post assign'd, / Through various Scenes with equal Virtue trod, / True to his Oath, his Order, and his God."[39] Wesley's cleric joins in one figure the two best kinds of charity, just as the verse joins them, too, in parallel clauses, "To cure the Body and to heal the Mind"; while the practical efficacy of his virtue is expressed through structures of negation that repeat and stress his elimination of multiple ills:

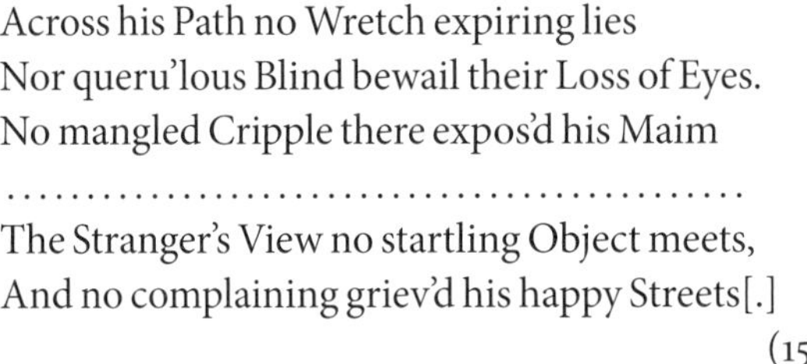

Across his Path no Wretch expiring lies
Nor queru'lous Blind bewail their Loss of Eyes.
No mangled Cripple there expos'd his Maim
. . . .
The Stranger's View no startling Object meets,
And no complaining griev'd his happy Streets[.]
(15)

The result is charity of comprehensive scope, and Wesley expresses this comprehensiveness by juxtaposing, in his subject's efforts "To raise the Friendless and support the Friend" (17), positive and negative forms of the same key term.

I mention this relatively prominent though now forgotten poem of the 1730s not to identify it as anything so direct as a source for or influence on Johnson's commemoration of Levet half a century later. There are numerous verse celebrations of unostentatious practical virtue to be found in the period, Pope's tribute to the man of Ross in the *Epistle to Bathurst* (1733) or his own father in the *Epistle to Arbuthnot* (1735) being just the most conspicuous examples. Comparison helps to demonstrate, however, how much more the mature Johnson could do, and how much more economically, with similar resources, and within the more intensive and exacting form of tetrameter. Where Wesley offers, for example, a somewhat extended parallelism in "To cure the Body and to heal the Mind," there is a more Marvellian kind of concentration to the same structure in Johnson, which arises several times in ways enhanced by emphatic midline caesurae: "The busy day, the peaceful night" (line 29), or, with more of a lexical surprise, "Obscurely wise, and coarsely kind" (line 10). The most memorable example comes in line 26, in which Levet "Nor made a pause, nor left a void," and here, too, the negation pattern is used with concentration, repeated not only from line to line but

39. Samuel Wesley, *The Parish Priest: A Poem, Upon a Clergyman Lately Deceas'd* (London, 1731), 4. Text references are to this edition. Wesley is thought to have been commemorating John Berry, vicar of Walton, Norfolk; see D. F. Foxon, *English Verse, 1701–1750: A Catalogue of Separately Printed Poems*, 2 vols. (Cambridge, 1975), 1:866.

also within the single line, and necessarily so, pauses and especially voids being—as Beckett perceived—qualities of maximal horror in Johnson's world. Negation is also stressed in the rather Miltonic pairing of successive un- prefixes ("Unfelt, uncounted") in line 30; think of Christ "Unmarkt, unknown" in *Paradise Regain'd* (1671), or again "unknown, unfriended."[40] There is variation in the repetition, then, and sometimes a studious avoidance of the obvious parallelism that might present itself, so that Wesley's somewhat predictable "raise the Friendless and support the Friend" is avoided in favor of Johnson's more compressed "Of ev'ry friendless name the friend" (line 8), with its air of rhythmic inevitability and gruff, undecorated truth. These variations only serve to emphasize the sameness of the subject they express, the unrelenting constancy of Levet's virtue as practiced, day in, day out: "The modest wants of ev'ry day / The toil of ev'ry day supplied" (lines 23–24).

Repetition is present as a stylistic feature of Johnson's poetry, then, in the service of thematic purpose, and there is some evidence that he rigorously strove to expunge repetition when that was not the case. In a passage from the *Life* dated to 1778, Boswell proudly reports his own detection of "a slight fault in [Johnson's] noble 'Imitation of the Tenth Satire of Juvenal,' a too near recurrence of the verb *spread*, in his description of the young Enthusiast at College":

> "Through all his veins the fever of renown,
> *Spreads* from the strong contagion of the gown;
> O'er Bodley's dome his future labours *spread*,
> And Bacon's mansion trembles o'er his head."[41]

When Johnson responds by gratefully instructing him to replace "spreads" with "burns" in the earlier line, Boswell congratulates himself not only for eliminating a clumsy repetition but also for intensifying the poem's meaning: "I thought this alteration not only cured the fault, but was more poetical, as it might carry an allusion to the shirt by which Hercules was inflamed."[42] What he neglects to mention, and probably realize, is that all Johnson was doing was to restore the original first-edition reading, which was "burns" all along but had been dropped in error from the second edition; he was not taking literary advice from Boswell—shirt of Nessus fire or no—but merely accepting his services as a detector of misprints. Even so, the anecdote handily demonstrates the care with which Johnson worked to strip his works of redundant verbal repetitions—a fact that might incline us to listen more closely to those he chose to retain.

Chief among these repetitions in *The Vanity of Human Wishes* as much as its predecessor *London* is of course the keyword "gold." In the earlier poem, as noted

40. John Milton, *The 1671 Poems: Paradise Regain'd and Samson Agonistes*, vol. 2 of *The Complete Works of John Milton*, ed. Laura Lunger Knoppers (Oxford, 2008), 5 (1.25); 31 (2.413).

41. *Life*, 3:357, italics in original.

42. *Life*, 3:358.

above, this runs from the "Thirst for Pow'r and Gold" that animates the unrestrained kleptocrats of line 62, via the smiling "Slaves to Gold" of line 178, to the "golden" pile of Orgilio (line 208), the "golden Coach" of his accomplices (line 235), and the heavily ironic "golden Reign" of King Alfred (line 248)—a memory now no less contaminated in the poem than the "silver Flood" at Greenwich. Perhaps surprisingly, there are only two occurrences in the original Latin text of *aureum* or its cognates, and financial corruption is just one among many targets at which Juvenal aims in his comprehensive satire on metropolitan decadence. Earlier translators or imitators such as John Oldham, Henry Higden, and John Dryden, too, had relatively little to say about gold, though they amply represent, and get some of their best comic passages from, elements of corruption that Johnson reduces or removes: witness the undiscriminating sexual voracity, entirely absent from Johnson's version, that makes Oldham's speaker warn that "All must go pad-lock'd: if nought else there be, / Suspect thy very Stables Chastity."[43] Where other poets faithfully reflect the scattershot nature of the original satire, Johnson turns it into something else, a concentrated poem about financial corruption and the deep complicity in it of the political elite. Whereas Dryden's lone mention of gold literally translates Juvenal ("But let not all the gold which Tagus hides / . . . Be bribe sufficient to corrupt thy breast"),[44] Johnson allows the gold to proliferate linguistically, and he makes it glisten: "Turn from the glitt'ring Bribe thy scornful Eye, / Nor sell for Gold, what Gold could never buy" (lines 87–88).

All of this is a dress rehearsal for perhaps the most remarkable passage in *The Vanity of Human Wishes* a decade later, in which "scarce observ'd the Knowing and the Bold / Fall in the gen'ral Massacre of Gold" (lines 21–22). This imaginatively compressed, rhythmically disrupted line has no close counterpart in Juvenal or earlier English versions, whose authors write slackly instead about "The greedy care of heaping Wealth" (Higden) or "heaps of money crowded in the chest" (Dryden).[45] No other translator or imitator has anything like the famous Johnsonian couplet that follows—"For Gold his Sword the hireling Ruffian draws, / For Gold the hireling Judge distorts the Laws" (lines 25–26)—in which the anaphoric opening "For Gold . . . For Gold" leads on to the mischievous repetition of "hireling," framed within the chiastic structure of "Sword . . . draws / . . . distorts . . . Laws." Inescapably, a sly equation is proposed in these patterns between villainy in the dock and on the bench, so that the expected antithesis between ruffian and judge turns out to be no antithesis at all. This is where the distinctive "force" of Johnson's poetry resides, in the complex, concentrated fusion of verbal and syntactical repetition in his couplet form.

In these poems the rhetoric of repetition is above all a polemical resource, a distillation of fashionable oppositional rhetoric—something Johnson would emphati-

43. *The Poems of John Oldham*, ed. Harold F. Brooks with Raman Selden (Oxford, 1987), 251 ("A Satyr, In Imitation of the Third of Juvenal," lines 169–70).

44. *Poems of Dryden*, 4:25 ("The Third Satire of Juvenal," lines 97–99).

45. Henry Higden, *A Modern Essay on the Tenth Satyr of Juvenal* (London, 1687), 4; *Poems of Dryden*, 4:98 ("The Tenth Satire of Juvenal," line 17).

cally renounce in such later works as the life of Thomson[46]—into the form of fierce political epigram. One finds the same effect in other poems of the Walpole era, such as the mock prophecy in *Marmor Norfolciense*, with its antipastoral vision of fruitful land despoiled by invaders who "Rob without fear, and fatten without toil," and its culminating vision of universal disorder: "Then o'er the World shall Discord stretch her wings, / Kings change their laws, and kingdoms change their kings."[47] Again the structures of linguistic repetition are used to remind us of actual historical repetition, the repetition of political usurpation now achieved by the House of Hanover but reaching back through the Glorious Revolution of 1688–89 to the inaugurating Williamite invasion of 1066. Artful echoes of Dryden and Pope reinforce this reminder, notably in the epanalepsis ("Kings . . . kings") of line 16. Most obviously this is a reminder of Dryden's reflection on the Glorious Revolution in his stylishly translated lament (from a neo-Latin source) for the defeated Jacobite loyalist Bonnie Dundee: "New people fill the land now thou art gone, / New gods the temples, and new kings the throne."[48] But Johnson also calls to mind Pope's *Windsor-Forest* (1713), in which, as with the ransacked landscape of *Marmor Norfolciense*, a scene of pastoral peace and plenty is usurped by new tyrants, literally the two Williams of the Norman conquest but by implication also William III—so leaving the people of England "To Savage Beasts and Savage Laws a Prey, / And Kings more furious and severe than they."[49] Rhythmic disruption—kings change their laws, and poets change their measure—intensifies the effect of disjuncture and discord. Here Johnson uses not only his own epanaleptic repetition, from "Kings" through "kingdoms" back to "kings" again, but also repeated formulae from Dryden and Pope to remind his readers that Hanoverian usurpation—like the tyranny of Sejanus-Wolsey-Walpole in *The Vanity of Human Wishes*—is just the most recent instance of a recurring evil.

I conclude with the mature Johnson, for whom political innuendo is a distant memory, and who instead returns—in yet another gesture of self-repeating—to the

46. "At this time a long course of opposition to Sir Robert Walpole had filled the nation with clamours for liberty, of which no man felt the want, and with care for liberty, which was not in danger" (Johnson, *Lives of the Poets*, 4:99). Consciously or otherwise, this dismissive parallelism—which implies, among other things, a retraction of *London*—recalls words that Johnson had put in Walpole's mouth decades earlier. In one of the parliamentary debates that Johnson wrote for the *Gentleman's Magazine* at the height of the opposition campaign, "Sir Retrob Walelop" charges the campaign's leaders with disingenuous posturing: "even in their own opinion, they are complaining of grievances which they do not suffer"; *Debates in Parliament*, vols. 11–13 of *YE*, ed. Thomas Kaminski and Benjamin Beard Hoover (2012), 12:579; first published in April 1743, concerning the proceedings of February 13, 1741.

47. Johnson, *Political Writings*, vol. 10 of *YE*, ed. Donald J. Greene (1977), 25 (*Marmor Norfolciense*, "To Posterity," lines 14, 15–16).

48. *Poems of Dryden*, 3:219 ("Upon the Death of the Viscount Dundee," lines 3–4).

49. Alexander Pope, *Pastoral Poetry and An Essay on Criticism*, ed. E. Audra and Aubrey Williams, vol. 1 of *The Twickenham Edition of the Poems of Alexander Pope*, 11 vols. (London and New Haven, Conn., 1961), 153 (*Windsor-Forest*, lines 45–46). Also perhaps lurking beneath Johnson's words is a mischievous—and in this case, somewhat incongruous—line of political innuendo that Pope parenthetically inserts in the *Essay on Criticism*: "(As *Kings* dispense with *Laws* Themselves have made)" (*Pastoral Poetry and An Essay on Criticism*, 259 [*Essay*, line 162]).

work of Horatian translation begun in his youth. The last poem we have from his hand is a translation from *Odes* 4.7, written within a month of his death in 1784. It is a poem, quoted in its entirety below, that makes recurrence not only its method but also its subject:

The snow dissolv'd no more is seen,
The fields, and woods, behold, are green,
The changing year renews the plain,
The rivers know their banks again,
The spritely Nymph and naked Grace
The mazy dance together trace.
The changing year's successive plan
Proclaims mortality to Man.
Rough Winter's blasts to Spring give way,
Spring yield[s] to Summer['s] sovereign ray,
Then Summer sinks in Autumn's reign,
And Winter chils the World again.
Her losses soon the Moon supplies,
But wretched Man, when once he lies
Where Priam and his sons are laid,
Is nought but Ashes and a Shade.
Who knows if Jove who counts our Score
Will toss us in a morning more?
What with your friend you nobly share
At least you rescue from your heir.
Not you, Torquatus, boast of Rome,
When Minos once has fix'd your doom,
Or Eloquence, or splendid birth,
Or Virtue shall replace on earth.
Hippolytus unjustly slain
Diana calls to life in vain,
Nor can the might of Theseus rend
The chains of hell that hold his friend.

If there survives any trace of the political here, it is in the image of sovereignty and reigning (with a halfhearted pun on autumnal rain) in lines 10–11 of the poem, which have no counterpart in the original Latin, nor so far as I know in any prior English translation. Issues of government or succession, however, now look local and trivial. What dominates this spare and rigorous last exercise is Johnson's stylistic intensification of Horace's mutability theme, specifically his use of patterns of repetition to enact meaning in subtle ways. The poem sets the recurrent rejuvenation of nature through the cycle of seasons in painful contrast with the relentless linear movement of an individual life toward—as Beckett would put it—annihilation. "The changing year renews the plain" in the poem's third line, and also renews itself in the progress of the poem, returning a few lines later as a point of contrast with the individual man, who will not rejuvenate like nature around him: "The changing year's successive plan / Proclaims mortality to Man." Just to rub it in, the anadiplodic effect of lines 9–12—anadiplosis being the rhetorical figure in which the closing term of one clause recurs in the opening of the next—reinforces the pattern of cyclical reanimation from which the poet is excluded: winter to spring, spring to summer, summer to autumn, winter again—at which point the poem gives way to a kind of desperate levity, introducing an effect that Smart, by comparison, misses. "Who knows if heav'n will give to-morrow's boon / To this our daily pray'r?"[50] is Smart's version of the lines that Johnson laconically renders "Who knows if Jove who counts our Score / Will toss us in a morning more?" Finally—given the striking absence from this Horace translation of the Christian consolation that Johnson had appended to Juvenal in *The Vanity of Human Wishes*—comes the grimmest recognition of all: that nothing can give to the individual life the immortality of nature in general. Not merit, not rank, not even eloquence: "Not you, Torquatus, boast of Rome, / When Minos once has fix'd your doom, / Or Eloquence, or splendid birth, / Or Virtue shall replace on earth."

Or might eloquence in fact do something to help? Johnson did not have the benefit of splendid birth, and he spent a lifetime berating himself for deficiencies in virtue of various kinds. Yet there can be little doubt about the eloquence, and the immortality conferred by verse—the compensatory capacity of the force of poetry in the face of decay and death—is a venerable poetic trope. Perhaps it is not only a joke at Rasselas's expense, but also a flourish of authorial self-recognition, when Johnson has his stranded hero "receive some solace of the miseries of life, from consciousness of the delicacy with which he felt, and the eloquence with which he bewailed them."[51] If so, the eloquence in Johnson himself is one that flows from his arts of repetition and enacts the repetitions of life.

I thank John Siferd for his able assistance in preparing this essay for publication.

50. Smart, *Works of Horace, Translated into Verse*, 127.
51. Johnson, *Rasselas and Other Tales*, vol. 16 of *YE*, ed. Gwin J. Kolb (1990), 14.

“A disposition to write”: Johnson as Correspondent

Jack Lynch

“WE HAVE BEEN SLOW TO RECOGNIZE the brilliance of Johnson’s epistolary output,” Tom Keymer points out, “and slower still to develop approaches adequate to it.”[1] The criticism is fair. Samuel Johnson’s letters can hardly be called neglected; anthologies have even made a few known, if not famous, outside narrow Johnsonian circles. Those few, however, are atypical. As Freya Johnston puts it, “two Johnsonian monuments have obscured the range and variety of his private correspondence. Two of his most famous letters, the vigorous denunciations of Lord Chesterfield and James Macpherson, are necessarily unrepresentative.”[2]

The other letters have not been completely ignored, either, but they have usually been mined for only two types of things: biographical nuggets, to supplement the third-person biographical accounts that figure so large in Johnsonian studies, as well as obiter dicta—a life radically wretched, the use of traveling is to regulate imagination by reality, and so on. We have a bias toward the grand generalities and resonant apothegms, but we need to remember how limiting this can be. Biographical data and grand pronouncements have their value—but so, too, do the less familiar letters, those with no profound wisdom to deliver, that were prompted by no extraordinary occasion.

This essay concerns Johnson’s attitudes toward letter writing itself—again, a subject that has not been entirely neglected. *Rambler* 152 is the most important source for Johnsonian meditations on epistolarity: “scarcely any species of composition deserves more to be cultivated than the epistolary stile, since none is of more various or frequent use, through the whole subordination of human life.”[3] We also remember the witticism Boswell recorded, that “It is now become so much the fashion to publish

1. Tom Keymer, “‘Letters about Nothing’: Johnson and Epistolary Writing,” in *The Cambridge Companion to Samuel Johnson*, ed. Greg Clingham (Cambridge, 1997), 224–39 at 225.

2. Freya Johnston, “Correspondence,” in *Samuel Johnson in Context*, ed. Jack Lynch (Cambridge, 2012), 21–28 at 21.

3. Johnson, *Rambler* 152, in *The Rambler*, vols. 3–5 of *The Yale Edition of the Works of Samuel Johnson* (hereafter cited as *YE*), ed. W. J. Bate and Albrecht B. Strauss (New Haven, Conn., 1969), 5:43 (August 31, 1751). Text references are to this edition.

letters, that in order to avoid it, I put as little into mine as I can."[4] While the essays and biographies give us some insights, though, the comments on letter writing that appear in Johnson's letters themselves have mostly been ignored.[5] In fact, few of the passages I discuss in this essay have ever been discussed in books or journal articles. These unfamiliar familiar letters may convey few great truths and resolve no biographical mysteries, but they do tell us who he was when he was at home.

We know much about Johnson as a writer, and have learned much in recent years about Johnson as a reader. Letters, however, make us both readers and writers in unfamiliar ways, making it difficult for us to discuss letters as literature.

For one thing, letters occupy a strange place on the continuum of private-to-public writing. Hugh Blair knew as much when he wrote, "Epistolary Writing . . . possesses a kind of middle place between the serious and amusing species of Composition."[6] This middle place—or *betweenity*, to use a word coined by another great eighteenth-century letter writer—has consequences for how we read.[7] Because letters stride the boundary between the "serious" and the "amusing," they are at the mercy of changing critical fashion. For much of the twentieth century, letters were neglected, used for biographical or cultural "background," but otherwise kept outside the neatly demarcated boundaries of the literary. Only in the 1980s did a redrawing of those boundaries begin.

Even when letters have been recognized as potentially literary, there has been an assumption that they deserve our attention only insofar as they address weighty subjects. Blair held that personal letters derive some of their worth from the grandeur of the topics they address: "If the subject of the Letters be important, they will be the more valuable" (*Lectures*, 2:298). Letters on mere domestic privacies, on the other hand, risk degenerating into unedifying trivialities. Hester Thrale knew that

4. *Boswell's Life of Samuel Johnson, Together with Boswell's Journal of a Tour to the Hebrides and Johnson's Diary of a Journey into North Wales*, ed. George Birkbeck Hill, rev. L. F. Powell, 6 vols. (Oxford, 1934–50), 4:102 (hereafter cited as *Life*).

5. They may have been ignored in more ways than one. The passages I dwell on in this essay come disproportionately from the letters that survive in manuscript. It is impossible to be certain, but it seems that many of Johnson's comments about letter writing are among the parts that are routinely omitted from unscholarly printed versions. In cases where no manuscript survives and we are forced to fall back on an early printed version or an extract in an auction catalogue, passages such as I discuss here appear very rarely. Perhaps literary history has decided they are the parts not worth preserving—which is one reason I am interested in them.

6. Hugh Blair, *Lectures on Rhetoric and Belles Lettres*, 3 vols. (London, 1785), 2:297. Text references are to this edition.

7. Horace Walpole coined *betweenity* in a letter to George Montagu, September 1, 1760, reprinted in *The Yale Edition of Horace Walpole's Correspondence*, ed. W. S. Lewis, 48 vols. (New Haven, Conn., 1937–83), 9:297.

> None but domestick and familiar events can be expected from a private correspondence; no reflexions but such as they excite can be found there; yet whoever turns away disgusted by the insipidity with which this, and I suppose every correspondence must naturally and almost necessarily begin—will here be likely to lose some genuine pleasure, and some useful knowledge of what your heroick Milton was himself contented to respect, as
>
> *That which before thee lies in daily life.*

She also knew, however, that genuine pleasure and useful knowledge had their own value: "[S]hould I be charged with obtruding trifles on the Publick," she wrote, "I might reply, that the meanest animals preserved in amber become of value to those who form collections of natural history, that the fish found in Monte Bolca serve as proofs of sacred writ, and that the cart-wheel stuck in the rock of Tivoli, is now found useful in computing the rotation of the earth."[8] Johnson agreed: there is much to learn from private letters, if only the reader is receptive and the writer is honest:

> Yet as much of life must be passed in affairs considerable only by their frequent occurrence, and much of the pleasure which our condition allows, must be produced by giving elegance to trifles, it is necessary to learn how to become little without becoming mean, to maintain the necessary intercourse of civility, and fill up the vacuities of action by agreeable appearances. It had therefore been of advantage if such of our writers as have excelled in the art of decorating insignificance, had supplied us with a few sallies of innocent gaiety, effusions of honest tenderness, or exclamations of unimportant hurry. (*YE*, 5:44)

Johnson was himself a master of effusions of honest tenderness, and he knew the value of filling up the vacuities of action.

Confusion easily works its way into discussions of epistolarity, since many things that are not properly letters have been treated as such. Blair excludes formal epistolary treatises from his discussion of letters proper: "Though they bear, in the title page, a Letter to a Friend, after the first address, the friend disappears, and we see, that it is, in truth, the Public with whom the Author corresponds. . . . There is no probability that they ever passed in correspondence, as real letters." For him, compositions that happen to bear some of the formal characteristics of the letter aren't "real": "Epistolary Writing becomes a distinct species of Composition, subject to the cognizance of Criticism, only or chiefly, when it is of the easy and familiar kind; when it is conversation carried on upon paper, between two friends at a distance" (*Lectures*, 2:297).

8. Hester Lynch Piozzi, *Letters to and from the Late Samuel Johnson, LL.D.: To Which Are Added Some Poems Never Before Printed: Published from the Original MSS. in Her Possession, by Hester Lynch Piozzi*, 2 vols. (London, 1788), 1:ii–iii.

It is easy to be confused over who "owns" a letter—a confusion inscribed in modern copyright law, which tries (not always successfully) to distinguish the ownership of the physical piece of paper from the ownership of the words written thereon. In *Thraliana*, it is sometimes unclear how to interpret Thrale's references to "my letters," by which she often means not "the letters I have written" but "the letters in my possession"—that is, letters written by others that she had with her. The problem is complicated further by the way in which private letters could become public. Johnson has much to say about the publication of putatively familiar letters. He acknowledges that letters on public matters are usually the ones that become public—"very few have endeavoured to distinguish themselves by the publication of letters, except such as were written in the discharge of publick trusts, and during the transaction of great affairs" (*YE*, 5:43)—but he acknowledges, too, that the line is not always clear. He gently chides one poet for the chicanery he used to get his letters into print: "It seems that Pope, being desirous of printing his Letters, and not knowing how to do, without imputation of vanity, what has in this country been done very rarely, contrived an appearance of compulsion; that when he could complain that his Letters were surreptitiously published, he might decently and defensively publish them himself."[9]

The letter's curious betweenity on the boundary of the public and the private has attracted attention, and with reason. The letter's seeming ability to present unvarnished truth without the artifice of public presentation is a perennial theme in eighteenth-century discussions of correspondence, particularly the letter as what Pope memorably called a "window in the bosom."[10] Blair knew better: "It is childish indeed to expect, that in Letters we are to find the whole heart of the Author unveiled. Concealment and disguise take place, more or less, in all human intercourse." Even Blair, though, expected some approximation of authenticity: "But still, as Letters from one friend to another make the nearest approach to conversation, we may expect to see more of a character displayed in these than in other productions.... Much, therefore, of the merit, and the agreeableness of Epistolary Writing, will depend on its introducing us into some acquaintance with the Writer" (*Lectures*, 2:298).

Johnson, on the other hand, found the very idea ridiculous. Laetitia Matilda Hawkins notes that he "spoke contemptuously of the habit of corresponding by letter, and of professing to *pour out one's soul* upon paper."[11] He makes that contempt clear in this ironic recitation of the familiar bromides:

9. "Pope," in *The Lives of the Most Eminent Poets: With Critical Observations on Their Works*, ed. Roger Lonsdale, 4 vols. (Oxford, 2006), 4:37. Text references are to this edition.

10. Alexander Pope to Charles Jervas, December 12, 1718, reprinted in Pope, *Correspondence*, ed. George Sherburn, 5 vols. (Oxford, 1956), 2:23. The scholarship on "authenticity" in epistolary correspondence is substantial; see, for example, Bruce Redford, *The Converse of the Pen: Acts of Intimacy in the Eighteenth-Century Familiar Letter* (Chicago, 1986), 46; and Cynthia Lowenthal, *Lady Mary Wortley Montagu and the Eighteenth-Century Familiar Letter* (Athens, Ga., 1994), esp. 20–21. For Johnson's practice, see Redford, *The Converse of the Pen*, 214–17, and Keymer, "'Letters about Nothing.'"

11. *Johnsonian Miscellanies*, ed. George Birkbeck Hill, 2 vols. (Oxford, 1897), 2:143, italics in original. Text references are to this edition.

> In a Man's Letters you know, Madam, his soul lies naked, his letters are only the mirrour of his breast, whatever passes within him is shown undisguised in its natural process. Nothing is inverted, nothing distorted, you see systems in their elements, you discover actions in their motives.
>
> Of this great truth sounded by the knowing to the ignorant, and so echoed by the ignorant to the knowing, what evidence have you now before you. Is not my soul laid open in these veracious pages? do not you see me reduced to my first principles? This is the pleasure of corresponding with a friend, where doubt and distrust have no place, and every thing is said as it is thought... These are the letters by which souls are united, and by which Minds naturally in unison move each other as they are moved themselves.... I have indeed concealed nothing from you, nor do I expect ever to repent of having thus opened my heart.[12]

Keymer's summary is astute: "By pushing to absurdity the claims implicit in the conventional language of undress, the po-faced pseudo-scientisms of Johnson's letter expose the fragility of the unexamined 'great truth' to which they explicitly seem committed."[13]

One more danger in reading letters is the tendency to treat them as discrete works. Even when personal letters have been subjected to more than merely biographical inquiry, critics have treated the individual letter, rather than the entire correspondence, as the unit of interest. This practice may be influenced by the New Critical habit of scrutinizing single lyric poems, divorced from the contexts in which they appeared; still, it is an interpretive practice poorly suited to correspondences. A poem, a play, a novel has a clear beginning and end; even if the work undergoes revision and expansion, at its moment of publication it has a defined shape. Letters, on the other hand, refuse to stand alone. They derive only part of their meaning from the words between "Dear Sir" and "Your humble servant"; much more comes from their place in a correspondence that can last months, years, or decades.

A full correspondence allows, even forces, us to see individual letters in new contexts. Perhaps the most important respect in which epistolary writing differs from other kinds is that it comes with an expectation, even an obligation, to produce more letters. In her study of one extended correspondence, Cynthia Lowenthal puts it well: "Partners in the epistolary cycle are also dependent on one another for the shape and substance of their letters; each document, whether a bridge or a record of absence, is a response to the letters that have gone before."[14] A poem may inspire other poems, but the existence of those later works is not really demanded by the original. A polemical

12. Samuel Johnson to Hester Lynch Thrale, October 27, 1777, reprinted in *The Letters of Samuel Johnson*, ed. Bruce Redford, Hyde Edition, 5 vols. (Princeton, N.J., 1992–94), 3:89–90 (hereafter cited in text as *Letters*).

13. Keymer, "'Letters about Nothing,'" 227.

14. Lowenthal, *Lady Mary Wortley Montagu*, 24.

pamphlet often engages in a discussion, but the pamphleteer hopes—or at least affects to hope—to end the debate with the definitive contribution. The letter writer, on the other hand, expects a response by return of post; a correspondence is open-ended, and always incomplete until death or irreconcilable enmity imposes finality upon it. Who, in a familiar exchange, wants to have the last word? What is more, the meaning of individual letters changes as new letters are added to the correspondence, and new evidence forces us to read old letters in new ways. Eighteenth-century writers of fiction who experimented with epistolary form knew this instinctively. When early English novelists such as Aphra Behn and Samuel Richardson pioneered influential fictional techniques by "writing to the moment," they took advantage of the fact that the imagined writers and readers did not know how their story was going to turn out.

With all these caveats out of the way, we can at last turn our attention to the letters themselves. To read through all of Johnson's letters in the Hyde Edition is a remarkable experience because they provide a kind of parallel track to his more familiar biography. They reveal the daily texture of life as Johnson experienced it at the time, and they show us sides of his character that do not come through in the more familiar sources. The things modern academic Johnsonians consider the most important in his life—the scholarship, the moral philosophizing, the political engagement—assume in the letters a much smaller part than they do in the works we usually read. Instead, we get to experience what occupied his mind from day to day, such as the extent of his suffering from physical and mental maladies. It is easy to exaggerate Johnson's handicaps; some commentators have been unable to withstand the urge to pile misery on misery and reduce him to a quivering bundle of syndromes. We must resist the desire to incapacitate him still further. The letters, though, leave no question that torment was often the dominant thing on his mind, crowding out everything else.

It is difficult to resist the temptation to look at Johnson's letters individually, since that is the form in which the evidence comes to us. We have a generous selection of letters written *by* Johnson, especially in his later years, but letters written *to* him have never been collected in one place: we have Johnson's *Letters*, not his *Correspondence*. True, we can piece some of that correspondence together. Hester Thrale published *Letters to and from the Late Samuel Johnson, LL.D.* in 1788; Boswell's *Life* includes hundreds of letters from Johnson and dozens to him; and R. W. Chapman's edition of 1952 is *The Letters of Samuel Johnson with Mrs. Thrale's Genuine Letters to Him*. And, conveniently, some of Johnson's most important correspondents and members of his circle have had their own letters published: James Boswell, Edmund Burke, Charles and Frances Burney, Robert Dodsley, David Garrick, Oliver Goldsmith, Thomas Percy, Hester Piozzi, Joshua Reynolds, Christopher Smart, Adam Smith, and Thomas Warton have all been the subject of more or less scholarly editions. Still, only a small fraction of the letters he received over his life have ever been published, and it would be difficult to read them through. A full *Correspondence of Samuel Johnson*, though a desideratum, would be no small effort.

In the absence of that full *Correspondence*, though, we can still try to understand the letters as part of reciprocal exchanges—and this is something Johnson makes fairly easy. Letter writing is one of the main subjects of Johnson's letters, and his comments on the subject provide a neglected perspective on his mind, his attitudes toward reading and writing, toward friendship, toward solitude.

Johnson wrote with an uncommon awareness of the exchanges prompted by his own writing. He so relished the back-and-forth quality of written exchanges that even attacks were welcome: "Abuse . . . is often of service: there is nothing so dangerous to an author as silence; his name, like a shuttlecock, must be beat backward and forward, or it falls to the ground" (*Johnsonian Miscellanies*, 1:407). The American outrage provoked by *Taxation No Tyranny* famously was not enough for him: "I think I have not been attacked enough for it," he mused. "Attack is the re-action; I never think I have hit hard, unless it rebounds" (*Life*, 2:384). That rebound was central to his conception of the literary life.

What he enjoyed, however, could also be a source of frustration. I focus in this essay on the obligation that correspondence imposed on both writer and recipient, a subject that appears everywhere in Johnson's letters. Perhaps a quarter of them—a quarter of those, at least, to his regular correspondents—devote one or more sentences to the duties imposed by correspondence, whether he was pleading for more letters from his friends or apologizing for failing to hold up his end of the bargain. No other subject comes close in terms of sheer volume. If Johnson's letters can be said to have a single theme, it is the obligation to write more letters.

Read his letters through, and you will be struck by the delight Johnson took in getting mail. Joy was all too rare in his life, and what happiness he did experience often arrived with the post. "You are a dear dear Lady," he wrote to Hester Thrale in 1779. "To write so often, and so sweetly makes some amends for your absence. Your last letter came about half an hour after my last letter was sent away, but now I have another" (*Letters*, 3:210). Just a few months before his death, Johnson wrote to Richard Brocklesby, "do not omit to write, for You cannot think with what warmth of expectation I reckon the hours of a post-day" (4:366).

Expectation disappointed, though, was terribly trying, and Johnson was genuinely pained when the post came and went without a letter for him. "Do not neglect to write to me," he begged Hester Thrale in 1777, "for when a post comes empty, I am really disappointed" (3:62). Again, two years later: "It is now past the Postman's time and I have no letter, and that is not well done, because I long for a letter, and you should always let me know whether you and Mr. Thrale and all the rest are, or are not well. Do not serve me so often, because your silence is always a disappointment" (3:198).

As a result, he made tremendous efforts to get his friends to write to him. A shocking amount of Johnson's epistolary output is given to wheedling, cajoling, scolding, hectoring, browbeating, or shaming his friends into writing letters to him. Examples are plentiful; this one from 1777 is all too typical: "Do you call this punctual correspondence?" he demanded of Hester Thrale. "There was poor I writing, and writing, and writing, on the 8th, on the 11th, on the 13th; and on the 15th I looked for a letter, but I may look and look." The problem? "Instead of writing to me you are writing the Thraliana" (3:66). Of course he is teasing; the letters, especially those to Thrale, are the place where his playful irony comes through most clearly. Even allowing for the irony, though, this is a pathetic performance, and there is no way Thrale could have avoided discomfort in reading a letter like this. Johnson treats the diary as a rival and comes across as peevish, pettish, and unpleasant to be around.

He could turn that petulance on any of his regular correspondents. Hester Thrale was a favorite target: "So many days and never a letter. . . . This is Turkish usage. And I have been hoping and hoping. But you [are] so glad to have me out of your mind" (1:405). Who would not be glad to be rid of such a grouch? (Hester Thrale learned to expect this treatment: "What a letter is this!" she writes in the middle of one of her own efforts; "but you would be angry were it shorter.")[15] No one was immune. Edmund Hector was told in 1757, "I rather take it unkindly that you do not from time to time let me hear from you" (1:153). In 1776 William Strahan was reprimanded, "I wrote to You about ten days ago, and sent you some copy. You have not written again. That is a sorry trick" (2:357). Even children could not escape. When in 1781 Hester Thrale wrote that "Queeney . . . says you did not bid her write to you; and you *used* to *bid* her write to you," Johnson replied with something hard to distinguish from bad nature: Queeney "is a naughty captious girl, that will not write because I did not remember to ask her" (3:364–65, 365n2).[16] Another one of his notes to Queeney is terribly off-putting to modern sensibilities. Queeney "has not written yet," he told her mother in 1771; "perhaps she designs that I should love Harry best" (1:375). Again, it is not to be taken seriously; the sly wink is unmistakable. Still, there is something unsettling about a man of sixty-one threatening to withhold affection from a six-year-old girl if she does not write often enough.

The scoldings were not limited to those who failed to write often enough; those who failed to write letters of sufficient length were also chastened: "When you write make your letters as long as you can," he told Lucy Porter in 1768, "for I always think them too short" (1:316). He said much the same to Thrale in 1773: "Never imagine that your letters are long, they are always too short for my curiosity; I do not know that I was ever content with a single perusal" (2:31). "A short letter to a distant friend," he wrote to Giuseppe Baretti, "is, in my opinion, an insult like that of a slight bow or

15. Piozzi, *Letters to and from the Late Samuel Johnson*, 1:193.

16. Johnson followed it up with a more gentle explanation to Queeney herself: "How could you suppose that by not asking you to write, I meant to show dislike or indifference. It had been more reasonable to suppose that having asked you often, and having had no reason to change my mind, I considered it as a general compact that we should write to one another" (3:369).

cursory salutation;—proof of unwillingness to do much, even where there is a necessity of doing something. Yet it must be remembered, that he who continues the same course of life in the same place, will have little to tell" (1:196).

Johnson was not the only letter writer who was pained by dilatory or lethargic correspondents. It is easy to find comparable passages in the letters of many other writers. In his account of early modern correspondence practices, Gary Schneider adduces a letter of 1523 from Antony of Guevara to Alonso of Albornoz, "wherein is touched, that it is a point of euill maner, not to aunswer to the letter that is written vnto him." Antony scolds Alonso: "Not without cause I saide, my pen was angrey with your slothfulnesse, since halfe a yeare past I did write vnto you, and you haue not as yet aunswered me." From anger Antony turns to finger-wagging: "Sir, you may take it for a rule, neuer to leaue him vnanswered, that hath taken paine to write vnto you. . . . To write to our better, is of necessitie, to answere our equall is of will, but to write vnto our inveriour, is of pure vertue."[17] Schneider, noting a number of passages like this in early modern letters, argues that "the maintenance of epistolary continuity was indeed the principal reason why certain letter-writing customs developed," with the dating of letters as his primary example. "Not acknowledging one's letters," he writes, "was, indeed, a source of tension, even anger. . . . prompt response constituted part of the conduct of a correspondence. That shame was inscribed in long-delayed letters attests to a feeling that one's epistolary duty had lapsed."[18]

Such scoldings had been formalized, even ritualized, by the eighteenth century. Many letter-writing manuals from the era include a model letter for nudging a negligent correspondent to reply. *The Compleat Secretary*, for example, an often-reprinted manual of 1704 by "G. F., Gent.," includes "A Letter to a Friend in the Country, for her neglecting to Write, according to her Promise," along with "The Gentlewoman's Answer."[19] James Wallace's *Every Man His Own Letter-Writer* (1782?) likewise includes a model letter "To a Friend on Neglect of answering Letters," along with an appropriate model reply. "A Considerable time having elapsed since I had the pleasure of hearing from you," Wallace advises his reader, "disagreeable doubts arise in my mind as to the continuance of your health." "I Blush to acknowledge the receipt of your four kind letters without returning an answer," the correspondent is to write back. "I must confess my neglect, submit myself to your candour, and promise the strictest attention to your epistolary favours in future."[20]

That such models exist indicates there was a need for them: eighteenth-century letter writers were self-conscious about their epistolary duties. Still, almost no one rivals Johnson in his insistence on prompt correspondence, or matches his crankiness when that correspondence does not come.

17. *The Familiar Epistles of Sir Antony of Guevara* (London, 1574), 110, 112, 113.

18. Gary Schneider, *The Culture of Epistolarity: Vernacular Letters and Letter Writing in Early Modern England, 1500–1700* (Newark, Del., 2005), 56, 57–58.

19. G. F., *The Compleat Secretary: In Four Parts* (London, 1704), 7, 9.

20. James Wallace, D.D., *Every Man His Own Letter-Writer; or, The New and Complete Art of Letter-Writing Made Plain and Familiar to Every Capacity* (London, 1782?), 120.

❀

Why the constant need for letters? Sometimes Johnson considered the possibility that no news was bad news, and that the lack of a letter meant that some misfortune had befallen the correspondent. "I am afraid that something has happened to occupy your mind disagreeably," he wrote to Thrale in 1775, "and hinder you from writing to me, or thinking about me" (2:187). He fretted about such things even when he knew he had no good reason: "If I have not a little something from you to day, I shall think something very calamitous has befallen us. This is the natural effect of punctuality. Every intermission alarms" (2:218). Mostly, though, he was not worried about his correspondents; he was worried about himself. Letters helped to stave off idleness when he was solitary, and to distract himself from himself. Letters guarded against the taedium vitae.[21] Unlike other things he might read, letters were produced specifically *for* him, proving that he was still loved—reminding and reassuring him that he mattered enough to make absent friends write to him. This explains the obligation he imposed on those friends, even when the obligation became burdensome.

Obligations, though, have an irritating habit of running two ways. As his *Dictionary* definition makes clear, *correspondence* is "reciprocal intelligence," and Johnson often had trouble with reciprocal relations. The burden of *having to write* could be oppressive. It was a genuinely lifelong concern. The very first sentence of Johnson's very first surviving letter, from October 1731, reads: "I have so long neglected to return You thanks for the favours and Assistance I received from you at Stourbridge that I am afraid You have now done expecting it" (1:3). The very last sentence of Johnson's very last surviving letter, apart from the formulaic valediction, from December 10, 1784, reads: "I am very unwilling to take the pains of writing" (4:446).

Writing to friends was not always painful; sometimes it served as a psychic analgesic. Johnson's letter to Hill Boothby at the end of 1755 is singularly evocative of the sorrow that could afflict him when he was alone at night, and it reveals that the inkwell was sometimes the only source of relief from his crushing loneliness: "It is again Midnight, and I am again alone. With what meditation shall I amuse this waste hour of darkness and vacuity. If I turn my thoughts upon myself what do [I] perceive but a poor helpless being reduced by a blast of wind to weakness and misery" (1:117). External evidence, moreover, tells us that Johnson could write fluently when the need arose. "Dr. Johnson wrote a long letter to Mrs. Thrale," Boswell writes in Banff on August 25, 1773. "I wondered to see him write so much so easily. He verified his own doctrine, that 'a man may always write when he will set himself *doggedly* to it'" (*Life*, 5:109–10, italics in original).[22] The evidence from Johnson himself, however, tells us that he was rarely

21. See Freya Johnston, "Correspondence," 24: "Johnson considered letters as 'fill[ing] up the vacuities of action by agreeable appearances' [*Rambler* 152]; therefore, 'when a post comes empty, I am really disappointed' [*Letters*, 3:62]. 'The vacuity of life,' Thrale noted, was his 'favourite hypothesis' [*Thraliana*, 1:179]."

22. Compare Boswell, *Journal of a Tour to the Hebrides with Samuel Johnson, LL.D., 1773*, ed. Frederick A. Pottle and Charles H. Bennett, new ed. (New York, 1961), 79.

so dogged, and that he saw himself as a bad correspondent. Of course, he saw himself as an idler in so many ways, unable to rise early, unable to go to church as often as he ought, unable to observe his resolutions, even unable to write enough. "When I miss a post," he wrote to Thrale in 1777, "I consider myself as deviating from the true rule of action. Seeing things in this light, I consider every letter as something in the line of duty" (*Letters*, 3:71).[23]

He failed in the line of duty disturbingly often, however, and the guilt over his irregular correspondence resulted in a long and impressive roster of apologies for delays. "That I have neglected so long to write to you," he told Thomas Percy in 1760, "is a reason why I should neglect no longer" (1:190). "I have for a long time intended to answer the Letter which You were pleased to send me," he told James Elphinston in 1749 (1:42). "It is a long time since I wrote to you," he told John Taylor in 1779 (3:163). "I beg pardon for having been so long without writing," he wrote to Lucy Porter in 1759 (1:187). He wrote her again twenty-one years later: "I am indeed but a sluggish Correspondent, and know not when I shall much mend; however I will try" (3:233). There are many more, even one in French: "Il faut avouer que la lettre que vous m'avez fait l'honeur de m'ecrire, a ete long tems sans rêponse. Voici mon Apologie" (1:321).

At times he worried that his silence would be interpreted as disrespect. "I hope You will not imagine from my Silence," he pleaded with Gilbert Repington in 1735, "that I neglected the kind offer which You[r] Brother was pleased to make" (1:7). In such cases his approach was usually to be apologetic. "It is but an ill return for the book with which you were pleased to favour me," he wrote to Thomas Warton as he worked on the *Dictionary*, "to have delayed my thanks for it till now. I am too apt to be negligent but I can never deliberately show any disrespect to a man of your character" (1:81). But just a few months later he was scolding Warton, albeit tongue in cheek, for committing the very sin for which he had just sought absolution: "Your Brother, who is a better correspondent than you, and not much better, sends me word . . . " (1:97).

Sometimes he tried justification. "[T]hough I am perpetually thinking on you, I could seldom find opportunity to write," he pleaded to Thrale early in the Hebrides outing. "I have in fourteen days sent only one Letter. You must consider the fatigues of travel, and the difficulties encountered in a strange Country" (2:54). A more common excuse was ill-health. "I would not have you think that I forget or neglect you," he told Lewis Paul, before explaining, "I have never been out of doors since you saw me. On the day after I had been with you I was seized with a hoarseness which still continues; I had then a cough so violent that I once fainted under its convulsions. I was afraid of my Lungs" (1:116). Besides, he insisted, even when he was physically able to write, his

23. Compare Schneider: "The language of duty was often negatively associated with the concept of idleness regarding letter writing. The adjective 'idle' to define one's letters was employed as in 'Idle blottes' or 'idle lines'—that served as an expression of politeness or deference. But . . . Anthony Wingfield characterizes letter writing as a very practical means of combating idleness, exhibiting social duty, and paying a debt. . . . This passage associates the act of letter writing with both spiritual and practical Protestant work, as a sort of check on idleness: not writing is tantamount to sinning" (*The Culture of Epistolarity*, 64).

correspondents would not welcome a chronicle of maladies. As he wrote to Lucy Porter in 1762, "If I write but seldom to you, it is because it seldom happens that I have any thing to tell you that can give you pleasure" (1:209). "If I have been long without writing," he told William Strahan in August 1784, "I have broken no laws of friendship. I have suppressed nothing that my friends could be glad to hear. My time has passed in the toil of perpetual struggle with very oppressive disorder" (4:371).

Often, though, he did not even bother with an excuse: "To enumerate the causes that have hindered me from answering your letter would be of no use" (1:169–70), he told Anna Maria Smart. "I will not trouble you with apologies," he wrote to Percy (1:190). One reason he did not always offer an excuse was that he often could not think of one. "I am almost ashamed to tell you that all your letters came safe," he wrote to Lucy Porter, "and that I have been always very well, but hindered, I hardly know how, from writing" (1:185).[24] And on occasion his only way out was an ironic joke that took the place of an apology: "That neither of us can in all these months find time to write to the other is very strange. We seem to try who can forbear longest. You see I have yielded at last" (1:391).

That he did not always have an excuse did not mean that he was willing to be subject to others' criticism. Johnson could be unpleasantly defensive about his dilatoriness. "I am grieved that you should think me capable of neglecting your letters," he wrote to Thomas Warton, "and beg that you never will admit any such suspicion again" (1:108). To Charles Burney, he protested, "If you imagine that by delaying my answer I intended to shew any neglect of the notice with which you have favoured me, you will neither think justly of yourself nor of me" (1:102).

Johnson, of course, was not the only letter writer to resort to formulas like this. In the *Lives*, he reprints a similar letter from James Thomson to his sister in 1747:

> I thought you had known me better than to interpret my silence into a decay of affection, especially as your behaviour has always been such as rather to increase than diminish it. Don't imagine, because I am a bad correspondent, that I can ever prove an unkind friend and brother. I must do myself the justice to tell you, that my affections are naturally very fixed and constant; and if I had ever reason of complaint against you (of which by the bye I have not the least shadow), I am conscious of so many defects in myself, as dispose me to be not a little charitable and forgiving. (*Lives*, 4:101–2)

Two and a half centuries later, the pace of modernity forces all of us to insert into our e-mail messages phrases like "Sorry to be so long in getting back to you." Again,

24. Compare Johnson's letter to Boswell on March 23, 1768: "I have omitted a long time to write to you, without knowing very well why" (*Letters*, 1:298).

however, few writers of the eighteenth century were more prone to such apologies as Johnson. The apology for unpunctual correspondence was a genre in which Johnson excelled.

One recurring excuse for not writing was that he had nothing to say, though on this subject he was of two minds. Sometimes having nothing to say was actually a reason to write. Keymer notes that "much of Johnson's epistolary output enacts his theoretical sense of the form as writing with nothing to say."[25] Johnson could occasionally bring himself to write when he had nothing to say: "Nothing new has happened," he wrote to Thrale, "and yet I do not care to omit writing" (*Letters*, 1:375). He praised her for writing an interesting letter with no matter: "Now you think yourself the first Writer in the world for a letter about nothing. Can you write such a letter as this. So miscellaneous, with such noble disdain of regularity, like Shakespears works, such graceful negligence of transition like the ancient enthusiasts" (3:237). He even took credit for being good at spinning letters out of nothing:

> You talk of writing and writing as if you had all the writing to yourself. If our Correspondence were printed I am sure Posterity, for Posterity is always the authours favourite, would say that I am a good writer too. Anch' io sonô Pittore. To sit down so often with nothing to say, to say something so often, almost without consciousness of saying, and without any remembrance of having said, is a power of which I will not violate my modesty by boasting, but I do not believe that every body has it. (3:89)

More often, though, he bemoaned the difficulty he felt in keeping up his side of a correspondence in the absence of news. "I promised to write to you," he told John Taylor in 1756,

> and write now rather to keep my promise than that I have any thing to say. . . . I know not how it happens, but I fancy that I write letters with more difficulty than some other people, who write nothing but letters, at least I find myself very unwilling to take up a pen only to tell my friends that I am well, and indeed I never did exchange letters regularly but with dear Miss Boothby. (1:139)

As he told Bennet Langton, "You that travel about the world have more materials for letters than I who stay at home, and should therefore write with frequency proportionate to your opportunities" (1:192). "It is usual," he wrote to Richard Congreve in 1735, "for Friends that have been long separated to entertain each other at their first meeting, with an account of that interval of Life which has pass'd since their last interview, a custom, which I hope you will observe, but as little has happen'd to me that You can receive any pleasure from the relation of, I will not trouble you" (1:9–10). In 1749, he had to

25. Keymer, "'Letters about Nothing,'" 231.

explain to James Elphinston, "I... know not why I have delayed it so long but that I had nothing particular either of enquiry or information to send You, and the same reason might still have the same consequence, but I find in my recluse kind of Life, that I am not likely to have much more to say at one time than at another" (1:42). "I know my Baretti will not be satisfied," he wrote in 1761, "with a letter in which I give him no account of myself: yet what account shall I give him? I have not, since the day of our separation, suffered or done any thing considerable" (1:199). Declining health exacerbated the problem. "Alas!" he lamented to John Taylor in 1779, "what have two sick old Friends to say to one another? commonly nothing but that they continue to be sick" (3:163). Indolence became an excuse for further indolence.

Having nothing to say was not entirely a manufactured excuse. Johnson was serious about not writing when he had nothing to say. He was encouraged to write about Spenser by no less a person than George III, but he thought Thomas Warton had said all that needed to be said, and so he turned his monarch down. The same applied to travel writing. Boswell "regretted, that he did not write an account of his travels in France" (*Life*, 2:389), but Johnson insisted he knew nothing special about the country. He did believe that a lack of material justified his silence, but he was unwilling to admit the same plea from others. "You have abundance of naughty tricks," he wrote in frustration to Francesco Sastres; "is this your way of writing to a poor sick friend twice a week? Post comes after post, and brings no letter from Mr. Sastres. If you know any thing, write and tell it; if you know nothing, write and say that you know nothing" (*Letters*, 4:425).

Johnson was aware of his double standard, or at least he could be on occasion. "Do not, dear Sir," he begged Bennet Langton, "make the slowness of this letter a precedent for delay, or imagine that I approved the incivility that I have committed" (1:107). Or, as he told Anna Maria Smart, "I must insist that you don't use me as I have used you, for we must not copy the faults of our friends" (1:170).

I have so far avoided discussion of Johnson's letters to Boswell. There are not as many of these letters as one might expect, and fewer still are in manuscript; most of those that survive were chosen by Boswell for publication in the *Life*, so they are probably not representative of the decades of exchanges. Still, in the surviving letters between the two we see the dynamic of Johnson's correspondence expressed with unusual clarity. Because the two men were so similar in their attitudes toward letter writing, we can see Johnson struggling with his own propensities when he writes to Boswell.[26]

All the usual hallmarks of Johnson's epistolary practice are there in the letters Boswell preserved. "Whether I shall easily arrive at an exact punctuality of correspondance," Johnson wrote in December 1763, "I cannot tell" (1:238). (It will surprise no one

26. For an essay specifically on this correspondence, see Lance E. Wilcox, "Edifying the Young Dog: Johnson's Letters to Boswell," in *Sent as a Gift: Eight Correspondences from the Eighteenth Century*, ed. Alan T. McKenzie (Athens, Ga., 1993), 129–49.

to hear he did not.) We find the same apologies for failing to write, and the same attempts to pressure Boswell into writing to him, but we also see the reverse. While Johnson wagged his finger at many sluggish correspondents, in Boswell he found someone who would chide him in return. As Boswell wrote from Edinburgh in June 1774, "You do not acknowledge the receipt of the various packets which I have sent to you. Neither can I prevail with you to *answer* my letters, though you honour me with *returns*" (*Life*, 2:279). Boswell could also write his own quasi-Johnsonian apologies. He could on occasion be a conscientious correspondent, at least insofar as it provided material for the biography he knew he wanted to write. "I generally kept copies of my letters to him," Boswell records, "that I might have a full view of our correspondence, and never be at a loss to understand any reference in his letters. He kept the greater part of mine very carefully" (2:2). Anything, of course, if it provided material for the magnum opus Boswell was always projecting. Usually, though, he rivaled Johnson for dallying, and he found himself writing the same kinds of excuses that Johnson wrote to so many of his friends. "Although my late long neglect, or rather delay, was truely culpable, I am tempted not to regret it, since it has produced me so valuable a proof of your regard. I did, indeed, during that inexcusable silence, sometimes divert the reproaches of my own mind, by fancying that I should hear again from you, inquiring with some anxiety about me, because, for aught you knew, I might have been ill" (3:105). Like Johnson, Boswell could both blame others for not writing to him while trying to dodge blame for failing to write: "I can now fully understand those intervals of silence in your correspondence with me," Boswell wrote, "which have often given me anxiety and uneasiness; for although I am conscious that my veneration and love for Mr. Johnson have never in the least abated, yet I have deferred for almost a year and a half to write to him" (2:139–40). That is an impressive bit of passive-aggressive rhetoric: claiming to understand when in fact chastising Johnson's silence, and seeming to apologize when in fact seeking to avoid blame.

How did Johnson respond to a taste of his own medicine? "To tell you that I am or am not well," he snapped, "that I have or have not been in the country, that I drank your health in the Room in which we sat last together and that your acquaintance continue to speak of you with their former kindness topicks with which those letters are commonly filled which are written only for the sake of writing I seldom shall think worth communication" (*Letters*, 1:237–38). Boswell's distinctive combination of insecurity and manipulativeness is matched only by Johnson's own.

When Boswell resorted to the "wicked tricks" of deflecting blame, many of which he might have adopted directly from Johnson, they served only to frustrate Johnson, even to rouse him to anger. Much of the reason is probably that these "tricks" drew attention to the obligation of writing, sometimes even resorting to the language of accounting. Boswell once noted that "My state of epistolary accounts with you at present is extraordinary. The balance, as to number, is on your side. I am indebted to you for two letters" (*Life*, 3:101). Johnson bristled at metaphors like this, resenting the implication that friendships could be reckoned with crude tallies—and yet he was himself a scorekeeper, as when he wrote to Lucy Porter: "Do not you owe me a Letter? . . . If you did not do it before you will owe me one now, and I hope you will not be long in paying it" (*Letters*, 1:318). Still, when Boswell turned his language on him he reacted with frustration.

On occasion, as we have seen, Johnson wrote with ease. The ever-jealous Boswell recorded with frustration that Johnson could summon the discipline when the need arose, as when he lost track of the time in writing a letter to Thrale: one morning in the Hebrides, "Dr. Johnson remained in his chamber writing a letter, and it was long before we could get him into motion. He did not come to breakfast, but had it sent to him. When he had finished his letter, it was twelve o'clock, and we should have set out at ten" (*Life*, 5:256). Boswell, though, usually got excuses, as in this letter of December 1763, not long after they parted for the first time: "You are not to think yourself forgotten or criminally neglected that you have had yet no letter from me—I love to see my friends to hear from them to talk to them and to talk of them, but it is not without a considerable effort of resolution that I prevail upon myself to write" (*Letters*, 1:237). Johnson likely would have felt he failed Hugh Blair's test: "The best letters, are commonly such as the Authors have written with most facility" (*Lectures*, 2:299).

One of the virtues of a letter is that it reminds the recipient of an absent friend and thereby keeps the friendship alive. At the same time, though, it can serve as a reminder of absence, and absence caused disquiet—as Alan T. McKenzie puts it, "only the letter can transcend the long and difficult distances between sender and recipient and that for many months or years the letter in hand will often have to take the place of the person who wrote it."[27] "Absence is the genesis of all letter writing," writes Lowenthal; "the correspondent, feeling the need to communicate with a friend or loved one, has only the letter to connect them."[28] Johnson says as much himself: "The purpose for which letters are written when no intelligence is communicated, or business transacted, is to preserve in the minds of the absent either love or esteem" (*YE*, 5:47). Yet this declaration is a reminder that relationships conducted over distance were subject to decay. Johnson reached out to John Taylor in 1756: "There is this use in the most useless letter, that it shows one not to be forgotten, and they may at least in the beginning of friendship, or in great length of absence keep memory from languishing" (*Letters*, 1:139–40). And yet, when Boswell made the exact same claims to him, he reacted pettishly: "Why should you importune me so earnestly to write? Of what importance can it be to hear of distant friends, to a man who finds himself welcome wherever he goes, and makes new friends faster than he can want them? If, to the delight of such universal kindness of reception, any thing can be added by knowing that you retain my good-will, you may indulge yourself in the full enjoyment of that small addition" (3:199–200).

27. McKenzie, "Introduction," *Sent as a Gift*, 7.
28. Lowenthal, *Lady Mary Wortley Montagu*, 24.

In fact, when Johnson was on the receiving end of the pleas for letters, he argued that such demands could be counterproductive. "I have received two letters from you," he told Boswell, "of which the second complains of the neglect shown to the first. You must not tye your friends to such punctual correspondence. You have all possible assurances of my affection and esteem; and there ought to be no need of reiterated professions" (3:118). It may be that Boswell's constant insecurity about his friendship hit a little close to home and reminded Johnson of his habit of doing the same to others. How else to account for letters like this? "I set a very high value upon your friendship," Johnson wrote to the ever-insecure Boswell, "and count your kindness as one of the chief felicities of my life. Do not fancy," he went on, "that an intermission of writing is a decay of kindness. No man is always in a disposition to write; nor has any man at all times something to say" (3:63–64).

Though Johnson depended on letters as evidence of affection, he warned Boswell that such tests were liable to backfire, and to damage the very friendship they were meant to shore up. "Are you playing the same trick again, and trying who can keep silence longest? Remember that all tricks are either knavish or childish; and that it is as foolish to make experiments upon the constancy of a friend, as upon the chastity of a wife" (3:181). This invocation of a troubled marriage serves to link letter writing to the jealousies and suspicions that come with marital strife. The advice did not help; in 1780, Johnson had to chide Boswell once again: "I find you have taken one of your fits of taciturnity, and have resolved not to write till you are written to; it is but a peevish humour, but you shall have your way" (3:303). Again, two years later: "At your long silence I am rather angry. You do not . . . think it worth your while to try whether you or your friend can live longer without writing, nor suspect after so many years of friendship, that when I do not write to you, I forget you. Put all such useless jealousies out of your head, and disdain to regulate your own practice by the practice of another, or by any other principle than the desire of doing right" (4:90).

It is hardly shocking to suggest Johnson could be needy and idle and Boswell could be annoying: these findings are not stop-press bulletins. These passages reveal no previously unknown side of Johnson, but they do give us new ways of seeing the familiar Johnson. They allow us to view him in a different literary context, one in which he is constantly negotiating his place in the give-and-take of epistolary exchange.

More important still, the letters show us Johnson lived most fully when his existence was acknowledged in the writing of others—published writing served to keep the shuttlecock of his name from falling to the ground, but personal letters were reminders that he was alive and that he was loved. Letters meant life, both his own and that of his correspondents; as long as he could keep them coming, he felt that he could stave off the horrors of death one more day. What better way, then, to express the horror of finality than in the "odd thought" that struck him on his deathbed: "we shall receive no letters in the grave" (*Life*, 4:413).[29]

29. Compare *Johnsonian Miscellanies*, 2:153.

"Hoot him back again into the common road": The Problem of Singularity, and the Human Comedy of the *Lives of the Poets*

David Nunnery

EDMUND "RAG" SMITH died from overdosing on a self-prescribed laxative:

> He found such opportunities of indulgence as did not much forward his studies, and particularly some strong ale, too delicious to be resisted. He eat and drank till he found himself plethorick: and then, resolving to ease himself by evacuation, he wrote to an apothecary in the neighbourhood a prescription of a purge so forcible, that the apothecary thought it his duty to delay it till he had given notice of its danger. Smith, not pleased with the contradiction of a shopman, and boastful of his own knowledge, treated the notice with rude contempt, and swallowed his own medicine, which, in July 1710, brought him to the grave. He was buried at Hartham.[1]

The pain must have been excruciating. Could Johnson, himself inclined to overeat (and, at times, to overdrink), harassed by bodily pains, and, more to the point, terrified of death and not glib about his inevitable encounter with the Infinite, possibly mean for readers to be amused by Smith's horrible one? I think so, and therein lies an argument about Johnson, humor, and the *Lives of the Poets* (1779–81).

This odd episode reflects two complementary impulses that animate the *Lives* and make the work such a lively and troubling achievement. They are not an exhaustive index to Johnson's mode of proceeding, but rather two keys among several to the unusual and profound pleasures of the *Lives*. Indeed, the reader's pleasure is a very serious business for him.[2] These impulses are, on the one hand, a deflationary humor

1. "Smith," *The Lives of the Most Eminent English Poets: With Critical Observations on Their Works*, ed. Roger Lonsdale, 4 vols. (Oxford, 2006), 2:177. Text references are to this edition.

2. As discussed later, in the literary-critical judgments from the *Lives* that drew the most anger—those of Milton, the "Metaphysical Poets," and Gray—Johnson accuses them of failing to please: reading *Paradise Lost* "is a duty rather than a pleasure"; the Metaphysicals' reader "sometimes admires,

that defends the social whole from the antisocial ravages of both ordinary self-puffery and what Johnson calls "singularity," and, on the other hand, a difficult, dubious sort of impulse that conditions the reader's mind by exercising the mental and moral faculties of humor—what one might call an epistemology and ethics of laughter.

Getting Away from "Jukebox Johnson"

Overlapping misunderstandings of Johnson's relationship to humor and the comic—Johnson the cranky Tory, the moral scold, the gloomy agonist, the laughable boor, the dispenser of crabby one-liners about oat-eating Scots and lady preachers—have dampened critical attention to his humor.[3] Likewise, each misunderstanding, in its pernicious way, has miscast him with regard to sociable, temporal happiness, a concern that connects his writing across time and genre and serves as the special focus, I believe, of the *Lives*. And the *Lives*, for all their pleasures, are his least-examined major work: a few individual lives have been much studied, and the *Lives* feature strongly in analyses of Johnson's literary criticism, but surprisingly few students of Johnson make claims about them as a biographical collection.[4] I want to toss a coin in all three fountains.

Johnson's comic method in the *Lives*, which ranges from the gentle twitting of human frailty to the jarringly humorous presentation of disaster, is part of a project of cultivating a reader who is sociably intelligent and an agile, probability-weighing risk assessor.[5] He does so in part by "hoot[ing] back" those who pridefully abandon the "common road" and thereby poison the social system, and in part (sometimes simultaneously) by presenting situations that challenge readers to figure out whether to laugh

[but] is seldom pleased"; and Gray's odes "strike, rather than please," though Johnson claims he is "one of those that are willing to be pleased," if only Gray would cooperate (1:290, 200, 4:183, 181). The massive scale of the *Lives* results from Johnson's being "led beyond [his] intention . . . by the honest desire of giving useful pleasure" (1:189). For a useful, brief discussion of this obligation to please, see Charles H. Hinnant, *"Steel for the Mind": Samuel Johnson and Critical Discourse* (Newark, Del., 1994), 103–7. For a more general discussion of Johnson's disapproving literary criticisms, see John Mullan, "Fault Finding in Johnson's *Lives of the Poets*," in *Samuel Johnson: The Arc of the Pendulum*, ed. Freya Johnston and Lynda Mugglestone (Oxford, 2012), 72–82.

3. The moniker "Jukebox Johnson" is taken from an unpublished play, *Two Sams*, by North Carolina playwright John Justice, staged by the company Shakespeare & Originals in the summer of 2003. The Sams in question are Johnson and Beckett. For a rollicking and learned exploration of Johnson's humor, see Kevin L. Cope, "Raising a Risible Nation: Merry Mentoring and the Art (and Sometimes Science) of Joking Greatness," in *Mentoring in Eighteenth-Century British Literature and Culture*, ed. Anthony W. Lee (Farnham, U.K., 2009), 131–47, esp. 137–43. Cope addresses Johnson's conversational humor as reported by Boswell, and so is not concerned with whether Boswell's relation is "even remotely accurate" (137).

4. Robert Folkenflik's *Samuel Johnson, Biographer* (Ithaca, N.Y., 1978) and Catherine N. Parke's *Samuel Johnson and Biographical Thinking* (Columbia, Mo., 1991) astutely examine Johnson's biographical career as a piece, and his "biographical thinking" across various genres, respectively, but Martin Maner's excellent *The Philosophical Biographer: Doubt and Dialectic in Johnson's "Lives of the Poets"* (Athens, Ga., 1988) is to date the only book-length study of biographical method in the *Lives*. Lonsdale's 185-page introduction to his 2006 edition, plus his generous annotation and indexing, is the sort of scholarship that should be accompanied by trumpets and parades.

5. I describe what I take to be Johnson's project in "Informational Biography and the *Lives of the Poets*," *The Age of Johnson* 22 (2012): 1–21.

at all, and if so, how that amusement is to be directed and circumscribed.[6] That is, for Johnson, temporal happiness requires the acknowledgment of healthy sociability as humankind's common need, and the search for happiness requires that one be able to perform the mental calculus necessary to confront the contingencies of real, rather than exemplary, lives. His humor affirms this need and engages these faculties, reminding the reader of the value of shared, social endeavor and promoting the fundamental mental operation of life and the *Lives*: addressing uncertainty by inducing, projecting, and revising patterns of expectation and interpretation. Serving as guide, Johnson repeatedly invites the reader to calculate the proper response to samples of experience, sometimes humorous experience.

Before diving in, I should offer working definitions of the simple but slippery terms on which the discussion relies, acknowledging per Johnson that such definitions are problematical, and for comedy, especially so.[7] For present purposes, I mean "comedy" mainly as Northrop Frye elaborated it, as an author's bringing about "the integration of society" within a story by "incorporating [the] central character" into a functioning social whole, as opposed to the disintegrative orientation of tragedy.[8] I am interested in comedy, then, as the narrative telos toward integrative resolution and the devices that enable this process, particularly humor. "Humor" here means simply the attempt to evoke laughter. And "laughter" has its usual meaning, though I include any reactions stronger and merrier than the mere intellectual satisfaction at perceiving felicities of language, what Shaftesbury associates with the "still, peaceful, serene, mild" reaction that "hardly is to be called laughter" at all.[9]

The "Forcible Hug" of Laughing Johnson

Humor is a vexed and vexing issue in long eighteenth-century literature and culture, in which laughing or not could be socially and politically fraught. Many who are delighted

6. Johnson's notion that a man's friends ought to "hoot him back again into the common road" is from *Adventurer* 131 (February 5, 1754), in *The Idler and the Adventurer*, vol. 2 of *The Yale Edition of the Works of Samuel Johnson* (hereafter cited as *YE*), ed. W. J. Bate, John M. Bullitt, and L. F. Powell (New Haven, Conn., 1963), 486. I should make clear that Johnson is not for hooting down those who make ambitious efforts, especially if designed to be useful. The flip side of healthfully normative group laughter is the tendency to sneer at anything new. An ambitious effort, Johnson writes, "may, therefore, expose its author to censure and contempt; and if the liberty of laughing be once indulged, every man will laugh at what he does not understand . . . and every great or new design will be censured as a project." Thus does the great builder (or lexicographer, editor of Shakespeare, and biographer) differ from the self-puffers and "the sanguinary . . . heroes and conquerors" whom he would see "huddled together in obscurity or detestation": *Adventurer* 99 (October 16, 1753), *YE*, 2:433–44.

7. See *Rambler* 125 (May 28, 1751): "The performances of art [are] too inconstant and uncertain, to be reduced to any determinate idea. . . . There is therefore scarcely any species of writing, of which we can tell what is its essence, and what are its constituents. . . . Comedy has been particularly unpropitious to definers"; in *The Rambler*, vols. 3–5 of *YE*, ed. W. J. Bate and Albrecht B. Strauss (1969), 3:300.

8. The phrases "the integration of society" and "incorporating a central character" are from Northrop Frye's description of the comic mode in *Anatomy of Criticism* (Princeton, N.J., 1957), 43.

9. Anthony Ashley Cooper, Earl of Shaftesbury, "Philosophical Regimen" (1698–1712), in *The Life, Unpublished Letters, and Philosophical Regimen of Anthony, Earl of Shaftesbury*, ed. Benjamin Rand (London, 1900), 226.

by the period's raucous stage comedies and the devilishness of Fielding, Smollett, Sterne, et alia, are surprised to be reminded of a vigorous antilaughter tradition, exemplified by such noble personages as Shaftesbury, Chesterfield, and the Marquis of Halifax. These were joined by upright divines like Richard Allestree, and even mordantly funny writers like Swift and Pope. Often the antilaughers did not forbid laughter altogether but defined its permissible forms almost out of existence, as is the case with Allestree, who noted soberly, "We read that *Christ* Wept over *Jerusalem* . . . and over *Lazarus*. But we never read of his Laughter."[10]

In this tradition, audible laughter was looked upon with suspicion and often outright disdain as vulgar, ugly, even immoral. Refusing to laugh was thus a sign of social refinement: Steele tells that a "*true Fine Gentleman*" expresses "good Humour without Noise." Similarly, Addison proposes that one might "distinguish a Gentleman as much by his Laugh, as his bow" and that "when we see the Footman and his Lord diverted by the same Jest, it very much turns to the Diminution" of the lord. Shaftesbury distinguishes "the well-bred people, those of a finer make . . . and raised above the vulgar" by how seldom and reservedly they laugh. Hearty laughter is for him the province of social inferiors and untouchables: servants, clowns, criminals, slaves, pillaging soldiers, and the insane. The approved "reserved, gentle" response, "hardly to be called laughter," must be "husbanded and kept only for places, persons, and things" in one's own polite sphere. Chesterfield had read warnings against laughter in his Castiglione as well as his Plato, Aristotle, Cicero, and Stoics, and so he disdained laughter as "ill-bred" and "the manner in which the mob express their silly joy at silly things." He thus famously boasted: "Since I have had the full use of my reason, nobody has ever heard me laugh." Even Hogarth warns that laughter makes faces "lose their beauty" and become "silly or disagreeable."[11]

This antilaughter tradition was emphatically not Johnson's own. His companions' accounts ring with his laughter, which Boswell describes as "a good humoured growl," and Tom Davies as a sound "like a rhinoceros." It was sometimes purely for his own enjoyment, as when the notion of Bennet Langton's solemnly making out his will left Johnson doubled over, holding onto a street post, convulsed with laughter that

10. Allestree, *The Government of the Thoughts* (London, 1694), 26. For an overview of this tradition, including its biblical and classical roots, its place in Renaissance and later European writing, and a broad sampling of British sources, see Virgil B. Heltzel, "Chesterfield and the Anti-Laughter Tradition," *Modern Philology* 26 (1928): 73–90, and the article to which he responds, E. Sprague Allen's "Chesterfield's Objection to Laughter," *Modern Language Notes* 38 (1923): 279–87. More recently, see Vic Gatrell, *City of Laughter: Sex and Satire in Eighteenth-Century London* (New York, 2006), 159–77. Swift's resistance to laughter is recorded in *Lives*, 3:55–56, Pope's at 3:202.

11. Richard Steele, *Guardian* 34 (1713), in *The Guardian*, ed. John Calhoun Stephens (Lexington, Ky., 1982), 143; Joseph Addison, *Tatler* 122 (1710), in *The Tatler*, ed. Donald Bond, 3 vols. (Oxford, 1985), 2:221; Shaftesbury, "Philosophical Regimen," 226–27. For Chesterfield, see the letter to his son, March 9, 1748, OS, in *Lord Chesterfield's Letters*, ed. David Roberts (Oxford, 1992), 72. For William Hogarth, see *The Analysis of Beauty*, ed. Ronald Paulson (New Haven, Conn., 1997), 98–99. The Marquis of Halifax likewise notes that laughing "throweth a Woman into a lower Form": *The Lady's New-Year's Gift* (1688), 15th ed. (London, 1765), 76–77. By contrast, William Congreve viciously satirizes this tradition via the character Lord Froth in *The Double-Dealer* (1693).

"resound[ed] from Temple-bar to Fleet-ditch." He had, says Fanny Burney, "more . . . comical humour, and . . . [love of] nonsense about him, than almost any body I ever saw." He was comfortable enough in his skin to roll bodily down a hill, kick off his slippers and fly past a young woman in a footrace, or bound about the room like a kangaroo.[12] Of all the impulses the mind can conjure on its own, the urge to laugh was one Johnson found particularly healthful, and, in most cases, irresistible.

So was the urge to share laughter. The Fleet-ditch episode notwithstanding, Johnson's laughter was social more often than solitary. David Garrick described its infectious power thus: "Johnson gives you a forcible hug, and shakes laughter out of you, whether you will or no." According to Hester Thrale Piozzi, "His laugh was irresistible, and was observed immediately to produce that of the company." Even the unclubable John Hawkins notes, perhaps not altogether approvingly, that Johnson "was a great contributor to the mirth of conversation" and that "in the talent of humour there hardly ever was [his] equal." For Johnson, to laugh with others was primarily to share pleasure, but in this context also a rejection of the proprieties that constrained sociability. Hannah More recalls standing with Johnson and Garrick "above an hour, laughing in defiance of every rule of decorum and Chesterfield."[13] To Johnson, laughter and sociability were natural and desirable—to refuse one was to pervert or diminish the other.[14]

This is not to say that Johnson was an indiscriminate laugher or that the impulse to laugh lay outside his frequent, familiar admonitions that happiness required

12. For the descriptions by Boswell and Davies, see *Boswell's Life of Johnson, Together with Boswell's Journal of a Tour to the Hebrides and Johnson's Diary of a Journey into North Wales*, ed. George Birkbeck Hill, rev. L. F. Powell, 6 vols. (Oxford, 1934–50), 2:378 (hereafter cited as *Life*). For the Langton anecdote, see 2:261–62. For the remaining quotations in the paragraph, see *The Early Journals and Letters of Fanny Burney*, vol. 3, *The Streatham Years: Part I, 1778–1779*, ed. Lars E. Troide and Stewart Jon Cooke (Kingston, Ontario, 1994), 255–56. The tumble downhill was related by Langton to Henry Digby Beste, who recorded it in his *Personal and Literary Memorials* (London, 1829), cited in *Life*, 1:477. The footrace with the young woman, which took place in Johnson's fifties, is recalled by Frances Reynolds and reprinted in *Johnsonian Miscellanies*, ed. George Birkbeck Hill, 2 vols. (Oxford, 1897; reprint, New York, 1966), 2:276. In another instance, Richard Green of Lichfield records Johnson's footrace with John Payne, a member of Johnson's Ivy Lane Club and later chief accountant for the Bank of England; Johnson won by catching "his little adversary up in his arms, and without any ceremony plac[ing] him upon the arm of a tree" (2:396). (*Johnsonian Miscellanies*, containing the recollections of many non-Boswell contemporaries of Johnson, is the richest trove of Johnson's shenanigans.) Also, at age sixty-six, Johnson won a footrace with his friend, the fifty-six-year-old Giuseppe Baretti; see *Life*, 2:386. The kangaroo anecdote, added in a note by Robert Carruthers to his edition of Boswell's *Journal of a Tour to the Hebrides* (London, 1852), 96, is appended to *Life*, 5:511. For Johnson's surprising intellectual and physical agility, see David Fairer's essay "The Agile Johnson" in this volume.

13. For Garrick, see *Life*, 2:231; for Hester Lynch Piozzi, see *Anecdotes of the Late Samuel Johnson, LL.D., during the Last Twenty Years of His Life*, 4th ed. (London, 1786), 298–99, hereafter referred to as Piozzi, *Anecdotes*; for Hawkins, see *The Life of Samuel Johnson, LL.D.*, 2nd ed. (London, 1787), 358; and for More, see *Memoirs of the Life and Correspondence of Mrs. Hannah More*, ed. William Roberts, 2 vols. (New York, 1836), 1:70. According to Boswell, Johnson and Samuel Foote conspired to write a play mocking Chesterfield's advice to his son (*Life*, 4:384).

14. For further discussion of Johnson as less gloomy than is often perceived, see Howard D. Weinbrot, "Johnson Rebalanced: The Happy Man, Supportive Family, and His Social Religion," in *Samuel Johnson: The Arc of the Pendulum*, 195–207.

regulating one's passions. Rather, his range of experience and capacity for sympathy gave him a strong sense of what was and what was not laughable, and his laughter proceeded naturally from those principles, though often to the embarrassment of the more laughter-resistant sensibilities of such companions as Hawkins, Goldsmith, and Boswell.[15] Understanding, then, what for Johnson was and was not legitimately laughable helps readers navigate the sometimes ambiguous and difficult humor of the *Lives*.

Some targets were out of bounds. Johnson could not bear jokes about the poor, who already existed at the margins of social sympathy. He considered Addison's ridicule of the Old Pretender's poverty indecent, worthy of "Milton's savageness, or Oldmixon's meanness," but "not suitable to the delicacy of Addison."[16] His anger at facile disregard for the pains of poverty drives his blasting of Soame Jenyns's Popean *Free Inquiry into the Nature and Origin of Evil* (1757) as well as his rebuke of Hester Thrale's glib joke about the smells of cheap food stalls along Porridge Island:

> Come, come (says he gravely), let's have no sneering at what is so serious to so many: hundreds of your fellow-creatures, dear Lady, turn another way, that they may not be tempted by the luxuries of Porridge-Island to wish for gratifications they are not able to obtain: you are certainly not better than all of *them*; give God thanks that you are happier.[17]

Johnson's rebuke is not meant to cut off the affable sociable intercourse between himself and Mrs. Thrale but rather to affirm that it not come at the expense of degrading the poor to a punch line, laughing them down and out of range of one's sympathy.

He likewise, and for the same reason, rejected humor directed at physical or mental infirmity, including his own. Once, at a dinner, Johnson was seated next to the hostess, and as a result of his nervous condition was "convulsively working his hand up and down." The lady, sensing a chance for a laugh,

15. For an argument that Johnson's humor rises out of "his sympathy for and love of humanity, and his sense of its basic folly," and the amiably comic notion that weakness unites the eminent and the ordinary, see Clarence Tracy, "Democritus, Arise! A Study of Dr. Johnson's Humor," *Yale Review*, n.s., 39 (1950): 294–310 at 302–3.

16. *Lives*, 3:15. Milton and Oldmixon mocked the poverty of the previous generation of exiled Stuarts during the Commonwealth. In "On Salmasius," attached to his *Defensio pro populo Anglicano* (1651), Milton accuses Salmasius of writing his *Defensio regia, pro Carolo I* (1649) for the last hundred Jacobuses of the exiled king; see Milton, *Complete Prose Works*, vol. 4, *1650–1655*, ed. Donald M. Wolfe (New Haven, Conn., 1966), 309. Oldmixon, in his *History of England, during the Reigns of the Royal House of Stuart* (London, 1730), reports speculation that an unnamed Londoner was "rich enough to have bought the whole Court of [exiled Stuarts at] *Bruges*" (419). It is unlikely that any of the Stuart royals could have been regarded as poor by any real-world standard; Johnson objects to poverty as a target for humor, whether accurately ascribed or not.

17. Piozzi, *Anecdotes*, 104. Johnson's review of Jenyns argues that Jenyns and Pope "perhaps never saw the miseries which they imagine thus easy to be borne. The poor, indeed, are insensible of many little vexations, which sometimes embitter the possessions and pollute the enjoyments, of the rich. They are not pained by casual incivility, or mortified by the mutilation of a compliment; but this happiness is like that of a malefactor who ceases to feel the cords that bind him when the pincers are tearing his flesh"; see *A Commentary on Mr. Pope's Principles of Morality, Or Essay on Man (A Translation from the French)*, vol. 17 of *YE*, ed. O M Brack (2005), 407.

> roguishly edged her foot within his reach, and . . . Johnson clenched hold of it, and drew off her shoe; she started, and hastily exclaimed, "O, fy! Mr. Johnson!" The company at first knew not what to make of it; but one of them, perceiving the joke, tittered. Johnson, not improbably aware of the trick, apologized: "Nay, madam, recollect yourself; I know not that I have justly incurred your rebuke; the emotion [that is, motion] was involuntary, and the action not intentionally rude."[18]

Johnson's response signals that her action, not his, has transgressed the bounds of sympathy. He was not "intentionally rude"; she has been, and her roguishness, rather than his tics, lies outside social acceptability, even though it is her table at which they sit. Johnson refuses to concede that the laughter she has produced is just, or that the social situation she has tried to create, in which it is permissible to make fun of his convulsions, is proper. His rebuke places her temporarily outside the social circle; his advice that she "recollect" herself is doubly apt.

And so, in the *Lives*, his detailed and poignant description of Pope's afflictions is in no way glib, certainly not cruel in the manner so many lampoons had been. He pokes no fun at the mental illness of Smart or Collins, forbears to moralize or sneer at Rochester's sorry decline, and is no less sensitive to Swift's ill-health than to Watts's, though his opinions of the two are very different. If this is unsurprising, given our notions of Johnson's general charitableness, it should at least be understood in its cultural context. In his day, jestbooks featuring cruel humor at the expense of the poor, elderly, and disabled were popular and prevalent, a mainstay of most booksellers' incomes. Nor were they a marginal, penny-press phenomenon; rather, the taste for jokes about starvation-level poverty, wife-beating, tumbling old men out of windows, and leading the blind into walls, *pace* Chesterfield, cut across class and gender lines. They appealed even to such members of the Johnson circle as Boswell, Garrick, and Mrs. Thrale.[19]

But what *was* good for a laugh? Pretentiousness and affectation in expression and habits were certainly fair game. The foibles of Langton along this line, even when they did not double Johnson over a street post, were a frequent target; when admonished about it by Boswell with a quotation out of Allestree, Johnson maintained that "the sense of ridicule is given us, and may be lawfully used."[20] Deflationary laughter in

18. The anecdote is recorded in Samuel Whyte's *Miscellanea Nova; Containing, amidst a Variety of Other Matters Curious and Interesting, Remarks on Boswell's Johnson; with Considerable Additions, and Some New Anecdotes* (Dublin, 1800), 50. The lady was Mrs. Chamberlaine, wife of Sheridan's brother-in-law. I thank Jack Lynch for providing the reference for this anecdote.

19. See Simon Dickie, "Hilarity and Pitilessness in the Mid-Eighteenth Century: English Jestbook Humor," *Eighteenth-Century Studies* 37 (2003): 1–22. For references to Boswell, Garrick, and Thrale as owners of crude jestbooks, or as purveyors of jestbook-style humor, see pp. 7, 9, and 15. Dickie expands this in his often-harrowing *Cruelty and Laughter: Forgotten Comic Literature and the Unsentimental Eighteenth Century* (Chicago, 2011). Gatrell, *City of Laughter*, provides over 700 glossy pages of evidence of the crudities Londoners in particular enjoyed.

20. *Life*, 3:379–80. In 1779, when Johnson was in the midst of writing the *Lives*, he defended the permissibility of ridicule against Boswell's quoting from Allestree's *Government of the Tongue* (Oxford,

matters of common intercourse, by which "arrogance is punished with ridicule," was natural and permissible.[21] And so in the *Lives* one finds the demi-booby Halifax, a "pretender to taste," demanding revisions to Pope's *Iliad* (1715–20), and upon Pope's later propitiating him and reading the passages unchanged, declaring, "*Ay, now they are perfectly right*." Swift fussily declares at dinner with the Earl of Orrery that his servant has, "*since we sat to the table, committed fifteen faults*." Johnson deadpans, "What the faults were Lord Orrery . . . had not been attentive enough to discover. My number may perhaps not be exact." And one of the finest comic touches in the *Lives* is the frequent reappearance of the ever-aggrieved John Dennis as a force of malignity, a trope that unites his targets like comrades in a siege, and that by means of repetition becomes thoroughly laughable.[22]

Within this broad category of deflationary humor, we find Addison gently mocked for climbing to stations that did not suit him, as in his flustered, fumbling inability to deliver news of the queen's death while secretary to the regency, and his ill-advised marriage to the countess dowager of Warwick. Of the latter, Johnson tells that the countess was "persuaded to marry [Addison], on terms much like those on which a Turkish princess is espoused, to whom the Sultan is reported to pronounce, 'Daughter, I give thee this man for thy slave.'" That Johnson clearly admires Addison, especially for his prosocial refining of the manners and pleasures of the age, lends the twitting a tone of bemusement rather than skewering. Further comment on the marriage draws readers into sympathy with Addison, whose noble wife "always remembered her own rank, and thought herself entitled to treat with very little ceremony the tutor of her son."[23] It is an irony of "Addison"—and the *Lives* abound with ironies, so frequently mapping the chasm between expectation and fulfillment, intent and result—that the quality Johnson most often criticizes in his subject is a haughtiness, an awareness of his own dignity and ability that sometimes curdled his relationships, notably with Steele.[24] The other qualities—a bashfulness that could lead to isolation and overdrinking and a zeal for political faction—are likewise socially corrosive.

[1667]) and Montagu Burrows's Good Friday sermon against "evil-speaking," which he and Boswell had just attended. The next year, Boswell records from Langton further dicta from Johnson on the subject: "The man who uses his talent of ridicule in creating or grossly exaggerating the instances he gives, who imputes absurdities that did not happen, or when a man was a little ridiculous, describes him as having been very much so, abuses his talents greatly. The great use of delineating absurdities is, that we may know how far human folly can go; the account, therefore, ought of absolute necessity to be faithful"; *Life*, 4:17.

21. *Adventurer* 131, *YE*, 2:485.

22. *Lives*, 4:24; 3:210. Johnson respected Dennis as a scholar and often as a critic, but his onion-thin skin and utter unclubability make him a comic figure à la Malvolio. For examples of Dennis in attack and complaint, see 2:77; 3:10–12, 27–37, 76, 142; 4:6–7, 11, 28, 34. Regarding Dennis's solitary dissent from the universal praise for Addison's *Cato*, Johnson notes drily that "The world was too stubborn for instruction" (3:11).

23. *Lives*, 3:14–15.

24. Paul Fussell, in *Samuel Johnson and the Life of Writing* (New York, 1971), argues that all the ironies in the *Lives* form a comic master trope. I believe Fussell casts his net too wide by reading as dark comedy, say, the starving Otway's choking to death on a mouthful of bread; I also think he renders Johnson too Suetonian with regard to presenting the horrible as humorous.

Thomson, one of five subjects added to the *Lives* at Johnson's request, is an especially frequent locus for this sort of sympathetic laughter; a few instances stand for the lot.[25] Thomson's life was short, punctuated by familial loss, professional struggle, and periods of serious poverty. As an author he was a modest success by early middle age, finally "at ease, but . . . not long to enjoy it": he died at forty-eight, never married, just three years after achieving a financial competence through a government appointment. In its broad outlines, then, Thomson's life appears tragic, in ways familiar to Johnson, given his own hardships.[26] Rather than have such gloomy elements overpower the rest, though, Johnson salts "Thomson" with humorous touches along the lines of what he found legitimately and sociably laughable.

For instance, he twits an instance of pretentious writing on Thomson's part:

> There was a feeble line in the play [*Sophonisba* (1729)]:
> "O Sophonisba, Sophonisba, O!"
> This gave occasion to a waggish parody:
> "O, Jemmy Thomson, Jemmy Thomson, O!"
> which for a while was echoed through the town. (4:98–99)

Johnson does not strike the deflating blow himself, but by letting it stand uncommented upon (save by the fairly neutral "waggish"), he invites the reader to regard it as legitimately amusing. In a similar instance, Johnson allows Thomson to appear ridiculous, if harmlessly so. His play *Agamemnon* (1738) "struggled with such difficulty through the first night that Thomson, coming late to his friends with whom he was to sup, excused his delay by telling them how the sweat of his distress had so disordered his wig, that he could not come till he had been refitted by a barber" (4:100).

Another humorous episode is of little consequence to the narrative of Thomson's life but demonstrates much about the craftiness of Johnson's humor: "He was once reading to [George Bubb] Doddington, who, being himself a reader eminently elegant, was so much provoked by his odd utterance, that he snatched the paper from his hand, and told him that he did not understand his own verses" (4:103). How do readers direct their amusement? The scene could be imagined such that we find one man ridiculous, or the other, or both. Note Johnson's characteristic manipulation of pronouns: eight third-person masculine pronouns flit from Thomson to Doddington and back without referents, conveying, arguably, the sense that laughter might be

25. The other lives Johnson recommended were of John Pomfret, Thomas Yalden, Isaac Watts, and Richard Blackmore. Johnson seems to have forgotten asking for Thomson's inclusion when introducing the life of Watts (4:105). George Birkbeck Hill once speculated that Johnson so forgot because the others are grouped in his mind by being, respectively, "[two] clergymen, . . . a Nonconformist minister, and . . . a writer of religious poetry"; see Johnson, *Lives of the English Poets*, ed. Hill, 3 vols. (Oxford, 1905), 3:302n1.

26. *Lives*, 4:101. Thomson, for example, found himself in need of a serviceable pair of shoes (4:97), a detail that no doubt elicited sympathetic memories from Johnson. For the story of Johnson's mortifying poverty while at Oxford, and his throwing away a gift of shoes left anonymously at his door, see *Life*, 1:76–77.

directed at either man, or both. There is no obvious target, and one may as well identify with Doddington's exasperation as Thomson's presumable bewilderment. Typically, Johnson ends without commenting on either man's actions. The reader makes what judgments he or she will and carries on.

In each example, and in many others not listed, an amicable social whole functions, even with the exasperated Doddington. In the first, Thomson is being mocked, but in a manner Johnson thought justifiable and beneficial: his name is echoing through the town, which beats the obscurity every struggling writer dreads.[27] Better, Johnson thought, to remain in the community than to grouse in one's grotto, a man apart. In the second, Thomson appears silly, but more so for his feeling the need to be refitted before seeing his friends; the anecdote moves from fear of professional failure to the sight of Thomson amid friends. In a similar instance of professional distress, he makes the joke himself. Having been introduced to the Prince of Wales, "and being gaily interrogated about the state of his affairs, [Thomson] said, '*that they were in a more poetical posture than formerly*,' and had a pension allowed him of one hundred pounds a year" (4:100). Here, his ability to find humor in hardship redounds to his material betterment, because a social whole operates in which those at various stations appreciate the value of sociable laughter.

Sometimes the humor is both general and gentle, as in this play on the word "gaping":

> [Thomson] had recommendations to several persons of consequence, which he had tied up carefully in his handkerchief; but as he passed along the street, with the gaping curiosity of a new-comer, his attention was upon every thing rather than his pocket, and his magazine of credentials was stolen from him." (4:97)

Johnson communalizes Thomson's foible, a frequent device in the *Lives* by which the fault is cast as a common failing rather than a personal vice or folly. Thomson does not get his pocket picked because he is uncommonly stupid or careless but because he is a naive newcomer, as presumably many readers will have been in some situation before encountering Thomson's. His failings are part of the common lot. In such cases, in laughing at them, we laugh at ourselves.

27. Johnson was of course himself the frequent target of mockery, which he accepted graciously. Hearing the defenders of Thomas Gray were laughing over one of James Gillray's caricatures insulting him, he replied, "I am very glad to hear this. I hope the day will never arrive when I shall neither be the object of calumny or ridicule, for then I shall be neglected and forgotten"; *Johnsonian Miscellanies*, 2:420. For Johnson's repeated disinclination to rise to the bait of satire and invective, and his pleasure at being criticized rather than ignored and forgotten, see *Johnsonian Miscellanies*, 1:270–72, 407; 2:354; and *Life*, 2:61, 335; 3:375; 4:55; 5:273, 400–401. For his frequent admonition in the *Lives* that authors do the same, see "Dryden," 2:83–88, 99–100, 113–15; "Addison," 3:12; "Blackmore," 3:76, 85; and "Pope," 4:6–7, 11, 35–36, 49–51. See also "Boerhaave" in *Early Biographical Writings of Dr. Johnson*, ed. J. D. Fleeman (Farnborough, U.K., 1973), 30–31.

In each instance, Thomson is made to look somewhat silly, in a manner uncommon to the tradition of previous biographies, except the forthrightly malicious. One cannot imagine Fulke Greville's superheroic Sidney looking like a bungler.[28] It is, though, common within the *Lives*—and a reader need not know of Johnson's regard for Thomson, nor his own failure as a dramatist, nor his being oft-disheveled, nor his having come to London from the provinces, nor his being materially secured by an enlightened monarch—to see that he does not present Thomson as a fool getting his comeuppance or as a hapless victim.[29] Thomson is no paragon: there are times when to be Thomson is to be foolish. The reader is not, however, situated above him; even if there is any temporarily Hobbesian "sudden glory . . . of some eminency in ourselves," Thomson's flaws and errors are seen as neither vicious nor extraordinary.[30] Anyone could be Thomson, or Thomson-like.

A more challenging, less readily legible anecdote appears in the life of John Gay. It features several elements from the lives of Addison and Thomson and elsewhere:

> [Gay] wrote a tragedy called *The Captives* [1724], which he was invited to read before the princess of Wales. When the hour came, he saw the princess and her ladies all in expectation, and advancing with reverence, too great for any other attention, stumbled at a stool, and falling forwards, threw down a weighty Japan screen. The princess started, the ladies screamed, and poor Gay after all the disturbance was still to read his play. (3:97–98)

The comic technique is apparent: the processional rhythm of the long sentence, with its portentous phrases, set off by commas, builds narrative tension that is released in Gay's pratfall, the calamity of the heavy screen falling, and the ladies' screaming. The comic denouement finds "poor Gay" in an impossible position, having to compose himself and read his tragic play to a thoroughly discombobulated audience.

28. Greville's *Life of the Renowned Sir Philip Sidney* (London, 1651) was written in 1610–12 but not published until forty years later. The most famous secular biography of the period, it presents Sidney as the ultimate English nobleman, soldier, courtier, and scourge of popery. Even Sidney's sniping match with the Earl of Oxford on a tennis court is cast as an act of exemplary political courage. Though Greville knew Sidney intimately, the biography is primarily a vehicle for praising Protestant rule and opposing alliance with France, not for helping the reader know Sidney as a person—except in his capacity as Protestant superhero.

29. One also sees Johnson's sympathy with Thomson in the following, which could well be read as autobiography: "He easily discovered that the only stage on which a poet could appear, with any hope of advantage, was London . . . where merit might soon become conspicuous, and would find friends as soon as it became reputable to befriend it" (*Lives*, 4:96–97). Notably, Richard Savage befriended Thomson upon his arrival and did the same for Johnson.

30. Thomas Hobbes, "Human Nature," in *The Elements of Law* (1640), in *Human Nature and "De Corpore Politico,"* ed. J. C. A. Gaskin (Oxford, 1994), 54–55: "The passion of laughter is nothing else but a sudden glory arising from sudden conception of some eminency in ourselves, by comparison with the infirmity of others, or with our own formerly."

But does Johnson mean for his readers to laugh *at* Gay? It is impossible to laugh *with* Gay, who surely is mortified. Johnson presents an interpretive, and ultimately ethical, challenge. Is Gay foolish or unlucky? Is the phrase "poor Gay" a sign of condescension or commiseration? Is Johnson mocking Gay for taking the affair too seriously? How does the reader decide? Given the portrait that Johnson constructs in the life—that of a meek, inoffensive, somewhat hapless man overshadowed by his more forceful, talented, and successful friends Swift, Pope, and Arbuthnot, who "regarded him as a play-fellow rather than a partner"—to laugh at him seems unkind, and not in keeping with Johnson's usual sympathetic practice (3:95).

Johnson also often stresses Gay's inability to sustain professional success, and his resulting deep dejection. Given that Gay, born "without prospect of hereditary riches," tries repeatedly to secure favor and employment at court, this disaster could well ruin his hopes there (3:95). Typically, Johnson neither offers explicit commentary nor tells the outcome of the misadventure, though later he notes that four years thereafter, Gay was offered a meager position in service to the toddler Princess Louisa, another in a long line of frustrations. The reader encountering the anecdote is given no clear direction of how to assimilate it. Would Johnson, who sympathized with a writer's struggle to keep fed and clothed, and the indignity of supplicating patrons, laugh Gay down? Could he regard the scene as having no ethical charge, to be enjoyed as a bit of slapstick? Is he offering it in the vein of "there but for the grace of God go we," with Gay the comic Everyman toppled by dumb luck?

Ultimately, so far as one can tell, this is no enterprise of great pith and moment: the nation does not hang in the balance, and the contemporary reader probably knew that Gay was to be rescued a few years later by *The Beggar's Opera* (1728). In any event, the reader is soon to learn this on subsequent pages, and of the kindness and prudent guidance shown Gay by the Duke and Duchess of Queensberry. Then, a reader might reasonably be tempted to view the catastrophe of *The Captives* through the softening lens of later success. But Johnson will not let even this reading rest comfortably, for as Gay finally seems established in security and comfort, "it is supposed that the discountenance of the Court sunk deep into his heart, and gave him more discontent than the applauses or tenderness of his friends could overpower. He soon fell into his old distemper." This depression, "though with many intervals of ease and cheerfulness[,] . . . hurried him to the grave" at age forty-four (3:100). Does this new information change our assessment of the anecdote? Did the tumble shorten Gay's life by humiliating him at court and driving him down in the princess's (later, queen's) esteem? Are we chagrined and compelled to "recollect" ourselves for having laughed at an event with tragic implications?

I do not think so; I think rather that Johnson found the fiasco laughable on its face, and that he found Gay sympathetic, though unlucky and something of a bungler. One may laugh without exulting in Hobbesian superiority, because anyone, trying to impress and show due deference to one's betters, in hope of future favors, might trip over the furniture. But I do not know this is right; Johnson has chosen not to tell me, and like every reader I must weigh my reaction to this anecdote against similar ones I encounter.

This sort of deflationary, sympathetic, "hoot[ing] back" humor is a valuable tool for Johnson in dealing with more fractious and often inscrutable subjects, such as Milton. It is evident in his light mocking of Milton's nephew Edward Philips, who, like other Milton biographers, felt the need to gloss over Milton's having, for a time, served as a schoolmaster:

> Philips, evidently impatient of viewing [Milton] in this state of degradation . . . has a mind to invest him with military splendour: "He is much mistaken," he says, "if there was not about this time a design of making him an adjutant-general in Sir William Waller's army. But the new modelling of the army proved an obstruction to the design." An event cannot be set at a much greater distance than by having been only *designed, about some time*, if a man *be not much mistaken*. Milton shall be a pedagogue no longer; for, if Philips be not much mistaken, somebody at some time designed him for a soldier. (1:253, italics in original)

Johnson found the situation itself laughable: "Let not our veneration for Milton forbid us to look with some degree of merriment . . . on the man who hastens home because his countrymen are contending for their liberty, and, when he reaches the scene of action, vapours away his patriotism in a private boarding-school" (1:248). But this laughter is directed at Milton's frustrated revolutionary zeal and his biographers' embarrassment. Johnson does not mock Milton for serving as a lowly schoolmaster, which he regards as "an honest and useful employment" undertaken for the most mundane and sensible of reasons, namely that Milton needed to earn a living. Would that he had remained such. Johnson makes his little gibe, defends Milton against his defenders, and thereafter writes of Milton as one former schoolmaster engaging another, commiserating about the difficulties of teaching and debating the proper curriculum for instructing young boys. Milton's fervor is deflated, Philips's unnecessary defensiveness is defanged, the mockery of Milton as a schoolmaster is debunked, and a functioning social whole operates, in which a man doing honest, socially productive work need not be ashamed that he is not instead leading a troop of cavalry against his king. Self-important dudgeon is hooted down on all sides.[31]

So, too, with the wily and often thin-skinned Pope. Johnson shows that the natural, sociable operations of sympathy, which lay at the heart of his biographical theory, depend upon one's not regarding oneself as a special case, immune to laughing and being laughed at. For example, rather than sharing the affronts of the self-important, much-complaining targets of the *Dunciad* (1728), people only laughed at their injuries, because "no man sympathises with the sorrows of vanity" that lie outside common

31. For an engaging, sympathetic account of Johnson's decades-long engagement with Milton that mixes scholarship, analysis, and judicious speculation, see Christine Rees, *Johnson's Milton* (Cambridge, 2010), esp. 211–39.

experience. Likewise, once Pope "thought himself one of the moving powers in the system of life," he did not suspect that people "went away and laughed" when he threatened to stop writing. Walled off by self-regard, he made himself as ridiculous as "an idiot who used to revenge his vexations by lying all night upon the [London] bridge." This humor does not signal antipathy, as it often does when leveled by Pope himself; rather, for Johnson it is a mechanism of social conciliation, for "hoot[ing] back" (4:32–36).

Importantly, Johnson considered himself a fair target for such laughter, believing that "a man should pass a part of his time with *the laughers*, by which means any thing ridiculous or particular about him might be presented to his view, and corrected."[32] Such laughter, in a genuinely sociable setting, is to be welcomed as helpful, or, if found to be groundless, dismissed rather than resented. In the *Lives* and beyond, for example, Johnson discourages feuds and grudges over perceived slights, especially in the literary world, in which authors repeatedly draw attention to attacks against themselves, giving them heat and life by answering them rather than letting them flicker and die. This hostility indeed is the *Lives*' most conspicuous trope for the destruction of sociability. Far better, by Johnson's example, to preserve and nurture a community of the similarly engaged, as he demonstrates in the Preface to his edition of Shakespeare (1765), in which he draws the famously antagonistic succession of editors out of their *odium academicum* and into a collegial partnership, according to "the Roman sentiment, that it is more honourable to save a citizen, than to kill an enemy."[33]

There are many instances of this deflationary, communalizing humor in the *Lives*, some readily legible and some less so. Together, they create and safeguard an amicable and sympathetic sociability among author, reader, and subject. It is an operation that mirrors the meeting of people Johnson favors outside the *Lives*, in which all are linked sympathetically with regard to their common humanity, even though materially they occupy different stations and inevitably their particular circumstances differ. Though Johnson generally supported a less-than-rigid system of social subordination as conducive to order, and thereby the peaceable pursuit of happiness, the *Lives*, unlike, say, the King's Library, are a forum in which all subjects meet equally, *sub specie humanitatis*, with the humbly born Cowley, Prior, and Akenside treated no differently from the high-born Halifax, Roscommon, and Sheffield.[34] All are "levelled with the

32. *Life*, 4:183. For an examination of the humaneness of Johnson's tendency to include himself as a target of humor, see W. J. Bate's "Johnson and Satire *Manqué*," in *Eighteenth-Century Studies in Honor of Donald F. Hyde*, ed. W. H. Bond (New York, 1970), 145–60.

33. Johnson, Preface to *Shakespeare* (1765), in *Johnson on Shakespeare*, vols. 7–8 of *YE*, ed. Arthur Sherbo (1968), 7:106. For Johnson's masterful collation of the editors from Nicholas Rowe to William Warburton (including the woeful Lewis Theobald) into a union in which "not one has left Shakespeare without improvement," see pp. 93–106 at 101.

34. Johnson was reading in the King's Library at the Queen's House, later Buckingham Palace, in February 1767, when King George entered and engaged him in conversation on a variety of topics, including his "desire to have the literary biography of this country ably executed, and [for] Dr. Johnson to undertake it." When asked how he had responded to a particularly kind compliment from the king, Johnson protested that it was "not for [him] to bandy civilities with [his] Sovereign"; *Life*, 2:33–41 at 40, 35. For a study of this episode in the context of similar ones in which a subject encounters royalty, though

general surface of life," so one may regard their experiences as analogous to one another's, and one's own.[35]

The Black Hole of Singularity

Some subjects strenuously resist this leveling, though, none more than Swift, whose personality gives Johnson the most trouble in the *Lives*. Johnson tries. Though not humorous, this instance shows an attempt to communalize and somewhat extenuate Swift's fractiousness: in the sorry episode with Esther "Vanessa" Vanhomrigh, when the middle-aged Dean failed to discourage "a passion which he never meant to gratify" on the part of the attractive young woman, it redounded eventually to the great unhappiness of all concerned, exposing Esther "Stella" Johnson to mortifying public comment and even imputedly causing young Vanessa's death from disappointment. Nevertheless, Johnson reasons, "recourse must be had to that extenuation which [Swift] so much despised, *men are but men*" (3:201, italics in original).

For Johnson, Swift embodies "singularity," a word that appears only three times in the life, but an idea that suffuses the *Lives* as a recurring concern, and especially in "Swift." As Adam Potkay has suggested, singularity is a "nodal" concept for Johnson, one that shows up in a variety of contexts and genres and seems to have special explanatory force.[36] It is not original or unique to him, of course—the illustrative quotations in the *Dictionary* for "singular" and "singularity" reach back to Shakespeare and Raleigh and forward to Charlotte Lennox, and a search for the words on Eighteenth Century Collections Online yields many thousands of entries. In the vast majority of cases, the senses are mostly mild, something along a continuum from "unique" to "mildly curious." In the *Dictionary*, it is only in the fourth definition for each that one sees singularity as in any way bad.[37]

often more awkwardly than did Johnson, see Howard D. Weinbrot, "Meeting the Monarch: Johnson, Boswell, and the Anatomy of a Genre," *The Age of Johnson* 18 (2007): 131–50. Cowley was the son of a grocer (*Lives*, 1:191), Prior was presumed to be the son of a joiner (3:48), and Akenside was the son of a butcher (4:171). Others whose impoverished upbringings Johnson notes include Rev. William Broome (3:215), David Mallet (4:167), and, of course, Richard Savage (3:121–14). As to whether Savage was cheated of a noble inheritance, we are content to remain agnostic.

35. *Idler* 84 (November 24, 1759), *YE*, 2:262.

36. Adam Potkay, "Johnson and the Terms of Succession," *SEL* 26 (1986): 497–509 at 498. As the title suggests, Potkay is analyzing Johnson's various uses of the word "succession."

37. The fourth definition for "singular"—"Having something not common to others"—is followed by the addition that "It is commonly used in a sense of disapprobation, whether applied to persons or things." To the fourth definition for "singularity"—"Character or manners different from those of others"—the first illustrative quotation, from Hooker, states that "The spirit of *singularity* in a few ought to give place to publick judgment," which is still pretty mild: Johnson, *Dictionary of the English Language*, 4th ed. (London, 1773), s.vv. "singular" and "singularity." In the *Dictionary*, it bears repeating, Johnson is describing current and sometimes historical usage, in both the definitions and quotations; beyond barring a few authors he believes morally dangerous, he does not bend definitions or select quotations so as to advance an agenda. For the most definitive essay on this point, see Howard D. Weinbrot, "What Johnson's Illustrative Quotations Illustrate: Language and Viewpoint in the *Dictionary*," in *Anniversary Essays on Johnson's Dictionary*, ed. Jack Lynch and Anne McDermott (Cambridge, 2005), 42–60. For further discussion of Swift and singularity, see also Weinbrot's "'Tis well an old age is out': Johnson, Swift, and His Generation" in this volume.

But for Johnson, when writing for his own rhetorical purposes, singularity is generally quite bad, which may help us understand "Swift." Johnson elaborates on singularity in *Adventurer* 131 (1754), which begins with Bernard Le Bovier de Fontenelle's praise of Sir Isaac Newton: though a genius, he "was not distinguished from other men, by any singularity either natural or affected." Johnson regards Newton as worthy of special praise for having "stood alone, merely because he had left the rest of mankind behind him, not because he deviated from the beaten tract." He did not neglect the "little things . . . the conduct of domestick affairs . . . the common intercourses of life . . . those trifles [by which] the ranks of mankind are kept in order, . . . the address of one to another is regulated, and the general business of the world carried on with facility and method."[38]

Johnson contrasts this with singularity, the "voluntary neglect of common forms," the "arrogant contempt of those practices, by which others endeavour to gain favour and multiply friendships." Those who "voluntarily consign themselves to singularity" are preeners, who "affect to cross the roads of life because they know that they shall not be jostled, and indulge a boundless gratification of will because they perceive that they shall be quietly obeyed." When better-willed people tolerate them, the singular "appear too frequently to consider the patience with which their caprices are suffered as an undoubted evidence of their own importance, of a genius to which submission is universally paid." They are bullies, and burdens: "He who expects from mankind, that they should give up established customs in compliance with his single will, and exacts that deference which he does not pay, may be endured, but can never be approved." Because of this, singularity is "in its own nature universally and invariably displeasing," as it implies a "rejection of the common opinion, a defiance of common censure." It is also irresponsible: to "comply with the notions and practices of mankind, is in some degree the duty of a social being; because by compliance only he can please, and by pleasing only he can become useful."[39] One thinks of Johnson's tempestuous, singular friend Savage.

This concern with singularity, the willful rejection of the accumulated wisdom of custom and the ties of sympathy, lies at the heart of the literary-critical judgments in the *Lives* that angered people most. In "Cowley," he writes that the Metaphysicals "endeavoured to be singular in their thoughts." In so doing they broke trust with the reader, delighting in "wit, abstracted from its effects upon the hearer," spinning out conceits that were ostentatious, but unjust, unnatural, and untrue. They "ransacked" art and nature, yoking ideas by violence—"they had no regard to that uniformity of sentiment which enables us to conceive and to excite the pains and the pleasure of other minds: they never inquired what, on any occasion, they should have said or done. . . . Their wish was only to say what they hoped had been never said before" (1:200–201).

38. *Adventurer* 131, *YE*, 2:482.

39. All quotations in this paragraph are from *YE*, 2:482–87. Johnson includes "To avoid all singularity" in a list of resolutions from October 1765; see *Diaries, Prayers, and Annals*, vol. 1 of *YE*, ed. E. L. McAdam Jr. with Donald and Mary Hyde (1958), 197.

This is the flaw he finds in Gray, who "thought his language more poetical as it was more remote from common use." His odes depend on "some violence both to language and sense" and are "marked by accumulations of ungraceful ornaments [that] strike, rather than please." Their "language is laboured into harshness. The mind of the writer seems to work with unnatural violence" (4:181–83). Johnson's objections often invoke violent assault: he sees the poetry of singularity as abusive. The poet's primary obligations are not to his own mind and art but rather to truth and the reader; singularity corrupts, even brutalizes, both. So elsewhere he complains of Dryden's "irregular and excentrick violence of wit" (2:149). The pastoral artificiality of Milton's *Lycidas* "forces dissatisfaction on the mind." He finds the poem "harsh . . . uncertain . . . unpleasing," and because it is a pastoral, "easy, vulgar, and therefore disgusting." This remark comes immediately after he argues that readers "prevail upon themselves to think that admirable which is only singular" (1:278–79).

But for all the concern with singular habits of writing, it is with singular habits of living that Johnson is most exercised, and thus with Swift. His character bothered Johnson immensely, and his withering verdict on Swift is the harshest in the *Lives*. Swift "was not a man to be either loved or envied. He seems to have wasted life in discontent, by the rage of neglected pride, and the languishment of unsatisfied desire. He is querulous and fastidious, arrogant and malignant." Johnson recoils from the "depravity of intellect [that] took delight in revolving ideas, from which almost every other mind shrinks with disgust" (3:212–13). He dislikes Milton as a person, on balance, and is sometimes exasperated with several other fellow travelers in the *Lives*; Swift, alone, fills him with a species of puzzled horror. Even Savage, who most fits the charge of having "wasted his life," so much the "slave of every passion" that "his friendship was therefore of little value," is at least legible; Swift is baffling, and Johnson does not like it (3:186–87). The "common intercourses of life" are the fields that Johnson gleans, gathering up samples that will allow him and us better to understand lives, and life, including our own. Swift's singularity, by contrast, is a rocky place, where Johnson's method can find no purchase.

At the root of his bafflement, and disapproval, is that Swift was "fond of singularity, and desirous to make a mode of happiness for himself, different from the general course of things and order of Providence" (3:204). Some singularities we can attribute to his final, sad decline into mental illness, such as his not speaking for much of the last two years of his life, refusing to eat until his servant, who had prepared and cut the food, had left, and then eating while walking, because it was his habit to be "on his feet ten hours a day." It might also explain his odd refusal to wear eyeglasses, such that in his lonely later life he could not read, leaving his mind "vacant to the vexations of the hour, till at last his anger was heightened into madness" (3:207).[40]

40. For an analysis of Swift's Ménière's disease, see Wanda J. Creaser, "'The Most Mortifying Malady': Jonathan Swift's Dizzying World and Dublin's Mentally Ill," *Swift Studies* 19 (2004): 27–48. Creaser notes that people afflicted with the disease commonly experience "anxiety, anger, grief, and depression," the vast majority become clinically depressed, and the symptoms of the disease make people "feel as if they are losing their minds" (33).

But there are other, earlier instances. Johnson explores two at particular length. One is Swift's secret marriage to Stella, which he describes with poignancy:

> She never was treated as a wife, and to the world she had the appearance of a mistress. She lived sullenly on, in hope that in time he would own and receive her; but the time did not come till the change of his manners and depravation of his mind made her tell him, when he offered to acknowledge her, that *it was too late*. She then gave up herself to sorrowful resentment, and died under the tyranny of him, by whom she was in the highest degree loved and honoured. What were her claims to this excentrick tenderness, by which the laws of nature were violated to retain her, curiosity will enquire; but how shall it be gratified? (3:205, italics in original)

Johnson finds no occasion for humor in this "excentrick tenderness"; it ruined lives, and unlike Swift's late-in-life oddities, was of long duration and required considerable planning and maintenance, making it seem entirely self-willed.

The other instance of special singularity, though, is darkly and perplexingly funny. Notably, it comes from Swift's close friend, Pope, via Joseph Spence's *Anecdotes* (1820):

> Dr. Swift has an odd, blunt way, that is mistaken, by strangers, for ill-nature. 'Tis so odd, that there's no describing it but by facts. I'll tell you the first one that comes into my head.
>
> One evening Gay and I went to see him; you know how intimately we are all acquainted.
>
> On our coming in, "Hey-day, gentlemen, says the Doctor, "what's the meaning of this visit? How come you to leave all the great lords that you are so fond of to come hither to see a poor Dean?"
>
> Because we would rather see you than any of them.
>
> "Ay, any one that did not know so well as I do might believe you. But since you are come I must get some supper for you, I suppose."
>
> No, Doctor, we have supped already.
>
> "Supped already! That's impossible—why, 'tis not eight o'clock yet."
>
> Indeed we have.
>
> "That's very strange. But if you had not supped I must have got something for you. Let me see, what should I have had? A couple of lobsters? Aye, that would have done very well—two shillings. Tarts—a shilling. But you will drink a glass of wine with me, though you supped so much before your usual time, only to spare my pocket?"
>
> No we had rather talk with you than drink with you.
>
> "But if you had supped with me as in all reason you ought to have

> done, you must then have drank with me: a bottle of wine—two shillings. Two and two is four, and one is five: just two and sixpence apiece. There, Pope, there's half a crown for you, and there's another for you, Sir, for I won't save any thing by you. I am determined."
>
> This was all said and done with his usual seriousness on such occasions, and in spite of everything we could say to the contrary, he actually obliged us to take the money. (3:211)[41]

This fits a pattern. Johnson notes elsewhere that when Swift's "friends of either sex came to him, in expectation of a dinner, his custom was to give every one a shilling, that they might please themselves with their provision" (3:207). It is not exactly stinginess, but what is it?

Given Pope's claim to intimacy, which we know to be true, and the compliments, fulsome but sincere, offered Swift by Pope and Gay, one naturally desires the scene to become what the visitors try to create: an amiable retreat from the busyness of the town, marked by pleasant conversation among intimates. Swift, though, turns that intimacy against his visitors—"Ay, any one that did not know you so well as I do, might believe you"—and resolutely rebuffs and distorts their intimacies, preferring a contest of wills marked on his part by suspicion, the deflection of pleasantries, and the vulgar intrusion of money. Each attempt at mollifying him is parried by insinuations that his visitors are haughty social climbers, dishonest men, and a burden on his time, household, and purse. He implacably refuses the pleasure of their company, and so prevents the reader from experiencing a sympathetic, vicarious pleasure in the reciprocation of good will among like minds. Whatever Swift wants, it seems not to be their friendship.

It is at least possible, though, that readers might try to read otherwise, that they might initially derive pleasure from the notion that the arch Swift is jousting with his friends in a game of wits, throwing them off-balance by feigning irritation while knowing that he can take such liberties precisely because they are intimates, and thereby perversely affirming rather than deflecting that intimacy.[42] It is the only avenue by which to find the anecdote enjoyable, I think. Laughing down his subject in a Hobbesian fashion is not something Johnson encourages, and it would itself be unpleasant given that these are all real people, not "humours" characters from the Old Comedy. The happiest and kindest reading, then, is that this is an instance of Swift's extraordinarily dry humor pushed to what seems to an outsider to be an unseemly extreme: we may think that

41. See Joseph Spence, *Observations, Anecdotes, and Characters of Books and Men: Collected from Conversation*, ed. James M. Osborn, 2 vols. (Oxford, 1966), 1:53–54. Neither Pope nor Spence dates the anecdote, but it presumably falls between September 1713—when Swift was made Dean—and September 1714, after which he returned to Ireland except for visits in 1726 and 1727. This is not, then, taken from the later period of Swift's life during which he was demonstrably mentally ill, though he probably suffered some ill effects of Ménière's disease most of his adult life.

42. This is the argument that John Vance makes about Johnson's own humor, especially as recorded by Boswell. See "The Laughing Johnson and the Shaping of Boswell's *Life*," in *Boswell's "Life of Johnson": New Questions, New Answers*, ed. Vance (Athens, Ga., 1985), 204–27.

Swift has decided on his joke and will not let it drop, his friends' feelings be damned, but we may also surmise that perhaps his friends know better and can see humor that we cannot. We are the strangers who mistakenly see ill-nature.

This is unfortunately the least supportable reading, though, as Pope opens by describing the story as a specimen of Swift's "odd, blunt way," not his "dry humor" or his "gift for playful absurdity," and his noting that it is not an anomaly but simply the first such that comes into his head. Pope may say that it is not ill-nature, but one wonders what to call it instead. The "odd" suggests Pope is at a loss himself. And after describing the action, he closes by noting Swift's "usual seriousness on such occasions": one does not know whether "such" refers to occasions involving money, or in which Swift forces a joke beyond which it might be funny, or in which he treats friends as intruders. None reads to his advantage. Any pleasantry withers with the repetitions of Swift's resolute unpleasantness. The tension he creates from the moment his visitors arrive is never relieved, but rather heightened until he is satisfied with total victory. There is no deviation from his "odd, blunt way" when pressing money on them, no wink-and-nod, no histrionic gesture to acknowledge the absurdity of the scenario. If Swift is in his own mind being funny, he regards humor as self-amusement rather than something to be sympathetically shared.

All this suggests strongly that Swift is entirely earnest. Pope does not recount what follows, and Johnson does not speculate, but one can scarcely imagine that intimacy was thereafter restored for the evening, if at all, except by Pope's and Gay's acquiescence and submission. If this is not to Pope's mind "ill-nature," that must mean simply that he intends by the term something like "genuine malice"; singular crassness and ill-temperedness in the face of friendship is not enough to warrant the term, even when habitual, as Pope implies it is for Swift.

But is it comical? I think it is. The accumulation of absurdity makes it funny from the outside, though Pope gives no reason to think it was pleasant up close. The laughter it elicits is defensive, like laughter at John Dennis's repeated critical thunderings, but, importantly, it is not solitary. The anecdote provides allies, Pope and Gay, who do all they can to create an amiable sociality, and to salvage it when Swift will not cooperate. They give him every chance, and when he resolutely refuses, they surrender and take his ill-offered money rather than invite more abuse. We are allowed sympathy with them, and though Swift refuses, we need not.

Conclusion: "Rag" Redux

The visit to Swift opens a line of sight into the humor in the Edmund Smith anecdote, how he was "brought ... to the grave" by the fatal purgative. Does Johnson mean for readers to laugh while imagining Smith's death, which must have been protracted and painful? Surely not. One must not be timid, though, where Johnson is bold, however "uneasy" it may make his readers.[43] In his composition of the anecdote, the play on

43. See Isobel Grundy, "On Reading Johnson for Laughs," *The New Rambler* 19 (1978): 21–25: "It's not news to us that Johnson makes us laugh, but it is an aspect of him which seems to make many readers and commentators uneasy" (21).

Smith's "swallow[ing] his own medicine" and the matter-of-fact denouement are demonstrably humorous devices pointing to Smith's folly and its consequences. Smith is clearly at fault for his gluttony and stubbornness, but how does Johnson mean for readers to read his death? As—please pardon me—his just des[s]erts, as criminal self-indulgence and foolishness that may legitimately be mocked? Unlike the Gay episode, it is prohibitively difficult to imagine Johnson's finding this situation inherently funny—a man dies, after all. So one looks for clues. Why does Johnson describe the ale as "too delicious to be resisted," rather than as "too delicious for Smith" (or "a man such as Smith") "to resist"? Does this communalize Smith's folly? Is the "rude contempt" Smith shows a social inferior enough to lose him the reader's sympathy, even in such an extremity? Does knowledge of Johnson's own life experiences offer guidance?[44]

A definitive answer, which Johnson could have chosen to provide, proves elusive. Shortly after this anecdote is a curious element of "Smith," one that is so obtrusive that it might signal Johnson's state of mind and intentions when reflecting on Smith. This is his extraordinary digression to eulogize his friends Gilbert Walmsley and David Garrick, which takes over the final five paragraphs of the life proper. Johnson notes that Walmsley was the source of much information about Smith, and that Walmsley considered him to be "*a man of great veracity*." He continues, "Of Gilbert Walmsley, thus presented to my mind, let me indulge myself in the remembrance." He recounts the many social kindnesses Walmsley did him, such that several decades later "it may be doubted whether a day now passes" in which Johnson does not feel "some advantage from his friendship." This in turn reminds him of the "many chearful and instructive hours" at Walmsley's table, "with companions such as are not often found," including Garrick, whom Johnson "hoped to have gratified with this character of [their] common friend: but what are the hopes of man!" Garrick's recent death had "eclipsed the gaiety of nations, and impoverished the publick stock of harmless pleasure" (2:178–79, italics in original).[45]

How does this remarkable chain of digression help us read the humor of the fatal anecdote? Johnson writes about Smith; doing so prompts him to reminisce about a mutual friend, who regarded Smith as an honest man and knew him well enough to

44. Regarding Johnson's likely attitude toward pathological eating, one might note that though Henry Thrale's strokes began just after the publication of the volumes containing "Smith," the overindulgence that brought them on was long established. Lee Morgan's biography, *Dr. Johnson's "Own Dear Master": The Life of Henry Thrale* (Lanham, Md., 1998), dates Thrale's decline in health from the spring of 1778, prior to the publication of the life of Smith. Unfortunately for present purposes, Morgan focuses on Thrale's depression brought on by money troubles, rather than his overindulgence as perhaps a longstanding symptom of depression, or as contributing to his ill-health and thereby exacerbating other worries. For a description of Thrale's pathological eating even as his health worsened, see p. 215.

45. Garrick died on January 20, 1779. As the volumes containing the life of Smith appeared in the spring of that year, it is likely that this relation of Garrick's death was inserted into proofs of the already-written life. We know, from a letter to John Nichols, that Johnson made an unrelated change to "Smith" as late as March 1: *The Letters of Samuel Johnson*, ed. Bruce Redford, 5 vols. (Princeton, N.J., 1992–94), 3:152. Garrick's widow included the "gaiety of nations" line on Garrick's funeral monument; see *Letters*, 3:150n1.

provide personal anecdotes. This reminiscence leads Johnson to think about an even closer friend and mourn his recent death, the news of which arrives with as much surprise as Smith's does in the anecdote. This does not precisely parallel Smith to Garrick; Smith was too small a figure to effect an eclipse. It does, though, subsume him in Johnson's thinking and writing within a network in which memorials of friendship are a primary conduit through which a person is remembered, and in which death is lamented. The first half of Johnson's life of Smith is taken from the account given by William Oldisworth, "with all the partiality of friendship" (2:165). Johnson "cannot much commend the performance," but he includes it nonetheless, as he frequently does with friendly encomia in the *Lives* (2:173). By means of these inclusions, the individual pains of a person's death are subsumed within a larger human narrative: "what are the hopes of man!"

And as in the Swift story, the anecdote gives us a conscientious interlocutor: the apothecary, who models the prosocial behavior Smith abjures. Then follow remembrances of close friends and "chearful" hours at table (which for Johnson tended to involve rhinoceros-laughter) and the "gaiety of nations." It could be that, in both "Swift" and "Smith," the challenges Johnson puts to his readers are couched in the comic so that the engine of comedy rescues them from the dark gravitational pull of singularity. The comic allows a social whole to function even in the face of the uniquely self-destructive. In this larger frame, one may shake one's head and chuckle at Swift's bad humor and Smith's fatal foolishness without abusing the bonds of sympathy that laughter should affirm rather than degrade. Laughter is thus prophylactic against mental torpor and social collapse; it is palliative and restorative, enjoyable in itself and also healthful, locating that pleasure and usefulness in the perception of humankind's shared condition.

As our fellow in this condition, Johnson invites us repeatedly to laugh, both to comfort us, and to spur our understanding, creating an active, flexible, analytical reader, not simply a receiver of confirmatory wisdom or a decoder of allegory. Johnson is seriously funny, and to miss or mischaracterize his humor is to lose an essential element of the seriousness of his project in the *Lives*. To suggest so is not merely an attempt to thrash the ghost of Chesterfield, nor to pick bones with the shades of Johnson-mockers such as James Gillray and Thomas Macaulay. It is, rather, an attempt to understand how humor in the *Lives* is, in Johnson's conception, lifelike.

PART III:
JOHNSON AND THE DULL DUTIES

Writing the *Dictionary of the English Language*: Johnson's Journey into Words

Lynda Mugglestone

FOR RENAISSANCE LEXICOGRAPHERS, the journey into words was a familiar trope. Thomas Blount's *Glossographia* of 1656, for example, was, he stated, the product of over twenty years' exploration in "a new world of Words."[1] Edward Phillips, Milton's nephew and a frequent Johnsonian source, provides a similar imaging of the lexical universe, appropriating Blount's phrase for his own work, the *New World of English Words* of 1658.[2] Even if, as Blount contended, Phillips's own investigative journeys had, in reality, been all too limited, the salience of this shared trope is clear. A globe, inscribed with the words "novis orbis verborum," appears prominently on Phillips's frontispiece, offering vivid illustration of the territories that readers can, courtesy of lexicography, now survey with ease.[3]

It is, however, in John Florio's earlier *Worlde of Words*, first published in 1598, that these connections are perhaps made most explicit. Florio's opening address "To the Reader" describes a "new voyage" in a "paper-sea" in which "discouerie," as befits a dictionary, "may happily profit other men." For Florio, dictionary-makers are indeed like "Sea-faring men," adventurers set sail for a realm that is both "deepe, and dangerous." Florio's imaging of his own solitary and hazardous journey is vivid. In contrast to other collective lexicographic enterprises, such as those in which the academicians of

1. Thomas Blount, *Glossographia: or A Dictionary, Interpreting all Such Hard Words . . . as are Now Used in Our Refined English Tongue* (London, 1656), sig. A3r.

2. Edward Phillips, *The New World of English Words; or, A General Dictionary* (London, 1658). See, for example, Johnson's entries for "BURROCK," n. ſ. "A small wear or dam, where wheels are laid in a river for catching of fish. *Phillips's World of Words*"; "BURSE," n. ſ. "An exchange where merchants meet, and shops are kept; so called, because the sign of the purse was anciently set over such a place; whence the Exchange in the Strand was termed Britain's Burse by James I. *Phillips*." Unless otherwise specified, all references to Johnson's *Dictionary* are taken from the first edition: Samuel Johnson, *A Dictionary of the English Language: in Which the Words are Deduced from Their Originals and Illustrated in Their Different Significations by Examples from the Best Writers*, 2 vols. (London, 1755).

3. See Thomas Blount, *A World of Errors Discovered in The New World of Words, or, General English Dictionary* (London, 1673), sig. A2r: "*Twelve months had not passed, but there appeared in Print this New World of Words . . . extracted almost wholly out of mine.*"

the Académie Française or Accademia della Crusca were engaged, he was "but one to turne and winde the sailes, to vse the oare, to sit at sterne" or "to watch vpon the upper decke." The solitary lexicographer, Florio stresses, must in this respect be "boute-swain, pilot, mate, and master." Bound on a journey across "a sea more diuers, more dangerous, more stormie, and more comfortlesse then any Ocean," he alone has to hold "all offices in one, and that in a more vnruly, more vnweildie, and more roome-some vessell, than the biggest hulke on Thames."[4]

Such narratives of risk and adventure can seem a world away from the dullness and drudgery in which Johnson's images of lexicography can operate. "To make dictionaries is *dull* work," Johnson famously notes under sense 8 of "DULL," further glossed as "Not exhilaterating [i.e., exhilarating]; not delightful." His "harmless drudge" (s.v. "LEXICOGRAPHER") commits not to Florio's expansive seas but moves in expectation of safety. "[A]s it was low, it likewise would be safe," Johnson remarks in his 1747 *Plan*.[5] Johnson's dictionary-maker traces a narrow and restrictive path in which he merely follows "the track of the alphabet with sluggish resolution" (*YE*, 18:26).

This is, however, by no means the only route or mode in which dictionary-making is seen to operate. As Paul Fussell reminds us, here in a further resonant image of movement and change, what Johnson's writing "means" is "to be searched where opposites and contradictions encounter each other."[6] The same proves true of Johnson's diverse narratives of lexicography. Johnson's metaphorical positioning—and repositioning—of the journey into words offers, in this light, yet another instance in which fruitful changes of direction allow us to examine both his critical departures as dictionary-maker, and his changing sense of the lexicographical enterprise per se.

Alongside the linear journey from A to Z, based in the textual pragmatics of the alphabet, we find therefore a range of configurations and alternative routes that reveal both continuity with and difference from Johnson's Renaissance forebears. Like Florio, it is clear that Johnson, too, can sail in a sea of words—an image that, for instance, underpins his 1747 identification of the dictionary-maker as "adventurer," engaged in a journey in which Florio's "discoverie" is also prominent: "I shall at least discover the coast, civilize part of the inhabitants, and make it easy for some other adventurer to proceed farther, to reduce them wholly to subjection, and settle them under laws" (*YE*, 18:58). While the dictionary-maker is, at this point, heading toward a shore of linguistic subjugation on a journey of conquest and control, the sense of the fluid expanse of language that must also be traversed is one to which Johnson repeatedly returns. "I now begin to see land," he writes on February 1, 1755, to Thomas Warton. "After having wandered, according to Mr. Warburton's phrase, in this vast Sea of words," the journey is, he indicates, almost at an end. In just over two months, the *Dictionary of the English Language* would be published, and the "Sea" crossed. A similar image of journey and

4. John Florio, *A Worlde of Wordes, or Most Copious, and Exact Dictionarie in Italian and English* (London, 1598), sigs. 6v–7r.

5. *Johnson on the English Language*, vol. 18 of *The Yale Edition of the Works of Samuel Johnson* (hereafter cited as *YE*), ed. Gwin J. Kolb and Robert DeMaria Jr. (New Haven, Conn., 2005), 27. Text citations are to this edition.

6. Paul Fussell, *Samuel Johnson and the Life of Writing* (London, 1972), 148.

return informs a further letter to Warton on March 25: "My Book is now coming *in luminous ora*" (unto the bright coasts of light).[7]

By this stage, moreover, Johnson's journey is also depicted as markedly far-reaching in both extent and scope. No longer following the fixed and linear path on land, Johnson's self-imaging now occupies a position akin to George Anson's recent *Voyage Round the World*, recounted by Richard Walter, chaplain of Anson's ship the *Centurion*, and serialized in the *Gentleman's Magazine* as Johnson worked on the *Dictionary* in 1749 and 1750. If Johnson's reading of Anson is reflected in a number of images within the contemporaneous *Rambler* essays, then, in terms of the *Dictionary*, Johnson is, he proclaims, now also a circumnavigator—"one who sails round," as the *Dictionary* defines this word.[8] Having traversed a world of words, Johnson had, as he stated to Garrick, "sailed a long and painful voyage round the world of the English language."[9] The nature of the journey, together with its location, range, and duration, have all changed in the years since the dictionary began.

As Richard Walter suggests, "A Voyage round the World is still considered an Enterprize of a very singular nature; and the Public have never failed to be extremely inquisitive about the various accidents and turns of fortune, with which this uncommon event is generally attended."[10] Johnson's lexicographic voyage, and interest in it, would, in this respect at least, be markedly similar. On one level, then, his metaphorical positioning strikes a noticeably contemporaneous note, as well as reaching back into the tropes of earlier lexicographic history. Like that of Anson, Johnson's journey would be far longer than originally envisaged, as well as similarly resonant of desire and expectation set against the rather different territories of actuality and experience.[11] Like Anson's, too, it would be marked by a language of discovery and observation, and a changing narrative of what had been found on the way. In Johnson's mapping of the spatial world of words, the journey as lexicographical progress can be strikingly apposite.

Though Johnson's interest in travel and travel writing has been extensively documented by such writers as Thomas Jemielity, Thursten Moore, and Tom Curley, the *Dictionary* itself tends to stay outside such discussions.[12] Curley focuses on Johnson's literary works as well as his letters, as does Jemielity; Moore's 1966 dissertation likewise

7. *The Letters of Samuel Johnson*, ed. Bruce Redford, 5 vols. (Princeton, N.J., 1992–94): 1:92, 101 (hereafter cited in text as *Letters*). Warburton's image of the "Sea of words" was, in fact, taken from Florio himself.

8. See Thomas M. Curley, *Samuel Johnson and the Age of Travel* (Athens, Ga., 1976), 117.

9. Arthur Murphy, "An Essay upon the Life and Genius of Samuel Johnson," *The Works of Samuel Johnson LL.D.*, 12 vols. (London, 1792), 1:74.

10. Richard Walter and Benjamin Robins, *A Voyage Round the World in the Years MDCCXL, I, II, III, IV, by George Anson*, ed. Glyndwr Williams (London, 1974), 9.

11. Anson's original objectives in terms of conquering at least part of the Spanish coast were abandoned; only 145 of the original crew returned home. Almost 1,500 died of disease. In diction resonant of Johnson's own narratives of the *Dictionary*, Anson's "scheme" as originally "projected" remained unfulfilled in "execution" (see, for example, *Voyage Round the World*, 19–20).

12. See Thomas Jemielity, "Dr. Johnson and the Uses of Travel," *Philological Quarterly* 51 (1972): 448–59; Thursten Maxwell Moore, "Samuel Johnson and the Literature of Travel" (PhD diss., University of Michigan, 1966); and Curley, *Johnson and the Age of Travel.*

offers a comprehensive reading of Johnson and travel while firmly removing the *Dictionary* and its making from consideration. As they all affirm, however, travel, as acts of reading and of writing, spans Johnson's literary career, from, say, the early translation of Lobo's *Voyage to Abyssinia* in 1735, to the later *Journey to the Western Isles of Scotland* (1775). Johnson's personal library, as they also note, was amply stocked with travels, a genre that Johnson identifies in a significant new sense division in his *Dictionary*: "Travels. Accounts of occurrences and observations of a journey into foreign parts."[13]

Johnson's changing metaphors of the journey into words nevertheless clearly resonate with his wider thinking on travel and the forms it might assume, as well as the values it might variously hold. As for Johnson's Renaissance predecessors, if dictionary-making is a journey, it has both a point of departure and an intended destination that may, of course, not necessarily be that which is eventually reached. Of interest, too, are the difficult years in between, in which the dictionary-maker may indeed find himself "at sea" in a variety of ways. To place the narrative trajectories of Johnson's *Dictionary* in this perspective can be rewarding. The fact that Johnson's lexicographic journey is repeatedly relocated from the initially static path on land to the instability of the sea is, for instance, by no means insignificant. Florio's unruly sea of words, as he early indicated, was not easily navigated, already throwing easy assumptions of lexicographical control into question. The location of the journey and the task the journey seeks to perform—colonization, control, discovery, exploration—offer radically different spaces in which the dictionary-maker might move.

By their very nature, for instance, the 1747 *Plan*, and the earlier "Scheme" of 1746 on which it depends, stand as the imagined or envisaged journey, detailing the course to be assumed and the "conquest" that is confidently expected to be made.[14] The past participles of the *Plan*, with their sense of intended achievement, represent the end point of a journey that is, in reality, still to be effected. "Thus, my Lord," Johnson writes to Chesterfield, "will our language be laid down . . . resolved into its elemental principles" (*YE*, 18:44). Here, as in Johnson's diction of "ascertained," "fixed," and "preserved," they merely contemplate a completed text in what remains the ease of hypothesis. In 1747, moreover, Johnson, like Anson, stood at the brink of a commissioned journey, directed on a certain course by the consortium of booksellers, just as Anson was, at least intentionally, sent off to attack the Pacific coast of Spanish America. In terms of the direction Johnson was to follow, the commercial opportunities for a work to accomplish what the *Dictionnaire* of the Académie Française had professedly done for French seemed self-evident. Advertisements published in 1747 make plain the normative intent of Johnson's forthcoming dictionary; it would be a work by which English words would be "regulated in their Construction" as well as "explain'd in all the Varieties of

13. This stands interestingly against Moore's assertion that "[t]here is no evidence in his writings that he considered travel writing to be a distinct literary genre (though it was a recognisable type)"; see "Samuel Johnson and the Literature of Travel," 68.

14. The holograph manuscript of Johnson's "Short Scheme for compiling a new Dictionary of the English Language" is reproduced in *YE*, 18:377–427.

their Meaning . . . according to the Authority of our purest Writers."[15] The calculated puff by William Strahan in the *Gentleman's Magazine* in 1749 shares a similar orientation in terms of what lexicography, in Johnson's hands, is to achieve: "It is hoped, that our language will be more fixed, and better established, when the publick is favoured with a new dictionary, undertaken with that view."[16]

As in Chesterfield's emendations of Johnson's drafted "Scheme" in 1746, this was moreover a course that, in particular aspects, was also influenced by Chesterfield himself. Johnson's original convictions about the acceptability and "settled propriety" of English spelling were, for instance, firmly displaced by Chesterfield's views. "[Y]our Lordship observes that there is still great uncertainty among the best writers," Johnson states in a revision added to the original text. His own earlier observations are deleted, while "uncertainty" is now rendered open to lexicographical redress (*YE*, 18:385). Such revisions further orient Johnson in one direction rather than another, steering him toward correctness and control and the intended imposition of power. It is "by his Lordship's opinion," as Johnson writes in the revised *Plan*, that he has "determined . . . to interpose my own judgment" in supporting "what appears to me most consonant to grammar and reason" (*YE*, 18:54). In what is an extensive addition to the original "Scheme," a new set of social relations informs the metaphorical journey to be made. Hierarchically rendered foot soldier to Chesterfield's "Caesar," Johnson becomes a participant dispatched on a journey of incursion in which, famously, he will also act as Chesterfield's "delegate," wielding "vicarious jurisdiction" (*YE*, 18:55) over the words and meanings that are encountered.[17]

A range of entries in the *Dictionary* do indeed reveal narratives of this kind. Command is, at least intentionally, assumed over "PRECARIOUS" and "PREJUDICE," "SHABBY" and "SHAMBLING." "VIZ," we are told, is "A barbarous form of an unnecessary word." Collocations such as "most peculiar" are condemned: "To join *most* with *peculiar*, though found in *Dryden*, is improper." Yet, the experiential reality of lexicography, and the complex journeys that the dictionary-maker must negotiate along the way, reveal other narratives as well. If opinion is offered, the facts of use remain, in line with Boswell's later emphasis on what he described as Johnson's "rational respect for testimony."[18] Dryden's testimony is given under "PECULIAR," alongside Johnson's reservations. Likewise, while Johnson's disapproval of "FINESSE" is clear, he does not deny its

15. See, for example, advertisements for Johnson's *Dictionary* in the *London Evening Post*, April 14 to 16, 1747.

16. W. S., "The Signification of Words Now Varied," *Gentleman's Magazine* 19 (1749): 65–66 at 66.

17. Johnson's reference here is to the Emperor Claudius, whose forces invaded Britain in 43 CE. In a similar classical framing of Chesterfield as Caesar, Johnson is also "Ausonius" (see *YE* 18:54–55, 55n4).

18. *Boswell's Life of Samuel Johnson, Together with Boswell's Journal of a Tour to the Hebrides and Johnson's Diary of a Journey into North Wales*, 6 vols., ed. George Birkbeck Hill, rev. L. F. Powell, 6 vols., 2nd ed. (Oxford, 1971), 1:406 (hereafter cited as *Life*).

increasing frequency and the ongoing momentum of change: "an unnecessary word which is creeping into the language." The present progressive ("is creeping") is prominent, rather than the expected auxiliaries of prescriptive control ("must not," "should not"). Similar is the evidence presented under "BLUSH" (n.) in phrases such as "at first blush." If the sense of "sudden appearance" for the latter "seems barbarous, yet," as Johnson adds, it is also "used by good writers." As in Johnson's entry for "ANACHRONISM," language practice can conspicuously triumph over what might have been expected to be normatively endorsed: "An errour in computing time, by which events are misplaced with regard to each other. It seems properly to signify an errour by which an event is placed too early; but is generally used for any errour in chronology."

Orthography, too, contrary to Chesterfield's intended remit, would prove its continuing "uncertainty" in the *Dictionary*. "In examining the orthography of any doubtful word, the mode of spelling by which it is inserted in the series of the dictionary, is to be considered as that to which I give, perhaps not often rashly, the preference. I have left, in the examples, to every authour his own practice unmolested, that the reader may balance suffrages, and judge between us," Johnson writes in 1755 of the practice he has, in fact, instituted (*YE*, 18:77). Yet, in examining the text, it is clear that definitions as well as citations testify to the range of possibilities that eighteenth-century spelling offered, requiring "suffrages" to be balanced in other ways as well. Alongside "RISK," given as headword, appears "risque," a form used in a range of definitions, as under "DANGER" ("Risque; hazard; peril"), "DANGERLESS" ("Without hazard; without risque; exempt from danger"); "To risque upon the success of an adventure" states sense two of "DEPONE." Headwords such as "SEARISQUE," defined as "hazard at sea," further illustrate ongoing variability rather than affirming the kind of orthographical conquest and concern for uniformity that we might have expected from the *Plan*. Spellings of "surgeon" are similar. "SEASURGEON" is "A chirurgeon employed on shipboard"; "LITHOTOMIST" is "A chirurgeon who extracts the stone by opening the bladder." While "SURGEON," as the *Dictionary* states, is the more modern form, language practice within the *Dictionary* instead attests the truth of coexisting norms. Chesterfield's "uncertainty" is not so much dispelled as soundly confirmed.[19]

In this respect, and in others, the fixed and, indeed, fixing destination of the *Plan* demonstrably recedes.[20] As in the embedded narratives and metalanguage of time that the *Dictionary* in reality comes to record, Johnson's lexicographic interest in the trajectories of unfixed change can be self-evident, as well as unmediated by negative comment. "KNIT," we are told, as used in the sense "To join; to unite," was "*formerly* a word of extensive use; it is *now* less frequent" (my emphases). Other narratives,

19. Further examples are easily located. "ORE" is given as headword for "Metal unrefined; metal yet in its mineral state," while, under "SMELT," the relevant definition appears as "To melt oar, so as to extract the metal"; dictionary practice likewise attests "SCREEN" ("Any thing that affords shelter or concealment") alongside "SKREEN" ("A skreen used in hot countries to keep off the sun, and in others to bear off the rain," under "UMBRELLA").

20. Johnson's engagement with prescriptive and descriptive approaches to language remains a fertile source of discussion. For a useful reprise of these arguments, see the essays by Geoffrey Barnbrook and Anne McDermott in *Anniversary Essays on Johnson's Dictionary*, ed. Anne McDermott and Jack Lynch (Cambridge, 2005), 92–128.

with equal objectivity, confirm changes in prepositional use or pronunciation (s.v. "COMMUNICATE." 3. "It had anciently the preposition *with* before the person, to whom communication either of benefits or knowledge was made. Now it has only *to*"; s.v. "ASPECT": "It appears anciently to have been pronounced with the accent on the last syllable, which is *now* placed upon the first"). Elaborating the meaning of "NEAT," Johnson hence describes rather than proscribes the momentum of usage. It is, he writes, "*now* used only in the cant of trade, but," he adds, was "*formerly* more extensive" (my emphases). Change is a staple of an eminently factual narration in the *Dictionary*. What is now is not what was previously. As Johnson stresses, words or senses move into obsolescence on the agreement of usage rather than the dictate of the lexicographer.[21]

That Johnson's *Plan* and Preface, together with the finished *Dictionary*, are disjunctive is, of course, nothing new.[22] Nevertheless, Johnson's interest in travel as trope—and not least as a pervasive device by which the disjunctions of imagination and reality can be revealed for what they are—emerges as particularly interesting in this respect. As in Johnson's own journeys to the Western Isles or in his fictional narratives by which Rasselas ventures outside the Happy Valley, or in which various protagonists in the *Rambler* essays, during the dictionary years, change their physical location or find out for themselves the deficits of received wisdom or the fallibilities of expectation, it is clear that the prime meanings of travel are, for Johnson, often located in movement and literal dislocation. Travel, in this sense, repeatedly reveals not what is expected but instead something that is, in Johnson's work, more complex, as well as more truthful.[23]

As the critic Carl Thompson confirms, travel's real value as device perhaps inheres above all in the ways in which the traveler may thereby be separated from "inherited norms and categories," disorientating expectation and revealing the necessary momentum of change.[24] Or, as Johnson would stress in the same vein to Hester Thrale during his own travels in the Western Isles in 1773, "The use of travelling is to regulate imagination by reality, and instead of thinking of how things may be, to see them as they are" (*Letters*, 3:78). The dictionary as journey can then beneficially operate in similar ways. This, too, is repeatedly seen from different perspectives as linguistic expectation is dislocated from reality and "inherited norms" are contested, as well as increasingly informed by realistic endeavor rather than the linguistic stabilities that imagination might readily confer. As the Preface to the *Dictionary* makes plain, the

21. See *YE*, 18:107–8.

22. See, for example, Howard D. Weinbrot, *Aspects of Samuel Johnson: Essays on His Arts, Mind, Afterlife, and Politics* (Newark, Del., 2001), 29–52.

23. See, for example, Bertrand Bronson on this principle in the *Journey to the Western Isles*: "I think it is clear that Johnson's primary purpose in undertaking the Highland expedition was to consolidate his opinions, test his earlier conjectures, and formulate his judgment by first hand observations of the merits and demerits of a system of life which he had long idealized"; "Johnson, Travelling Companion, in Fancy and Fact," *Johnson and His Age*, ed. James Engell, Harvard English Studies 12 (Cambridge, Mass., 1984), 163–87 at 169.

24. Carl Thompson, *Travel Writing* (London, 2011), 66.

kind of journeys that Johnson once contemplated have, in reality, not been effected, whereas Johnson's destination—the end point of 1755—is, we realize, also by no means where it was supposed to be. Johnson, as he admits, has not been able to "take a voyage to perfect my skill in the dialect of navigation," nor to "visit caverns to learn the miner's language" (*YE*, 18:102). In a similar image of deflected course, and once-intended conquest, the "recesses of northern learning" have not, he states, been able to be ransacked (*YE*, 18:100). Other departures are enacted, too. Sounds are not ascertained but, Johnson realizes, "are too volatile and subtile for legal restraints" (*YE*, 18:105). "Cant" is not cast aside (s.vv. "BILINGSGATE," "BAMBOOZLE," "MUGGISH"). The diction of professions and trade is included rather than excluded (see, for example, Johnson's entries for such words as "COMB-MAKER," "HODMAN," and "HANDSEL").[25] It is the failure of the French Academy to fix their own language that now acts as firm—and factual—corrective for the ostensibly utopian visions of the *Plan*. "The *French* language has visibly changed under the inspection of the academy," Johnson reminds readers of his own *Dictionary*; "[T]he embodied criticks of *France*, when fifty years had been spent upon their work, were obliged to change its oeconomy, and give their second edition another form" (*YE*, 18:105, 112, italics in original).

The dictionary-maker of 1755 in turn emerges as markedly different from the kinds of identities assumed in 1747. Missives to patrons are, as Johnson later observed, often highly ambiguous documents. "In patronage, [an author] must say what pleases his patron," he states; it is "an equal chance whether that be truth or falsehood."[26] Some of the tensions observable even in the finished *Plan* are certainly reflective—and arguably, also productive—of this kind of ambiguity; if Johnson subordinated himself as foot soldier, he also ventured to comment on the "madness" of invasions, and the kinds of journeys in which power and suppression are paramount (*YE*, 18:58). Outside the confident participles by which language was to be fixed and ascertained, the outcome of the projected conquest could already seem framed in doubt. Seen from the later vantage point of the Preface, the *Plan* can in fact seem like a journey within a different genre entirely, with marked resemblances to, say, the traveler's tale, with the fabrication and exaggeration that this narrative type often involves. "[C]onquests . . . are now very rare," the Preface instead reminds us (*YE*, 18:105). The projected journeys of the *Plan* conversely suggest affinities with archetypal quest narratives, here in search of the holy grail of linguistic stability. "[O]ne great end of this undertaking is to fix the English language," as Johnson had stressed in 1747 (*YE*, 18:38). If his diction was, at that point, strikingly in alignment with Swift's 1712 *Proposal for Correcting, Improving, and Ascertaining the English Tongue*, the 1755 Preface regulates expectation in this respect, too, and not least in its firm rejection of Swift's work as a "petty treatise" (*YE*, 18:107).

The *Dictionary*, as Johnson attests, has in fact come to be based on a very different set of journeys. Rather than conquest and invasion, it is a series of "fortuitous and unguided excursions" into books that instead provide the evidence on which the *Dictionary* must depend (*YE*, 18:84). In terms of the processes that Johnson adopts in

25. For Johnson's discussion of this, see *YE*, 18:102.
26. *Life*, 5:59.

crafting the dictionary text, these, too, can be seen as collective acts of departure, as the *Dictionary* also makes plain. "Excursions" are, by definition—and here, of course, Johnson's own—located in "the act of deviating from the stated or settled path." As Johnson's choice of "fortuitous" indicates, such ventures are guided by chance, and by the cumulative nature of experience gathered across a range of journeys into words.

The reality of reading for the dictionary, as W. K. Wimsatt affirms, can in this way vividly emblematize the capacities for divergence, for choice, and for movement outside any previous and predetermined path. "Imagine yourself half-way through Johnson's program of reading for the *Dictionary*, arriving at [a] page of Bacon's *Natural History*," he writes; "Which of the words and passages on the page would you mark in black lead pencil for your amanuenses to copy? Which would you pass over? By what norms would you make your selection? How many minutes would you need to reach your decisions on one page?"[27] In the recovered journeys that extant copies of Johnson's marked-up books still allow us to trace, it is this capacity for variation, and for a range of possible routes rather than a settled or narrow path through words, that is transparent. If we look at Johnson's reading of page 67 of his copy of Robert Burton's *Anatomy of Melancholy*, for example, "concupiscible" is underlined, but adjacent words such as "appetite" are not. "Twists" is underlined, but not, say, "wring," nor indeed "horsemill," a word that does not appear in the *Dictionary* at all. Reading page 69, Johnson marks out "damp," "dote," and "macerate," yet "running," which appears on the same page, remains unmarked and unrecorded in this sense in the *Dictionary*.[28] As in Florio's journey across the sea of words, the trajectories of evidence can move in a range of possible directions, caught by the pull of one form rather than another. It is the sheer variety of ways in which one might, in reality, move from A to Z that is perhaps, above all, confirmed by these surviving testimonies of Johnson's verbal excursions.

To *read*, as the *Dictionary* itself attests, is therefore not only "to peruse any thing written" but is, importantly, a process by which one might also "learn by observation." This conjunction—of study and education, of reading and equally of beneficial transformation by such activity—likewise informs Johnson's own processes of change between *Plan* and Preface. As Locke contends, for example, "The widest excursions of the mind are made by short flights frequently repeated; the most lofty fabricks of science are formed by the continued accumulations of single propositions." In a form of words to which Johnson also drew attention in the dictionary years, Locke's image of the beneficial excursion can, in terms of the *Dictionary*, be seen to ally observation, reading, and the iterated journeys into words with the salience of empirical possibilities, and the testing that experience rather than simple expectation will bring.[29] Or, as

27. W. K. Wimsatt, "Johnson's Dictionary," in *New Light on Dr. Johnson*, ed. Frederick W. Hilles (New Haven, Conn., 1959), 69–71; cited in Fussell, *Samuel Johnson and the Life of Writing*, 200.

28. "Running" was not included as a headword in 1755. Added to the fourth edition in 1773, with a quotation from William Law, it was defined as "Kept for the race," a signification that does not explain its use in Burton's "out of a running wit." Johnson's copy of Burton's *Anatomy of Melancholy* is now in the Bodleian Library.

29. See *Rambler* 137, in *The Rambler*, vols. 3–5 of *YE*, ed. W. J. Bate and Albrecht B. Strauss (1969), 4:361 (July 9, 1751). Text references are to this edition.

Johnson argues in *Rambler* 180 (December 7, 1751), here from a vantage point midway through the *Dictionary*, "it is only from the various essays of experimental industry, and the vague excursions of minds sent out upon discovery, that any advancement of knowledge can be expected" (*YE*, 5:183).

Learning, knowledge, and travel during the dictionary years are here brought into careful symbiosis. Rather than conquest, such excursions of the mind, realized in the *Dictionary* by iterated "short flights" of reading and accumulated evidence, can in such ways be seen to ally Johnson's lexicographic journey with the kind of philosophic enterprise commended by the Royal Society in which "excursion" is salient and "discovery" centers on a new understanding—and documentation—of what might hitherto have been uncharted or unknown. Such patterns of movement and departure—between known and unknown, between received wisdom and knowing things as they are—repeatedly inform the divide between *Plan* and Preface/*Dictionary*, and the journeys that are envisaged against those that are, in reality, undertaken. As the Preface confirms, the litany of well-established opinions about language and ascertainment, abundantly voiced across recent decades by such writers as Defoe, Swift, Addison, and Sheridan, are discarded. As for Florio, the sea serves to confirm the limits of human power. In terms of both reason and experience, change in language, as Johnson emphasizes, is "as much superior to human resistance, as the revolutions of the sky, or intumescence of the tide" (*YE*, 18:105–6). The dictionary-maker can traverse but not control the sea of words. As in the citation from Dryden that Johnson includes in his entry for "FREE," it is important to get the direction of power and subjugation right: "What do'st thou make a-shipboard? To what end / Art thou of Bethlem's noble college *free*? / Stark-staring mad, that thou shou'dst tempt the sea?"[30] Johnson thus concludes, "I have indulged expectation which neither reason nor experience can justify" (*YE*, 18:104). The illusions of control are unambiguously revealed for what they are.

By this point, the journey is, like Johnson's commendation of travel writing in Lobo's *Voyage to Abyssinia*, also commendably real. As in Johnson's 1735 preface to Lobo, it is the "diligent and impartial enquirer" who has "described things as he saw them" who is to gain greatest praise. For Lobo, facts displace the diction of "romantick absurdities" and "incredible fictions."[31] The grandiose and exaggerated claims that characterize less rigorous narratives are displaced. Observation is careful and precise. As here, travel writing and its attendant metaphors can be a means of engaging with truth, and the careful documentation by which real knowledge is brought into view.[32] It brings, too, a

30. See sense 13, which Johnson defines as "invested with franchises; possessing any thing without vassalage; admitted to the privileges of any body."

31. *A Voyage to Abyssinia*, vol. 15 of *YE*, ed. Joel J. Gold (1985), 3.

32. As Johnson notes, Lobo's emphasis on facts results in a "modest and unaffected narration" in which, for example, "he meets with no basilisks that destroy with their eyes, his crocodiles devour their prey without tears, and his cataracts fall from the rock without deafening the neighbouring inhabitants" (*YE*, 15:3).

necessary responsiveness to what is actually experienced rather than to what was merely expected or foreseen. As Johnson had stated already in *Rambler* 5 (April 3, 1750), "[I]t ought to be the endeavour of every man to derive his reflections from the objects about him; for it is to no purpose that he alters his position, if his attention continues fixed to the same point" (*YE*, 3:28). To maintain a position in which language is to be fixed while a series of "fortuitous excursions" inexorably attest flux and mutability through both time and text is futile.

Across the *Dictionary* and its making, Johnson's series of identities (invader, discoverer, circumnavigator, one who has taken countless excursions into books), articulated though a range of travel narratives, certainly suggest one way into this sense of transformativity, as do the changing destinations of *Plan* and *Dictionary* itself. If travel as metaphor illuminatingly focuses attention on lexicography as process, as well as upon transition between these different states, it therefore also explores the need for change in the human as well as linguistic subject. Being receptive to experience is important; and, after nine years of working on a dictionary, Johnson's attention is, as we have seen, by no means fixed to the same point.

This sense of individual movement—and its absence—is, however, additionally revealing if we return, in conclusion, to Johnson and his soon-to-be erstwhile patron. To read Chesterfield's letters in the *World*, published in November and December 1754, is, of course, to return to a point from which Johnson had long ago departed. Chesterfield's diction maintains intact the discourse of power and conquest, of control and subordination of 1747. Johnson, for Chesterfield, occupies a role as incipient dictator, able to wield a power that, as Johnson's writings reveal, he himself now knows to be fallible. Swift is still constructed, and commended, as "ingenious."[33] Chesterfield's words echo and reinforce the *Plan*, and Johnson's thinking of seven years before. "Nothing can be more rationally imagined," as Chesterfield continues to affirm. Johnson's Preface meanwhile adopts the diction of the *Vanity of Human Wishes*, in which nature and the human desire for control are once again set at odds, and the sea becomes the location of overweening ambition. "The waves he lashes, and enchains the wind," as Johnson stated of Xerxes in 1749.[34] "[T]o enchain syllables, and to lash the wind, are equally the undertakings of pride, unwilling to measure its desires by its strength," Johnson concludes, here with reference to language, in the 1755 Preface (*YE*, 18:105).

Whether in Xerxes or the lexicographer, such expectations lead merely to disillusion and disappointment. Xerxes, "with humbler thoughts," must henceforth sail in "[a] single skiff" at the mercy of "Th'insulted sea" (*YE*, 6:103, lines 237–38). Likewise, for Johnson, "may the lexicographer be derided, who being able to produce no example of a nation that has preserved their words and phrases from mutability, shall imagine that his dictionary can embalm his language, and secure it from corruption and decay" (*YE*, 18:105). In Chesterfield's vision of prescriptive process, and Johnson's hard-won

33. Chesterfield's letters to the *World* are reprinted in *Samuel Johnson: The Critical Heritage*, ed. James T. Boulton (London, 1971), 95–101 at 97, 95.

34. *The Vanity of Human Wishes*, in *Poems*, vol. 6 of *YE*, ed. E. L. McAdam Jr. with George Milne (1964), 103, line 232.

conclusions since he ventured forth in the published *Plan*, the lack of accord could not be clearer.

It is the journey into words to which, significantly, Johnson would once more return in his famous letter to Chesterfield. As he makes plain, far from working on a dictionary "written under the protection of greatness," he was in fact denied such assistance and had been drowning in a sea of words (*YE*, 18:27). As he states in what is a further pointed act of redefinition: "Is not a Patron, My Lord, one who looks with unconcern on a Man struggling for life in the water, and when he has reached ground, encumbers him with help" (*Letters*, 1:96). The dictionary, as this letter also makes plain, is emphatically a journey to be completed on Johnson's own terms, as well as one from which Chesterfield is now excluded. Identities also undergo a further metaphorical shift. Chesterfield is no longer "Caesar" but the owner of a "cock-boat" cast aside as Johnson makes his way into harbor. "Does he now send out two cock-boats to tow me into harbour?" Johnson asks Garrick.[35] Or, in the version recounted by William Shaw that makes similarly extensive use of these interrelated metaphors: "after making a hazardous and fatiguing journey round the literary world, I had fortunately got sight of the shore, and was coming into port with a pleasant tide and a fair wind, when my Lord Chesterfield sends out two little cock-boats to tow me in."[36] There could be no greater cutting down to size.

As Johnson's entry in the *Dictionary* confirms, "travel" is, in essence, a "[j]ourney of curiosity or instruction" (s.v. "TRAVEL," sense 2). "Nothing tends so much to enlarge the mind as *travelling*," a citation from Isaac Watts states in illustration. "A man not enlightened by *travel* or reflexion, grows as fond of arbitrary power, to which he hath been used, as of barren countries, in which he has been born and bred," Addison affirms in a further quotation, placing lack of knowledge and assumptions of unreasonable power in a similar context. Chesterfield, deprived of the "fortuitous excursions" into books by which Johnson's sense of the experiential reality of words comes to change is, in this light, allied with the untraveled and hence unenlarged mind, and rooted into the theoretical excursus of the "Scheme" and *Plan*. Yet, as Johnson's writings repeatedly stress, theory and experience are, of necessity, very different entities. "Difference . . . will always be found between notions borrowed from without, and notions generated within," as he would write to Boswell in September 1769 (*Letters*, 1:329). "Nothing is more subject to mistake and disappointment than anticipated judgment concerning the easiness or difficulty of any undertaking, whether we form our opinion from the performances of others, or from abstracted contemplation of the thing to be attempted," he posited in May 1751, four years before the *Dictionary* was at an end (*YE*, 4:286). In a principle applicable both to life and the life of words, it was experience alone, as Johnson concluded, that remained "the great test of truth."[37]

35. Arthur Murphy, "An Essay upon the Life and Genius of Samuel Johnson," 1:74.

36. See William Shaw and Hester Lynch Piozzi, *Memoirs of the Life and Writings of the Late Dr. Samuel Johnson* [*by*] *William Shaw. Anecdotes of the Late Samuel Johnson, LL.D. During the Last Twenty Years of His Life* [*by*] *Hester Lynch Piozzi*, ed. Arthur Sherbo (London, 1974), 121.

37. *Life*, 5:454.

"The dreams of a poet": Vocational Self-Definition in Johnson's *Dictionary* Preface

Stephen Fix

WE MIGHT EXPECT THE PREFACE TO A DICTIONARY to provide a rather straightforward commentary—written in an impersonal and largely dispassionate voice—on the book's purposes and design.[1] But the preface to Samuel Johnson's *Dictionary of the English Language* (1755) surprises by being something more than that. It comes to us as a kind of autobiography, raising the question of why Johnson himself is so intensely and persistently present in his own text. This essay attempts to provide one possible answer to that question.

I briefly remind readers of the basic facts regarding the creation of Johnson's *Dictionary*. In 1746, Johnson contracted with a group of booksellers to produce a comprehensive dictionary, whose scope and purpose he spelled out in the *Plan of a Dictionary of the English Language*. Published in 1747, the *Plan* was addressed to the powerful secretary of state, Philip Stanhope, the fourth Earl of Chesterfield, whose support for the project Johnson's booksellers had actively solicited.

Johnson thought that he could accomplish the task quickly, perhaps even in three years; but he had several false starts, and in the end, the work took about seven years. Johnson wrote the preface and other introductory materials in late 1754. In February 1755, on the eve of the *Dictionary*'s publication, Johnson's famous letter complained to Chesterfield about his effort to associate himself with a work that, in the end, he had done little to encourage.

When the *Dictionary*'s two-volume folio edition was published in April 1755, it was immediately recognized as a prodigious act of scholarship. It contained definitions

1. That is exactly what Johnson's audience would have found in prefaces to the two earlier dictionaries that were probably most familiar to them: the 1720 edition of John Kersey's *The New World of Words: or, Universal English Dictionary*, and the 1736 edition of Nathan Bailey's *Dictionarium Britannicum*. Kersey's short preface amounts to a table of contents and a summary of changes made to earlier editions. Bailey's preface—longer than Kersey's, but considerably shorter than Johnson's—provides a commentary on the history and particular characteristics of the English language. Both prefaces are written in an impersonal, scholarly voice, and they are devoid of any effort to feature the lexicographer or dramatize the struggles he faced in creating the dictionary.

for nearly 43,000 words, illustrated with 114,000 quotations. Three more folio editions appeared in Johnson's lifetime (1755–56, 1765, and 1773); changes to the preface itself were minor and not critically significant.

In the *Plan*, the letter to Chesterfield, and the *Dictionary*'s preface, Johnson frequently deploys images, metaphors, and analogies to explain the nature and value of his work. I wish first to examine two such forms of self-definition, and the changes they underwent from 1747 to 1755—namely, those moments when Johnson compares dictionary writing to military activities, and when he attempts to analogize the creation of his book to the creation of a child.

The best-known comparison of a lexicographer to a military hero comes toward the end of the *Plan*. Johnson is addressing Chesterfield:

> When I survey the plan which I have laid before you, I cannot, my Lord, but confess, that I am frighted at its extent, and, like the soldiers of Caesar, look on Britain as a new world, which it is almost madness to invade. But I hope, that though I should not complete the conquest, I shall at least discover the coast, civilize part of the inhabitants, and make it easy for some other adventurer to proceed farther, to reduce them wholly to subjection, and settle them under laws.[2]

The paragraph hedges its claims but only out of modest deference to Chesterfield. The hedging, if anything, suggests something of Johnson's real confidence: It is "madness to invade" the English language—"almost." Johnson is "frighted" by the "extent" of the enterprise, but not, apparently, by its nature. He does not forsake the notion of "conquest"; he says only that it will be incomplete—and in a lovely proleptic irony that looks forward to the mid-1750s, Johnson suggests that the final conquest will belong to "some other adventurer."

At other points in the *Plan*, Johnson again deploys the language of military conquest and governance. He refers to lexicography as the "province allotted me," and to his dictionary as a sort of citadel that, he says, might "secure our language from being overrun with *cant*" (*YE*, 18:26, 42).

2. *Johnson on the English Language*, vol. 18 of *The Yale Edition of the Works of Samuel Johnson* (hereafter cited as *YE*), ed. Gwin J. Kolb and Robert DeMaria Jr. (New Haven, Conn., 2005), 58. Italics in quotations from the *Plan* and the preface are in Johnson's text. In the introductions to this volume and to the individual texts within it, Kolb and DeMaria provide concise overviews of the context, composition, and reception of the *Plan* and preface. For more detailed commentaries on these subjects, see two seminal studies: James H. Sledd and Gwin J. Kolb, *Dr. Johnson's Dictionary: Essays in the Biography of a Book* (Chicago, 1955); and Allen Reddick, *The Making of Johnson's Dictionary, 1746–1773* (Cambridge, 1990). For a bibliography of major modern scholarship on the *Dictionary*, see Jack Lynch, "Studies of Johnson's *Dictionary*, 1955–2009: A Bibliography," in "Johnson after Three Centuries: New Light on Texts and Contexts," ed. Thomas A. Horrocks and Howard D. Weinbrot, special issue, *Harvard Library Bulletin* 20 (2009): 88–131.

So it was in 1747. But seven years later, Johnson rewrites and abandons these images of military power and authority, and confesses his own subjugation to the enterprise. The change is tartly imaged in the letter to Chesterfield, in which Johnson tells the belated patron that he now no longer cherishes the hope of being "Le Vainqueur du Vainqueur de la Terre"—the conqueror of the conqueror of the world.[3]

In the preface itself, Johnson systematically recasts the imperial images he had deployed in the *Plan*. Explaining one reason why it now seems impossible to stabilize and purify language, Johnson admits that "commerce" with other nations necessarily "corrupts the language" and forces travelers to "learn a mingled dialect, like the jargon which serves the traffickers on the *Mediterranean* and *Indian* coasts" (*YE*, 18:106). The coasts that Johnson once imagined as the starting place of the lexicographer's civilizing efforts have now become the locus and unconquerable domain of the problem his project was intended to address.

A few months later, in a letter to Thomas Warton, Johnson again invokes this image but in a more personal and troubled way. Equating the publication of the *Dictionary* with a sailor's arrival on shore, Johnson confesses his fears about what he will "find upon the coast" and adds: "I hope however the criticks will let me be at peace for though I do not much fear their skill or strength, I am a little afraid of myself, and would not willingly feel so much illwill in my bosom as literary quarrels are apt to excite."[4]

Elsewhere in the preface, in a passage to be examined later in more detail, Johnson describes and dismisses the other heroic analogies that had once underwritten his dictionary project—a project that he had thought would allow him, he says, to "enter and ransack" the "obscure recesses of northern learning" (*YE*, 18:100). Along similar lines, Johnson abandons his earlier image of the dictionary as a citadel when he mocks the false ambitions of the French and Italian academies, which, he says, vainly tried "to guard the avenues of their languages, to retain fugitives, and repulse intruders" (*YE*, 18:105).[5]

For the purposes of self-description, Johnson not only abandons these earlier images; he adopts their opposites. Looking at his project through the eyes of the world, Johnson defines the lexicographer, at the start of the preface, "not as the pupil, but the slave of science, the pioneer of literature, doomed only to remove rubbish and clear obstructions from the paths through which Learning and Genius press forward to conquest and glory" (*YE*, 18:73). The invading soldier has now become a "slave." Reduced to a dependent and subservient status, the lexicographer neither conquers the coasts nor

3. Johnson to Chesterfield, February 7, 1755, in *The Letters of Samuel Johnson*, ed. Bruce Redford, 5 vols. (Princeton, N.J., 1992–94), 1:94–97 at 95 (hereafter cited as *Letters*).

4. Johnson to Thomas Warton, February 1, 1755, *Letters*, 1:91–92 at 92. For further discussion of the preface as an aspect of Johnson's lexicographic journeying, including remarks on the letter quoted here, see Lynda Mugglestone's essay in this volume, "Writing the *Dictionary of the English Language*: Johnson's Journey into Words."

5. Years later, in his life of Swift, Johnson mocks Swift's *Proposal for Correcting, Improving, and Ascertaining the English Tongue*: "The certainty and stability which, contrary to all experience, he thinks attainable, he proposes to secure by instituting an academy; the decrees of which every man would have been willing, and many would have been proud to disobey." See *The Lives of the Poets*, vols. 21–23 of *YE*, ed. John H. Middendorf (2010), 22:984.

triumphantly advances inland; rather, he picks up litter from the beach, so that the real conquerors, who come later, may come ashore in a tidy and gracious place. The lexicographer is merely literature's "pioneer"—a word drained of creative overtones in the *Dictionary*, in which Johnson defines the term as "one whose business is to level the road" in advance of an invading army.

The general direction of my argument on this point is significantly indebted to Scott Elledge and Howard D. Weinbrot, who have written important, convincing articles about how Johnson transforms these images between 1747 and 1755.[6] Elledge and Weinbrot treat such changes as signs of Johnson's shifting views on the stability and definability of language. They are certainly that, but I would argue that they suggest something more deeply personal that carries us to the heart not only of Johnson's idea of language but also of his idea of *himself*.

To explore that claim, I will turn to a related, but less frequently examined, set of images—images that also undergo a change between 1747 and 1755, and that seem to voice a more personal concern about Johnson's authority and creativity as a dictionary writer.

Among the more persistent tropes of self-characterization that Johnson uses in the preface is that of parenthood. That he should do so is in many ways unsurprising, since one goal of Johnson's historical dictionary is to identify linguistic origins and progeny. But it is surprising how often Johnson's phrasing and diction place the issue before us. A lexicographical genealogist, Johnson is always questioning what engenders what, always defining and adjusting familial relations: "I am not yet so lost in lexicography, as to forget that *words are the daughters of earth, and that things are the sons of heaven*" (*YE*, 18:79). Later Johnson writes, "I have therefore inserted *Dutch* or *German* substitutes, which I consider not as radical but parallel, not as the parents, but sisters of the *English*" (*YE*, 18:83). He tells us that "sometimes the meaning of derivatives must be sought in the mother term" (*YE*, 18:92). He warns us "not to disturb, upon narrow views, . . . the orthography of their fathers" (*YE*, 18:78).

At such moments, Johnson sounds like a faithful, deferential son, cautious not to assume the prerogatives of the originators who have gone before him. But as the preface comes toward its end, Johnson edges up to a claim that is at once more assertive and more compromised. Drawing on the language of childbirth, Johnson says that he is finally prepared to "deliver" his book "to the world," a book for which, "having laboured it with so much application, I cannot but have some degree of parental fondness" (*YE*, 18:110, 104).

"I cannot but have some degree of parental fondness": the phrasing could be a form of modesty, but it also sounds like a statement of reservation and uncertainty, as if the parental pride were foisted on him in that helpless moment when fondness overwhelms judgment. Johnson sounds unconvinced of his implicit claim to fecundity and

6. See Scott Elledge, "The Naked Science of Language, 1747–1786," in *Studies in Criticism and Aesthetics, 1660–1800: Essays in Honor of Samuel Holt Monk*, ed. Howard Anderson and John S. Shea (Minneapolis, 1967), 266–95; and Howard D. Weinbrot, "Johnson's *Plan* and Preface to the *Dictionary*: The Growth of a Lexicographer's Mind," in *Aspects of Samuel Johnson: Essays on His Arts, Mind, Afterlife, and Politics* (Newark, Del., 2005), 29–52.

creativity, just as he became unconvinced of the powerful and authoritative metaphors of military conquest. For shortly after lodging this tentative claim to parenthood, Johnson closes the preface with this lament: "I have protracted my work till most of those whom I wished to please, have sunk into the grave, and success and miscarriage are empty sounds" (*YE*, 18:113). Johnson seems uncertain whether he has engendered a live birth; and the possibility that his labors have produced only a miscarriage is deepened, I think, by the proximate image of family and friends sinking into the grave.[7]

This moment is all the more interesting and significant if we contrast it with a part of the *Plan* where identical terms are in play. Talking prospectively about the difficult task of writing definitions, Johnson says: "The great labour is yet to come, the labour of interpreting these words and phrases with brevity, fulness and perspicuity; a task of which the extent and intricacy is sufficiently shewn by the miscarriage of those who have generally attempted it" (*YE*, 18:46). In 1747, Johnson sounds confident enough about the product of his labor that he associates the idea of "miscarriage" with those *other* lexicographers whose work Johnson's will supersede. But by 1755, that confidence has evaporated, and Johnson at least considers the possibility that his work is an instance of failed creativity.

The examples I have examined might suggest, then, that the more Johnson worked on his dictionary project, the less comfortable he was with images of his own authority and creative power. As those claims fade, they are replaced and overtaken by images that have a more troubled valence—images that report Johnson's anxiety and dislocation. In fact, in the most personal and compelling parts of the preface, Johnson presents himself as embattled, powerless, isolated, and besieged by disease and regret.

Of the instances we could explore, none more fully encompasses Johnson's mood than the preface's extraordinary final paragraph, which performs a complicated calculus of gain and loss, defense and surrender:

> In this work, when it shall be found that much is omitted, let it not be forgotten that much likewise is performed; and though no book was ever spared out of tenderness to the authour, and the world is little solicitous to know whence proceeded the faults of that which it condemns; yet it may gratify curiosity to inform it, that the *English Dictionary* was written with little assistance of the learned, and without any patronage of the great; not in the soft obscurities of retirement, or under the shelter of academick bowers, but amidst inconvenience and distraction, in sickness and in sorrow. It may repress the triumph of malignant criticism to observe, that if our language is not here fully displayed, I have only failed in an attempt which no human powers have hitherto completed. If the lexicons of ancient tongues, now immutably fixed, and comprised in a few volumes, are yet, after the toil of successive ages, inadequate and

7. For an illuminating discussion of Johnson's frequent use of family images throughout his writings, see Howard D. Weinbrot, "Johnson and the Domestic Metaphor," in *Aspects of Samuel Johnson*, 146–75.

> delusive; if the aggregated knowledge, and co-operating diligence of the *Italian* academicians, did not secure them from the censure of *Beni*; if the embodied criticks of *France*, when fifty years had been spent upon their work, were obliged to change its oeconomy, and give their second edition another form, I may surely be contented without the praise of perfection, which, if I could obtain, in this gloom of solitude, what would it avail me? I have protracted my work till most of those whom I wished to please, have sunk into the grave, and success and miscarriage are empty sounds: I therefore dismiss it with frigid tranquillity, having little to fear or hope from censure or from praise (*YE*, 18:111–13).

There is, of course, combativeness amid this confession. And here, as elsewhere in his writings, Johnson shows a talent for inoculating himself against objections by raising them first himself. But we should not be too quick to see that strategic move as the heart of the story, for we would be likely then to undervalue or diminish the distress Johnson is reporting as he constructs this final portrait of his lexicographical identity.

Johnson opens the preface by saying that the world will not even bestow "a smile" on this "humble drudge" of a lexicographer (*YE*, 18:73). He returns to this theme of isolation and injury at the end but now in more earnest and urgent tones. He expects no "tenderness" and anticipates little solicitude. From the gentle sound and kind meaning of these words, Johnson sees himself excluded, just as he is excluded from the easier tones of a life he might have led in "the soft obscurities of retirement" or "under the shelter of academick bowers." The sort of criticism that awaits his *Dictionary* is depicted as especially virulent: it is "malignant"—a term Johnson uses once earlier in the preface, when he speaks of the "malignity" that he knows will "fasten" on his work (*YE*, 18:88).[8]

But it hardly matters now whether this malignity hits its mark, for Johnson is—he tells us—already sick in body, mind, and heart: The *Dictionary* was written "amidst inconvenience and distraction, in sickness and in sorrow." Johnson had prepared us for this claim just a few paragraphs before: "Much of my life has been lost under the pressures of disease" (*YE*, 18:109–10). One gathers a sense that something more than a dictionary is approaching its end.

What is perhaps most striking of all in this passage is Johnson's isolation. He is without a patron, and almost without learned helpers. He systematically locates himself outside the scholarly citadels in which other dictionary writers work. He is

8. The kind of criticism worrying Johnson here—criticism that is malicious almost to the point of injuring the body—is vividly figured a decade later in his Preface to *Shakespeare* (1765). Commenting on William Warburton's 1747 edition of Shakespeare, Johnson calls Warburton a man of "genius and learning" but strongly objects to many of his editorial practices. Johnson's rhetorical fury, however, is saved for "those who could exalt themselves into" Warburton's "antagonists." Warburton's "chief assailants," Johnson writes, "are the authours of *The Canons of Criticism* and of the *Revisal of Shakespeare's Text*; of whom one ridicules his [Warburton's] errours with airy petulance, suitable enough to the levity of the controversy; the other attacks them with gloomy malignity, as if he were dragging to justice an assassin or incendiary. The one stings like a fly, sucks a little blood, takes a gay flutter, and returns for more; the other bites like a viper, and would be glad to leave inflammations and gangrene behind him." See *Johnson on Shakespeare*, vols. 7–8 of *YE*, ed. Arthur Sherbo (1968), 7:98–100.

excluded from "academick bowers." He stands apart from the "aggregated knowledge, and co-operating diligence of the *Italian* academicians," apart from "the embodied criticks of *France*." The adjectives are significant: while others cooperate, Johnson is abandoned and alone. While the French critics are "embodied," Johnson is diseased.

That he stands alone is, of course, a matter of some pride to Johnson—a modest device for forgiving his shortcomings and for claiming the singular credit he knows he deserves. But as soon as he implicitly lodges this claim, he dismisses it, too. The solitariness that, early in the paragraph, could be interpreted as a source of pride soon becomes engulfed by "gloom"; and "in this gloom of solitude," praise of any kind—even praise that he gives himself—is useless.

The profound poignancy of the final sentence flows in part from the sense Johnson creates of lost possibilities. Having forsaken the comfortable academies, and having found the wider world to lack tenderness, Johnson conjures up—for a fleeting moment—a smaller, more private and personal world. But even here the landscape is barren. Those whose praise he would truly value have sunk out of sight. Even the "sounds" of words—the very substance of the *Dictionary* itself—are "empty." And at the end of a paragraph that faults others for being so eager to blame, Johnson finally blames himself: "I have protracted my work till most of those whom I wished to please, have sunk into the grave."

In the final phrases, Johnson takes his leave with an always-startling gesture of injured serenity. He no longer "deliver[s]" his *Dictionary* to the world; he dismisses it. The warmth of "parental fondness" has now been transmuted into "frigid tranquillity." Not knowing what he, or the rest of the world, will make of what he has created, he urgently proclaims his indifference.

Johnson's attempt at closure only opens a new set of questions, for we know that his "tranquillity" is not tranquil at all. Why—at the end of this great project—does the dictionary maker leave us, and himself, on such a note of cool suspension? Why is it that at the end of the preface—unlike, say, the end of *The Vanity of Human Wishes* (1749)—the value of making something is so much called into question, and the created product is so little able to calm the mind?[9]

We should not make the mistake of bypassing the obvious answers to these questions. Certainly Johnson is concerned about the criticism his book will get; no writer is more vulnerable to claims of error or omission than a lexicographer. And yet, in the letter to Warton quoted earlier, Johnson had pointed in another direction. "I do not much fear" the "skill or strength" of the critics, Johnson said. His real fear is lodged elsewhere: "I am a little afraid of myself."

Perhaps picking up on this hint, Boswell's gloss on the end of the preface is cast in terms of personal psychology:

> It must undoubtedly seem strange, that the conclusion of his Preface should be expressed in terms so desponding, when it is considered that

9. The closing couplet of *The Vanity of Human Wishes* is: "With these celestial wisdom calms the mind, / And makes the happiness she does not find." See Johnson, *Poems*, vol. 6 of *YE*, ed. E. L. McAdam Jr. with George Milne (1964), 109, lines 367–68.

> the authour was then only in his forty-sixth year. But we must ascribe its gloom to that miserable dejection of spirits to which he was constitutionally subject, and which was aggravated by the death of his wife two years before.[10]

Again, true enough. Johnson's wife, Tetty, who had died in 1752, is clearly first on the list of those whom Johnson was too late to please.[11] Boswell is also surely correct in linking the sentiments of the preface to the wider complex of doubts and fears that shaped Johnson's psyche and emerged regularly in his writings.

But there is another, less articulated possibility embedded in Boswell's remark. What—he seems to be wondering—could prompt a man who is only at the midpoint of his life and career to leave us on a note of such loss and regret, especially at the end of this remarkable project?

I both accept Boswell's answers to this question and propose another of my own. Before doing so, however, I should emphasize that I have no doubt that Johnson thought he had written a great dictionary. What he said of the *Dictionary* project to Boswell in 1779 was true in 1755: "I knew very well what I was undertaking,—and very well how to do it,—and have done it very well" (*Life*, 3:405). Rather, I see Johnson's worries coalescing not around the quality of the work he produced but around the implications of the fact that he produced this kind of work—good or bad—at all.[12]

As we read the *Plan* and especially the preface, Johnson's personal voice is remarkably prominent, even intrusive; he appears to be unusually eager to explain to us, in metaphor and in more prosaic ways, exactly who he is and what he is about. That alone would suggest that writing the *Dictionary* was, for Johnson, an important act of self-

10. *Boswell's Life of Johnson, Together with Boswell's Journal of a Tour to the Hebrides and Johnson's Diary of a Journey into North Wales*, ed. George Birkbeck Hill, rev. L. F. Powell, 6 vols. (Oxford, 1934–50), 1:298 (hereafter cited as *Life*).

11. The deep sense of loss that Tetty's death engendered is powerfully expressed in the funeral sermon Johnson wrote in her memory. There, he praises her "intellectual excellence," "the extent of her knowledge," and "the accuracy of her judgment"—qualities that would have made her an ideal audience for the *Dictionary*. See Sermon 25, in *Sermons*, vol. 14 of *YE*, ed. Jean Hagstrum and James Gray (1978), 261–71 at 268.

12. The sense of personal loneliness and vocational anxiety that I have been describing in the pages above resurfaces as Johnson concludes his revisions for the *Dictionary*'s fourth edition, published in 1773. In 1772, he writes a Latin poem, "Post Lexicon Anglicanum Auctum et Emendatum" (see *YE*, 6:271–74 for the Latin and Arthur Murphy's 1792 English translation). After reflecting that even Joseph Scaliger—a scholar of greater powers—found dictionary making a valuable but life-sapping endeavor, Johnson depicts himself as exhausted and vacant, afflicted with "Black melancholy," repairing to a restless and "lonely bed" where "I mourn all night, and dread the coming day." He describes his life as "A dreary void, where fears with grief combin'd / Waste all within, and desolate the mind." Howard D. Weinbrot observes that, in this poem, "Johnson wonders whether he has used his talents well . . . and whether he can indeed survive his postpartum depression. From 1755 on, he was known as 'Dictionary Johnson,' Britain's most distinguished man of letters. . . . Is that enough? Is it all? Is that what he is designed for?" (*Aspects of Samuel Johnson*, 83).

definition. And as he performs that act, Johnson struggles repeatedly with questions about his own creative authority and the judgments that might be rendered on the value of his work. At its most intense, the struggle comes to this: Johnson seems anxiously to understand that he has chosen—or perhaps slid into—the life of the scholar and critic rather than the life of the poet.

We will come shortly to the evidence for this claim in the preface itself, but should first contextualize the argument by brief reference to other aspects of Johnson's life and work from 1747 to 1755. Always conscious of the parable of the talents, Johnson spent at least half his life deciding what to be: a teacher, perhaps a lawyer, finally a writer. He was good at that, and it put bread on the table.

But what kind of writing? Fourteen years elapsed between his start on his only play, *Irene*, and its production in 1749. That it was staged at all, Johnson perhaps understood, was a tribute less to its poetic and theatrical merits than to the loyalty of his former student, David Garrick. As for his poems, only two could be called popular or critically regarded, both of them imitations of Juvenal. *London*, published anonymously in 1738, had five separate editions. Eleven years later, and with his name on the title page for the first time, Johnson published *The Vanity of Human Wishes*. It was received with respect and even enthusiasm but still had "no second separate edition" (*YE*, 6:xix). Thereafter, with the exception of a fine prologue for *Comus*, Johnson stopped writing poems entirely during the 1750s—and wrote very few more thereafter.

Moral and critical prose was what was absorbing Johnson's energies and talents. He was writing not only the *Dictionary* but also *The Rambler* and other periodical essays in the early 1750s. By the time he wrote the *Dictionary*'s preface, *The Rambler* was a resounding success, and it promised—along with the *Dictionary*—to be the basis of Johnson's fame. In this regard, Allen Reddick nicely points to the citation used by Oxford's vice-chancellor when awarding Johnson's honorary degree in 1755, on the eve of the *Dictionary*'s publication. Johnson, the vice-chancellor said, had "very eminently distinguished himself by the publication of a series of essays, excellently calculated to form the manners of the people, and in which the cause of religion and morality is every where maintained by the strongest powers of argument and language; and . . . [he] shortly intends to publish a Dictionary of the English Tongue, formed on a new plan, and executed with the greatest labour and judgement." As Reddick observes, it "is significant that in the Vice-Chancellor's summation Johnson's popular poetical achievements, specifically 'London' . . . and 'The Vanity of Human Wishes,' are not even mentioned: the great projects of *The Rambler* and *Dictionary* have eclipsed his other performances in the eyes of the public."[13]

In Johnson's correspondence during this period, we find his preoccupations to be largely of a critical and scholarly nature. Writing to encourage Thomas Warton to complete his new book on Spenser, Johnson is at once scholarly cheerleader and Dean of the Faculty: "Where hangs the new volume? can I help? let not the past labour be lost for want of a little more, but snatch what time you can from the hall and the pupils and the coffeehouse . . . to complete your design" (*Letters*, 1:94). And Johnson nags Samuel

13. As quoted in Reddick, *The Making of Johnson's Dictionary*, 80–81.

Richardson to make over his novel into a sort of scholarly work by creating an index to the incidents in *Clarissa*—a work, Johnson says, that "will be occasionally consulted by the busy, the aged, and the studious" (*Letters*, 1:48).

A brief quotation from another letter to Richardson, in 1753, hastens us to the point. Sending Richardson some notes he had written about English spelling, Johnson pays the novelist this compliment: "I shall be glad if these strictures appear to you not unwarrantable, for whom should we who toil in settling our language desire to please but him who is adorning it" (*Letters*, 1:70).

"We who toil in settling our language" *versus* "him who is adorning it": This is the distinction that I believe strongly affects Johnson's sense of himself and his career as he writes the *Dictionary*. Something close to this distinction crops up a year later in the preface: I "do not form, but register the language," Johnson writes. I "do not teach men how they should think, but relate how they have hitherto expressed their thoughts" (*YE*, 18:102). The self-identifying labels Johnson chooses for himself in the preface are noteworthy: "I have endeavoured to proceed with a scholar's reverence for antiquity, and a grammarian's regard to the genius of our tongue" (*YE*, 18:78).

In these and other ways, Johnson presents himself as having a sort of secondary relation to the language he is recording. He "facilitates" the "Learning and Genius" of others (*YE*, 18:73). He sees his own work primarily as a vehicle through which his and later ages may understand achievements greater than his own. "I shall not think my employment useless or ignoble," Johnson writes of the *Dictionary*, "if by my assistance foreign nations, and distant ages, gain access to the propagators of knowledge, and understand the teachers of truth" (*YE*, 18:110).

While not regarding his work as either useless or ignoble, Johnson sees himself as engaged in a project that lacks the primary power of original writing. He places his work as a lexicographer at one remove from the sort of creativity that allowed others to write the works he quotes. His distance is apparently greatest from poetry. As a dictionary maker, he tells us, he is engaged in what the world understands as "artless industry" (*YE*, 18:26). On Parnassus, he writes elsewhere, poets wear the "laurels of eternal verdure."[14] But in the terrain of lexicography, he says, "not even the barren laurel" can be found (*YE*, 18:27). The word "barren"—which connects to the metaphors of lost fertility examined above—appears once more in the preface, when Johnson locates himself in "the dusty desarts of barren philology" (*YE*, 18:94).

As the *Dictionary* project unfolds, then, Johnson struggles with issues of vocational identity, and in the process of modifying or abandoning his claims to authority and creative power, he seems conscious—above all—of his distance from being a poet. His diction and self-presentation, his images and metaphors, seem to acknowledge that a transition has occurred in his career.

What is especially striking, though, is that Johnson—in complex ways—continues to associate himself with the claims of poetry. We can see this best by focusing on another of those remarkable passages that serve as the nerve centers of the preface:

14. Johnson, *The Rambler*, vols. 3–5 of *YE*, ed. W. J. Bate and Albrecht B. Strauss (1969), 4:201 (*Rambler* 106, March 23, 1751).

> When first I engaged in this work, I resolved to leave neither words nor things unexamined, and pleased myself with a prospect of the hours which I should revel away in feasts of literature, the obscure recesses of northern learning, which I should enter and ransack, the treasures with which I expected every search into those neglected mines to reward my labour, and the triumph with which I should display my acquisitions to mankind. When I had thus enquired into the original of words, I resolved to show likewise my attention to things; to pierce deep into every science, to enquire the nature of every substance of which I inserted the name, to limit every idea by a definition strictly logical, and exhibit every production of art or nature in an accurate description, that my book might be in place of all other dictionaries whether appellative or technical. But these were the dreams of a poet doomed at last to wake a lexicographer. I soon found that it is too late to look for instruments, when the work calls for execution, and that whatever abilities I had brought to my task, with those I must finally perform it. To deliberate whenever I doubted, to enquire whenever I was ignorant, would have protracted the undertaking without end, and, perhaps, without much improvement; for I did not find by my first experiments, that what I had not of my own was easily to be obtained: I saw that one enquiry only gave occasion to another, that book referred to book, that to search was not always to find, and to find was not always to be informed; and that thus to persue perfection, was, like the first inhabitants of Arcadia, to chace the sun, which, when they had reached the hill where he seemed to rest, was still beheld at the same distance from them.
>
> I then contracted my design . . . (*YE*, 18:100–101)

In important ways, the first paragraph reenacts the same transitions I have charted in his metaphors of conquest and paternity. Here, as before, Johnson conjures up two states, as different as sleeping and waking. The first, itself almost Arcadian in its innocent rambunctiousness, is marked by the bold metaphors of military conquest, of confident forays into recesses, depths, and mines. The second is defined as a time "too late to look"—a belated time when effort produces only endless replication, as "book" refers "to book," and our chase brings us no closer to the elusive sun. Read in this sense, that "dreams of a poet" sentence bridges Johnson's movement from one world to another. His confession is both straightforward and true: My expansive ambitions were those of a poet, but my contracted product is only a dictionary.

On further reflection, though, we might realize that Johnson's paragraph is trickier than that. "These were the dreams of a poet doomed at last to wake a lexicographer": In a couple of ways, the claim is oddly untrue. Johnson had to know that he came, in fact, remarkably close to realizing the dreams he outlines in the first half of this paragraph. When he wrote the *Dictionary*, he left very few "words" and "things" "unexamined"; he indeed "enquired into the original of words"; and he paid extraordinary attention to all kinds of sciences.

The claim might be called untrue in another way: the dreams that the first half of the paragraph specifies would not strike us, or many of Johnson's contemporaries, as the dreams of a *poet*. They sound more like the dreams of a scholar, a critic, a scientist, and—indeed—a lexicographer. If these are the dreams of a poet, he is a poet who has already become something else.[15]

Since he decided to set up the passage in exactly this way, it seems reasonable to suggest that Johnson was looking for a way to declare a particular sort of transition in himself. He is accomplishing two things at once: he declares that he has awakened to find himself something other than a poet, but at the same time, he defines the poet's dreams in the very language of the lexicographer's awakened state.

We need to interpret the paragraph, then, in a way that respects the complexity of Johnson's assertions about himself. Even as he overtly abandons the claims of being a poet, Johnson—writing in highly imagistic, rhythmic language that connects his prose to the resources of poetry—seems unwilling or unable to disassociate himself completely from poetic activity. He remains anxious to assert a creative dimension to his work, if only by imperfect analogy. When I began this project—Johnson seems to say—I was, at least, like a poet. My capacious knowledge, and my mastery of words, would together allow me to create a definitive sort of book—a book perhaps not unlike an epic poem, a book that "might be in place of all" others by encompassing all of the culture's verbal and physical artifacts. My dream resembled the poet's dream of mastery over language. But, in the end, I had to settle not only for something less, but for something different—a vocation to which I am "doomed at last."

The "at last" suggests that Johnson has been engaged in a long struggle with himself, whose final result he is now reporting. Johnson, here and always, refuses to accept the world's careless dismissal of dictionary making as an "artless" activity. He knows its value, and he knows—as this passage shows—its proximate relation to the impulses and activities of poetry. But finally that knowing does little to diminish the sense that he is, nonetheless, "doomed"—"doomed," as he had said when he used the word at the start of the preface, "doomed only to remove rubbish and clear obstructions from the paths through which Learning and Genius press forward to conquest and glory" (*YE*, 18:73). Whatever kingdom he rules, he rules by what he calls "a kind of vicarious jurisdiction"

15. This interplay between poetry and learning is evident in Johnson's presentation of Imlac in *Rasselas* (1759). Imlac—often taken as a figure for Johnson himself—is "desirous to add" his "name" to the "illustrious fraternity" of poets, and it is as a poet that Imlac is first introduced. But as he describes his own education and activities as a poet, Imlac—"a man of uncommon knowledge"—repeatedly speaks the language of learning, the language of a scholar whose first task is "study" and whose goal is "knowledge." Poetry requires lexical breadth, but lexical breadth does not make a poet. Indeed, by the time he reaches the summary point of his "dissertation upon poetry" in chapter 10, Imlac seems to dissociate "the business of a poet" from the kind of work a lexicographer must do: The poet "must neglect the minuter discriminations" and "does not number the streaks of the tulip, or describe the different shades in the verdure of the forest." See Johnson, *Rasselas and Other Tales*, vol. 16 of *YE*, ed. Gwin J. Kolb (1990), esp. chaps. 7–11 (29–46), quotations at 40–41, 37, 44, and 43.

(*YE*, 18:55). His is an art that enables the art of others; his is an art of narrowing down, an art of accurate recording, an art of settling rather than adorning.

Readers of Johnson have always understood that the desire to fix the language—stabilizing its identity and locating its place—was central to Johnson's ambition in the *Dictionary*. My claim is that he was also engaged in the project of fixing himself, stabilizing his own identity and locating his place in relation to the talents and opportunities he had at midlife. In this act of vocational definition, the *Dictionary* itself is the first illustration, to be followed later by the edition of Shakespeare (1765), *The Lives of the Poets* (1779–81), and other works of scholarship and criticism.

I want to end where Johnson began. Not much attention has been paid to the Latin epigraph Johnson selects for the title page of the *Dictionary*—a text that is, in a sense, the book's first preface.[16] It is taken from Horace's *Epistles* 2.2. The epistle opens with the speaker, who is about to sell a slave, telling the buyer exactly what he is getting. He wants to forestall later complaints, should the buyer discover some small defects in the slave. "You bought him with your eyes open—fault and all," the speaker says; "the condition was told you; do you still pursue the seller and annoy him with an unjust suit?"[17]

The speaker goes on to declare himself a poet—but a beleaguered one. He says that poverty drove him to writing verses; that the shifting fortunes of his life are contriving to "wrest" him from his poems; and that "amid all my cares and all my toils"—such as commenting on the verses of others, caring for sick friends, and enduring the noise and distractions of the city—he is now virtually unable to write good poems (429).

For a moment, he tries to console himself by imagining some different version of his life—a creatively fruitful life of retirement in Athens. But that imagined poet, too, is beleaguered and misunderstood. In Horace's presentation of him, this poet sounds a lot like Johnson: "A gifted man, that has chosen for home sequestered Athens, that has given seven years to his studies and grown grey over his books and meditations, when he walks abroad is often more mute than a statue and makes the people shake with laughter" (431).

Recalled mentally to his own time and place, the speaker then complains about the puffery with which hack poets praise each others' works, and, if necessary, their own. The speaker finds strength by separating himself from those self-flattering and self-satisfied hacks, and by associating himself instead with those men "whose aim is to have wrought a poem true to Art's rules" (433).

16. See, however, Lawrence Lipking's brief but helpful commentary on Johnson's choice of this epigraph in *Samuel Johnson: The Life of an Author* (Cambridge, Mass., 1998), 132–33.

17. Horace, *Satires, Epistles, and Ars Poetica*, trans. H. R. Fairclough (London and Cambridge, Mass., 1970), 425–27 (hereafter cited in text).

The speaker's subsequent description of that true poet's activity becomes the source for the *Dictionary*'s epigraph, and it is easy to see why these words must have struck Johnson as an apt preface to his book:

> [*at qui legitimum cupiet fecisse poema,*]
> *cum tabulis animum censoris sumet honesti;*
> *audebit, quaecumque parum splendoris habebunt*
> *et sine pondere erunt et honore indigna ferentur,*
> *verba movere loco, quamvis invita recedant*
> *et versentur adhuc intra penetralia Vestae;*
> *obscurata diu populo bonus eruet atque*
> *proferet in lucem speciosa vocabula rerum,*
> *quae priscis memorata Catonibus atque Cethegis*
> *nunc situs informis premit et deserta vetustas*;

> [But the man whose aim is to have wrought a poem true to Art's rules,] when he takes his tablets, will take also the spirit of an honest censor. He will have the courage, if words fall short in dignity, lack weight, or be deemed unworthy of rank, to remove them from their place, albeit they are loth to withdraw, and still linger within Vesta's precincts. Terms long lost in darkness the good poet will unearth for the people's use and bring into the light—picturesque terms which, though once spoken by a Cato and a Cethegus of old, now lie low through unseemly neglect and dreary age. (432–35, lines 109–18, my brackets)

Like Johnson's longer preface, this passage asserts the value of sorting out the language, recovering and rehabilitating what has been lost. Horace calls this the activity of the true poet. But by placing these words at the start of his *Dictionary*, Johnson converts a poet's self-definition into a description of the lexicographer's mission and talent. As in the "dreams of a poet" passage, Johnson again seems to conflate and merge the language of poetry and the language of lexicography.

But amid this conflating and merging, there is a distinction—and a declaration as well. Look closely at what Johnson has done with, and to, Horace's passage. Starting his *Dictionary* epigraph in midsentence, Johnson leaves off the words that I have placed in brackets above:

> *at qui legitimum cupiet fecisse poema,*
> But the man whose aim is to have wrought a poem true to Art's rules,

In the epigraph, as in the preface, the "dreams of a poet" are both preserved and lost, recorded and left behind. The "gifted man" who "has given seven years to his studies" awakens again to find himself proud, troubled, and on the other side of his lexicographical sentence. Horace's epigraph is meant to define the *Dictionary*, but as the *Dictionary*'s author uses it, what it ultimately defines is Johnson himself.

Fragments and Disquisitions: Johnson's *Shakespeare* in Context

Marcus Walsh

SAMUEL JOHNSON'S 1765 *Shakespeare* was delayed by his other writing commitments as well as by ill-health. It was published in the middle of a pivotal decade, in which a number of editors were already involved in scholarly and critical advances that would soon substantially change the textual representation and contextual understanding of Shakespeare. The latter years of the decade would see early fruits of those advances, including George Steevens's four-volume *Twenty of the Plays of Shakespeare* (1766), which was based on the surviving early quarto editions, and Edward Capell's ten-volume *Mr William Shakespeare, His Comedies, Histories, and Tragedies* (1768), in which Capell chose, from the quartos and folios, what he considered the best of those early texts as copy for each play.

Johnson's 1765 edition of course was a monument and epochal moment of criticism and scholarship in itself. Its Preface provided a groundbreaking analysis of neoclassical dramatic theory based on mimetic first principles, and the fullest and most telling analysis of text-critical method since Lewis Theobald's *Shakespeare Restored* (1726). Johnson's edition was the first exercise, in the editing of vernacular English texts, in recognizably and extensive variorum form, inheriting a methodology of seventeenth-century Dutch classical editing and establishing what would be the dominant methodology of learned Shakespearean editing for the rest of the eighteenth century and beyond.

In a number of respects, however, Johnson's editorial practice was not state-of-the-art for the 1760s. His running commentary is often thin, whole pages of text passing without notes, falling well short of the level of explanatory completeness aimed at within the next few years by Steevens and Edmond Malone. Johnson's variorum method certainly involves close interpretative engagement with predecessors, but sometimes it amounts to no more than citation without remark, especially of some of Theobald's longer annotations. Referencing of citations is incomplete or absent. He makes occasional conjectures and frequent interpretative assertions with little or no support.[1] From the larger, formal, point of view, Johnson's eight volumes are light in the apparatus that vernacular, as well as classical, editions were beginning regularly to accrue: there is no contents list, no index, no glossary. Even Sir Thomas Hanmer's 1744 edition has a glossary.

Johnson clearly understood, and aspired further to improve, the central principles and methods developed by his forebears in eighteenth-century vernacular editing. In the *Proposals* for the edition, published in 1756, he demonstrates his involvement in theoretical thinking about editing, claims special expertise in Elizabethan diction and literary context, promises the use of variorum method, and drafts a hermeneutic approach. He states that "critical sagacity" must be employed when all the books are "evidently vitiated"; that no conjectural change shall be "imposed . . . without notice"; and that while "many alterations may be proposed as eligible, very few will be obtruded as certain." He insists that emendatory criticism must not be undertaken by any critic "who is not particularly versed in the writings of that age, and particularly studious of his authour's diction." He announces a significant methodological advance, promising to move from the predominating concern of previous critics—specifically, that of Theobald, the apostle of Richard Bentley—with the text, toward "the elucidation of passages obscured by accident or time." As maker of the *Dictionary of the English Language* (1755), he can boast that he has had "more motives to consider the whole extent of our language than any other man from its first formation." He hopes that "by comparing the works of Shakespeare with those of writers who lived at the same time, immediately preceded, or immediately followed him, he shall be able to ascertain his ambiguities, disentangle his intricacies, and recover the meaning of words now lost in the darkness of antiquity." He undertook that "in this edition all that is valuable will be adopted from every commentator."[2]

These proposals, then, promise an advanced—in significant respects, an innovative—edition, providing interpretation and explanation of the Shakespearean text based firmly on Johnson's extensive, and distinctive, knowledge of Shakespeare's literary and linguistic contexts. What subscribers received did not entirely fulfill that promise. Johnson indeed provides numerous references to the sixteenth- and seventeenth-century authors who provide illustrative, and at least potentially interpretative, context for Shakespeare's words: Hakluyt, Donne, Spenser, Bacon, Digby, Drayton, Sackville, Milton, Dryden, Waller, Walton, Ben Jonson, Ascham, Butler, Camden, and many others. He makes frequent references to less literary kinds, for example, to balladry, quoted from Thomas Percy's *Reliques* as well as from earlier sources and, especially, to proverbs.[3] Johnson puts both literary and nonliterary contemporary contexts to some use in the validation of interpretations. He "easily explained" Lear's expression "Look'd black upon me" (2.4.158) as "to 'look clowdy or

1. For example, on Ophelia's exclamation "By Gis" (4.5.56), Johnson remarks, "I rather imagine it should be read, By Cis,— That is, by St Cecily"; in *Johnson on Shakespeare*, vols. 7–8 of *The Yale Edition of the Works of Samuel Johnson* (hereafter cited as *YE*), ed. Arthur Sherbo (New Haven, Conn., 1968), 8:995. Text citations are to this edition.

2. Samuel Johnson, *Proposals for Printing, by Subscription, the Dramatick Works of William Shakespeare* (London, 1756), 6–7; in *YE*, 7:55, 56, 58.

3. For Johnson's use of proverbs, see, for instance, *YE*, 8:943, 962, 984.

gloomy,'" with telling support from Milton: "So frown'd the mighty combatants, that hell / Grew darker at their frown" (*Paradise Lost* [1674], 6:68; *YE*, 8:679).[4] When Juliet reports that "Some say, the lark and loathed toad chang'd eyes" (3.5.31), Johnson remembers that "this tradition of the toad and lark I have heard expressed in a rustick rhyme, 'To heav'n I'd fly, / But the Toad beguil'd me of my eye'" (*YE*, 8:951). Such new uses and applications of context are, however, surprisingly unusual in Johnson's commentary. Rather more frequently, Johnson speculates or asserts without contemporary corroboration: "I believe 'modern' is only 'foolish' or 'trifling'"; "the meaning seems to be"; "This, I believe, is a metaphor taken from a mine" (*YE*, 8:790, 976, 1001). Thus Iago's complaint that his jealousy of Othello "[d]oth, like a poisonous mineral, gnaw my inwards" (2.1.290) elicits from Johnson an assertion without any informing source: "This is philosophical. Mineral poisons kill by corrosion" (*YE*, 8:1026). Johnson not only explains fewer difficulties than Steevens or Malone in their editions, achieving far less comprehensive explanatory coverage, but also cites supporting evidence far less frequently. Often Johnson depends, as these later learned editors distinctively and characteristically would not, on the authority of an ipse dixit.

Nor does Johnson very often make interpretative resort to Shakespeare's own writing.[5] The principle of parallel passages, already developed in classical and, especially, biblical criticism, had been clearly restated in relation to vernacular editing by Theobald in *Shakespeare Restored*: "every Author is best expounded and explain'd in *One* Place, by his own Usage and Manner of Expression in *Others*."[6] Theobald had learned this vital and powerful hermeneutic tool from Bentley, and it would be fruitfully and extensively used by Capell, Malone, and, especially, Steevens. Despite his considerable if measured respect for Bentley, Johnson does not regularly follow in this essential methodological tradition.

The staple of Johnson's commentary is not the adduction of parallel passages but the paraphrase. Johnson avowedly used paraphrase in the *Dictionary* as a mode of definition. He regularly used paraphrase in his *Shakespeare*, both to define unfamiliar individual words and to disentangle passages. So, when Timon says that to pay the reputed value of a jewel "would unclew me quite" (1.1.171), Johnson remarks that "To 'unclew' is to 'unwind' a ball of thread. To 'unclew' a man, is to draw out the whole mass of his fortunes" (*YE*, 8:711).[7] Johnson uses paraphrase for critical—that is, for interpretative—purposes, typically to justify an original reading and hence avoid the need for conjectural emendation. Thus, where William Warburton and Hanmer had

4. Similarly, where Hamlet puns on the circumstantial "as'es of great charge" of Claudius's kingly letter to his English tributary (5.2.44), Johnson adds this note, in 1773: "A quibble is intended between 'as' the conditional particle, and 'ass' the beast of burthen. That 'charg'd' anciently signified 'loaded', may be proved from the following passage in *The Widow's Tears*, by Chapman, 1612. / Thou must be the *ass charg'd with crowns* to make way" (*YE*, 8:1005, italics in original).

5. For instances of exceptions, see *YE*, 8:968, 987.

6. *Shakespeare Restored; or, a Specimen of the Many Errors as Well Committed as Unamended, by Mr. Pope in His Late Edition of This Poet* (London, 1726), viii. Compare Theobald's preface to the *Works of Shakespeare*, 7 vols. (London, 1733), 1:xliii.

7. The word is given in Johnson's *A Dictionary of the English Language: in Which the Words are Deduced from Their Originals and Illustrated in Their Different Significations by Examples from the Best Writers*, 2 vols. (London, 1755), defined simply as "To undo."

felt compelled to change Timon's indignant response to Apemantus, "What! a knave too?" (4.3.239), Johnson disentangles several lines of dialogue to show Timon's meaning: "I before only knew thee to be a 'fool', but I now find thee likewise a 'knave.' This seems to be so clear as not to stand in need of a comment" (*YE*, 8:735). More commonly, however, Johnson uses paraphrase not for text-critical but for explanatory purposes: so the Friar's adjuration as he hands Juliet the phial, "If no unconstant toy, nor womanish fear, / Abate thy valour in the acting it" (4.1.119–20) is paraphrased, "If no 'fickle freak,' . . . no 'change of fancy,' hinder the performance" (*YE*, 8:953). As in the modern Arden *Shakespeare*, the predominance of paraphrase in Johnson tells of an edition aiming in no small part to clarify the text for the reader, not least the younger reader, as well as to engage in critical arguments concerning readings and meanings.

Recent Johnsonian scholarship accepts that there was a close and continuing relationship, amounting to symbiosis, between Johnson as lexicographer and Johnson as textual critic.[8] If Johnson's 1765 *Shakespeare* included no glossary, it had, after all, its own enormous, organized, and sophisticated glossary in the *Dictionary* that had been published ten years earlier. The *Dictionary* and the *Shakespeare* were major projects of his professional life over nearly three decades, from the *Miscellaneous Observations on the Tragedy of Macbeth* (1745) and *Plan* (1747) for the *Dictionary*, through the first edition of the *Dictionary* (1755), the Shakespeare *Proposals* (1756) and the *Shakespeare* itself, and the publication in 1773 of both the second edition of the *Shakespeare* and the revised fourth edition of the *Dictionary*. The text of Shakespeare provided Johnson with some thousands of headwords for his dictionary, noted on index slips from the 1740s onward. The *Dictionary* in effect provided annotations and illustrations of each of these Shakespearean uses, by its sense divisions, its definitions, and, at least in some cases, its parallel illustrative passages. Indeed, Johnson explicitly remarked on the value of the *Dictionary* for the understanding of Shakespeare's literary predecessors and contemporaries:

> The Reason why the authours which are yet read of the sixteenth Century are so little understood is that they are read alone, and no help is borrowed from those who lived with them or before them. Some part of this ignorance I hope to remove by my book[.][9]

Working on the *Shakespeare* allowed Johnson further opportunity for thought on Shakespeare's words, and the footnotes of the *Shakespeare* gave him further scope to

8. For the most detailed and analytical discussion of this relationship, see Simon Jarvis, *Scholars and Gentlemen: Shakespearian Textual Criticism and Representations of Scholarly Labour, 1725–1765* (Oxford, 1995), chap. 6.

9. Johnson to Thomas Warton, February 1, 1755, in *Letters of Samuel Johnson*, ed. Bruce Redford, 5 vols. (Princeton, N.J., 1992–94), 1:92.

comment on their sense, their usage, and their authority. The 1773 revisions of the *Dictionary* and the *Shakespeare* should have afforded Johnson, and his Shakespearean coadjutors, another occasion to consider and record the outcomes of their continuing lexicographical and explanatory efforts.

Certainly, there are many places among Johnson's annotations in the 1765 *Shakespeare* more or less strongly underpinned by Johnson's work as lexicographer. Hamlet fears that Laertes makes "a wanton of me"; Johnson glosses "wanton" as "a man feeble and effeminate," not far from the sense given in the *Dictionary* (with this passage from *Hamlet*, and another from *King John* as illustrations): "A trifler; an insignificant flutterer." The word "lynstock" in the prologue to act 3 (line 32) in *Henry V* had been illustrated in the *Dictionary* with that very passage, and glossed there from Hanmer, as it is here, as the gunner's matchstick. Timon wishes the whores, "Yet may your pains six months be quite contrary" (4.3.143); Johnson amends the line (which indeed requires amending)[10] to read "quite *contraried*," encouraged by what he had already shown in the *Dictionary*, that the use of "contrary" as a transitive verb could be demonstrated from Hugh Latymer's sermons (*YE*, 8:732–33).[11]

The additions that Johnson himself made to the 1773 *Shakespeare* annotations, though sporadic and often clustered,[12] are frequently lexical in character, and on a few occasions are also recorded, at least in part, in the fourth edition of the *Dictionary*. Thus in 1773 Johnson adds, to a line (4.2.49) in *1 Henry VI*, that "A rascal deer is the term of chase for lean poor deer," though he provides no evidence (*YE*, 8:574); in the fourth edition of the *Dictionary* he adds to the headword RASCAL a second sense of the word, "still mentioned for lean deer," though he gives neither this Shakespearean line, nor any other source, as illustration. Banquo's reference to the "coigne of 'vantage" (*Macbeth*, 1.6.7) where the martlet makes its nest is glossed "[c]onvenient corner" (*YE*, 8:765), the first sense of the word COIGNE given in the 1755 *Dictionary*, but only illustrated, with Banquo's line, in the fourth edition.

Nevertheless, the relationship between the *Dictionary* and the *Shakespeare* is variable and unresolved. If work on the *Shakespeare*, over many years, fed into the *Dictionary*, work on the *Dictionary* fed into the *Shakespeare* rather less consistently. Though many of Johnson's Shakespearean notes assert the definition of a word, illustrative quotation is rare, though he had such illustrative quotation, at least potentially,

10. See Stanley Wells and Gary Taylor, with J. Jowett and W. Montgomery, *William Shakespeare: A Textual Companion* (Oxford, 1987), 506.

11. Hugh Latymer, *Seventh Sermon Preached before King Edward the Sixth* (1549). For other instances, see *YE*, 8:805 ("power"; *Coriolanus*, 2.3.4), 976 ("escot"; *Hamlet*, 2.2.342); 978 ("moble"; *Hamlet*, 2.2.496); and 1002 ("loggats"; *Hamlet*, 5.1.90). There is a demonstrable relation between new lexical discoveries Johnson made in preparing his 1765 *Shakespeare* and additions made to the fourth edition of the *Dictionary*; thus, he adds to the *Dictionary* in 1773 the headword FORGETIVE ("That may forge or produce"), from *1 Henry IV*, 4.3.98 (glossed in 1765 as "from 'forge'; inventive, imaginative"). For other, similar, examples, see Jarvis, *Scholars and Gentlemen*, 154–55.

12. For instance, around the first act of *Hamlet*; for the remainder of that play, there is relatively little, and for *Othello*, nothing.

readily to hand in the great dictionary he had just finished. He rarely draws on lexicographical expertise in the making of text-critical decisions;[13] the analytical relation between Johnson's text of Shakespeare on the one hand, and the headwords, definitions, and illustrations in his *Dictionary* on the other, is arguably less close than, for instance, the relation among Capell's text of Shakespeare, his Notes, *School of Shakespeare*, and Glossary. A number of Johnson's lexicographical additions to the *Shakespeare* in 1773 were for words or senses that he had already noted in the first edition of the *Dictionary*, but of which he had failed to avail himself in the 1765 Shakespearean apparatus: so "tag," in the sense "the lowest and most despicable of the populace" (*Coriolanus*, 3.1.248; *YE*, 8:810); so "romage," in the sense "tumultuous hurry" (*Hamlet*, 1.1.107; *YE*, 8:959). Where a new note in the 1773 *Shakespeare* is lexical, it is not in fact either normally or commonly as a result of information new to the 1773 *Dictionary*. Equally, Johnson often draws in the Shakespeare annotations, in his explanations and sometimes in his conjectures, on word senses recorded in neither the first nor the fourth edition of the *Dictionary*: so "gimmal," in the western countries dialect sense "a 'ring'" (*Henry V*, 4.2.49; *YE*, 8:556); so "lightly," in the sense "commonly, in ordinary course" (*Richard III*, 3.1.94; *YE*, 8:622); so the conjectural "brabe," in the sense "prize" or "reward," "found in Holyoak's *Dictionary*,"[14] but not in fact in Johnson's (*Cymbeline*, 3.3.23; *YE*, 8:890–91).

It seems clear that, as he annotated his *Shakespeare*, Johnson did not work with his personal lexicographical filing system to hand, or indeed, with any consistency, with a copy of the *Dictionary* itself.[15] If he sometimes remembered how he had defined and illustrated a word, very frequently he did not. Johnson's own notes in his edition rarely cross-refer, at points of difficulty, to parallel passages from Shakespeare, or to the validating body of the writings by authors of Shakespeare's own time (less, certainly, than do the variorum notes he cites from Theobald and Warburton). He does not often cross-refer even to the illustrative passages he had himself already used in the *Dictionary*. His edition is not, to use his own notorious words from the *Dictionary*, "reticulated or decussated"; Johnson does not network his text for the reader. Johnson's *Shakespeare*, certainly in 1765, and so far as his own work was concerned, in 1773, never threatens to become an elaborated hypertextual machine, such as we find exemplified in Capell's edition, or indeed in the subsequent variorum editions of Steevens and Malone.

13. Among the exceptions might be noted "o'er-raught"—that is, "over-reached"—at *Comedy of Errors*, 1.2.96. Johnson gives in the *Dictionary*, under OVERWROUGHT, a particular third meaning: "It has in *Shakespeare* a sense which I know not well how to reconcile to the original meaning of the word, and therefore conclude it misprinted for *overraught*; that is, *overreached* or cheated."

14. Johnson's reference is to Francis Holyoake, whose *Dictionarie Etymologocall* first appeared in John Rider's 1606 edition of *Riders Dictionarie* and was later published under Holyoake's own name as *Dictionarium etymologicum Latinum* (1633 and later editions).

15. Similarly, Johnson's footnote glosses of individual words in his edition of Sir Thomas Browne's *Christian Morals* depend on context and do not call on the validating authority of the dictionary that he had published just the previous year; see *Christian Morals: by Sir Thomas Browne, Of Norwich, M. D. and Author of Religio Medici. The second edition. With a life of the author, by Samuel Johnson; and explanatory notes* (London, 1756). I owe this point to O M Brack Jr.

This is a fundamental difference, and it is a difference of process as much as of product. We do not know how Theobald or Capell or Steevens recorded and recollected their information, but their information was so extensive, and its application so methodical, that they must all have used filing systems of some kind. The complex interconnections of Capell's text and *Notes and Various Readings*, and, more especially, the long lists of parallel passages that are the staple methodology of Theobald's *Shakespeare Restored* and of Steevens's critical notes, absolutely depend on data ready-organized in some sophisticated and large-scale paper arrangement.

Johnson's data, by contrast, appear very often to have been drawn not from paper file systems but from memory. Examples of inaccurate quotation are numerous in the *Shakespeare*, as they had been in the *Rambler* (1750–52) and would be in the *Lives of the Poets* (1779–81). At various places in his *Shakespeare*, Johnson omits words from Herbert, substitutes a reading in Waller, misquotes Gilbert Burnet, invents lines from *Paradise Lost*, changes Cornelius Celsus, misremembers the *Essay on Man*, alters an epigram by Ben Jonson, changes a word in the conclusion of Sir John Davies's *Nosce teipsum*, and approximately recalls Dryden's *Defence of the Epilogue*. In two separate notes on *Henry VIII* (1.1.28 and 1.2.32), his memory rewrites lines from Dryden's *Palamon and Arcite* (3.8, 3.544–45), though he had got the quotations right in the *Dictionary*, under CHIEF and MANY. Several such remembered passages involve small errors that do not damage Johnson's interpretative case. Other slips of the mind, however, affect the provenance or even the substance of his evidence. In his note on Hamlet's insistence that his companions "swear by my sword," Johnson remembers a source at second hand: "Mr. Garrick produced me a passage, I think, in Brantôme, from which it appeared, that it was common to swear . . . upon the cross which the old swords always had upon the hilt"; the reference is to the *Rodomontades* (1665?) of Pierre de Bourdeille, Seigneur de Brantôme, translated by John Ozell in 1741, but Arthur Sherbo tells us that no such passage has been found in Brantôme.[16] A final instance exposes Johnson's uses of memory in extreme and exceptional form. Attempting to edify Osric's term of art "impon'd" in his own margin, Johnson at first tentatively suggests, "Perhaps it should be, 'deponed,'" citing as from Samuel Butler's *Hudibras* (1663–78) the line "I would upon this cause *depone*"; but what he quotes from *Hudibras* is apparently a memorial misconstruction of three of Butler's lines (part 3, canto 3, lines 689–91) that do not contain the word *depone* at all. Johnson had in fact already provided a different memorial misconstruction of the line from *Hudibras*, as "On this I would *depone,*" in the 1755 *Dictionary*, for his sole validating illustration of a proposed sense 2 of the word: "To risque upon the success of an adventure." This proposed sense was apparently as imaginary as Butler's use of the word had been. Johnson's quotation in his *Shakespeare* of the passage in Butler was evidently checked neither against the text of *Hudibras*, nor against the text of his own *Dictionary* (*YE*, 8:1007).

16. *YE*, 7:132, 152, 185; 8:577, 633, 635, 639, 642, 749, 805, 898, 956, 972. Greg Clingham suggests that, in one of the quotations from *Palamon and Arcite* (*YE*, 8:635), Johnson's misremembering amounts to a "critical 'adjustment'" that "adds a certain balance to the thought which apparently takes its form from the lines in Shakespeare"; see "'The Inequalities of Memory': Johnson's Epitaphs on Hogarth," *English* 35 (1986): 221–32 at 222.

So to describe Johnson's editorial processes and outcomes is to identify the 1765 *Shakespeare* as consistent, in several if not in all aspects, with normal editorial science of its time. If he did not seek to annotate all Shakespearean cruces, nor had anyone before him. If his identification of references is vague or absent, so had been that of all his predecessors and contemporaries, and indeed so would be that of most of his immediate successors, including even Steevens and Malone. (The exception to this rule is Capell, whose documentation of his references in his massive commentary, published separately as *Notes and Various Readings to Shakespeare*,[17] is significantly more exact and more informative.) It is not possible for an editor at every moment to grapple with whole libraries; if Johnson depended on his memory, it was in part because his phenomenal intellectual powers allowed him to use the first kind of knowledge, what he knew of a subject himself, and often to spare himself pursuit of the second kind of knowledge, of where he could find information upon it.[18] More importantly, so to describe Johnson's editorial practices may give a possible direction for study of the relation of his 1765 *Shakespeare* to the scholarly and intellectual traditions and possibilities that were and had been available to him.

Johnson of course had early and substantial experience of literary and bibliographical scholarship. He had worked with one of the early eighteenth century's most remarkable antiquarians and literary scholars, William Oldys, for the bookseller Thomas Osborne, in the preparation of both the *Catalogus Bibliothecae Harleianae* (1743–44) and the *Harleian Miscellany* (1744–46). He had shared with Oldys the examination and cataloguing of the wide variety and vast number of old and learned books in one of the preeminent British book collections, for which he wrote content and bibliographical notes. The relative contributions of Oldys and Johnson as coauthors of the *Catalogus* and *Miscellany* are not readily ascertainable, and it is entirely possible that Johnson's contributions to these works were comparable in scope and expertise with those of Oldys.

Oldys exemplified the dedicated literary scholar, from whom Johnson could, and in some ways evidently did, learn much. Oldys was a bibliophile, a book collector, an obsessive collector of knowledge. Before he met Johnson, Oldys had already completed several significant works of literary scholarship. He made detailed manuscript annotations in two copies of Gerard Langbaine's *Account of the English Dramatick Poets* (Oxford, 1691), the first bought by Oldys in 1724, the second, after his landlord had disposed of the first copy in Oldys's absence, bought by him in 1727. Both of these copies would circulate among other scholars, in effect enjoying a limited but distin-

17. Edward Capell, *Notes and Various Readings to Shakespeare*, 3 vols. (London, 1779–83; part 1 is a reissue of the 1774 edition).

18. See *Boswell's Life of Johnson, Together with Boswell's Journal of a Tour to the Hebrides and Johnson's Diary of a Journey into North Wales*, ed. George Birkbeck Hill, rev. L. F. Powell, 6 vols. (Oxford, 1934–50), 2:365 (April 18, 1775), hereafter cited as *Life*.

guished, and influential, manuscript publication. The first copy passed to Thomas Coxeter, and thence to Theophilus Cibber, forming the basis of Cibber's additional notes in the five-volume *Lives of the Poets of Great Britain and Ireland in the Time of Dean Swift* (1753). The second copy, with marginal and interlinear notations added over a lifetime, was bought on Oldys's death by Thomas Birch, and was used, copied, and extracted by Percy, Malone, Reed, and Steevens, who printed "Anecdotes of Shakespeare, from Oldys's Mss. &c." in the 1778 variorum *Shakespeare*.[19] Oldys's first important printed publication was an edition of Sir Walter Raleigh's two-volume *History of the World* (1736), with Oldys's "Life of the Author, newly compil'd, from materials more ample and authentick than have yet been publish'd." In 1737 Oldys began publication of *The British Librarian*, a collection of his researches into rare and early books and manuscripts found in a number of private libraries. As a reason for discontinuing the work in 1738, he lamented the "vast and unseen Mass of Reading" required to produce a "small quantity of Writing."[20] No words could more plangently summarize the necessary and perpetual condition of the true literary scholar.

Oldys's methods were shaped by such influential English scholars as Bentley, and latterly by a wider Enlightenment movement toward comprehensive research, careful analysis of data, and full running documentation. That movement was driven especially by Pierre Bayle's *Dictionnaire historique et critique* (1697), which aimed to correct Louis Moréri's *Grand dictionnaire historique* (1674) by a copious running commentary of footnotes, "a miscellany of proofs and discussions," which skeptically interrogated the narrative of received truth. Interest in Bayle was particularly strong in 1734, in which year the first volumes of two rival English versions of Bayle's *Dictionary* were published.[21] Oldys himself contributed to one of these, the *General Dictionary*, and would later enthuse, in *Biographia Britannica*, that Bayle's work had turned Moréri's work from "a *Library* for the *Ignorant*" into "the *Treasure* of the *Learned*."[22]

Oldys's research methods, his care for completeness of reading and detail of documentation, for proof and demonstration, in part derived from Bayle, may well have influenced Johnson in turn, especially no doubt in the relatively systematic process by which Johnson, and his amanuenses, gathered, recorded, and ordered information in card-index form for the composition of his *Dictionary of the English Language*. The chronological arrangement of illustrative quotations, sense by sense, headword by headword, enabled a process of dictionary construction not merely scholarly but analytical and hermeneutic. The influence, however, went beyond, and

19. For fuller discussion of the Oldys Langbaines, see Marcus Walsh, "Literary Scholarship and the Life of Editing," in *Books and Their Readers in Eighteenth-Century England: New Essays*, ed. Isabel Rivers (London and New York, 2001), 191–215 at 207–8; *ODNB*, s.v. "Oldys, William (1696–1761)," by Paul Baines, last modified January 2008, http://www.oxforddnb.com/view/article/20699.

20. Oldys, *The British Librarian* (London, 1738), 375.

21. *The Dictionary Historical and Critical of Mr Peter Bayle* (London, 1734); *A General Dictionary, Historical and Critical: in which a New and Accurate Translation of that of the Celebrated Mr. Bayle . . . is included* (London, 1734). For discussion of Bayle, see Anthony Grafton, *The Footnote: A Curious History* (Cambridge, Mass., and London, 1997), 190–214.

22. *Biographia Britannica*, ed. Oldys, vol. 1 (London, 1747), xvi.

lasted longer, than the *Dictionary*. Oldys's projected life of Shakespeare, incomplete at his death in 1761, "may have furnished bits of information for Johnson's edition."[23] In preparing his *Lives of the Poets*, Johnson benefited from access to Oldys's annotations on Langbaine, probably via Steevens's own annotated transcript. From this source, for instance, Johnson derives his account of the letters written by Abraham Cowley when in Paris as Lord Jermin's secretary.[24] The form of the *Lives* was also indirectly influenced through works in which Oldys played some contributory part, including Theophilus Cibber's *Lives of the Poets of Great Britain and Ireland* (1753) and Mrs. Cooper's *The Muses Library* (1737).[25]

There remained, however, deep practical and philosophic differences between Oldys and Johnson, as scholarly readers and writers. Oldys wrote compulsively and continuously in the margins and between the lines of his own books, most famously in his two copies of Langbaine, but also in copies of *Englands Parnassus* (1600), *Hudibras*, Edward Phillips's *Life of Mr. John Milton* (1694), William Nicolson's *English, Scotch and Irish Historical Libraries* (1736), and Thomas Fuller's *History of the Worthies of England* (1662), and no doubt others.[26] He pursued through his life, and left at his death, a wide variety of organized manuscript materials: commonplace books, and notes on libraries in London, English poets, engraved portraits, natural history, and memoirs of the Oldys family.[27] Johnson recommended the compiling of notebooks and commonplace books, but it is unclear that in practice he did so. He heavily and systematically, if cryptically, marked up the books he used in the preparation of the *Dictionary*, but most of Johnson's books were unmarked or only lightly marked.[28] Indeed, and significantly, Johnson protested against the refrigeration of the reading mind, the interruption of the reader's experience of narrative or argument, necessarily involved in breaking off to make notes. In the *Idler*, Johnson observes that:

> It is the practice of many readers, to note in the margin of their books, the most important passages, the strongest arguments, or the brightest sentiments. Thus they load their minds with superfluous attention, repress the vehemence of curiosity by useless deliberation, and by frequent interruption break the current of narration or the chain of reason, and at last close the volume, and forget the passages and marks together.[29]

23. Lawrence Lipking, *The Ordering of the Arts in Eighteenth-Century England* (Princeton, N.J., 1970), 72.

24. *Lives of the Poets*, ed. Roger Lonsdale, 4 vols. (Oxford, 2006), 1:78, 194, 376nn17–20.

25. See Lipking, *Ordering of the Arts*, 71.

26. This habit of marginal writing can be paralleled in Richard Bentley and his Dutch scholarly predecessors. See John K. Hale, "Paradise Purified: Dr Bentley's Marginalia for his 1732 Edition of *Paradise Lost*," *Transactions of the Cambridge Bibliographical Society* 10 (1991): 58–74; and Kristine Louise Haugen, *Richard Bentley: Poetry and Enlightenment* (Cambridge, Mass., and London, 2011), 98, 99, 281n45, 294n96, 315n50.

27. See *ODNB*, "Oldys, William (1696–1761)."

28. For discussion, see Robert DeMaria Jr., *Samuel Johnson and the Life of Reading* (Baltimore and London, 1997), 24–25, 37–38, 40–43, 47.

29. Johnson, *The Idler and The Adventurer*, vol. 2 of *YE*, ed. W. J. Bate, John M. Bullitt, and L. F. Powell (1963), 231 (*Idler* 74, September 15, 1759).

This difference between Oldys and Johnson is a matter not only of reading practice, important though that is, but of fundamental intellectual direction. This was well enough understood at the time. A writer to the *Gentleman's Magazine*, in 1784, wrote of Oldys that "He was an excellent picker-up of facts and materials; but had [little power] of arranging them, or connecting them by intermediate ideas."[30] In strikingly similar terms, Hawkins wrote, just three years later, that Johnson:

> was never a sedulous inquirer after facts or anecdotes, nor very accurate in fixing dates: Oldys was the man of all others the best qualified for such an employment; Johnson's talent was disquisition; a genious like his, disdained so servile a labour.[31]

Oldys was an heir to a powerful and developing Enlightenment movement toward a philological and historical scholarship centering on textual evidence and its documentation. He did not do narrative or extended and structured argument. His characteristic products were catalogues, collections, remarks, above all the "perpetual commentary" of validating documentation, in the manner of Bayle, to be found in his annotated copies of Langbaine. One instance of his formal and methodological legacy is Thomas Warton's *History of English Poetry*, where the narrative is continuously interrupted by long bibliographical and documentary digressions and never approaches its end-point.[32] Another, yet more appropriate and dramatic, is the life of Shakespeare that Malone presents in the prolegomena of his 1790 edition; here Nicholas Rowe's fabling biography of the bard is made to serve as thin Morérian narrative to the Baylcian debunkings of Malone's page-dominating footnotes.[33] Johnson by contrast valued the "current of narration" and continuous disquisition or (as he defined and Hawkins understood the word) "disputative enquiry."[34] For all of Johnson's enormous knowledge and voracious reading, he was not, for most of his life, and in relation to most of his enterprises, obsessed with scholarly detail. As Robert DeMaria Jr. has tellingly put it, Johnson "did not have a habit of research."[35] If Johnson used some of Oldys's materials in the *Lives of the Poets*, he did not there use Oldys's validating methods.

Johnson's *Shakespeare* similarly demonstrates the difference between the methodologies of the two men. Scholarly annotation of literary texts has, characteristically and historically, been concerned with local issues, of textual reading and textual

30. *Gentleman's Magazine* 54 (1784): 260; quoted by Lipking, *Ordering of the Arts*, 72.

31. Sir John Hawkins, *The Life of Samuel Johnson, LL.D.* (London, 1787), 533.

32. Warton himself remarks, "I have chose to exhibit the history of our poetry in a chronological series: not distributing my matter into detached articles, of periodical divisions, or of general heads. Yet I have not always adhered so scrupulously to the regularity of annals, but that I have often deviated into incidental digressions; and have sometimes stopped in the course of my career"; see *The History of English Poetry, from the Close of the Eleventh to the Commencement of the Eighteenth Century*, vol. 1 (London, 1774), iii–iv.

33. *The Plays and Poems of William Shakspeare*, ed. Edmond Malone, 10 vols. (London, 1790), 1:102–54.

34. Johnson's full definition, in the first edition of the *Dictionary*, and in the unaltered entry for the word in the fourth edition (1773), is "examination; disputative enquiry."

35. DeMaria Jr., *Samuel Johnson and the Life of Reading*, 59.

meaning, and with local textual phenomena, such as variant readings, or material or verbal allusions. Annotation is characterized by local explanatory procedures, such as the adduction of contextual evidence or of parallel passages, or the clarification of difficult original expressions by paraphrase. Its primary concern has been interpretative. Theobald, in the preface to his 1733 *Shakespeare*, in entire conformity with contemporary understanding, defines three possible editorial responsibilities: "the Emendation of corrupt Passages; the Explanation of obscure and difficult ones; and an Inquiry into the Beauties and Defects of Composition." Theobald here sets out his own agenda, and the central agenda of scholarly editing of Shakespeare as of other poets in his century, by insisting that "this Work is principally confin'd to the two former Parts," of textual emendation and explanation.[36] Johnson's notes to the 1765 *Shakespeare* certainly follow that agenda repeatedly and extensively, examining problematic verbal readings, engaging with previous editors, addressing particular interpretative problems, using some at least of the most familiar explanatory methods (notably, paraphrase). It is nevertheless remarkable that Johnson brings less that is new to the evolving textual understanding of Shakespeare than his wide literary knowledge, and his special lexicographical expertise, might have promised. The restrained use of the parallel passage, the relatively thin added layer of new interpretative contextual materials, the occasional tendency to assert explanations without documented demonstration, are all diagnostic.

As Theobald had already shown, and as Johnson had agreed in his 1756 *Proposals*, in order to amend Shakespeare's text and recover his meaning it was essential to compare his works in detail "with those of writers who lived at the same time, immediately preceded, or immediately followed him." This would be a major feature of Capell's *Notes and Various Readings* and of the great variorum editions of Steevens and Malone. Johnson, however, adds little of such narrow-class evidence in 1765, and very little indeed of Theobald's "reading [that] was never read." Where Johnson adduces passages from sixteenth- and seventeenth-century writers, they are generally drawn from the "well of English undefiled." Frequently he cites classical writers and European humanist writers. The result is often less interpretative or explanatory than illustrative, educational, analogical, or moral. Mercutio's reference to "Spanish blades" (*Romeo and Juliet*, 1.4.84) prompts the remark that "[a] sword is called a 'Toledo', from the excellence of the Toletan steel," and the quotation of an epigram by Grotius, which expands the resonance of Shakespeare's phrase but explains a word Shakespeare does not use from an author Shakespeare did not know: "*Ensis Toletanus / Unda Tagi non est alio celebranda metallo*" (*YE*, 8:944). Johnson identifies Lady Capulet's "book . . . [t]hat in gold clasps locks in the golden story" (*Romeo and Juliet*, 1.3.93) as the *Golden Legend*, and he gives the lines a color, though not an interpretation, by speaking of it as "a book in the darker ages of popery much read . . . but of which Canus . . . proclaims the author to have been '*homo ferrei oris, plumbei cordis.*'"[37] The critical debate about Hamlet's "suit of sables"

36. *The Works of Shakespeare*, ed. Lewis Theobald, 7 vols. (London, 1733), 1:xl–xli.

37. "A man with a mouth of iron and a heart of lead"; *YE*, 8:943. Sherbo points out that the reference is to *De locis theologicis* (1563) by Francisco Melchior Cano, an author Johnson read on his journey to France. See *Life*, 2:391.

(3.2.125) irritates Johnson so much that he gives a Greek quotation from Erasmus's *Adagia* to the effect that the dead do not bite, and a Latin quotation from Horace's *Art of Poetry* to the effect that we are all doomed to die ("*debemur morti*"). This is salutary and poignant advice for all editors, though it sheds no direct light on Hamlet's words.

Johnson's edition is characterized and distinguished in rather different ways. Beside the always local fragments of emendation and explanation, his commentary offers the meal of disquisitory criticism, less in the form of "Inquiry into the Beauties and Defects of Composition," than of analogy, illustration, moral application, and imaginative response. These are moments that move from local interpretation of determinate meaning in the text toward a concern with the larger external significance of the text. So Johnson pours moralizing cold water on King Henry's vaunt that the English will be eternally remembered in the name of Crispin Crispian (*Henry V*, 4.3.57–59):

> It may be observed that we are apt to promise to ourselves a more lasting memory than the changing state of human things admits. . . . Late events obliterate the former. (*YE*, 8:557)

So famously and movingly Johnson provides, on the Duke's metaphor of life as an "after-dinner's sleep" in *Measure for Measure* (3.1.33), an aesthetic appreciation and an explanatory paraphrase that develops into lyrical moral disquisition:

> This is exquisitely imagined. When we are young we busy ourselves in forming schemes for succeeding time . . . when we are old we amuse the languour of age with the recollection of youthful pleasures . . . so that our life . . . resembles our dreams after dinner, when the events of the morning are mingled with the designs of the evening. (*YE*, 7:193)

At such moments Johnson the annotator is concerned with empathetic as well as moral response, and he credits his reader with his own intensity of imaginative engagement with the words of the text. In such notes are echoes of his account in the Preface of how Shakespeare's drama moves its audience in the theater, as "a just picture of a real original; as representing to the auditor what he would himself feel, if he were to do or suffer what is there feigned" (*YE*, 7:78). Often a quotation from a classical author serves as the occasion for moral elaborations. Commenting on King Henry's judgment of the traitor Scroop's seeming wisdom, Johnson cites Juvenal and generalizes the character:

> The king means to say of Scroop, that he was a cautious man, who knew that *fronti nulla fides*, that a specious appearance was deceitful . . . Surely this is the character of a prudent man.[38]

38. *Henry V*, 2.2.135 (*YE*, 8:539–40). The citation is of Juvenal, *Satires* 2.8.

The allusion to Juvenal does not claim to identify a source, or in itself validate an interpretation. Rather, as Robert DeMaria Jr. has put it, in such notes Johnson is "responding on his own terms to Shakespeare's meaning . . . accommodating Shakespeare to his own rhetorical world."[39]

Johnson's longer notes in particular tend to the literary critical, the generalizing, and the moral, not to the strictly text-critical or exegetical. The classic example is the discussion of the character of Polonius, who is, Johnson insists, not "a character only of manners," as Warburton had argued, but "a mixed character of manners and of nature," the experienced and able public man insensibly entering old age. The emphatic repetitions of Johnson's rhetoric insist upon Polonius as the type of "dotage encroaching upon wisdom":

> Such a man is positive and confident, because he knows that his mind was once strong, and knows not that it is become weak. Such a man excels in general principles, but fails in the particular application. (*YE*, 8:973–74)

This brilliant passage is of a piece with Johnson's Preface to *Shakespeare* not only in idea, in its representation of Shakespeare as the great mimetic poet of general nature, depicting characters who recall originals to every bosom ("*such* a man"), but also in mode, not fragmentary or local, but discursive and universal.

Such moments in Johnson's commentary set out to tell a broader story. Though they appear infrequently among his more detailed and focused responses to the issues raised by the Shakespearean text, they nevertheless illuminate his more general attitudes to the business of explanatory commentary, and its value and uses for the reader. They have a close if oblique relation to one of the most celebrated, and resonant, passages of the Preface:

> Notes are often necessary, but they are necessary evils. Let him, that is yet unacquainted with the powers of Shakespeare, and who desires to feel the highest pleasure that the drama can give, read every play from the first scene to the last, with utter negligence of all his commentators. When his fancy is once on the wing, let it not stoop at correction or explanation. When his attention is strongly engaged, let it disdain alike to turn aside to the name of Theobald and of Pope. Let him read on through brightness and obscurity, through integrity and corruption; let him preserve his comprehension of the dialogue and his interest in the fable. And when the pleasures of novelty have ceased, let him attempt exactness, and read the commentators. (*YE*, 7:111)

Johnson is ambivalent about detailed, line-by-line annotation, whether its aim be textual emendation or textual explication, and that ambivalence echoes his uneasy relation

39. Robert DeMaria Jr., *The Life of Samuel Johnson* (Oxford and Cambridge, Mass., 1993), 228.

to the new philology and its evidential methods. For the reader "unacquainted" with Shakespeare—a reader probably young, and certainly the intended beneficiary of Johnson's predominantly paraphrasing explanatory methodology—Johnson insists that reading be an act of the imagination, of continuing engagement with the horizontal progress of the Shakespearean "fable" and the dialogue in which it is enacted, rather than with the vertical fragmentation of adduced interpretative evidence. Nonetheless, the surrender to continuous disquisition is a pleasure of "novelty," a state of innocence beyond which the reader must pass. The young and the inexperienced reader especially require explanatory notes.[40] Understanding after all is necessary, and textual accuracy matters. "Exactness" is achieved not through intuitive comprehension, through the flight of the imagination, but through a focused and particular engagement with the text, and the explanatory knowledge brought to the places of the text by its commentators. In the 1765 *Shakespeare*, for all his reservations, Johnson is also a commentator. In the "Blinking Sam" of Reynolds's 1775 portrait, now at the Huntington Library, we find not only the rapt and imaginative reader of such scenes as the conclusion of *King Lear*, but also the intensely engaged student of the Shakespearean textual crux.

Lawrence Lipking has told in the most convincing terms the story of the evolution through the eighteenth century of the genres of literary history and biography, and more especially the invention, not least in Johnson's *Lives of the Poets*, of appropriate discursive forms distinct from those of the Enlightenment encyclopedia or catalogue. Lipking argues that the forms of the encyclopedia as practiced by Bayle, and of the life as written by Oldys, could not satisfy the narrative requirements of literary biography:

> The decisive condition for the development of English literary history . . . was not antiquarian research, but the accommodation of that research to . . . a way of ordering. . . . the establishment of proper documentation must be the beginning, not the end of the biographer's task. When Oldys adopted perpetual commentary as his method, he ensured a sound scholarly procedure, but he forfeited the flexibility and concentration of interest which give life to biographical writing.[41]

The literary biography, however, is not the exclusive or ideal or inevitably privileged end product of literary scholarship. In close chronological parallel, another model, that of the text-critical and exegetical commentary in English literary editing, was gaining its own identity, form, and refinement. The learned edition was already becoming both an established and leading mode of learned literary activity and an essential basis of textual study and understanding. It would reach a high point of

40. There is a parallel here with Jean Le Clerc's complaint about "some Criticks, who think it beneath them to make such Notes; they say that they are only good for young Men, and that those who have made some Progress, may easily be without 'em: But neither of them is altogether true." See Le Clerc, *Parrhasiana: or, Thoughts upon Several Subjects, . . . Done into English* (London, 1700), 168.

41. Lipking, *Ordering of the Arts*, 74, 80.

methodological sophistication, cultural significance, and intellectual power in the variorum editions of Steevens and Malone. It is true that in the 1765 *Shakespeare* Johnson made a pivotal contribution to the development of this second discourse, in his introduction to vernacular editing of variorum form, and in his perpetual strenuous engagement with his editorial predecessors in matters of textual reading and meaning. The striking and powerful presence in his editorial commentary of moralizing and generalizing application, however, and the relative absence of new contextual evidence and validating documentation, suggest that Johnson was not fully invested in the methods and discourses of the new editorial approach and methodology. Johnson's talent indeed was disquisition. Though he did not, as Hawkins alleged, disdain the servile pursuit of "facts and anecdotes," of parallels and contexts, of documents and documentation, the imperatives of that pursuit did not outweigh his concern for Shakespeare's drama as the mirror of life.

PART IV:

JOHNSON AND POLITICS

"To preserve order and support Monarchy": Johnson's Political Writings

F. P. Lock

JOHNSON'S POLITICAL CONVICTIONS ought not to be a subject of doubt or controversy. He wrote extensively about politics, and his writings are supplemented by a rich biographical record. Yet no aspect of his thought has provoked more acrimonious debate.[1] Evidence alone cannot settle the matter, for much of the evidence is itself contested. No short or summary answer is likely to do justice to the complexity of Johnson's ideas, to their development, or to their relation to the politics of his day. Nor are even his overtly political writings self-explanatory. All were published anonymously, and some employ a distinct persona. All are occasional, and therefore require knowledge of context for their understanding. All are rhetorical, concerned to make a case, adjusting arguments and language to an immediate audience, and not necessarily the unconstrained expression of his own dispassionate convictions. Most are negative, recording more strongly what he reprobated than what he approved. Some are satirical, employing the exaggerations characteristic of satire. Some are, or appear to be, the work of an angry man, and they may not represent the settled opinions of calmer moments. Finally, they span a period of forty years, years of considerable change in British politics.

Should we attempt to impose order on such disparate material? Can we do so without committing one of the fallacies that Quentin Skinner identifies as "mythologies," the search for an author's "doctrines" and for "coherence" in the totality of a

1. Donald J. Greene, *The Politics of Samuel Johnson* (New Haven, Conn., 1960; 2nd ed., Athens, Ga., 1990; citations are to the 1990 edition); Greene, introduction, *Political Writings*, vol. 10 of *The Yale Edition of the Works of Samuel Johnson* (hereafter cited as *YE*), ed. Greene (New Haven, Conn., 1977; text references are to this edition); Howard Erskine-Hill, "The Political Character of Samuel Johnson," in *Samuel Johnson: New Critical Essays*, ed. Isobel Grundy (London, 1984); John Cannon, *Samuel Johnson and the Politics of Hanoverian England* (Oxford, 1994); J. C. D. Clark, *Samuel Johnson: Literature, Religion, and English Cultural Politics from the Restoration to Romanticism* (Cambridge, 1994); essays by Greene, Erskine-Hill, Clark, Thomas M. Curley, Howard D. Weinbrot, and Michael Caldwell published in "Samuel Johnson and Jacobitism," *The Age of Johnson* 7 (1996): 1–212, and 8 (1997): 1–148; a series of articles on Jacobitism and eighteenth-century English literature published in *ELH* 64, no. 4 (1997): 903–1066; and Weinbrot, *Aspects of Samuel Johnson: Essays on His Arts, Mind, Afterlife, and Politics* (Newark, Del., 2005), 301–400 (condensing earlier contributions).

writer's work?[2] A biographer might be content, might even prefer, to record what Johnson said about politics as a series of discrete propositions, each to be explained in context as a response to a particular conjuncture of events and circumstances. But some attempt at a synthesis is surely needed, even in a biography. In Johnson's case, the problem is compounded by his dialectical habit of mind, his ability to see both sides of a question and his willingness sometimes to argue both, even at the cost of what Boswell tactfully calls his "varying from himself."[3] In such cases, can we properly distinguish between what Johnson "really" believed, and what he said while talking for victory? Can we claim that a statement in one work represents his "genuine" conviction, while what he writes in another is no more than a sally of wit or anger? Such procedures invite subjectivity and special pleading in favor of what we want Johnson to have believed.

A possible solution is to borrow a distinction from speech act theory and to ask not only what Johnson says, but also what he was doing, or thought he was doing, on a particular occasion.[4] In the search for Johnson's political convictions, statements and occasions when expressing his convictions was his explicit purpose will then carry greater evidential force than texts in which other purposes predominated. There may, of course, be disagreement about particular instances. But the principle offers a means of at least attempting to validate what may otherwise appear arbitrary judgments about when Johnson "really means" what he says.

Johnson's political writings can be divided into two groups: those written before and after 1760. The most important pre-1760 texts are concentrated in the years 1738 and 1739, at the height of the opposition to the administration of Sir Robert Walpole; the most important later texts were written between 1770 and 1774, during the early years of Lord North's ministry. While there are continuities between them, these groups are marked by stronger contrasts. Briefly, in the 1730s, Johnson wrote as the indignant scourge of a corrupt political elite and of an unpopular ministry and monarch. In the 1770s, he defended the policies of a ministry that was no less unpopular than Walpole's had been, his declared aim being "to preserve order and support Monarchy."[5] Superficially, then, he appears to have changed his side, or at least his point of view. Strikingly different pictures of Johnson's politics emerge from privileging one or the other of these periods. In what has been the most influential study, Donald Greene gives greater weight to the first. He analyzes the early pamphlets in detail and claims that Johnson never repudiated their principles. On the other hand, he asserts, to the "serious student" of Johnson's political thought, the later pamphlets "may not seem entirely to deserve the

2. Quentin Skinner, "Meaning and Understanding in the History of Ideas," *History and Theory* 8 (1969): 3–53, esp. 7–22.

3. *Boswell's Life of Johnson, Together with Boswell's Journal of a Tour to the Hebrides and Johnson's Diary of a Journey into North Wales*, ed. George Birkbeck Hill, rev. L. F. Powell, 6 vols. (Oxford, 1934–50), 3:155 (September 17, 1777), hereafter cited as *Life*.

4. Quentin Skinner, "Interpretation and the Understanding of Speech Acts," in *Visions of Politics*, 3 vols. (Cambridge, 2002), 1:103–27.

5. Johnson to Robert Chambers, April 19, 1783, in *Letters of Samuel Johnson*, ed. Bruce Redford, 5 vols. (Princeton, N.J., 1992–94), 4:124. The context is a gloomy retrospect on the last twenty years of British politics.

isolated pre-eminence that their notoriety accorded them." Their arguments can be found in the earlier writings, while "a large proportion of their content is made up of special pleading about incidents that do not now seem quite so exciting as they did then."[6] Greene's strategy is overtly revisionist: he seeks to overturn the conventional view of Johnson's politics as "Tory" or "reactionary," and to promote an interpretation more in accord with modern, liberal, social democracy. His Johnson is a populist firebrand. This is the view that I propose to controvert. The early writings appear to me a treacherous source for the elucidation of Johnson's mature politics, to which the pamphlets of the 1770s, authoritarian in tone and hostile to popular participation in politics, provide a surer guide.

In 1738 and 1739, Johnson published three pamphlets markedly antagonistic to the ministry of Sir Robert Walpole and broadly in support of the opposition.[7] They are brilliant and often entertaining, and there is no reason to doubt that they represent his genuine convictions at the time of writing. Yet several considerations suggest caution in taking them as paradigmatic of his mature political opinions. First, there is their early date. They are likely to reflect youthful exuberance and enthusiasm more than deliberate thought. That Johnson would gravitate to the opposition was, if not predetermined, at least influenced by extraneous factors. He was a poor, angry, disappointed young man, and therefore disposed to believe that much was wrong with the world, and to suspect the worst of the government. He was a poet, and he hoped that his tragedy would prove a passport to fame and fortune. The Walpole administration, and Walpole himself and the king in particular, were notoriously indifferent to literature, while the literary establishment was strongly tied to the opposition. In addition, Johnson's combative temperament is likely to have biased him in favor of opposition to the governing oligarchy, before he had the time or the opportunity to examine the issues with dispassionate detachment.[8] Later, he came to judge Walpole more favorably.[9] For all these reasons, his early works are less likely than his later to embody his deepest convictions.

6. Greene, *Politics of Samuel Johnson*, 204–5.

7. The three pamphlets are *London* (1738); *Marmor Norfolciense* (1739); and *A Compleat Vindication of the Licensers of the Stage* (1739).

8. A further consideration is his Lichfield background. While still in Lichfield, Johnson sharpened his wits by arguing with Gilbert Walmsley, whom he later described as "a Whig, with all the virulence and malevolence of his party" ("Smith," *Lives of the Poets*, vols. 21–23 of *YE*, ed. John H. Middendorf [2010], 22:532). After Walmsley's death, Johnson "felt my Toryism much abated" (reported by Boswell [s.v. November 10, 1773], in *Life*, 5:386). The identification of Walmsley as the Whig in question is Boswell's but appears plausible. According to Sir John Hawkins, Johnson's father was a Jacobite; see Hawkins, *The Life of Samuel Johnson, LL.D.*, ed. O M Brack Jr. (Athens, Ga., 2009), 3. Given Johnson's rebellious temperament, this would not have made him a Jacobite sympathizer. But in Lichfield he encountered a range of Tory and Jacobite opinions and sentiments; see Paul Monod, "A Voyage out of Staffordshire: Samuel Johnson's Jacobite Journey," in *Samuel Johnson in Historical Context*, ed. Jonathan Clark and Howard Erskine-Hill (Basingstoke, U.K., 2002), 11–43. This exposure probably reinforced his personal reasons for siding with the opposition.

9. Hawkins, *Life of Samuel Johnson*, 308–9. A passage in the life of Thomson supports the idea (*YE*, 23:1283).

Second, Greene's stricture about the pamphlets of the 1770s, that they contain "special pleading about incidents that do not now seem quite so exciting as they did then," applies with greater force to the anti-Walpole squibs. They contain more personal and topical satire and are more closely bound to the specific events and conditions of the 1730s. Thus, while the *Compleat Vindication of the Licensers of the Stage* (1739) does make some general points about censorship, it is much more concerned with a particular measure, Walpole's Licensing Act. The later pamphlets show a greater power of generalization, about questions that remain current: the relations between electors and the legislatures they elect; international law; and the nature of the sovereign state.

A third argument against deriving Johnson's views from the early pamphlets is that all are literary exercises. All employ satire, irony, and exaggeration. This makes them dangerous guides to his serious political convictions. In the *Compleat Vindication*, for example, the parody is energized by massive overstatement. For the purposes of the satire, the Licensing Act becomes the first move in a plot that would in due course have outlawed literacy. In this respect, the parallel that Greene draws with *Areopagitica* is misleading.[10] Milton's pamphlet is a serious and nuanced argument against censorship before publication; Johnson's is a reductio ad absurdum, from which the precise nature of his views on censorship cannot safely be inferred. Further, to the extent that they are written in the idiom of the opposition, these pamphlets are less completely the product of Johnson's own mind. Allowance has to be made for the extent to which they are exercises in which he was more concerned to exhibit his own virtuosity than to formulate his personal political creed.

The pamphlets of 1738 and 1739 were written with great panache and conviction. There can be no doubt of their sincerity. But they are rooted in a particular political context, the last years of the Walpole administration, and they reflect the conditions and political configuration of that moment. They show clearly the strength of Johnson's political convictions, and they sufficiently refute the notion that he was not especially interested in politics.[11] They are excellent literary compositions, among the best examples of his work as a satirist.[12] As satires, they are largely preoccupied with particulars, and with distributing blame rather than exercising judgment. Highly topical, they are little concerned with general principles. Greene, as part of his strategy of promoting the importance of the pamphlets of 1738 and 1739, seeks to minimize this topicality. He formulates a series of general propositions that, he asserts, are implicit in *Marmor Norfolciense* (1739) and in the *Compleat Vindication*: that "the only satisfactory basis for a political system must be the enlightened minds of free and responsible

10. This parallel is developed by Greene in *Politics of Samuel Johnson*, 101, 144; and *YE*, 10:55.

11. Patrick O'Flaherty, "Samuel Johnson's Politics: Some Points of Disagreement," review of Greene's *Politics of Samuel Johnson* in *Dalhousie Review* 72 (1992): 382–98 at 398; Cannon, *Samuel Johnson and the Politics of Hanoverian England*, 63; David Nokes, *Samuel Johnson, a Life* (London, 2009), 164.

12. In "Johnson and Satire Manqué," W. Jackson Bate argues that Johnson had a "hatred and fear of satire" and "did not dare to release the satiric impulse partly because it was so strong"; see *Eighteenth-Century Studies in Honor of Donald F. Hyde*, ed. W. H. Bond (New York, 1970), 145–60 at 150. Yet a strong satiric "impulse" is a notable feature of Johnson's political writings, both early and late.

individuals"; that "the individual has an inalienable responsibility to examine and judge all human matters for himself"; that Johnson could never have "preferred any system of government which does not rest on the rational exercise of the minds of free and responsible individuals," a system that he believed really existed in Britain; and that Johnson was "one of the most effectual propagators of democracy in the eighteenth century."[13] Yet no such propositions are to be found in Johnson's texts. Johnson was much too intelligent and well informed to imagine that the political system of eighteenth-century Britain rested on anything so utopian as the "rational exercise of the minds of free and responsible individuals." On the contrary, he knew that it was dominated in normal times by patronage, influence, and corruption, subject to occasional control by a volatile and irrational public opinion, itself more often reflecting unthinking mob hysteria than the collective reasonings of well-informed individuals.[14]

Greene adduces a few passages in which Johnson appears to approve the existence and influence of a vigorous "public opinion."[15] In each case, however, attention to what Johnson was doing in each text, as well as to what the text says, suggests that these are all acknowledgments of fact rather than expressions of approval. The earliest of these supposed affirmations of principle occurs in the preface to the *Gentleman's Magazine* for January 1743. "Under a Form of Government like ours," the preface declares, "which makes almost every Man a secondary Legislator, Politicks may justly claim a more general Attention than where the People have no other Duty to practise than Obedience, and where to examine the Conduct of their Superiors, would be to disturb their own Quiet, without Advantage."[16] This preface, however, is not a personal statement by Johnson but an editorial manifesto.[17] Even if it were a personal statement, the

13. Greene, *Politics of Samuel Johnson*, 106, 108, 243, 244.

14. In his life of Butler, Johnson claims that "the wisdom of the nation is very reasonably supposed to reside in the parliament," not in anything so volatile as public opinion. Parliament derived that respect from its being composed largely of men of property and education. From a proposal in one of Cromwell's parliaments to burn the records in the Tower, efface the memory of the past, and begin a new system of life, Johnson concludes that nothing like "wisdom" can be expected of "the lower classes of the people" (*YE*, 21:223). Roger Lonsdale surveys the politics of the *Lives*, and recent scholarship on the subject, in his edition (*Lives of the Most Eminent English Poets: With Critical Observations on Their Works*, ed. Lonsdale, 4 vols. [Oxford, 2006], 1:166–75). Johnson's mainly incidental comments provide a valuable supplement to his more sustained arguments in the *Political Tracts*, on which this essay concentrates.

15. In a note on the opening of "Observations on the Present State of Affairs," Greene cites, as "equally forthright assertions of the right of the people to know," the preface to the *Harleian Miscellany*, the *Compleat Vindication*, the preface to the *Preceptor*, and the "Speech on the Rochefort Expedition" (*YE*, 10:262–65). Such passages, he claims, refute "the legend of Johnson the blind authoritarian" (*YE*, 10:185–86n1). I concur that Johnson was no "blind" authoritarian: he was authoritarian by conscious and rational conviction.

16. *Gentleman's Magazine* 13 (January 1743): iii.

17. The same objection applies to treating the preface to the *General Index to the First Twenty Volumes of the Gentleman's Magazine* (1753), even if wholly Johnson's composition, as an expression of his opinions. Greene calls this an "important document" in which Johnson "casts his eye over the outstanding public events in the history of the nation" and "an emphatic public pronouncement"; see "Johnson: The Jacobite Legend Exhumed," *The Age of Johnson* 7 (1996): 73–74. Johnson's own views cannot safely be inferred from an anonymous preface spoken in the editorial voice and with the intention of persuading readers to buy the *General Index*.

preface as a whole is rather equivocal about this aspect of the British system. It begins by reporting that "those who are most eminent among us for their Understanding and Politeness" have "for many Years lamented" that party politics has so engrossed public attention, to the exclusion of other subjects. The characterization of the British system of government is sequestered in a subordinate clause, in a sentence in which the main clause affirms that "Life requires many other Considerations," and that politics "may be said to usurp the Mind" when it monopolizes public attention. This declaration leads to a defense of the editorial policy of the *Gentleman's Magazine*, which has been to "diversify our Work," by including articles on morality, commerce, and philosophy.

The following paragraph particularizes the subject of the manufacture of wool, "the most important Part of our Commerce." On this subject, the *Magazine* has "collected and abridg'd all the Schemes that have been proposed for preventing its Exportation," as well as publishing many curious letters. A fair interpretation of the purport of this preface is that people pay too much regard to "the Struggles of opposite Parties" and insufficient to informing themselves about matters of real substance and importance, such as trade and commercial regulation. The woolen trade is a political issue in the sense that its regulation is a proper subject of parliamentary, and therefore of public, concern. But it is not amenable to being settled by popular opinion. If this preface indeed reflects Johnson's views, it suggests that, as early as 1743, he had moved away from his inflammatory journalism of 1738–39 toward a more responsible kind of writing, designed to inform and educate the public.

A passage in Johnson's introduction to the *Harleian Miscellany* (1744) echoes the preface to the *Gentleman's Magazine*. "The *Form* of our *Government*," he observes, "gives every Man . . . the Right of enquiring into the Propriety of publick Measures." As a consequence, those entrusted with the government are obliged "to give an Account of their Conduct, to almost every Man, who demands it." This being the case, "*innumerable* Pamphlets" have been written and published, such as could never have appeared under "*arbitrary* Governments." So far, so good. But in the following paragraph, Johnson notes "another Source of unexhaustible Publication" in "the Multiplicity of *Religious Sects* tolerated among us."[18] No one would cite that paragraph to illustrate Johnson's views on religious toleration. Neither should the paragraph on political pamphlets be taken as more than a statement of historical fact. Nor should the rhetorical purpose of the introduction be ignored. It was written as a puff for a collection of reprinted pamphlets, sold in weekly parts. Its purpose was to persuade readers to purchase a collection of obsolete and largely forgotten ephemera, and it should not be taken as an expression of Johnson's considered opinion of the merits of the British system of government.

A similar caveat may be entered with regard to the preface to Robert Dodsley's *Preceptor* (1748). A study of "the Principles of *Laws* and *Government*" is there said to

18. In Allen T. Hazen, *Samuel Johnson's Prefaces & Dedications* (New Haven, Conn., 1937), 54, italics in original.

form a necessary subject to qualify a man "to act and judge as one of a Free People." Again, this is not a voluntary expression of Johnson's independent opinion but an explanation of the rationale for an educational textbook. In any case, the "Principles" are formulated to emphasize duties rather than rights. They are principles "by which Men are taught to whom Obedience is due, for what it is paid, and in what Degree it may justly be required." An Englishman "professes to obey his Prince according to the Law," and gives his consent, "by his Representative, to all the Laws by which he is bound." Johnson does concede "a Right to petition the great Council of the Nation, whenever he thinks they are deliberating upon an Act detrimental to the Interest of the Community."[19] But he confines the right both in time (while a measure is under consideration) and in scope (to the interest of the community). The tone and wording of this passage, together with its emphasis on obedience, make it, for 1748, a decidedly minimalist statement of the political rights of an Englishman.[20]

The high-sounding opening of "Observations on the Present State of Affairs" (1756) has also been adduced to illustrate Johnson's support for the "right to know." "The time is now come," the observer asserts, "in which every Englishman expects to be informed of the national affairs, and in which he has a right to have that expectation gratified" (*YE*, 10:185). This sounds like, and has been interpreted as, a general principle.[21] But the paragraph proceeds to distinguish between "counsels yet unexecuted, and projects suspended in deliberation" and the situation "when a design has ended in miscarriage or success." In the following paragraph, Johnson switches to "the general subject of the present war" and a long discussion of the disputes between the British and the French in North America. The essay ends abruptly with "To be continued," but no continuation ever appeared. The opening paragraph provides an awkward introduction to what immediately follows, which turns from secrets of state to recent history that was common knowledge. It must therefore have been relevant to some topic in the intended continuation. The most likely subject is the recall of Admiral Byng. Johnson took a keen interest in this controversy and subsequently reviewed several pro-Byng pamphlets (*YE*, 10:213–60). The first paragraph of the "Observations" makes good sense as an allusion to the ministry's attempt to make a scapegoat of Byng by manipulating, indeed falsifying, the information that was made public.[22] If this interpretation is correct, "The time is now come" is not a general assertion of the public's "right to know" but a protest against a cover-up, made in the interest of natural justice.

19. In Hazen, *Prefaces & Dedications*, 187–88.

20. Johnson's "Life of Dr Francis Cheynel" (first published in *The Student, or the Oxford and Cambridge Monthly Miscellany* in 1751), though primarily concerned with religion and education, is markedly authoritarian in tone, hostile to the rebellion of the 1640s, and zealous for "subordination"; see *Early Biographical Writings of Dr Johnson*, ed. J. D. Fleeman (Farnborough, U.K., 1973), 389–405 at 391.

21. That is, by Greene. In addition, Greene elides the important distinction Johnson makes between "is doing" and "has done" (*YE*, 10:185–86n1).

22. Johnson's "Observations" appeared in *Literary Magazine* no. 4, which was published about August 15, 1756. Byng's fleet fought the French on May 20; news of the encounter reached London on June 3. Byng was immediately recalled, and the affair soon became a leading topic of comment and controversy in the newspapers.

The same limitation of public enquiry to situations "when a design has ended in miscarriage or success" is seen in Johnson's "Speech on the Rochefort Expedition" (1757, *YE*, 10:262–65).[23] All this speech asserts is that "the people have a right to address his Majesty, for an enquiry into the conduct of the late expedition." But the "right" here asserted is no engine of democracy. On the contrary, Johnson avers that "There is, perhaps, no nation in the world where individuals have not the right to address their king, if they think themselves injured." The propriety of any enquiry, and any redress that may follow, are implicitly left in the hands of the king and his advisers.

The ease and rapidity with which the ministry was able to exploit public prejudice against Byng probably contributed to Johnson's growing skepticism about popular participation in politics. The germ of this skepticism is already present in *London* in 1738, and it was probably nourished by the developments that followed the fall of Walpole. To find it forcefully expressed in Johnson's political pamphlets of the 1770s will therefore occasion no surprise. Nevertheless, between Johnson's earlier and later political writings, there is at least a shift of emphasis. Nor is such a development in the least unexpected. The times changed, and Johnson changed, though in another direction. His initial gravitation to the opposition was overdetermined by a variety of considerations: his religion and his commitment to the established church; Oxford; his poverty and outsider status; his personal connections in London; Walpole's inattention to the patronage of literary men; George II's unpopularity; and a youthful belief in the possibility of changing the world. By the 1770s, all these factors had been neutralized or reversed. North's ministry was perceived as more supportive of the established church, a perception that was reflected in North's own election as chancellor of the University of Oxford in 1772.[24] George III himself was more popular and respected than his grandfather had been, and he was not accused of subordinating British to Hanoverian interests. Though still by temperament an outsider, Johnson was a state pensioner. As early as *Rasselas* (1759), he had acknowledged the ineradicability of corruption.[25] In the 1760s, factious parties, popular discontents, and insubordination in the American colonies had all contributed to political instability. Johnson was not alone in believing

23. First published in 1785, the "Speech" is said to have been dictated extempore by Johnson "at the Desire of a Friend," by whom it was delivered. How far it represents Johnson's own convictions is therefore open to doubt. It may have been dictated in a spirit of "if you want to move for an address, these are some arguments that you could use." The same caveat could be applied to Johnson's sermons and to Chambers's law lectures. But Johnson might have allowed himself greater latitude in dictating an opinion on the political topic of the day than in a sermon or lecture. I am confident that he would not, even in a sermon or lecture written for another, have said anything he did not believe.

24. G. M. Ditchfield, "Ecclesiastical Policy under Lord North," in *The Church of England, c. 1689–c. 1833: From Toleration to Tractarianism*, ed. John Walsh, Colin Haydon, and Stephen Taylor (Cambridge, 1993), 228–46. Ditchfield warns against accepting too readily the notion of a resurgence of High Church politics in the 1770s. Even so, the defeats inflicted on such initiatives as the Feathers Tavern petition suggest that contemporary observers, including Johnson, are likely to have believed that Dissent was, at least, no longer being officially encouraged. On several occasions in the Commons, North spoke boldly in defense of the Church and its privileged position; see James J. Sack, *From Jacobite to Conservative: Reaction and Orthodoxy in Britain, c. 1760–1832* (Cambridge, 1993), 79–80.

25. Johnson, *Rasselas and Other Tales*, vol. 16 of *YE*, ed. Gwin J. Kolb (1990), 32.

that such threats to the established political order required strong government. The most potent danger now came from below, not from oppression and corruption above. He was far from idealizing Lord North, but North represented the lesser evil.

The first of the four pamphlets, *The False Alarm*, was written at great speed, on January 10 and 11, 1770 (*YE*, 10:313; text at 317–45). Its immediate concern is with the controversy that followed the election of John Wilkes as MP for Middlesex in March 1768. The question in dispute was whether the House of Commons had the power not only to expel a member but also to declare him ineligible for reelection to the same Parliament. Soon, however, the issue became a partisan struggle between the ministry and the opposition. The opposition mobilized extraparliamentary opinion in its favor through a campaign of meetings and petitions in London and in the provinces. Johnson took the ministerial side. In the first two-thirds of the pamphlet, he provides a reasoned and dispassionate consideration of the original question, appealing to logical arguments and legal precedents to demolish the opposition's case. The exclusion of Wilkes is no great grievance, he argues: a "false alarm" has been fomented by unscrupulous demagogues for their own selfish ends. This part of the pamphlet exhibits the "subtlety of disquisition," for which Johnson regarded it as the best of the series.[26]

The last third of the pamphlet is markedly different in tone and method. Instead of "subtlety of disquisition," Johnson launches a sustained diatribe against popular agitation on political issues, one that is not limited to the Wilkes case. He caricatures the petitioners as a motley crew of tailors, drapers, and blacksmiths who meet at the local alehouse to "consider the state of the nation." In a virtuoso piece of satire, he ridicules "the progress of a petition," which he denigrates as inspired by opposition malcontents and signed by their ignorant dupes. He excoriates the venal and materialistic electors who lack the capacity to reach intelligent decisions on political questions, who are easily bribed by free food and drink, and who revel in a brief and illusory moment of self-importance. In contrast to this "rabble," Johnson introduces two responsible characters, both of whom try to educate the uninformed so that they have a clearer understanding of the question.[27] But their best efforts are unsuccessful. Johnson takes every opportunity to besmirch the social origins and motives of the discontented. They are "pedlars," a "despicable faction" distinguished only by "plebeian grossness, and savage indecency," motivated by "the desire of levelling," their political zeal a pretense hiding

26. Conversation with Boswell, March 21, 1772 (*Life*, 2:147).

27. Johnson uses the term "rabble" in all four pamphlets (and elsewhere), and always pejoratively. In his *Dictionary of the English Language,* he defines the term as "A tumultuous croud; an assembly of low people." Boswell, however, reports him as saying (in the context of a discussion of social subordination) that only "opinion, by which we have a respect for authority" prevents "us, who are the rabble, from rising up and pulling down you who are gentlemen from your places" (March 21, 1772; *Life*, 2:153). This must have been spoken with playful irony. Though Johnson exhibited great compassion for the poor and for "low people," politically he always identified himself with the "gentlemen" and never evinced any respect for the political opinions or capacity of the "rabble" or the "croud."

"the natural malignity of the mean against the great" (*YE*, 10:341). At the end of the pamphlet, Johnson dismisses the movement as a temporary fit of inebriation or madness from which the people will soon recover. If the court will only stand firm and "despise" this agitation, its factious nature will become apparent, and its impotence will be exposed. The two voices of the pamphlet serve complementary rhetorical purposes. The rational and historical arguments demonstrate that the Wilkes case represents, at worst, a "small irregularity," not a constitutional crisis. But having scotched the "false" alarm, in the latter part of the pamphlet, with its powerfully emotive language, Johnson sounds a genuine alarm at a real danger to the constitution, from popular agitation, exploited by self-interested, factious politicians.

The second pamphlet in the series, *Thoughts on Falkland's Islands*, published in March 1771, exhibits a similar contrast (*YE*, 10:349–86). Initially, Johnson provides a dispassionate narrative of the history of the islands, and of Britain's recent dispute with Spain on their account. He argues that the islands are of minimal value or importance; that the ministry has acted properly and successfully throughout, gaining every essential point that was contested; that to have risked war to extort further concessions from Spain would have been folly; and that the opposition wanted war, not for the ostensible reason of humbling Spain, but to undermine the ministry in order to obtrude itself into power. To this end, the war faction employed the same methods as it had in the case of Wilkes: using exaggeration and misrepresentation to create a false sense of crisis, and fomenting discontent and disaffection among those too ignorant to know better. Having settled the immediate issue, Johnson proceeds to generalize on the horrors of war and the wisdom of avoiding it, as a way of reinforcing his particular point. As in *The False Alarm*, the language in this latter part becomes more emotive, especially in two remarkable passages, the tone of which can be judged from a few characteristic expressions. Again, Johnson's contempt extends equally to the rabble and to those who mislead them, whom he compares to vendors of poison and to Milton's Satan. But most of his strongest language is reserved for the rabble, which he reviles in the most opprobrious terms. The shouting of the rabble is as mindless as the illumination of windows. Composed of "the cits of London, and the boors of Middlesex," the rabble displays "plebeian malignity." Junius, a leading opposition journalist, is compared to a meteor "formed by the vapours of putrefying democracy" (*YE*, 10:376–78). The "howl of plebeian patriotism" may have given foreigners the idea that a new Peasants' Revolt was in prospect. But the rabble is only formidable because it has been "pampered into impudence" by the lenity of the ministry; government can no more be "subverted by the rabble" than a city can be "drowned by the overflowing of its kennels" (*YE*, 10:385–86).[28]

In Johnson's view, the ministry has allowed the selfish and factious opposition leaders to pose as patriots, and the rabble has been misled by them. Popular agitation

28. Johnson's contempt for the "rabble" is apparent from his letters to Hester Thrale at the time of the Gordon Riots (June 9, 10, and 12, 1780, in *Letters*, 3:267–74). Their motivation is either plunder (268) or the "high sport" of burning the jails, a "good rabble trick" (271).

should therefore be ignored—indeed, repressed—for it does not genuinely represent the people. Rather, it merely echoes the lessons that they have learned by rote from unscrupulous demagogues. The pamphlet thus enforces the same lessons as *The False Alarm*. There is no crisis. If there was one, or the threat of one, it has been ably defused by the ministry. More generally, the remarkable degree of popular interest and participation in politics that characterizes the British system may be not, as is sometimes supposed, its strength and its glory, but its weakness, and the most probable cause of its decline. Popular discontent is mostly ill informed and unjustified. But since passions have been aroused, the best way of calming them is to provide more accurate information, as Johnson's own pamphlet does.

The third pamphlet, *The Patriot*, was written even more rapidly than *The False Alarm*: on October 1 or 8, 1774 (*YE*, 10:387). Its purpose was to influence the general election that had just been called. For this end, it redefines the term "patriot." In the 1730s, this title had been usurped by those in opposition to the court. Johnson denies the validity of their claim to it and reappropriates it for the supporters of the present constitutional order. In an electioneering pamphlet, we would expect any criticism of "the people," or of their participation in the political process, to be muted or suppressed. Indeed, Johnson at one point venerates the elector as holding "a high dignity and important trust" (*YE*, 10:390). But most of the pamphlet is devoted to vilifying the false patriots and the gullible "people" whom they so easily delude. In pursuit of popularity, pretended patriots promise wild constitutional reforms, such as shorter parliaments or an extended franchise, or undertake to obey the dictates of their constituents. In contrast to these dangerous schemes, Johnson highlights the single recent improvement to the constitution, George Grenville's Elections Act of 1770, made perpetual in 1774, which provided a more equitable mode of settling controverted elections.[29] The only bright spot in an otherwise gloomy political landscape, this reform was the work, not of the self-styled "patriots," but of the self-denying members of the last Parliament, men whom the "patriots" have traduced as "worthless, venal, and prostitute, slaves of the court, and tyrants of the people" (*YE*, 10:399). The inference is that further reform (and Johnson does not deny that the existing system is capable of amelioration) is more likely to come from above, from the wise and the prudent, rather than from below.

"The people," Johnson observes, "is a very heterogeneous and confused mass of the wealthy and the poor, the wise and the foolish, the good and the bad." A candidate for Parliament who is a true patriot will appeal to the "higher ranks" and seek through their influence to "regulate the lower." He will associate chiefly with "the wise, the temperate, the regular and the virtuous." The false patriot, on the contrary, will address himself "to the indigent, who are always inflammable; to the weak, who are naturally suspicious; to the ignorant, who are easily misled; and to the profligate, who have no hope, but from mischief and confusion." To appeal to these groups, the pretended patriot will employ not argument but the tricks of low popularity. The true patriot, in

29. Philip Lawson, "Grenville's Election Act, 1770," *Bulletin of the Institute of Historical Research* 53 (1980): 216–28.

contrast, suspects, with becoming diffidence, that "of his constituents, as of other numbers of men, the smaller part may often be the wiser." Of this truth, discouraging for democracy, Johnson himself entertains no doubt. Even in an election address, he cannot conceal his contempt for the ignorant majority, whose opinions "are not propagated by reason, but caught by contagion"; for their mindless support of self-seeking "patriots"; and for the rhetoric of "patriotism" that has clouded and enflamed political discourse (*YE*, 10:393–94, 395, 391).

Taxation No Tyranny, the last and longest of the four pamphlets, was written over several months and published on March 8, 1775 (*YE*, 10:401–2). In this tract, Johnson strongly defends, against the claim of "no taxation without representation," both the legality and the equity of Parliament's power of taxing the colonies. The primary concern of *Taxation No Tyranny* is thus not with British domestic politics but with relations between the mother country and the colonies. Nevertheless, there are strong parallels with the earlier pamphlets. Johnson presents the conflict as one between superior and inferior parties, and he resolves it by invoking a natural hierarchy. The Americans are cast in the role played earlier by the local rabble. During the course of his argument, Johnson manifests a disbelief in the reality of the American "grievances" and attributes the agitation about them to the work of self-interested fomenters of sedition, figures familiar from the earlier pamphlets. These factious pseudopatriots, the "zealots of anarchy," in Britain as well as in the colonies themselves, exploit and magnify the supposed "grievances," inventing remote consequences in which they do not really believe, in order to fuel public alarm. As he had previously argued in other contexts, governors should ignore the complaints of the disaffected, which he characterizes as "the abortions of Folly impregnated by Faction" (*YE*, 10:412). Public business is best conducted by the wise, who should not be deflected from doing what is right by the "yelps" of hypocritical libertarians.

Johnson rejects the notion that representation is required for political "liberty." Indeed, he dethrones "liberty" from the pride of place that it typically occupies in eighteenth-century political discourse. "Liberty," he imagines his opponents contending, "is the birthright of man, and where obedience is compelled, there is no liberty." Against this assertion, he retorts that "Government is necessary to man, and where obedience is not compelled, there is no government." Society requires an absolute power, first to make laws, and then to enforce them (*YE*, 10:448). Thus Johnson privileges government and subordination over liberty, and duties over rights. Had America been discovered and the colonies founded in "days of laxity," between the fourth and the tenth centuries, they might indeed have formed independent states. But by the fifteenth century, Europe had regained the "settled form" lost in the ages following the decline and fall of Rome. Columbus and later adventurers were thus constrained to proceed as the agents of one or other of the European sovereigns. The colonies founded were considered "mere extensions or processes of empire." Johnson applies the same absolutism to the domestic sphere. "All government," he argues, "is ultimately and essentially absolute," for "[i]n sovereignty there are no gradations."

The supreme power, wherever it is placed, is irresistible, except by rebellion, "an act which makes it questionable what shall be thenceforward the supreme power" (*YE*, 10:420–23).

Taken by itself, as a theoretical account of political sovereignty, Johnson's statement is unexceptional, even a "commonplace of the time."[30] But Johnson deduces from it practical implications that were not universally accepted. In fact, it underlies his denial of legitimacy to the exercise on the legislature of the pressure of public opinion. Political power in Britain, he acknowledges, originates with the people, or rather with the body of electors, most of whom were property owners.[31] He further accepts the right to petition. But he denies that electors have any right to control or coerce their members once elected, and he deplores the way in which the right to petition was being interpreted as a right to exert constant pressure on elected representatives. The expansion of this "right" was gradual. But an important stage was marked, just at the time of Johnson's active pamphleteering, by the failure in 1771 of the last attempt to prohibit the reporting of parliamentary debates in the press. This failure led to a significant shift in the relations between members and their constituents. Sovereignty became more "circular," not only originating in popular choice but also requiring constant or at least intermittent validation by public opinion.[32] Today, even where there is no formal requirement to this effect, modern legislatures are typically heedful of what "the people" think or are reported to think. Johnson viewed this as a deplorable development, one that threatened to undermine the constitution: the many, who were likely to be foolish, would be able to overrule the few, who were more likely to be wise—hence the hostility, manifest in all four pamphlets, to the influence of popular opinion on legislative deliberation.

As a record of Johnson's political beliefs and opinions, the pamphlets of the 1770s enjoy formidable credentials. They are unquestionably works of his maturity: they were produced in his early sixties, after about thirty years of observation of the working of actual politics. Written over a period of about five years, they belong to nearly the same context and form a coherent body of writing. They deal for the most part directly, not

30. Greene (*YE*, 10:422n8), citing parallels from Addison and Blackstone. Other instances could be added.

31. In the county electorates, the qualification was possession of a 40s. freehold. In the boroughs, it varied considerably, and many voters were not freeholders. See Sir Lewis Namier and John Brooke, *The House of Commons, 1754–1790*, 3 vols. (London, 1964), 1:10–46; and Frank O'Gorman, *Voters, Patrons, and Parties: The Unreformed Electoral System of Hanoverian England, 1734–1832* (Oxford, 1989), 28–58.

32. This change is not easy to date precisely. After the Septennial Act of 1717, parliaments were normally allowed to run nearly to their new legal limit of seven years. But in 1774, Lord North called an early election at what he thought would be a favorable opportunity to obtain popular support. In 1784, George III dissolved Parliament, avowedly to allow "the people" to pass judgment on the Coalition's India Bill, much as a modern prime minister might seek a "mandate" on a policy issue.

through irony or satire, with urgent practical issues, yet they also appeal to general principles. Finally, Johnson himself collected the four pamphlets into a volume, *Political Tracts*, published in 1776. This is the only occasion on which he took the initiative in gathering his shorter pieces. He distributed presentation copies, some to people he did not know especially well, suggesting the importance he attached to the collection as representing his political principles.[33] *Political Tracts* has thus the best claim to be regarded as his political testament.

There are grounds on which this claim might be questioned. Like the earlier pamphlets, they were all published anonymously, as was *Political Tracts* itself. They are all rhetorical, and their arguments are mixed with a good deal of invective, abuse, and polemic. In two of them at least, Johnson was writing at the behest of the ministry.[34] Yet none of these objections undermines their evidential value as expressions of Johnson's opinions. Anonymity remained the norm in political writing in the 1770s, when only a few eccentric pamphleteers signed their works. Johnson makes no attempt, as was often done, to create a persona or a fictive situation that would establish distance between the actual writer and the speaker of the pamphlet. Nor did he try to conceal his authorship, which was recognized immediately on publication and constantly assumed in discussions in the press. That the pamphlets are rhetorical is undeniable, but so were all political pamphlets. That Johnson's rhetoric was passionate and often emotive evinces the conviction with which he wrote. The pamphlets are the work of an angry man who cares deeply about the questions he is addressing—so deeply that he is more concerned with strength of expression than with the probability of persuasion. A self-conscious rhetorician in perfect control of his writing would have written differently: more dispassionately, and with greater attention to the likely means of influencing his opponents. Likewise, although at least two of the pamphlets were commissioned by the ministry, in both cases Johnson wrote too strongly for them.[35] As with the abusive parts of all the pamphlets, this tendency to excess suggests that he was writing primarily from conviction, which happily coincided with his brief.

By collecting these pamphlets into a volume, Johnson invited readers to regard them as an authoritative statement of his political creed. Its leading articles can be briefly summarized. Preeminent is the theoretical and practical need for a strong political authority able and willing to act wisely, even in the face of popular opposition. In

33. Seven such copies are recorded; see J. D. Fleeman, *A Preliminary Handlist of Copies of Books Associated with Dr Samuel Johnson* (Oxford, 1984), 39–40; and *A Bibliography of the Works of Samuel Johnson*, comp. Fleeman, 2 vols. (Oxford, 2000), 2:1269. Wetherell's copy is now in the Samuel Johnson Birthplace Museum at Lichfield. In addition, Johnson gave copies to two Benedictine monks who were visiting London (Johnson to Hester Thrale, June 8, 1776, in *Letters*, 2:343).

34. That *Thoughts on Falkland's Islands* and *Taxation No Tyranny* were commissioned is clear from the submission of their texts to ministerial scrutiny. *The Patriot* was "called for by my political friends" (Johnson to Boswell, November 26, 1774, in *Letters*, 2:155). The genesis of *The False Alarm* is unknown: it too may have been written at the suggestion of political friends.

35. In *Thoughts on Falkland's Islands*, a jibe aimed at George Grenville was suppressed (Johnson to Bennet Langton, March 20, 1771, in *Letters*, 1:356; *YE*, 10:349, 383). The conclusion of *Taxation No Tyranny* was rendered more conciliatory (Johnson to William Strahan, March 1 and 3, 1775, in *Letters*, 2:184–86; *YE*, 10:401–2).

keeping with this belief, Johnson deprecates the participation in politics of the ill informed and the uneducated. He opposes constitutional innovation and dismisses or minimizes the imaginary popular "grievances." He identifies genuine "patriotism" with support for the present establishment and the present ministry. No less striking is his recurrent rhetorical strategy of polarizing political questions as stark moral oppositions between good and bad. He concedes no ground to his opponents and makes no gestures toward compromise or reconciliation. His antagonists are invariably wrong, usually in several ways and from several points of view. His characteristic tone is aggressive, sometimes unnecessarily so. These pamphlets, then, provide no support for the notion that Johnson was in politics a "moderate."[36] Nor was this moral polarizing merely a polemical strategy. Biographical evidence confirms that he genuinely conceived the issues in these terms.

At Oxford in 1776, in conversation with Boswell, and in Johnson's presence, Dr. Nathan Wetherell, Master of University College, averred that "I would have given him a hundred guineas if he would have written a preface to his "Political Tracts," by way of a Discourse on the British Constitution." Boswell added his view that Johnson ought to write "expressly" in support of the constitution in church and state. Johnson was annoyed rather than flattered.[37] His failure to add a preface to *Political Tracts* is readily explicable as an instance of his habitual reluctance to write. In addition, he may well have thought that the tracts themselves already contained a sufficient exposition of his principles. Nevertheless, Wetherell was right to regret the lack of a general account by Johnson of the constitution. In its absence, most accounts of Johnson's politics rely to a degree on inference. There are dangers in this procedure. Fortunately, we possess two sources of constitutional statements uncontaminated by the partisan rhetoric of the political pamphlets: Johnson's sermons, and the law lectures on which he collaborated with Robert Chambers.[38] Neither source is wholly unexceptionable. The sermons were written for others to deliver, and their freestanding generalizations appear such only because we are ignorant of the occasions for which they were written, not because they are really independent of those occasions. Additionally, in the case of the law lectures, Johnson's precise contribution is uncertain. Yet since neither source is likely to contain material with which he disagreed, both can be used, with proper caution, as expressions or at least reflections of his views.

Johnson's political sermons voice the distrust of popular participation in politics that is so notable a feature of the *Tracts*. In Sermon 5, he describes the ideal state as a morally benevolent hierarchy, which would be "powerful without faction." Its governors,

36. Cannon, *Samuel Johnson and the Politics of Hanoverian England*, 7; Nicholas Hudson, *Samuel Johnson and the Making of Modern England* (Cambridge, 2003), 8.

37. *Life*, 2:441 (March 20, 1776).

38. Johnson, *Sermons*, vol. 14 of *YE*, ed. Jean H. Hagstrum and James Gray (1978); and Sir Robert Chambers, *A Course of Lectures on the English Law*, ed. Thomas M. Curley, 2 vols. (Madison, Wis., 1986).

undisturbed by "the turbulence of the people," can pursue "steady" counsels and undertake "vigorous" actions. In such a utopia, "no man would either have false friends, or publick enemies" (*YE*, 14:60–61). This sermon idealizes political subordination and paternalism. In Sermon 7, Johnson observes that periods of despotism tend to alternate with periods of political licentiousness. The present age is characterized by a "spirit of scepticism and captiousness, of suspicion and distrust, a contempt of all authority, and a presumptuous confidence in private judgement." Johnson traces this spirit to the "warm assertion of the right of judging for themselves," a right supposedly beyond question because "God himself gave us a claim to it." Controverting such assertions, Johnson redescribes this supposed "right" as a "privilege." It has been "ill understood" and has caused "very dangerous and pernicious mistakes" (*YE*, 14:75–77). The immediate context is religion, but the explicitly political opening of the sermon suggests that the criticism of "rights" extends to political rights. In Sermon 23, written for a January 30 service, he identifies "envying and strife" as political evils. The allusions in this sermon to popular agitation suggest that it may belong to the same years as the *Tracts*. The civil wars of the 1640s are characterized as "a war of the rabble against their superiours," in which "those who were grown impatient of obedience, endeavoured to obtain the power of commanding." This is more than a historical observation, for "[s]uch evils surely we have too much reason to fear again" (*YE*, 14:247).[39]

Finally, in Sermon 24, Johnson identifies "the great demand" of the people for "the security of property, the confirmation of liberty, and the extension of commerce." All three, he argues, the people of England already possess. There is therefore no justification for popular agitation or for any further devolution of political power. Since all government is "power exerted by few upon many," nations "cannot be governed but by their own consent." The first duty of subjects is therefore "obedience to the laws." This obedience is the effect not of compulsion but of "reverence" for government, founded on a conviction of "the necessity of some coercive power." To preserve "the proper influence of government . . . even the errours and deficiencies of authority must be treated with respect." Government is difficult not only to administer but even to understand, and "where very few have capacity to judge, very few have a right to censure." Subjects have a duty to obey the laws and respect the chief magistrate (*YE*, 14:254, 258–59).

None of these sermons can confidently be assigned to a precise context. But all belong to a period in which the tendency of political discourse was toward a concern for individual rights, in which more extensive political rights were being demanded for a greater proportion of the population, and in which respect for authority was being eroded. In these sermons, as in the pamphlets of the 1770s, Johnson deplores and opposes these trends and seeks to promote an alternative culture of willing obedience

39. Howard D. Weinbrot tentatively assigns Sermon 23 to 1745–46; see "The Thirtieth of January Sermon: Swift, Johnson, Sterne, and the Evolution of Culture," *Eighteenth-Century Life* 34 (2010): 45. As I read the sermon, civil war is presented as a more distant possibility than it would have appeared in 1745–46. I interpret it rather as a warning against popular agitation and therefore incline to place it in the same period as the pamphlets (1769–75).

and subordination, based on a recognition that few members of society are equipped to make sensible political decisions. In *Rambler* 52 (September 15, 1750), Johnson does acknowledge that "the common voice of the multitude uninstructed by precept, and unprejudiced by authority," is "more decisive" than the opinion of the learned. But he limits this popular wisdom to "questions that relate to the heart of man," such as how to comfort the afflicted.[40]

The law lectures that Johnson helped Chambers to compose have the advantage over the sermons in that they can be precisely dated (1767–73), and their context is known. They were intended to instruct prospective lawyers in the principles of the English legal system. They were delivered at Oxford, where their audience was predominantly young men who belonged to, or aspired to join, the social stratum of the gentry.[41] Chambers himself was an example of a young man eager to climb the professional ladder, as in due course he did. Some allowance should certainly be made for this audience. Such lectures, we might predict, would articulate satisfaction with the status quo and would be most unlikely to identify deep flaws in the present constitutional arrangements. Much of what Chambers says about the constitution is indeed conventional and uncontroversial, so that deducing the political philosophy that informs the lectures is not easy. Even so, attention to emphasis and tone, and to the contemporary context, is revealing. Given the prominence in contemporary political discourse of British "liberties" as the hallmark of the constitution, Chambers is restrained in his references to liberties and rights, rarely referring either to Magna Carta or to the Revolution of 1688. In his account, duties take precedence over rights, and the general welfare of society requires the subordination of rights to authority.[42]

Conventionally enough, Chambers locates sovereignty in Parliament, but he privileges the monarchy with regard to the other branches of the legislature, and even to the people, though this privileging is more a matter of respectful tone than substance. Rebellion and civil war he presents as the worst of evils. Only necessity can justify rebellion. But short of the extreme cases in which necessity justifies rebellion, Chambers offers no alternative to obedience. In a dispute with Sir Adam Fergusson, Johnson likewise took a dismissive view of "all this childish jealousy of the power of the crown." In extreme cases, "If a sovereign oppresses his people to a great degree, they will rise and cut off his head."[43] Neither Johnson nor Chambers was an apologist for divine right or a mystical view of kingship. The king's status derives rather from history,

40. *Rambler* 52, in *The Rambler*, vols. 3–5 of *YE*, ed. W. J. Bate and Albrecht B. Strauss (1969), 3:280.

41. By 1700, barristers ranked as esquires, irrespective of their social origins; see Geoffrey Holmes, *Augustan England: Professions, State, and Society, 1680–1730* (London, 1974), 170. This was not true of the lower branch of the law, the attorneys; see Michael Birks, *Gentlemen of the Law* (London, 1960), 188. Those of Chambers's auditors who intended to make the law their profession would all have been aspiring barristers.

42. Chambers, introduction to *A Course of Lectures*, 1:31–32, 41–46.

43. *Life*, 2:170 (March 31, 1772).

and from a convenient legal fiction.[44] For its time, this is a stronger, because more credible, argument than indefeasibility could be: the monarchy is a useful institution, serving a necessary social purpose, a purpose unaffected by the personal character of the monarch. Monarchy is strongly linked to the preservation of social order.

This pragmatic appreciation of monarchy as an institution is entirely compatible with the personal hostility to George II found in *London* and *Marmor Norfolciense.* Since hereditary, personal monarchy has largely disappeared from the modern world, today's readers are likely to view it with scant respect as an outmoded anachronism, and to interpret negative or satiric references to kings as implying antimonarchical views. But such a view is unhistorical. In the eighteenth century, before the establishment of the United States, there was no example of a large state without a monarchy.[45] Even the French revolutionaries at first assumed that they needed a king. Johnson certainly believed that hereditary monarchy was both fundamental to the British constitution and politically useful. Its utility was not affected by the character or behavior of individual monarchs. If a king acted intolerably, he would provoke a rebellion. Such a rebellion would usually end, not in the foundation of a republic, but in the restoration of the monarchy under a different monarch. The British experience from 1640 to 1660 is an example. The Great Rebellion failed to establish a republic, and the Restoration of the monarchy in 1660 was generally welcomed.[46] When Johnson describes the Revolution of 1688 as having "broke our constitution," he probably means that the constitutional settlement went too far in disturbing the hereditary succession, and by making the crown to a degree elective, tipped the balance of power toward the popular element.[47] In 1689, many took this view, having advocated either a regency on behalf of James II, or the succession of his daughter Mary.[48] For pragmatic reasons, neither course was adopted. Instead, by making William and Mary joint sovereigns, the settle-

44. Chambers, *A Course of Lectures*, 1:45–46.

45. Montesquieu argues that republics are necessarily small (*L'esprit des lois*, 8.16, in *Oeuvres complètes*, ed. Roger Caillois [Paris 1949–51], 2:362). Hume disagreed, while acknowledging that such was the "common opinion"; see "The Idea of a Perfect Commonwealth," in *Essays*, ed. Eugene P. Miller, rev. ed. (Indianapolis, 1987), 527–28. Before the publication of Thomas Paine's *Common Sense* (1776), few Americans were opposed to a monarchical element in a mixed government; see Cecelia M. Kenyon, "Republicanism and Radicalism in the American Revolution: An Old-Fashioned Interpretation," *William and Mary Quarterly* 19 (1962): 153–82, esp. 165–68; and Jerrilyn Greene Marston, *King and Congress: the Transfer of Political Legitimacy, 1774–1776* (Princeton, N.J., 1987), 1–63.

46. Not everyone welcomed the Restoration. But in his life of Milton, Johnson asserts that Charles II was restored "with the irresistible approbation of the people" (*YE*, 21:144). In conversation with Boswell, he claimed that the Restoration was greeted with "exuberance of joy"; see *Life*, 2:370 (April 18, 1775). Ronald Hutton accepts the popular rejoicing, of which there are many reports, as genuine; see *The Restoration: A Political and Religious History of England and Wales, 1658–1667* (Oxford, 1985), 125–26, 185. Malcontents prudently kept quiet, and there is no way of estimating their true number.

47. *Life*, 4:170–71 (March 22, 1783). The context is a comment on the opinion, expressed by James Oglethorpe, that "Government is now carried on by corrupt influence, instead of the inherent right in the King." Johnson attributes the loss of "inherent right" to the Revolution.

48. The legal and theological case against the transfer of the crown was formidable: see G. L. Cherry, "The Legal and Philosophical Position of the Jacobites, 1688–1689," *Journal of Modern History* 22 (1950): 309–21; and Mark Goldie, "The Political Thought of the Anglican Revolution," in *The Revolutions of 1688*, ed. Robert Beddard (Oxford, 1991), 102–36.

ment weakened the hereditary principle and therefore the authority of the crown. Viewed in this context, Johnson's severe attacks on George II can be seen as reflecting a belief that George's failure to embody the monarchical ideal was reducing the respect due to monarchy as an institution.

A long passage in *Marmor Norfolciense* does appear to satirize kings in general for their indifference to the interests of posterity. This "comprehensive sarcasm," together with other remarks, has been alleged to show that Johnson "was by no means the devotee of monarchism that legend makes him out to be."[49] That *Marmor* treats George II—and by extension, other "foreign" kings such as William III—with offensive scurrility, is true. Yet this need not imply a criticism of monarchy as an institution.[50] In *Marmor*, the prime example of the disregard of kings for posterity is their annual demands for money from Parliament in "gracious speeches delivered from the throne, and received with the highest gratitude and satisfaction by both Houses of Parliament." Yet the object of the satire here is not the king, but the absurd ritual with which sessions of Parliament were opened. The "gracious speech" was known to be the composition of the ministry, and to reflect ministerial rather than royal policy. The debates in the two houses on an address of thanks in reply to the speech from the throne were the first tests of strength between ministry and opposition. A page or so later, the speaker notes how quickly politicians "by a kind of contagion, catch the regal spirit of neglecting futurity." What cures the disease is often "the frown of a prince, and the loss of a pension," which are wonderfully effective "to abstract men's thoughts from the present time, and fill them with zeal for the liberty and welfare of ages to come" (*YE*, 10:31–32). This observation is the more remarkable, as the speaker for a moment steps outside the standard rhetoric of the opposition to undercut the pretenses of opposition politicians to "patriotism." The passage as a whole satirizes the cant and corruption of the political system. It is not an attack on monarchy as an institution.

Johnson's critical comments on kings should not be allowed to occlude his belief in the constitutional value of monarchy. When Oliver Goldsmith controverted the maxim that "the King can do no wrong," Johnson retorted that "in our constitution, according to its true principles, the King is the head; he is supreme; he is above every thing, and there is no power by which he can be tried."[51] These remarks have

49. Greene, *YE*, 10:32n8. Strangely, despite his habitual denigration of the value of Boswell's evidence, Greene cites the index to Boswell's *Life* for instances of Johnson's low opinion of kings. But these obiter dicta, if fairly examined, are by no means uniformly unfavorable. Some of the most virulent, such as the characterization of William III as "one of the most worthless scoundrels that ever existed" (*Life*, 2:342), are momentary ebulliences of passion, not to be taken seriously as historical or political judgments.

50. In *London*, contempt for George II is balanced with praise for four earlier English monarchs, invoked to provide a contrasting ideal.

51. This statement may appear inconsistent with the retort to Fergusson, that a grievously oppressed people will rise and cut off the king's head. To Goldsmith, Johnson was speaking of constitutional procedures. To Fergusson, he was acknowledging a people's last (admittedly unconstitutional) resort. Edmund Burke would later elaborate this distinction between a constitutional remedy and a rebellion. Burke denies that there is any constitutional procedure to try the king but reluctantly acknowledges the case of armed rebellion, which he calls "an extraordinary question of state, and wholly out of the law" and "the very last resource of the thinking and the good" (*Reflections on the Revolution in France* [1790], ed. J. C. D. Clark [Stanford, Calif., 2001], 180–81).

important implications for Johnson's interpretation of the events of 1649 and 1688–89. To prevent the tyranny or despotism of a monarch above the law, the constitution provides that redress may be had against those who advised or executed illegal or improper actions. "Political institutions," Johnson generalizes, "are formed upon the consideration of what will most frequently tend to the good of the whole, although now and then exceptions may occur."[52] Hereditary monarchy is such an institution: it provides stability and avoids the evils of disputed successions. In the pejorative sense of the word, Johnson was no "devotee" of monarchy. His reverence for monarchy was based on a rational belief in its utility as an institution, and especially in its function as the foundation of social order and political stability.[53]

Much of what Chambers argues, especially with regard to the monarchy, reflects the theory rather than the contemporary practice of the constitution. Parliament, politicians, and public opinion had all achieved considerably greater importance and influence than would be deduced from his account, in which the monarchy appears the central political institution. In Walter Bagehot's distinction, Chambers emphasizes the "dignified" rather than the "efficient" parts of the constitution.[54] In the same way, Johnson's sermons describe what politics ought to be like, rather than their practical operation. Yet this consideration enhances the value of the lectures and sermons as repositories of his political thinking, unconstrained by the need to adjust to recent unwelcome developments that had in practice weakened the monarchy as an institution and that had elevated rights above duties.

The topical pamphlets collected in *Political Tracts*, supported by the general principles expressed in the sermons and law lectures, provide a consistent and coherent body of political opinions tending, in Johnson's own formulation, to "preserve order and support Monarchy." Johnson was no enemy to "liberty," properly defined. But he rejected claims that the established "liberties" were in any danger, and he believed that the current threat to constitutional stability came from innovations mischievously proposed as affirmations or extensions of these "liberties." These pamphlets have the best title to be regarded as representing his mature opinions. They do not, to be sure, represent the whole of his political thinking. They tell us, for example, more about his aversions than his predilections, and they need to be placed in larger political and biographical contexts than I have been able to develop in this essay. Nevertheless, for the reasons here adumbrated, they, rather than the squibs of the 1730s, deserve to be regarded as embodying the main tenets of his political thought.

I am grateful to Howard Weinbrot for his helpful comments on early drafts of this essay, and to Robert DeMaria Jr. for several valuable suggestions.

52. *Life*, 1:423–24 (July 6, 1763). Even Greene acknowledges that Johnson regarded kings as "necessary"; see *Politics of Samuel Johnson*, 309n24.

53. Nicholas Hudson argues that "the need to maintain reverence for kingship represents a central tenet in his political attitudes"; see "Johnson and Revolution," *Harvard Library Bulletin* 20 (2009): 9–28 at 13.

54. Walter Bagehot, *The English Constitution* (1867), in vol. 5 of *Collected Works*, ed. Norman St. John-Stevas (London, 1974), 206.

Three Contexts for Reading Johnson's Parliamentary Debates

Thomas Kaminski

JOHNSON WROTE THE PARLIAMENTARY DEBATES in the *Gentleman's Magazine* from July 1741 to March 1744. These were years of considerable political and historical turmoil. In 1739 the clamors of the nation's merchants and the incessant attacks of the "Patriot" opposition had forced Sir Robert Walpole to go to war with Spain over that nation's attempts to restrict British trade to the West Indies. But Walpole was no war minister, and things had gone badly. During Johnson's tenure as a debate writer, a British army would suffer a humiliating defeat at Cartagena in Spanish America. The nation would be thrust into a second war—this time on the Continent—as the death of the Holy Roman Emperor Charles VI precipitated the War of the Austrian Succession. Here, too, the Walpole ministry would prove itself indecisive or incompetent. As a result, Walpole would fall from power and his old enemies seek to prosecute him for corruption—and fail in their attempts. Lord Carteret, who had been among Walpole's fiercest opponents, would succeed him as the dominant figure in the new administration, only to find himself, within a year, as hated as his predecessor.

All of these events were of immediate interest to Parliament, and all occupied Johnson's attention as the reporter of the debates. But the debates themselves are complex documents. They provide accounts of real events, but accounts based on information of uncertain reliability and tricked out in rhetorical finery that Johnson thought suitable to the dignity of a national legislature. For modern readers, who generally lack any context for reading Johnson's debates, they are likely to be reduced to a series of rhetorical flourishes—one speaker's passionate attack on a supposedly corrupt ministry, another's dignified defense of the government's programs, and so forth. The purpose of this essay is to provide three contexts for reading Johnson's debates. The first section of the essay focuses on their immediate parliamentary context and considers the accuracy of the debates as historical documents. The second compares Johnson's debates with the rival series being published concurrently in the *London Magazine*. The third considers the debates in terms of the broader historical and political background. My goals in all three portions of this essay, though, are limited: I shall not attempt to show what Johnson has to teach us about Parliament or journalism or history, but what some knowledge of these matters can tell us about how to read Johnson's debates.

I shall begin with the debates' authenticity, the extent to which Johnson captured the actions, the arguments, and the expressions of those who spoke on the floor of the Lords or the Commons. This matter has long been obscured by Johnson's own reflections on the project, for a mere few days before his death, he spoke disparagingly of the debates to John Nichols: "He said, that the Parliamentary Debates were the only part of his writings which then gave him any compunction: but that at the time he wrote them, he had no conception he was imposing upon the world, though they were frequently written from very slender materials, and often from none at all,—the mere coinage of his own imagination."[1] If we take Johnson at his word, we should expect little correspondence between the reports of the debates in the magazine and the fragmentary historical record of the actual events, but that is not the case. The debates have a better grounding in fact than Johnson's rigorous adherence to truth or the anxiety arising from his approaching death allowed him to admit. Sir John Hawkins, who is perhaps the best informed of Johnson's biographers on the subject, tells us that Edward Cave, the publisher of the *Gentleman's Magazine*, attended the debates with some associates, took notes when possible, and then adjourned to a tavern where the small group of conspirators attempted to reconstruct what they had seen and heard, especially the names and the order of the speakers, the arguments made by each, and perhaps even some memorable phrases.[2] At the time it was illegal to report parliamentary information of any sort, so Cave and his associates were forced to act with discretion. Taking notes, for instance, was not permitted in the gallery of either House. Afterward Cave provided the materials he had assembled to his hired author, first William Guthrie, then Johnson, and finally John Hawkesworth. When we compare Johnson's debates with eyewitness accounts that have survived, we find that Cave's information was sketchy in some instances, but surprisingly complete in others.

The question of the debates' accuracy and authenticity has in fact received significant scholarly attention. Benjamin Hoover devoted nearly half of his book *Samuel Johnson's Parliamentary Reporting* to an analysis of the factual basis for the debates, and I have offered a briefer treatment in the introduction to the new edition of the *Debates* in the *Yale Edition* of Johnson's works.[3] Rather than reproduce that

1. Nichols's conversation with Johnson is quoted in *Boswell's Life of Samuel Johnson, Together with Boswell's Journal of a Tour to the Hebrides and Johnson's Diary of a Journey into North Wales*, ed. George Birkbeck Hill, rev. L. F. Powell, 6 vols. (Oxford, 1934–50), 4:408–9 (hereafter cited as *Life*).

2. Sir John Hawkins, *Life of Samuel Johnson, LL.D.*, 2nd ed. (London, 1787), 94–96.

3. See Benjamin B. Hoover, *Samuel Johnson's Parliamentary Reporting* (Berkeley, Calif., 1953), 55–130; and Johnson, *Debates in Parliament*, vols. 11–13 of *The Yale Edition of the Works of Samuel Johnson* (hereafter cited as *Debates*), ed. Thomas Kaminski, Benjamin B. Hoover, and O M Brack Jr. (New Haven, Conn., 2012), 11:xxvii–xxxii. Text references are to this edition.

work here, let me summarize the basic findings but then elaborate on several aspects of Johnson's practice.

First, there is no evidence that Johnson ever wrote a debate without significant information provided by Cave. For a number of debates we have collateral materials in the form of notes, diaries, and letters written by persons who attended or participated in the debates. The most important and extensive of these are Bishop Thomas Secker's notes. As bishop of Oxford, Secker sat in the Lords, and his record of the debates offers a substantial and detailed account of who spoke and what each person said. When Johnson's debates are compared with Secker's notes, we often find extensive overlaps between the two. Johnson's accounts generally capture only a portion of the material Secker preserved, but they often include the most important arguments and sometimes echo individual phrases. Similarly, Secker often lists more speakers than Johnson can accommodate, but Johnson usually places his selected speakers in the proper order. At times, though, a comparison with Secker reveals the dearth of Johnson's information. Some of his speeches clearly have no basis in fact, and others are liable to elaborate an idea or argument differently from what we find in the bishop's record. But for a debate like that on the indemnity bill, an attempt to indemnify from prosecution anyone who would give evidence against Walpole after his fall, it is clear that Johnson worked from a remarkable amount of reliable information. In a debate that fills seventy-five pages in the *Yale Edition*, we find more than fifty passages where Johnson's text echoes some idea, argument, or phrase preserved in Secker's notes and attributes that material to the appropriate speaker. In Lord Hervey's speech alone, there are thirteen correspondences in eight pages of text.[4] Although the rhetoric throughout is wholly Johnson's, the debate itself is firmly anchored in the events and the arguments of the day.

The debates are not all as faithful as that on the indemnity bill, but in every case for which we have independent historical records, those records confirm various aspects of Johnson's account. From this it seems safe to conclude that none of the debates was in fact the mere coinage of his imagination; he always worked from notes. By examining those debates for which we have substantial information, we can also draw some inferences about his overall practice.

First, Johnson does not appear to make up examples or tell anecdotes on his own authority. In a speech in support of the indemnity bill, for example, Johnson has the Duke of Argyll tell of an attempt by his political enemies to prosecute him using a false witness who had been bribed and granted immunity for his own previous crimes.

4. In Johnson's debates, the speakers appeared in "Lilliputian" disguise, with Lord Hervey actually styled the Hurgo Heryef. Because it was illegal to publish debates, each magazine adopted a ruse to avoid prosecution. The *London Magazine* (hereafter cited as *LM*) claimed that its reports were merely the debates of a Political Club and hid the identity of its speakers behind classical names. Cave, on the other hand, loosely adapted the terminology of *Gulliver's Travels*, with Britain renamed "Lilliput" and France, "Blefuscu." Other names were anagrams or travesties, so that Walpole became "Walelop" and Chesterfield "Castroflet." Since the Lilliputian disguise is not on the whole relevant to this essay, I employ the speakers' real names throughout.

The anecdote corresponds closely with the duke's own story as Secker recorded it (*Debates*, 12:957–58, 958n9). In the debate on the spirituous liquors bill—the attempt to replace a high-but-unenforceable tax on gin with a lower tax that could be collected more efficiently—Johnson's Chesterfield argues against the new law on the grounds that the lower levy will encourage rather than discourage drunkenness. When the law's proponents retort that the amount of the tax could be raised over time, resulting in a gradual decrease in the consumption of gin, Chesterfield tells the story of a certain Webb, known for his abstemious regimen, who had counseled a friend to forgo wine. The friend replied that he would attempt to do so by degrees: "By degrees, says [Webb] with indignation, if you should unhappily fall into the fire, would you caution your servants not to pull you out but by degrees?" In a truncated note Secker verifies the story: "It is said, raise it by degrees. If you should fall into the fire, would you bid your servant pull you out by degrees?" (*Debates*, 13:1410 and n4).[5] Whenever we encounter an anecdote or illustrative tale of this kind, if collateral evidence is available, we can expect to find the anecdote in that material. Johnson did not invent such stories or supply them from his own experience.

The same is true of some of the more surprising, or less compelling, arguments that appear in the debates. In a speech against the indemnity bill, Lord Hervey suggests that criminals of all sorts will abuse the offer of immunity: "housebreakers, highwaymen, and pickpockets, will come up in crouds to the bar, charge the Earl of [Orford] as their accomplice, and plead this bill as a security against all enquiry."[6] He then offers an example:

> A man whom the consciousness of murder has for some time kept in continual terrors, may clear himself for ever, by alleging, that he was commissioned by the [Earl of Orford], to engage, with any certain sum, the vote or interest of the murdered person; that he took the opportunity of a solitary place to offer him the bribe, . . . but that finding him obstinate and perverse, filled with prejudices against a wise and just administration, . . . he could no longer restrain the ardour of his loyalty, but thought it proper to remove from the world a man so much inclined to spread sedition among the people, and that therefore finding the place convenient, he suddenly rush'd upon him, and cut his throat.

Here, if anywhere, Johnson might appear to be indulging his imagination: he had run out of sense, and so Lord Hervey was made to talk nonsense. But Secker quickly dispels that notion. He records the following from Hervey's speech: "If any person can interweave a confession of his own crime with an accusation of the person mentioned in the Bill, he is safe, provided any question leads at all to such a confession. So that to confess

5. Although Secker does not mention Webb, the account in the *LM* confirms this part of the story.

6. Here and in all subsequent quotations, the Lilliputian terms are replaced with their proper names set in brackets.

his own guilt would be all a man would aim at in his answer. 'Did lord Orford give 5 guineas at such an election?' 'Yes, for I saw the man take it, and I murdered him'" (*Debates*, 12:944–45, 945n7). The argument is undoubtedly Hervey's, with some elaboration by Johnson. This is typical: the more eccentric or surprising the argument, the more likely we are to find it in the collateral records. In debates for which we have no such records, then, we should be wary of attributing such arguments to Johnson. In the debate on the seamen's bill (January 27 to March 23, 1741), William Pulteney suggests that charity-school boys could provide a permanent supply of future seamen for the navy if they were sent to sea at an early age. Nowhere does Johnson force proposals of this sort on his speakers. We should presume the plan to be Pulteney's rather than Johnson's (*Debates*, 11:274–75, 275n7).[7]

Finally, Johnson does not use Latin phrases or cite classical examples without some sanction from the speakers themselves. In a speech opposing the indemnity bill, Johnson's Carteret uses three Latin phrases: before a man can be accused, he asserts, there must be "a *corpus delicti*, a crime really and visibly committed" (12:925); speaking of what we would call "due process," he notes that "*rectum recte, legitimum legitime faciendum*"—that is, right must be done properly and the lawful lawfully (12:931); and finally, he complains that the Commons were administering oaths to witnesses "*coram non judice*," before a magistrate who lacked proper authority (12:932). Secker records each of these phrases in Carteret's speech, as well as a subsequent exchange between Chesterfield and Lord Chancellor Hardwicke, where the former asserts that even if there is no *corpus delicti* in Walpole's case, there is *corpus suspicionis* (12:973), to which the great lawyer Hardwicke replies, "*Corpus suspicionis* is a new term, it is the body of a shadow: that is the foundation of the Bill" (12:975n1). Johnson captures not only the exchange between Chesterfield and Hardwicke, but Hardwicke's precise formulation in his dismissal: "as to the words *corpus suspicionis*, I do not comprehend what they mean: it is an expression indeed which I never before heard, and can signify, in my apprehension, nothing more than the *body of a shadow*, the substance of something which is itself nothing" (12:975).

And so what are we to think when Carteret, in the debate on spirituous liquors, is made to assert that "luxury is . . . *ad modum possidentis*, of different kinds, in proportion to different conditions of life, and one man may very decently enjoy those delicacies or pleasures to which it would be foolish and criminal in another to aspire" (13:1350)? Secker offers only a brief record of Carteret's speech; he makes no mention of luxury and does not record the Latin phrase. But we must nevertheless suspect that Carteret rather than Johnson was responsible for the Latin. The phrase itself, which translates "according to one's means," echoes a passage from Tacitus's *Annals* where a senator, Gallus Asinius, argues against a sumptuary law on the grounds that luxury

7. The proposal had appeared in a contemporary pamphlet, *An Essay on Ways and Means for . . . Increasing the Number of Sailors in Great-Britain* (London, 1741), 35. It seems much more likely that Pulteney would have been aware of such a pamphlet, which professed on its title page to be "humbly offered to the consideration of Parliament," than that Johnson should be.

and parsimony are relative to the means of the individual.[8] Carteret himself was not shy of displaying his learning, and he undoubtedly knew his Tacitus. In 1730 Constantia Grierson had dedicated her edition of Tacitus to him, noting that she had undertaken the work at his suggestion and carried it out under his guidance and protection ("tuis auspiciis").[9] And within a year of the debate on spirituous liquors, in a debate not reported by Johnson (December 9, 1743), Carteret complained of the false rumors being spread among the British and Hanoverian troops on the Continent, illustrating his point with a story from the *Annals* of a soldier whose lies stoked a mutiny.[10] Everything here suggests that the original echo was Carteret's and that Johnson merely reported what Cave's spies had carried away from the debate.[11]

This is not to suggest that all of Johnson's speeches merely rephrase what was actually said in Parliament. He was under pressure to fill pages in the magazine, and when Cave's notes failed him, his imagination did not. In such cases he seems to have picked up a general topic—for instance, whether the "voice of the people" is to be followed or disregarded by the legislature—and expounded it for paragraphs, if not pages. He might then allow another speaker to challenge the earlier arguments. In some cases, the topic had emerged somewhere in the debate itself, but not always.[12]

At times Johnson used his authorial control to shape the debate. A good example occurs in the Commons debate on the motion requesting that the king "remove Sir Robert Walpole from his presence and councils for ever" (February 13, 1741). An

8. The passage reads, "Neque in familia et argento quaeque ad usum parentur nimium aliquid aut modicum nisi ex fortuna possidentis" (*Annals*, 2.33). The Loeb edition translates it as follows: "In slaves or plate or anything procured for use there was neither excess nor moderation except with reference to the means of the owner" (Tacitus, *Annals*, books 1–3, trans. John Jackson [London, 1931], 431).

9. *C. Cornelii Taciti Opera Quae Extant*, 3 vols. (Dublin, 1730), 1:i–ii. The work had been undertaken while Carteret was Lord Lieutenant of Ireland.

10. See the excerpts from Philip Yorke's parliamentary journal in *Cobbett's Parliamentary History of England*, vols. 12 and 13 (London, 1812), 13:276 (hereafter cited as *PH*). The reference was apparently to *Annals*, 1.22–23.

11. That Secker failed to record the remark is no sure indication that it was inauthentic, for his notes are clearly incomplete. He failed to record, for instance, a classical allusion made by Lord Chancellor Hardwicke in the Lords debate on the state of the army (December 9, 1740). The Duke of Argyll, a hero of the War of the Spanish Succession, had attacked Walpole for treating commissions in the army as a form of political patronage. In Johnson's debate, Hardwicke, a lawyer by training, wishes to dispute some of Argyll's points but fears to expose himself "to the censure of having harangued upon war in the presence of Hannibal." He is clearly recalling the story of Phormio, a Peripatetic philosopher at the court of Antiochus who had lectured foolishly on war with Hannibal in the audience. The tale is recounted by Cicero in *De oratore*, 2.75. Although Secker missed the allusion, another spectator of the debate did not. The French ambassador in London, recounting the debate in a letter to his superiors in Paris, preserves Hardwicke's concession that he was speaking "*coram Hannibale*"—that is, in Hannibal's presence. Johnson's statement is undoubtedly authentic, though no trace of it is to be found in Secker. See *Debates*, 11:99 and n1.

12. For a brief discourse on the importance of heeding the voice of the people, see *Debates*, 11:427–29. The argument, attributed to the Duke of Argyll, is not found in Secker's notes to his speech, but the idea may have been suggested by several other opposition speakers who point out the popular discontent with Walpole's policies.

identical motion had been offered in the Lords on the same day, and Johnson wrote a long account of the Lords debate for the July issue of the magazine. Since the two debates had covered the same matters, the report of the Commons debate was put off for another eighteen months, not appearing until February 1743. Overall, this debate contains numerous historically accurate elements. It records the failed effort of the opposition to force Walpole to leave the House while his conduct in office was discussed, and it includes speeches against the motion by Edward Harley and Lord Cornbury, two Tories who abandoned the opposition cause on the grounds that the motion was inherently unjust. But in the body of the debate, Johnson availed himself of a shortcut: he devoted more than half the debate to two grand speeches, one of indictment by Samuel Sandys, and one of defense by Stephen Fox. Sandys, we know, began the debate with a long speech of accusation, but Fox appears merely to have made a few miscellaneous remarks on the injustice of the proceedings.[13] Johnson, though, has Fox provide a complete defense of Walpole's policies, both foreign and domestic, for the previous twenty years (*Debates*, 12:520–48). It seems clear that Johnson wished to balance the debate and clarify the issues: he already had Sandys's indictment, but he needed a defense. This he wrote himself and put in Fox's mouth. Many of the arguments he includes were undoubtedly employed by Walpole's supporters, but Fox did not utter them. The speech is almost certainly a fiction, but the extent to which it misrepresents what was said in the Commons that day is a more difficult matter.

The second context is also complicated by Johnson's statement that the debates were largely the product of his imagination. This has led some to assume that the competing series in the *London Magazine* must be more authentic, for the author of those debates, whoever he may have been, must certainly have relied more closely than Johnson on his source material.[14] This assumption, as I now wish to argue, is largely without merit.

13. We possess an important eyewitness account of this debate by Thomas Tower, a Whig backbencher: see I. G. Doolittle, "A First-hand Account of the Commons Debate on the Removal of Sir Robert Walpole, 13 February 1741," *Bulletin of the Institute of Historical Research* 53 (1980): 125–40. For Sandys's speech, see pp. 128–31; for Fox's, p. 134.

14. A. S. Turberville, for instance, asserted that when one is forced to choose between the two series, "the *London* should always be preferred to the *Gentleman's Magazine*": *The House of Lords in the XVIIIth Century* (Oxford, 1927), 517. The author of the debates in the *LM* is sometimes said to be Thomas Gordon, the translator of Tacitus. Gordon was named by John Wright in the preface to volume 9 of *PH* (1811), [ii], but I can find no earlier evidence to support this claim. Although Gordon had been an active political essayist during the 1720s, attacking the Walpole administration in *Cato's Letters* (published in the *London Journal*, 1720–23), he was soon bought off by Walpole with the job of first commissioner of the wine licenses; see *ODNB*, s.v. "Gordon, Thomas (d. 1750)" by Leslie Stephen, rev. Emma Major, last modified January 2008, http://www.oxforddnb.com/view/article/11083. At this point he devoted himself to translation. He even dedicated his Tacitus (1728) to Walpole. He also married a wealthy widow, which made it unnecessary for him to write for bread. In these circumstances, it seems highly unlikely that Gordon would have involved himself in the illegal and burdensome activity of reporting debates.

The two sets of debates differ somewhat in their overall character. The series in the *London Magazine* tends to emphasize historical background; Johnson provides general arguments. In reading the *London Magazine* debates, one is often impressed by the large amount of information they contain: in the debate on the mutiny bill, one learns the history of quartering and victualling the home forces in Britain since the reign of William III; and in various attacks on Walpole's foreign policy, one is treated to a veritable history of European politics for the preceding two decades. The accumulation of facts often gives these debates an air of authority that Johnson's more rhetorical efforts can seem to lack. But an abundance of historical detail in a published debate is no guarantee that the actual participants presented that information in support of their arguments, and when we compare debates from both series with authentic records, we find that Johnson's generalities can sometimes be more authentic than the "facts" that fill the rival version. Consider the following example.

On March 9, 1742, a month after Walpole's fall, James Hamilton, Viscount Limerick, moved in the Commons that a "committee be appointed to enquire into the conduct of affairs at home and abroad during the last twenty years" (*Debates*, 12:847). But Walpole's supporters had come out in force, and the motion was defeated by two votes. The new ministry, however, knew that it could not let the matter drop without losing public support, and so two weeks later, on March 23, Limerick moved another inquiry, this one to focus on Walpole's management of the Treasury, and for only the last ten years. The second motion was successful and a committee of inquiry established.

These attempts by the Commons to investigate Walpole aroused great public interest, and both magazines carried versions of both debates. The *London Magazine* ran its reports from December 1742 to January 1743, with the *Gentleman's* offering its versions several months later, beginning in May. Limerick, though, was disdainful of what he read in the magazines, and in September he published his own account of what he had said. A prefatory letter asserted that "there has never yet been any authentic Copies published of the two inclosed Speeches," adding in a contemptuous footnote, "Except such as are made by Scribblers, hired by the Publishers of *Magazines* at so much *per* Sheet; that no one Member in the House can charge his Memory with a single Sentence of those palmed Speeches, and which may as properly be father'd upon *Chinese* as *British* Speakers."[15] Limerick's pamphlet, then, gives us a direct means of testing the accuracy of the magazine debates.

If we start with the *London Magazine*, we find that Limerick's first speech, from the debate of March 9, 1742, is typical of that series. After some opening remarks on the Commons' duty to tell the king of the people's discontent and a brief digression on Walpole's "corrupt Influence, both at Elections and in Parliament," this "Limerick" takes us through a long and detailed survey of Walpole's errors and misdeeds, including the South Sea Scheme, the misuse of Civil List funds, the Treaty of Hanover (1725),

15. *Two Speeches on the Late Famous Motion, By the Right Honourable the Lord L—k* (London, 1743), 2, hereafter cited in text as *Two Speeches*. The folio pamphlet was advertised for sale in the *Daily Advertiser* for September 7, 1743.

the hiring of foreign troops in the 1720s without sufficient cause, the Treaty of Seville (1729), the excise scheme, the dismissal of officers from their places for opposing the excise, the tepid response to Spanish attacks on British merchants in the West Indies, and the Convention of the Pardo (1739). The Civil List alone is mentioned nine times, and we are treated to a brief but confusing relation of the increases in the appropriations for the Civil List between 1720 and 1727.[16]

There is, I suspect, nothing in this speech that the real Lord Limerick did not agree with, but the speech that he published as his own is, nevertheless, very different. It is much more general and considerably shorter, only one-quarter the length of the *London Magazine* speech. As in the magazine, Limerick is greatly concerned with the corruption of the Commons, but he first reflects on governmental finance: "It is owing to this [that is, the Commons' subservience to Walpole], that during a long and profound Peace, our Taxes have not been *diminish'd*, nor our Debts *paid*." His reflections on Walpole's foreign policy through the 1720s and 1730s are brief and general: "We plunged ourselves into inconsistent Treaties, and contradictory Engagements, till we had negociated away our most important Interests." He only descends to specifics when criticizing the conduct of the war with Spain, begun in 1739, and the failure of the ministry to support Britain's ally, Austria, in the great war overspreading the Continent, the War of the Austrian Succession: "We have had the Honour," he tells us with a touch of irony, "to compleat the Ruin of the House of *Austria*, and to raise the House of *Bourbon* to be Masters of the Fate of *Europe*" (*Two Speeches*, 4). There is no mention of the Civil List, no enumeration of treaties, no deploring the excise. Insofar as the *London Magazine* account talks about corruption, it cannot help but echo Limerick's main concern, but once it descends to particulars, it has nothing in common with the speech that Limerick published.

Johnson's speech, on the other hand, captures a number of the general assertions we find in Limerick's original. Here, too, the heavy costs of an extended peace are lamented: "But peace has in this nation by the wonderful artifices of our ministers been the parent of poverty and misery. . . . We have been so far from seeing any part of our taxes remitted, that we have been loaded with more rigorous exactions to support the expences of peace, than were found necessary to defray the charges of a war." Treaties, we are told, "have been concluded without any regard to the interest of [Great Britain]." Unlike the authentic speech, Johnson does not single out the disastrous war policies of recent years, but he echoes nevertheless the contrast between the relative strengths of the Bourbon and Austrian dynasties: "If we survey the condition of foreign nations, we shall find, that the power, and dominions of the family of [Bourbon] . . . have been daily encreased. We shall find, that they have encreased by the declension of the House of [Austria], which treaties and our interest engage us to support" (*Debates*, 12:846–47). Johnson's report is by no means a paraphrase of Limerick's published text, but it much more closely approximates the overall character of his speech than does the rival version in the *London Magazine*.

16. *LM* 11 (1742): 587–91 at 587; in *PH*, 12:448–56.

With respect to Limerick's second speech (March 23, 1743), the *London Magazine* dropped its litany of Walpole's errors and abuses, providing a broader, less detailed accusation. This report seems marginally more accurate than Johnson's, for it directly echoes a few statements found in the printed speech, even though it continues to elaborate these with material not to be found in the original.[17] Johnson's version seems to have been written from very limited information. He suggests some of Limerick's main points, especially his concern for the constitution, but he provides no strong parallels or clear verbal echoes. There exists nonetheless one extended parallel between Limerick's published speech and Johnson's debate, though it does not occur where one would expect.

Toward the end of the published speech, Limerick defends the policy of appointing a "secret committee" to investigate political malfeasance:

> I have heard a Secret Committee treated as the most terrible Thing in Nature; but surely, Sir, Gentlemen either don't know, or don't consider what it is they seem so much to fear. Secret Committees are not to *judge*, they are not even to *accuse*; they are only to *search* and *enquire* after Facts, they are to *collect* and *sort* them, and lay them before the House. To *judge* is the Province of the *Lords*, to *accuse* belongs to the *Commons*; and diligently to *search* and *enquire* is the Business and Duty of a *Committee*. This is the mighty Power, this is the dreadful Object; dreadful indeed it may be to the *Guilty*, but to the Guilty *only*. (*Two Speeches*, 8)

In Johnson's debate we find these ideas elaborated not under Limerick's name but in the seconding speech attributed to Sir John St. Aubyn:

> But in every consideration of this kind, great terrors have been raised at the mention of a secret committee. It is called a most dangerous delegation; and to intimidate the assertors of justice it is represented so formidable, as to be able to controul that very body from which it derives its powers; and foreign examples are produced, no ways similar, under different constitutions, to support this allegation. It has been called a committee of accusation, tryal and judgment.
>
> But, Sir, it is a constitutional appointment, always practised when high offenders are to be called to justice.... It is a committee of enquiry which is only to proceed no farther than the extent of their commission, revocable at your pleasure. It is only to collect and digest the materials of evidence, to produce facts supported by such evidence, facts afterwards to be canvass'd, to undergo a strict examination in the House, before you will found upon them a vote of accusation.
>
> You yourselves are but accusers, and your accusation must be carried to an higher assembly for tryal and judgment. (*Debates*, 12:892)

17. *LM* 11 (1742): 655–57; in *PH*, 12:532–36.

The parallels are numerous and clear. It appears that Johnson was given accurate information about what was said, but a faulty indication of who said it. It is also possible that Johnson felt that this point was not appropriate for a speech moving the creation of a secret committee, and so he relegated it to the seconder, who might more properly attempt to sweep away potential objections. In such matters we are in the dark.

Perhaps the most important lesson to be learned from comparisons of the competing series is that both magazines were subject to the same limitations in compiling information, and both resorted to fictional representations when that material failed. For example, Horace Walpole's maiden speech in the Commons took place on March 23, 1742, in the debate that I have just been discussing. The next day he sent Horace Mann a "copy" of what he said. Johnson did not report the speech, but the *London Magazine* did, and some years later, while preparing his letters for publication, Walpole added the following note to the copy of his speech: "There is a fictitious speech printed for this in several Magazines of that time, but which does not contain one sentence of the true one."[18] A comparison of the two versions bears out his claim. The speech in the magazine was the mere coinage of its author's imagination, and that author was not Johnson.

Johnson's debates are often more accurate in recording who spoke in a debate and what he said, for the *London Magazine* usually presented fewer speeches overall.[19] This practice, as one might expect, frequently led to misattributed arguments, as significant statements made by those whose speeches had been left out were simply put into the mouths of others. Since its debates took this digested form, the *London Magazine* sometimes paid little attention to the proper order of the speakers—a failing that, in any attempt to give a realistic account of what had happened on the floor of the House, could be a matter of some significance. For example, in the *London Magazine*'s version of the debate on the indemnity bill, Hardwicke speaks before Chesterfield, yet we learn from Secker that Hardwicke not only followed Chesterfield but responded to his arguments.[20] Johnson gets the order of the speakers right and includes some of the apposite responses. (The passage quoted above, where Hardwicke dismisses the term *corpus suspicionis*, is the most important example.) Cave, of course, was aware of his rival's shortcomings and quick to point them out to his readers. In the prefatory material to Johnson's account of the indemnity-bill debate, he intruded a paragraph listing the errors in the competing version.[21] Cave in fact had good reason to boast that his magazine's account had come much closer to the truth.

18. For Walpole's speech, see *Horace Walpole's Correspondence with Sir Horace Mann*, ed. W. S. Lewis, Warren Hunting Smith, and George L. Lam, in *The Yale Edition of the Correspondence of Horace Walpole*, ed. W. S. Lewis, 48 vols. (New Haven, Conn., 1937–83), 17:376–77. This edition fails to print Walpole's note, which first appeared in *Letters of Horace Walpole . . . to Sir Horace Mann*, ed. George Agar Ellis, Baron Dover, 3 vols. (London, 1833), 1:136.

19. This portion of the essay is indebted to Benjamin Hoover's comparison of Johnson's debates with both the *LM* debates and Bishop Secker's notes; see *Samuel Johnson's Parliamentary Reporting*, 58–123, esp. 111–20.

20. *LM* 11 (1742): 368, 375; *PH*, 12:650–53.

21. Cave there criticized the *LM* for leaving out speakers, confusing their order, and putting "the Words of one Statesman in the Mouth of another," which, he said, "is with these People a common

In some debates, though, especially when the speakers turn to historical matters or international politics, the writer for the *London Magazine* shows a firmer grasp of the issues. For example, by 1742 Britain was involved in the war on the Continent, supporting Austria against the attacks of the new Holy Roman Emperor, Charles VII, and his French allies. In late summer that year, the Carteret ministry agreed to take sixteen thousand of the king's Hanoverian troops into British pay, an action that provoked a great popular outcry. Among other complaints, Carteret's enemies asserted that these troops were useless, for the king could not send them to fight against the emperor without exposing himself to the "imperial ban," a formal interdict that could deprive an electoral prince of his territory. This charge, it turned out, was unfounded. The emperor could not impose the ban at will; it could only be employed against those officially declared enemies of "the emperor and empire." Only the imperial diet could make such a declaration, and this would not be forthcoming while states of the empire were engaged on opposing sides in the current war. Nevertheless, members of the opposition brought up the ban during the Lords debate on dismissing the Hanoverian troops (February 1, 1743). Asserting the popular belief, they claimed that the king's electoral troops could not be used against the emperor. It is clear from Secker's notes that Carteret refuted these claims: "I am authorized by the king to say, that these troops shall march into the empire, which is not acting against the emperor and empire. France assists the emperor only as elector. If he calls France in as emperor, he breaks his Capitulation Oath" (*PH*, 12:1061). The *London Magazine* debate offers a generally accurate version of Carteret's assertion and spells out the conditions necessary for imposing the ban: "no law can hinder any prince of the Germanick body to assist [Austria] in repelling force by force. This, I shall grant, would be acting *contra imperatorem*, but it would not be *contra imperatorem et imperium*, and the latter only is what subjects a member to the ban of the empire."[22] Johnson never clarifies the issue in this way. His Carteret asserts that the king will march his troops into the empire, and his Hardwicke declares that the emperor himself cannot impose the ban, but Johnson nowhere explains the conditions necessary for imposing it; that is, he fails to articulate the distinction made by Carteret in the actual debate.[23] One suspects that Johnson did not fully understand the issues—few did—and that he made no effort, beyond reading the sketchy notes that he had been given, to learn what he did not know.

In addition, competitive pressures forced the *London Magazine* to adopt some of the practices of the *Gentleman's*. Its debate on the spirituous liquors bill (February 22–25, 1743) contains a more complete roster of speakers than usual and marshals them in the proper order.[24] The speeches in the *London Magazine* also echo an

Mistake" (*Gentleman's Magazine* 12 [1742]: 512). The *LM* account had appeared between July and September 1742; Johnson's report began in October. Cave thus had been able to examine the rival version in its entirety.

22. *LM* 12 (1743): 580. The Latin phrases mean "against the emperor" and "against the emperor and empire."

23. For Johnson's most important references to the ban, see *Debates*, 13:1145–46, 1150, 1261.

24. The *LM* covered only two sessions of what in Johnson's version is a three-day debate. It also omitted a subsidiary debate on the second day when opposition Lords attempted to have the final

unusually large number of particular phrases that we find in Secker's notes—an ironic situation, perhaps, since the two speeches that Johnson wrote in Chesterfield's name for this debate were subsequently printed in Chesterfield's *Miscellaneous Works* as examples of his lordship's eloquence.[25] The speeches in the *London Magazine*, though less impressive rhetorically, adhere more closely to the content and expression of the original speeches. And so after Chesterfield's death, his reputation as an orator was allowed to depend more on Johnson's style than on the *London Magazine*'s substance.

Finally, let me add a note about bias in the debates. Johnson himself led his readers to expect biased accounts. As Arthur Murphy recalled, when Johnson first revealed to the company at a dinner party that he had written the debates, one of those present "praised his impartiality; observing, that he dealt out reason and eloquence with an equal hand to both parties. 'That is not quite true,' said Johnson; 'I saved appearances tolerably well; but I took care that the WHIG DOGS should not have the best of it.'"[26] I have argued elsewhere that this was largely a bit of conversational high spirits, for the debates themselves are remarkably evenhanded.[27] The same, though, cannot be said for the debates in the *London Magazine*, which clearly favored the opposition parties. Neither Walpole nor Carteret got a fair shake in its pages.[28] Perhaps the most glaring example of bias in the *London Magazine* is its introduction to the Commons debate on taking Hanoverian troops into British pay (December 10, 1742). In his speech at the opening of Parliament, the king had announced that he was sending sixteen thousand of his electoral troops to join the coalition army that Britain was assembling in the Austrian Netherlands. In the prefatory matter to this debate, the editor of the *London Magazine*, with obvious irony, tells of the joy that every friend of the "present happy Establishment" felt in learning that Hanover was finally going to contribute to the common good, "for none of us at first imagined, that we were to pay for these *Hanover* Troops. . . . But how greatly were we surprised, how greatly disappointed, and in our Turn abashed, when among the Estimates presented to the House of Commons, we found an Estimate of the Expence of those 16,000 *Hanover* Troops, . . . and even that

reading of the bill postponed for five days. Johnson often reported supplemental debates on procedural matters of this sort; the *LM* generally did not. As a result, Johnson's debates often present a more complete picture of what had gone on in Parliament. For the portions of this debate covered by the *LM*, its list of speakers is marginally more accurate than Johnson's. See also Hoover, *Samuel Johnson's Parliamentary Reporting*, 117–20.

25. See *Miscellaneous Works of the Late Philip Dormer Stanhope, Earl of Chesterfield*, ed. Matthew Maty, 2 vols. (London, 1777), 1:242–60. For Johnson's amused reaction upon discovering that his speeches had been published in Chesterfield's works, see *Life*, 3:351.

26. *Essay on the Life and Genius of Samuel Johnson, LL.D.*, in *Johnsonian Miscellanies*, ed. George Birkbeck Hill, 2 vols. (Oxford, 1907), 1:379.

27. See Thomas Kaminski, *The Early Career of Samuel Johnson* (Oxford, 1987), 132–39; and *Debates*, 11:xxxvii–xliii.

28. As Benjamin Hoover has noted, in the Lords debate on the removal of Walpole, the *London Magazine* devoted more than 70 percent of its text to speeches attacking the Great Man, and less than 30 percent to his defense. Johnson also allotted more text to the opposition, but his division of about 60/40 was more in keeping with the balance of the actual debate. See Hoover, *Samuel Johnson's Parliamentary Reporting*, 77–78.

Estimate charged higher in Proportion, than ever this Nation had before paid for any foreign Troops taken into its Service."[29] This was the opposition line presented as editorial background. Nothing similar is to be found anywhere in Johnson's debates.

The third context for Johnson's debates is easily the broadest. It offers us the opportunity to examine the ways in which Johnson responded to immediate historical events and to the broader political culture. We can begin with a curious set of anachronistic statements within the debates that confirm something that has long been presumed about Johnson's methods of composition. There was always a delay of at least four or five months, and sometimes as much as two years, between the actual debate in Parliament and Johnson's report of it in the *Gentleman's Magazine*. Because publishing debates was illegal, both magazines thought it wise, despite their disguised reports, to defer printing recent material until the current session of Parliament had come to an end, usually between April and June.[30] At that time, debates on the most controversial issues of the recent session would be rushed into print while older material would be put off indefinitely.[31]

These delays had one noticeable effect: Johnson sometimes mentioned recent events that had not yet taken place at the time of the actual debate. Lapses of this sort are most easily recognizable in two debates where the subject is the conduct of the current wars, first the war with Spain, which began in 1739, and later the great Continental war that began in December 1740. The first examples arise in the Commons debate on raising new regiments of marines for an attack on the Spanish West Indies (December 10, 1740). Johnson's account of this debate would not appear for two years, until the magazine's annual Supplement for 1742.[32] When the actual debate had taken place, Britain was at war only with Spain and had no part in the new Continental war. Johnson's speakers, though, articulate the concerns and anxieties of late 1742. General Wade talks of the possibility of a French invasion, and Sir William Yonge argues that Britain must bear the high cost of these new regiments as a means of showing its allies that it is committed to the war (*Debates*, 11:140, 148). In 1740, Britain had nothing to fear from France, and it had no allies in its war with Spain; two years later, all this had changed. Similarly, in the debate of April 8, 1741, on whether Britain should support Maria Theresa of Austria in her struggle to maintain the Habsburg inheritance, Johnson's

29. *LM* 12 (1743): 209–10.

30. On the magazine's disguised reports, see above, note 4.

31. The briefest delay was about four months, for the Lords debate on dismissing the Hanoverian troops (February 1, 1743), which began in the June 1743 issue of the magazine. The Lords debate on the removal of Walpole (February 13, 1741) and the debate on the indemnity bill (May 25, 1742) were each delayed for five months. The Commons debates on raising new regiments (December 10, 1740) and on the removal of Walpole (February 13, 1741) each had to wait about two years.

32. The Supplement was published in January of the new year; thus, the Supplement for 1742 appeared in January 1743.

speakers fulminate against the French, who "pour troops into [Germany]" in support of the new emperor, Charles VII (*Debates*, 12:661). The French, though, did not cross the Rhine until August of that year, four months after the debate took place. By June 1742, when this debate was published, Johnson had apparently forgotten the order of events.

Trivial as these details may be, they are useful because they confirm for us that Johnson did not write up the debates immediately after they took place, but delayed until copy was called for. Scholars had long assumed this to be the case, based largely on Sir John Hawkins's vivid description of Johnson at work: the debates "were written at those seasons when he was able to raise his imagination to such a pitch of fervour as bordered upon enthusiasm, which, that he might the better do, his practice was to shut himself up in a room assigned him at St. John's gate, to which he would not suffer any one to approach, except the compositor or Cave's boy for matter, which, as fast as he composed it, he tumbled out at the door."[33] This sounds like a man trying to keep ahead of the presses, and it is good to have confirmation in the texts themselves.

Overall, though, the debates' broader political and historical context is much too large to consider in a single essay, so let me examine one case in which Johnson's debates not only responded to events but may have contributed to shaping the popular perception of them. The immediate context is the virulent anti-Hanover sentiment of the years 1742 to 1744. Although the British people were undoubtedly committed to the Protestant succession, many resented the clear preference that both of the first two Georges showed for their German homeland, and whenever war threatened on the Continent, the opposition complained that British policy was being guided by concerns for the safety of Hanover. Such sentiment had last been widely felt during the late 1720s, when tensions with Austria led the Walpole administration to pay for twelve thousand Hessian auxiliaries as a force that could be mobilized on short notice. The opposition in both Parliament and the press complained that Britain had no interests on the Continent, and that the forces had been hired to protect Hanover. Despite the administration's denials, popular resentment over the Hessians lasted for nearly five years, until Britain was reconciled with Austria and the Hessian subsidy ended.[34]

In 1741 Britain again found itself entangled in Continental politics as the king declared his support for Maria Theresa against her Bavarian and French enemies. In August, France moved an army across the Rhine to threaten Hanover, and George lost his nerve. As elector he was committed by treaty to send four thousand Hanoverian regulars to Austria; he did not send them. In addition, Britain had hired twelve thousand Danish and Hessian auxiliaries also intended for Austria; these, too, were retained by the king in the electorate. It was a scandalous violation of Parliament's intent and a breach of the Act of Settlement, the fundamental law by which the king held his crown.

33. Hawkins, *Life of Johnson*, 99.

34. See Jeremy Black, "Parliament and Foreign Policy in the Age of Walpole: The Case of the Hessians," in *Knights Errant and True Englishmen: British Foreign Policy, 1660–1800*, ed. Black (Edinburgh, 1989), 41–54. Black argues that, despite administration denials, the Hessian forces were in fact hired to protect Hanover (47–48).

But the king was not through. When the immediate danger passed, he told his British ministers that he now found his Hanoverian troops too expensive, and that he intended to disband a portion of them. Carteret, who was now at the head of the ministry, had been engaged in putting together a coalition of nations to oppose France, and he feared that disbanding the king's electoral troops would signal to all Europe that George and thus Britain were not committed to the war. As a result, he proposed that Britain pay for sixteen thousand of the king's Hanoverian troops, well over half of the entire electoral army.[35] The move was deeply unpopular. As elector of Hanover, George had reneged on his treaty commitments with Austria, and now Britain was being asked to pay for the bulk of his troops. Even the most vigorous supporters of the Protestant succession might feel that Britain was being exploited by Hanover.[36]

The general discontent over hiring the Hanoverians not only found its way into Johnson's debates but also took an unprecedented form—direct criticism of the king. In parliamentary matters generally, the king was exempt from criticism, based largely on the constitutional doctrine that "the king can do no wrong." Although lawyers argued about the precise implications of the concept, in practice it had come to mean that whenever wrong was done, the king's ministers, not the king himself, were to blame.[37] We find this principle operating throughout the earlier debates, where Walpole and his ministerial colleagues are attacked even for policies over which they had little or no control.[38] But in the debates on the Hanoverian troops, the tone seems to have changed, and even when the king is not attacked directly, he is sometimes touched by implication.

In the first of the debates that Johnson wrote on the topic, the Lords debate of February 1, 1743, the Earl of Sandwich complains of the cost of the Hanoverian troops, for which he blames the ministry: "It must be indeed, confessed that if an estimate is to be made of our condition, from the conduct of our ministers, the fear of exhausting our treasure must be merely panic, and the precepts of frugality which other states have grown great by observing, are to us absolutely unnecessary" (*Debates*, 13:1139). But he then turns to the most explosive topic of the debate, the payment of levy money to the elector. It was typical in subsidy treaties for the nation hiring foreign troops to pay part of the cost of raising them, even if those regiments were already in existence.

35. See the letter of Newcastle to Hardwicke (October 24, 1743) in Philip Yorke, *Life and Correspondence of Philip Yorke, Earl of Hardwicke*, 3 vols. (Cambridge, 1913), 1:318–19; see also *Debates*, 13:1077.

36. For the fierce opposition to taking the Hanoverian troops into British pay, see Robert Harris, *A Patriot Press: National Politics and the London Press in the 1740s* (Oxford, 1993), 122–77.

37. See, for instance, *Craftsman* 855 (November 13, 1742). Two decades later Blackstone would express this same understanding of the phrase: "whatever may be amiss in the conduct of public affairs is not chargeable personally on the king; nor is he, but his ministers, accountable for it to the people"; see William Blackstone, *Commentaries on the Laws of England*, 4 vols. (London, 1765–69), 3:254–55.

38. In the debate of December 9, 1740, the Duke of Argyll explicitly exempts the king from any blame for policies that Argyll considered damaging to the army (*Debates*, 11:92). Even when the king was clearly responsible for a flawed policy—as in his pursuit of a neutrality agreement between Hanover and France in 1741—speakers in the debates blame the Walpole administration (see *Debates*, 12:738 and n. 5, 741–42).

In the contract now submitted to Parliament, the king, like a mercenary foreign prince, was to be paid an additional £139,313 for levying the forces that he had only recently intended to disband. Sandwich now assumes a new tone:

> This demand of levy-money shocks every [British subject] yet more strongly, on considering by whom it is required; required by that family whom we have raised from a petty dominion for which homage was paid to a superior power, . . . by a family whom from want and weakness we have exalted to a throne, from whence, with virtue equal to their power, they may issue their mandates to the remotest parts of the earth. . . .
>
> I should imagine, my Lords, that when [a king] of the House of [Hanover] surveys his navies, reviews his troops, or examines his revenue, beholds the splendor of his court, or contemplates the extent of his dominions, he cannot but sometimes, however unwillingly, compare his present state with that of his ancestors; and that when he gives audience to the ambassadors of princes, who, perhaps, never heard of [Hanover], and directs the payment of sums, by the smallest of which all his ancient inheritance would be dearly purchased; and reflects, as surely he sometimes will, that all these honours and riches, this reverence from foreign powers, and his domestick splendor, are the gratuitous and voluntary gifts of the mighty people of [Great Britain], he should find his heart overflowing with unlimited gratitude, and should be ready to sacrifice to the happiness of his benefactors, not only every petty interest, or accidental inclination, but even his repose, his safety, or his life; . . . that he should consider his little territories as only a contemptible province to his [British] empire, a kind of nursery for troops to be employed without harrassing his more valuable subjects. (*Debates*, 13:1140–41)

This attack is not against the ministers but the king; its focus is not mistaken policy or corrupt practice but ingratitude. And yet it is unclear who was primarily responsible for this outburst, Sandwich or Johnson. There is no exact parallel in Secker's notes, but there are hints and suggestions of disapproval of the king's conduct. At the very start of the speech, Sandwich asserted that taking the Hanoverians into British pay "shakes the affections of the people at home" (Secker's notes, *PH*, 12:1059). Later, he objected that the contract required the British to pay for a troop of the king's Hanoverian Life Guards: "Why should not the king," he asks, "trust himself to the fidelity and courage of English Guards?" (*PH*, 12:1060). Near the end he brought up the levy money, complaining (in an anecdote repeated by Johnson) that Louis XIV, when hiring Hanoverian forces in 1672, had refused to pay levy money except for the portion that had in fact been newly raised: "Surely, then, we should not have been made to pay the whole for troops not intended to assist us" (*PH*, 12:1061). In this last matter, blame might properly have fallen upon the ministers, who should have told the king that levy money was inappropriate in these circumstances, but in accepting it, the king had certainly done nothing to earn the affection of his people.

A more outrageous example of disrespect occurs in the Commons debate on this same topic (December 10, 1742). The speech that Johnson wrote in Pitt's name focuses on the king's failure to send electoral troops to Austria's aid, as required by treaty. In a remarkable piece of Johnsonian irony, he attributes the king's dereliction to the "pernicious counsels" of his advisers, yet one cannot read the passage without recognizing the speaker's overwhelming contempt for the king:

> To what can we impute this negligence of treaties, this disregard of justice, this defect of compassion, but to the pernicious counsels of those men who have advised His Majesty to hire to [Great Britain] those troops which he should have employed in the assistance of the queen of [Hungary];[39] for it is not to be imagined that His Majesty has more or less regard to justice as [king of Great Britain] than as elector of [Hanover], or that he would not have sent his proportion of troops to the [Austrian] army, had not the temptations of greater profit been industriously laid before him. (*Debates*, 13:1108)

Surely, Pitt says with a derisive smile, the king would have acted honorably—if only his ministers had not appealed to his avarice. In quoting this passage, the historian Uriel Dann calls it "a sneer at the sovereign that seeks its equal in the history of Parliament."[40] But Pitt (or Johnson) is not done. He turns to the great matter of the Hanoverian exploitation of Britain:

> If therefore our assistance [to Austria] be an act of honesty, and granted in consequence of treaties, why may it not equally be required of [Hanover]? and if it be an act of generosity, why should this nation alone be obliged to sacrifice her own interest to that of others? Or why should the elector of [Hanover] exert his liberality at the expence of [Great Britain]?
>
> It is now too apparent, that this great, this powerful, this formidable kingdom is considered only as a province to a despicable electorate, and that in consequence of a scheme formed long ago, and invariably persued, these troops are hired only to drain this unhappy nation of its money; that they have hitherto been of no use to [Britain], or to [Austria], is evident beyond controversy; and therefore it is plain, that they are retained only for the purposes of [Hanover]. (*Debates*, 13:1109)

There is perhaps a residual ambiguity in the speech: the "scheme formed long ago" to enrich Hanover at British expense may indeed have been executed by treacherous

39. That is, Maria Theresa, queen of Hungary and archduchess of Austria.
40. Uriel Dann, *Hanover and Great Britain, 1740–1760* (Leicester, U.K., 1991), 56.

ministers intent on maintaining the king's favor, but the ingratitude and fecklessness of the king is everywhere apparent.

Once again, it is difficult to know just how to apportion credit for these remarks. Anti-Hanover polemics were indeed fierce, but the rhetoric of these attacks tended to be less directly insulting to the king. Perhaps the most inflammatory pamphlet of the day was *The Case of the Hanover Forces in the Pay of Great-Britain, Impartially and Freely Examined*, unsigned, but now generally attributed to the Earl of Chesterfield and Edmund Waller. The authors suggest that the king should not expect to receive payment for the entire force of sixteen thousand troops:

> The *British* Nation presume to hope and expect that either the 4000 Men which *Hanover* was to furnish the Queen of *Hungary* with, will be deducted from the 16000, or, that at least, we shall only pay the Difference between their own Pay and that which is necessary for their Service abroad. . . . For no Man thinks so meanly of his Majesty, as to imagine he designs, whatever his Ministers may do, to save and pocket what would be their own Pay at home, as well as the entire Expence of the 4000 Men, due from *Hanover* to the Queen of *Hungary*.[41]

There may be some irony here, for some men did "think so meanly of his Majesty," but there is no obvious contempt. And when he spoke in the actual debates, as recorded by Secker, Chesterfield was coy. He criticized Hanover for its failure to live up to its treaties: "It is astonishing that Hanover is not one of the powers engaged to guarantee the Pragmatic Sanction. It hath not given even its quota [that is, its 4,000 men]." But in the matter of taking the Hanoverians into British pay, he exonerated the king and blamed his ministers: "the king knows his interest too well to be moved by such considerations, but ministers may mistake and flatter this way" (*PH*, 12:1066).

Even Pitt, for whom we have authentic records of subsequent remarks on this matter, nowhere else shows contempt for the king. A year later, in December 1743, the Hanoverians once again came up for parliamentary approval, and Pitt once again had his say. But in this case, Philip Yorke, the eldest son of Lord Chancellor Hardwicke, kept notes of Pitt's speeches. Yorke's accounts portray Pitt as an implacable enemy of Carteret but not demonstrably hostile toward the king. In the debate of December 6, 1743, Pitt sees the king as endangered by Carteret's policies: "his Majesty yet stands on the firm ground of his people's affections, though on the brink of a precipice: it is the duty of parliament to snatch him from the gulph where an infamous minister has placed him, and not throw paltry flowers on the edge of it to conceal the danger: it may be a rough, but it is a friendly hand which is stretched out to remove him."[42] Pitt abuses Carteret, though, in language similar to that which he had used against Walpole: he is "an execrable, a sole minister, one who had renounced the British nation, and seemed to have drunk of the potion described in poetic fictions, which made men forget their

41. *The Case of the Hanover Forces* (London, 1743), 78–79.
42. *PH*, 13:141–42. Yorke's accounts, like Secker's, are included in *PH*.

country" (*PH*, 13:136). Like many of his countrymen, Pitt had been incensed by reports that the king had favored his Hanoverian officers at Dettingen, but even here he is less critical of the king than he appears in Johnson's debate. Pitt averred—in Yorke's condensed phrasing—that he "could prove that the invariable rules of service had been neglected with regard to the English officers. General of the English army not advised with: the great person [that is, the king] hemmed in by German officers, and one English minister; how could he then be informed of the sense of the army, or of the people, almost exasperated to despair" (*PH*, 13:142). Once again the blame is deflected from the king to his advisers. Nor was Yorke unwilling to mention intemperate remarks. He described the general disturbance in the House brought on by "the inconsiderate warmth of Stanley,[43] who charged the king (by name) with having shewed a notorious partiality to his electoral troops"; and he recorded the dark insinuation of the Jacobite John Hynde Cotton that "to get rid of the Hanover yoke will be difficult" (*PH*, 13:464, 145).

From the evidence, then, it appears that Pitt fiercely opposed any measures by which Hanover benefited financially from its connection with Britain, but he, like almost all his contemporaries in Parliament, refrained from blaming the king directly for these actions. He probably noted, as he does in Johnson's account, that Hanover had failed to meet its treaty commitments; as we have already seen, Chesterfield had made the same complaint in the Lords. In the authentic reports, though, Pitt attacks Carteret rather than the king. The minister had abetted the king's attempts to evade his commitments and had hidden the people's discontent from him. The counselor, not the king, was at fault.

In these matters, I wish to suggest, Johnson's essential characterization of Pitt's complaint—his indignation that various military and financial costs had been transferred from Hanover to Britain—was accurate, but its focus and its tone were distorted. Johnson's Pitt despises the king, but the Pitt we find in the authentic records rails only at his minister. And it may well have been Johnson rather than Pitt who lamented that Britain had been reduced to "a province to a despicable electorate." Writing in the early months of 1744, Johnson would have fed off the anti-Hanover polemics that had dominated political discourse for more than a year. Unlike those who wished well to the present royal family, he did not have to find ways to blame the king's follies on his ministers. His hatred for George II is well attested,[44] and it appears to have spilled over into Pitt's speeches.

If my inferences here are correct, Johnson's distorted account had two powerful effects. First, to Pitt's contemporaries the speech would have provided an exaggerated picture of his audacity. He appeared to be the only Member of Parliament willing to scorn the constitutional fiction that the king can do no wrong, daring even to insult the king on the floor of the House. The debates, we must remember, were read by many,

43. Hans Stanley (1721–1780), the member for St. Albans, was only twenty-two years old at the time of the debate (January 18, 1744) and apparently unaccustomed to parliamentary restraint.

44. See *Life*, 1:147, 2:342.

while only a few would have heard the actual speech from the gallery of the Commons. The contemptuous reference to Hanover as a "despicable electorate" may even have contributed to the king's long refusal to admit Pitt to office. The second effect is on the writing of history. This particular speech has generally been used to characterize Pitt's opposition to "Hanoverian measures." In a recent essay, the historian Brendan Simms refers to it as "[Pitt's] famous diatribe against the Hanoverian connection, which did so much to colour contemporary and subsequent perceptions of him as a diehard critic of the Personal Union."[45] It stands as a prime example of the vehemence of the young, reckless Pitt. A century ago Lord Rosebery suggested that the tone was itself one of the signs of the speech's genuineness: "it is scarcely possible to conceive sarcasms more calculated to afflict the sovereign in his tenderest susceptibilities than those which Pitt now launched, even as we read them in an imperfect report; they are, indeed, so masterly in this way as almost to prove their authenticity. This is the first speech of real point and power delivered by Pitt of which we have any record."[46] But the tone, I am suggesting, was Johnson's, not Pitt's, and so any conclusions drawn from it are likely to skew our understanding of Pitt's early political character. The willingness of historians to accept this speech as genuine is, of course, readily understandable. Johnson's speech is the only record we have of what Pitt said in this important early debate, and so they have a choice: Johnson's evidence, or no evidence at all.[47] Since Johnson's speech is sneering and contemptuous and allows them to tell a more compelling story than they could otherwise, they are happy to tell Johnson's story. Whatever the case, it seems inescapable that the "historical" Pitt is at least in part the creation of Johnson's pen.

In this essay I have argued three very different things. First, Johnson's debates are more firmly rooted in fact than he led his contemporaries to believe. Although quite a few speeches bear little resemblance to the recoverable historical record, many, perhaps most, rest on reliable source material. In addition, features that catch the reader's attention—eccentric arguments, anecdotes, Latin phrases, classical allusions—generally have some basis in statements actually made on the House floor. Next, the idea that Johnson's debates must have been less reliable than the rival series in the *London Magazine* does not stand up to scrutiny. If Johnson sometimes wrote speeches wholly from his imagination, so did his competitor. In such matters as the number and order of participants and the overall completeness of a report, his debates are, in general, superior. But if he did not know much about an issue, he did not go off in search of knowledge: he made what sense he could of the notes that Cave provided, and he left it

45. Brendan Simms, "Pitt and Hanover," in *The Hanoverian Dimension in British History, 1714–1837*, ed. Simms and Torsten Riotte (Cambridge, 2007), 32.

46. Archibald Philip Primrose, Earl of Rosebery, *Lord Chatham, His Early Life and Connections* (New York, 1910), 173.

47. The *LM* published a report of the debate, but it did not include a speech by Pitt.

at that. Finally, Johnson's debates did not merely reflect the political world they were intended to report; they also influenced that world. The public perceptions of Walpole, Carteret, Chesterfield, and perhaps most of all, Pitt, were shaped, at least in part, by the speeches that Johnson wrote in their names. This was not just the influence of a fleeting moment, for these speeches found their way into histories of Parliament and, in the cases of Chesterfield and Pitt, into biographies and other collections whose readers would have had little reason to suspect their dubious origins.[48] From the remarks of more recent historians, it appears to be an influence that continues to this day.

48. For example, several speeches written by Johnson in Pitt's name were included in the first volume of John Almon's *Anecdotes of the Life of the Right Honourable William Pitt, Earl of Chatham*, 4 vols. (London, 1792).

PART V:
JOHNSON, RELIGION, AND PHILOSOPHY

Reflections on Johnson's Churchmanship

William Gibson

THE HISTORIOGRAPHY OF JOHNSON'S CHURCHMANSHIP in the twentieth and twenty-first centuries has been somewhat checkered. In the last thirty years, the nature of Johnson's churchmanship has been hotly contested, but in the preceding half-century, he was widely accepted as an equivocal or ambiguous churchman. The aim of this essay is to consider the sources of presumed ambiguity in Johnson's churchmanship and to trace the more seismic fault lines that developed in Johnsonian scholarship in the last quarter of the twentieth century. It will also consider wider aspects of the eighteenth-century religious context within which Johnson—and others—found precise and exact consistency in churchmanship impossible to maintain. And it will conclude with some thoughts about the exceptional nature of Johnson and with a suggestion that there may be greater consensus among Johnson scholars than they sometimes concede.

Johnson's Inconsistencies

In 1930, S. C. Roberts challenged John H. Overton and Frederic Relton's extraordinary and implausible claims that Johnson was both a "representative man" of the eighteenth century and one who "was not bound to the Church by any ties." Overton and Relton argued that, though Johnson was "very comfortable in his seat in St Clement Danes," he was unshocked by his friend John Taylor's apparent secularism.[1] Roberts claimed that Overton and Relton had presented a "profoundly misleading" picture of Johnson, one that he corrected.[2] Roberts reclaimed Johnson's family religious affiliation, suggesting that the roots of Johnson's faith reached into his father's High Church Jacobitism and his mother's evangelicalism. Roberts showed how seriously Johnson took religion and how deep were his concerns about death and salvation. Much of Roberts's view was derived from Boswell, whose own religious views were complex and migratory, but he

1. John H. Overton and Frederic Relton, *The English Church from the Accession of George I to the End of the Eighteenth Century*, History of the English Church 7 (London, 1906), 284–86. Overton and Relton's views were entirely consistent with their now-discredited pessimistic perception of the eighteenth-century Church.

2. S. C. Roberts, "Dr Johnson as Churchman," *Church Quarterly Review* 156 (1930): 372.

also drew on other sources, notably Johnson's own *Prayers and Meditations*, published posthumously, in 1785. Roberts argued that there was an unresolved inner conflict in Johnson, which meant that he was as comfortable in the Mitre or a club as in St. Clement Danes. For Roberts, Johnson was a "spiritual hypochondriac" caught between his father's melancholy and his mother's preoccupation with sin. Religion may have been a source of comfort for Johnson, but it was not easily found. For Roberts the poles of gloominess and cheerfulness that dominated Johnson's religion were symptomatic of other binaries: he was a staunch Anglican with sympathies for other groups; he was a Tory High Churchman who was drawn to progressive thinking; he regarded Satan's rebellion against God as the first Whig act but recognized the necessity of the Revolution of 1688; and he was an Anglican partisan who said that he thought "all Christians, whether Papist or Protestant, agree in the essential articles and that their differences are trivial and rather political than religious."[3] Thus, Johnson appeared as a figure whose religious views were liminal and ambiguous.

Roberts also saw the need to take Johnson's public utterances with large pinches of salt. He identified two such occasions. The first was when, in Sir Robert Chambers's garden in Oxford, Johnson saw Chambers throw snails into his neighbor's garden and reproached him, to which Chambers replied, "My neighbour is a Dissenter," and Johnson commented, "Oh, if so, toss away."[4] The second was his comment "I would be a Papist if I could. I have fear enough but an obstinate rationality prevents me"—though Roberts showed that Johnson prefaced this comment with the view that the attraction of Catholicism was that it had "so many helps to get to heaven."[5] Equally, Roberts claimed that Johnson's apparent antipathy for Dissent and sympathy for Catholicism should not be taken seriously; such remarks were at odds with other statements Johnson made.

Roberts replaced Boswell's description of Johnson as "a steady Church-of-England man"[6] with "a steady prayerbook man," noting Johnson's claim that he knew of "no good prayers except those in the Book of Common Prayer," and the fact that his last poem, written eight days before his death, was a Latin paraphrase of the Anglican Communion service. Yet, while Johnson embraced the prayer book as a touchstone of Reformation Anglicanism, he also elevated the nature of Anglican priesthood and sacraments to the point of dreading communicating more than once a year and agonizing whether to accept an invitation to dinner with a bishop during Holy Week.[7]

3. Roberts, "Johnson as Churchman," 380.

4. This anecdote was originally found in *Lord Eldon's Anecdote Book*, ed. Anthony Lincoln and R. Lindley McEwen (London, 1960), 17–18.

5. *Boswell's Life of Samuel Johnson, Together with Boswell's Journal of a Tour of the Hebrides and Johnson's Diary of a Journey into North Wales*, ed. George Birkbeck Hill, rev. L. F. Powell, 6 vols. (Oxford, 1934–50), 4:289 (hereafter cited as *Life*).

6. Dr. James Caudle of the Yale Boswell project reminds me that the full quotation reads, "It is to the mutual credit of Johnson and Divines of different communions, that although he was a steady Church-of-England man, there was, nevertheless, much agreeable intercourse between him and . . . Moravian[s], . . . the English Benedictines, at Paris, . . . His Catholick Majesty's Chaplain of Embassy at the Court of London, . . . [and] a Presbyterian" (*Life*, 4:410–11).

7. Roberts, "Johnson as Churchman," 378–79. Roberts quoted the sermon Johnson wrote for Taylor on the sacrament (Sermon 9), in which he advocates receipt of Communion "not transiently and

W. T. Cairns's book *The Religion of Dr. Johnson, and Other Essays* (1946) also argued that the young Johnson was immersed in Anglican cultural identity. Indeed, as a boy Johnson learned the collects by heart. He read *The Whole Duty of Man* (1658) and claimed that studying the other great Anglican devotional work, William Law's *A Serious Call to a Devout and Holy Life* (1729), was the first occasion of his "thinking in earnest of religion." His personal observance of the religious calendar was deeply imbued with Anglican identity, as was his preparation for Communion. Yet Cairns hinted at an evolving Latitudinarian element in Johnson: his prayers, such as those on his mother's death, were remote and restrained, shying away from emotional expression. Cairns also suggested that the sermons Johnson wrote for Dr. Taylor of Market Bosworth indicated some of Johnson's opinions—and of course Taylor was a Whig Latitudinarian.[8] Like Roberts, Cairns recognized Johnson's ability to live in two worlds: in his own conversation, for example, Johnson could be vulgar and crude, but he reproved it in others, as Sir Joshua Reynolds claimed.[9]

Hiram Bennett's 1958 study advanced the view that Johnson was "a faithful son of the Church, whose religion was sincere, who was a frequent communicant and a firm believer in the ancient creeds." Like Roberts and Cairns, Bennett saw the contradictions in Johnson, not least that he was a Tory who accepted a pension from George III. But, following Boswell, he had no doubt that Johnson's rejection of holy orders when offered a parish was motivated not only by scruple but also by a sense that he was unfit for the life of a clergyman and that he would not be prepared to live outside London. What, in Bennett's view, made Johnson the quintessential Anglican was how well versed he was in the "catholic character of the Ecclesia Anglicana." His prayers were, claimed Bennett, modeled on the collects of the Church, and his thought strongly influenced by the prose sonnets of the Book of Common Prayer. What Bennett found curious therefore was not Johnson's attendance at St. Clement Danes but his extreme scruple about receiving the sacrament. He recounted Johnson's own account of the unsettling experience of Easter 1770 when he prayed against "bad and troublesome thoughts; [and] resolved to oppose sudden incursions of them," right up to the point at which he went to the table to receive Communion. When he got home, Johnson recited the prayer of general thanksgiving as well as other parts of the Communion service. And he asked, "Shall I ever receive the Sacrament with tranquillity? Surely the time will come." These might have been the scruples of a man concerned about the legitimacy of the Church, but they sound more like those of a man acutely aware of his own unworthiness. This was a fairly common eighteenth-century concern, which

carelessly," which explains Johnson's own infrequent receipt of it. For Johnson and the prayer book, see Bishop Edward Williamson, "Dr Johnson and the Prayer Book," *Theology* 53 (1950): 363–72.

8. Johnson's sermons, those of "a very devout Tory High Churchman," were used to support himself financially; he claimed to have written about forty, though only twenty-eight have survived. One was for Reverend Henry Hervey Aston to preach to the Sons of the Clergy; another was for William Dodd at Newgate. The remainder were for his friend John Taylor. Johnson seems to have drafted sermons for his clients, and they amended what he wrote to accord with their own views. See O. C. Edwards Jr., *A History of Preaching* (Nashville, Tenn., 2004), 418.

9. William Thomas Cairns, *The Religion of Dr. Johnson, and Other Essays* (Oxford, 1946), 4, 9, 12, 21.

Victorians mistook for religious indifference, but was in fact evidence of deep religious introspection and scruple. Bennett also regarded Johnson as an Anglican partisan, ready to "defend the most minute circumstance connected with the Church of England."[10] Sir John Hawkins put this down to the "tincture of enthusiasm" in Johnson's religion, though Bennett provided sufficient evidence of Johnson's wariness of evangelicalism to rule this out.[11]

Maurice J. Quinlan's 1964 study, *Samuel Johnson: A Layman's Religion*, claimed that Johnson was "on the whole . . . an orthodox member of the Church of England." But he introduced greater equivocation into the discussion than previously. Quinlan argued that Johnson's main struggle was not between faith and doubt but between the worldly and spiritual values of his age, and he ascribed Johnson's irregular church attendance to his deafness, his preference for private devotion, his childhood fear of stones falling from the church in Lichfield, and his preference for prayer over sermons. In this latter he was not a typical Anglican. Drawing on Boswell, Quinlan traced William Law's influence on Johnson, not least in the number of quotations from Law that Johnson used. Law's attraction to Johnson was in the idea of Christian perfectionism, and prayer as a means to achieve it—a lifelong struggle for Johnson. In this, Law was influential for both Johnson and John Wesley, as well as for some evangelicals. But while Johnson did not accept Law's High Church doctrines of the Eucharist, he shared Law's suspicion of prayer as liable to become formulaic and also a wariness of direct petitions to Christ, although he adopted penitential prayer and prayer for the dead—both High Church tropes.[12]

Quinlan also analyzed the strong influence of Samuel Clarke on Johnson. Johnson owned two sets of Clarke's sermons and recommended them to others as among the best in the English language. Naturally, Boswell could not understand Johnson's taste for Clarke, who was regarded with suspicion as a crypto-Arian.[13] However, Johnson was wary of Clarke's heterodoxy, which he parodied in chapter 22 of *Rasselas*. He was careful to recommend Clarke except where he was not orthodox, and he disliked Clarke's elevation of reason, which he preferred to replace with the Holy Spirit. What Johnson liked about Clarke was his method: simplicity, clarity, resignation in illness, desire for improvement, and fear of sin and lack of forgiveness. Johnson especially valued Clarke's sermon on "The Shortness and Vanity of Humane Life," and he frequently echoed its sentiments.[14]

10. Hiram R. Bennett, "Samuel Johnson, Churchman," *Anglican Theological Review* 40 (1958): 302, 304, 306, 307–8.

11. Bennett concluded that Johnson was "a curious man . . . and a good man" ("Churchman," 309).

12. Maurice J. Quinlan, *Samuel Johnson: A Layman's Religion* (Madison, Wis., 1964), ix, xi, 5–25.

13. *Boswell's Life of Johnson*, ed. R. W. Chapman (Oxford, 1980), 913. Opinions about Clarke are changing, however. See, for example, Thomas C. Pfizenmaier, *The Trinitarian Theology of Dr. Samuel Clarke (1675–1729): Context, Sources, and Controversy*, Studies in the History of Christian Thought 75 (Leiden, 1997); and Pfizenmaier, "Why the Third Fell Out: Trinitarian Dissent," in *Religion, Politics, and Dissent, 1660–1832: Essays in Honour of James E. Bradley*, ed. William Gibson and Robert D. Cornwall (Farnham, U.K., 2010).

14. Quinlan, *A Layman's Religion*, 27–44.

Quinlan saw evidence of Johnson's inconsistencies in his definition of atonement. In 1773 Boswell claimed that Johnson did not accept that Christ had expiated the sins of man, but that Christ had made a perpetual propitiation to enable man to achieve perfection. By 1784 Johnson had shifted to the view that atonement was merely an exemplary act by Christ. Yet by the end of his life, both Hannah More and Dr. Brocklesby testified that Johnson had spoken of Christ's propitiation and sacrifice.[15] Probably, therefore, his opinions fluctuated and perhaps were not always clear to himself. Quinlan argued that Johnson's attitudes toward repentance also show his ambiguities. Johnson embraced both the Protestant teaching of contrition (sorrow derived from divine love) and the Catholic view of attrition (sorrow based on fear of damnation). The latter was strongly opposed by Latitudinarians such as Clarke and Gilbert Burnet. But Johnson also adhered to the Protestant doctrine of regeneration, which tested continuous contrition and the view that charity was a response to repentance. Like Benjamin Hoadly, Johnson accepted the validity of deathbed repentance; this was clearly echoed in "The Convict's Address," which he wrote for William Dodd.[16]

Quinlan also thought Johnson's sermons showed change and development over time, from his first in 1745, written for Henry Hervey Aston, to the series he wrote in the 1780s. Though he repeatedly returned to such familiar themes as brotherly love and charity, the sermons show the maturing of Johnson's churchmanship. Johnson was also highly committed to benevolence and charity, which he saw as a religious duty, a view held by High, Low, and evangelical churchmen. Yet Johnson's charitableness was partly emotional and secular as well as religious in motivation. Above all, Johnson admired sincerity and energy: he admired it in Wesley, and he appreciated the fervor of Methodism, though he did not like what he saw as misdirected evangelical zeal. He especially disliked the Methodist claim to personal spiritual direction from God and the "enthusiasm" of claims to divine inspiration.[17]

Quinlan claimed that Johnson veered between Anglican, Dissenting, and even Catholic identities. Johnson objected to lifting the Test for universities (Quinlan cited his oft-quoted comment about a cow being a very good thing in a field but not for the garden, which was a reference to the Methodists expelled from Oxford in 1768).[18] Yet Johnson's position was shot through with inconsistencies: he sternly upheld the Thirty-Nine Articles but openly derided the seventeenth, on predestination;

15. Quinlan, *A Layman's Religion*, 33–35; *Johnsonian Miscellanies*, ed. George Birkbeck Hill, 2 vols. (Oxford, 1897), 205–6. See also S. C. Wilks, "True and False Repose in Death," *Christian Observer* 310 (October 1827): 581–92. This was the London version of the *Christian Observer* and was confusingly collected together and bound in volumes with different numbers so that Wilks's piece was also in volume 27 of the collected *Christian Observer*, published in 1828. I am indebted to Howard D. Weinbrot for drawing my attention to Donald Greene's essay "Dr. Johnson's 'Late Conversion': A Reconsideration," in *Johnsonian Studies*, ed. Magdi Wahba (Cairo, Egypt, 1962), 61–92.

16. *Sermons*, vol. 14 of *The Yale Edition of the Works of Samuel Johnson* (hereafter cited as *YE*), ed. Jean Hagstrum and James Gray (New Haven, Conn., 1978), 300–313.

17. See in particular Donald H. Ryan, "Dr Samuel Johnson, the Wesley Family and Methodism," in *Proceedings of the Wesley Historical Society* 58 (2011): 1.

18. Johnson speaking to Boswell, April 15, 1772, in *Boswell for the Defence, 1769–1774*, ed. William K. Wimsatt Jr. and Frederick A. Pottle (New Haven, Conn., 1959), 127.

he similarly refused to hear William Robertson preach in Edinburgh because he was a Calvinist. After Johnson's death, some people claimed that he flirted with Catholicism, and Boswell also fueled this belief—suggesting that Johnson "leaned" toward Rome, that he liked monasticism, that he often defended Catholics. Yet Johnson often tilted at Catholicism as having snatched the Bible from the hands of the people, as being abusive in promoting purgatory and prayers for the dead, and as being dogmatic.[19]

High Church or Low Church

After Quinlan, the issue of Johnson's theological ambivalence gave way to more focused discussion of whether he could be categorized as a Latitudinarian or a High Churchman, Whig or Tory. One of the questions about Johnson's churchmanship derives from his father's position. Boswell and Hawkins both regarded Michael Johnson as a Tory Jacobite, albeit one who swore the oaths of abjuration and allegiance. Chester F. Chapin argued that Johnson's attachment to the Church of England was derived in part from his father's influence.[20] He also acknowledged that Law's influence on Johnson was as profound as on Wesley but in a different direction, not toward evangelicalism but toward earnestness and "seriousness."[21]

For Chapin, Johnson's attitude toward subscription at Oxford exemplified his contradictory views. Johnson believed that subscription for its undergraduates amounted to making boys subscribe to what they did not understand, but he still endorsed subscription and defended the religious Test for universities. Chapin claimed that Johnson was complex enough to comprehend the rationalism of the tradition of Richard Hooker, Clarke, John Tillotson, and Joseph Butler as well as mystical Anglican eschatology. Nevertheless, Chapin argued that Johnson was a "modern" who was liberal and progressive, a partisan Anglican who accepted the toleration of Dissent, as long as it did not encroach on rights of the Church, and who disliked persecution for belief.[22] Chapin's Johnson admired William Warburton's Erastian position on the

19. Quinlan, *A Layman's Religion*, 49–64, 69–82, 85–92, 101–20, 130–46, 150–93. The myriad Johnson deathbed claims are considered in a series of articles in the British publication *Christian Observer* from 1817 to 1839, the most significant of which are "Last Days of Dr. Johnson—The *Quarterly Review* and Hannah More," *Christian Observer* 35 (January 1835): 51–62; "The Last Days of Dr. Johnson," *Christian Observer* 37 (January 1837): 35–36; and "Dr. Johnson's 'Conversion,'" *Christian Observer* 37 (November 1837): 683–85. See also Joseph Milner, "Resignation: An Original Letter from the Late Rev. Joseph Milner to the Late Rev. Isaac Milner, Dean of Carlisle," *Church of England Magazine* 16 (1844): 421–22 at 422, in which Milner claimed Johnson was "unfaithful to his convictions." That Johnson experienced an evangelical conversion on his deathbed has been suggested by William Roberts, *Memoirs of the Life and Correspondence of Mrs. Hannah More*, 2 vols. (London, 1834–35), 1:377–80, 392–94; and W. Field, *Memoirs of the Life, Writings, and Opinions of the Rev. Samuel Parr*, 2 vols. (London, 1828), 1:154. T. B. Shepherd, in *Methodism and the Literature of the Eighteenth Century* (London, 1940), 229, discussed Johnson's friendly links with evangelicals.

20. Chester F. Chapin, *The Religious Thought of Samuel Johnson* (Ann Arbor, Mich., 1968), 3–4, 10. This attachment led Johnson to desire the restoration of Convocation, which would strengthen the Church against heterodoxy. See Chapin, "Samuel Johnson and the Church's Convocation," *Cithara* 46, no. 2 (2007): 16–24.

21. Chapin, *The Religious Thought of Samuel Johnson*, 37–38.

22. Chapin, *The Religious Thought of Samuel Johnson*, 118–19.

alliance of church and state and believed in establishment for the majority denomination. He supported the Church of England in England but sympathized with Catholics in Ireland.

Chapin also pointed out that in *The False Alarm* (1770), Johnson attacked Dissent for its slide into Arianism and Socinianism and for its alignment with the "Wilkes and Liberty" campaign. In doing so, Johnson revealed his emphasis on social stability; he appreciated the role of religion in the transmission of culture and values but recognized the need for the Church to exert social control over the poor and to regulate what was taught to the people—hence one reason for Johnson's regard for Methodism: however much he disliked its "enthusiasm," he admired its orthodoxy and commitment to an established church. Chapin was not alone in arguing that Johnson was progressive. Nicholas Hudson has also questioned Johnson's Toryism and especially his subordination to government, seeing Johnson's thought as containing elements of modernity.[23] He also regards Johnson's churchmanship as far more sympathetic to Latitudinarians such as Clarke, Tillotson, Isaac Barrow, and even Benjamin Hoadly.[24]

Chapin returned to the issue of Johnson's churchmanship in an article in 1990.[25] Here, Chapin argued that Johnson's *Dictionary* definition of a Tory was an accurate reflection of Johnson's own views.[26] Yet, Chapin continued to point out the subtleties and complexities in Johnson's apparent Tory High Churchmanship. For example, Chapin went beyond Johnson's oft-quoted comment that a wise Tory and a wise Whig would agree, including the remainder of the quotation from Boswell that "a High Tory makes government unintelligible: it is lost in the clouds. A violent Whig makes it impractical: he is for allowing so much liberty to every man, that there is not power enough to govern a man."[27] This sounds much more like "a plague on both your houses." The evidence of Johnson's equivocal Toryism was clear: he was more a detractor than an admirer of the Stuarts, but he regarded the Glorious Revolution as breaking the constitution. Chapin argued that Johnson's Toryism relied heavily on his belief in social order and in popular assent to religion. In Scotland he was prepared to accept the establishment, however much he regarded Presbyterianism with horror. His pragmatism also applied to English Dissent: he admired the Dissenters' zeal but regretted their separation from the Church.[28] Chapin argued that it would be wrong to assume that Johnson's churchmanship was purely pragmatic: he was contemptuous of Socinians and Unitarians because of their theology—though even here, there was equivocation

23. Nicholas Hudson, *Samuel Johnson and the Making of Modern England* (Cambridge, 2003).

24. Nicholas Hudson, "Johnson, Socinianism, and the Meaning of Christ's Sacrifice," *Notes and Queries* 32 (1985): 238–40; and Hudson, *Samuel Johnson and Eighteenth-Century Thought* (Oxford, 1990), 221.

25. Chester Chapin, "Religion and the Nature of Samuel Johnson's Toryism," *Cithara* 29, no. 2 (1990): 38–54.

26. In the *Dictionary of the English Language* (1755), Johnson defines a Tory as "one who adheres to the antient constitution of the state, and the apostolical hierarchy of the church of England, opposed to a whig."

27. Boswell, quoted in Chapin, "Religion and the Nature of Samuel Johnson's Toryism," 38.

28. Chapin, "Religion and the Nature of Samuel Johnson's Toryism," 39, 40–41.

in his admiration of Clarke. Theology lay at the core of his suspicion of Dissenters also.[29] Chapin's view that Johnson's politics arose from his churchmanship is clear. In Sermon 24, Johnson argued that there were equal dangers in the tyranny of rulers and the rule of the mob, but he saw the greatest danger in the latter. This was what led him to oppose the American Revolution. It was also what led him to argue against eroding the Anglican monopoly in the state—something that he saw as instilling respect for authority.

Chapin also considered the character of Johnson's supposed Latitudinarianism. In an article in 2001, he concluded that Johnson was a High Churchman, but this was a qualified view. Chapin's Johnson was wary of extremes of churchmanship and was especially so of High Churchmanship. In particular, Johnson did not seek to exclude or persecute Dissenters, having by the 1770s accepted their permanence as part of the fabric of English society. Johnson also drew on ideas of seventeenth-century Nonconformists like Richard Baxter, so his High Churchmanship was not akin to that of Francis Atterbury and the High Church party of Queen Anne's reign. Chapin even saw Johnson as eirenic and ecumenical in outlook and argued that he may well have—at some point—shared Hoadly's view of the Eucharist as a "bare memorial." Thus, Chapin's view of Johnson's High Churchmanship is cautious and highly contingent.[30]

The conflict over Johnson's churchmanship was reflected in work such as James Gray's *Johnson's Sermons,* published in 1972. Gray recognized that there were some distinctive and whiggish elements in Johnson's thought. Johnson wrote sermons, some of which were for his Whig friend John Taylor, despite Johnson's comment "I hate to see a Whig in a parson's gown." Johnson also acknowledged the value of Tillotson's sermons, and although he thought they lacked beauty, he relied on Tillotson's arguments against transubstantiation. Like Quinlan, Gray saw the ambiguity in Johnson's attitudes toward Clarke. Gray also cited William Seward's claim that Clarke's sermons had made Johnson a Christian. Johnson liked Clarke's rationalism and clarity as well as his emphasis on sincerity and private judgment, and he used Clarke's methods when it came to reservations about revelation and recommended Clarke's *Prayers and Meditations*. Despite not being an optimist, Johnson adopted a selectively Pelagian view that religion and morality were aimed at the development of human happiness.[31] Johnson also saw the sermon as an instrument of persuasion—both Low Church attitudes.[32]

Charles Pierce's *The Religious Life of Samuel Johnson* (1983) emphasized a neurotic element in Johnson's churchmanship and harked back to earlier ideas of Johnson-

29. See, for example, G. M. Ditchfield, "Dr Johnson and the Dissenters," *Bulletin of the John Rylands Library* 68 (1986): 373–409.

30. Chester F. Chapin, "Samuel Johnson: Latitudinarian or High Churchman?" *Cithara* 41, no. 1 (2001): 35–43.

31. As James E. Bradley has pointed out to me, Donald Greene denied Johnson's Pelagianism in his article "How 'Degraded' was Eighteenth-Century Anglicanism?" *Eighteenth-Century Studies* 24 (1990): 93–111, in which he also marshalled considerable evidence of the profoundly religious character of eighteenth-century society, something absent from his later debates with Jonathan Clark.

32. James Gray, *Johnson's Sermons: A Study* (Oxford, 1972), 24, 66, 67–90, 141, 150–66, 186.

ian ambiguity. Pierce suggested that reading Law had fueled Johnson's anxiety and hypocrisy, and he linked Johnson's faith to his illnesses and anxieties. Pierce listed Johnson's frequent resolutions to attend church more regularly, but Johnson often failed to do so, blaming poor eyesight and hearing. Pierce argued that Johnson had a high view of the Eucharist but was only an irregular and erratic communicant. He quoted Hawkins that Johnson was conversant with Church Fathers but knowledgeable also of Hooker, James Ussher, Henry Hammond, and Robert Sanderson. Pierce also argued that between 1760 and 1767 Johnson had a religious crisis, and that reading the Dissenter Richard Baxter brought Johnson out of this breakdown. Finding that Baxter had experienced similar scruples and anxieties seemed to help Johnson.[33]

The character of Johnson's politics and churchmanship remained compelling to scholars. In 1994 John Cannon showed some of the subtleties of Johnson's religious politics in *Samuel Johnson and the Politics of Hanoverian England*. Cannon analyzed Johnson's Tory credentials: he believed Convocation should be recalled; he supported the expulsion of Methodists from Oxford; he had no sympathy for the Feathers Tavern petition, which he called supplying our enemies with "arms from our arsenal"; he held that an established church was good for stability and social order.[34] Johnson's Toryism was derived from a paternalist view of society and the need to control the poor. Cannon recalled that at a dinner with the Dissenting booksellers Edward and Charles Dilly in May 1773, Johnson argued that freedom of conscience was different from freedom to preach and teach, which was against the interests of the established church and lessened the Church's authority and therefore should not be tolerated. Seven years later Johnson said that the state had the right to regulate the religion of the people who were "the children of the state."

Cannon speculated that 1714 was the perfect ecclesiastical moment for Johnson, with the Stuart Queen Anne on the throne and a High Church Tory government in power. Yet there was much that Cannon did not explain: he recognized the ambiguity of Johnson's assertion to Boswell "I would be a Papist if I could" and his defense of the Roman Catholic church in Ireland. Ultimately Cannon, perhaps unsatisfactorily, decided that Johnson's churchmanship was "conventional and middle of the road." He did not adjudicate in the paradox summed up in Charles Churchill's couplet on Johnson's acceptance of a pension from George III in 1761: "He damns the pension which he takes / And loves the Stuarts he forsakes." Yet Cannon conceded that Hannah More called him "Jacobite Johnson," and Charles Petrie claimed that Johnson was even blackmailed about his Jacobitism. Cannon made the point that Jacobitism was hotly contested in Lichfield, not least in the 1718 by-election, in which there were Jacobite protests in the streets. But he acknowledged that Johnson had friends who were Whigs.

33. Charles E. Pierce Jr., *The Religious Life of Samuel Johnson* (Hamden, Conn., 1983), 23, 69, 70–71, 76, 131–42.

34. John Cannon, *Samuel Johnson and the Politics of Hanoverian England* (Oxford, 1994), 17–18; Cannon suggested that Lichfield's suffering in the Civil War left Samuel Johnson with a keen desire for social order.

Cannon was also cautious in interpreting Johnson's poem *London* (1738) as a Jacobite essay on exile and his *Marmor Norfolciense* (1739) as "Jacobite Sedition"; he felt it was easy to read too much into Johnson's Jacobitism, though he conceded that Johnson had sympathy for the Stuarts and disregard for the Hanoverians.[35]

The Recent Fault Lines in Johnson's Churchmanship

There have therefore been subtle and nuanced differences in the treatment of Johnson's churchmanship; Johnson scholars accepted that there were unresolved and perhaps unresolvable ambiguities and inconsistencies in his views. But before the publication of Donald Greene's *Politics of Samuel Johnson,* in 1960, the approach to Johnson's churchmanship was largely theological. After Greene, scholars have treated Johnson's churchmanship as inseparable from his political views. Moreover, scholars have sought to establish a consistency in Johnson's thought and to iron out, explain, or resolve ambiguities. Scholars have also become proprietorial about Johnson, claiming him exclusively for one view or another, and they have abandoned contingency in favor of certainty. Greene identified a different Johnson from those who saw him as a conflicted and inconsistent Tory High Churchman. Greene's polemical work, with an introduction that was extensively redeveloped for the second edition in 1990, took issue with the identification of Johnson as a Tory, Jacobite, and Non-juror.[36] Greene denied that Johnson approved of the Young Pretender, and he attacked such views as "nonsense resuscitated in the 1980s by serious historical scholars." He criticized Jonathan Clark's claim that Johnson left Oxford to avoid the oaths as "hardly credible" and denied that Johnson deliberately declined the oaths.[37]

Greene denied that Johnson absorbed Non-juring with the Royal Touch in 1713 and suggested that Clark simply made Johnson guilty by association for living close to the Jacobite club in St. Clement Danes. Greene also chastised Howard Erskine-Hill for so frequently claiming Johnson was a Non-juror. Greene argued that Johnson's dislike of Walpole did not make him, or Walpole's many other opponents, Jacobites or Non-jurors.[38]

In part, the chasm between Greene and Clark and Erskine-Hill opened because of the use of sources. Greene claimed that Clark and Erskine-Hill relied too heavily on Boswell, and in turn Greene denied that he brushed Boswell aside in favor of other sources. Nevertheless, both sides marshalled literary and historical artillery in their support. As evidence against Johnson's Jacobitism, Greene cited "The Political State of Great Britain" in the *Literary Magazine* in 1756, in which Johnson denounced James II

35. Cannon, *Samuel Johnson and the Politics of Hanoverian England,* 19–23, 36, 37, 42, 51–54. See also Charles Petrie, *The Jacobite Movement,* 3rd ed. (London, 1959), 479.

36. Much of the discussion that follows draws on the second edition of Greene's book, in which he developed his views and replied to many of the critics of the first edition.

37. Donald Greene, "Introduction," *The Politics of Samuel Johnson,* 2nd ed. (Athens, Ga., 1990), xi–xxxiii. Jonathan Clark responded to Greene's second edition in "The Heartfelt Toryism of Dr Johnson," *Times Literary Supplement,* October 14, 1994, 17–18.

38. Greene, "Introduction," *The Politics of Samuel Johnson,* xxxiii–xxxviii.

and claimed that it had been necessary for Britain to depose him. In reply, Erskine-Hill argued that this was Johnson's prudent conformity to the establishment. Greene argued strongly that Boswell's account of Johnson was erroneous and made misattributions and inventions; and that Erskine-Hill had used Boswell naively and selectively. For Greene, "Johnson was neither a card-carrying Tory nor a card-carrying Jacobite. . . . he was a hard-headed skeptical independent observer."[39] In short, Greene sought to present Johnson as a pragmatist rather than an ideologue.

The principal response to Greene's view of Johnson came from Jonathan Clark's *Samuel Johnson: Literature, Religion, and English Cultural Politics from the Restoration to Romanticism*, published in 1994. Clark sought to reverse what he saw as the orthodoxy of Johnson as a pragmatist who was unideological. Clark's book challenged Johnson scholars on two fronts. First, he claimed it was the first historical analysis of Johnson that did not rely on the speculative literary forms of existing scholarship. Second, he presented Johnson as deeply ideologically committed. Stripped of years of pragmatic interpretation, Johnson emerged from Clark's book as a Tory, Non-juror, and Jacobite who carried these principles into his role at the center of literary activity and English cultural politics. Clark also defended Boswell as a source for Johnson's life and opinions and sought to show that much of Boswell's interpretation of Johnson was corroborated by others such as Hawkins.[40] In an accompanying article in the *Times Literary Supplement*, Clark was more explicit in his analysis that "the Johnson pictured by many students of English literature is fundamentally different from Johnson as he appears to the latest historians." Clark also suggested that "armed with . . . powerful solvent, Greene . . . strip[ped] away what he saw as layers of Romantic or Victorian varnish" to reveal Johnson as a progressive figure, a "latitudinarian, at most a proto-Evangelical." In contrast, Clark reclaimed Johnson through the pages of both Boswell and Hawkins. For Clark, it was clear that progressive liberal academics regarded such a regressive and retrospective Johnson as a diminished figure. Nevertheless, Clark advanced a considerable weight of circumstantial evidence that Johnson had specifically evaded the oaths of allegiance and abjuration on at least four occasions.[41]

The *TLS* was briefly the location of the pursuit of this furious debate. Donald Greene replied to Clark, claiming that "The Heartfelt Toryism of Dr Johnson" was an ad hominem attack. He denied that he supported the Whig interpretation of history and insisted that eighteenth-century Toryism was far less ideological and polarized than Clark had maintained. Greene questioned Clark's view that the British press in the mid-eighteenth century had treated Johnson as a Jacobite and also argued that Johnson's school friends did not seem to be aware of such a tendency. Greene also claimed that the one role Johnson had taken on in his early career, that of schoolmaster, required the oaths of allegiance and abjuration, and consequently Clark's claims about

39. Greene, "Introduction," *The Politics of Samuel Johnson*, xl–xli, xliii, xliv, lvi.

40. J. C. D. Clark, *Samuel Johnson: Literature, Religion, and English Cultural Politics from the Restoration to Romanticism* (Cambridge, 1994).

41. Clark, "The Heartfelt Toryism of Dr Johnson," 17–18.

Johnson's evasion of the oaths were based on circumstantial evidence only. Greene summarized his position thus:

> the problem seems to be summed up in his [Clark's] comment that I find that "Johnson was a moderate, a realist, intelligent and well informed, responding to the political complexities of his age, neither a bigot nor a reactionary." Clark is right; that is exactly how, after many years of immersing myself in Johnson's voluminous writings, I do find him.[42]

The principal battleground of the dispute, however, was the 1996 volume of *The Age of Johnson*, which was largely devoted to essays on Johnson's politics and churchmanship. The tone of the articles was angry and personal.[43] Naturally, the nature of evidence came to the fore: the debate addressed such issues as the reliability of Boswell and Hawkins and the degree to which they confirmed or contradicted each other. Jonathan Clark continued to maintain that by adopting a Lewis Namier–influenced view of English politics in the eighteenth century as unideological, Greene had committed himself to a position that had been roundly rejected by subsequent historical research. Thus, a view of Johnson that suggested he was indifferent to political ideology or simply responding to prejudices was insufficient in a world that now accepted the continuity of an effective Tory ideology and organization between 1714 and 1760.[44] Clark accused Greene of adopting an anachronistic, "timeless" view of Johnson, whereas Clark took the view that Johnson reconciled himself to George III without renouncing his earlier principles. For Clark, Boswell may have portrayed Johnson as a man of political expediency rather than of principle; nevertheless, Boswell's depiction of Johnson as a Tory was widely corroborated. Clark also considered the issue of the circumstantial evidence of Johnson's Non-juring and argued that the sheer volume of such evidence was in favor of Johnson being a Non-juror.[45]

Greene was having none of it. His essay in *The Age of Johnson* was easily the longest, running close to eighty pages.[46] Greene advanced seven propositions: John-

42. Donald Greene, "Was Dr Johnson Really a Jacobite?" *Times Literary Supplement,* August 18, 1995, 13–14. A month later, Eveline Cruickshanks contributed a letter to the *TLS,* September 8, 1995, 17, in which she argued that the evidence indicated not just that the Tory party was strongly committed to Jacobitism in the mid-eighteenth century but also that "some North American scholars adhere to the Whig interpretation of history as if it were God-given." Greene's reply in the *TLS,* October 13, 1995, 19, denied any adherence to the Whig interpretation of history and also concluded that Lewis Namier had not found much evidence of "gut religious" politics in eighteenth-century England.

43. Howard Erskine-Hill commented of Donald Greene that "my own fighting spirit should in some measure rise to meet his." See Erskine-Hill, "Johnson the Jacobite? A Response to the New Introduction to Donald Greene's *The Politics of Samuel Johnson,*" *The Age of Johnson* 7 (1996): 3–26 at 3.

44. J. C. D. Clark, "The Politics of Samuel Johnson," *The Age of Johnson* 7 (1996): 27–56 at 29.

45. Clark, "The Politics of Samuel Johnson," 31–43.

46. Donald Greene, "Johnson: The Jacobite Legend Exhumed, A Rejoinder to Howard Erskine-Hill and J. C. D. Clark," *The Age of Johnson* 7 (1996): 57–135 at 58, 60, 61.

son was not identified by his contemporaries as a Jacobite; his father may have been a Jacobite, but he certainly took the oath of obedience and abjuration in 1712; Johnson did not embrace the divine right of kings, a vital Jacobite principle; Johnson's apparent failure to take any oaths was not due to scruples; Johnson's early writings have been misconstrued as Jacobite; Johnson was a monarchist but not a Stuart supporter; and Johnson repeatedly praised George III and the Hanoverian monarchy after 1760. Greene attacked Clark and Erskine-Hill as ideologues who ignored the evidence. Locating Johnson in a direct relationship with eighteenth-century American politics, given his rejection of the colonists' argument in *Taxation No Tyranny*, Greene nevertheless claimed Johnson for Lockean and progressive thinking. He cited Johnson's denunciation of Thomas Jefferson and Patrick Henry: "How is it that we hear the loudest yelps for liberty among the drivers of Negroes?" Moreover, in a lengthy postscript, written to respond to the *TLS* spat, Greene asked what sort of Tory Johnson was when he denounced the Tories for their "frigid neutrality" over the Wilkes issue.[47] Greene clearly did not believe that Johnson experienced a "permanent split" in his political thinking. This enabled Greene to attack the view that Johnson could be suspected of having been present (at the very least) at the 1745 rebellion and denounce it in his writings; it also allowed him to deny that Johnson's tour of the Western Isles was a pilgrimage to pre-Reformation sites inspired by a secret interest in Catholicism.

Greene's essay was buttressed by Thomas M. Curley's article "Johnson No Jacobite; or, Treason Not Yet Unmasked," in which Curley endorsed Greene's view that the evidence of Johnson's Jacobitism was insufficient for a formal diagnosis.[48] Curley's conclusion was that Johnson had to be innocent until proven "guilty" of Jacobitism. Drawing on Johnson's collaboration with Sir Robert Chambers on his Vinerian law lectures, Curley found no evidence of Jacobite influences in what Johnson contributed to the voluminous lectures. He asked where Clark had "positive proof for such a positive pronouncement" of Johnson's Jacobitism, and he compared it to Johnson's defense of the oaths for Dissenters in March 1772.[49] Moreover, Curley suggested that some of Johnson's early political writings, including *Marmor Norfolciense*, were only anti-Walpole rather than anti-Hanoverian or pro-Tory.[50]

Howard D. Weinbrot concluded the essays in *The Age of Johnson* on Johnson's Jacobitism by defending Greene and subjecting Clark's work to forensic analysis.[51] Weinbrot declared himself openly for a progressive and forward-looking Johnson, asserting that Johnson was essentially pragmatic rather than ideological in his politics.

47. Greene, "Johnson: The Jacobite Legend Exhumed," 98, 112.

48. Curley was careful to explain that he neither knew nor collaborated with either Greene or Clark.

49. Thomas M. Curley, "Johnson No Jacobite; or, Treason Not Yet Unmasked," *The Age of Johnson* 7 (1996): 137–62 at 150–51.

50. Curley subjected Erskine-Hill and Clark to Johnsonian textual analysis, comparing sections of their published opinions in the following issue of *The Age of Johnson*: Thomas M. Curley, "Johnson No Jacobite; or, Treason Not Yet Unmasked: Part II, a Quotable Rejoinder from A to C," *The Age of Johnson* 8 (1997): 127–31.

51. Howard D. Weinbrot, "Johnson, Jacobitism, and the Historiography of Nostalgia," *The Age of Johnson* 7 (1996): 163–211.

Johnson, wrote Weinbrot, even owed a debt to Locke. Weinbrot also suggested that Johnson's reconciliation to the Hanoverians after 1760 was typical of other Tories. But his principal position was that Clark needed to prove his case more conclusively: "The question under review, after all, is not whether Professor Greene is wrong, but whether Dr Clark is right."[52] He challenged Clark's view that the eighteenth century was greatly influenced by classical traditions, which drew Johnson to Toryism. Weinbrot refused to concede the influence of the classical tradition on Johnson, citing strong German and Protestant influences. Weinbrot also argued that Clark had misread some writers, notably Hawkins, and transformed subjunctives into certainties, piling up many *may haves*. He also struck at Clark's claims by asserting that Johnson probably *did* take the oaths at Oxford and did not take them for the London-trained bands only because, as a sick, half-blind, fifty-year-old writer, he could reasonably provide a substitute.

Clark did not let the matter rest, and in 2002 he published an impressive collection of essays, coedited with Howard Erskine-Hill, called *Samuel Johnson in Historical Context*.[53] The Johnson who emerged from *Samuel Johnson in Historical Context* was much more complex and contradictory than scholars in the debate had until then conceded. In the introduction, Erskine-Hill grappled with the problem of two Johnsons: a progressive, pragmatic, and enlightened Johnson but also an unenlightened Johnson who drew deeply on dynasticism, lore, superstition, and classical education. Paul Monod addressed the issue of Johnson's Jacobitism, defending Johnson from Boswell's depiction of him as a sentimental or romantic Jacobite like Hester Thrale or Hannah More. Instead, Monod argued that Johnson was not a hypocrite but experienced a variegated Jacobitism that fluctuated in intensity—the same could be said for Dryden, Pope, Savage, and Gibbon. He also particularized Johnson's Jacobitism to Staffordshire, in which Jacobitism had a stronger flavor (and for longer) than in much of Britain. So Johnson's early life was tainted by Jacobitism and influenced such works as his poem *London* and *Marmor Norfolciense*; yet the play *Irene*—written in 1737 but not performed until 1749—showed an occlusion of Johnson's views. Monod's conclusion was that "Johnson was never quite the Jacobite he wanted later in life to appear to be"; his was an emotional as well as intellectual Jacobitism that was not constant throughout his life.[54] In examining claims of Johnson's Non-juring, Richard Sharp collected some significant circumstantial evidence of Johnson's worship at St. Clement Danes, a church that attracted such Non-jurors as John Byrom, William Bowyer, and Archibald Campbell as well as a group of Non-juring printers. The patronage and worship of the parish were strongly Jacobite and Non-juring. This was the parish in which Johnson chose to worship.[55] Eirwen Nicholson pointed out the 1726 controversy in the parish—

52. Weinbrot, "Johnson, Jacobitism, and the Historiography of Nostalgia," 163–66, 170.

53. *Samuel Johnson in Historical Context,* ed. Jonathan Clark and Howard Erskine-Hill (Basingstoke, U.K., 2002).

54. Paul Monod, "A Voyage out of Staffordshire; or, Samuel Johnson's Jacobite Journey," in *Samuel Johnson in Historical Context,* 11–44.

55. Richard Sharp, "The Religious and Political Character of the Parish of St. Clement Danes," in *Samuel Johnson in Historical Context,* 44–55. Of course the incumbent was a juring member of the Church of England.

the depiction of St. Cecilia on the altarpiece was a portrait of Maria Sobieski, wife of the Old Pretender—which further endorsed the parish and vestry as a nest of Jacobites.[56]

Clark's own essay took the issue of Johnson and oaths to its furthest extent, arguing that England was "a polity defined by oaths." He suggested that, as an undergraduate at Pembroke College, Oxford, Johnson swore the oath of uniformity but not those of allegiance or abjuration, which only scholars and foundationers were required to do. Perhaps scruple over the oaths that would have been required on graduation, as much as poverty, drove Johnson from Oxford, and scruple—as much as health—played a role in Johnson's failure to serve in the London-trained bands. Clark argued that, well into the 1750s, Johnson was a convinced and committed Tory who clapped himself sore at a Jacobite speech in Oxford in 1759. Yet Clark recognized that the 1760s were a period of political transition for Johnson—as much as for the Tories generally. Gradually it was possible for Johnson to support Tory Hanoverian policy. Perhaps Clark's most significant suggestion is that throughout his life Johnson sought, to some degree, to evade political definition, and hence to define him is complex and contentious.[57] In his conclusion, Clark warned against anachronistic views of Johnson's Jacobitism or dynastic loyalty to the Stuarts as "nostalgic"—a form not available to Johnson as a pre-Romantic figure. Clark insisted that Johnson's politics and religion were a matter of choice.[58] Other essayists showed Johnson's partisanship in seeking patrons, his pragmatism in foreign policy, his love-hate fascination with Scotland, his delicate Latin verse, and his sense of the divine right of kings.[59]

The theme of Johnson's Toryism was taken up in an unexpected area by Robert Mayhew, who concluded that Johnson used landscape in his writing as a means to express moral ideas. Johnson's landscape language was sharply contrasted with that of the Latitudinarians: Robert Boyle, for example, developed a landscape description that drew on an understanding of nature and rational ideas of landscape.[60] However, Johnson's description of landscape was binary, focusing on polarities like town and countryside, past and present, civilized and savage. These poles resonated with those of Catholic–Protestant, English–Spanish, and they had political and religious overtones. Place for Johnson determined state of mind. His language was more emblematic than empirical, and it developed a patriotic rhetoric. Words like *path*, *prospect*, and *tempest* were moral terms. For Mayhew, Johnson's Tory High Churchmanship was the "moving force" behind an emphasis on the scriptural routes to faith. These were views Johnson shared with fellow High Churchmen such as John Hutchinson

56. Eirwen E. C. Nicholson, "The St. Clement Danes Altarpiece and the Iconography of Post-Revolutionary England," in *Samuel Johnson in Historical Context*, 55–76.

57. J. C. D. Clark, "Religion and Political Identity: Samuel Johnson as a Nonjuror," in *Samuel Johnson in Historical Context*, 79–146.

58. J. C. D. Clark, "Conclusion: Literature, History, and Interpretation," in *Samuel Johnson in Historical Context*, 295–307.

59. See the important essays by Eveline Cruickshanks, Jeremy Black, Murray Pittock, and David Money in *Samuel Johnson in Historical Context*.

60. Robert J. Mayhew, *Landscape, Literature, and English Religious Culture, 1660–1800: Samuel Johnson and the Languages of Natural Description* (Basingstoke, U.K., 2004).

and William Jones of Nayland. Nature was dependent on God, not on man, and it was a form of revelation.

The movement in the direction of Johnson as an ideological Tory and a principled High Church Non-juror and Jacobite was challenged forcefully by Howard D. Weinbrot in *Aspects of Samuel Johnson,* which supported some of the views Greene had asserted in *The Politics of Samuel Johnson.* Weinbrot sought to rescue Johnson from the lens of Boswell. He quoted Johnson's comment that "a wise Tory and a wise Whig . . . will agree. Their principles are the same, though their modes of thinking are different." And he pointed out Johnson's approval of Tillotson, even preferring him to Robert South. For Weinbrot, Johnson was empirical, skeptical, and unideological; he adopted some decidedly Whiggish views, such as those on property, which were derived from Locke. Weinbrot also considered Johnson to be deeply conflicted on the Glorious Revolution—fundamentally committed to the Stuart cause but accepting of the revolution as a necessity to defend the constitution. Thus, for Weinbrot, "Johnson was . . . eclectic in selecting from different political systems." Yet Weinbrot denied in the strongest terms the possibility that some of that eclecticism came from Jacobitism, and he did so in what he claimed was a defense of "the canons of scholarly method, the nature of evidence and the sorts of inferences that such evidence allows one legitimately to draw."[61] On the matter of oaths, Weinbrot was unequivocal: Johnson swore the oath of supremacy in December 1728, many Oxford Jacobites, such as Thomas Hearne, swore the oaths of allegiance and abjuration with mental reservation, why would Johnson not have done so? More likely was that Johnson could not face continuing at Oxford in poverty. Moreover, Johnson's age and poor eyesight meant he could not serve in the London-trained bands and had no principled objection to the role and oaths.[62] In a later essay, Weinbrot claimed some of Johnson's views were consistent with Whiggism and Latitudinarianism, and Johnson derived much of his thinking on civil government from the Low Church strand of English churchmanship represented by Hooker and Hoadly. For Weinbrot, Johnson was much more like an "old Whig" than a Tory, as he married royal prerogative with the liberty of the people. Citing Johnson's twenty-fourth sermon and his views of 1763 on the legitimacy of the people to reclaim their rights, Weinbrot constructed Johnson as often whiggish, someone whose High Churchmanship was nothing like the existing models of Atterbury and those who elevated Charles I as a king and martyr.[63]

61. Howard D. Weinbrot, *Aspects of Samuel Johnson: Essays on His Arts, Mind, Afterlife, and Politics* (Newark, Del., 2005), 20–21, 55–56, 303, 305–7.

62. Weinbrot, *Aspects of Samuel Johnson*, 312–30.

63. Howard D. Weinbrot, "Johnson and the Modern: The Forward Face of Janus," in *Johnson after 300 Years*, ed. Greg Clingham and Philip Smallwood (Cambridge, 2009), 55–72. Two further volumes regarding Johnson appeared too late to be considered for this study: *The Politics of Samuel Johnson,* ed. Jonathan Clark and Howard Erskine-Hill (Houndmills, U.K., 2012), and *The Interpretation of Samuel Johnson*, ed. Jonathan Clark and Howard Erskine-Hill (Houndmills, U.K., 2012).

The Myth of Johnson's Exceptionalism

It is an irony that both "sides" in the Greene/Weinbrot versus Clark/Erskine-Hill debate have overlooked key points of agreement. Both regard Johnson as more complex and prone to inconsistency than scholars have previously conceded. Erskine-Hill's introduction to *Samuel Johnson in Historical Context* is an elegant argument for a comprehensive analysis of Johnson in which he can be seen as embracing more than one dimension of politics and religion. In his concluding essay, Clark called for a treatment of Johnson that did not use categories "imposed on people in the past" and recognized that historians and literary scholars had problems with Johnson because he often obscured his meaning. Clark has argued for Johnson to be seen as holding complex political views that complicate the easy use of the terms *Tory* and *Whig* and that collide Tory Jacobite sympathies with de facto acceptance of the Hanoverian succession.[64] Weinbrot made a comparable request in his paper for the Samuel Johnson at 300 Years conference, held at Pembroke College, Oxford, in September 2009. In an essay entitled "Johnson Rebalanced: The Happy Man, the Supportive Family, and His Social Religion," Weinbrot urged a more rounded view of Johnson, a complex fusion of "smiling Sam" and "sad Sam," a metropolitan, enlightened, and progressive Johnson and a provincial, traditionalist Johnson.[65] Weinbrot also asked scholars to abandon simple views of Johnson as dour, pessimistic, and depressive when he was also capable of great optimism and laughter. Johnson was an inclusive figure capable of holding both High Church and Latitudinarian views. Such comprehending opinions have found support from other scholars. The volume of essays based on the tercentenary conference opened a new contingency in opinions about Johnson. Fred Parker indicated how much Johnson disliked large and overarching systems of thought and philosophy.[66] Clement Hawes argued that Johnson's politics are much more difficult to pin down than scholars have acknowledged.[67] And Chester Chapin's 2001 essay on Johnson's churchmanship goes some way to exploring the complexity of the categorization.[68]

Nevertheless, a "both/and" resolution would be intellectually unsatisfactory, a scholarly "quantitative easing" or intellectual "raising of the debt ceiling" that simply accepts that Johnson was a big enough figure and sufficiently complex to hold contradictory and conflicting positions at the same time. While this is likely to have been the case to some degree, it does not do justice to the context within which Johnson developed his churchmanship. Perhaps the question about Johnson's life and work that most readily accommodates the "both/and" position is whether he was a progressive and enlightenment thinker, or retrospective and traditionalist in outlook. Not only do

64. Clark, "Conclusion: Literature, History, and Interpretation," 295–307.

65. This essay appears in *Samuel Johnson: The Arc of the Pendulum,* ed. Freya Johnston and Lynda Mugglestone (Oxford, 2012), 195–207.

66. Fred Parker, "'We are Perpetual Moralists': Johnson and Moral Philosophy," in *Samuel Johnson after 300 Years*, 1–14.

67. Clement Hawes, "Samuel Johnson's Politics of Contingency," in *Samuel Johnson after 300 Years*, 73–94.

68. Chapin, "Samuel Johnson: Latitudinarian or High Churchman?"

long lives lend themselves to inconsistency of this nature, but so do turbulent times. Johnson was born into a kingdom in which it was entirely reasonable to expect that there might be a reversal of the Act of Settlement of 1701 and a Stuart restored to the throne; he died at a time when this was unthinkable. In such circumstances, there were many people who held beliefs in 1760 that they might have found impossible to contemplate in 1720 and vice versa. As Clark noted, "The drama of Johnson's public life was exactly that of the changing dilemmas with which Englishmen were confronted from Anne, through the Hanoverian accession and successive unsuccessful conspiracies, to grudging reconciliation after 1760."[69] That is the nature of history—people change their minds, or find themselves caught between two views that appear to be in conflict, and even agree with two opposing views at the same time. Clark indicated that positing a "rational" Johnson who found himself at odds with a "nostalgic" Johnson is perhaps an anachronism, and that may be so. But it may also be that Johnson found himself, especially after the 1740s, unable to find a single polarity for his churchmanship and politics.

A further aspect of the debate is the way in which the two sides have applied a laser-like scrutiny to him. Johnsonians have consequently tended to regard him as exceptional. Johnson was remarkable, but he lived in an age of remarkable people, and some consideration should be given to whether he was exceptional in his contested characteristics. Three examples of similarly long-lived figures in the eighteenth century offer interesting comparisons with Johnson: John Wesley, Benjamin Hoadly, and David Hume. The case of John Wesley provides some instructive evidence of the problem not just of political and religious categorization, but also of changes of views over time. Wesley can be treated as an Anglican who inherited a seventeenth-century High Church theology and whose implicit criticism of the Church of England in the eighteenth century was made from this perspective. He was a Tory in politics, and his mother was a fairly open Non-juror.[70] Certainly there was much in Wesley's churchmanship and politics that was highly "conservative." Like Johnson, Wesley was often wary of expressions of popular opinion; he was suspicious of the poor and sought to buttress authority in church and state. Yet there are those who regard Wesley as progressive, and some evidence can be marshalled for this. He flouted episcopal authority, improvised and innovated in church organization, and laid aside the doctrine and traditions of the Church in ordaining clergy. He supported the antislavery movement, and there are theologians who even claim Wesley as the originator of liberation theology and emancipation in American thought.[71]

Wesley was also capable of significant changes of mind. His about-face over the issue of support for the American colonists in 1774–76, in which he plagiarized Johnson's *Taxation No Tyranny*, shows that deeply held principles often led to significantly different conclusions. In 1774, Wesley had endorsed a defense of the American colonists

69. Clark, "The Heartfelt Toryism of Dr Johnson," 17.

70. See Charles Wallace Jr., *Susanna Wesley: The Complete Writings* (New York, 1997).

71. See, for example, Theodore W. Jennings Jr., *Good News to the Poor: John Wesley's Evangelical Economics* (Nashville, Tenn., 1990).

entitled *An Argument in Defense of the Exclusive Right Claimed by the Colonies to Tax Themselves*. The Bristol Baptist minister Caleb Evans was among those who forced Wesley to concede not only that he had plagiarized Johnson in a subsequent tract but also that he had supported the American colonists up to 1775, when he decided that they represented a danger to Britain. But of course there must have been many people in 1774, when there was no evidence of widespread disobedience to the Crown in America, who were sympathetic to the claim of "no taxation without representation"; but that was a very different thing from supporting armed insurrection in 1776.[72]

Benjamin Hoadly lived for eighty-five years, and he also straddled the era of the Stuarts and the Hanoverians. For Hoadly the central concern was the reunion of the Church and Dissent. From 1703 to 1708 he engaged in a furious controversy with the Dissenter Edmund Calamy on "the reasonableness of conformity" for Dissenters, placing the onus on them to accept episcopacy and Anglican liturgy. It was a debate that brought Hoadly some admiration from fellow Anglicans. By 1716, however, he had concluded that the onus now lay on the Church of England to change if it was to attract and comprehend Dissenters. Such a change did not negate Hoadly's desire for Dissenters to accept episcopacy and the Book of Common Prayer, but it did mean that many regarded him as a traitor to the church in which he was a bishop.[73]

Another important and instructive comparison for Johnson is with David Hume. Some have assumed him to have been either atheist or theist, but like Johnson, Hume still evades definition. His "reversal" in the final part of the *Dialogues Concerning Natural Religion*—a posthumous publication in 1779 that might be assumed to reveal his authentic views—confuses scholars by seeming to endorse faith. As with Johnson, concealment and partial self-revelation were modes of thought and expression that Hume embraced. The choice of the dialogue form in both their writings perhaps captures more than one inner voice in conflict with another. Like Johnson, moreover, Hume was a man of friendships and sociability. Both had circles of friends with differing opinions. Hume certainly seems to have been influenced by his friends in two directions: first, he sometimes did not speak or write his opinions as bluntly as he might have, for fear of offending them; second, he amended his opinions in response to those of his friends. These discrete influences of pragmatic friendship undoubtedly affected Hume's work,[74] and perhaps the same tugs of pragmatic friendship also affected Johnson.[75]

72. Henry Abelove, "John Wesley's Plagiarism of Samuel Johnson and Its Contemporary Reception," *Huntington Library Quarterly* 59, no. 1 (1996): 73–79.

73. William Gibson, *Enlightenment Prelate: Benjamin Hoadly, 1676–1761* (Cambridge, 2004), xx.

74. Jonathan Dancy, "'For Here the Author is Annihilated': Reflections on Philosophical Aspects of the Use of the Dialogue Form in Hume's *Dialogues Concerning Natural Religion*," in *Philosophical Dialogues: Plato, Hume, Wittgenstein*, ed. Timothy Smiley (Oxford, 1995), 29–60; Richard Dees, "Morality above Metaphysics: Philo and the Duties of Friendship in *Dialogues* 12," *Hume Studies* 28 (2002): 131–48; Terence Penelhum, "Hume's Views on Religion: Intellectual and Cultural Influences," in *A Companion to Hume*, ed. Elizabeth S. Radcliffe (Oxford, 2010), 323–38.

75. Of course, as with Hume, generations of friends, correspondents, editors, biographers, and critics have appropriated Johnson for their particular purposes. I am indebted to Dr. Dan O'Brien for this point.

A further problem for Johnson scholars is also the slipperiness of the terms *Whig* and *Tory* and of the nature of church politics in the eighteenth century. Much as Johnson liked to give clear-cut dictionary definitions—which might have been more reasonable after 1760—such terms could not be easily defined earlier in the century. Tories, theoretically adherents of hereditary monarchy and a sacerdotal view of the character of the monarch, were nevertheless scathing of James II and admiring of Mary II and Anne—and later so of George III. Even *Jacobite* was an ambiguous term. John Byrom, himself a Jacobite, wrote the verse:

> God bless the King, I mean the Faith's Defender,
> God bless—no harm in blessing—the Pretender,
> But who Pretender is, or who is King,
> God bless us all—that's quite another Thing.[76]

The society Samuel Johnson was born into was deeply ideological—Clark is right in this. The character of the ideologies in England between 1688 and 1745 was complex and surprising, not least because they did not always create opposing polarized positions. This is partly because there were two ideological axes, those of religious doctrine and monarchical principle. For many people, when these ideologies competed, they created a topsy-turvy world. So it was a paradox in 1688–89 that Tory Anglican bishops who had proclaimed passive obedience to a ruler as a cornerstone of the Church found themselves actively resisting James II.[77] But oaths of obedience and loyalty were no small things, and five of the seven bishops whom James had put on trial chose to stick by him rather than replace him with William and Mary. Equally, it was profound scruple that led William Sherlock and Robert Nelson to equivocate between Non-juring and conformity. Sherlock, widely expected to become a Non-juror in 1689, shocked his friends by conforming on the last day permitted by law;[78] and Nelson, having become a Non-juror, returned to the Church in 1710 despite remaining a committed Jacobite. It was not therefore absence of scruple or ideological commitment that caused men to change their minds and adopt ambiguous positions; it was superabundance of it. Such scruples encouraged individuals to circumscribe their own idiosyncratic positions, so that John Sharp—later archbishop of York—agreed to swear the oaths to William III but refused to receive an appointment to any bishopric from which a Non-juror had been ejected.

Religious politics in church and state in this period were similarly complex. The modern analogy to two-party politics is anachronistic, and it fails to capture the sense of ideological permeability between two loose groupings of interests and connections. Again, this was not expediency but the product of deeply held principles. In religious terms, this can be seen in the churchmanship of two leading bishops in the second

76. Timothy Underhill, "John Byrom," in *British Writers: Supplement XVI,* ed. Jay Parini (New York, 2010).

77. William Gibson, *James II and the Trial of the Seven Bishops* (Basingstoke, U.K., 2010).

78. *ODNB,* s.v. "Sherlock, William," by W. E. Burns.

decade of the eighteenth century, William Talbot and George Smalridge. Talbot and Smalridge were highly committed Whig Latitudinarian and Tory High Churchman, respectively, except that they did not conform to the usual principles of their "parties." Despite being Atterbury's High Church ally, Smalridge was suspected of heterodoxy and even of Arianism, so that his friends had to deny it after his death.[79] Talbot's Whig Latitudinarianism had been clearly evidenced both by his acceptance of the deanery of Worcester after the Non-juror George Hickes was ejected from it and by his time as bishop of Worcester. Talbot nonetheless held some deeply High Church theological opinions that placed him alongside some of the most altitudinarian churchmen of his day.[80] In other words, looks in Johnson's day could be deceiving, and stereotypes simply did not work. It might be the case that there were a few, highly consistent Tories who were also Non-jurors and Jacobites, but there were far more variants of these combinations, including those with mental reservations, both in their support for the Stuart cause and in their conformity to the Church and their loyalty to the Crown.[81]

An example in Johnson's theology is his attitude toward the Eucharist. While this undoubtedly changed and developed over his lifetime, there is also no doubt that Johnson had a high sacramental view of receipt of Holy Communion. His preparation for it, and his anxieties over his unworthiness for it, were common in eighteenth-century England and a powerful reason for infrequent communication. Johnson's writing showed him to be strongly guided by the Book of Common Prayer, which combined Thomas Cranmer's sense of the Eucharist as a memorial and as a sacrament imparting grace. Johnson stood foursquare with the Anglican theology of the Eucharist, but his anxieties led him to resist the Church's teaching on its receipt.[82]

The danger of overanalyzing every saying and quotation of Johnson's is evidenced in Chester Chapin's 2001 article, in which he tried to second-guess why Johnson used anti-Jacobite quotations from Addison's work in the *Dictionary*. Chapin asked whether Johnson quoted anti-Jacobite material from *The Freeholder* "to be acceptable to people of very different political opinions," or whether he might have endorsed all the quotations he used in the *Dictionary* without espousing other Whig opinions. Such are the convolutions that scholars can recognize in this dispute.[83] Johnson's own writings

79. William Gibson, "Altitudinarian Equivocation: George Smalridge's Churchmanship," in *Religious Identities in Britain, 1660–1832*, ed. William Gibson and Robert G. Ingram (Aldershot, U.K., 2005), 43–60.

80. William Gibson, "William Talbot and Church Parties, 1688–1730," *Journal of Ecclesiastical History* 58, no. 1 (2007): 26–48.

81. A good example is Susanna Wesley, mother of John and Charles Wesley, who was a Non-juror and a Jacobite but who remained a Dissenter by baptism and did not share her husband's high views on the nature of the priesthood. She was a curious mixture of Puritan-Dissenting Jacobite Non-juror.

82. See, for example, Jane Steen, "Literally Orthodox: Samuel Johnson's Anglicanism," *Enlightenment and Dissent* 11 (1992): 87–106.

83. Chester Chapin, "Samuel Johnson and Joseph Addison's Anti-Jacobite Writings," in *Notes and Queries* (2001): 38–40. For the record, Chapin concluded, "although far from conclusive, the bit of evidence here presented weighs the scale somewhat, I believe, in favor of those who see Johnson as always a Tory but never a Jacobite" (40). For more on Johnson's illustrative quotation, see Howard D. Weinbrot, "What Johnson's Illustrative Quotations Illustrate: Language and Viewpoint in the *Dictionary*," in

and voices are also an ingredient in this debate. Erskine-Hill identified four forms of Johnsonian writing: constrained Jacobite writing, crypto-Jacobite writing, open Jacobite writing, and non-Jacobite writing.[84] In each of these voices, Johnson could of course be ironical, parodying, serious, sardonic, or all manner of other attitudes and sentiments.

Conclusion

In his gossipy biography of Samuel Johnson, Charles Norman wrote that "as a man, Johnson is more complicated than his obvious and outward physical defects have indicated."[85] Perhaps understandably, Johnson scholars have developed a myth of Johnsonian exceptionalism. They have done so, in part, because neither the theological analyses of the first half of the twentieth century nor the political lens of more recent scholarship has provided a completely satisfactory explanation of Johnson's complex and contradictory churchmanship. Like most claims to exceptionalism, that for Johnson is a myth. Many of Johnson's contemporaries found themselves grappling with the multifaceted dynastic, theological, and political ideas of the eighteenth century and, like Johnson, found that complete consistency was impossible to achieve.

I am grateful to Professor J. C. D. Clark and Professor Howard D. Weinbrot for their comments on earlier drafts of this essay; responsibility for its opinions remains my own.

Anniversary Essays on Johnson's "Dictionary," ed. Jack Lynch and Anne McDermott (Cambridge, 2005), 42–60; and Allen Reddick, "Vindicating Milton: Poetic Misprision in Johnson's *Dictionary of the English Language*," in "Johnson after Three Centuries: New Light on Texts and Contexts," ed. Thomas A. Horrocks and Howard D. Weinbrot, special issue, *Harvard Library Bulletin* 20 (2009): 61–72.

84. Erskine-Hill, "Johnson the Jacobite?" 9.

85. Charles Norman, *Mr. Oddity, Samuel Johnson LL.D* (London, 1952), 1.

The Active Soul and *Vis Inertiae*: Change and Tension in Johnson's Philosophy from *The Rambler* to *The Idler*

Nicholas Hudson

IT IS WIDELY ACCEPTED that in *The Rambler* and *The Adventurer*, published between 1750 and 1754, Johnson articulated a distinctive philosophy of life that remained consistent throughout his career and that was relatively uncomplicated by doubts or contradictions. The "pure wine" of *The Rambler*, as Johnson described these essays,[1] has seemed an expansion in prose of the outlook condensed in *The Vanity of Human Wishes* (1749), and it has dominated discussion of his moral and philosophical attitudes. The series of essays he wrote at the end of the 1750s, *The Idler*, has received relatively little attention. Patrick O'Flaherty's stated intention in 1970 to inaugurate a wave of scholarship about these essays resulted in little more than a trickle. Even for O'Flaherty, *The Idler* differed from the earlier essays less in content than in Johnson's more "detached" and satirical style.[2] For many readers, *The Idler* has seemed at best "light" and "amusing satire," only occasionally serious and aimed to gratify the tastes of the wider audience of *The Universal Chronicle*, the newspaper in which it appeared weekly as the opening essay.[3] There have been occasional dissenting voices. Though generally agreeing with O'Flaherty that *The Idler* differs from *The Rambler* mostly in its satirical form, James F. Woodruff also noted a new darkness in these essays, "an underlying vision of human activity everywhere as vanity and idleness."[4] In an important book on Johnson's thought, Isobel Grundy agreed: noting an unacknowledged "bleakness" in these essays, she concluded that "The *Idler* amounts to a sustained ironic reversal of the *Rambler*'s position."[5]

1. *Boswell's Life of Samuel Johnson, Together with Boswell's Journal of a Tour to the Hebrides and Johnson's Diary of a Journey into North Wales*, ed. George Birkbeck Hill, rev. L. F. Powell, 6 vols. (Oxford, 1934–50), 1:210n1 (hereafter cited as *Life*).

2. Patrick O'Flaherty, "Johnson's *Idler*: The Equipment of a Satirist," *ELH* 37, no. 2 (1970): 211–25.

3. James L. Clifford, *Dictionary Johnson: Samuel Johnson's Middle Years* (New York, 1979), 194–96; J. P. Hardy, *Samuel Johnson: A Critical Study* (London and Boston, 1979), 102–3.

4. James F. Woodruff, "Johnson's *Idler* and the 'Anatomy of Idleness,'" *English Studies in Canada* 6 (1980): 35.

5. Isobel Grundy, *Samuel Johnson and the Scale of Greatness* (Leicester, U.K., 1986), 248n19, 93.

In this essay, I will take up these hints that something happened to Johnson's outlook in *The Idler* beyond a supposed shift to a more jocular or popular style. In *The Idler*, I will argue, Johnson was rethinking the understanding of human nature characteristic of *The Rambler* and *The Adventurer*, and by extension *The Vanity of Human Wishes*. It may seem strange to claim that Johnson's outlook became more pessimistic over the course of the 1750s, as he was never especially optimistic or sanguine. Like *The Vanity of Human Wishes*, however, the earlier essays portray human beings as tragically heroic in their restless aspiration and implacable ambition. In *The Idler*, on the contrary, human beings are defined much less by their vain ambition for greatness than by what, in both these essays and *The Rambler*, Johnson called *vis inertiae*, inert force, the physical pull toward stillness made famous by Sir Isaac Newton's theory of gravitation. For Johnson, "idleness" also meant a diffusion of mental energy into useless and aimless bustle. As Woodruff commented, "idleness" in *The Idler* is something more than an amusing leitmotif; it is a serious and even obsessive theme reconfigured and "anatomized" in essay after essay.[6]

The impression that *The Idler* differs from the earlier essays in being more vernacular and popular seems less convincing when read, as it seldom has been, as part of *The Universal Chronicle*. This newspaper was not a light journal on miscellaneous literary matters. It was what we might call a "war paper," whose columns were filled, week after week, with accounts of Britain's escalating war against France in North America and on the Continent. In pointed ways, Johnson was commenting on the content of *The Universal Chronicle* itself, often drawing material from the newspaper of the same day, which he seems to have read before writing his essay. Most depressing for Johnson was the patriotic fervor whipped up by the "Great Commoner," William Pitt, who, having finally secured a dominant place in George II's cabinet, committed British troops to the Continent and revamped American policy just at the time this newspaper was launched. Although Johnson himself began his career as a journalist for *The Gentleman's Magazine*, often reporting on the conflicts of the early 1740s, he became deeply disillusioned by the spectacle of hack writers repeating mendacious reports on what he regarded as purposeless human slaughter. His animus was directed against not only the reporters who supplied this paper but also the gullible, "patriotic," and idle readers who consumed this propaganda because, as he implied in the ironic pose of a fellow "idler," they could find nothing else with which to fill their empty minds. Paradoxically, that most strenuous of human activities, war, epitomized a human tendency toward "idleness," as understood in Johnson's sense as meaningless and, in this case, murderous agitation.

The difficult question that arises is whether this evident crisis in Johnson's philosophical outlook represents a permanent change or a temporary reaction to these historical events, intensified by Johnson's growing frustration with his own indolence in the late 1750s. My judgment is that *The Idler* marks less a transformation of his outlook than a shift of emphasis from one side of his assessment of human nature to another. Even in *The Rambler*, Johnson often recoils in the face of human malignity

6. Woodruff, "Johnson's *Idler*," 22.

and stupidity. Similarly, in the late 1750s, he could still present humans as celestial beings restlessly driven toward a fulfillment possible only in the afterlife, a common and persuasive interpretation of *Rasselas* (1759). As we will consider, however, even *Rasselas* implies a doubtful wavering between opposed views of human nature, for this work is filled with much deflating satire of human fatuity, and it draws significantly toward "The conclusion, in which nothing is concluded."[7] We should perhaps reflect on this warning against conclusions. Boswell's biography continues to influence the view of Johnson as an inherently unified "self" whose erratic moods only superficially deviated from a consistent underlying philosophy. Yet Boswell met Johnson as an already famous literary figure in his mid-fifties who had gone through many difficult transitions and experiences. Contrary to a tendency of Johnsonian scholarship, we might question Boswell's habit of gleaning various statements across the wide field of Johnson's career as merely stylistically colored expressions of an unchanging, core philosophy. Evidence suggests, on the contrary, that Johnson went to his grave undecided on the question of whether the outlook of *The Rambler* was essentially truer than the bleaker attitude of *The Idler*. Certainly Johnson had consistent beliefs, but like most intelligent people, he could change his mind.

Empiricism and Dualism in *The Rambler*

It has been conventional for several decades to situate Johnson's thought squarely in the tradition of empiricism. According to a long line of scholars, he essentially endorsed John Locke's analysis of the mind in *An Essay Concerning Human Understanding* (1690), a work that Johnson frequently cited to illustrate philosophical terms in the *Dictionary*.[8] Adam Potkay has presented the challenging thesis that Johnson generally differed from David Hume by "degree only," despite Johnson's frequent expressions of disdain for this most skeptical and heterodox heir of Locke's empiricism.[9] In many respects, Johnson's empiricism is indisputable. He rejected belief in innate ideas, believing that all knowledge came from the senses. He also believed that passions rather than some autonomous "will" motivated human actions, and that the role of reason was to regulate or discipline the passions toward enlightened self-interest. Nevertheless, particularly with relation to *The Rambler* and *The Adventurer*, I would qualify this consensus by stressing that Johnson's characteristic emphasis on the insufficiency of sensory ideas and bodily pleasure, the endless leaping ahead of the "soul" toward imagined states of fulfillment, has no significant equivalent in the philosophy of either Locke or Hume. My identification of this theme will not seem especially novel to scholars who know W. J. Bate's *The Achievement of Samuel Johnson* (1955), once a

7. Johnson, *Rasselas and Other Tales*, vol. 16 of *The Yale Edition of the Works of Samuel Johnson* (hereafter cited as *YE*), ed. Gwin J. Kolb (New Haven, Conn., 1990), 175.

8. Jean H. Hagstrum, *Samuel Johnson's Literary Criticism* (Minneapolis, 1952), 3–20; Paul K. Alkon, *Samuel Johnson and Moral Discipline* (Evanston, Ill., 1967), 85–108; William Edinger, *Samuel Johnson and Poetic Style* (Chicago, 1977), 31–32; Robert DeMaria Jr., *The Life of Samuel Johnson: A Critical Biography* (Oxford and Cambridge, Mass., 1993), 77.

9. Adam Potkay, *The Passion for Happiness: Samuel Johnson and David Hume* (Ithaca, N.Y., and London, 2000), 215.

work of enormous influence on Johnson studies. Highlighting Imlac's phrase in *Rasselas*, the "hunger of the imagination" (*YE*, 16:118), Bate stressed the theme of endless yearning in Johnson's thought and life.[10] Bate nonetheless wished to present Johnson as a precursor of Freud rather than as an orthodox defender of Christian dualism. His book set off a wave of biographical speculation about Johnson's thwarted desires and sexual repression while exerting relatively little influence on studies of his moral and religious thought.[11]

In contrast with Johnson, eighteenth-century empiricists generally had little interest in the "hunger of the imagination" or the immaterial soul. Although Locke declared that he believed in the existence of the soul, he found himself embroiled in a bitter controversy with the bishop of Worcester, Edward Stillingfleet, for arguing that God could make matter think.[12] As Locke's orthodox opponents detected, this position was consistent with what he set out to establish in his *Essay*. All of human knowledge and behavior, Locke contended, could be explained without recourse to any principles besides ideas derived from the senses and the basic drive to pursue pleasure and avoid pain. Against the view that human action reflected the existence of an autonomous faculty called the "will," Locke argued that all human action is prompted by what he called "uneasiness," a desire for renewed sensual satisfaction or relief from discomfort. Apart from these sensory stimulations, Locke imagined the mind as essentially quiescent. As he observed, "indeed in this life there are not many, whose happiness reaches so far, as to afford them a constant train of moderate mean Pleasures, without any mixture of *uneasiness*; and yet they could be content to stay there for ever." Locke repeated this observation a little later in the *Essay*: "The indolency and enjoyment we have, sufficing for our present Happiness, we desire not to venture the change: Since we judge that we are happy already, being content, that is enough." As we will see, Johnson was much struck by Locke's judgment that the mind does not always "think," for even waking thoughts may be so "dim and obscure . . . that they are very little removed from none at all."[13] This position again cast doubt on the assumption that thinking evinced the existence of a perpetually active, immaterial soul.

Given that Hume advanced the eighteenth century's most forceful case against belief in an immaterial soul, it is significant that he avoided the sensory reductionism of Locke's *Essay*. In Hume's analysis, the mind is animated not just by pleasure and pain but also by the passions, especially pride, humility, love, and malice. These basic passions underlie their particular variations, such as ambition, envy, beneficence, and revenge.

10. Walter Jackson Bate, *The Achievement of Samuel Johnson* (Oxford, 1955), 63–64.

11. Although influenced by Bate, for example, T. F. Wharton's *Samuel Johnson and the Theme of Hope* (London, 1984) pays little attention to Johnson's Christianity, the inadequacy of temporal hopes, or the hope for fulfillment in the afterlife. See, however, Fred Parker, "'We are Perpetually Moralists': Johnson and Moral Philosophy," in *Samuel Johnson after 300 Years*, ed. Greg Clingham and Philip Smallwood (Cambridge, 2009), 15–32. Parker discusses Johnson's critique of classical and Enlightenment philosophies grounded in the objective of an ultimate worldly goal or telos.

12. See John Locke, *An Essay Concerning Human Understanding*, ed. Peter H. Nidditch (Oxford, 1975), bk. 4, chap. 3, par. 6, 542. Stillingfleet attacked Locke in *A Discourse in Vindication of the Doctrine of the Trinity* (London, 1697), which led to Locke's reply and a further exchange of pamphlets.

13. Locke, *Essay*, bk. 2, chap. 21, par. 261; bk. 2, chap. 21, par. 9, 273; bk. 2, chap. 19, par. 4, 228.

All these passions draw from the common well of "sympathy," the inherent sociability of human beings and their interest in the passions and comparative well-being of others. As Hume argued in *A Treatise of Human Nature* (1739–40), however, the emotional life of human beings is not fundamentally different from that of animals: "All the internal principles, that are necessary in us to produce either pride or humility, are common to all creatures."[14] Nor did he believe that human beings were incapable of satisfaction with their present condition. Indeed, "Men generally fix their affections more on what they are possess'd of, than on what they never enjoyed."[15] Hume sometimes suggested that humans have a natural propensity to be idle. As he wrote in his essay "Of Taxes," "men naturally prefer ease before labour, and will not take pains if they can be idle."[16] For that reason, he strongly promoted the virtues of commercial society, which spurred "the spirit of industry" and gave people new opportunities to increase their self-esteem and live in social interaction. He often stressed the inherent pleasure of activity, but he did not claim that indolence was an evil. As Hume wrote in "Of the Refinement of the Arts," the ideally happy life should combine "action, pleasure, and indolence" in just proportions.[17] Throughout his essays, Hume repeatedly linked "happiness" with "security."[18] Though not ignoring the human capacity for envy and malice, he generally portrayed humans as capable of sociable, benign, and contented interaction when they are secure of their possessions and legally protected from violence.

Roughly speaking, Johnson shared Hume's ideal of a prosperous, legally secure society in which people have opportunities for social interaction and the pursuit of many kinds of pleasure. But Johnson was not nearly so sanguine as Hume. Isobel Grundy is surely correct to state that, at least in *The Rambler*, Johnson "regards all human activity as competitive, as a struggle to become . . . greater or higher or brighter than one's neighbour."[19] As Adam Potkay has acknowledged, "sympathy" plays a less important role in Johnson's moral system than it does in Hume's, and it is by no means a natural and universal foundation of human selfhood.[20] Johnson's frequent portraits of gratuitous cruelty in *The Rambler*, the pleasure that people take merely in humiliating the unfortunate and those in their power, might seem to suggest that his view of human nature owed much to Thomas Hobbes. Yet Hobbes was a thoroughgoing materialist who saw humans as driven by the constant desire for earthly power and sensual pleasure. Johnson, on the contrary, traced human behavior to an inherent drive to achieve a fulfillment that this world and the senses cannot finally provide. This drive is often misdirected toward behavior that is cruel or immoral, but it also energizes our most admirable accomplishments.

14. David Hume, *A Treatise of Human Nature*, ed. L. A. Selby-Bigge, rev. P. H. Nidditch (Oxford, 1978), bk. 2, pt. 1, sec. 12, 328.

15. Hume, *Treatise*, bk. 3, pt. 2, sec. 1, 482.

16. Hume, *Essays, Moral, Political, and Literary*, ed. Eugene F. Miller (Indianapolis, 1985), 344.

17. Hume, *Essays*, 270.

18. See, for example, Hume, "Of Parties in General" and "Of the Rise and Progress of the Arts and Sciences," in *Essays*, 55, 124.

19. Grundy, *Scale of Greatness*, 8.

20. Potkay, *Passion for Happiness*, 101–2.

For Johnson in *The Rambler*, unlike Locke, mere ease cannot be equated with happiness or contentment: "Ease, if it is not rising into pleasure, will be falling towards pain."[21] The stimulation of human activity is not just from "want to want," as in Hobbes.[22] "The natural flights of the human mind are not from pleasure to pleasure, but from hope to hope" (*Rambler* 2, *YE*, 3:10). Although Johnson does not explicitly cite Locke's opinion that the mind does not always think, as he will in *The Idler*, he makes clear that the "incessant cogitation" of the "soul" marks its fundamental difference from the senses and the body, which is often idle:

> That the soul always exerts her peculiar powers, with greater or less force, is very probable, though the common occasions of our present condition require but a small part of that incessant cogitation; and by the natural frame of our bodies, and general combination of the world, we are so frequently condemned to inactivity, that as through all our time we are thinking, so for a great part of our time we can only think. (*Rambler* 8, *YE*, 3:42)

This essay's theme, "the inequality of our corporeal to our intellectual faculties" (*YE*, 3:41), distinguishes Johnson's form of empiricism from that of both Locke and Hume. Johnson is not suggesting that human beings have innate ideas or denying that passion or self-interest, in some form, impels human endeavor. His conviction is rather that the mere pursuit of sensual pleasure or self-esteem is never enough in what he calls "our present condition." Johnson believes that humans typically engage in a "restless pursuit of enjoyments, which they value only because unpossessed" (*Rambler* 78, *YE*, 4:46). This statement represents something more than a difference of "degree" from Hume. It points to a fundamental disagreement between a free-thinking philosopher who saw no reason to introduce the soul to explain human behavior and a committed Christian dualist who, in turn, saw no explanation for human behavior without assuming that we have aspirations *beyond* the senses or worldly passions.

The difference between Johnson's form of empiricism and that of Locke or Hume is made clear in many essays in *The Rambler*. In *Rambler* 41, for example, Johnson introduces a key concept, "vacuity of being," as evidence of an immortal soul:

> So few of the hours of life are filled up with objects adequate to the mind of man, and so frequently are we in want of present pleasure or employment, that we are forced to have recourse every moment to the past and future for supplemental satisfactions, and relieve the vacuities of our being, by recollection of former passages, or anticipation of events to come. (*YE*, 3:221)

21. Johnson, *The Rambler*, vols. 3–5 of *YE*, ed. W. J. Bate and Albrecht B. Strauss (1969), 4:83 (*Rambler* 85). As Johnson certainly believed that all human behavior is self-interested, his understanding of the will is easily confused with Locke's sensory hedonism. See Claudia L. Johnson, "Samuel Johnson's Moral Psychology and Locke's 'Of Power,'" *SEL* 24, no. 3 (1984): 563–82.

22. See Potkay, *Passion for Happiness*, 66–67.

The incessant inadequacy of the sensory world is "strong proof of the superior and celestial nature of man."[23] The minds of brutes, by contrast, seem "exactly adapted to their bodies, with few other ideas than such as corporeal pain or pleasure impress upon them" (*YE*, 3:222). Because of the disproportion between the soul and the body, humans face special dangers and challenges. Johnson warns insistently against the temptation of filling up the vacuity of being with mere fantasies. This is a "disease" or an "infection" that needs to be checked immediately (*Rambler* 89, *YE*, 4:107). Idle thoughts are dangerous because "the intellect . . . will embrace any thing, however absurd or criminal, rather than be wholly without an object" (*Rambler* 89, *YE*, 4:86). On the other hand, "It is always pleasing to observe, how much more our minds can conceive, than our bodies can perform" (*Rambler* 17, *YE*, 3:97). The yearning for some fulfillment beyond mere sensual contentment has been responsible for humanity's most heroic efforts and greatest achievements, indeed for the rise of civilization itself. Dissatisfied with mere sensual pleasure, humans have created "artificial wants" such as wealth, power, and fame. The desire for fame, for example, can lead to pernicious self-aggrandizement and cruelty. Yet it derives not merely from a Hobbesian lust for dominance or from a desire to augment self-esteem, as Hume thought. It is a sign of the soul's immortal destiny: "the soul of man, formed for eternal life, springs forward beyond the limits of corporeal existence, and rejoices to consider herself as co-operating . . . with endless duration" (*Rambler* 49, *YE*, 3:266). The desire of fame and other drives are essentially fallacious, for they will not ultimately fulfill the vacuity of being. In this life, however, they can be usefully disciplined and directed toward useful and even virtuous activity.

At the core of Johnson's thinking in *The Rambler*, then, is a dualism that reflects not just Christian orthodoxy but also a real philosophical conviction. Though indebted to empiricism, especially Locke's, Johnson is also quite consciously correcting that tradition's reduction of human behavior to sensory stimulation and pleasure. The great challenge of human life, according to *The Rambler*, is to channel the soul's perpetual forward drive toward beneficial ends, and to achieve what he himself calls a "healthy" relationship between the immaterial spirit, the physical body, and the material world.

The Soul, the Body, and the Material World in *The Rambler*

In a famous incident reported in Boswell's *Life*, Johnson "refuted" a third great figure in eighteenth-century empiricism, George Berkeley, by "striking his foot with mighty force against a large stone, till he rebounded from it."[24] Since Berkeley set out specifically to uphold the existence of an immaterial soul, his philosophy was perhaps less offensive to Johnson's Christian sensibilities than the skepticism of David Hume. Johnson apparently considered writing a life of Berkeley.[25] But Johnson's dramatic rebuttal

23. As shown by Robert G. Walker, Johnson's observations on the endlessness of human desire correspond with arguments for the immortality of the soul common particularly in the early part of the eighteenth century. See *Eighteenth-Century Arguments for Immortality and Johnson's "Rasselas"* (Victoria, Canada, 1977), 26–34.

24. *Life*, 1:471.

25. See Clifford, *Dictionary Johnson*, 125. This was reported by the philosopher's son George Berkeley, whom Johnson so offended at some point that he refused to cooperate with the projected life.

of Berkeley by kicking a stone, traditionally cited as evidence of Johnson's lack of philosophical acumen, suggests an important feature of his moral thought. The material world, whose existence Berkeley denied, is essential to Johnson's philosophy, for he thought of the "self" as shaped by the conflict between the mind's boundless desires and the limitations imposed by external reality. This is a less naive position than might initially appear, for it anticipates the nineteenth-century philosophies of Destutt de Tracy, Hegel, and Freud, who in their different ways also regarded the self as constructed through the dialectical interaction between subjectivity and the external world.[26]

This collision between the forward movement of the soul and material resistance is captured in the language and imagery of *The Rambler*, giving these essays an air of vigorous activity and challenge virtually absent from *The Idler*. The imagery of *The Rambler* dramatizes the forward drive of the soul through analogies derived from areas of experience not usually counted among Johnson's primary interests. In many cases, his analogies draw from a reservoir of metaphors that we easily ignore because they are so conventional. Johnson was hardly unique in describing life as a sea voyage through tempests and around whirlpools and hidden rocks, or as a journey down a road flanked by tempting landscapes, both of which are among his favorite sources of extended imagery and allegory. Johnson's frequent recourse to imagery of profit, investment, and financial speculation similarly connects him with a large body of imagery insisting on the need to maximize the capital of time and action. *Rambler* 8, on the disproportion between "real action" and "seeming possibilities of action," is one of several essays that impress the need to direct the "force" of the soul toward profitable goals: "Lest a power so restless should be either unprofitably, or hurtfully employed, and the superfluities of intellect run to waste, it is no vain speculation to consider how we may govern our thoughts, restrain them from irregular motions, or confine them from boundless dissipation" (*YE*, 3:42). Images of profitability often lead to agricultural analogies urging readers to avoid allowing their time, compared to an estate, "to lie waste by negligence, to be over-run with noxious plants, or laid out for shew rather than for use" (*Rambler* 108, *YE*, 4:214). Although Johnson usually has in mind intellectual endeavors, these comparisons embrace a much broader readership and implicitly endorse useful human activity of all kinds. The traveler, the banker, the landowner, and the intellectual are joined in their common impulse toward endeavor and challenge.

26. Johnson's reflections on the dialectical construction of identity are comparable to those of the nineteenth-century empiricist Antoine-Louis-Claude Destutt, comte de Tracy, who argued that the distinction between the self (*le moi*) and the body emerged from the experience of resistance to physical desire by outward objects. See *Élémens d'idéologie*, 5 vols. (Bruxelles, 1826–27), 1:98–103. This version of selfhood should be distinguished from G. W. F. Hegel's argument that self-consciousness constructs itself in dialectical relation to the assumed consciousness of the human Other, as famously set out in his chapter "Lordship and Bondage" in *The Phenomenology of Spirit* (1807). For Freud, notoriously, the ego emerges as a screen of resistance in response to the failure of libidinal desire, the id, to achieve immediate fulfillment. Although Johnson is not utterly different from Freud in thinking that the self is formed dialectically, he did not think that human desires were even largely sexual, and he did not think that these desires were limited to what this world could even possibly fulfill. It is this difference that makes Johnson an essentially dualistic and Christian thinker, not the proto-Freudian imagined in the 1960s.

Johnson's repeated use of imagery drawn from conquest, war, and military activity was similarly conventional in the eighteenth century, though rather more surprising: he always hated war, though the Seven Years' War later in the 1750s made his antimilitarism more explicit and angry. Perhaps because Britain was more or less at peace in the early 1750s, as sniping with the French over possession of America was just beginning, he felt able to exploit the natural comparison between intellectual endeavor and imperial conquest: "It is the proper ambition of the heroes in literature to enlarge the boundaries of knowledge by discovering and conquering new regions of the intellectual world" (*Rambler* 137, *YE*, 4:362).[27] "Heroes of literature" was an expression he used elsewhere in the effort to endow intellectual ambition with the glory usually reserved for conquerors: "The garlands gained by the heroes of literature must be gathered from summits equally difficult to climb with those that bear the civic or triumphal wreaths" (*Rambler* 21, *YE*, 3:117). War, however morally abhorrent in itself, vividly illustrated the soul's forward charge against the resistance of the material world: "The resolution of the combat is seldom equal to the vehemence of the charge. He that meets with an opposition which he did not expect, loses his courage. The violence of his first onset is succeeded by a lasting and unconquerable languor" (*Rambler* 43, *YE*, 3:234).

Less conventional was Johnson's expansive use of imagery drawn from natural science. In a book written many decades ago, W. K. Wimsatt set out his detailed thesis that the Latinate or "inkhorn" vocabulary of *The Rambler* derived in large part from the language of such scientists as Boyle, Newton, and Ray.[28] This feature of *The Rambler* is rather surprising because, both in these essays and later, Johnson applauds Socrates's supposed achievement of showing that moral instruction was far more important than the study of the physical world.[29] Moreover, Johnson's heavy use of scientific vocabulary seems to conflict with his consistent assumption that the soul is immaterial. According to an ancient tradition, however, the operations of the soul cannot be imagined except through ideas derived from the senses, the classic example being the derivation of "spirit" from "air" or "breath." Johnson greatly expands these analogies, which often show a considerable interest in recent scientific theory, by comparing the operations of the soul with a wide range of phenomena in the material world. "The old peripatetick principle, that 'Nature abhors a Vacuum'" (*Rambler* 85, *YE*, 4:86), illustrated his belief in the soul's ceaseless desire for new objects. Other scientific analogies recall what he later criticized as "metaphysical" conceits in the poetry of Donne and Cowley. In *Rambler* 8, for example, he yokes the atomic theory that even the hardest bodies are porous with the inequality between what the soul imagines and the body performs. Opportunities for material endeavor are few, scattered like atoms across the spaces of a mental life predominated by thinking and projecting. *The*

27. Johnson uses a similar analogy between intellectual endeavor and conquest in the *Plan of a Dictionary of the English Language* (1747), in *Johnson on the English Language*, vol. 18 of *YE*, ed. Gwin J. Kolb and Robert DeMaria Jr. (2005), 58.

28. W. K. Wimsatt, *Philosophic Words: A Study of Style and Meaning in the "Rambler" and "Dictionary" of Samuel Johnson* (New Haven, Conn., 1948).

29. See *Rambler* 24, *YE*, 3:132; "Milton," *The Lives of the Most Eminent Poets: With Critical Observations on Their Works*, ed. Roger Lonsdale, 4 vols. (Oxford, 2006), 1:248–49.

Rambler is also filled with images of optics, telescopes, and microscopes to illustrate the problems faced by "the eye of the intellect" in judging distant obstacles and challenges, or assessing the soul's own capacity in relation to the world (*Rambler*s 28, 176, and 203).

These scientific analogies have an ordering function in Johnson's analysis of the soul or intellect. Boyle and Newton showed that the physical world obeys a set of consistent laws; Johnson indicated that the soul obeys analogous laws. Very many of the essays in *The Rambler* begin with an observation on the natural world and then move immediately to a comparison with human nature. For instance, just "as the feathers and strength of a bird grow together," so the individual's ability to resist temptations increases with age (*Rambler* 159, *YE*, 5:81). Just as the most long-lived animals have a long gestation, so the best compositions or "offspring of the mind" derive from long meditation (*Rambler* 169, *YE*, 5:130). But Johnson always makes clear that these are only inexact analogies, for the laws of the soul are ultimately different from those of the material world or the body. He decisively limits his observation in *Rambler* 78 that the mind grows insensitive to familiar events just as the body becomes numb to repeated sensations: "Thus far the mind resembles the body, but here the similitude" ends (*YE*, 4:46). The mind has control over its own ideas, whereas the body is passively subject to sensation. In *Rambler* 151, he compares "the effects of time upon the human body" and "the climactericks of the mind" (*YE*, 5:37–38). But the upshot of this comparison is that whereas the body changes through time only by being satiated by familiar sensations, the mind ultimately seeks beyond the senses, creating imaginary pleasures and rushing endlessly toward distant goals. Crucially, Johnson wishes to diffuse any impression that by using scientific or physical metaphors for the soul he means that the soul is itself material or merely an extension of physical needs. The greatest challenges and dangers of life result instead from the "present state of union" (*YE*, 5:39) between the soul and body. In this present state, we must attend assiduously to this union, never allowing the senses to overwhelm the soul or, on the contrary, allowing the soul to luxuriate dangerously in imaginary realms, as it is apt to do. What Johnson calls "health" in our earthly condition requires that the body and the soul both remain active and vigorous (see *Ramblers* 85 and 112). Nothing is more pitiable, he writes in *Rambler* 48, than "an active and elevated mind, labouring under the weight of a distempered body" (*YE*, 3:260).

What physical science helped to illustrate was, above all, the collision between the movement of the immaterial soul and the unsuspected obstacles presented by the material world. The soul is like an object projected through an atmosphere that continually slows it, or across an apparently smooth surface marked by invisible inequalities: "The advance of the human mind towards any object of laudable persuit, may be compared to the progress of a body driven by a blow. It moves for a time with great velocity and vigour, but the force of the first impulse is perpetually decreasing, and though it should encounter no obstacle capable of quelling it by a sudden stop, the resistance of the medium through which it passes, and the latent inequalities of the smoothest surface will in a short time by continued retardation wholly overpower it" (*Rambler* 127, *YE*, 4:312). As this statement implies, we are always faced with the temptation of falling back into exhausted or frustrated idleness. Like an overambitious general, the aspiring mind might lose courage at the first setback or defeat. As Johnson repeatedly reminds the reader, however, idleness is essentially *unnatural* to the soul. "The putrefaction of stagnant life" must be cured by renewed activity, new hopes and desires (*Rambler* 47, *YE*, 3:258).

Only at one point in *The Rambler* does Johnson indicate the existence of another principle of the soul. As he observes in an essay on procrastination, "we every day see the progress of life retarded by the *vis inertiae*, the mere repugnance to motion, and find multitudes repining at the want of that which nothing but idleness hinders them from enjoying" (*Rambler* 134, *YE*, 4:347). Once again, Johnson is drawing from the language of science. Although the term *vis inertiae* was not original to Newton, this founder of modern physics first demonstrated the importance of recognizing that the inertia of matter was not just dead weight but a *force*. Although Johnson's phrase "repugnance to motion" does not quite capture Newton's revolutionary insight that matter has gravitational force, he does indicate that the force of the soul is counteracted by an opposite tendency toward stillness. This is the tendency that would come to dominate his vision of human nature in *The Idler*. In *Rambler* 134, however, Johnson still characterizes the pull toward indolence as contrary to any possibility of contentment or mental health: "Idleness never can secure tranquillity; the call of reason and of conscience will pierce the closest pavilion of the sluggard" (*YE*, 4:348).

I have perhaps belabored the point that Johnson believed in an immaterial soul. I have done this because Johnson's dualism most sets him apart from the empiricism of Locke, Hume, and Berkeley, a difference that has been widely neglected or underrated in studies of his moral and philosophical thought. *The Rambler* is more distinctive and provocative than might appear in our secular age, for Johnson is advancing an implicitly Christian counterargument against the reductive empiricism of Locke and Hume. He is also denying Berkeley's idealism by insisting that the creation of personal identity can result only from the conflict between all the spirit desires and external resistance to its relentless forward movement. Perception cannot be equated with being, as Berkeley contended, because we desire far more than we can perceive. Johnson differed from other moralists of his time in describing "moral discipline of the mind" (*Rambler* 8, *YE*, 3:42) as not just the regulation of passions, though this is a conventional part of his program, but as a coming to terms with the essential incompatibility between the immortal soul and the limitations imposed by our attachment to a physical body and a transient physical world. This incompatibility of what the soul desires and what we can achieve is a main source of all our damaging and futile vanities. But *The Rambler*, like *The Adventurer* that followed it, generally presents an ennobling vision of humans as essentially spiritual beings striving in this material world to achieve a fulfillment ultimately available only in heaven.

The Adventurer in Johnson's Development

Although Johnson never forgets the human capacity for cruelty and pettiness in *The Rambler*, a more general pessimism spreads over the last months of these essays.

Until his essay of November 19, 1751, *Rambler* 175, Johnson had not pronounced that "the majority are wicked" or suggested that "depravity" was an inherent feature of human nature (*YE*, 5:160). This gloom may have been connected with the final decline of his wife, Tetty, whose death in March 1752 spelled the end of *The Rambler*. Johnson closed the series with an indignant declaration of his neglected commitment to morality, religion, and the English language. Tetty's death plunged Johnson into a debilitating grief that at least severely slowed his work on the *Dictionary* and may have prompted his friends at the Ivy Lane Club, particularly John Hawkesworth and John Payne, to encourage him to contribute to a new journal, *The Adventurer*. Johnson made a heroic recovery, writing twenty-nine rather than the twenty-seven essays solicited for this periodical, all the while completing the bulk of the *Dictionary*.

His determination to lift himself from grief and misanthropy is reflected by the generally upbeat tone of his *Adventurer* essays. Isobel Grundy has plausibly interpreted his essay of August 14, 1753, on "the Admirable Crichton" as ironic, for it is curious to find Johnson exalting a man not only for his scholarly excellence but also for his prowess as a fighter and a dancer.[30] Nonetheless, Johnson's desire to rescue his audience from "torpid despondency" by promoting a "favorable opinion of the powers of the human mind" corresponds with the general tone of these essays.[31] One often feels that Johnson was trying to sustain his own courage as he faced the challenge of finishing the great work of the *Dictionary*. He must have been addressing himself as well as the reader when he wrote that "To strive with difficulties, and to conquer them, is the highest human felicity" (*Adventurer* 111, *YE*, 2:455). But Johnson did not wish to restrict this ennobling message to the "heroes of literature." In *The Rambler*, as we have seen, Johnson's financial analogies suggested that even the busy merchant, whatever his personal narrowness, demonstrated the aspiring spirit of human nature and the graduation of desire from basic sensual pleasures to the artificial wants that motivate commercial society. Generally speaking, however, Johnson was less fullhearted than Hume in his endorsement of commercial culture. "The whole practice of buying and selling," he writes in Sermon 18, "is indeed replete with temptation, which even a virtuous mind finds it difficult to resist."[32] He was seldom so unqualified in his endorsement of the free-market economy than in *Adventurer* 68, where he suggests that the petty tradesman who fashions a gilded candlestick or a fancy pipe is engaged in a socially valuable activity. As he writes, "There is . . . no employment, however despicable, from which a man may not promise himself more than competence." The perpetual busyness of commercial society counteracts the dangers of idleness: "Not only by these popular and modish trifles, but by a thousand unheeded and evanescent kinds of business, are the multitudes of this city preserved from idleness" (*YE*, 2:385).

As these statements imply, Johnson's *Adventurer* essays impatiently reject intellectual pride and an arrogant disdain for vulgar activities. In *The Rambler*, he had sometimes included "letters" from fictional correspondents who counted him among

30. See Grundy, *Scale of Greatness*, 113–19.

31. Johnson, *The Idler and the Adventurer*, vol. 2 of *YE*, ed. W. J. Bate, John M. Bullitt, and L. F. Powell (1963), 401 (*Adventurer* 81).

32. Johnson, *Sermons*, vol. 14 of *YE*, ed. Jean Hagstrum and James Gray (1978), 197.

"those who exalt themselves into the chair of instruction" (*Rambler* 72, *YE*, 4:12) while neglecting the modest arts of politeness, good humor, and worldly prudence. In *The Adventurer*, however, he takes direct aim at what he calls the "unreasonable distribution of praise and blame" (*Adventurer* 99, *YE*, 2:430). This essay makes clear that Johnson's comparison between conquest and intellectual endeavor in *The Rambler* did not imply a serious admiration for military heroes. He argues that the praise bestowed on such figures as Alexander the Great, Julius Caesar, or, more recently, Peter the Great and Charles XII of Sweden, reflects the distortion of the standards of fame: "I would wish Caesar and Catiline, Xerxes and Alexander, Charles and Peter, huddled together in obscurity or detestation" (*YE*, 2:433). Yet this attack on the glory of conquerors leads to his defense of a frequently maligned group, scientific projectors. "From such men, and such only," he protests, "are we to hope for the cultivation of those parts of nature which lie yet waste, and the invention of those arts which are yet wanting" (*YE*, 2:434). Johnson's concern to adjust the standards of praise and blame also characterizes other *Adventurer* essays that assail contempt for common pleasures: "I cannot . . . but consider the laborious cultivation of petty pleasures, as a more happy and more virtuous disposition, than that universal contempt and haughty negligence, which is sometimes associated with powerful faculties" (*Adventurer* 128, *YE*, 2:477). The worst kind of idleness is the arrogant bantering of those who ridicule all kinds of activity that do not meet their own professed and self-satisfied standards of importance: "To find some objection to every thing, . . . to laugh at those who are ridiculously busy without setting an example of more rational industry, is no less in the power of the meanest than of the highest intellects" (*YE*, 2:478). "By a partial and imperfect representation," he goes on, "may every thing be made equally ridiculous" (*YE*, 2:478).[33] Struggling to maintain a conviction in his own worth, laboring daily with the impoverished men who served as his amanuenses, Johnson was in no mood for the satire and pessimism that apparently engulfed him about four years later when he started *The Idler*.

Johnson's Philosophical Reassessment in *The Idler*

It is difficult to reconcile the statements that I have just cited from *The Adventurer* with Johnson's attitude in *The Idler*. Not only does he apparently adopt the role of the haughty moralist laughing at those who are "ridiculously busy," but the aspiring human being who dominates the earlier essays, the restless spirit absorbed with securing his or her fulfillment and immortality, has evidently dwindled into a being defined by the desire to avoid any kind of effort whatsoever. He continues to use analogies derived from natural science. The opening *Idler* considers various definitions of "the human species" as the reasonable animal or the laughing animal before proposing that our species is best defined as "an idle animal." "That the definition may be complete," he writes, "idleness must be not only the general, but the peculiar characteristic of man; and perhaps man is the only being that can properly be called idle, that does by others what he might do himself, or sacrifices duty or pleasure to the love of ease" (*YE*, 2:4). The persistence of

33. For Johnson's defense of petty activities and pleasures at many points in his career, see Freya Johnston, *Samuel Johnson and the Art of Sinking, 1709–1791* (Oxford, 2005).

Johnson's concentration on this theme in the following essays undermines any original impression that he is being merely playful or offering a lighter alternative to his previous gravity. Some readers apparently understood the *Idler* as inviting a celebration of indolence. In perhaps the first genuine letter Johnson ever included in his essays, a correspondent complains wittily that the *Idler* has not lived up to his name, for he has failed to praise the consummate joys of sitting all day in an "elbow-chair . . . vacant of thought" (*Idler* 9, *YE*, 2:30). Johnson's reaction to this letter is disconcertingly serious. He advances a long description of the *vis inertiae*, briefly mentioned in *The Rambler*, but now a force of increasing and all-consuming power:

> The *vis inertiae*, the quality of resisting all external impulse, is hourly increasing; the restless and troublesome faculties of attention and distinction, reflection on the past, and solicitude for the future, by a long indulgence of idleness, will, like tapers in unelastic air, be gradually extinguished; and the officious lover, the vigilant soldier, the busy trader, may, by a judicious composure of his mind, sink into a state approaching to that of brute matter; in which he shall retain the consciousness of his own existence, only by an obtuse langour, and drowsy discontent. (*YE*, 2:31)

Roughly speaking, this passage continues themes found in *The Rambler*. There Johnson warned that "Idleness never can secure tranquility; the call of reason and of conscience will pierce the closest pavilion of the sluggard." But the piercing calls of reason and conscience seem much more acute than "drowsy discontent." In *The Idler,* the gravitation of human nature toward "a state approaching to that of brute matter" seems not only possible but pervasive. As he writes in a later essay, there are many who "have long ceased to live, and at whose death the survivors can only say, that they have ceased to breathe" (*Idler* 31, *YE*, 2:96).

Though he often couches his views in a deceptively detached and ironic tone, Johnson seems to be reassessing his previous philosophic outlook at many points in *The Idler*. In *Idler* 24, for example, Johnson explicitly addresses Locke's question in *An Essay Concerning Human Understanding* on "whether the soul always thinks" (*YE*, 2:76). Locke had decided that it did not, but Johnson left little doubt in *The Rambler* that the soul is always restively active. In *The Idler*, on the contrary, Johnson indicates that many humans think no more than animals: "If it be impossible to think without materials, there must necessarily be minds that do not always think; and whence shall we furnish materials for the meditation of the glutton between his meals, of the sportsman in a rainy month, of the annuitant between days of quarterly payment, of the politician when the mails are detained by contrary winds" (*YE*, 2:77). In *The Rambler*, Johnson challenged Locke's view that the will is satisfied with mere ease. "Ease," he wrote, "if it is not rising into pleasure, will be falling towards pain." In *The Idler*, by contrast, few seem to desire anything but ease, and are roused to activity only by the sharpest motives: "The mind is seldom quickened to very vigorous operations but by pain, or the dread of pain. . . . He that is happy, by whatever means, desires nothing but the continuance of happiness, and is no more sollicitous to distribute his sensations into their proper species, than the common gazer on the beauties of the spring to separate light into its original rays" (*Idler* 18, *YE*, 2:57). It is worth noting the scientific allusion here to Newtonian optics, an analogy that also appears in *The Rambler*. But here the scientific reference to the division of sunlight into its constituent rays illustrates all that the common viewer cannot be bothered to know.

Contrary to the message of *The Vanity of Human Wishes,* a form of low-grade contentment seems possible in *The Idler*, but it is the contentment of ignorance and self-delusion. Here is an important distinction: in these essays, "idleness" does not usually mean total inertia, but more frequently an empty and purposeless bustle, as exemplified by Johnson's portraits of Jack Whirler and Will Marvel, among others. These characters seem satisfied with petty, short-term agitation. While the domestic world of *The Idler* is less disturbed by the tragically vain and disruptive drives of pride, envy, greed, and ambition, this relative calm comes at the expense of making life less significant and noble. In *Idler* 31, Johnson wonders whether "idleness may maintain a very doubtful and obstinate opposition" against "pride" as the most all-embracing of human vices. Most "fill the day with petty business" and "have always something in hand which may raise curiosity, but not solicitude, and keep the mind in a state of action, but not of labour" (*YE*, 2:95, 97). The pursuit of fame and wealth ends not in spiritual calamity but in indifference, and even the impoverished person struggling to stay alive "had rather live in ease than in plenty" (*Idler* 9, *YE*, 2:32). As in *The Rambler* and *The Adventurer*, Johnson traces the development of artificial wants after the satisfaction of basic physical needs. This theme seems echoed in *Idler* 30: "Where necessity ends curiosity begins, and no sooner are we supplied with every thing that nature can demand, than we sit down to contrive artificial appetites" (*YE*, 2:92). But this statement does not lead to the optimistic vision in *Adventurer* 68 of a society in which every person may find useful employment in an economy generated by the constant production of new luxuries. In *Idler* 30, the invention of useless articles feeds not the restless desire for novelty but the effortless diversion of the rich and bored: "The idle and the luxurious find life stagnate, for want of desire to keep it in motion. This species of distress furnishes a new set of occupations, and multitudes are busied from day to day, in finding the rich and the fortunate something to do" (*YE*, 2:93).

Across a wide range of issues, therefore, Johnson seems deliberately to undermine philosophical and social positions characteristic of his essays earlier in the 1750s. What caused this dramatic change of outlook? One obvious explanation is biographical. *The Rambler* and *The Adventurer* were written during the most intense and productive period in Johnson's career. His vision of the questing scholar, beset with challenges and setbacks, corresponded with his heroic efforts as he first revamped his approach to the *Dictionary* during the composition of *The Rambler* and then churned out the entire lexicon from K to the end of the alphabet in little more than a year while he contributed to *The Adventurer*.[34] This great accomplishment, along with his lasting

34. See Allen Reddick, *The Making of Johnson's Dictionary, 1746–1773* (Cambridge, 1990), 72–81.

grief over Tetty, evidently took its toll, and after 1755 Johnson fell into one of the darkest periods of his life. Having received a contract to do a new edition of Shakespeare, Johnson often seemed unable to rouse himself from bed or the tea table, and he was apparently found by a visitor without even pen, ink, or paper.[35] Even during the composition of the *Dictionary* he had prayed for help to overcome idleness, but during the time of *The Idler* this self-recrimination becomes constant and desperate.[36] As has been often observed, the portrait of Sober in *Idler* 31, another character who fills up his days with idle activities, seems based on Johnson himself. But the relative lightness and indulgence of this self-portrait belies the mental sufferings of a man who thought that idleness was a damnable sin.

Johnson's own guilty struggle with indolence is nonetheless hardly an adequate explanation of why he would transform his vision of human nature in general. His torpor or useless dawdling was reflected in society at large. Unlike his previous periodicals, *The Idler* was what we would call a column in a newspaper, *The Universal Chronicle*, whose appearance seemed timed to correspond with William Pitt's commitment of British troops to the Continent in the spring of 1758 and his overhaul of British military strategy in North America. The common impression of *The Idler* as a light journalistic bagatelle is less convincing when these essays are read in the context of a newspaper that, in issue after issue, recounts troop movements, deployments, and battles along with lists of thousands of casualties. With keen irony, Johnson juxtaposes his ruminations on idleness with a world that seems to have exploded into frenetic, murderous, and essentially empty activity.

The Idler in the Context of *The Universal Chronicle*

Like *The Rambler* and *The Adventurer*, *The Idler* stemmed from Johnson's association with men who belonged to the Ivy Lane Club. When he first agreed to write these essays, it was under the editorship of a former member of that club, John Payne, who had published *The Rambler*. Payne was a businessman, and he decided that Johnson, who was now famous as the author of both *The Rambler* and the *Dictionary*, could usefully contribute an essay that would begin a weekly paper largely devoted to reporting on the war. Johnson's agreement to this plan was deftly ironic and reflected his newfound authority. Many of *The Idlers* comment obliquely on the news in the same issue, which Johnson often seems to have scanned before writing each essay. "One of the principal amusements of the Idler," he acknowledges, "is to read the works of those minute historians the writers of news" (*Idler* 7, *YE*, 2:22).

The issue of *The Universal Chronicle* for August 19, 1758, for example, contains General Amherst's long account of one of Britain's first great successes against the French, the taking of the naval base of Louisbourg, Cape Breton Island, in July. In *The Idler* that begins the issue, Johnson imagines how this victory, which was being cel-

35. Sir John Hawkins, *The Life of Samuel Johnson, LL.D.*, ed. O M Brack Jr. (Athens, Ga., and London, 2009), 219; Arthur Murphy, *An Essay on the Life and Genius of Samuel Johnson, LL.D.*, in *Johnsonian Miscellanies*, ed. George Birkbeck Hill, 2 vols. (Oxford, 1897), 1:416.

36. See Johnson's prayers from 1756 to 1761 in *Diaries, Prayers, and Annals*, vol. 1 of *YE*, ed. E. L. McAdam Jr., with Donald and Mary Hyde (1958), 63–73.

ebrated with great official pomp, would be reported differently by British and French historians in the future (*Idler* 20, *YE*, 2:63–65). All the details of Johnson's parody are lifted from Amherst's report, except that the general's lionized account of British heroism is corrected by the equally plausible French description of this victory as sheer good fortune in the face of dauntless defenders. After a six-week siege, the unfortunate explosion of a powder keg in a French ship spread fire through the whole fleet. In *Idler* 7, having compared news writers to spiders spinning out webs of titillating nonsense, Johnson parodies a breathless report on the sea battle between a French ship and a British one, the *Friseur* and the *Bull-dog*. He apparently had in mind the battle between the *Raisonnable* and the *Devonshire*, reported in the sixth number of *The Universal Chronicle*. While in the original report only twelve English are killed, in Johnson's parodic battle this number climbs to ninety-five.[37]

Johnson's implied suspicion that casualty numbers were being manipulated in the press for propagandistic effect seems accurate. In the issue of September 9, 1758, *The Universal Chronicle* reported on "the late glorious Victory obtained by the King of Prussia" at the battle of Zorndorf, in which "fifteen thousand Russians had been left on the battlefield; along with 3000 Prussians."[38] In fact, the militaristic Prussian king now known as Frederick the Great lost about 13,000 troops in a battle that ended not in a "glorious Victory," as Frederick himself vaunted, but a bloody stalemate.[39] In the same issue Johnson published an essay so bitter and contrary to the patriotic spirit of the paper that it was suppressed in the first collected edition of *The Idler* in 1761. In this, the original *Idler* 22, a circle of vultures reflect with grave perplexity on why humans leave piles of food on the battlefield, especially when led by a frantic human "eminently delighted with a wide carnage" (*YE*, 2:320).

Many other examples could be cited of Johnson's bitterly sarcastic commentary on a war promoted with glorious fanfare in the columns that followed each number of *The Idler*. His first target in these essays was the idle fanaticism of war itself, and its reduction of human beings to beasts or meat on a battlefield. One can hardly suspect that the orthodox Johnson ever questioned his dualistic conception of human nature; these essays nonetheless raise serious questions about whether most human activity is really more rational than the actions of animals or even machines. At the battle of Zorndorf, thousands of men were literally reduced to "brute matter," and the wisest vulture speculates that humans "had only the appearance of animal life, being really vegetables with a power of motion" (*YE*, 2:320). Johnson repeatedly ridicules the recent failures of the British army and the perceived nobility of military life. In *Idler* 5, he wonders why the troops do not include fashionable ladies, as ladies can surrender and retreat as well as men (*YE*, 2:18). In *Idler* 8, he proposes that English troops might be beneficially prepared for battle like dogs by filling up mock cities with beef and ale (*YE*, 2:27–28).

But for Johnson the quintessence of idleness is displayed by the reporters of military news and by readers, like those of *The Universal Chronicle,* who feed like vultures on mendacious accounts of slaughter. In *Idler* 30, Johnson anticipates the famous

37. *The Universal Chronicle* 6 (May 13, 1758): 44.

38. *The Universal Chronicle* 23 (September 9, 1758): 178.

39. See Franz A. J. Szabo, *The Seven Years War in Europe, 1756–1763* (Harlow, U.K., 2008), 167–68.

maxim attributed to various twentieth-century figures that truth is the first casualty of war: "Among the calamites of war may be justly numbered the diminution of the love of truth" (*YE*, 2:95). Although Johnson had lectured journalists in the first issue of *The Universal Chronicle*, reminding them of their duty to truth, he seems in fact to have made up his mind about the moral character of these "petty historians."[40] The "news-writer," he writes in *Idler* 30, "is 'a man without virtue, who writes lies at home for his own profit.' To these compositions is required neither genius nor knowledge, neither industry nor sprightliness, but contempt of shame, and indifference to truth are absolutely necessary" (*YE*, 2:94). The news writer had only to know that "scarce any thing awakens attention like a tale of cruelty" (*YE*, 2:95). As this statement implies, the guilt of the news writer is shared by the multitudes who fill their empty minds with reports of sieges, cannonades, charges, and mass scalpings, delighting in pain, and too idle to consider whether the reports are accurate. In *Idler* 3, Johnson comments on his readership with a feigned sympathy that can only be read, in context, as the most withering sarcasm:

> When I consider the innumerable multitudes that, having no motive of desire, or determination of will, lie freezing in perpetual inactivity, till some external impulse puts them in motion; who awake in the morning, vacant of thought, with minds gaping for the intellectual food, which some kind essayist has been accustomed to supply; I am moved by the commiseration with which all human beings ought to behold the distresses of each other, to try some expedients for their relief, and to inquire by what methods the listless may be actuated, and the empty replenished. (*YE*, 2:11)

As Johnson goes on to suggest, his role is to think for readers "who will not take the trouble to think for themselves" (*YE*, 2:11–12). Despite his frequent pretense of being a fellow idler with his readers, Johnson's writing in *The Idler* represents in many respects his most bitter and disillusioned commentary on the stupidity of the modern public and on the degradation of human reason.

The Idler and *Rasselas*

The stark difference between *The Idler* and Johnson's earlier essays raises the question of whether his own indolence, along with the public's consumption of news about British military glory, led him to question or even abandon a vision of human nature that we now tend to characterize as consistently "Johnsonian." This is the fundamentally ennobling vision of *The Vanity of Human Wishes* and *The Rambler*: human beings inexorably quest for a fulfillment not available in this world, deluded and often cruel, but nobly tragic in their visionary and hopeless aspiration for earthly happiness. Certainly the shift in *The Idler* is not simply stylistic. Contrary to Patrick O'Flaherty's reading of *The Idler*, Johnson's satire in these essays is not usually "detached" or what Bate

40. "Of the Duty of a Journalist," *The Universal Chronicle* 1 (April 8, 1758): 1–2.

famously called *manqué,* initial mockery softened by ultimate compassion.[41] Johnson was genuinely enraged by the stupidity of war and the idle patriotic fanfare that surrounded it, and he was not in the mood to forgive it.

He does nonetheless imply his shared guilt with those he condemns. In these essays Johnson adopts a real persona, "the Idler," in a way that he did not in *The Rambler*. Although there is no consistent "Mr. Rambler," "the Idler" is a sustained persona who outwardly indulges the reader's desire for mere ease. But it is a pose filled with covert scorn and even anguish. It is interesting that Johnson has not discarded his belief that the soul requires sustained jolts of activity; but this need now seems easily satisfied by the chemistry experiments of Sober, the silly county rambles of Will Marvel, or the fatuous critical dicta of Dick Minim. These are relatively harmless figures, but Johnson elsewhere suggests that it is not visionary ambition but useless agitation that generates the worst human evils. In contrast with his heroic analogies in *The Rambler*, he suggests in *The Idler* that conquest is motivated paradoxically by the idle desire for something to do. As a retired "soldier" confesses in *Idler* 21, "I suppose every man is shocked when he hears how frequently soldiers are wishing for war." But this conventional moralism gives way to bitter irony: "The wish is not always sincere, the greater part are content with sleep and lace, and counterfeit an ardour which they do not feel" (*YE*, 2:67). The idle violence of war is repeated on a domestic level by the dissection of live animals, as denounced in *Idler* 17. The gruesome curiosity of vivisection seems all the more atrocious because humans themselves seem little better than animals. Imagery of stars and telescopes, of voyage and discovery, gives way in *The Idler* to imagery of brute matter and animality.

Nevertheless, the conclusion that Johnson really has embraced this deeply pessimistic reassessment of human nature is complicated by the publication of *Rasselas* in April 1759. It is hard to dispute that this tale gives narrative form to the central themes of *The Rambler*. In the Happy Valley, the prince feels his inherent difference from the surrounding animals: "'What,' said he, 'makes the difference between man and all the rest of the animal creation? Every beast that strays beside me has the same corporal necessities with myself; he is hungry and crops the grass, he is thirsty and drinks the stream, his thirst and hunger are appeased, he is satisfied and sleeps; he rises again and is hungry, he is again fed and is at rest. I am hungry and thirsty like him, but when thirst and hunger cease I am not at rest'" (*YE*, 16:13). This is evidently the vision of humanity set out in Johnson's earlier work—restless, unfulfilled, and irreducible to the sensory or worldly motivations that constitute human nature in empiricist philosophy. It seems that the Johnson of *The Rambler* is back, along with his imagery of vacuity, repletion, quest, and astronomy. The Nile rises and falls, correlating symbolically with the hero's desire to be filled up spiritually. Rasselas, like Johnson the son of a merchant, quests forward across a philosophical landscape to find that happiness cannot be achieved even outside the Happy Valley, though his search will never end in this life. The astronomer has fallen prey to the hunger of the imagination and, deluded into the belief that he

41. W. J. Bate, "Johnson and Satire Manqué," in *Eighteenth-Century Studies in Honor of Donald F. Hyde*, ed. W. H. Bond (New York, 1970), 145–60.

controls the weather, needs to be brought back to earth by socializing with the travelers. The tale draws to a close with an affirmation of the immateriality of the soul.

Johnson's apparent return to his previous philosophy seems again connected with circumstances in his life. He conceived of *Rasselas* in January 1759, while his mother was approaching death, and his thoughts were turned away from the war and toward more universal themes. While portraits of idleness continued in later essays, direct references to the war became much less frequent over the remainder of *The Idler*, which continued until April 1760. During this period, Britain's fortunes against France considerably improved, and Johnson may have felt the uselessness of opposing the rising wave of patriotic elation. He nonetheless did allow himself one last attack on militarism right at the crescendo of this fanfare. James Wolfe's taking of Quebec was reported in the October 27 issue of *The Universal Chronicle*, which included poems on Wolfe's posthumous glory and a congratulatory address by the Lord Mayor to the king.[42] In the next issue, Johnson's *Idler* delivered a searing condemnation of the colonial war from the perspective of an Indian chief, who hopes to drive both the British and French from his land: "When they shall be weakened with mutual slaughter, let us rush down upon then, force their remains to take shelter in their ships, and reign once more in our native country" (*Idler* 81, *YE*, 2:254). The contrast between this essay and the contents of the newspaper could not have been more stark and bitter. One can only imagine Johnson's reaction to the letter that followed this *Idler*, a plea from a patriotic citizen that the inscription on the monument planned for Wolfe be in English rather than Latin so it could be read by "well dress'd Gentlemen and Ladies."[43]

It is arguable, nonetheless, that *Rasselas* does not entirely contradict the pessimistic outlook on human nature characteristic of the essays Johnson was writing in its immediate background. Prince Rasselas takes himself to be the exemplar of human nature in general, yet the tale makes clear that he is the only one of the royal family, with the exception of Nekayah, who feels the inadequacy of the Happy Valley. "Few of the princes," we are told, "had ever wished to enlarge their bounds, but passed their lives in full conviction that they had all within their reach that art or nature could bestow." The "singularity" of the prince's "humour made him much observed" (*YE*, 16:12), finally attracting the attention of his tutor, who is left perplexed by the prince's discontent. Imlac assures the prince that all the artificers of pleasure brought from outside rue the day when they entered captivity, but as their "minds have no impression but of the present moment," they "are either corroded by malignant passions, or sit stupid in the gloom of perpetual vacancy" (*YE*, 16:55). Once outside the valley, the travelers encounter various forms of idleness or meaningless activity. The "young men of spirit and gaiety" laugh at the prince when he delivers a *Rambler*-like sermon on the dignity of human nature (chapter 16). When Nekayah goes out to visit families, she returns with a depressing report on the empty thoughts and desires of the daughters: "every thing floated in their mind unconnected with the past or future, so that one desire easily gave way to another" (*YE*, 16:92). In the harem of Pekuah's Arab captor,

42. See *The Universal Chronicle* 82 (October, 27 1759): 337–38.
43. *The Universal Chronicle* 83 (November 3, 1759): 345.

similarly, the girls "ran from room to room as a bird hops from wire to wire in his cage. They danced for the sake of motion, as lambs frisk in a meadow" (*YE*, 16:138).

These glimpses of human nature reduced to sensuality or petty agitation are peripheral to the main characters' quest for spiritual fulfillment. They nonetheless introduce a nagging doubt about whether the experience of the prince and his friends is quite as typical of human nature as they assume or rather the spiritual ambition of a few especially noble souls. Johnson certainly preferred to agree with Imlac that "we always rejoice when we learn," and that all wish to avoid the "vacuity in which the soul sits motionless and torpid for want of attraction" (*YE*, 16:49). But *The Idler* provides evidence that he had deeply considered the possibility that human beings are not generally very ambitious, and that the public is quite satisfied with the petty stimulus provided by artificers of pleasure and the sensational untruths delivered by writers of the daily news. Filled with people duped by propaganda and the love of easy pleasure, Britain was to this extent a Happy Valley. Johnson's own deepening lethargy, which reached a crisis at the end of the 1750s, increased his suspicion that the active, questing human spirit is in fact counteracted by the even more powerful force of *vis inertiae*, a desire for mere ease, and the inexorable gravitation toward brute matter. I do not believe that Johnson ever exchanged one philosophy for another, the outlook of *The Rambler* for that of *The Idler.* But these visions are not fully compatible, and they represent two explanations of human nature that create an important, underlying tension in his mature thought.

Boswell was certainly right to observe that the famous writer he met in 1763 had much *vivida vis*.[44] Johnson wrote to Boswell in the voice of *The Rambler* in 1771: "Whatever philosophy may determine of material nature, it is certainly true of intellectual nature, that it *abhors a vacuum*: our minds cannot be empty."[45] The older Johnson continued to sound like *The Rambler* in his conviction that life can never be happy in the present moment and in his promotion of aspiration and achievement. As in *The Rambler*, he most admired the greatest literary endeavors, as exemplified by Shakespeare, Dryden, Pope, and Milton's *Paradise Lost*. But Boswell also met a man of deepened political conservatism who distrusted the frivolous agitation of Wilkite radicals and the clamor for war over the Falkland Islands. "The notion of liberty amuses the people of England," Johnson scoffed, "and helps to keep off the *taedium vitae*." Although he believed theoretically that "rational" happiness was the highest pleasure, he tended to believe that most people would opt for the continued satisfaction of their sensual appetites, for "the greatest part of men are gross."[46] But Johnson did not distinguish himself from "the greatest part of men" as arrogantly as this statement might suggest. Beneath the animated and social man whom Boswell encountered was a private man deeply anguished by his own indolence to the point of believing that he had wasted his life. As he confided to his diary in 1772, "In life little has been done, and life is very far advanced. Lord have mercy upon me" (*YE*, 1:152). Deep in Johnson's soul and in his philosophy, the Idler continued to contend with the Rambler and the Adventurer.

44. *Life*, 4:425.

45. Johnson to Boswell, June 20, 1771, *The Letters of Samuel Johnson*, ed. Bruce Redford, 5 vols. (Princeton, N.J., 1992–94), 1:363.

46. *Life*, 1:394; 3:246.

PART VI:
JOHNSON AFTER JOHNSON

FIGURE 1. Sir Joshua Reynolds, *Blinking Sam*, oil on canvas, 1775. Huntington Library, Art Collections, and Botanical Gardens, Gift of Frances and Loren Rothschild.

Blinking Sam, "Surly Sam," and "Johnson's Grimly Ghost"

Robert Folkenflik

IN THE PORTRAIT known as *Blinking Sam*, displayed in the Huntington Art Gallery in San Marino, California (fig. 1), Sir Joshua Reynolds represents Samuel Johnson in his familiar brown coat intensely reading a book or pamphlet, perhaps in a brown-paper wrapper, its pages doubled over. In this half-length portrait surrounded by a dark oval, light falls on Johnson's face and hands, accented by the whiteness of his sleeves, cuffs, neckcloth, and book. The buttons on his coat are muted. Nothing else appears in the picture. Indeed, several writers from the eighteenth century through the Victorian period referred to it as "unfinished."[1] Inevitably, the portrait elicits Boswell's well-known quotation of a claim about Johnson: "'He knows how to read better than any one (said Mrs. Knowles;) he gets at the substance of a book directly; he tears out the heart of it.'"[2] The portrait also suggests Topham Beauclerk's teasing remark to his Irish friend James Caulfeild, first Earl of Charlemont: "Johnson shall spoil your books."[3] Certainly any book collector can sympathize with David Garrick's hesitance to lend his rare volumes to collate for Johnson's edition of Shakespeare (*Life*, ed. Hill, 2:192).

Blinking Sam is not the name Reynolds gave the portrait, nor is it the name by which Johnson would have wanted it to be known. He did not want it to be known at all. Johnson liked to nickname his friends—Bozzy, Goldy, Mund, Murph, Renny—this last not Sir Joshua Reynolds but his sister Frances—and he also nicknamed some of his other portraits. This one might be titled "Portrait of a Man to Whom One Should Not Lend a Book," or, perhaps, "The Close Reader," though not in the twentieth-century

1. See, for instance, Alexander Napier's description in James Boswell, *The Life of Samuel Johnson, LL.D.: Together with The Journal of a Tour to the Hebrides*, ed. Napier, 4 vols. (London, 1884), 4:406 (hereafter cited as *Life*, ed. Napier).

2. *Boswell's Life of Johnson, Together with Boswell's Journal of a Tour to the Hebrides and Johnson's Diary of a Journey into North Wales*, ed. George Birkbeck Hill, rev. L. F. Powell, 6 vols. (Oxford, 1934–50), 3:284–85 (hereafter cited as *Life*, ed. Hill). Alexander Napier was perhaps the first of many to note the pertinence of Mrs. Knowles's comment: "So intent is his eager gaze on the volume he holds in his hands, that he seems as if he would tear out its very heart" (*Life*, ed. Napier, 4:406).

3. Topham Beauclerk to Lord Charlemont, November 20, 1773, *The Manuscripts and Correspondence of James, First Earl of Charlemont*, 2 vols. (London, 1891–94), 2:359–60 at 360.

sense. Reading was a popular subject for portraits in the eighteenth century. Reynolds himself portrayed his niece Theophila Palmer reading *Clarissa*, and his painting of Giuseppe Baretti reading plays a role in the story that follows. Such paintings represented interiority, inwardness, and the intellect.[4] In the portrait of Johnson, the act of reading also provides a suitable activity for hands that were often clenched or cramped. None of Reynolds's portraits of Johnson shows him with unbent fingers.

Despite Johnson's comments on some of the results, he sat willingly for portraits, and he even criticized a friend's parents for refusing to sit: "Sir, among the anfractuosities of the human mind, I know not if it may not be one, that there is a superstitious reluctance to sit for a picture" (*Life*, ed. Hill, 4:4). A room of his Bolt Court house functioned as a gallery of engraved portraits. Johnson sat for a wide range of artists, was given a number of portraits, and never paid for any. "These things have never cost me any thing," he told his stepdaughter, Lucy Porter, referring to a plaster bust sculpted by Joseph Nollekens. Whether Johnson sat for this particular portrait by Reynolds is one major question surrounding it.[5]

The last few years have been difficult for Reynolds's portraits of Johnson. Like the National Portrait Gallery's *Samuel Johnson* (1756–57)—Reynolds's first portrait of him (fig. 2)—*Blinking Sam* needed restoration, for it was accidentally damaged at the top while in the possession of its prior owner. This damage, now repaired, affected neither the image of Johnson nor the illusionistic oval surround. *Blinking Sam* also received an intellectual bashing at the beginning of this century. Traditionally, on the basis of published statements by Hester Lynch Piozzi, formerly Mrs. Thrale, and by James Northcote, Reynolds's student and assistant from 1771 to May 1776, it has been dated 1775, with the name *Blinking Sam* attached to it. David Mannings's excellent *Sir Joshua Reynolds: A Complete Catalogue of His Paintings*, however, claims on the basis of an inscribed statement on the first engraving of this portrait, signed "E. E." (plausibly Edward Edwards), that the painting was "probably posthumous" and assigns it to around 1786.[6] That engraving, by John Hall, was published on January 1, 1787 (fig. 3). Johnson died in 1784. The implication is that this portrait has no claim to the name *Blinking Sam*. It has never been considered anything but an autograph Reynolds, and Mannings does not dispute that.

4. Nadia Tscherny, "Reynolds's Streatham Portraits and the Art of Intimate Biography," *The Burlington Magazine* 128, no. 994 (1986): 4–11. For an intelligent account of the reader-as-subject in paintings, with an eye to the novel, see William Beatty Warner, "Staging Readers Reading," in "Reconsidering the Rise of the Novel," special issue, *Eighteenth-Century Fiction* 12 (2000): 391–416. For the role of reading in Johnson's life, see Robert DeMaria Jr., *Samuel Johnson and the Life of Reading* (Baltimore, 1997).

5. Johnson's *Dictionary of the English Language*, 2 vols. (London, 1755) defines *anfractuousness* as "Fulness of windings and turnings." For Johnson's collection of engravings, see Robert Folkenflik, "Samuel Johnson and Art," in Paul Alkon and Robert Folkenflik, *Samuel Johnson: Pictures and Words* (Los Angeles, 1984), 63–118 at 83. For the Nollekens bust, see Johnson's letter to Porter on February 19, 1778, *The Letters of Samuel Johnson*, ed. Bruce Redford, 5 vols. (Princeton, N.J., 1992–94), 3:108–9 (hereafter cited as *Letters*).

6. *Sir Joshua Reynolds: A Complete Catalogue of His Paintings*, ed. David Mannings, 2 vols. (New Haven, Conn., 2000), 1:282. Edwards (1736–1806) is well known to art historians as the author of the

There are, then, several unresolved issues regarding the portrait at the Huntington. I hope to clarify some of them and to offer plausible answers to the following questions: First, when was the painting traditionally known as *Blinking Sam* painted, does it have a right to that name, and what was the meaning of Johnson's offended response to it? Second, what is the painting's provenance? Third, what was its afterlife in terms of copies, too few of which have been discussed? And fourth, what has been *Blinking Sam*'s reception, from its appearance to the twenty-first century?

Creation and Response

The phrase "blinking Sam" comes from Mrs. Piozzi's *Anecdotes of the Late Samuel Johnson, LL.D.*, written in 1786—the year, according to Mannings, in which the Huntington portrait was painted:

> When Sir Joshua Reynolds had painted [Johnson's] portrait looking into the slit of his pen, and holding it almost close to his eye, as was his general custom, [Johnson] felt displeased, and told me "he would not be known by posterity for his *defects* only, let Sir Joshua do his worst." I said in reply, that Reynolds had no such difficulties about himself, and that he might observe the picture which hung up in the room where we were talking, represented Sir Joshua holding his ear in his hand to catch the sound. "He may paint himself as deaf if he chuses (replied Johnson); but I will not be *blinking Sam*."[7]

As Mannings notes, Mrs. Piozzi does not date the work in question. Requiring a lifetime portrait of Johnson to attach to the anecdote, Mannings suggests that *Blinking Sam* is actually that now at Tate Britain, which Reynolds painted for the Thrales' library at Streatham (fig. 4).[8] Since Johnson was obviously not referring to a posthumous painting, the choice of one in the same room as Reynolds's self-portrait (fig. 5), also mentioned in the anecdote, has a certain plausibility. Yet, Mrs. Piozzi's words do not suggest that the portrait she is speaking of is in the same room. She might also have called attention to the portrait of another nearsighted reader, Giuseppe Baretti, among the

posthumously published *Anecdotes of Painters, Who Have Resided or Been Born in England* (London, 1808), intended to supplement Horace Walpole's four-volume *Anecdotes of Painting in England* (Strawberry-Hill, 1762–80).

7. Hester Lynch Piozzi, *Anecdotes of the Late Samuel Johnson, LL.D., During the Last Twenty Years of His Life* (London, 1786), 248.

8. *Reynolds*, ed. Mannings, 1:281. L. F. Powell notes that "[John Wilson] Croker clearly confused this picture [of Johnson holding a book] with the [Streatham portrait]: he dates it 1778 and describes it as 'Mrs. Piozzi's picture'" (*Life*, ed. Hill, 4:450); Croker corrects this error in his second edition and dates it 1775. See James Boswell, *Life of Samuel Johnson*, ed. John Wilson Croker, 5 vols. (London, 1831), 5:379 (hereafter cited as *Life*, ed. Croker). Kai Kin Yung carefully suggests that the painting's "vigor and vitality is so akin to [James] Barry's . . . that the possibility that the portrait was finished at a later date cannot be absolutely ruled out." See *Samuel Johnson, 1709–84: A Bicentenary Exhibition*, ed. Kai Kin Yung (London, 1984), 112. Barry painted his oil sketch of Johnson in 1778–80. Before this time, Reynolds had tired of Barry's attacks on portrait painters and of other aspects of his behavior.

FIGURE 2. Sir Joshua Reynolds, *Samuel Johnson*, oil on canvas, 1756–57. © National Portrait Gallery, London, NPG 1597.

FIGURE 3. John Hall after Sir Joshua Reynolds, *Blinking Sam*, line engraving, 1787. Prints and Drawings, British Museum.

FIGURE 4. Sir Joshua Reynolds, *Samuel Johnson*, oil on canvas, 1778. Painted for the Thrales' library at Streatham. © Tate, London 2014.

FIGURE 5. Sir Joshua Reynolds, *Self-Portrait as a Deaf Man*, oil on canvas, 1775. Painted for the Thrales' library at Streatham. © Tate, London 2014.

paintings in the room.[9] Indeed, given the error she makes in describing the subject ("looking into the slit of his pen"), we might wonder whether she actually saw the painting or only heard what Johnson and perhaps others had to say of it.

Mrs. Piozzi may have mistaken what Johnson was "holding . . . almost close to his eye," but she cannot have mistaken that action for Johnson's pose in the Streatham portrait, where he has no prop whatsoever, nor is his eyesight more markedly problematic than in Reynolds's first portrait of Johnson (see fig. 2).[10] Johnson's eyes are closed in Reynolds's second portrait of him (1769), now at Knole in Kent, which Johnson liked best of Reynolds's depictions (*Letters*, 1:372). The Huntington portrait, as well as the one Mrs. Piozzi incorrectly describes, involve nearsighted intensity of focus. In the anecdote, Johnson clearly speaks of a recently finished portrait. Edmond Malone's biography of Reynolds dates his self-portrait, to which Mrs. Piozzi refers, to about 1775; Mannings largely agrees, though he does not specify the basis for his dating.[11]

Furthermore, her diary, *Thraliana*, which begins in 1776 and lasts until 1809, does not mention *Blinking Sam*, a fact consistent with the work having been painted in 1775. Her amusing and typical anecdote poses some problems. Even if we regard Mrs. Piozzi as wrong about Johnson's nearsighted attention, rather than referring to a different portrait, she gives no date. Only her reference to Reynolds's self-portrait in her house at Streatham suggests that the painting of Johnson must be from 1775 or later. It remained for James Northcote to date *Blinking Sam* in his 1813 biography of Reynolds.

Northcote identifies the portrait of Johnson reading as the one Mrs. Piozzi refers to in her *Anecdotes*, even though she speaks in error about Johnson "looking into the slit of his pen, and holding it almost close to his eye." Northcote states confidently, "In this same year [1775] Reynolds painted that portrait of his friend Dr. Johnson, which represents him as reading and near-sighted," and he gives an anecdote of his own concerning Johnson's response to Reynolds: "This was very displeasing to Johnson, who when he saw it, reproved Sir Joshua for painting him in that manner and attitude, saying, 'It is not friendly to hand down to posterity the imperfections of any man.'"[12] This is a version of what Johnson said to Mrs. Thrale. Annotating Northcote's comments in her own copy of his book, she rightly takes issue with his characterization of Reynolds in his self-portrait (see fig. 5) as holding an ear trumpet but protests neither the identification of the object in Johnson's hands nor the date of his portrait.[13]

9. Richard Wendorf, *The Elements of Life: Biography and Portrait-Painting in Stuart and Georgian England* (Oxford, 1990), 254.

10. Bruce Redford, however, refers to the Streatham portraits of Johnson, Reynolds, and Baretti as the "disability sub-group"; see *Dilettanti: The Antic and the Antique in Eighteenth-Century England* (Los Angeles, 2008), 109.

11. Edmond Malone, "Some Account of the Life and Writings of Sir Joshua Reynolds," in *The Literary Works of Sir Joshua Reynolds*, ed. Malone, 3 vols. (London, 1798), 1:lxxvii note; *Reynolds*, ed. Mannings, 1:50.

12. James Northcote, *Memoirs of Sir Joshua Reynolds* (London, 1813), 218, hereafter cited as *Memoirs* (1813).

13. Loren Rothschild notes the relevance of Mrs. Piozzi's silence on the date of the painting and the activity of its subject in "Blinking Sam: The True History of Sir Joshua Reynolds's 1775 Portrait of

Northcote also inaccurately puts in her mouth Johnson's bitter reproof of Reynolds: "Of this circumstance Mrs. Thrale says, 'I observed that he (Johnson) would not be known by posterity, for his defects only, let Sir Joshua do his worst.'" Mrs. Thrale, now Piozzi, protests in her marginalia to the biography and corrects Northcote, "I did not say it as here represented—laying Blame on Reynolds; I excused him—in the manner Mr. Northcote says but there was no Trumpet in Sir Joshua's Picture, he is painted holding his Ear to catch the Conversation."[14] Although she notes that Northcote makes it seem as though she reproves Reynolds by quoting Johnson's words as hers ("let Sir Joshua do his worst") and that the ear trumpet does not appear in the self-portrait, she does not notice that Northcote turns her remark into "He may paint himself as deaf *as* he chuses" (my italics), an even more Johnsonian *mot* but not one for which there is any evidence.[15]

Northcote erred concerning the gesture in Reynolds's self-portrait, attributed to Mrs. Thrale one of Johnson's comments, and botched the wording of Johnson's reproof of Reynolds. Hence, he may seem too unreliable to credit. But the difference here is that Northcote's own knowledge of Johnson's initial reaction allows him to date Mrs. Piozzi's anecdote; whereas Northcote was not at Streatham for Johnson's encounter with Mrs. Thrale, Johnson is likely to have upbraided Reynolds in his own house, where Johnson probably first saw the portrait, and where Northcote resided. Johnson almost certainly would have complained directly to Reynolds as well as to Mrs. Thrale, and the protest that it was not "friendly" to paint such a portrait plausibly expresses Johnson's wounded pride.[16]

Northcote defends Reynolds as an artist and as a friend of Johnson. In response to Johnson's claim that "it is not friendly to hand down to posterity the imperfections of any man," Northcote continues, "But, on the contrary, Sir Joshua himself esteemed it as a circumstance in nature to be remarked as characterizing the person represented,

Samuel Johnson," *The Age of Johnson* 15 (2004): 141–50, originally published as a privately printed pamphlet (Los Angeles, 2002). Reynolds does hold an ear trumpet in Johan Zoffany's *Academicians of the Royal Academy* (1771–72).

14. Mrs. Piozzi owned the second edition, in which the anecdote reappears: James Northcote, *The Life of Sir Joshua Reynolds*, 2 vols. (London, 1818), 2:3–4, hereafter cited as *Memoirs* (1818). Her copy is at the Houghton Library. For a facsimile of page 3, see Richard Wendorf, "'Well said Mr. Northcote': Hester Thrale Piozzi's Annotated Copy of James Northcote's Biography of Sir Joshua Reynolds," *Harvard Library Bulletin*, n.s., 9 (1998): 29–40 at 37.

15. *Reynolds*, ed. Mannings, 1:282. Many art historians, including Mannings, have erred in following Northcote's rather than Piozzi's actual words. This misquotation is found in the long-standard biography as well as in Mannings's predecessors: Charles Robert Leslie and Tom Taylor, *Life and Times of Sir Joshua Reynolds*, 2 vols. (London, 1865), 2:143; and Algernon Graves and William Vine Cronin, *A History of the Works of Sir Joshua Reynolds*, 4 vols. (London, 1899–1901), 2:523. See also, among others, Derek Hudson, *Sir Joshua Reynolds: A Personal Study* (London, 1958), 187; and Tscherny, "Reynolds's Streatham Portraits," 9.

16. Northcote's *Memoirs* is compromised and should be used with care. This anecdote remains the same in both the first and second editions. See *ODNB*, s.v. "Northcote, James," by Martin Postle: "as Northcote later told William Hazlitt, he had employed a certain Mr Laird to edit the book and see it through the press. Moreover, the publisher, Henry Colburn, employed researchers to gather anecdotal material relating to Reynolds, which was incorporated unacknowledged and verbatim in Northcote's text."

and therefore as giving additional value to the portrait." He adds, "It is evident, however, that Sir Joshua meant not to hurt his feelings."[17] Johnson's objections both to Reynolds and to Mrs. Thrale draw upon the terminology of art theory. Johnson read Jonathan Richardson's *Theory of Painting* "by chance" at Oxford and observed that "truly I did not think it possible to say so much upon the art." Richardson asserted that "Nature with all its Beauties has its . . . Defects, which are to be avoided."[18] Given Johnson's capacious and retentive memory, he might have recalled these words in his protest to Mrs. Thrale, just as his complaint of "imperfections" could allude to Reynolds's own words in *Discourses on Art* (1770), which Johnson helped him revise: "All the objects which are exhibited to our view by nature, upon close examination will be found to have their blemishes and defects. The most beautiful forms have something about them like weakness, minuteness, or imperfection. . . . The painter, who aims at the greatest style . . . corrects nature by herself, her imperfect state by her more perfect. His eye being enabled to distinguish the accidental deficiencies, excrescences, and deformities of things, from their general figures, he makes out an abstract idea of their forms more perfect than any one original."[19] Reynolds writes that one needs to "correct nature," not display it, as Johnson complains he had.

Other than Northcote's description and date, Mannings says, "there is no real evidence" for the identification of the Huntington portrait as the one Mrs. Piozzi is talking about. Instead, Mannings believes that E. E.'s inscription on the engraving's mount is correct regarding the date of 1786 for Reynolds's portrait of Johnson. Both points need reconsideration. Even if E. E. is Edward Edwards, his undated comment on when the portrait was painted is not "real evidence" but assertion, with neither source nor date for the inscription, and no details whatever. His inscription does not help to date the claim: "The head was painted by Sir Joshua from Memory after the death of the Doctor."[20]

The assumption that E. E. is right about the date requires Mannings to seek another Reynolds portrait to designate as *Blinking Sam*. It is unlikely that the Streatham portrait (see fig. 4), which Johnson had before him every time he entered his friends' library, is actually *Blinking Sam*, as Mannings suggests. Nothing is held "almost close to his eye" in this portrait. There is something wrong with Johnson's left eye in the Streatham, but that is also true of Reynolds's first portrait of Johnson (see fig. 2). Johnson fairly enough refers to the engraved version of the Streatham as "Surly Sam," a different unflattering characterization.[21]

17. Northcote, *Memoirs* (1813), 218.

18. Northcote, *Memoirs* (1818), 1:236; Jonathan Richardson, *An Essay on the Theory of Painting* (London, 1715), 192.

19. Sir Joshua Reynolds, "Discourse III" (December 14, 1770), *Discourses on Art*, ed. Robert R. Wark (New Haven, Conn., 1975), 44.

20. *Reynolds*, ed. Mannings, 1:282. The inscribed engraving is in the British Museum, Department of Prints and Drawings, 1838,0714.29.

21. In James Boswell, *Boswell, Laird of Auchinleck, 1778–1782*, ed. Joseph W. Reed and Frederick A. Pottle (New York, 1977), 369.

Edwards's comment could have been written any time between 1787 and his death in 1806—that is, before Northcote published his biography of Reynolds. If we did not have Mrs. Piozzi's anecdote, but only Northcote's concerning Johnson and Reynolds, there would be little controversy about the Johnson portrait or its date. But there is another early comment that has gone unremarked in this context. Frances Reynolds, in one of her four manuscripts for "Recollections of Dr. Johnson," begun as early as 1791, describes Johnson's response to portraits thus: "When asked for his opinion of the likeness of any portrait of a friend, he has generally evaded the question, and if obliged to examine it, he has held the picture most ridiculously close to his eye, just as he held his book. But he was so unwilling to expose that defect, that he was much displeased with Sir Joshua, I remember, for drawing him with his book held in that manner, which, I believe was the cause of that picture being left unfinished."[22] Frances, who died in 1807, identified the subject of the painting that "displeased" Johnson before Northcote's *Memoirs* appeared in 1813.

The weight of the evidence for dating, then, is on the side of Northcote and 1775 as the date of the painting. To this we might add Reynolds's willingness that year to portray disability, in his self-portrait. As Mrs. Piozzi's anecdote mentions (see fig. 5), Reynolds there cupped his hand around his ear.

Provenance

The early provenance of the Huntington painting is murky. Though we know that Edmond Malone was one of its first owners, there is no evidence that Reynolds painted *Blinking Sam* specifically for him. Johnson met Malone in 1764, but Malone was in Ireland from 1766 to 1778. We do not know when this portrait came into Malone's possession, but Johnson sat for Reynolds in 1778, and Johnson and Malone did not become close friends until 1779. This timing suggests that the work was not painted for Malone, though it might have been given or sold to him. Perhaps it was the painting Malone chose in 1792, when Reynolds in his will left £200 "to be laid out . . . in the purchase of some picture at the sale of his Collection, 'to be kept for his sake.'"[23] In 1812, when Malone died, the portrait went to his older brother Richard Malone, Baron Sunderlin. The provenance indeed is clear-cut only from the time of Sunderlin's ownership onward. He died in 1816, after which time his widow bequeathed it to her nephew, the Reverend Thomas Richard Rooper (1782–1866). His son, the Reverend William Henry Rooper, sold it to Agnew's in 1883. It was bought in the same year by Archibald Philip Primrose,

22. Frances Reynolds, "Recollections of Dr. Johnson," in *Life*, ed. Croker, 5:390. Three of the manuscripts are in the Hyde Collection at the Houghton Library, but the fourth draft, now lost, which Croker followed.

23. Leslie and Taylor, *Sir Joshua Reynolds*, 2:223. Mannings follows Leslie and Taylor. See also Graves and Cronin, *Reynolds*, 2:522; Wendorf, *Elements*, 253; and Susan Rather, "Stuart and Reynolds: A Portrait of Challenge," *Eighteenth-Century Studies* 27 (1993): 61–84 at 68n22. L. F. Powell writes, "the portrait was purchased by Malone and given or bequeathed to his brother Lord Sunderlin" (*Life*, ed. Hill, 4:450). For the details of Reynolds's will, see Malone, "Some Account," 1:cxviii note.

fifth Earl of Rosebery, and, after a detour back through Agnew's, was bought by Edward Cecil Guinness, first Earl of Iveagh, in 1891. He bequeathed it to his brother A. E. Guinness in 1927, following whose death it was sold at auction by Christie's in 1953 to Barclay and Perkins, the brewery in a direct line of descent from Henry Thrale's. The company later merged with another eighteenth-century brewer, Courage, Ltd. In 1987, Hanson Trust, the successor to Courage, sold the portrait to Loren Rothschild, who, with his wife, Frances, gave it to the Huntington in 2006.[24]

Another aspect of the provenance deserves consideration. If this portrait was in Malone's possession before 1791, why did Boswell not mention it in the *Life*, published that year? Malone, his close friend since 1785, was at his elbow prodding him along much of the time he was writing the *Life*. Boswell was very interested in portraiture and art more generally. Although he notes "the extraordinary zeal of the artists to extend and perpetuate [Johnson's] image," he only mentions the Knole portrait and the portrait that Reynolds gave him (see fig. 2). That is, among the "several pictures by Sir Joshua Reynolds," Boswell mentions neither *Blinking Sam*, which appeared as the frontispiece to Johnson's *Works* (1787), edited by Sir John Hawkins, and was strikingly mentioned in Mrs. Piozzi's *Anecdotes,* nor the Streatham portrait that hung in her library (see fig. 4). That is, he omits paintings associated with his biographical rivals. Since the Hall engraving of *Blinking Sam* in volume one of Hawkins's edition of the *Works* served effectively as the frontispiece to Hawkins's *Life of Johnson*, I believe that Boswell silently sets up a duel of the portraits and favors his own. Boswell says that upon meeting Johnson for the first time, "I found that I had a very perfect idea of Johnson's figure, from the portrait of him painted by Sir Joshua Reynolds soon after he had published his Dictionary, in the attitude of sitting in his easy chair in deep meditation, which was the first picture his friend did for him, which Sir Joshua very kindly presented to me, and from which an engraving has been made for this work" (fig. 6). Engraved by James Heath, it served as the frontispiece to the *Life*, a book dedicated to Reynolds. The neat story of the portrait's coming full circle certainly bests Sir John Hawkins's use of *Blinking Sam*, but it is unlikely. Boswell did not meet Reynolds until 1769. Had he seen the portrait at Reynolds's studio, it is hard to believe that Boswell would not have memorialized the event in his journals and trumpeted it in his letters. Boswell registers in his *London Journal* (1763) what he actually thought of Johnson when he met him: "Mr Johnson is a man of a most dreadful appearance." There is no sign of any expectations raised by viewing Reynolds's first portrait of Johnson.[25]

24. For accounts, see *Life*, ed. Hill, 4:450; *Reynolds*, ed. Mannings, 1:282; and Rothschild, "Blinking Sam," 144–45, which includes prices and a fuller provenance than in Mannings.

25. *Life*, ed. Hill, 4:421n1; 1:392; James Boswell, *Boswell's London Journal, 1762–1763*, ed. Frederick A. Pottle (New York, 1950), 260. Irma S. Lustig suggests that Boswell had the opportunity to see the portrait before or shortly after meeting Johnson, but I do not find the argument convincing; see Lustig, "Facts and Deductions: The Curious History of Reynolds's First Portrait of Johnson, 1756," *The Age of Johnson* 1 (1987): 161–80 at 173–74.

FIGURE 6. James Heath after Sir Joshua Reynolds, *Samuel Johnson*, stipple engraving, 1791. Used as the frontispiece to Boswell's *Life*. Huntington Library, Art Collections, and Botanical Gardens.

Henry Crabb Robinson's posthumously published *Diary, Reminiscences, and Correspondence* (1869) may explain Boswell's silence on *Blinking Sam*. Crabb Robinson visited T. R. Rooper to see the portrait in 1831; a detailed note, undoubtedly by Crabb Robinson's editor, Thomas Sadler, asserts that it was a lifetime portrait: "This portrait was originally painted for Mrs. Thrale, but rejected by Johnson.... After some time and much solicitation, Dr. Johnson allowed Mr. Malone to become the purchaser of it."[26] The notion that Malone owned it before Johnson died in 1784 probably derives from W. H. Rooper's understanding of the provenance, which does not appear in Frances Reynolds's version of the anecdote. In a letter to Edward Walford in 1883, W. H. Rooper says it was "painted for Mrs. Thrale, but *spurned* by the Doctor, when the face only was finished, and after a while permitted to pass into the hands of Edmond Malone." Alexander Napier's more elaborate account may come from this letter or, more likely, W. H. Rooper himself. If accurate, such a transition would explain why the portrait was not available to Boswell: "This portrait, rejected and unfinished, Mr. Malone was allowed to buy for his brother, Lord Sunderlin of Baronston in Ireland, with whom it remained till his death in 1816." *Blinking Sam*, which reflects Reynolds's typical handling of the backgrounds of oval portraits, is certainly not "unfinished" as we now have it. It was exhibited twice when W. H. Rooper owned it: in 1867, with the portrait dated 1784, and in 1883, dated 1775.[27]

Assuming, rightly, I believe, that the Huntington portrait was painted in 1775, its location from then until Malone owned it remains unknown. Perhaps it remained in Reynolds's atelier until 1792, when Malone may have purchased it.

Copying Sir Joshua

The evidence of the early copies of the Huntington painting is also relevant, and it should be assessed in any attempt to overthrow the painting's seemingly settled identification. In a few cases, the copies are interesting in their own right, and one of them helps to determine the painter of an important late portrait of Johnson long thought to be by Reynolds. Mannings's entry for the painting now at the Huntington mentions only one copy, a "crude," "untraced" version owned by Dr. G. Pierce and exhibited in Boston in 1923.[28] There are, though, at least five known early copies, one each thought to be by Frances Reynolds, her niece Theophila Palmer, the American painter Gilbert Stuart, and Northcote himself. Additionally, a copy was recently discovered by John Stone in a private collection owned by descendants of the Boswell family. This one

26. Henry Crabb Robinson, *Diary, Reminiscences, and Correspondence*, ed. Thomas Sadler, 2nd ed., 3 vols. (London, 1869), 2:526n.

27. W. H. Rooper to Edward Walford, June 3, 1883, in Walford, "Dr. Johnson, Painted by Reynolds," *The Antiquarian Magazine & Bibliographer* 4, no. 19 (1883): 1–8 at 7; *Life*, ed. Napier, 3:557. Graves and Cronin mention the exhibitions in *Reynolds*, 2:522–23. The first dating is consistent with the claim in the footnote to Crabb Robinson.

28. *Reynolds*, ed. Mannings, 1:282.

seems to derive from the putative Gilbert Stuart painting at the Houghton Library, discussed below. The reading material is doubled over and unfinished, as in the Houghton copy.[29]

Johnson sat to Frances Reynolds ten times or so between 1780 and 1783, and the copy at the Albright-Knox Art Gallery in Buffalo, New York, is thought to be the result of those sittings (fig. 7), but the evidence and arguments for its provenance are unconvincing. The unpublished letter of J. Pearson, a dealer, to the foremost Johnson collector of the day, R. B. Adam, who purchased it, quotes Johnson's letter to Mrs. Thrale on August 20, 1783, from the second edition of Northcote's *Memoirs* (1818), about Johnson's sittings for Frances Reynolds. Pearson asserts that the painting offered to Adam is the late portrait mentioned in Johnson's letter. The last owner is unnamed, and the provenance is not discussed, though Pearson quotes Northcote's note, which only appears in the second edition, mentioning that John Hatsell owned the portrait in 1818. This attribution long remained unquestioned. Adam bought the painting, and his widow gave it to the Buffalo Fine Arts Academy, now the Albright-Knox, in 1905.

When the foremost Reynolds scholar of the last generation, Ellis Waterhouse, visited the Albright-Knox in 1975, the chief curator reports him as saying that he did "not know of many pictures securely attributed to Frances Reynolds, but thinks that this one is probably 'bad enough to be the real thing!'"[30] He also knew of "no portraits of Johnson identical with this one." If Steven A. Nash, then chief curator, was aware of *Blinking Sam* at the time, he did not say so, but the Albright-Knox portrait is a very free copy. It is a somewhat longer half-length, without an oval. The coat is darker, with a dozen bright gilt buttons, and the sleeves are lacy rather than plain. The book is open, not doubled over; although the edge of the book is not much farther from Johnson's face, its print appears to be farther away: he is less nearsighted. Johnson's hands are almost in the same plane here, whereas his right hand is lower in Sir Joshua's portrait. In *Blinking Sam,* the wig is fluffy; in the copy, it is frizzy, and an ear is visible. The Albright-Knox painting could use a cleaning: the complexion is sallow, perhaps from old varnish. *Blinking Sam* is more pink, and the thrust of Johnson's head is downward, as opposed to the more upright position in the Albright-Knox. Altogether, Sir Joshua's

29. Loren Rothschild, *Blinking Sam*'s previous owner, reasserts that the painting is a lifetime portrait. He accepts the traditional identification and date and makes the salient point that Piozzi's marginalia in her copy of Northcote's biography of Reynolds corroborates his dating. See Rothschild, "Blinking Sam," 141–50.

30. Letter of J. Pearson to Adam, January 16, 1895; "Notes of S. Nash," on Waterhouse's opinion, May 5, 1975, both Albright-Knox archives. For Northcote's quotation of Johnson's letter, see *Memoirs* (1818), 2:159–60, 159n. Northcote painted a portrait of Hatsell, who died in 1820. If Northcote is right about Hatsell's ownership, the portrait discussed in Johnson's letter cannot be the portrait now at Haverford College, with its unbroken line of descent from John Taylor to Haverford. It could be another, such as the portrait of Johnson attributed to the circle of Sir Joshua Reynolds; see Sotheby's, London, sale L11030 (April 14, 2011), http://www.sothebys.com/en/auctions/ecatalogue/2011/old-master-early-british-paintings-l11030/lot.242.html.

portrait of Johnson is more concentrated, intense, and compelling than the copy. Nash is more circumspect in his catalogue of the Albright-Knox holdings. He cites Johnson's letter, recognizes that the portrait's provenance is "uncertain" before Pearson owned it, acknowledges that Pearson "may have based [his] statement solely upon James Northcote," and says that the pose is close to that of *Blinking Sam*.[31]

But the identification with the Albright-Knox painting is not persuasive if we look at it in context. Johnson wrote to Mrs. Thrale: "I sat to Mrs. Reynolds yesterday for my picture, perhaps the tenth time, and I sat near three hours, with the patience of *Mortal born to bear.* At last She declared it quite finished and seems to think it fine. I told her it was Johnson's *grimly ghost*. It is to be engraved, and I think, *in glided* etc. will be a good inscription."[32]

The details of Pearson's letter have never been examined skeptically. For a start, would Frances Reynolds, even with her "habitual perplexity of mind, and irresolution of conduct," as Fanny Burney put it, need some ten sittings between 1780 and 1783 to paint a free copy of one of Sir Joshua's portraits? She was a known copyist of her brother's paintings, but after he dismissed her from her position as his housekeeper in 1779, she left his household. Even more significantly, this portrait is a version of *Blinking Sam*. It is not likely that Johnson would write in good humor to Mrs. Thrale, to whom he had complained so vociferously of the original, or that he would sit on ten occasions, as much as three hours at a time, in a pose fairly similar to the one he found so humiliating in Sir Joshua's representation. Additionally, as we have seen, Frances was familiar with the portrait of Johnson reading nearsightedly and his response to it. Would she have had the temerity to suggest such a pose? Moreover, Northcote, who quotes Johnson's letter and says that he knows where the painting to which Johnson refers is located, does not link it to the anecdote of "blinking Sam."[33] Finally, there is no reason why the vigorous reader portrayed in *Blinking Sam*, even in the Albright-Knox version, should be characterized as "Johnson's *grimly ghost*." This analysis does not eliminate Frances Reynolds as the artist of the Albright-Knox portrait of Johnson—she may have painted both—but it does eliminate any claims based on Johnson's 1783 letter.

There is, however, an important portrait at Haverford College, long thought to be by Sir Joshua, that may be the one by Frances Reynolds for which Johnson sat

31. Steven A. Nash with Kary Kline, Charlotta Kotik, and Emese Wood, *Painting and Sculpture from Antiquity to 1942* (New York, 1979), 191.

32. Johnson to Mrs. Thrale, *Letters*, 4:188. It was not engraved. Bruce Redford says that this "may be the portrait attributed to Frances Reynolds, which now hangs in the Albright-Knox" (Johnson to Frances Reynolds, June 16, 1780, *Letters*, 3:278). The allusion is to David Mallet's revision of a gothic ballad, "William and Margaret." See Mallet, *The Excursion* (London, 1728), 75. Johnson probably knew the poem from his friend Thomas Percy's *Reliques of Ancient English Poetry*, 3 vols. (London, 1765), 3:311 ("Margaret's Ghost"); lines 3–4 read: "*In glided* Margaret's grimly ghost, / And stood at William's feet."

33. Madame d'Arblay [Fanny Burney], *Memoirs of Doctor Burney*, 3 vols. (London, 1832), 1:332; Northcote, *Memoirs* (1818), 2:159.

FIGURE 7. Frances Reynolds? [copy after Sir Joshua Reynolds], *Portrait of Dr. Samuel Johnson*, oil on canvas, 1783? Albright-Knox Art Gallery / Art Resource, NY.

(fig. 8). Although L. F. Powell called it the "finest of all the portraits of Johnson" (*Life*, ed. Hill, 4:452), the long-accepted attribution has been questioned more recently by Waterhouse and others.[34] Waterhouse suggests that this portrait "might be" by Benjamin Wilson, as Mannings reports, but that is unlikely. Wilson was Waterhouse's default choice for portraits misattributed to Reynolds: the two painters were competitors early in Reynolds's career; Wilson and Reynolds were both in Thomas Hudson's studio; and contemporaries sometimes confused works by the two of them.[35]

The line of provenance of the Haverford portrait of Johnson is unbroken, known from its possession by Johnson's old, close friend John Taylor of Ashbourne, down to the Johnson collector A. Edward Newton, whose daughter gave it to Haverford. Taylor's possession was in keeping with Johnson's idea of the purpose of a portrait: "Every man is always present to himself, and has, therefore, little need of his own resemblance; nor can desire it, but for the sake of those whom he loves, and by whom he hopes to be remembered."[36] The notion that the painting was indeed by Sir Joshua and the false provenance of the Albright-Knox portrait kept researchers from seeing any connection to the letter detailing the sittings. None of those recently mentioning the good possibility that Frances Reynolds painted the Haverford portrait support the attribution with evidence. Martin Postle, who calls his attribution "highly speculative," has suggested in conversation with me that the thinly painted surface led him to suspect that Sir Joshua's sister was the painter. Frances Reynolds's portraits were considered

34. Ellis Waterhouse, manuscript notes to Graves and Cronin, *Reynolds*, Archives, Paul Mellon Centre, London; Yung, *Samuel Johnson*, ed. Yung, 135–36; *Reynolds*, ed. Mannings, 1:283; and Peter Martin, *Samuel Johnson: A Biography* (London, 2008), 502. Along with Martin, others have suggested that Frances Reynolds is the painter, though without argument or evidence; see John Kerslake, "Portraits of Johnson," *The New Rambler* C 25 (1984): 32–34; Helen Ashmore, "'Do Not, My Love, Burn Your Papers': Samuel Johnson and Frances Reynolds: A New Document," *The Age of Johnson* 10 (1999): 165–94; and Martin Postle, "Johnson, Joshua Reynolds, and 'Renny Dear,'" *The New Rambler* E 8 (2004–5): 13–21.

35. I once thought that the Haverford work was the last lifetime portrait of Johnson and that its painter was the young James Roberts. His signed sketch for Sarah Adams, the daughter of Johnson's friend William Adams, the master of Pembroke, was executed on Johnson's last trip to Oxford in 1784 and still is extant. Kai Kin Yung finds Roberts a possibility, though he misses the Sarah Adams connection. Yung is cautious in part because Roberts, later known for his theatrical representations, painted few oil portraits. He notes that Roberts's portrait of Sir John Hawkins has a "similar coarseness" but differs in coloring (1786, in the collection of the Faculty of Music, Oxford University). The similarities go farther. Both portraits show jowls and sagging flesh. Both look a bit as though the subjects wear waxy masks. Both contain curtains to the left, though differently handled. Johnson's wig is very like that in the sketch. But there are limits to the similarities. There is no indication that Roberts, having willingly offered "Slim" Adams a sketch of anything she would like after painting a portrait of her father, went on to offer her or Johnson a free oil portrait, and the sketch looks in pose and expression unlike the Haverford portrait. For Roberts's sketch, see *Life*, ed. Hill, 4:533–34; and Robert Folkenflik, "Representations," *Samuel Johnson in Context*, ed. Jack Lynch (Cambridge, 2012), 62–82 at fig. 14. See also *Samuel Johnson*, ed. Yung, 135–36.

36. Johnson, *The Idler and The Adventurer*, vol. 2 of *The Yale Edition of the Works of Samuel Johnson*, ed. W. J. Bate, John M. Bullitt, and L. F. Powell (New Haven, Conn., 1963), 140 (*Idler* 45, February 24, 1759).

FIGURE 8. Frances Reynolds?, *Samuel Johnson*, oil on canvas, 1783. Courtesy of Special Collections, Haverford College, Haverford, PA, HC09-4061.

imitations of her brother's manner. Her portraits are becoming better known; they include one of Anna Williams (Dr Johnson's House, London), one of Hannah More (Bristol Museum and Art Gallery), and a triple portrait of herself and her sisters (formerly, Collection of Dr. John Edgcumbe), among others.[37] The Johnson of the Haverford portrait who looms sickly before us might well be characterized self-satirically as "Johnson's *grimly ghost*."

The Haverford work is an important portrait of Johnson. The British caricaturist and author Max Beerbohm annotated his copy of A. Edward Newton's frontispiece to *A Magnificent Farce*: "Where is this portrait? Not in America, I do hope—for I've never seen it, and should like to, inasmuch as it's far more convincing and *telling* than any of the others. This is the man that said those things. This is how he looked when he was saying them. This is intimately the dear man himself—not the legendary monster." I neither find it on the level of Sir Joshua's portraits, nor do I agree with Beerbohm's sentimental account, but in its pathos, in its presentation of the vulnerable, old, sick, stooped man, it may be the best likeness. The stooping, which is characteristic of Johnson, as we know from verbal descriptions, is something that Reynolds avoids in his portraits, probably because such a detail would demean his subject.[38]

The unfinished version of *Blinking Sam*, now at the Houghton Library and said to be by Gilbert Stuart, is a more interesting case (fig. 9). In 1775, Stuart went to London, where he painted Sir Joshua Reynolds in 1784 and seems to have met Johnson. Anecdotes of exchanges between them are extant but difficult to trace back to their sources. Their mutual friend Benjamin West may have introduced them. Stuart remained in England until he left for Ireland in 1787. This copy of the portrait hung at Heale House, the seat of William Bowles, a young friend of Johnson who met him by 1780. The painting could have been made before or after the contested date of 1786, if Stuart painted it, which therefore sheds no light on the dating of its original.

The attribution of this copy to Stuart, however, is untenable; it rests on the portrait's inscription: "Dr. Samuel Johnson, LLD, painted by Stuart for Wm Bowles, Esq., of Heale House, his intimate friend, and thought so good a likeness he would not allow it to be finished. Given to Sir J. P. Boileau, B^{t} By Admiral Bowles." The Houghton Library, which lists the date of the painting as "1783?," the year of Johnson's visit to Heale,

37. The triple portrait is illustrated in Richard Wendorf, *Sir Joshua Reynolds: The Painter in Society* (Cambridge, Mass., 1996), plate 13.

38. *Life*, ed. Hill, 4:452 (with provenance). For Beerbohm, see John Overholt, "Not the Legendary Monster," *Hyde Collection Catablog*, September 25, 2006, http://blogs.law.harvard.edu/hydeblog/2006/09/25/not-the-legendary-monster/. Fanny Burney writes, "Dr. Johnson was announced. He is, indeed, very ill-favoured,—he is tall & stout, but stoops terribly,—he is almost bent double"; Burney to Samuel Crisp, March 27–28, 1777, in *The Early Journals and Letters of Fanny Burney*, vol. 2, *1774–1777*, ed. Lars E. Troide (Oxford, 1990), 225. The coarse version said to be by Theophila "Offy" Palmer, Reynolds's niece, is a cruder version of the Albright-Knox. She came to live with Reynolds following the death of her father in 1770 and stayed until her marriage in 1781. Had she copied the portrait, these years would have been the likely period. I have, however, only seen a photograph at the Heinz Archive of the National Portrait Gallery and have no basis for deciding its status.

FIGURE 9. Gilbert Stuart? copy after Sir Joshua Reynolds, *Samuel Johnson*, oil on canvas, date unknown. Houghton Library, Harvard University, *2003JM-15.

identifies the inscription as "added sometime after 1838," the year Boileau became a baronet, but William Bowles, the son of Johnson's friend, did not become a rear admiral until 1841. I take the inscription as the source for Mary Hyde's claim that Bowles "had his young friend, Gilbert Stuart, . . . paint Johnson's portrait at Heale House" when Johnson visited from August 28 to September 17, 1783. There is no reason to believe the inscription, and Carrie Rebora Barratt, the foremost of Stuart scholars, informs me that, on the basis of seeing the portrait itself, there is no reason to think it his. Her view parallels that of Charles M. Mount, Stuart's biographer, in correspondence with the Hydes the year they bought it. A color photograph of the portrait led him to respond on September 26, 1964: "Nowhere on it can I find anything that would resemble the work of Gilbert Stuart."[39] As the inscription states, the painting is unfinished. The head alone is complete, though the design of the full portrait is clear. The left hand is roughly indicated, and the shadowy reading material is doubled over, making it apparent that this copy does not derive from the Albright-Knox or its fellows, which depict an open book.

The last of the copies deserving of attention here is the one ascribed to Northcote. Although my analysis keeps me from attributing any of the copies physically known or known through photographs to those for whom they are claimed, the unchallenged representation of Northcote as the source of Ignace Joseph de Claussin's engraving (1813, fig. 10) of Johnson during Northcote's lifetime (he died in 1831) argues that Northcote copied *Blinking Sam*. L. F. Powell mentions having seen the painting in private hands (*Life*, ed. Hill, 4:457–58). De Claussin's engraving is my candidate for the ugliest image of Johnson. It substitutes an open book for the doubled-over reading matter of *Blinking Sam*, as did the Albright-Knox (see fig. 7) and the copy putatively by Theophila Palmer. Additionally, if any of those claimed as copyists except for Stuart actually copied the portrait, the dates of composition would most likely have been prior to their departures from Reynolds's household: Northcote, by 1776; Frances Reynolds, by 1779; Theophila Palmer, by 1781—which again suggests that it was painted earlier. Mrs. Piozzi was in the best position to deny the identity or date of *Blinking Sam* but did not.

The Reception of *Blinking Sam*

Blinking Sam has been both praised and deprecated from its own time forward, frequently the latter, on the basis of Mrs. Piozzi's anecdote alone. William Fordyce Mavor's unsigned "Life of Dr. Samuel Johnson" prefaced James Harrison's edition of Johnson's *Dictionary* in the same year in which her *Anecdotes* appeared (1786). According to Mavor, "With the clumsy, vulgar portrait, by his friend, Sir Joshua Reynolds, [Johnson]

39. Mary Hyde, *The Impossible Friendship: Boswell and Mrs. Thrale* (Cambridge, Mass., 1972), 84; Barratt, correspondence with the author; Charles M. Mount to Mary Hyde, Hyde Collection, Houghton Library. Susan Rather notes the unlikelihood of such a copy of *Blinking Sam* in "Stuart and Reynolds," 69n.

FIGURE 10. Ignace Joseph de Claussin after James Northcote, *Samuel Johnson*, etching, 1813. © National Portrait Gallery, London, NPG D16487.

is known to have been exceedingly disgusted."[40] Such satirical representations of Johnson as James Gillray's *Old Wisdom Blinking at the Stars* (1782, fig. 11) remind us that he had a visual public identity as nearsighted before Mrs. Piozzi's anecdote appeared.[41] Johnson's *Dictionary* (1755) defines "blink" in this sense as "to see obscurely." Given that when William Hogarth, Ozias Humphry, and others met Johnson, they took him for an "ideot" (*Life*, ed. Hill, 1:146), Johnson's choice of illustration for this word in his *Dictionary* would have cut close to the bone: Shakespeare's "What's here! the portrait of a *blinking* idiot" (*Merchant of Venice*, 2.9.54).

Since *Blinking Sam* was rarely seen in the eighteenth or nineteenth centuries, the anecdote regarding Johnson's annoyance was often used to point a moral. As an example of "Some Observations Respecting the Infirmities and Defects of Men of Genius" (1795), Isaac D'Israeli instances this portrait: "Even the strong-minded Johnson would not be painted *Blinking Sam.*" A number of contemporaries take their cue from D'Israeli. *The Hive* (1796) reprinted D'Israeli's long footnote as "Remarkable Traits of Vanity in Celebrated Literary Characters," and Mavor in *The British Tourists* (1798–1800) closely paraphrases D'Israeli's comment on Johnson. Henry Angelo mentions *Blinking Sam* in the context of caricature and "personal deformity," saying, "The wisest men are not always proof against these attacks."[42]

Opinions have followed the divergent directions taken by Johnson and Reynolds. William Hazlitt, arguably the best English art critic of the Romantic era, claims that the finest portraits fully represent "individual nature." These visual biographies supply "most of the peculiarities and details, with most of the general character." Praising Boswell's scene of Johnson's dinner with Wilkes, he compares it to "blinking Sam."[43]

Ironically, Hazlitt defends the painting on the same grounds as Reynolds does in Northcote's account, effectively as part of his attack on Reynolds's theory of art, which, as we have seen, is closer to Johnson's objections to this portrait than to Reynolds's defense of it. Johnson himself is quoted a number of times as counseling something like Reynolds's position in the case of biography, though the depiction may not be "friendly." Similarly, Allan Cunningham's six-volume *Lives of the Most Eminent British Painters,*

40. [William Fordyce Mavor], "The Life of Dr. Samuel Johnson," in Johnson, *A Dictionary of the English Language* (London, 1786), f1r–g2v.

41. The head of Johnson in the Gillray etching comes from a Thomas Trotter profile engraving, not from an engraving of Reynolds's dignified and idealized Knole portrait of Johnson, as is commonly thought. Note the opposition of Johnson's head to those of Pope, Milton, and an unidentified poet.

42. Isaac D'Israeli, "Some Observations Respecting the Infirmities and Defects of Men of Genius," *An Essay on the Manners and Genius of the Literary Character* (London, 1795), 115–16n; *The Hive: A Selection from Modern Writers* (Edinburgh, 1796), 85; William Fordyce Mavor, *The British Tourists; or, Traveller's Pocket Companion*, 6 vols. (London, 1798–1800), 6:159; *The Reminiscences of Henry Angelo*, 2 vols. (London, 1828), 1:428.

43. William Hazlitt, "On the Imitation of Nature" (1814), *The Complete Works of William Hazlitt*, ed. P. P. Howe, after the edition of A. R. Waller and Arnold Glover, 21 vols. (London, 1930–34), 18:75.

FIGURE 11. James Gillray, *Old Wisdom Blinking at the Stars*, hand-colored etching, 1782. Huntington Library, Art Collections, and Botanical Gardens.

Sculptors, and Architects (1830–33), modeled on Johnson's *Lives of the Poets* (1779–81), claims that Reynolds "was right—he gave individuality and character to the head."[44]

In 1831 Henry Crabb Robinson and his friend the portrait painter John James Masquerier visited T. R. Rooper, who then owned *Blinking Sam*. Crabb Robinson reports that Masquerier was "greatly delighted" by the portrait, which he thought "the best he has ever seen of Johnson by Sir Joshua. The Doctor is holding a book, and reading like a short-sighted man. His blind eye is in the shade. There is no gentility, no attempt at setting off the Doctor's face, but no vulgarity in the portrait." This judgment parallels Hazlitt's preference. Sir Walter Armstrong, like Hazlitt, praises Reynolds for being without a "rival" as a portraitist of "masculine personalities," especially Johnson in *Blinking Sam*, as well as Lord Heathfield, David Garrick, Giuseppe Baretti, Laurence Sterne, and Oliver Goldsmith.[45]

Blinking Sam's reception remained mixed in the twentieth century. Reynolds's biographer Derek Hudson oddly saw *Blinking Sam* as a cautionary tale about "the danger of excessive reading by candle-light." Herman W. Liebert's study of lifetime portraits of Johnson judged this portrait to be "not a noble one; indeed, I think it is an ugly one, though it is not idealized and probably represents Johnson as he appeared." This brings to the surface a central problem. Johnson was notorious for ugliness in his own day, and though Liebert recognizes the portrait as realistic, unlike Hazlitt, he does not rate it highly on such grounds. The fullest account of representations of Johnson is Morris R. Brownell's *Samuel Johnson's Attitude to the Arts*, which devotes only half a sentence to *Blinking Sam*.[46]

Johnson's biographers generally have ignored or merely mentioned the portrait. John Wain is a significant exception. He sees in it "the mature critic of literature and society." Like Reynolds's first portrait of Johnson, at his *Dictionary* desk (see fig. 2),

> it shows him working; not sitting at a desk producing a daily stint of words but holding up to his fierce, near-sighted gaze a book that in the rapture of attention he is grasping and forcing out of shape, the covers back to back (it will never be the same again). Once again one notices the

44. Robert Folkenflik, *Samuel Johnson, Biographer* (Ithaca, N.Y., 1978), esp. chap. 2; Allan Cunningham, *The Lives of the Most Eminent British Painters, Sculptors, and Architects*, 2nd ed., vol. 1 (London, 1830), 283. Hazlitt is often sharply critical of Reynolds but nonetheless admires his portraits, especially those of men. Among them he instances "Reynolds's intimate acquaintance" and mentions first "Dr. Johnson": "he painted them as pure studies from nature, copying the real image existing before him, with all its known characteristic peculiarities; and, with as much wisdom as good-nature, sacrificing the graces on the altar of friendship. They are downright portraits, and nothing more" ("Character of Sir Joshua Reynolds," in *Complete Works*, ed. Howe, 18:54, 55). That is, they are not ideal but real.

45. Crabb Robinson, *Diary*, 2:526–27 (December 13, 1831); Sir Walter Armstrong, *Sir Joshua Reynolds* (London, 1900), 170.

46. Hudson, *Sir Joshua Reynolds* (1958), 187; Herman W. Liebert, "Portraits of the Author: Lifetime Likenesses of Samuel Johnson," in Liebert and J. Douglas Stewart, *English Portraits of the Seventeenth and Eighteenth Centuries* (Los Angeles, 1974), 56; Morris R. Brownell, *Samuel Johnson's Attitude to the*

> hands: large, strong, actively participating in the thrust towards knowledge and ideas, as if wisdom were a juice that could be literally squeezed out of dry paper and ink.[47]

This is a generally admirable account, as in its final metaphor, which captures Johnson's muscular reading. In speaking of Johnson's "fierce, near-sighted gaze," Wain may have remembered Mrs. Piozzi's description of his remarkable eyes: "his eyes, though of a light-grey colour, were so wild, so piercing, and at times so fierce, that fear was I believe the first emotion in the hearts of all his beholders." Gray is indeed the predominant color of his eyes in *Blinking Sam*, though years earlier, in her diary, *Thraliana*, she had described them in the same way, but called their color "light blue," which is how they appear in a number of portraits.[48] The painting may not be Johnson at work. It shows Johnson turning his laser beam on a text that he is just as likely to let drop in a few moments, despite being in the middle of it. This is the Johnson who responded to a friend's asking "if he had read" a book: "'I have looked into it.' 'What' (said Elphinston,) 'have you not read it through?' Johnson . . . answered tartly, 'No, Sir; do *you* read books *through*?'" (*Life*, ed. Hill, 2:226).

More recently, several art historians have provided valuable broader contexts for understanding *Blinking Sam*. Nadia Tscherny looks at the painting as part of "the art of intimate biography." She argues that "the first of numerous copies and variations of Reynolds's *Johnson reading* were done by artists of the next generation, such as Gilbert Stuart, and by the nineteenth century the representation of a sitter reading, in an informal close-up head and shoulders format, had become extremely popular." Readers were popular painter's subjects in the eighteenth century, and, as we have seen, her assertion is not accurate concerning the copies, but it does suggest that Reynolds's portrait anticipated a trend of the period following Johnson's death. A sharper contextualization is Martin Postle's convincing hypothesis that Reynolds's portraits of writers and artists in the 1750s were experimental: "In such intimate, idiosyncratic portraits, Reynolds celebrated friendship, and the visual representation of 'genius', as well as his own innovative painting technique."[49] Postle speaks of Reynolds's first portrait of

Arts (Oxford, 1989), 87. L. F. Powell's important 1933 appendix "The Portraits of Johnson," in *Life*, ed. Hill, 4:447–64, represents the developed knowledge of Johnson's portraits beginning with Boswell and expanded and corrected by editors of the *Life*. Its section on this portrait deals with various problems but does not characterize it.

47. John Wain, *Samuel Johnson* (New York, 1974), 221. Margaret Lane calls the portrait "kindly" but says nothing else; *Samuel Johnson and His World* (New York, 1975), 206n. Peter Martin sees it as "a penetrating study, . . . [showing Johnson] as if in the act of reading some political pamphlet which he was about to attack with relish"; *Samuel Johnson*, 480.

48. Piozzi, *Anecdotes*, 344; *Thraliana: The Diary of Mrs. Hester Lynch Thrale (later Mrs. Piozzi), 1776–1809*, ed. Katharine C. Balderston, 2 vols. (Oxford, 1942), 1:205. The manuscript of *Thraliana* is at the Huntington Library.

49. Tscherny, "Reynolds's Streatham Portraits," 10; Postle, "Reynolds in the 1750s: Technical Matters" (paper given at Samuel Johnson Colloquium, National Portrait Gallery, June 5, 2008).

Johnson, but the idea is valuable for considering *Blinking Sam*. Johnson may not have cared for this unofficial, uncommissioned portrait, but its intimate depiction expresses fondness, knowledge, and perhaps amusement.

Other recent assessments have focused on Johnson the reader. For Richard Wendorf, the portrait "should remind us of the many passages in the *Life of Johnson* in which Boswell comments on Johnson's unusual reading habits, especially his ability to grasp 'at once what was valuable in any book, without submitting to the labour of perusing it from beginning to end.'" Robert DeMaria Jr. also pays close attention to Reynolds's portrait as part of his larger consideration of Johnson's different kinds of reading, which here "is not study, although it is highly attentive, engaged, and searching. His posture and intensity suggest that it is not curious reading; he is not lost in a book."[50]

One last perspective is worth attention. Reynolds on occasion demonstrably thought of his paintings in pairs: Oliver Goldsmith and Edmund Burke, the Irishmen among the Streatham worthies, even Johnson (the Knole portrait) and Reynolds himself similarly cloaked in mezzotint engravings by James Watson (both 1770).[51] As we have seen, Reynolds's self-portrait as a deaf man cupping his hand to his ear was painted around the same time as his portrait of the nearsighted Johnson. In referring to Reynolds's self-portrait as analogous to *Blinking Sam*, Mrs. Piozzi may have been seeing exactly what Reynolds wished his viewers to see. Wendorf notes some of the similarities: "Both pictures are small, half-length images in which the subject is shown at close range . . . , and both draw attention to their subjects' physical limitations."[52] I think, however, that Reynolds is also wittily alluding to the topos, familiar in both art and literature throughout Europe, of the five senses. In England, he probably knew of Francis Hayman's series of single-figure representations of the senses, engraved in mezzotint by Richard Houston (all 1753, fig. 12) the year after Reynolds's return from Italy. The senses of hearing and sight are conveyed in the portraits of Reynolds and Johnson, however, not by their presence but by their absence. Hayman's figures are female, but male figures were frequently used. Reynolds's studies in Italy were likely to have exposed him to other examples of the genre.[53]

The art historian John Ingamells calls *Blinking Sam* "the least satisfactory of Reynolds's portraits of Johnson," though he does not specify why.[54] I do not see *Blinking*

50. Wendorf, *Elements*, 254, quoting *Life*, ed. Hill, 1:71; DeMaria, *Johnson and the Life of Reading*, 12.

51. Wendorf, *Elements*, 253.

52. Wendorf, *Sir Joshua Reynolds*, 44.

53. See Folkenflik, "Representations," 68–70, for an overview of portraits, statues, caricatures, halfpennies, and shop signs depicting Johnson. For the topic of the five senses, see *Immagini del sentire: i cinque sensi nell'arte*, ed. Sylvia Ferino-Pagden (Milan, 1996). For Hayman's Five Senses series, see Brian Allen, *Francis Hayman* (New Haven, Conn., 1987), 142–44. A copy of *Hearing* is in the British Museum, Department of Prints and Drawings, 2010,7081.549. For single-figure male examples of the genre, see the series by Jusepe de Ribera. In some ways, Reynolds's wit in representing the senses was anticipated by Ribera, who uses the image of a blind man feeling a sculpted head to illustrate the sense of touch (*The Sense of Touch*, ca. 1615–16, Norton Simon Museum, Pasadena, Calif.), whereas such a sculpture sometimes was used to illustrate sight.

54. See Ingamells, *National Portrait Gallery: Mid-Georgian Portraits, 1760–1790* (London, 2004), 294.

FIGURE 12. Richard Houston after Francis Hayman, *Hearing*, mezzotint, 1753. Prints and Drawings, British Museum. © Trustees of the British Museum.

Sam in this way. This image of Johnson is manifestly different from Reynolds's other three, and it emphasizes aspects of the subject not found in them. The Streatham library portraits have been considered "intimate" portraiture, but they are social, and this one is more intimate yet. It is the visual equivalent of being overheard. The painting has no setting, no background. The focus is entirely on the reader, and his focus is entirely on the text. We do not know if there is anyone else in the room, and unlike Reynolds's portrait of Baretti, there is no indication of a room. We can infer the artist's presence, but the painting does not appear to be posed. If Reynolds took it from life, he might have sketched it surreptitiously, as Johnson's wounded response suggests. It seems to me unlikely that Johnson sat for it. It could have been done from a sketch from life or from Johnson's frequent presence in Reynolds's company. Reynolds did have an unfinished portrait of Johnson, the first he painted of him, in his house until 1789, when it was in James Heath's studio for engraving (see figs. 2 and 6).

Inferences

I hope to have clarified the issues I raised earlier in this essay. *Blinking Sam* probably was painted in 1775. Though its original ownership is unclear, it passed from Edmond Malone or his brother through a series of owners until it was sold in 1987 to Loren and Frances Rothschild, who generously presented it to the Huntington Library. There are several more copies of *Blinking Sam* than art historians have acknowledged. *Blinking Sam* has been both praised and blamed from its appearance around 1775 to the present. I would side with those who praise it.

The slack presentation of the Albright-Knox free copy, with its more upright reader at greater length, his book open, and no oval surround, enables us better to appreciate *Blinking Sam*'s dynamism. The half-length portrait confines its force within an oval; the light focuses on the face and hands; the image is close to the picture surface; the reading matter is bent back beneath Johnson's good eye, surrendering its information to the single-minded reader. Johnson brings energy and concentration to reading—clearly not for him a leisure activity. He is a reader, the portrait implies, like no other.

I am indebted to Brian Allen, John Andries, Carrie Rebora Barratt, Peter Martin, Laura McGrane, John Overholt, Diane Peterson, Martin Postle, Loren Rothschild, Lisa Saltzman, Jacob Simon, John Stone, Guilland Sutherland, and Richard Wendorf. I am grateful for the funding of the Edward A. Dickson Emeritus Professorship at the University of California, Irvine, and grants from the Paul Mellon Centre for Studies in British Art and the University of California-Catalonia Visiting Scholar Fund. I am also indebted to audiences at the National Portrait Gallery, London, Haverford and Bryn Mawr colleges, Harvard University, and the University of Barcelona. The Heinz Archive, Mellon Centre, Houghton Library, and Huntington Library proved invaluable. I draw on a few paragraphs in Folkenflik, "Representations," *Samuel Johnson in Context*, 62–82.

Byron's Johnson

Freya Johnston

LORD BYRON LOVED DOGS. And it is perhaps Byron, the most questing of poetic characters, who makes good William Empson's "absurd but half-true" claim that, for eighteenth-century skeptics, "dog," rather than "God," became "the last security behind human values." Empson adds that:

> it gives one a sense of Voltaire's real qualifications to discover England when one finds him, in old age, with wary but genial admiration, shaking his head over Dr. Johnson to Boswell and calling him ("in the English phrase") "a superstitious dog." The stress, of course, is on *superstitious*; with the stress on *dog* it would have seemed as rude then as it does now. *Dog* is unstressed because the phrase assumes that everybody is *some* kind of dog. . . . It is the pastoral idea, that there is a complete copy of the human world among dogs, as among swains or clowns.

Like a dog, as Empson describes that creature, Byron repeatedly "blows the gaff on human nature."[1] But he appeals to us to love and trust him all the same. Dogs, after all, are sincere. The family motto was "*Crede Byron*."

If Byron is a dog, however, in T. S. Eliot's reading he is a dead one:

> Of Byron one can say, as of no other English poet of his eminence, that he added nothing to the language, that he discovered nothing in the sounds, and developed nothing in the meaning, of individual words. I cannot think of any other poet of his distinction who might so easily have been an accomplished foreigner writing English. . . . Just as an artisan who can talk English beautifully while about his work or in a public bar, may compose a letter painfully written in a dead language bearing some resemblance to a newspaper leader, and decorated with words like "maelstrom" and "pandemonium": so does Byron write a dead or dying language.[2]

1. William Empson, *The Structure of Complex Words* (London, 1951; reprint, London, 1995), 158–74 at 168–69. "Blowing the gaff" is criminal slang for revealing a secret without permission.
2. T. S. Eliot, "Byron," in *On Poetry and Poets* (London, 1957), 193–206 at 200–201.

Eliot's tone is discouraging, but he makes a point that deserves to be taken seriously. Byron's language was "dead or dying" because he considered himself to be writing in what he bewailed as "the declining age of English poetry": a period in which the worst sign for national taste, to his mind, was the widespread "depreciation of Pope."[3]

In the fourth canto (1818) of *Childe Harold's Pilgrimage*, Byron—who tended to promote the idea of himself as a master of division and opposition—instead described his poetic art as one of combination. This is Byron "about his work," as Eliot might put it:

I twine
My hopes of being remembered in my line
With my land's language[.][4]

"In my line" achieves the typical Byronic splicing of the casual and the precise, giving a colloquial, perfunctory spin to earnest aspirations. Deftly encompassing "my line of work" (whether vocational, occupational, or mere pastime), "my poetic line," and "my line of inheritance," it is a phrase that the *Oxford English Dictionary* dates back to the late eighteenth century. Yet "my land," as opposed to "my line," is strangely possessive language at this point in Byron's career; he had been in exile since signing the deed of separation from Lady Byron in April 1816. Two years later he wrote, "every step nearer England—would be to me disgusting."[5]

So what did it mean for Byron to speak of "my land," or its language, from abroad? Was English still, in fact, his language? Or was he merely, as Eliot would have it, an "accomplished foreigner writing English"? Byron suggests that his poems combine the hope of being remembered with the exercise of his native tongue—exercise that was, in itself, an effort of memory for one who now went whole months at a time without speaking English at all. In one of many furiously combative letters on *Don Juan* (1819–24), Byron wrote that his poem "may be bawdy—but is it not good English?" (*LJ*, 6:232). Yet he could see the dangers of his own manner and of its influence on others. He did not exempt his works from the charge of being written in what he called "that false stilted trashy style which is a mixture of all the styles of the day—which are *all bombastic.*" "[N]o one" had done more than he "through negligence to corrupt the language." The prevailing style in 1820, Byronic trappings included, was "neither English nor poetry" (*LJ*, 7:182, italics in original).

So how could his style be at once "good English" and "neither English nor poetry"? Even if mixture and bombast seemed, to Byron, fatal flaws in Romantic verse (so much of which concerns fatal flaws), all poetic lines—at any rate, all English ones—are ancestrally and culturally mixed beasts. In 1821, Byron again described himself as

3. George Gordon, Lord Byron, *The Complete Miscellaneous Prose*, ed. Andrew Nicholson (Oxford, 1991), 149, 143 (hereafter cited in text as *CMP*).

4. George Gordon, Lord Byron, *The Complete Poetical Works*, ed. Jerome McGann, 7 vols. (Oxford, 1980–93), 2:127 (hereafter cited in text as *Poetical Works*).

5. George Gordon, Lord Byron, *Byron's Letters and Journals*, ed. Leslie A. Marchand, 12 vols. (Cambridge, Mass., 1973–82), 6:31 (hereafter cited in text as *LJ*).

"amongst the builders of this Babel attended by a confusion of tongues." But this time he added, by way of self-exculpation, that he had never been "amongst the envious destroyers of the classic temple of our Predecessor" (*CMP*, 148).[6] In other words, unlike most of his contemporaries, Byron had not sought to malign Pope or his eighteenth-century admirers and imitators, but to honor their example. What Byron contributed to his "land's language" arose partly from his study and appreciation of Johnson, and hence from Johnson's study and appreciation of Pope, a writer whom Byron described as "the greatest moral poet of any age—or in any language" (*CMP*, 163).

Byron may have viewed himself as partly responsible for the degeneracy of public taste—and hence, in typically lurid terms, with "all the remorse of a murderer." But it is one of many paradoxes about his work that—in the absence of Johnson, who he wished could rise from the dead "to crush" the Lakers and the Cockneys—he also thought himself qualified to contribute to its redemption (*LJ*, 7:175). Byron's "good English," then, invites us to apply it to the literary and critical conduct of the man who writes it; to one who serves as an honest, self-divided witness of the damage he has helped to inflict on his own linguistic medium.

James Boulton commented on the "relatively small . . . attention paid to Johnson by the Romantics and—except for Byron, . . . how completely adverse their judgement."[7] In his second prose contribution to the Bowles controversy of the 1820s, Byron hailed Johnson as "the great Moralist" and "the noblest critical mind which our Country has produced" (*CMP*, 125n, 138n). To those considering Byron's and Johnson's careers from an unsympathetic vantage point, nobility of rank might easily be contrasted with nobility of mind. You can imagine Johnson's "short Song of Congratulation" (1780) ("Long-expected one and twenty . . . ")[8] being redirected with minimal alterations at Byron, who wrote shortly before his twenty-first birthday of having debts amounting to "perhaps twelve thousand pounds." In the preface to his first collection of poems, *Hours of Idleness*, published in 1807 when he was nineteen, the young lord concludes by citing "The opinion of Dr. JOHNSON on the Poems of a noble relation of mine"—the Earl of Carlisle—"'That when a man of rank appeared in the character of an author, his merit should be handsomely acknowledged.'" Byron insists that he would rather "incur the bitterest censure of anonymous criticism" than avail himself of such a privilege (*Poetical Works*, 1:34). His wish was duly granted. Henry Brougham's devastating unsigned review, measuring Byron against Pope's juvenile publications to the discredit of the former, also leapt on

6. On Byron, Pope, and Johnson, see Tony Howe, "Uncircumscribing Poetry: Byron, Johnson, and the Bowles Controversy," in *Liberty and Poetic Licence: New Essays on Byron*, ed. Bernard Beatty, Tony Howe, and Charles E. Robinson (Liverpool, 2008), 206–18.

7. "Introduction," *Johnson: The Critical Heritage*, ed. James T. Boulton (London, 1971), 34.

8. Johnson, *Poems*, vol. 6 of *The Yale Edition of the Works of Samuel Johnson* (hereafter cited as *YE*), ed. E. L. McAdam Jr. with George Milne (New Haven, Conn., 1964), 307. Text references are to this edition.

> Dr Johnson's saying, that when a nobleman appears as an author, his merit should be handsomely acknowledged. In truth, it is this consideration only, that induces us to give Lord Byron's poems a place in our review, beside our desire to counsel him, that he do forthwith abandon poetry, and turn his talents, which are considerable, and his opportunities, which are great, to better account.[9]

One reason Byron was enraged by this was that he more than half-agreed, resolving time and again to turn his back on scribbling. And yet, "Lords too are Bards," as he asserted in *English Bards and Scotch Reviewers* (1809), his attempt at a new *Dunciad* (1728–44) (*Poetical Works*, 1:251). But the opposition of nobility to poetry remained throughout his life and characterized the aftermath of his death. In 1824, the dean refused an application to inter him in Westminster Abbey, so he was buried in the family vault near Newstead. A cortège of forty-seven carriages accompanied the hearse from London. "He was buried like a nobleman," John Cam Hobhouse wrote, "since we could not bury him as a poet." A century later, despite the backing of Thomas Hardy, Rudyard Kipling, and three former prime ministers, a petition for a Byron memorial in Westminster Abbey was also refused. "The Abbey is not a mere literary Valhalla," the dean announced: "Byron, partly by his openly dissolute life and partly by the influence of licentious verse, earned a world-wide reputation for immorality among English-speaking people."[10] (Byron's reply could well have been that his "world-wide reputation for immorality" extended far beyond those who spoke English.)

It might come as a surprise that such a writer, one whose "whole life" was, as he put it, "at variance with propriety, not to say decency," should have so admired Johnson (*LJ*, 2:92). Born four years after Johnson's death, Byron owned editions of the *Dictionary of the English Language* (1755), the *Lives of the Poets* (1779–81), "which I think the type of perfection" (*LJ*, 6:72), and Boswell's *Life* (1791). The 1816 sale catalogue of his books includes near-complete collections of Johnson's verse and periodical essays.[11] The list of constitutional similarities between these two writers turns out to be, potentially, a very long one. It would have to include the following:

First, a love of truth. Hence, a principled resistance to the vagaries and indulgence of imagination, and a strong dislike of mere fiction. For Byron, truth became synonymous not with imagination or beauty, but with plain fact. He was a more sober empiricist than any of his contemporary poets. And he drew on Johnson to buttress his move away from literary invention to common sense, hard cash, and real life. Neither wished to argue from books; both of them defended traveling, and the need to see things for oneself.

9. Henry P. Brougham, *Edinburgh Review*, February 1801, 285–89, in *Byron: The Critical Heritage*, comp. Andrew Rutherford (London and New York, 1970), 28.

10. *ODNB*, s.v. "Byron, George Gordon Noel, sixth Baron Byron (1788–1824)," by Jerome McGann, last modified October 2009, http://www.oxforddnb.com/view/article/4279.

11. *A Catalogue of a Collection of Books, Late the Property of a Nobleman About to Leave England on a Tour . . . Which Will Be Sold by Auction by Mr. Evans, at His House, No. 26, Pall Mall, on Friday, April 5, and Following Day* (London, 1816).

They shared a love of anecdote and biography, as well as an endless desire for verifiable human testimony, as opposed to mere news, and a resistance to the merest whiff of cant. Both were instinctively suspicious of intellectual systems. Each had a strong tendency to melancholy, which they thought hereditary, and an equally strong tendency to indolence. Against that indolence, Johnson, like Byron, resisted stagnation. Each man prided himself on his facility for speedy composition and bursts of productive activity. Byron's recollection of himself at school makes him sound the intellectual spitting image of Johnson:

> I was . . . remarked for the extent and readiness of my *general* information —but in all other respects idle—capable of great sudden exertions— (such as thirty or forty Greek Hexameters) . . . but of few continuous drudgeries.—My qualities were much more oratorical and martial— than poetical—and . . . our head-master . . . had a great notion that I should turn out an Orator—from my fluency—my turbulence—my voice—my copiousness of declamation—and my action. (*LJ*, 9:42–43, italics in original)[12]

Other similarities include a voracious appetite and a fondness for crash diets. Both of them, in various ways, were lovers of extremes. They shared a history of physical suffering from birth: Byron had a club foot; Johnson endured scrofula and many other painful afflictions. Both men were sensitive about their bodies and prone to show off through feats of physical prowess (Byron's preference was for swimming and wrestling). Both were attracted to Catholicism, and susceptible to ghosts. In canto 16 of *Don Juan*, Byron dwells on one of his favorite themes—what Jerome McGann identifies as "to doubt if doubt itself be doubting."[13] Such an activity is the more confusing when you bear in mind that "to doubt" was a more assertive, more positive activity for Byron and his contemporaries than it might be for us. In his work, "to doubt" as often means "to suspect" or "apprehend" that something is the case as it means to waver or feel uncertain; this positive sense of doubt seems to expire around the end of the nineteenth century. But here, in canto 16, Byron squares up to rational, skeptical readers inclined to question the existence of ghosts, and calls on Johnson's shade for authoritative support:

6

And therefore, mortals, cavil not at all;
Believe:—if 'tis improbable, you *must*;
And if it is impossible, you *shall*:
'Tis always best to take things upon trust.

12. Compare *Boswell's Life of Samuel Johnson, Together with Boswell's Journal of a Tour to the Hebrides and Johnson's Diary of a Journey into North Wales*, ed. George Birkbeck Hill, rev. L. F. Powell, 6 vols., 2nd ed. (Oxford, 1971), 1:56–60 (hereafter cited as *Life*).

13. Jerome McGann, *Don Juan in Context* (London, 1976), 137.

I do not speak profanely, to recall
    Those holier mysteries, which the wise and just
Receive as gospel, and which grow more rooted,
As all truths must, the more they are disputed.

7

I merely mean to say what Johnson said,
    That in the course of some six thousand years,
All nations have believed that from the dead
    A visitant at intervals appears;
And what is strangest upon this strange head,
    Is, that whatever bar the reason rears
'Gainst such belief, there's something stronger still
In its behalf, let those deny who will.

(*Poetical Works*, 5:620–21, italics in original)

Byron versifies a mixture of Imlac and Boswell, borrowing Johnson's attitudes as well as his vocabulary: caviling, belief, thousands of years, the arguments for and against. In chapter 31 of *Rasselas*, Pekuah is—unsurprisingly—not reassured to be told, on the brink of the pyramid, that

> "There is no people, rude or learned, among whom apparitions of the dead are not related and believed. This opinion, which, perhaps, prevails as far as human nature is diffused, could become universal only by its truth: those, that never heard of one another, would not have agreed in a tale which nothing but experience can make credible. That it is doubted by single cavillers can very little weaken the general evidence, and some who deny it with their tongues confess it by their fears."[14]

In Boswell's *Life*, Johnson, "Talking of ghosts," says:

> "It is wonderful that five thousand years have now elapsed since the creation of the world, and still it is undecided whether or not there has ever been an instance of the spirit of any person appearing after death. All argument is against it; but all belief is for it."[15]

For good measure, Byron slaps an extra thousand years on top of Johnson's "five." This is probably because he is quoting from memory. But he is trying to be faithful to the spirit of his original: "I merely mean to say what Johnson said." Byron, himself so imitated, also cast about for models and resemblances. He was a good mimic and fatherless, therefore perhaps doubly keen to discern likenesses of others in himself. "I do not

14. Johnson, *Rasselas and Other Tales*, vol. 16 of *YE*, ed. Gwin J. Kolb (1990), 116.
15. *Life*, 3:230.

know that I resemble John Jacques Rousseau," he wrote to his mother in 1808 (*LJ*, 1:171). Later, he announced, "certes I am not Johnson," but the announcement was partly regretful: he went on to cite Johnson as a "fair precedent" for his own verses on "Drury-Lane," which were partly modeled on the earlier poet's prologue (*LJ*, 2:212–14). Leigh Hunt recalled that Byron "liked to imitate Johnson, and say, 'Why, Sir,' in a high, mouthing way, rising, and looking about him."[16] Imitations of Johnson's imitations feed into the early verse, too. The *Elegy on Newstead Abbey* (1807) attempts the mid-century style of *The Vanity of Human Wishes* (1749)—that is, Pope filtered through Johnson. Even if Byron is writing here in stanzas rather than in heroic couplets, he retains some of the qualities and structures of Johnson's verse and strikes the same note of dark inevitability regarding fate:

> Years roll on years; to ages, ages yield;
> Abbots to Abbots, in a line succeed;
> Religion's charter, their protecting shield,
> Till royal sacrilege their doom decreed.
> (*Poetical Works*, 1:108)

Compare:

> Year chases year, decay pursues decay,
> Still drops some joy from with'ring life away;
> New forms arise, and diff'rent views engage,
> Superfluous lags the vet'ran on the stage,
> Till pitying Nature signs the last release,
> And bids afflicted worth retire to peace.
> (*The Vanity of Human Wishes*; *YE*, 6:106)

The treatment of succession in the *Elegy on Newstead Abbey*—a line apparently interminable, until it is abruptly concluded by the animated abstraction of "royal sacrilege"—is indebted to Johnson, as is the general atmosphere of "doom decreed." Byron sounds more like Pope than Johnson does; "Years . . . years," "ages, ages," and "Abbots to abbots" summon up the compact, boxed-in maneuvers of *The Rape of the Lock* (1714)—"Where Wigs with Wigs, with Sword-knots Sword-knots strive, / Beaus banish Beaus, and Coaches Coaches drive"—as well as Pope's sense of himself in *Epistle II.ii* (1734) as an "unweary'd Mill," "Years foll'wing Years" as he turns "ten thousand Verses."[17] Byron progressively frees himself from the confinements of the couplet form, even as he repeatedly laments his inability to write as Pope did. In ottava

16. *His Very Self and Voice: Collected Conversations of Lord Byron*, ed. Ernest J. Lovell Jr. (New York, 1954), 328.

17. Pope, *The Rape of the Lock and Other Poems*, ed. Geoffrey Tillotson, vol. 2 of *The Twickenham Edition of the Poems of Alexander Pope* (London and New Haven, Conn., 1966), 152 (hereafter cited as *TE*); *Imitations of Horace*, ed. John Butt, vol. 4 of *TE* (1953), 171.

rima, he discovers a kind of writing sufficiently flexible to accommodate his speaking voice. But he was never oppressed by Johnson's or Pope's example. What the young Byron lacks, by comparison with his eighteenth-century predecessors, is energy.

Echoes of *The Vanity of Human Wishes* recur in some unpublished lines "To a Youthful Friend" (1808):

> Such is the common lot of man:
> Can we then 'scape from folly free?
> Can we reverse the general plan,
> Nor be what all in turn must be?
> (*Poetical Works*, 1:220)

The source for which is:

> Yet hope not life from grief or danger free,
> Nor think the doom of man revers'd for thee:
> (*The Vanity of Human Wishes*; *YE*, 6:99)

It is easy to smile at such precocious despondency: but that is the strain in which Johnson's poetic career began, too. His earliest surviving work, "On a Daffodill, the first Flower the Author had seen that year" (probably written at the age of fifteen) hastens to wither its youthful ambitions into despair. No sooner has Johnson raised the "fair omens" of his flower's "unusual glories" than he sees it "shrivel" into eternal obscurity. Like the daffodil, the author is doomed to fade: "Alike must fall the poet and his theme" (*YE*, 6:3–4). Lawrence Lipking has observed that the poem displays two related, contradictory aspects of Johnson's authorial character: a vast appetite for success, and a preemptive despondency that snatches defeat from the jaws of prospective victory.[18] Byron affected less ambition and enjoyed spectacular early success; but, as teenagers, he and Johnson are in many ways close allies on the page.

John Gibson Lockhart dwells on Byron's and Scott's love of Johnson, dismissing as "the cant of our day" the claim that "Johnson was no poet." Scott, Lockhart reports (via James Ballantyne), "had more pleasure in reading *London*, and *The Vanity of Human Wishes*, than any other poetical composition he could mention; and I think I never saw his countenance more indicative of high admiration than when reciting aloud from those productions."[19] Correspondence and poems reveal Scott's friend Byron toying receptively and appreciatively throughout his later years with fragments from *The Vanity of Human Wishes*. The ways in which he deploys Johnson support Christopher Ricks's suggestion that Byron "dissipates" his sources: "With allusion, he breaks lines or phrases down, and his poetry is then shard-borne."[20] Where Johnson

18. Lawrence Lipking, *Samuel Johnson: The Life of an Author* (Cambridge, Mass., and London, 2000), 34–38.

19. J. G. Lockhart, *Memoirs of the Life of Sir Walter Scott, Bart.*, 7 vols. (Edinburgh, 1837–38), 2:307–8, 308n.

20. Christopher Ricks, *Allusion to the Poets* (Oxford, 2002), 149.

energetically compresses and intensifies, Byron relaxes and scatters. What he admires in his later reading of *The Vanity of Human Wishes* is, he says, "all the examples and mode of giving them" (*LJ*, 8:19). He treats the poem as a miscellaneous collection of individual people and phrases, the "examples" to be picked up and thrown across other works and other contexts. Writing, for instance, of Scrope Davies, a gambler and drunkard who went temporarily missing, Byron asks, "what can have become of Scrope? . . . it is sad that he should 'point a moral and adorn a tale' unless of his own telling" (*LJ*, 7:100). The phrasing here, "a tale . . . of his own telling," suggests an independent-minded attitude to allusion as well as to morals. Byron was scrupulous about acknowledging the debts of his writing to other poets, and his vision of literary self-sufficiency entails telling a tale that is yours even when repeating other people's words and phrases. Every source is made his own. In *The Corsair* (1814), the same Johnsonian couplet shapes the final lines of the poem: "He left a Corsair's name to other times, / Linked with one virtue, and a thousand crimes" (*Poetical Works*, 3:214).

Byron's Johnsonian strain, as it manifests itself in his early verse imitations, is not particularly inventive; it has none of the deft mobility, the lightning adaptation to circumstance, of *Don Juan*. But nor does it show any hallmarks of the anxiety of influence, unlike the responses to Johnson exhibited by William Hazlitt (ten years Byron's senior) or John Ruskin (thirty-one years Byron's junior). Ruskin appreciated Johnson's *Idler* (1758–60) and *Rambler* (1750–52) for their "adamantine common-sense" but felt he had to liberate himself from Johnson's style: "the turns and returns of reiterated Rambler and iterated Idler," he wrote,

> fastened themselves in my ears and mind; nor was it possible for me, till long afterwards, to quit myself of Johnsonian symmetry and balance in sentences intended, either with swordsman's or paviour's blow, to cleave an enemy's crest, or drive down the oaken pile of a principle.[21]

Against the background of this fearful symmetry, Ruskin describes Byron's stylistic influence in wholly contrasting, amenable terms:

> One word only . . . I must permit myself about [Byron's] rhythm. Its natural flow in almost prosaic simplicity and tranquillity interested me extremely, in opposition alike to the symmetrical clauses of Pope's logical metre, and to the balanced strophes of classic and Hebrew verse. But though I followed his manner instantly in what verses I wrote for my own amusement, my respect for the structural, as opposed to fluent, force of the classic measures, supported as it was partly by Byron's contempt for his own work, and partly by my own architect's instinct for "the principle of the pyramid," made me long endeavour, in forming my prose style, to keep the cadences of Pope and Johnson for all serious statement. . . . had it not

21. *Praeterita and Dilecta*, vol. 35 of *The Works of John Ruskin*, ed. E. T. Cook and Alexander Wedderburn (London and New York, 1980), 225.

> been for constant reading of the Bible, I might probably have taken Johnson for my model of English. To a useful extent I have always done so.[22]

Ruskin still appears unsure that he has escaped Johnson, or indeed that he ever sought to imitate his style. But one thing he is sure about is that "I never for an instant compared Johnson to Scott, Pope, Byron, or any of the really great writers whom I loved."[23] Byron and Johnson stand at opposite ends of a spectrum: one of them natural, simple, relaxed, and fluent, a happy combination of public voice with private prose; the other, declamatory and "structural." Biography enters into Ruskin's analysis here, as it enters invited or uninvited into most of Byron's verse: the poet's professed "contempt for his own work" is something that weighs against Johnson's apparent seriousness of purpose and of cadence. Disenchanted Romanticism is married to a real speaking voice; and a real speaking voice, at least in poetry, is not what one associates with Johnson.

Perhaps Ruskin also felt, as Thomas Macaulay had suggested in 1831, that Byron was an index of the sheer distance between Romantics and Augustans—a writer who brings Johnson to mind because he is so far away from him. Or rather, Byron straddled two eras, attracting and comprehending them both, to the satisfaction of neither:

> [Byron] was the man of the last thirteen years of the eighteenth century, and of the first twenty-three years of the nineteenth century. He belonged half to the old, and half to the new school of poetry. His personal taste led him to the former; his thirst of fame to the latter;—his talents were equally suited to both.... He was the representative, not of either literary party, but of both at once, and of their conflict, and of the victory by which that conflict was terminated. His poetry fills and measures the whole of the vast interval through which our literature has moved since the time of Johnson. It touches the *Essay on Man* at the one extremity, and *The Excursion* on the other.[24]

Byron saw himself as both observer and cause of the decline of literature since Johnson. Like Macaulay, he was shocked at the vastness of the "distance" between himself and Pope (and, by extension, Johnson). He was fitted neither by character nor experience to superintend literary proprieties. He did not seek to change the direction of what he castigated as wrongheaded or declining literature; rather, he sought to bear witness to it from abroad. But he came closest to fulfilling the role of superintendent when he recognized that he would himself be condemned according to eighteenth-century standards—standards he often hailed as superior, most obviously during his involvement in the so-called Bowles controversy. He emerges victorious from that contest by virtue of repeatedly measuring "the whole of that vast distance" Macaulay invokes.

22. Ruskin, *Praeterita and Dilecta*, 151, 225.
23. Ruskin, *Praeterita and Dilecta*, 225.
24. Macaulay, quoted in *Byron: The Critical Heritage*, 296–316 at 308.

The sonneteer William Lisle Bowles had, in 1806, provoked a public quarrel over the status of Pope by publishing a new, ten-volume edition of the works, in which he discussed the poet's moral character in unsympathetic, uncomplimentary terms and deprecated his range and capabilities as a writer.[25] This performance generated some rude lines in Byron's *English Bards and Scotch Reviewers* (*Poetical Works*, 1:240). Then, in his *Specimens of the British Poets* (1819), Thomas Campbell condemned Bowles's treatment of Pope as exaggerated and unjust.[26] Bowles responded, as did Isaac D'Israeli and others. Byron's name was cited on both sides, and eventually he could not resist joining in. This was partly because defending Pope meant attacking cant—"the grand 'primum mobile' of England," as Byron put it in his first published contribution to the quarrel, "Cant political—Cant poetical—Cant religious—Cant moral—but always *Cant*, multiplied through all the varieties of life" (*CMP*, 128, italics in original). Such an effort naturally involved getting Johnson on his side; Byron told Thomas Medwin that he "had occasion to study [Johnson] when I was writing to Bowles," and that Johnson was "the profoundest of critics."[27]

Like Johnson, Byron was vigorously committed to the idea that literature should be continuous with and directly applicable to real life. He writes with brilliant relish and sensational immediacy in reply to Bowles's criticism of a poetic line about ships, asking: "Did M^{r}. B. ever gaze upon the Sea?" and arguing that he, Byron, was more entitled than most writers to discuss the subject, given that

> I have *swum* more miles—than all the rest of them together now living ever *sailed*—and have lived for months and months on Shipboard;—and during the whole period of my life abroad—have scarcely ever passed a month out of sight of the Ocean.—Besides being brought up from two years till ten on the brink of it. (*CMP*, 130–31, italics in original)

The discussion is reminiscent of "Thomson," in which Johnson writes:

> The biographer of Thomson has remarked, that an author's life is best read in his works: his observation was not well-timed. [Richard] Savage, who lived much with Thomson, once told me, how he heard a lady remarking that she could gather from his works three parts of his character, that he was a *great Lover, a great Swimmer*, and *rigorously abstinent*; but, said Savage, he knows not any love but that of the sex; he was perhaps

25. For a full account of the dispute, see Jacob Johan van Rennes, *Bowles, Byron, and the Pope-Controversy* (New York, 1966).

26. Thomas Campbell, *Specimens of the British Poets; with Biographical and Critical Notices, and an Essay on English Poetry*, 7 vols. (London, 1819), 1:262–71.

27. Thomas Medwin, *Medwin's Conversations of Lord Byron*, ed. Ernest J. Lovell Jr. (Princeton, N.J., 1966), 198.

> never in cold water in his life; and he indulges himself in all the luxury that comes within his reach.[28]

Like Byron, Johnson trounces a rival interpretation of literature with an appeal to the testimony of experience. In his endeavor to see through poems to their human originators and measure one against the other, he differs neither from Thomson's earlier biographer nor from his female reader. But he has the superior witness in Savage—one who shows, in fact, how the author's life is not necessarily, or at least not always, "best read" in his works (a moral that Byron's readers, in particular, have found difficult to swallow). Poems are not invariably trustworthy as records of their authors' lives, morals, or experiences. And Johnson's comment on this fact—"his observation was not well-timed"—is studiously neutral. He refuses to provide any further conclusions. We will carry on reading literary works and the private lives of their authors in relation to one another, but we have to acknowledge that such a relationship will not be straightforward.

This was a touchstone in the dispute about Pope, largely thanks to Pope himself, who had repeatedly insisted that bad authors were bad people.[29] Byron, naturally sensitive to this line of argument, could not forgive Bowles for having charged the poet with "Envy—duplicity—licentiousness—avarice" (*CMP*, 147). His counterblast takes the form of insisting that Pope was as good a man as he was a near-faultless writer—rather than suggesting, as he might have done, that to focus on the man himself, and his moral failings, was a fruitless way of proceeding, especially given the length of time that had elapsed since Pope's death.[30] In his attack on Bowles in *English Bards and Scotch Reviewers*, Byron was rather less confident about Pope's life: "The first of poets was, alas! but man!" (*Poetical Works*, 1:240); Campbell went further than this, conceding that "The vindictive personality of [Pope's] satire is a fault of the man, and not of the poet."[31]

On Pope's character, as he reviews it in the letters on Bowles, Byron differs markedly from Johnson, who could never have written, as Byron did, that Pope's "moral is as pure—as his poetry is glorious"; who wrote, in fact, of *The Dunciad*, "That the design was moral, whatever the author might tell either his readers or himself, I am not convinced" (*CMP*, 144; *Lives of the Poets*, 4:75). Byron hailed the *Essay on Man* (1732–34) as a work of genius, the poem of which Johnson wrote: "Never were penury of knowledge and vulgarity of sentiment so happily disguised. The reader feels his mind full, though he learns nothing" (*Lives of the Poets*, 4:76). In spite of these hefty stumbling blocks, Byron readily acknowledged Johnson's "Pope" as "the finest critical work extant," one that "can never be read without instruction and delight" (*CMP*,

28. Johnson, *The Lives of the Most Eminent English Poets: With Critical Observations on Their Works*, ed. Roger Lonsdale, 4 vols. (Oxford, 2006), 4:103. Text references are to this edition.

29. See, for instance, *An Essay on Criticism*: "each *Ill Author* is as bad a *Friend.*" In *Pastoral Poetry and An Essay on Criticism*, vol. 1 of *TE*, ed. E. Audra and Aubrey Williams (1961), 296.

30. See also *LJ*, 7:217.

31. Campbell, *Specimens of the British Poets*, 1:270.

150n). And Johnson, whatever else he might have thought of the noble lord, would in a reciprocal bow have endorsed Byron's claim in the *Letter to Murray* (1821) that "the highest of all poetry is Ethical poetry—as the highest of all earthly objects must be moral truth" (*CMP*, 143).

Perhaps the most affecting moment in both Johnson's and Byron's discussions of Pope arrives when they consider Martha Blount's role in Pope's last years. Here, too, the object of the writing in both cases is "moral truth." Johnson's account is full of the benefit of the doubt, rather than of hindsight:

> She is said to have neglected him, with shameful unkindness, in the latter time of his decay; yet, of the little which he had to leave, she had a very great part. Their acquaintance began early; the life of each was pictured on the other's mind; their conversation therefore was endearing, for when they met, there was an immediate coalition of congenial notions. Perhaps he considered her unwillingness to approach the chamber of sickness as female weakness, or human frailty; perhaps he was conscious to himself of peevishness and impatience, or, though he was offended by her inattention, might yet consider her merit as overbalancing her fault; and, if he had suffered his heart to be alienated from her, he could have found nothing that might fill her place; he could have only shrunk within himself; it was too late to transfer his confidence or fondness. (*Lives of the Poets*, 4:52)

The continually self-revising but quiet, composed propriety of this appraisal derives from the fact that it refuses to gossip, even when speculating about people who have died. And it progressively becomes a kind of free indirect style, written as if from Pope's viewpoint, exhibiting charitable motives toward one who might have been described by the biographer in his own voice in much balder, harsher terms. We see the poet, reanimated by Johnson, charging himself with faults and imputing "female weakness, or human frailty" to one of whom we have already heard a fiercer diagnosis: "shameful unkindness."

Johnson's doubtful language—"she is said to"; "perhaps"; "though"; "might yet"; "if"; "could have"—puts us back in the position of a vulnerable, lonely, still-living individual, as he nears his death. Weighed against all these doubts, "it was too late." Nonetheless, as we read, the process of adjudication seems, temporarily, unfinished, because we feel, for a moment and as if from the inside, just that sense of uncertainty that we are invited to believe Pope experienced. As ever with Johnson, multiple attempts are in play to arrive at a kind of equilibrium, a just distribution of praise and blame, but (equally characteristically) the process of adjudication is left incomplete.

Byron responded to Bowles's lewd insinuations about Pope's relationship with Martha Blount, about his disabilities and possible impotence, with a cool but tender assessment of the evidence. It seems likely to have been informed by Johnson's sympathetic tact in the earlier biography. Just below the surface of this writing is the challenge to dare to read into it Byron's own profligacy and disability, and to snigger at the "useless Needle" as a prurient image for Pope's impotence (in its solitary weakness, it sounds like Donne's compass gone wrong):

> To me it appears of no very great consequence whether Martha Blount was or was not Pope's Mistress—though I could have wished him a better. ——She appears to have been a cold-hearted—interested—ignorant—disagreeable—woman upon whom the tenderness of Pope's heart in the desolation of his latter days was cast away, not knowing whither to turn as he drew towards his premature old age, childless and lonely—like the Needle which approaching within a certain distance of the Pole—becomes helpless & useless—& ceasing to tremble, rusts.—She seems to have been so totally unworthy of tenderness that it is an additional proof of the kindness of Pope's heart to have been able to love such a being.—But we must love something. (*CMP*, 166)

For what it's worth, that image of a rusting needle gradually ceasing to tremble may have been inspired by just the kind of newspaper column that Eliot accused Byron of resembling. In his notes to the *Complete Miscellaneous Prose*, Andrew Nicholson cites an 1820 issue of *Blackwood's*, regarding evidence of the "loss of magnetic virtue" in a pair of ships' compasses "whenever they approached within 5 or 6 miles of the north shore" of Lancaster Sound (*CMP*, 464–65).

Byron is far more overtly present in this writing than Johnson is in "Pope," but that is partly because Byron is writing a polemical assault on Bowles, righting a perceived injustice to the memory of a poet he loved. He also writes far more explicitly against Martha Blount; the dash just before "woman" looks as if it might be covering an expletive as the alternative name for what she truly was. The achievement of Johnson's writing on this subject is not to make us feel sympathy for her, but sympathy for Pope's view of her, and by extension primarily for Pope. It seems possible that, when Byron writes, "it is an additional proof of the kindness of Pope's heart to have been able to love such a being," he is responding to Johnson's imaginative characterization (itself, perhaps, "an additional proof"?) of Pope's thought processes. The conclusion of both passages is essentially the same, except that Johnson emphasizes "nothing" and Byron "something": "if he had suffered his heart to be alienated from her, he could have found nothing," and "we must love something."

Another touchstone in the Bowles controversy was the relationship of nature to art. Byron asserted, with increasing panache and disdain, the insufficiency of mere nature to the poet—an argument that allowed him to swipe at "Turdsworth," his preferred name for the monarch of the Lakes, and "The Scoundrels of Scribblers" who were "trying to run down *Pope*" (*LJ*, 7:253, italics in original). "Nature,—exactly, simply, barely, Nature,—will make no great Artist of any kind," he writes, "and least of all a poet—the most artificial perhaps of all artists" (*CMP*, 137). Art is, in fact, superior to nature, at least as far as poetry is concerned; and here, again, Byron enlists Johnson as a key supporting witness. Citing his extravagant praise, in the *Lives of the Poets*, of a declamatory passage from William Congreve's *Mourning Bride* (1697), "the whole of whose merit consists in artificial imagery," Byron writes:

> Here is the finest piece of poetry in our language so pronounced by the noblest critical mind which our Country has produced,—& the whole imagery of this quintessence of poetry is unborrowed from *external* nature.——I presume that no one can differ from Johnson that as description it is unequalled.—For a controversy upon the subject the reader is referred to Boswell's Johnson. (*CMP*, 138n)

Many people have begged to differ from Johnson's praise of *The Mourning Bride*, but that is another story. Byron seems to have construed his anti-Bowles polemic as a natural extension of Johnson's response to Joseph Warton, whose revised 1782 two-volume *Essay on the Genius and Writings of Pope* (the first volume appeared in 1756) had paved the way for Bowles by asserting that Pope's verse "lies more level to the general capacities of men, than the higher flights of more genuine poetry."[32] (In 1818, Byron referred to "the unjustifiable attempts at depreciation [of Pope] begun by Warton—& carried on to & at this day by the new School of Critics & Scribblers who think themselves poets because they do *not* write like Pope"; *LJ*, 6:31, italics in original). Johnson was determined to parry such attacks, famously asserting in what is the last paragraph of the *Lives of the Poets*, disregarding the appended letter and reprinted comments on Pope's epitaphs, that

> After all this, it is surely superfluous to answer the question that has once been asked, Whether Pope was a poet? otherwise than by asking in return, If Pope be not a poet, where is poetry to be found? To circumscribe poetry by a definition will only shew the narrowness of the definer, though a definition which shall exclude Pope will not easily be made. (*Lives of the Poets*, 4:79–80)

If we take this paragraph in its entirety as the final word of the *Lives*, it is a conclusion that triumphantly refuses to be conclusive on the nature of the art it has been discussing. For a lexicographer, or perhaps *as* a lexicographer, Johnson was strikingly ambivalent about the value and remit of any "definition," preferring instead to emphasize the limits of its applicability.

Byron embraced an overtly political, globalized version of Johnson's insistence that criticism could not hedge poetry about with such definitions as Warton had attempted in his *Essay*, when he demarcated the "MAN OF WIT" and the "MAN OF

32. Joseph Warton, *An Essay on the Genius and Writings of Pope*, 4th ed., 2 vols. (London, 1782), 2:410.

SENSE" from the "TRUE POET."[33] In Byron's reading, to foist such categorizations on the reader becomes a form of tyrannical oppression. So Bowles's "principles of poetry," humbly proposed to the world as "invariable" and "unanswerable," prompted Byron to declare: "I do hate that word '*invariable*.'— —What is there of *human*—be it poetry—philosophy—wit, wisdom—science—power—glory—mind—matter—life—or death ——which is '*invariable*?'" (*CMP*, 129). Johnson helped him to that conclusion, but Johnson had also helped him to arrive at the opposite one, and in the same year (1821). Of *The Vanity of Human Wishes*, Byron wrote in January:

> 'tis a grand poem—and *so true*!—true as the 10th of Juvenal himself. The lapse of ages *changes* all things—time—language—the earth—the bounds of the sea—the stars of the sky, and every thing "about, around, and underneath" man, *except man himself*, who has always been, and always will be, an unlucky rascal. The infinite variety of lives conduct but to death, and the infinity of wishes lead but to disappointment. All the discoveries which have yet been made have multiplied little but existence. An extirpated disease is succeeded by some new pestilence; and a discovered world has brought little to the old one, except the p[ox]—first and freedom afterwards—the *latter* a fine thing, particularly as they gave it to Europe in exchange for slavery. But it is doubtful whether "the Sovereigns" would not think the *first* the best present of the two to their subjects. (*LJ*, 8:19–20, italics in original)

So all human things are variable, and all human things are invariable. Inconsistencies cannot both be right; but, imputed to Byron, they may both be true.[34] Perhaps the general point to derive from this is that human beings are invariable at least in their variability.

Byron's reading of *The Vanity of Human Wishes* is quick to move from appreciating the eternal truth of Johnson's verse to more immediate outrage at the injustice of human sovereigns. For Byron, as for many political and humanitarian campaigners from the 1790s onward, Johnson's name and example pointed a moral very different from that suggested by Macaulay—who, citing Edmund Burke, claims that Johnson "appears far greater in Boswell's books than in his own"—and by Thomas Carlyle, for whom Johnson's character was fixedly, immutably great.[35] Johnson encouraged Byron in his resist-

33. Warton, *Essay*, 1:v–vi.

34. See *Rasselas and Other Tales*, *YE*, 16:33: "'Inconsistencies . . . cannot both be right, but, imputed to man, they may both be true.'"

35. Thomas Carlyle, review of Croker's edition of Boswell's *Life* in *Fraser's Magazine*, May 1832, 379–413, in *Johnson: The Critical Heritage*, ed. Boulton, 432–48. On Johnson's reputation in the 1790s, see Isobel Grundy, "What is it about Johnson?," in *Samuel Johnson: The Arc of the Pendulum*, ed. Freya Johnston and Lynda Mugglestone (Oxford, 2012), 168–80 at 175–77.

ance to definitions and limitations of all kinds, a resistance that ultimately made him impatient with the whole business of literature: "As to defining what a poet *should* be, it is not worth while," he wrote, again in January 1821 and echoing Johnson's "Pope," "for what are *they* worth? what have they done?" (*LJ*, 8:41). Instead, he imagined for himself a reformist political career; but his impatience with all rules, systems, and institutions made such a hope impossible to realize.

If Hazlitt and Ruskin sought to escape Johnson, Byron construed him as a liberating precedent. He authorized Byron's use of English. Byron appealed to Johnson's work when accused of language that was too strong, passionate, or indecent. He dug up examples of coarse terms in Johnson when arguing the case for *Don Juan* (*LJ*, 6:253). And he quoted Johnson's argument that Matthew Prior, subsequently proscribed as lewd, was in fact perfectly safe reading (*LJ*, 6:208). Johnson's model of professional authorship freed Byron to participate in the combative games of the literary market (*LJ*, 7:175; 8:103; 9:67–68). When aspiring authors sought his advice, he quoted Johnson in order to demonstrate the risks and trials of the writer's life, and the necessity of financial and literary independence (*LJ*, 2:90, 179; 3:66–67; 4:69). Johnson's critical precepts, as rehearsed in writing and in spoken exchanges, licensed Byron to follow his own instincts in the teeth of powerful contemporary opposition (*LJ*, 1:162–63; 2:214; 4:93, 314–15).

In their writings on Pope, both Johnson and Byron, each of them lavishly biographized, repeatedly circle around the relationship between an author and his works. Celebrity is part of the mythology of their lives. If it is a declared aim of this volume to consider Johnson independently of Boswell's *Life*, one reason why Byron's perceptions are valuable is that, although they have been inflected by Boswell, they have not been read through or against Macaulay and Carlyle. Despite his love of biography, Byron instinctively thought about Johnson's writing before he considered Johnson the human being. His was no vision of Johnson the lofty, unaltering Great Man. While it is clear that Byron knew whole passages of Boswell by heart, for him the *Life* coexists with the works. It has not superseded them.

Johnson and Scott, England and Scotland, Boswell, Lockhart, and Croker

James Engell

THIS ESSAY ENLARGES on the literary relations between Samuel Johnson and Sir Walter Scott. It also examines an analogy: as Johnson came to represent England and English culture, so Scott, though in somewhat different ways, came to embody Scotland and Scottish culture. The essay treats their biographers, Boswell and Lockhart, and explores how they shaped their subjects as national representatives, as well as how Lockhart employed Johnson's presence to enhance his portrait of Scott.

Warm Esteem

Late in life, having doggedly and brilliantly written himself and others largely out of massive debt during the six previous years but now broken in health and seeking a climate in which to recover, Sir Walter Scott, before leaving for Italy, sends to the press the last line of manuscript he will ever submit. It is by Samuel Johnson. With grace, Scott writes that he hopes it may not apply to himself: "Superfluous lags the veteran on the stage."[1] He had always loved *The Vanity of Human Wishes* (1749) and may have also had in mind Johnson's *Rambler* 207 (March 10, 1752), on the folly of remaining too long on the stage. Scott also has recourse to Johnson's poem in his letters, one of which John Gibson Lockhart includes in the *Memoirs* (3:14). There Scott cites the "fears of the brave, and follies of the wise." Elsewhere he remarks that Johnson's poem "has often extracted tears from those whose eyes wander dry over pages professedly sentimental."[2] For Scott, the poem concerns, in his wonderfully suggestive phrase, "the debt of humanity" (5:370). Its lines occur to him on personal occasions, with solemn thoughts of the limitations of life, its insecurity and illnesses, and the need for compassion and benevolence.

1. John Gibson Lockhart, *Memoirs of the Life of Sir Walter Scott*, 5 vols. (Boston, 1901), 2:186 (hereafter cited as *Memoirs*); see also 5:370. The line was, at least, the last one Scott wrote that Lockhart himself submitted for publication. Lockhart did not submit *The Siege of Malta* or *Bizarro*. See Donald E. Sultana, "*The Siege of Malta*" *Rediscovered: An Account of Sir Walter Scott's Mediterranean Journey and His Last Novel* (Edinburgh, 1977); see also *Castle Dangerous*, ed. J. H. Alexander (Edinburgh, 2006), 194–216, for Lockhart's decisions regarding publication of Scott's late works.

2. Walter Scott, *Miscellaneous Prose Works*, 6 vols. (Edinburgh, 1827), 3:288.

Gwin Kolb remarks that "Scott's warm esteem for Samuel Johnson and his works, including *Rasselas*, is a solidly established fact in literary history,"[3] but specialization in literary studies has driven the two writers apart. The paucity of anything treating the two is remarkable. Kolb's brief article twenty years ago is a rare exception. He contends that Scott wrote the advertisement and acted as "editor" of *Rasselas*, for which I have found corroborating evidence: the author of the advertisement mentions Johnson reflecting "deeply upon the vanity of human wishes" and associates "Lobo's History of Abissinia" with the "royal family of Gondar."[4] In a note Scott wrote for Boswell's *Journal of a Tour to the Hebrides* (1785), he connects "Bruce, the Abyssinian traveller," with "a king named *Brus*" in that region, and the Scottish-sounding link "occasioned some mirth at the court of Gondar."[5] Scott's notes to the *Tour* were first published in 1831.[6]

Of a dozen biographies of Scott in the past century, only three mention Johnson with any pertinence (those of Moray McLaren and John Sutherland, cited below, and that of A. N. Wilson), and then only to quote Scott's reverting to some of Johnson's words, or to make a brief comparison. None acknowledge what Kolb calls Scott's "warm esteem" for Johnson. We still hear Thomas Macaulay's essay on Johnson quoted regularly, but how often Scott's appreciative "Memoir"—what Lockhart calls "his Sketch of Johnson's Life"? Citing it, Lockhart also relays Byron's favorable, sensitive reflections on *The Vanity of Human Wishes* (*Memoirs,* 2:186).

For a century or more, the common estimate was that the two greatest biographies in the language were by Boswell and Lockhart. In one of many instances, Leslie Stephen in the *Dictionary of National Biography* (1893) states that Lockhart turned his "admirable materials . . . to such account that the biography may safely be described as, next to Boswell's 'Johnson,' the best in the language. He handed over all the profits to Sir Walter Scott's creditors."[7] H. J. C. Grierson, the most accomplished biographer of Scott in the earlier twentieth century and also editor of his letters, affirms that Lockhart's biography "as a work of art is rivalled only by Boswell's *Johnson*, and [James Anthony] Froude's *Carlyle*, while it has pages which in beauty of feeling and style rise to a higher level than anything in these works."[8]

Scott himself had long ago praised Johnson and Boswell's *Life* in print:

3. Gwin J. Kolb, "Sir Walter Scott, 'Editor' of *Rasselas*," *Modern Philology* 89, no. 4 (1992): 515–18 at 515.

4. Kolb, "Sir Walter Scott," 518.

5. *Boswell's Life of Johnson, Together with Boswell's Journal of a Tour to the Hebrides and Johnson's Diary of a Journey into North Wales*, ed. George Birkbeck Hill, rev. L. F. Powell, 6 vols., 2nd ed. (Oxford, 1964–71), 5:123–24n3 (hereafter cited as *Life*, ed. Hill).

6. Boswell, *The Life of Samuel Johnson: Including A Journal of a Tour to the Hebrides*, ed. John Wilson Croker, 10 vols. (London, 1839 [1831]) (hereafter cited as *Life*, ed. Croker, with silent deletion and slight variation).

7. *Dictionary of National Biography*, ed. Sir Leslie Stephen and Sidney Lee, 63 vols. (London, 1885–1901), 34:29.

8. H. J. C. Grierson, *Lang, Lockhart, and Biography* (London, 1934), 17 (originally the Andrew Lang Lecture at St. Andrews, December 6, 1933).

> Of all the men distinguished in this or any other age, Dr. Johnson has left upon posterity the strongest and most vivid impression, so far as person, manners, disposition, and conversation are concerned. We do but name him, or open a book which he has written, and the sound or action recall to the imagination at once his form, his merits, his peculiarities, nay, the very uncouthness of his gestures, and the deep impressive tone of his voice. We learn not only what he said, but form an idea how he said it; and have, at the same time, a shrewd guess of the secret motive why he did so, and whether he spoke in sport or in anger, in the desire of conviction, or for the love of debate . . . he is, in our mind's eye, a personification as lively as that of Siddons in Lady Macbeth, or Kemble in Cardinal Wolsey. All this, as the world knows, arises from his having found in James Boswell such a biographer as no man but himself ever had, or ever deserved to have. . . . Considering the eminent persons to whom it relates, and the quantity of miscellaneous information and entertaining gossip which it brings together, his Life of Johnson may be termed, without exception, the best parlour-window book that was ever written.[9]

"Parlour-window book" echoes a letter sent earlier to Scott and quoted in Lockhart's *Memoirs.* When Scott's *Minstrelsy of the Scottish Border* (1802–3) appeared, George Ellis wrote to him that it was "a collection which must form a parlor-window book in every house in Britain which contains a parlor and a window" (1:322). There is no slight in Scott's designation of a "parlour-window book," just as there was none in Ellis's compliment. It meant a volume achieving popular fame that rests on real merit.

Later, conscious of but not self-satisfied with his own literary fame, Scott directed in his will that Lockhart, his son-in-law, should take up the task of recording his life. Lockhart, like his subject, knew and esteemed Boswell's *Life.* Yet, for all the shadows cast by these twinned biographies, as far as I can tell no one has examined them, their authors, or their subjects, in any comparative way in the last forty-five years, and before that only Ian Jack in his 1965 essay, "Two Biographers: Lockhart and Boswell," a study of the temperaments, merits, and techniques of the two biographers.[10]

A crucial link exists between the two great books. In 1831 John Wilson Croker's edition of Boswell's *Life* appeared. Lockhart reviewed it in November of that year for the *Quarterly Review*, where he served as editor—and lived in London, not Scotland—for almost thirty years. Scott's will assigning Lockhart in 1832 the undertaking of his biography may not have been the first time Lockhart considered that task; but the appearance of Croker's edition about a year earlier did not prompt Lockhart to

9. *Life*, ed. Croker, Publisher's Preface, 1:xvi–xvii. The full reference is Walter Scott, *Biographical Memoirs*, 3 vols., vols. 3–4 of *The Miscellaneous Prose Works of Sir Walter Scott* (Edinburgh, 1834), 1:260–61.

10. Ian Jack, "Two Biographers: Lockhart and Boswell," in *Johnson, Boswell, and Their Circle: Essays Presented to Lawrence Fitzroy Powell* (Oxford, 1965), 268–85.

indicate he had ever entertained the possibility. Reviewing Croker's edition, Lockhart encountered Croker's notes that paint Johnson as an Englishman who held harsh views of Scotland. Lockhart's review calls Boswell's *Life* "that English [not British] book which, were this island to be sunk tomorrow . . . would be most prized in other days and countries, by the students 'of us and of our history.'" Lockhart credits Boswell as a founding genius of subsequent memoirs.[11] Some of Macaulay's most negative statements about Johnson came in *his* review of Croker's edition of Boswell's *Life*, as if Croker, not Johnson, had elicited them.[12]

Yet, Lockhart said that for his own part he "never thought of being a Boswell." He would not cooperate with literary gentlemen who "designed to *Boswellize* Scott."[13] Near the end of the *Memoirs*, he states, "I am not going to 'peep and botanize' upon his grave" (5:442). The phrase is from Wordsworth, "A Poet's Epitaph," asking if one is a "slave, / One that would peep and botanize / Upon his mother's grave?" (lines 18–20). While this may distance him from Boswell's technique and temperament, it does not rule out writing a biography of similar scope.

A great deal might be said about Johnson and Scott, Boswell and Lockhart, though for nearly half a century next to nothing has been.[14] This essay highlights one aspect of the two writers and their biographers: the way in which Johnson and Scott, in part through those biographical writings, came to stand as embodiments and limit cases of national character and identification, English and Scottish. This is only one aspect. There are other reasons why Johnson, Scott, Boswell, and Lockhart claim our attention: history, morality, preservation, politics, and the life of authorship.

The issue of national identification is complicated and enriched by the fact that Boswell and Lockhart were both Scots, both Tories, and both spent time in London—Lockhart, for decades. Ian Jack explores these and other intersections of their careers. The national aspect is strongly inflected by Johnson's apparent opinions of Scotland and the Scots, opinions reported by Boswell, sometimes provoked by him, at other times aimed at him in humor or mild exasperation.

More than two decades prior to Croker's 1831 edition of Boswell's *Life*—for which, in the section devoted to *A Tour to the Hebrides*, Scott would provide copious notes—the Wizard of the North had decided how he would deal with Johnson's attitudes to Scotland. With characteristic generosity, Scott called on Johnson's own moral sentiments. In 1810, quoting from memory, he consoled his dear friend J. B. S. Morritt on the deaths of Morritt's brother-in-law and another close friend:

> The beautiful and feeling verses by Dr. Johnson to the memory of his humble friend Levett [*sic*], and which with me, though a tolerably ardent Scotchman, atone for a thousand of his prejudices, open with a

11. John Gibson Lockhart, "Croker's Edition of Boswell," *Quarterly Review* 46, no. 91 (November 1831): 1–46 at 11.

12. Nicholas Hudson, *Samuel Johnson and the Making of Modern England* (Cambridge, 2003), 3.

13. See Jack, "Two Biographers," 281.

14. Carol Ray Berninger, "Across Celtic Borders: Johnson, Piozzi, Scott" (PhD diss., Drew University, 1993), treated the attitudes of these writers to older Celtic cultures in Scotland and, for Mrs. Piozzi, in Wales. Scott's *Waverley* (1814), *The Antiquary* (1816), and *Rob Roy* (1817) chiefly represent his views.

sentiment which every year's acquaintance with this *Vanitas Vanitatum* presses more fully on our conviction.

"Condemn'd to Hope's delusive mine,
As on we toil from day to day,
By sudden blast[s,] or slow decline
Our social comforts melt [drop] away."

I am sure Mrs. Morritt must have deeply felt these repeated strokes of misfortune.[15]

The "vanity of vanities" recalls Scott's admiration of the poem that in 1749 commenced Johnson's decade of moral writing, a period that ended with another of Scott's favorites, *Rasselas*. The tenderness Scott expresses over Johnson's poem on Levet was no passing straw. He felt Johnson's power as a moral historian who could examine not only the ambitious Charles XII of Sweden but also Richard Savage and Robert Levet, two of Johnson's personal acquaintances. Savage desired recognition and literary reward. Levet was an obscure medical practitioner who knew he would never have either, yet attained them through Johnson's tribute to his anonymous charity and patient care that asked no remuneration.

Thirteen years later, in 1823, Scott confronted the death of Dr. Matthew Baillie, brother of Joanna Baillie, an author whom he admired—as did Wordsworth—and judged among Scotland's finest. Scott wrote to John Richardson:

There is a sort of firmness which arises even out of the extent of such a calamity, much like that which enables men to start up and exert themselves after receiving a dreadful fall; the extent of the injury received is not perceived till long after. I am truly concerned about Joanna. . . . He is himself an inestimable loss to society, and . . . always put me in mind of Johnson's beautiful lines, though made for a humbler practitioner:—

"When fainting nature called for aid,
And hovering Death prepared the blow,
His powerful [vig'rous] remedy displayed
The force [power] of art without the show."[16]

Again, Scott's memory of the lines is imperfect, yet ready and apposite. For him, this sentiment in Johnson far outweighs any prejudices against Scotland.

Johnson and Scotland

The crudest and, for some readers, most memorable way in which Boswell portrays Johnson as quintessentially English is in his reporting what Johnson said about Scotland and the Scots. Boswell takes a cue from statements such as Johnson's *Dictionary*

15. Walter Scott to J. B. S. Morritt, October 3, 1810, *Familiar Letters of Sir Walter Scott*, ed. David Douglas, 2 vols. (Boston, 1894), 1:192, quoting Johnson's "On the Death of Dr. Robert Levet" (1782), lines 1–4.

16. *Familiar Letters*, 2:177.

definition of "oats" as a food that in England is fed to horses "but in Scotland supports the people."[17] Conscious of his own pedigree as a Scot, yet in awe of Johnson, Boswell primes, induces, or openly invites Johnson to counter with some quip or criticism imputing to Scotland a lack of sophistication, learning, cleanliness, or culture. Johnson is often happy to oblige. He likes to pique Boswell, pull his leg, or score a point when Boswell prods.[18] It is as if Boswell wants him to say provocative things, to reply brusquely, though on the *Tour*, Boswell wants to show off Scotland and a select group of its citizens, too. A far better guide to Johnson's attitude to Scotland is not Boswell's prose, engaging as it is, but Johnson's *Journey to the Western Islands of Scotland* (1775). Johnson on Scotland differs a great deal from Boswell on Johnson on Scotland.

The best place to begin assessment of Johnson's attitude to Scotland in his *Journey* is the final paragraph. After admitting that in England he has "passed my time almost wholly in cities" and "may have been surprised by modes of life and appearances of nature" more familiar to others, he concludes his book: "Novelty and ignorance must always be reciprocal, and I cannot but be conscious that my thoughts on national manners, are the thoughts of one who has seen but little."[19] It is no false modesty. Aside from his concern with England, Johnson wrote more on, thought more about, and spent more time in Scotland than any other nation. Yet, he concludes with self-admonition. If we distrust Boswell as the complete guide to Johnson, in part because Boswell spent no more than a year in his company, we might follow Johnson in distrusting his own reaction to Scotland, where he spent less than a third of that time.

Johnson's *Journey* has elicited divergent judgments about his attitudes. No wonder, for as Mary Lascelles points out, "Johnson's sympathies, and antipathies, were closely engaged" with what the "deliberate counterpoise of evidence" means not only for Scotland's past but also for her future (*YE*, 9:xv). Balancing his words "ancient," "ruins," "declining," "small or straggling market-towns," "waste of reformation," and "a place of little trade" are their opposites: "new," "civility, elegance, and plenty," "trade," and "great civility." Affrighted at some villagers' "very savage aspect of wildness and manner" (42), in other locations he enjoys "true pastoral hospitality" (33). He finds certain dwellings smoky and cramped, yet other structures are "well built, airy, and clean" (12). He questions his own "English vanity" (7) and overturns the well-worn idea that England is always clean, Scotland dirty: an inviting lane "would have had the appearance of an English lane, except that an English lane is almost always dirty" (31–32). He is more likely to praise than to blame Scottish letters;

17. Samuel Johnson, *A Dictionary of the English Language*, 2 vols. (London, 1755), s.v. "Oats."

18. For their larger personal relationship, see John B. Radner, *Johnson and Boswell: A Biography of Friendship* (New Haven, Conn., 2012).

19. *A Journey to the Western Islands of Scotland*, vol. 9 of *The Yale Edition of the Works of Samuel Johnson* (hereafter cited as *YE*), ed. Mary Lascelles (New Haven, Conn., 1971), 164. For Johnson's complex attitudes to Scotland, see two valuable essays by Murray Pittock: "Johnson and Scotland," in *Samuel Johnson in Historical Context*, ed. Jonathan Clark and Howard Erskine-Hill (New York, 2001), 184–96; and "Scotland," in *Samuel Johnson in Context*, ed. Jack Lynch (Cambridge, 2012), 329–36; see also Pat Rogers, *Johnson and Boswell: The Transit of Caledonia* (Oxford, 1995), chap. 8, "Johnson, Boswell, and Anti-Scottish Sentiment," 192–215, esp. 202–15.

for example, "Literature is not neglected by the higher ranks of the Hebridians" (54), who commonly have books in two or more languages. Freya Johnston analyzes Johnson's *Journey* with acuity. She stresses his "scrupulous indecision," an uncertainty how to judge what he sees and witnesses, something characteristically un-Johnsonian.[20]

Two major points permeate his text. First, the prosperous middle state that Johnson sees as a prized hallmark of England struggles to emerge in Scotland—not enough people are yet comfortable and leisured. He wonders if this will happen, which raises the second point: the changes sweeping over Scotland are so powerful, rapid, and often painful that, in addition to the loss of a native oral culture, forced emigration and the specter of poverty are all too real. "The true state of every nation," Johnson remarks with distilled political wisdom, "is the state of common life" (*YE*, 9:22). That state in Scotland hangs in the balance. The Scots, for example, have "attained the liberal, without the manual arts" (28). Absent the latter, their economy and prosperity remain in jeopardy.

Lascelles closes her introduction to the *Journey* by comparing Scott's views on the depopulation and possibility of improvement in the Border and Highlands with Johnson's views on the same subject in the Highlands and the Hebrides, though Johnson is on one occasion skeptical about declining population (66). They do not quite see eye to eye—Lascelles says Scott puts trust in "the pride of some landlords and the compassion of others," while Johnson looks "for the intellectual capacity and energy which might make good will effectual" (xxvi). Yet, she sees that Scott and Johnson identify very similar problems.

Boswell's advertisement to the second edition of the *Life* (1793) lauds Johnson as a defender of English values against "that detestable sophistry which has been lately imported from France, under the false name of *philosophy*."[21] That comment carries political insinuations about a French revolution unknown to Johnson. For Boswell to compare Johnson's views not with French or Italian ones, but with Scottish, proved more effective as a nursery for what Nicholas Hudson calls the virtually "iconic" identification of Johnson with England.[22] A *contrast* closer to home would be stronger and, for many readers, more rousing—or maddening—though Scott himself would never rise to the bait.

Johnson Champions the English by *Contrast*

Boswell records Johnson drawing national contrasts, generally to English advantage. Here are two with France, and in the second, Johnson even relegates the French below the Scots: "An eminent foreigner . . . was very troublesome with many absurd inquiries. 'Now there, Sir, (said he,) is the difference between an Englishman and a Frenchman. A Frenchman must be always talking, whether he knows any thing of the matter or not; an Englishman is content to say nothing, when he has nothing to say'" (*Life*,

20. Freya Johnston, *Samuel Johnson and the Art of Sinking, 1709–1791* (Oxford, 2005), 17. Chapter 3, "Diminishing Returns: *A Journey to the Western Islands of Scotland*," 126–81, is most pertinent and quotes William Empson's phrase "an indecision and a structure" (132).

21. James Boswell, *The Life of Samuel Johnson, LL.D.*, 2nd ed., 3 vols. (London, 1793), 1:xv.

22. Hudson, *Samuel Johnson and the Making of Modern England*, 133.

ed. Hill, 4:14–15). Johnson also observes, "France is worse than Scotland in every thing but climate. Nature has done more for the French; but they have done less for themselves than the Scotch have done" (2:402–3). A pointed jibe comes in this comment reported by Boswell about "a Scotchman," which Johnson clinches by invoking, with irony, Dryden's line praising Milton:

> I put him in mind that the landlord at Ellon in Scotland said, that he heard he [Johnson] was the greatest man in England,—next to Lord Mansfield. "Ay, Sir, (said he,) the exception defined the idea. A Scotchman could go no farther:
> 'The force of nature could no farther go.'" (2:336)

William Murray, Earl of Mansfield, was born in Perthshire, Scotland, but became a prominent English jurist and political figure.

Yet, Johnson also is determined to catch Boswell thinking too much about his apparent "prejudice against the Scotch," as Boswell dutifully records:

> And as to his prejudice against the Scotch . . . he said . . . "When I find a Scotchman, to whom an Englishman is as a Scotchman, that Scotchman shall be as an Englishman to me." His intimacy with many gentlemen of Scotland, and his employing so many natives of that country as his amanuenses [for the *Dictionary*], prove that his prejudice was not virulent; and I have deposited in the British Museum . . . the following note in answer to one from me, asking if he would meet me at dinner at the Mitre, though a friend of mine, a Scotchman, was to be there:—
> "Mr. Johnson does not see why Mr. Boswell should suppose a Scotchman less acceptable than any other man. He will be at the Mitre." (2:306–7)

Is Johnson probing Boswell's own sense of inferiority? Or teasing him about assuming that Johnson is prejudiced? Later in their friendship, Boswell retaliates. He mentions a Scotsman who

> had the same contempt for an Englishman compared with a Scotsman, that he had for a Scotsman compared with an Englishman; and that he would say of Dr. Johnson, "Damned rascal! to talk as he does of the Scotch." This seemed, for a moment, "to give him pause." It, perhaps, presented his extreme prejudice against the Scotch in a point of view somewhat new to him, by the effect of *contrast*. (3:170)

Boswell is no match, however, for the agility of Johnson's "extreme prejudice." He reports that an Irish friend once expressed to Johnson "an apprehension, that if he should visit Ireland he might treat the people of that country more unfavourably than he had done the Scotch." Johnson answered "with strong pointed double-edged wit, 'Sir, you have no reason to be afraid of me. The Irish are not in a conspiracy to cheat the world by false representations of the merits of their countrymen. No, Sir; the Irish are a FAIR PEOPLE;—they never speak well of one another'" (2:307). Johnson formulates the response at Boswell's expense. Everyone loses except the English, but the Scots lose the most. Next to Boswell, the condescending estimate of Sir John Hawkins takes the color and nuance out of Johnson's views concerning Scotland.[23]

Johnson "a stern *true-born Englishman*" and "*John Bull*"

Invoking a phrase from *Richard II*, Boswell qualifies Johnson's "prejudice" as one of "no ill will":

> That he was to some degree of excess a *true-born Englishman*, so as to have ever entertained an undue prejudice against both the country and the people of Scotland, must be allowed. But it was a prejudice of the head, and not of the heart. He had no ill will to the Scotch; for, if he had been conscious of that, he would never have thrown himself into the bosom of their country, and trusted to the protection of its remote inhabitants with a fearless confidence. (*Life*, ed. Hill, 2:300–301)

And Boswell leavens the *true-born Englishman* with a sense that Johnson can criticize his own compatriots for their frigid reserve:

> Though a stern *true-born Englishman*, ... he had ... candour enough to censure, the cold reserve too common among Englishmen towards strangers: "Sir, (said he,) two men of any other nation who are shewn into a room together ... will immediately find some conversation. But two Englishmen will probably go each to a different window, and remain in obstinate silence. Sir, we as yet do not enough understand the common rights of humanity." (4:191)

By the 1830s, however, Johnson had become a popular caricature. The *Monthly Magazine* comments on Croker's edition of Boswell's *Life* and *Tour*: "The doctor was a first-rate John Bull, that is, a first-rate bull-dog, and nothing could be more formidable

23. Hawkins writes: "Johnson's prejudices were too strong to permit him to extend his philanthropy much beyond the limits of his native country, and the pale of his own church; and, that he was unable to conquer his habits of thinking and judging, is the only apology that can be offered for his asperity towards the people whose country and manners he, in his journey above spoken of [to Scotland], has taken upon him to describe; or that he has forborne to display any such generous sentiments respecting the inhabitants of Scotland as others have done who have visited that country"; Sir John Hawkins, *The Life of Samuel Johnson, LL.D.*, ed. O M Brack Jr. (Athens, Ga., 2009), 292. It is impossible to give Johnson's *Journey* a fair reading and agree with this sentiment.

than his gripe [*sic*], when he once took the trouble to tear down his antagonist."[24] Boswell is much to blame. In his exuberance, especially in the *Tour*, he couples Johnson as "*true-born Englishman*" with "*John Bull*" (*Life*, ed. Hill, 5:20). Boswell handles neither phrase well. He is supposedly cautious—"if I may be allowed the phrase"—about Johnson as "much of a *John Bull*." But there it is. The phrase originated with John Arbuthnot, a Scot, and Boswell seems unaware of this. He also seems unaware of Daniel Defoe's satiric poem *The True-Born Englishman* (1701), which points out that many among the nobility and gentry descended from foreign invaders. Scott later did not care for John Bull. In 1830 he wrote to Lady Louisa Stuart bemoaning that the simplistic views of the time gull "the ass's ears of John Bull" (*Memoirs*, 5:279).

Johnson Praises English Intellects

In the all-important semiotic systems of mathematics and of words, Boswell provides two instances in which Johnson does champion English thinkers: "In a Latin conversation with the Père [Roger Joseph] Boscovitch . . . I heard him maintain the superiority of Sir Isaac Newton over all foreign philosophers, with a dignity and eloquence that surprized that learned foreigner" (*Life*, ed. Hill, 2:125–26). In *The Advancement of Learning* (1605), Bacon called for a science of semiotics, and Johnson praises Bacon's grasp of English as the supreme practice of semiotics manifested as national language. Boswell relays Johnson's comment that Bacon "was a favourite authour," one he had not read until compiling the *Dictionary*, in which Johnson often quotes him. William Seward recollects Johnson having mentioned "that a Dictionary of the English Language might be compiled from Bacon's writings alone," and that Johnson had once considered giving an edition of Bacon's English works, and "writing the Life of that great man" (3:194).

Johnson's emphasis on Bacon as a master of English and his concomitant interest in him suggest the most important factor in Johnson's reputation as the epitome of English culture: his earned authority in the language itself. The first example of this, however well worn, is telling, for it combines *contrasting* another nation with control over one's native tongue. Dr. Adams and Johnson discuss the *Dictionary*, and Adams asks how he can complete it in three years when forty members of the French Academy took forty years to compile their dictionary. Johnson replies with a witty ratio: "This is the proportion. Let me see; forty times forty is sixteen hundred. As three to sixteen hundred, so is the proportion of an Englishman to a Frenchman" (1:186).

Again, language is the essential element in national identity, and for Johnson its use can help or hinder a larger integration of the United Kingdom. Holding to one's own dialect tends to promote provincialism or clannishness, the implication of which Lockhart will later absolve Scott. Yet Johnson is unaware of the hegemonic implications of his attitude. Perhaps it is, as he says in the *Journey*, his "English vanity" at work:

> He observed that "The Irish mix better with the English than the Scotch do; their language is nearer to English. . . . They have not that extreme

24. "Johnson, Boswell, and Croker," *Museum of Foreign Literature, Science and Art* 19 (July to December 1831): 449–53 at 449, quoting from the *Monthly Magazine*.

> nationality which we find in the Scotch. I will do you, Boswell, the justice to say, that you are the most *unscottified* of your countrymen. You are almost the only instance of a Scotchman that I have known, who did not at every other sentence bring in some other Scotchman." (2:242)

The most telling remark that Boswell reports, however, suggests that Johnson was so intimate with the English language that the *Dictionary* had grown in his own mind "insensibly." This is not strictly true—Johnson relied on "the best authors" to illustrate and to provide many of its words and, by inference, their definitions. Then again, judging and selecting those authors required a mind saturated in literature of the English language, all imaginative *or* learned works in any genre or field of knowledge. When Boswell asked him how he had acquired such a grasp of English and then planned to compile the *Dictionary*, "He told me, that 'it was not the effect of particular study; but that it had grown up in his mind insensibly'" (1:182).

Transcending Nationality

With Johnson, any reader should frequently find resort in *yet*, *but*, or *however*—words that provide the pivots for *The Vanity of Human Wishes*, many essays, and the Preface to *Shakespeare*. And so, Boswell in his inclusiveness reveals a figure belonging to a nation but promoting uppermost the ideal of a republic of letters, a confederacy of knowledge that transcends boundaries. Boswell tells how, according to Sir William Forbes, several friends proposed translated emendations to Johnson's fine Latin epitaph for Goldsmith. "'Sir Joshua agreed to carry it to Dr. Johnson, who received it with much good humour and desired Sir Joshua to tell the gentlemen, he would alter the Epitaph in any manner they pleased, as to the sense of it; but *he would never consent to disgrace the walls of Westminster Abbey with an English inscription*'" (*Life*, ed. Hill, 3:84–85). Though we no longer regard Latin as the language of universal learning, the point remains, and we recall that his conversation championing Newton was in Latin. For Johnson, there exists a geography of intellect and morality whose territory is bounded only by the human mind and whose most common language should be as widely understood as possible.

The pith of this attitude Peter Levi states well:

> He was committedly on the side of American Indians, Negro slaves, the British poor, and every other underdog he knew. It is important to realize that these attitudes could go together with the most progressive analysis of human society. There is a crucial sense in which Johnson belongs outside an English context, to the European Enlightenment. . . . Johnson believed utterly in the republic of letters, the community of learning, with . . . all human enterprise and improvement depending on it. His roots were in the renaissance.[25]

25. Samuel Johnson and James Boswell, *A Journey to the Western Islands of Scotland and The Journal of a Tour to the Hebrides*, ed. Peter Levi (London, 1984), 21. For Johnson's relation to Renaissance

To this admirable and accurate assessment may be added Nicholas Hudson's acute statement, which returns us to Johnson's reputation as "*true-born Englishman*" and "first-rate John Bull." Hudson remarks that while Johnson "was skeptical of English contemporaries prejudiced in favor of their homeland," he "did become a virtually iconic Englishman for the Victorians, a tradition that still endures. . . . Nor did any author of his time contribute so much to . . . a self-reflexive image of nationhood constructed above all in dictionaries, editions of canonized authors, histories, works of fiction, and all the publicly disseminated products of 'print-culture.'"[26]

Only the largest of figures, cultural or political, can be identified so closely with their own cultures or systems, yet also transcend, even criticize, such nationalities to help pay, as Scott says, "the debt of humanity." This paradox is true of Virgil, for example, Cervantes, Goethe, and Tolstoy. Ben Jonson praises Shakespeare as "Soul of the age!" Yet in the same poem, "To the Memory of My Beloved, The Author, Mr. William Shakespeare, and What He Hath Left Us," Jonson asserts, "He was not of an age, but for all time!" (lines 17, 43).

Enter Croker

Between Boswell's first edition of his *Life of Johnson* in 1791 and that of George Birkbeck Hill, the most important is that by John Wilson Croker in 1831. Croker included Boswell's *Tour*, which its author had printed separately (1785–86). Croker obtained notes for the *Tour*, seventy-seven by Scott and a few by Lockhart. They repay study, though Boswell's later editors largely ignored them.[27] Many of Scott's notes to the *Tour* are informative, with his own eyewitness travels as warrant for his statements.

Thanks to Jack Lynch's *Bibliography of Johnsonian Studies, 1986–1998*, I located a study of Scott's notes published by Ann Bowden and William B. Todd in 1995.[28] It prints all of Scott's notes and annotates their fate in five subsequent editions of the *Tour* from 1835 through 1964. Having reconstructed some of this history, I was relieved to see my hunch about Scott's notes already verified by Bowden and Todd. "As it was once observed for Johnson," they comment, "so it now appears for Scott: early notes since disregarded are occasionally more informative than later discourse." After Croker's edition, Scott's notes enjoyed only "sporadic recurrence." Croker's invitation to Scott to contribute produced on January 30, 1829, "a highly evocative letter" and "numerous other communications, most of which, in one form or another, also found their way

humanists, see Robert DeMaria Jr., *Samuel Johnson and the Life of Reading* (Baltimore, 1997), 8, 10, 39–40, 49, 69, 84, 73–75, 97–100, 114, 116–21, 124–25, 217.

26. Hudson, *Samuel Johnson and the Making of Modern England*, 133; see also 3, 226.

27. Peter Levi's superb 1984 reading edition does not seem to avail itself of them. R. W. Chapman's 1924 edition bypasses Croker's edition and its notes. Frederick Pottle and Charles Bennett in 1936 quote a few notes by Croker but less than half a dozen by Scott, dismissing one this way: "like all Scott's *Boswelliana*, it should be read as historical fiction, not as a record of fact." This comment seems ungenerous and itself something of an ahistorical fiction; see James Boswell, *Boswell's Journal of a Tour to the Hebrides*, ed. Frederick A. Pottle and Charles H. Bennett (New York, 1936), 375–76n2.

28. Jack Lynch, *Bibliography of Johnsonian Studies, 1986–1998* (New York, 2000), 13.

below the text." Scott's seventy-seven notes and a few he wrote for the *Life* were "widely publicized" and reviewed "as the principal feature of the 1831 edition."[29]

Reviewing Croker's edition, Lockhart was convinced that the notes "will never be divorced from the text which they so admirably illustrate, and indeed, invest with a new interest throughout." Although Lockhart admits that the note concerning Johnson and Adam Smith arguing over David Hume may be specious, his prediction concerning Scott's notes proved false. In 1860 Robert Carruthers suppressed fifty-three notes entirely, gave his own in place of twenty-two, and indirectly printed but two. Hill and Powell use twenty-seven of Scott's notes in full, but only seven others are variously employed.[30] Many valuable ones slipped away. The reasons given—if any—for stinting Scott are meager. Any future editor of the *Tour* should consult Bowden and Todd's study. They provide one other fascinating item I have not seen mentioned elsewhere.

The now-established practice of including Boswell's *Tour* with his *Life* "may not have originated with Croker," nor the idea of including notes by Scott. On January 19, 1829, eleven days before Croker's invitation to Scott, Lockhart wrote to John Murray, publisher of Croker's edition, "Pray ask Croker whether Boswell's account of the Hebridean Tour ought not to be melted into the book. Sir Walter has many MS. annotations in his 'Boswell,' both 'Life' and 'Tour,' and will, I am sure, give them with hearty good will."[31] Lockhart seems the first to hatch the idea not only of including notes by Scott but also of folding Boswell's *Tour* into any edition of the *Life*, something Bowden and Todd call "a radical innovation," and one that has lasted.

Croker, who used the notes by Scott and Lockhart, often appears combative concerning Boswell, Johnson, and Scotland. When Boswell states that Johnson "was to some degree of excess *a true-born Englishman*," but that his prejudice against "the people of Scotland . . . was a prejudice of the head, and not of the heart," Croker retaliates by asking if Boswell thinks he helps his case by regarding "Johnson's dislike of Scotland as the result not of *feeling* but of *reason*? In truth, in the printed Journal of his Tour, there is nothing that a fair and liberal Scotchman can or does complain of; but his conversation is full of the harshest and often most unjust sarcasms against the Scotch, nationally and individually" (*Life*, ed. Croker, 5:234n1).

Latching on to Boswell's observation about Johnson's "wonder at the extreme jealousy of the Scotch," Croker alters "jealousy" and in turn wonders at "the *extreme* prejudice of Johnson against Scotland and the Scotch . . . because he was himself a *Jacobite*, and many of his earliest acquaintances and some of his nearest friends were Scotch." Croker concludes, "I have a strong suspicion that there was some *personal* cause for this unreasonable and, as it appears, *unaccountable* antipathy" (5:240n2). Croker grasps for an ad hominem cause when the situation, complicated by Boswell's

29. Ann Bowden and William B. Todd, "Scott's Commentary on *The Journal of a Tour to the Hebrides with Samuel Johnson*," *Studies in Bibliography* 48 (1995): 229–48 at 229–30.

30. Bowden and Todd, "Scott's Commentary," 230–32, quoting Lockhart's November 1831 review; see note 11 above.

31. Bowden and Todd, "Scott's Commentary," 229n3, quoting Samuel Smiles, *A Publisher and His Friends*, 2 vols. (London, 1891), 2:288.

interventions, would have been enlightened by reference to Johnson's *Journey*, which Croker earlier has named but here ignores.

Croker's tone, occasionally sniping, often carries implicit or explicit criticism of Boswell (for example, 4:226–27, 245) and a self-confident exposition of Johnson's views. He dismisses Boswell's account of Johnson's comments on religion, particularly Boswell's characterization of Johnson's trust in the efficacy of "*deathbed repentance*." Croker ascribes Boswell's readiness to infer that Johnson had such a belief to the "personal or national offence which he took at Dr. Johnson's deprecation of the Scottish clergy" (4:277n1), a motive that seems doubtful. However innovative the inclusion of the *Tour* in an edition of Boswell's *Life*—Croker accepted Lockhart's suggestion to Murray—his own notes are erratic.

Scott's notes to the *Tour*, largely informative, reflect an awareness of how long ago the tour took place. If Scott corrects, he does so gently. On Johnson's doubt about the ability of a Scotch family to "tell of themselves a thousand years ago," Scott counters, "More than the Doctor would suppose" and gives as evidence his own reading of that family's history dating to 1263, "modestly drawn up, and apparently with all the accuracy which can be expected when tradition must be necessarily much relied upon" (4:242n1). Scott identifies landmarks. He largely avoids commenting on Jacobite issues and rarely imputes views to Johnson. Indeed, one of Scott's anecdotal notes assumes reconciliation and honor to be above politics (4:330n1). His most severe "correction" of Johnson is mild: "It is strange that Johnson should not have known that the 'Adventures of a Guinea' was written by a namesake of his own, Charles Johnson" (4:307n1). Johnson may be excused. The work (1760–65) originally was anonymous, and the actual author was Charles Johnstone (*Life*, ed. Hill, 5:275n2).

Scott validates the danger Johnson and Boswell experienced when they sailed in a small boat between islands. His authority stems from his own experience in the Hebrides, where he knows travel is risky: "Indeed, the whole expedition was highly perilous, considering the season of the year, the precarious chance of getting seaworthy boats, and the ignorance of the Hebrideans, who, notwithstanding the opportunities, I may say the *necessities* of their situation, are very careless and unskilful sailors—Walter Scott" (*Life*, ed. Croker, 5:7n1).

One of Scott's notes, the veracity of which Carruthers calls into question on the grounds it was a story told by others, should be reproduced at least in part.[32] L. F. Powell admits it may be accurate. It involves Boswell's father, Johnson, and Boswell himself, and it depicts the conflict between Scottish Whig and English Tory when Johnson visited Lord Auchinleck. "'There's nae hope for Jamie, mon,'" Boswell's father "said to a friend," and continued:

> "Jamie is gaen clean gyte. . . . He's done wi' [Pasquale] Paoli . . . and whose tail do you think he has pinned himself to now, mon?" Here the old judge summoned up a sneer of most sovereign contempt.

32. *Boswell's Journal of a Tour to the Hebrides*, ed. Robert Carruthers (London, 1852), 305 and n.

> "A *dominie*, mon—an auld dominie; he keeped a schŭle, and cau'd it an acaadamy" [Johnson's school at Edial]. . . . the controversy between Tory and Covenanter raged with great fury, and ended in Johnson's pressing upon the old judge the question, what good Cromwell, of whom he had said something derogatory, had ever done to his country; when, after being much tortured, Lord Auchinleck at last spoke out, "God, doctor! he gart kings ken that they had a *lith* in their neck"—he taught kings they had a *joint* in their necks. Jamie then set to mediating between his father and the philosopher, and availing himself of the judge's sense of hospitality, which was punctilious, reduced the debate to more order.—Walter Scott (*Life*, ed. Croker, 5:131n1; see *Life*, ed. Hill, 5:382n2)

Scott reports a witty reply to Johnson's infamous definition of oats, for England was renowned for the quality of its horses: "Lord Elibank made a happy retort on Dr. Johnson's definition of oats as the food of horses in England and of men in Scotland: 'Yes,' said he; ;and where else will you see *such horses* and *such* men?'—Walter Scott" (*Life*, ed. Croker, 5:136n1).

I have dwelt on Scott's notes to the *Tour* because for 180 years they have been lost in the shuffle. Nearly all deserve to rejoin the deck as valid cards, not jokers. And Lockhart deserves credit as the originator of folding the *Tour* into the *Life*.

~ Johnson's Presence in Scott's Life and Lockhart's *Memoirs*

Lockhart's *Memoirs of the Life of Scott* is cast with Boswell's biography in mind as a broad formal model and, to a certain extent, a thematic one—the development and career of a writer whose eminence became clear decades before his death and whose fame while alive shaped a national culture. There are key differences, with the richness of conversation in Boswell's *Life* perhaps the most significant one, as Ian Jack notes. However, Jack assumes that Boswell prints Johnson's "*ipsissima verba*."[33] We now know that Boswell altered some of Johnson's language. Scott was not the talker Johnson was, nor Lockhart the eager stenographer. His devotion took other forms. Lockhart begins his study by printing Scott's own autobiographical essay, the "Ashiestiel Fragment," of 1808. Its second paragraph includes a clear reference to Johnson's *Life of Mr Richard Savage* (1744). Scott presents it in the context of admonitions drawn from the lives of writers, failings against which his own habits he hopes will prove defense. He says Thomas Percy's *Reliques of Ancient English Poetry* (1765) shaped his sensibility, a collection by an editor he admired and whom he almost certainly knew had received aid from Johnson, despite Johnson's occasional antipathy to the ballad form. Scott writes: "But above all, I then first became acquainted with Bishop Percy's Reliques of Ancient Poetry. [Scott omits "English" from the title.] . . . I remember well the spot where I read these volumes for the first time" (*Memoirs*, 1:31–32).

33. Jack, "Two Biographers," 285.

When, after Scott's self-portrait of several dozen pages, the autobiography turns to biography, Lockhart soon quotes and extends a parallel that Scott mentions in his preface to *Guy Mannering* (1815). It refers to Johnson's boyhood memory of being touched by the queen in order to cure the king's evil, his scrofula or tubercular infection. Lockhart frames his quotation from Scott's preface with a particular parallel:

> "As Dr. Johnson had a shadowy recollection of Queen Anne as a stately lady in black, adorned with diamonds," so his own [Scott's] memory was haunted with "a solemn remembrance of a woman of more than female height, dressed in a long red cloak, who once made her appearance beneath the thatched roof of Sandy-Knowe." . . . This was Madge Gordon, grand-daughter of Jean Gordon, the prototype of Meg Merrilies [in *Guy Mannering*]. (1:61–62)

Scott states in his autobiographical essay that he suffered "constitutional indolence," to which Lockhart soon provides another Johnsonian parallel by juxtaposing an anecdote in which William Gifford quotes Johnson's own confession that "he knew little Greek," to which Jacob Bryant counters, "but how shall we know what Johnson would have called much Greek?" Lockhart makes an analogy with Scott's experience by concluding, "What Scott would have called constitutional diligence, I know not; but surely, if indolence of any kind had been inherent in his nature, even the triumph of Socrates was not more signal than his" (1:117).

Lockhart also quotes James Ballantyne's "Memorandum," written after Scott's death. It reveals how Scott's publishing partner recognized the parallels that Scott and his career might suggest with Johnson and Boswell. In 1796 Ballantyne and Scott met in a coach and renewed their friendship, Forty years later, Ballantyne congratulates himself: "'I doubt if Boswell ever showed himself a more skilful *Reporter* than I did on this occasion'" (1:232). Ballantyne never wrote a valuable biography of Scott. Boswell, the famous Scottish predecessor, did not intimidate Lockhart. Rather, he seems to have steeled Lockhart, perhaps because Lockhart admired Boswell's subject and knew that his own temperament and technique differed from Boswell's.

Having virtually disowned his younger brother Daniel, whose bad behavior worsened when he was sent to Jamaica, Scott later regretted his own pride and coldness. Dan returned home, soon to die, but Scott refused even to see him. In *The Fair Maid of Perth* (1828), in the character of Conachar, he addresses this history obliquely. Scott told Lockhart that Conachar expressed his own remorse and expiation. He confessed that the characterization of Conachar was his version of Johnson standing bareheaded in the rain many long minutes at Uttoxeter, where as a youth he had refused to accompany his father to help sell books.[34] Such acts of penance in the marketplace were associated with the punishments of ecclesiastical courts, but for Johnson it was self-imposed.

No doubt, too, Scott remained throughout his life conscious that Johnson had in 1773 discussed and perhaps visited his high school six years before Scott attended it

34. Moray McLaren, *Sir Walter Scott: The Man and Patriot* (London, 1970), 210; *Life*, ed. Hill, 4:373.

(*Life*, ed. Hill, 5:80, also 2:144n2).[35] William Strahan, Johnson's publisher, was also a graduate.

In other places, Johnson's or Boswell's shade intervenes. Johnson said he loved biography above all other forms of composition because it could be put to use. Lockhart includes one of Scott's letters of 1803 to Anna Seward, "the Swan of Lichfield," in which Scott states that biography is "the most interesting perhaps of every species of composition," though spoiled if done inaccurately (quoted in *Memoirs*, 1:348). Seward personally knew and generally admired Johnson and Scott, and Lockhart relates that after Scott visited Seward in Lichfield, she wrote to Henry Francis Cary, the translator of Dante: "'Not less astonishing than was Johnson's memory is that of Mr. Scott; like Johnson, also, his recitation is too monotonous and violent to do justice either to his own writings or those of others'" (quoted in *Memoirs*, 2:9). Lockhart does not qualify the parallels others draw between Johnson and Scott; he emphasizes and augments them.

As one example, Lockhart stresses that Scott helped minor writers: "This part of Scott's character recalls by far the most pleasing trait in that of his last predecessor in the plenitude of literary authority—Dr. Johnson" (2:59). Lockhart overlooks the fact that Scott seems to have underestimated and perhaps underserved such a writer as James Hogg.[36] There are other Johnsonian comparisons, too (for example, 1:215 and n; 2:56–57). One parallel is that Scott not only provided notes for Croker's edition of Boswell's *Life* including Boswell's *Tour* but also in 1814 took a lengthy Johnsonian excursion, a "Vacation," prompted by curiosity about the culture of native inhabitants of the far north, the folk populating the Shetland Islands, Fair Isle, the Orkney Islands, Harris, and the Hebrides. Though his journal of the voyage, kept in "five little paper books," is not comparable to Boswell's *Tour* or Johnson's *Journey*, it is attractive in its own right, and Lockhart includes it entire (2:401–512 at 401), much as Croker had included Boswell's *Tour* in his edition of the *Life*—following Lockhart's suggestion.

Scott and Johnson converge, perhaps unexpectedly, in their judgments of *Ossian* and of James Macpherson, so much so that it becomes hard to distinguish their opinions.[37] Scott writes in 1808 that, when young, he read Shakespeare and "became intimate with Ossian and Spenser" but preferred Spenser: "The tawdry repetitions of the Ossianic phraseology disgusted me rather sooner than might have been expected from my age" (1:30). In 1805 he had written to Anna Seward, "I should be no Scottishman if I had not very attentively considered" the Ossian dispute. However, he concludes, "I am compelled to admit that incalculably the greater part of the English Ossian must be ascribed to Macpherson himself, and that his whole introductions, notes, etc., etc., are an absolute tissue of forgeries" (1:437).

Scott avers that Macpherson knew originals in an oral tradition but emphasizes that the Highland Society, trying to defend Macpherson, found instead "that

35. John Sutherland, *The Life of Walter Scott: A Critical Biography* (Oxford, 1995), 22.

36. Ian Duncan, *Scott's Shadow: The Novel in Romantic Edinburgh* (Princeton, N.J., 2007), chap. 6, "Hogg's Body," esp. 151–54. See also James Hogg, *Anecdotes of Scott: Anecdotes of Sir W. Scott and Familiar Anecdotes of Sir Walter Scott*, ed. Jill Rubenstein (Edinburgh, 2004), xi–xxix.

37. See, however, Duncan, *Scott's Shadow*, 279–80.

there were no real originals—using that word as is commonly understood." Macpherson was "a man of high talents, and his poetic powers as honorable to his country, as the use which he made of them, and I fear his personal character in other respects, was a discredit to it" (1:439–40). Scott does not mention Johnson on Ossian in this letter to Anna Seward, but his conclusions are nearly identical with Johnson's. He confirms this verdict years later in a note to Croker's edition, where he acknowledges and validates Johnson's view (*Life*, ed. Croker, 4:264n2).

Scotland and Britain

Boswell highlighted Johnson's national attitudes by the method of contrast, especially England versus Scotland. Lockhart modifies this tack to reflect that Scott endeavored to be—and was—thoroughly successful in England as well as Scotland. Here he follows Scott's lead in the autobiographical essay, for example, where Fielding, an Englishman, and Smollett, a Scot, are both among "our best novelists." Lockhart will similarly speak of "our earlier dramatic authors," when he means chiefly English ones. Lockhart records Scott's interest in Norse and German fables, "but for the treasures of diction he was content to dig on British [not 'Scottish'] soil. He had all he wanted in the old wells of 'English undefiled' [another echo of Johnson], and the still living, though fast shrinking, waters of that sister idiom which had not always, as he flattered himself, deserved the name of a dialect" (*Memoirs*, 1:32, 135, 114).

In place of Boswell's contrast between England and Scotland, Lockhart, knowing how securely Scott was fixed in the Scottish heart, employs what Scott intimated—and lived—a literary citizenship in both worlds. Of course, Lockhart also knew that, as Nicholas Hudson remarks, no one would mistake Scott for an English writer.[38] The point is Scott's cosmopolitan attitude and popularity, his roots in native soil yet his branches extending everywhere: "His works were the daily food, not only of his countrymen, but of all educated Europe. His society was courted by whatever England could show of eminence," yet "whoever had Scotch blood in him, 'gentle or simple,' felt it move more rapidly through his veins when he was in the presence of Scott" (3:236).[39]

This national hybrid vigor Lockhart establishes early in the biography when he quotes Jane Anne Cranstoun. Hearing Scott's rhymed translation of *Lenore* in 1795, she effuses, "'Walter Scott is going to turn out a poet—something of a cross, I think, between Burns and Gray.'" Lockhart emphasizes that Scott possessed "minute and accurate knowledge of the leading persons and events both of Scotch and English history" (1:217, 2:136).

No stronger symbolic instance of Scott's British as well as Scottish literary appeal and importance—and of his generosity to a fellow writer, Robert Southey—can be found than his decision to decline the place of poet laureate and to suggest Southey as the better choice. Scott declines the laureateship on grounds that it requires regular,

38. Hudson, *Samuel Johnson and the Making of Modern England*, 150.

39. See Ann Rigney, *The Afterlives of Water Scott: Memory on the Move* (Oxford, 2012); and *The Reception of Sir Walter Scott in Europe*, ed. Murray Pittock (London, 2006).

frequent publication and expressions of commemoration. The former is not his habit, and the latter he feels he cannot perform as well as others. He notes his two offices in government affording decent income, and he says that the laureateship might more appropriately be held by someone whose exclusive work and remuneration are connected with literature. Scott probably could not imagine himself the person most fit "to commemorate the events of his Royal Highness's administration" (2:350—his letter to the Marquis of Hertford, September 4, 1813), and feared that the honor would detract from, even damage, his role as a poet of Scotland's traditions and history. Of course, he would not breathe a word of this in declining the honor.

For his self-identity and career, the better decision was to decline. Yes, he may have had Southey in mind—and so what might look like ingratitude he turns to credit his own generous nature without stain of hypocrisy. This view gains reinforcement from Scott's letter to Byron of November 6, 1813: "I am somewhat an admirer of royalty, and in order to maintain this part of my creed, I shall take care never to be connected with a court, but stick to the *ignotum pro mirabili*" (2:366). The maxim means to remain unacquainted or at a distance in order to admire or marvel. It is an extrication, yet a triumph. He did not despise the honor. His much-loved Dryden, whom he edited, was first to hold it (his treatment of Dryden in some respects surpasses Johnson's, which Scott knew), but Scott was wary of it. Privately he wrote to Joanna Baillie: "If the Regent means to make it respectable, he will abolish the foolish custom of the annual [birthday] odes, which is a drudgery no person of talent could ever willingly encounter—or come clear off from, if he was so rash. And so, peace be with the laurel,

'Profaned by Cibber and contemned by Gray.'" (2:362)

Lockhart lets Scott's correspondence and that of others relate details. He notes only that "the Regent had good sense and good taste enough" soon to hold the custom of the birthday ode "'more honored in the breach than the observance,'" and, as a result, "the whole fell completely into disuse" (2:356). This validates Scott's opinion. Southey did not seem to mind being second choice, and Lockhart, in a note added in 1839, quotes Southey's praise of Scott's conduct as "characteristically generous, and in the highest degree friendly" (2:356n). Sometimes a biographer does best when letting documents speak for themselves. In this manner, Lockhart achieves a dignity and usually an accuracy that surpasses encomium or protest. He so admired Scott—he returned from Italy himself to die in the room next to the one in which more than twenty years earlier Scott had died, and he is buried at his feet—that his veneration and Scott's advice checked Lockhart's youthful satirical bent and set the course for his entire life.

Scott and National Culture

By the time of Scott's death, identification of him with Scottish history and culture was so pervasive, popularly acknowledged, and, by scholars, already championed, that Lockhart needed to do nothing to encourage it. He had exerted himself to establish it a dozen years earlier. In *Peter's Letters to His Kinsfolk* (1819), Lockhart articulates what Ian Duncan calls "the first programmatic account of the ideological formation of a romantic cultural nationalism in Great Britain,"[40] something that, I would add, Lockhart had impetus to do from his study of modern German literature. Duncan ventures that, for Lockhart, Scott represents the "hero as a man of letters" who can perform what Macpherson botched. Lockhart, writing as Peter Morris, might describe the landscape near Scott's Abbotsford as "bare and sterile." However, as Duncan explains, for Lockhart, "Scotland, Abbotsford, and Scott's poetry all stand for one another."[41] Lockhart's praise is high: "this great genius seems to have been raised up to counteract . . . this unfortunate tendency of his age ["mere speculative understanding"] by re-awakening the sympathies of his countrymen for the more energetic characters and passions of their forefathers."[42]

Duncan analyzes such recovery of a national culture, however, as "a Frankenstein operation,"[43] something almost ghoulish. Nevertheless, when we encounter Lockhart's *Memoirs*, written more than fifteen years after *Peter's Letters*, Lockhart's view is no less sympathetic but more tempered and balanced—a shift from his earlier, almost blind hero worship of Scott. In the biography, Lockhart sets about to give evidence that Scott's identification with Scotland was earned, genuine, and present from Scott's early childhood to his last days. Commenting on the *Border Minstrelsy*, Lockhart says that Scott's "taste and fancy" were formed "as early as his moral character." Even before he became an author, he had "assembled about him, in the uncalculating delight of native enthusiasm, almost all the materials on which his genius was destined to be employed" (1:355). This "uncalculating delight" is Lockhart's equivalent to Boswell's reporting Johnson's use of "insensibly" for the manner of conceiving the *Dictionary*.

The materials left by Scott—his sketch of Johnson's life, his notes to Boswell's *Tour*, his references to Johnson in his letters, his comments on Boswell's *Life*, his quotations from Johnson and the context of those quotations—all encouraged Lockhart to employ the *completeness* demonstrated by Boswell. Lockhart plays upon the analogy of Johnson as the prime representative of English culture, significantly embodied by Boswell, in order to illustrate how Scott fused old, romantic Scotland with modern Scottish life; how Scott blended Scottish lore and British literature in a culture larger, perhaps, than Johnson had envisioned sixty years earlier. In this task Lockhart neither strains nor exults. He lets the written words of Scott and others do the work. He does not engage or repeat Croker's less charitable views about Johnson on Scotland.

Playing off Scott's statement in his autobiographical essay that "Every Scottishman has a pedigree" (1:2), Lockhart weaves that pedigree, and the places Scott lived

40. Duncan, *Scott's Shadow*, 47.

41. Duncan, *Scott's Shadow*, 48–49, 65.

42. J. G. Lockhart, *Peter's Letters to His Kinsfolk*, 3 vols. (Edinburgh, 1819), 2:348, quoted in Duncan, *Scott's Shadow*, 68.

43. Duncan, *Scott's Shadow*, 69.

and knew, with the content of Scott's own literary efforts, so that the man, his works, and his native heritage are amalgamated as a larger whole (1:51–61). Just as one instance: "So long as Sir Walter retained his vigorous habits, he used to make an autumnal excursion, with whatever friend happened to be his guest at the time, to the Tower of Harden, the *incunabula* of his race. A more picturesque scene for the fastness of a lineage of Border marauders could not be conceived," and Scott had nearly renovated "the dilapidated *peel* [fortified house or tower] for his summer residence" (1:55).

As Lockhart reports, Scott later jokes about his ancestors. His "grandfather was a horse-jockey and cattle-dealer, and made a fortune; my great-grandfather a Jacobite and traitor (as the times called him), and lost one; and after [that is, before in time] him intervened one or two half-starved lairds, who rode a lean horse, and were followed by leaner greyhounds . . . fought duels; cocked their hats,—and called themselves gentlemen" (2:308). Lockhart, too, harbors a healthy suspicion of pedigrees: "It hardly needed Swift's biting satire to satisfy the student of the past, that the very highest pedigrees are as uncertain as the very lowest" (5:442).

Yet, Lockhart also quotes Scott's verse epistle to William Erskine, famous lines that describe Scott's early fascinations, which Lockhart dates to Scott's third year! Scott recounts "feelings rous'd in life's first day," which "Glow in the line and prompt the lay." By the winter hearth he heard "patriot battles won of old / By Wallace Wight and Bruce the Bold," how later Highland clans broke "the scarlet ranks," and how as a boy "stretched at length upon the floor," he laid out "Pebbles and shells" in mimic conflict: "And onward still the Scottish Lion bore, / And still the scattered Southron fled before" (1:69–70).

Those "feelings rous'd in life's first day" of loyalty to an older order are exemplified by an anecdote concerning Scott's father, who in his own home met a political enemy, Murray of Broughton, privately on business. Murray had borne evidence against one of Prince Charles Stuart's adherents. Intruding and curious about the guest, Scott's mother brought Murray a cup of tea as refreshment. Scott's father later smashed the cup and told his wife, "I can forgive your little curiosity, madam, but you must pay the penalty. I may admit into my house, on a piece of business, persons wholly unworthy to be treated as guests by my wife. Neither lip of me nor of mine comes after Mr. Murray of Broughton's" (1:162).

Lockhart includes Scott's statement about the author of *Sir Tristram*, that "Philo-Tomas, whoever he was, must surely have been an Englishman; when his hero joins battle with Moraunt, he exclaims—

> 'God help Tristrem the Knight,
> *He fought for Ingland*.'

This strain of national attachment," concludes Scott, "would hardly have proceeded from a Scottish author, even though he had laid his scene in the sister country." Regarding Scott's work on *Border Minstrelsy*, Lockhart mentions "the patriotic enthusiasm which mingled with all the best of his literary efforts" (1:309, 317). *The Field of Waterloo* apparently "disappointed" the public, but Lockhart adds: "The burst of pure native enthusiasm upon the *Scottish* heroes that fell around the Duke of Wellington's person bears, however, the broadest marks of the 'Mighty Minstrel'" (3:76).

In literary societies Scott joined when young, Lockhart reports that he spoke of Anglo-Saxon and Norse sagas but "was deep . . . in . . . all the Scotch chronicles; and his friends rewarded him by the honorable title of *Duns Scotus*," a sobriquet he employed to sign at least one letter (1:135, 139). In part because Scott translated works from the German (for example, Goethe's *Götz von Berlichingen*), Lockhart goes out of his way to state that *Glenfinlas* is based on "Gaelic tradition" and "far more likely to draw out the secret strength of his genius, as well as to arrest the feelings of his countrymen, than any subject with which the stores of German *diablerie* could have supplied him" (1:281). We need to suppose the word *therefore* inserted before "far more likely." That is Lockhart's reasoning. And we might bear in mind that Lockhart admired German literature. His first conversation with Scott centered on his own visit to Goethe, and Lockhart translated Friedrich Schlegel's lectures on the history of literature.

Perhaps the most dramatic instance of Scott's love of country comes in 1806. It carries a clear but not rancorous political tinge, and it involves not literature but law, another deep interest he shared with Johnson. Scott engages in Tory politics and fights Whig innovations, especially those to alter "the courts of law and the administration of justice." After one meeting, walking on the way to Castle Street, "between Mr. [Francis] Jeffrey and another of his reforming friends," even as they compliment him and suggest treating matters "playfully," Scott is overcome and exclaims,

> "No, no—'t is no laughing matter; little by little, whatever your wishes may be, you will destroy and undermine, until nothing of what makes Scotland Scotland shall remain." And so saying, he turned round to conceal his agitation—but not until Mr. Jeffrey saw tears gushing down his cheek—resting his head until he recovered himself on the wall of the Mound. (1:487–88)

Jeffrey reappears later when he reviews *Marmion*. Lockhart says the review mentions "'manifest neglect of *Scottish* feelings'"—perhaps, Lockhart guesses, leveled as a criticism because the poem also expresses "the boldness and energy of *British* patriotism." Jeffrey's charge exasperates Lockhart for years after the review, for Lockhart insists that Scott "had just poured out all the patriotic enthusiasm of his soul in so many passages of Marmion, which every Scotchman to the end of time will have by heart" (2:42, 35). As if to answer Jeffrey's charge again, Lockhart remarks that *The Antiquary*, like Scott's previous novels, *Waverley* and *Guy Mannering*, is "the transcript of actual Scottish life" (3:105).

As a symbol of respecting older loyalties, Lockhart describes how Scott had a lock of hair from the head of Charles I encased in a large ring specially made, "and for some years he constantly wore the ring, which is a massive and beautiful one, with the word REMEMBER surrounding it in highly relieved black-letter" (2:373). At times Scott is playful, writing J. B. S. Morritt on November 11, 1814, concerning *The Lord of the Isles*: "I think you will like it: it is Scottified up to the teeth" (3:10). Interestingly, Johnson felt no need to write long works chronicling or glorifying English culture. His fame and commercial success spread for other reasons.

Language and a Larger Culture

Just as Johnson's authoritative relation to the English language proved crucial for his stature as quintessentially English, so Lockhart tackles Scott's relation to English, a tricky negotiation for almost every Scottish writer.[44] Edwin Muir early in the twentieth century concluded that "the Scots language," "the Scottish literary tradition," and "the political and social state of Scotland" were "all three . . . unsatisfactory as bases for a *genuinely autonomous* literature."[45] Muir's chief example was Scott. Lockhart had felt obliged to say this about Scott:

> His pronunciation of words, considered separately [not in total rhythm and phrasing, but as pronounced syllabically], was seldom much different from that of a well-educated Englishman of his time; but he used many words in a sense which belonged to Scotland, not to England, and the tone and accent remained broadly Scotch, though, unless in the *burr*, which no doubt smacked of the country bordering on Northumberland, there was no *provincial* peculiarity about his utterance. (1:76)

Yes, language was an issue. Suffice it to say that the categories of minority and majority cultures and literatures may be applied to Scott's predicament, and Lockhart knew as much. He reports that Scott stated to him (almost as a confession) that, regarding a young lady at Mertoun, he counted "not as the least" among her kindnesses and helps "the lady's frankness in correcting his Scotticisms, and more especially his Scottish *rhymes*" (1:229). We now know that in helping Lockhart prepare his biography for the press, J. B. S. Morritt excised many of Lockhart's Scotticisms.[46]

Language remains a primary marker in the minds of everyone. The more that English became standardized—thanks in part to Johnson—the more any deviance from its norms suggested something foreign. Scott adjusted to this situation, identifying with Scotland and yet, through the English he employed, claiming British identity. In language, too, hybrid vigor: a grafting of minority to majority.

44. James G. Basker, "Scotticisms and the Problem of Cultural Identity in Eighteenth-Century Britain," *Eighteenth-Century Life* 15, nos. 1–2 (1991): 81–95; Rogers, *Transit*, chap. 7, "Boswell and the Scotticism," 171–91, esp. 189–90 and 190n47.

45. Edwin Muir, *Scott and Scotland: The Predicament of the Scottish Writer* (London, 1936), 176, emphasis added.

46. Jack, "Two Biographers," 278.

We have seen how Lockhart emphasizes Scott's appeal to "all educated Europe." Perhaps this is because, at bottom, though most at home in Scotland, and then most in certain locales, Scott was fascinated by human interest, by traditions and old stories wherever he found them. Scott's romantic appeal was universal. Mark Twain famously claimed that Scott—not Harriet Beecher Stowe, as Lincoln had remarked—was the writer responsible for starting the Civil War: Scott's fictions of chivalry permeated Southern households. In Natchez, Mississippi, in old homes open to the public, I have noticed invariably a set of Scott's novels. Twain satirizes all this in such novels as *Huckleberry Finn*. Yet, it is a humane sense of a lost past being rescued and made dramatically urgent again that gives Scott popularity without borders. And in this is something of the moral historian who realizes the vanity of human wishes, the "fears of the brave, and follies of the wise," another line from Johnson that Scott found reason to quote (3:14). The context of the line is revealing, for it deals, respectively, with the last days of a great warrior *and* of a great writer:

> In life's last scene what prodigies surprise,
> Fears of the brave, and follies of the wise?
> From Marlb'rough's eyes the streams of dotage flow,
> And Swift expires a driv'ler and a show.[47]

In the final analysis, then, it is as a representative and epitome not so much of national character but of national culture *and* the larger *res publica* of letters that Johnson remains presiding—and brooding—over England, Great Britain, and the English-speaking world, seated as a statue in Lichfield, looking over the Midlands and beyond, or standing in St. Paul's, fixed in marble and muscular thought. The memorial inscription there (1796) is in Latin. Similarly, Scott in his statue presides and broods over Edinburgh and Scotland, looking over Lowlands and Highlands, over the United Kingdom and beyond. By their own works they achieved this vision. Yet, were it not for Boswell and Lockhart, whatever their shortcomings, the lives of their subjects as prime embodiments and shapers of their cultures, and of ours, would be poorer and less secure. Scholars and critics should separate Johnson's views from Boswell's, Scott's from Lockhart's, but for a common cultural inheritance—and for the common reader—this is a harder goal to expect.

During the Tour in 1773, Johnson turns to the Rev. Donald Macqueen and to Boswell, who records:

> Talking of Biography, he said, he did not think that the life of any literary man in England had been well-written. Beside the common incidents of life, it should tell us his studies, mode of living, the means by which he attained to excellence, and his opinion of his own works. He told us, he

47. *Vanity of Human Wishes*, in *Poems*, vol. 6 of *YE*, ed. E. L. McAdam Jr. with George Milne (1964), 106, lines 315–18.

> had sent [Samuel] Derrick to Dryden's relations, to gather materials for his Life; and he believed Derrick had got all that he himself should have got; but it was nothing. (*Life*, ed. Hill, 5:240)

Both Boswell and Lockhart supplied what Johnson had said was missing from English biography. Johnson in his complaint overlooked his own *Life of Savage*, which Scott had identified as formative on the first page of his own autobiographical essay. Perhaps the only other candidate when Johnson made the remark would be Robert Lowth's *Life of William of Wykeham* (1758), though Wykeham might not be considered a "literary man."

In Scott's lifetime a stage musical of *The Lady of the Lake* appeared. The character of James Fitz-James, the king in disguise, is drawn after James V of Scotland. But the figure of Roderick Dhu, a highland chief, enjoys an accompanying melody now associated with another head of state. When asked his favorite song, John F. Kennedy replied, probably without knowing its origin, that he had always been partial to "Hail to the Chief."

Yet, where are the American statues to poets and moralists? They are not well known. There is no poets' corner or poets' plot in Arlington National Cemetery; no poet or novelist graces the Mall in Washington, D.C. Helen Keller rests at the National Cathedral, but few know this. Its most famous statue is a gargoyle of Darth Vader. No poet or writer is buried in Poets' Corner in the Cathedral of St. John the Divine in New York City. The Literary Walk in Central Park has statues only of Shakespeare, Walter Scott, Burns, and Fitz-Greene Halleck, an American poet largely forgotten. What writer has found Washington, D.C., a home, as Johnson did London, or Scott Edinburgh? Perhaps Lincoln, or Walt Whitman during the Civil War.

Imagination and the Biographies of Writers

Neither Boswell nor Lockhart was a poet, at least not a good one. Their monuments are in prose. Yet it seems appropriate here to quote verse, the medium in which Johnson and Scott first revealed themselves by name in their literary works. William Cowper's epitaph in 1785 already registers national identification:

> Here Johnson lies—a sage, by all allow'd,
> Whom to have bred may well make England proud . . .

For Scott we have a sonnet by his friend Wordsworth, who in 1803 emphasized to Scott how seriously he regarded that word "friend" (1:377–78; 461). He wrote "On the Departure of Sir Walter Scott from Abbotsford, for Naples" when Scott, seriously ill, prepared to leave in 1831. Wordsworth mentions "Eildon's triple height" near Abbotsford, as well as Scott's beloved Tweed. As Scott departs, Wordsworth proclaims, "the whole world's good wishes with him goes." Wordsworth implores "winds of ocean, and the midland sea," the Mediterranean, to be true, "Wafting your charge to soft Parthenope," the ancient name, through Virgil, for Naples (lines 3, 9, 13–14).

Wordsworth knew that the imagination Scott exercised had first found its home in the local. Despite the gorgeous rhyme and climax it supplies, Parthenope is the least important place in the poem. The Eildon Hills and the Tweed are vital, and Abbotsford is in the title. Scott and Wordsworth had climbed Helvellyn together and walked near Abbotsford. Each knew the hills the other loved, from which came their strength and craft.

About this Lockhart is explicit (as is Scott), for Scott often states his love for those hills, and for Tweedside, however unremarkable and bare they might appear to other eyes. In the "Conclusion" to the *Memoirs*, Lockhart makes the case for family, clan, and locale as the guiding stars of Scott's imaginative voyage. He wished to rescue the fading past, and he held such associations with ancestors and family, and with the landscape of his home, that these were not only of supreme personal value but also fuel for his reconstructions of other worlds:

> An imagination such as his . . . soon shaped out a world of its own—to which it would fain accommodate the real one. The love of his country became indeed a passion. . . . But the Scotland of his affections had the clan Scott for her kernel. . . . The author of the Lay would rather have seen his heir carry the Banner of Bellenden gallantly at a foot-ball match on Carterhaugh, than he would have heard that the boy had attained the highest honors of the first university in Europe. . . . [H]e desired to plant a lasting root, and dreamt not of personal fame, but of long distant generations rejoicing in the name of "Scott of Abbotsford." By this idea all his reveries—all his aspirations—all his plans and efforts, were overshadowed and controlled. (5:444–45)

Lockhart says that even when Scott "had reached the summit of universal and unrivalled honor, he clung to his first love with the faith of a Paladin," a faith that "was at least a different thing from the modern vulgar ambition of amassing a fortune. . . . The lordliest vision of acres would have had little charm for him, unless they were situated on Ettrick or Yarrow, or in

—'Pleasant Tiviedale,
Fast by the river Tweed'—

—somewhere within the primeval territory of "the Rough Clan" (5:445). The verse is from *Chevy Chase*.

Lockhart remained devoted to Scott and portrays him favorably, though at times inaccurately—for example, at the expense of James Hogg and the Ballantyne brothers, a slant owing in part to how Robert Cadell, the publisher, handled the proof sheets.[48] Yet, Lockhart's final comments strike a tone altered from his earlier *Peter's*

48. Duncan, *Scott's Shadow*, 152–54; Jack, "Two Biographers," 279, who cites Francis Russell Hart, "Proofreading Lockhart's *Scott*: The Dynamics of Biographical Reference," *Studies in Bibliography* 14 (1961): 3–22 at 20.

Letters. While exculpating Scott from his financial missteps, Lockhart remarks on his "rashness about buying land, building, and the like" (5:448), the very actions that helped create Abbotsford as a symbol of Scotland and Scott's writing.

Lockhart has no illusions now about what he had admired in 1819: "The whole system of conceptions and aspirations, of which his early active life was the exponent, resolves itself into a romantic idealization of Scottish aristocracy." Lockhart continues, "I can, therefore, understand that he may have, from the very first, exerted the dispensing power of imagination very liberally, in virtually absolving himself from dwelling on the wood of which his ladder was to be constructed" (5:448–49). It is a remarkable sentence. It counters Ian Duncan's sense that Lockhart's *Memoirs* are based on "the circular logic that sustains modern literary biography, whereby the works generate the meaning of the life supposed to be their explanatory ground."[49] This is for Scott and his works a "circuit" in which, as Duncan invokes Clifford Siskin, "author, reader, and nation" are folded "into a unified organic formation" that "comes decisively together in Romanticism under the disciplinary title of 'literature.'"[50] Yet, Lockhart realizes this; he critiques it at the end of the *Memoirs*. Scott was engaged, he says, in "a romantic idealization." Scott's imagination acted as dispensation and absolution. Lockhart acknowledges that "the author of such a series of romances as his, must have, to all intents and purposes, lived more than half his life in worlds purely fantastic." Here, "fantastic" means imaginative. Scott was, as Lockhart puts it, "willing, in his ruminative moods, to veil, if possible, from his own optics the kind of machinery by which alone he had found the means of attaining his darling objects" (5:449–50).

What import do Lockhart's statements carry? All great imaginative and experiencing natures create *formative* illusions. Self-potentiating, their inventive aspirations are necessary heralds for the fulfillment of their creative acts. To anatomize what Coleridge calls "a semblance of truth sufficient to procure for these shadows of imagination that willing suspension of disbelief . . . which constitutes poetic faith" is to break the spell and banish its magic. Only by a "negative faith" does any artist create such illusions.[51] The circular logic of imaginative achievement yoked to personal life is, like the circular logic of much faith, to be fully expected. Coleridge remarks that faith and "all spiritual truths" exhibit always something of a "seeming argumentum in circulo."[52] The writer's life is largely a life of imagination, and so the works and primarily the works become the high road to see the landscape of that life, especially that part of the life dedicated to their creation. Lockhart knew this. So did Johnson; moreover, Johnson had no qualms about identifying the works of gifted authors as indispensable to national identity. He states in the preface to his *Dictionary*, "The chief glory of every people arises from its authors." This is what Wordsworth means in his

49. Duncan, *Scott's Shadow*, 276.

50. Duncan, *Scott's Shadow*, 277–78.

51. Samuel Taylor Coleridge, *Biographia Literaria*, ed. James Engell and W. Jackson Bate, 2 vols. (Princeton, N.J., 1983), 2:6, 134.

52. Coleridge, *Biographia Literaria*, 2:244.

sonnet, quoted above, when he claims of Scott: "Blessings and prayers in nobler retinue / Than sceptred King or laurelled Conqueror knows, / Follow this wondrous Potentate."

Johnson was terse and to the point about his own home. "You find no man, at all intellectual, who is willing to leave London. . . . When a man is tired of London, he is tired of life; for there is in London all that life can afford" (*Life*, ed. Hill, 3:178). Yet Johnson was fascinated by Scotland from his youth and traveled there at an advanced age under adverse conditions, to see what he could of its older culture and disappearing ways of life. When young, Johnson devoured romances, and the opening of *The Vanity of Human Wishes* is rife with romantic images—"the clouded maze of fate," "As treach'rous phantoms in the mist delude," "Walks the wild heath," "The rustling break alarms, and quiv'ring shade" (*YE*, 6:92–93). Where does Johnson make the decision to write his *Journey to the Western Islands*? Overcoming his aversion to the bare, treeless landscape of much of Scotland, he seems near Anoch as struck with his surroundings as Scott later was with his near the Tweed. Johnson relates:

> I sat down on a bank, such as a writer of romance might have delighted to feign. I had indeed no trees to whisper over my head, but a clear rivulet streamed at my feet. The day was calm, the air soft, and all was rudeness, silence, and solitude. Before me, and on either side, were high hills, which by hindering the eye from ranging, forced the mind to find entertainment for itself. Whether I spent the hour well I know not; for here I first conceived the thought of this narration.

He admits that he and Boswell "had no evils to suffer or to fear" there, then reverts to the power that informs his great poem: "yet the imaginations excited by the view of an unknown and untravelled wilderness are not such as rise in the artificial solitude of parks and gardens. . . . The phantoms which haunt a desert are want, and misery, and danger . . . man is made unwillingly acquainted with his own weakness, and meditation shews him only how little he can sustain, and how little he can perform" (*YE*, 9:40–41). The setting and Johnson's reflections on it strongly echo in vocabulary and theme his account in chapter 4 of *Rasselas*: "One day, as he was sitting on a bank, he feigned to himself" a romantic tale. Soon, however, Rasselas "recollected himself" and then raised "his eyes to the mountain," which by its barrier had forced him to invent such entertainments.[53]

53. *Rasselas and Other Tales*, vol. 16 of *YE*, ed. Gwin J. Kolb (1990), 18. Rogers, *Transit*, 110, draws attention to Johnson's letter to Hester Thrale of September 21, 1773, written during the Tour regarding the spot where he reports in the *Journey* to have "first conceived the thought" of that book: "I sat down to make notes on a green bank, with a small stream running at my feet, in the midst of savage solitude, with Mountains before me" (*The Letters of Samuel Johnson*, ed. Bruce Redford, 5 vols. [Princeton, N.J., 1992–94], 2:73). Earlier in his letter Johnson states, "the place at which we now are, is equal in strength of Situation, in the wildness of the adjacent country, and in the plenty and elegance of the domestick entertainment, to a Castle in Gothick romances" (2:71).

Near the end of Scott's life, when he had completed his *Tales*, writing their preface and quoting from Johnson's *Vanity*, he reflects on "an uncommon share" of blessings, but he must now experience life's "usual proportions of shadow and storms." He wishes, in effect, for "a healthful mind"—"that the powers of his mind . . . may not have a different date from those of his body!"—and hopes that he may again meet his friends, "if not exactly in his old fashion of literature, at least in some branch, which may not call forth the remark, that—

> 'Superfluous lags the veteran on the stage.'" (*Memoirs*, 5:369–70)

Scott's last personal line given to the public is by his much-esteemed Johnson.

Several years before this, Scott had discovered that he and others were on the brink of financial disaster and grave embarrassment. In his own *Journal*, to whom does he turn to brace himself for the task of working off the debts? What writer gives him courage to confront the worst? Scott faces "absolute ruin." He considers leaving the United Kingdom. Then, he turns: "I will not yield without a fight for it. It is odd, when I set myself to write *doggedly*, as Dr. Johnson would say, I am exactly the same man as ever I was, neither low-spirited nor *distrait*."[54]

Scott is remembering Johnson's remark that "a man may write at any time, if he will set himself *doggedly* to it." Boswell invokes this statement in the *Life* to illustrate how Johnson overcame "constitutional indolence, his depression of spirits," and his work on the *Dictionary* to write the *Rambler* essays "twice a week." But Boswell had first reported Johnson's statement, with "*doggedly*" italicized, in the *Tour*. Reading that book, Scott would have noticed where Johnson made the remark. It was in the building in Edinburgh where "the records of Scotland . . . are deposited" (*Life*, ed. Hill, 1:203, 5:40).

James Ballantyne related that Johnson had always been Scott's support and pleasure:

> "He had often said to me that neither his own nor any modern popular style of composition was that from which he derived most pleasure. I asked him what it was. He answered, Johnson's . . . and I think I never saw his countenance more indicative of high admiration than while reciting aloud from those productions." (*Memoirs*, 2:186)

The longer that literary history is around, the more we feel we know its lessons when, in fact, the more opportunity this affords to suffer amnesia and suffer the consequences. Johnson valued such history. Scott venerated it. Literary history and biography find their appeal in their application to present life and present circumstances. This Johnson and Scott held fervently. I hope to have brought the two authors closer to modern readers in that warm relation that Scott felt, and which honors Johnson. If

54. Quoted in McLaren, *Sir Walter Scott*, 187.

this essay rekindles interest in literary biography and in pairing Boswell and Lockhart, whose subjects came to epitomize English and Scottish culture, this may add something, too.

I am indebted to Joshua Wilson and Nicole Miller for research assistance; to Matthew Ocheltree and Richard Johnston for helpful comments; to Sol Kim-Bentley and Nicole Miller for manuscript preparation; to many scholars of Johnson and Scott, in particular to Ian Duncan, Freya Johnston, and—as catalyst and better craftsman of this effort—Howard D. Weinbrot, none of whom bear responsibility for errors. The Long Eighteenth-Century and Romanticism Colloquium at Harvard provided salutary critique. Finally, recalling that Sir Walter Scott kept at his writing desk "arranged in careful order" small objects that he associated with his parents (*Memoirs*, 5:454), I recall mine, in whose modest home library I spent happy hours as a child, among its volumes reading Boswell's *Tour* and Scott's *Ivanhoe*.

A History of the Collected Works of Samuel Johnson: The First Two Hundred Years

Robert DeMaria Jr.

WHILE STUDYING the history of Johnson's collected works at the Houghton Library, home of Harvard's Hyde Collection, I encountered a venerable predecessor: David Fleeman's "A Critical Study of the Transmission of the Texts of the Works of Dr. Samuel Johnson."[1] Fleeman's dissertation surveys all the editions of Johnson's works, from that of Sir John Hawkins (1787) to the so-called Oxford edition (1825). The Hyde copy of this dissertation, uncatalogued when I arrived at Houghton, is a carbon copy on onionskin paper. It is tenderly inscribed, "To the onlie begetter of these ensuing pages, Dr. L. F. Powell, with grateful affection from David Fleeman—14 January 1965." This 463-page text clearly provided the foundation for Fleeman's lifelong work, *A Bibliography of the Works of Samuel Johnson*.[2]

The most laborious part of Fleeman's great *Bibliography* is its technical description, including full collations, of each separate edition of each of Johnson's individual and collected works from their first publication through 1984, the bicentenary of Johnson's death. In his treatment of *Rasselas* (1759), for example, Fleeman is obliged to provide bibliographical formulae and full collations for over four hundred editions or issues of the same text. The *Bibliography* shows in the fullest possible way how Johnson's writing has been disseminated in print. In his dissertation, Fleeman was concerned only with editions of Johnson's collected works, but his method is similarly thorough. The conclusions of his study are general and severe: "that no reprinted text, unless there is evidence of authorial revision, can or ought to be trusted; that there are apparently no limits to the degree of corruption which a reprint cannot reach, and that none of the extant collected editions of Johnson's Works supplies a reliable text" ("A Critical Study," vii). Fleeman is particularly hard on the Oxford edition of 1825, partly because of its eminence as the standard text for the previous 140 years. He says definitively: "Textually

1. Fleeman, "A Critical Study of the Transmission of the Texts of the Works of Dr. Samuel Johnson" (PhD diss., Oxford, 1965), hereafter cited in text.

2. *A Bibliography of the Works of Samuel Johnson: Treating His Published Works from the Beginnings to 1984*, comp. Fleeman, prepared for the press by James McLaverty, 2 vols. (Oxford, 2000), hereafter cited in text.

the 1825 edition is valueless. It should never be quoted" (407). As sufficient evidence, Fleeman points out that the editor's "extravagant punctuation allowed him to add fifty-five superfluous commas to Chapter 1 of *Rasselas*" (407n27). Waxing philosophical in a bibliographical way, Fleeman offers the Oxford edition only a backhanded reprieve: "Its only value is that it is an object lesson in the delusive fascination which printed copy-text has exerted over generations of printers and editors" (407).[3]

When Fleeman wrote his dissertation, only two volumes of the *Yale Edition* had been published. He was hopeful that "the progress of the new Yale edition of Johnson's Works has and is continuing to make it of less moment to depose the 1825 edition from the eminence which it had unworthily enjoyed" (iii). Although Fleeman was critical of the *Yale Edition*, he endorsed its basic approach to establishing the text by returning to the earliest publications of each of Johnson's works.[4] The *Yale Edition* is now drawing to a close, with only two of its twenty-three volumes unfinished. Although the work of editing Johnson will not end with the completion of the *Yale Edition*, it will reach an important milestone. In anticipation of that achievement, it is fitting to ask how Johnsonian editing arrived at its current state and where it might go in the future.

My account is deeply indebted to Fleeman's dissertation. Access to the Hyde Collection enabled me to examine all the evidence myself, but most of the knowledge presented here was originally gathered by Fleeman, and many of the opinions are his. The story of editions of Johnson's works is largely bibliographical, but a part of it is also biographical. It is a story about a chain of books, but it is also about a filiation of editors. The series begins with Johnson himself, goes through Hawkins, Boswell, and many less famous editors, and carries on into the present time with editors, several of whom are known or have been known to many readers of this essay.

Samuel Johnson

Reporting on Johnson's arrangements for publishing *The Vanity of Human Wishes* (1749), Boswell says, "It will be observed, that he reserves to himself the right of printing one edition of this satire, which was his practice upon occasion of the sale of all his writings; it being his fixed intention to publish at some period, for his own profit, a complete collection of his works."[5] In a footnote, Boswell printed a copy of the receipt for the sale of the copyright, provided by James Dodsley in 1786. The original receipt, now in the Hyde Collection, shows that Johnson inserted the clause "reserving to my self the right of printing one Edition."[6] Fleeman's study of Johnson's earnings confirms

3. The "delusive fascination" and "eminence" of the Oxford edition were still in evidence as recently as 2009 when Harvard University Press published *Samuel Johnson: Selected Writings*, ed. Peter Martin, with a text "sourced from the 1825 Oxford edition" (vii).

4. For Fleeman's criticism of the *Yale Edition*, see, for example, "Some Notes on Johnson's Prayers and Meditations," *Review of English Studies*, n.s., 19 (1968): 172–79. Of the *Idler* in the *Yale Edition*, Fleeman noted, "The value of the work of these editors is confined to the text: their introduction is unsound and misleading" ("A Critical Study," vii note 4).

5. *Boswell's Life of Johnson, Together with Boswell's Journal of a Tour to the Hebrides and Johnson's Diary of a Journey into North Wales*, ed. George Birkbeck Hill, rev. L. F. Powell, 6 vols. (Oxford, 1934–50), 1:193 (hereafter cited as *Life*).

6. Houghton Library, MS Hyde 50 (52).

that "he regularly retained the right to print one edition for himself."[7] However, though Hawkins also mentioned this in the advertisement to his edition of the *Works* (1787),[8] he added that Johnson's "intention . . . to publish . . . a complete collection of his works" was not very "fixed." He "seems to have parted with his copyrights soon after the first editions," as Fleeman notes, and "the plan came to nothing."[9]

Perhaps the most important step that Johnson took toward establishing an edition of his works was to acknowledge to Boswell many of the works he had published anonymously. His acknowledgments support Boswell's "Chronological Catalogue of the Prose Works of Samuel Johnson, LL.D." (*Life*, 1:16–24), which is an important source for all future bibliographies and hence all future editions of his collected writings. Johnson's own moves in the direction of collecting his works were tentative and modest. He added his lives of Sir Francis Drake (1740–41) and Admiral Blake (1740) to the third edition of his *Life of Richard Savage* (1767), and to the third edition of the *Idler* (1767), he added the "Essay on Epitaphs" (1740), the "Dissertation on the Epitaphs of Pope" (1756), and the "Essay on the Bravery of the English Common Soldier" (1760). Since both books were published in 1767, it is tempting to believe that Johnson was then beginning to collect his scattered works, as Robert W. Chapman and Allen T. Hazen suggested.[10] However, as Fleeman points out in his *Bibliography*, Johnson did not "edit" the additions to the *Idler* or the *Life of Savage*, and that indicates that he did not make the additions himself.[11] The texts undoubtedly come from their previous publication in periodicals (not from manuscripts), and the minor changes in them all seem to be the work of compositors: some changes in italics, some differences in pointing and spelling, but nothing substantive.

Even the evidence that Johnson ever intended to collect his works is scant. Apart from Boswell's remark about the contract for *The Vanity of Human Wishes*, mentioned above, for Fleeman the most suggestive evidence regarding such a collection is an item in the sale catalogue of James Boswell the younger's library: "A Blank Book, inscribed in Johnson's hand, HISTORIA STUDIORUM, May, 1753. In it is contained a 'Scheme of J——-n's Works,' and the mark he used in the margin of his books."[12] It sold for £2/5, much less than the first draft of the *Plan* of the *Dictionary*, which fetched £17/6/6, to be sure, but more than the £2 fetched for two letters from Edmund Hector accompanied

7. J. D. Fleeman, "The Revenue of a Writer: Samuel Johnson's Literary Earnings," in *Studies in the Book Trade: In Honour of Graham Pollard*, ed. R. W. Hunt, I. G. Philip, and R. J. Roberts (Oxford, 1975), 211–30 at 218.

8. See p. 350 below.

9. Fleeman, "Revenue of a Writer," 218.

10. R. W. Chapman and Allen T. Hazen, *Johnsonian Bibliography: A Supplement to Courtney*, Proceedings of the Oxford Bibliographical Society 5 (London, 1938), 117–66; in William Prideaux Courtney and David Nichol Smith, *A Bibliography of Samuel Johnson* (New Castle, Del., 1984), 142; cited by Fleeman in *Bibliography*, 1:744.

11. Fleeman, *Bibliography*, 1:744. Fleeman notes that Alexander Chalmers thought these pieces not included by Johnson himself (1:745n1).

12. *Bibliotheca Boswelliana* (London, 1825), item 3161 (Fleeman, "A Critical Study," 9*n4); the Houghton Library copy (B 1827 230*) is marked with the price and buyer of each item.

by the manuscript of Johnson's poem "To a Lady who Gathered a Sprig of Myrtle."[13] The price suggests that the notebook had some interesting matter, and Fleeman thought it may, if discovered, provide evidence that Johnson "intended to prepare an edition [of his works]" ("A Critical Study," 9*n4). Yet 1753 seems an unlikely date for such ambitions: Johnson was preparing to complete the *Dictionary of the English Language* and must have felt his schedule was full. In 1767, the other date proposed for his attention to an edition of his works, he was relatively comfortable: his edition of Shakespeare was finished, and his pension was keeping him safe. But for either date there is only shaky evidence that Johnson was serious about collecting his works.

One other small collection of Johnson's works in his lifetime merits brief mention: *Political Tracts. Containing, The False Alarm. Falkland's Islands. The Patriot; and Taxation No Tyranny* (London, 1776). Johnson clearly authorized the publication because he presented copies to friends,[14] and there are minor substantive changes in the texts (*Bibliography*, 2:1269). The epigraph to the volume also seems authorial because it comes from Claudius Claudianus, one of Johnson's favorite poets.[15] On the other hand, Johnson probably did not view this volume as a serious step in the direction of a collected edition of his works because he did not put his name on the title page.

Late in Johnson's life, several people urged him to assemble his works. On July 15, 1783, Hawkins asked Bennet Langton to approach Johnson about collecting his works, as Hawkins says he himself had done a little earlier. His arguments to Johnson were that an edition would "perpetuate and prevent injury to his memory," and that it would provide an annuity for Mrs. Williams.[16] Hawkins's approach shows how well he knew his old friend: appealing to Johnson's sense of responsibility to others had been a way to get him to work since his old friend Edmund Hector and the Birmingham publisher Thomas Warren had spurred him on to finish his translation of Father Lobo's *Voyage to Abyssinia* (1735) by telling him the pressmen were languishing for work. But Johnson could not be moved in this case.

John Nichols, Johnson's neighbor and editor of the *Gentleman's Magazine*, says he also spoke to Johnson about collecting his works "not long before his death."[17]

13. *Bibliotheca Boswelliana*, item 3158.

14. There are copies in the Hyde Collection that were presented to Anthony Chamier and James Boswell, respectively. Boswell says the work was entitled "Political Tracts by the Author of the Rambler," but no such language is on the title page of the copy given him by Johnson or in the description in Fleeman (*Bibliography*, 2:1268; both Hyde copies reverse the contents of sigs. A1 and A2, as Fleeman describes them).

15. "Fallitur, egregio quisquis sub principe credit / Servitium, nunquam Libertas gratior extat / Quam sub Rege pio" (*De Consulate Stilichonis*, 3.1.113–15): "He errs who thinks that submission to a noble prince is slavery; never does liberty show more fair than beneath a good king" (*Claudian*, trans. Maurice Platnauer, 2 vols. [London, 1922], 1:51). Johnson's copy of Claudianus, with annotations, is now in the Hyde Collection (*2003J-SJ956 [case 7, shelf 2]). Johnson also used a passage from Claudianus as the epigraph for *Rambler* 199 (February 11, 1752).

16. Bertram H. Davis, *A Proof of Eminence: The Life of Sir John Hawkins* (Bloomington, Ind., 1979), 317.

17. Fleeman, "A Critical Study," 9*, citing John Nichols, *Literary Anecdotes of the Eighteenth Century*, 9 vols. (London, 1812–15), 2:552, and *Life*, 4:409.

Then, on the very day of Johnson's death, the book dealer and publisher George Nicol wrote to John Hoole, a man to whom Johnson was particularly close in his last days:

> I take this method of saying a few Words to you on the Affairs of our Worthy & respected Friend Dr. Johnson.——Since the delicacy of his Mind will not permit him to do, what I think both Law & Equity entitle him to do, His Friends must take the next best step to serve him—that is—to press the Booksellers to make an offer for his Works—if that offer shoud be any thing in reason to close with them at once, which will make his circumstances easy, & save his Mind, now turn'd to other Subjects, from future suspence.
>
> Though I cannot be concern'd in any Scheme to take this business out of their hands, yet I am very willing to use every endeavour for Dr. Johnson's advantage, that something near the Value may be offerd—But above all they shoud be pressed to make their offer soon—because I am apprehensive, it is intended to procrastinate the Business, in hopes of getting that for nothing, for which they are bound both by Justice & gratitude to pay the value.[18]

The bonds of justice and gratitude were unfortunately broken along with the vital chain of Johnson's life. Once the great man was dead and buried, the booksellers wasted no time. A mere four days after his interment, they met at the Chapter Coffee House and agreed that they would engage Hawkins "for his Life of Dr Johnson, and as Editor of his Works." The agreement stipulated that "a complete and elegant Edition of the Works of Dr Johnson shall be printed," and that, in their opinion, it should be "printed on a full sized Medium Octavo."[19]

Thomas Davies

Hawkins was not Johnson's first identifiable collector, and he did not wholly deserve the name of editor. The bookseller and actor Thomas Davies was in fact the first to collect a number of Johnson's works. In 1773–74 he published three volumes called *Miscellaneous and Fugitive Pieces*. The first two volumes were small octavos hastily assembled while Boswell had Johnson safely away on their Scottish tour. As Fleeman observes, the books came out on December 23, less than a month after Johnson returned from Scotland ("A Critical Study," 1*). Characteristically, Johnson did not object to this invasion of his literary property. Two years later, for example, when John Wesley stole from him en bloc in his *Calm Address to Our American Colonies* (1775), Johnson reacted by

18. Houghton Library, MS Hyde 10 (507); cf. Fleeman, "A Critical Study," 9*–10*.

19. Fleeman ("A Critical Study," 8*) quotes this document, which was then in the possession of Arthur A. Houghton Jr. and is now in the Houghton Library (MS Eng 1386 [75]). For a transcription, see O M Brack Jr., "The Publishers' Agreement for Sir John Hawkins's *Life of Samuel Johnson, LL.D.* and the *Works of Samuel Johnson* (1787)," *Johnsonian News Letter* 62, no. 2 (2011): 22–24 at 23–24.

thanking Wesley for agreeing with him.[20] Johnson was almost as understanding with Davies. In the *Anecdotes* (1785), Hester Thrale Piozzi writes:

> When Davies printed the Fugitive Pieces without his knowledge or consent; How, said I, would Pope have raved, had he been served so? "We should never (replied he) have heard the last on't, to be sure; but then Pope was a narrow man: I will however (added he) storm and bluster *myself* a little this time;"—so went to London in all the wrath he could muster up. At his return I asked how the affair ended: "Why (said he), I was a fierce fellow, and pretended to be very angry, and Thomas was a good-natured fellow, and pretended to be very sorry: so *there* the matter ended: I believe the dog loves me dearly."[21]

Perhaps Davies was nevertheless cautious about offending Johnson. He did not use Johnson's name on the title page, and he did not include Johnson's embarrassing essays in support of William Lauder (1747, 1750), the forger who falsely accused Milton of plagiarizing *Paradise Lost*.[22] *Miscellaneous and Fugitive Pieces* includes works not by Johnson in volume 2, and volume 3 is entirely composed of works by other writers. Davies cobbled his volumes together from diverse sources, but the many pieces by Johnson in the first two volumes constitute an attempt to collect his works, and later compilers often used Davies's attributions and his texts. In volume 1, Davies includes many of Johnson's best fugitive pieces, and in most cases he takes them responsibly from their first appearances in the press: the review of Soame Jenyns's *Free Enquiry into the Nature and Origin of Evil* from the *Literary Magazine* (1757); the revised life of Boerhaave from Robert James's *Medicinal Dictionary* (1742), the lives of Sydenham (1742), Burman (1742), and Cave (1754) from the *Gentleman's Magazine*. For the oft-reprinted "Vision of Theodore," however, Davies went to the "fifth" edition (1769) of *The Preceptor* (1748), a merely expedient choice of the copy-text that was at hand.

In compiling volume 2, Davies printed Johnson's introduction to the *Harleian Miscellany* (1744–46) as "An Essay on the Origin and Importance of Small Tracts and Fugitive Pieces." He gathered the introduction to *Proceedings of the Committee to Manage Contributions for Cloathing French Prisoners* from the original pamphlet (1760), and he rescued several other pieces from Johnson's contributions to the *Literary Magazine* (1756–58). Davies also made mistakes. For example, he tacitly attributed "Thoughts concerning Agriculture" to Johnson, although it is by Richard Rolt.

Despite its errors, Davies's collection is important for at least three reasons: first, he worked in the most vexing and difficult area of the Johnsonian canon—the periodi-

20. See Henry Abelove, "John Wesley's Plagiarism of Samuel Johnson and Its Contemporary Reception," *Huntington Library Quarterly* 59, no. 1 (1996): 73–79 at 79; cf. Fleeman, *Bibliography*, 2:1245.

21. *Anecdotes of the Late Samuel Johnson, LL.D., during the Last Twenty Years of his Life* (London, 1786), 55–56, italics in original.

22. See Fleeman, "A Critical Study," 7*.

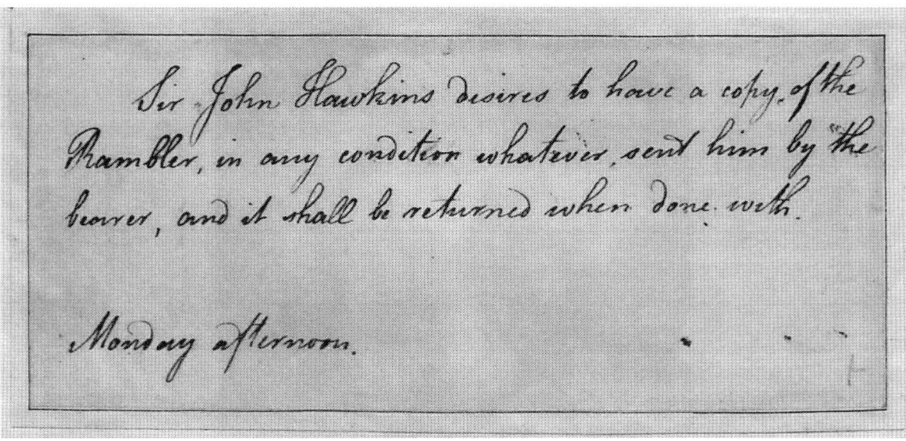
Sir John Hawkins desires to have a copy of the Rambler, in any condition whatever, sent him by the bearer, and it shall be returned when done with.

Monday afternoon.

FIGURE 1. Letter sent on behalf of Sir John Hawkins to John Nichols, in an extra-illustrated copy of John Wilson Croker, *Johnsoniana* (1836). Houghton Library, Hyde Collection, 2003SJ-SJ1169, f: 1.115.1.

cal pieces; second, he was sometimes discriminating in his choice of texts; and third, his edition provided the copy-texts for many Johnsonian works that were to appear in later collected versions.

Sir John Hawkins

Hawkins's edition of the *Works* appeared three years after the Christmas Eve 1784 meeting of the booksellers; it included most of the works that would be recognized as Johnson's by later editors; and in many, many cases, for better or worse, it supplied the relevant texts for later editors. There are eleven volumes in the edition, but the first volume is devoted wholly to Hawkins's life of Johnson. The biography clearly took most of Hawkins's time during these brief three years, and the editorial work, if it deserves that name, got short shrift. Bertram Davis, Hawkins's sympathetic biographer, says, "Hawkins was the supervisor rather than the editor" of the edition. As evidence, Davis cites a letter from Hawkins to John Nichols, then editor of the *Gentleman's Magazine*:

> I have no Copy of the miscellaneous Lives; they may be found by the Help of the enclosed Paper. If Newton's cannot be found it must be omitted. Such of them as are in your Magazine should be printed from it or at least examined therewith. Let me see them as you proceed that I may be assured that none are omitted.[23]

Fleeman ("A Critical Study," 20*n38) cites a letter from Hawkins to a bookseller that indicates a similar disregard for editorial responsibility (figure 1): "Sir John Hawkins

23. Davis, *A Proof of Eminence*, 317.

desires to have a copy of the Rambler, in any condition whatever, sent him by the bearer, and it shall be returned when done with."

Even more damaging from the point of view of modern editorial responsibility is a letter from Hawkins's son, John Sidney Hawkins, outlining his father's method: "A list of the pieces, which each volume was to contain, was therefore delivered out by my father for the Printers; and, as in many instances they had before been printed, it was the bookseller's business to borrow, as he did, from such persons as happened to possess them, the original works in which the different compositions had at first appeared."[24] Apparently Hawkins in many cases did not even supply the publisher with the texts to be reprinted. Nevertheless, in his advertisement to the edition, he declared, "I have . . . taken upon myself the office of his Editor, and accordingly here present to view as complete a collection of the various writings of Dr. Samuel Johnson as I was able to form, and the directions he left behind him would permit me to publish."[25]

It is not clear what "directions" Hawkins had from Johnson, but Hawkins oddly neglected to include many works that his biography shows he knew were Johnson's. Hawkins's daughter Laetitia, whom he hired as proofreader, was surprised, for example, to find *Marmor Norfolciense* omitted ("A Critical Study," 28*). It is impossible to tell if he was following "directions" now lost or was just being careless.

Whether or not he was following Johnson's "directions," Hawkins deserves credit for rounding up a large number of Johnson's fugitive pieces. He was deeply indebted to Davies and only rarely went back to original sources, but he is the sole authority for several of Johnson's minor pieces, including "Considerations on the Plans Offered for the Construction of Blackfriars Bridge" (1759), the prayer on the death of Anna Williams (1783), "The Ant" (1766), and the "Portrait of Mrs Montagu" (1779) ("A Critical Study," 35n86). Going forward, Hawkins's edition was, to say the least, immensely influential.

Fleeman's examination of Hawkins's treatment of specific texts further illuminates his casual procedures in editing. Fleeman concludes his discussion of Hawkins's version of the *Adventurer* by writing: "The treatment of the text points either to extreme carelessness by Hawkins, or to the possibility [penciled in, "Likelihood"] that Hawkins himself had little to do with the editing of the texts in the edition which bears his name" ("A Critical Study," 19). Fleeman is similarly critical of Hawkins's *Idler*, and to cinch his point on Hawkins's treatment of the *Rambler*, Fleeman has merely to point out that he used the tenth edition as his copy-text.[26]

24. *Gentleman's Magazine* 84 (1814), pt. 1, pp. 551–53 at 552.

25. The advertisement is in the preliminary matter of *The Works of Samuel Johnson, LL.D. Together with His Life and Notes on His Lives of the Poets*, 11 vols. (1787), 1:[vii].

26. Fleeman is equally critical of the treatment of the *Idler* in the *Yale Edition*. "But, alas," he writes, "it cannot be said that the problem [with Hawkins's *Idler*] is in any way diminished by the discussion of the Yale editors [W. J. Bate and J. M. Bullitt]: their account is marred by gratuitous error (Cave, not Faden, was the printer of the *Rambler*), and by a failure to make use of typographical analysis in their notes on the printers and publishers. The student of the bibliography of the *Universal Chronicle* will not find his ideas clarified by the muddy thinking of these editors" ("A Critical Study," 27). On the blank facing page in the Hyde copy of his dissertation, Fleeman wrote in six points, with the heading

Hawkins not only missed some works obviously by Johnson but also included some obviously not by him. The most puzzling of these erroneous attributions is "The Apotheosis of Milton, A Vision," on which Fleeman comments, "It is well-nigh impossible to give a satisfactory reason for the inclusion of this piece in Hawkins's edition of the *Works*" ("A Critical Study," 246). Hawkins also included a review of Edmund Burke's *A Philosophical Inquiry into the Origin of Our Ideas of the Sublime and Beautiful* (1757) and "Thoughts concerning Agriculture" (1756), both of which he found in Davies. Those inclusions are understandable, but the inclusion of the "Vision of Milton" is strange. In genre, the "Vision" is a dialogue of the dead that takes place among the pantheon of writers, into which Milton is about to be inducted. The speaker describes various authors, from Chaucer to Dryden, Shadwell, Otway, and others. When Milton is brought in, Cowley objects to his politics; there is a murmur in the crowd; and the piece leaves off with a Swiftian *caetera desunt*. It is un-Johnsonian in every way, from its genre, to its treatment of Milton, to its self-conscious incompleteness. This attribution suggests another of the many ways in which Hawkins was not thoughtful in composing his edition of Johnson's *Works*.

John Stockdale, Isaac Reed, George Gleig

The faults of Hawkins's edition did not long go undetected. Arthur Murphy reviewed the edition severely in *The Monthly Review* (April–August, 1787). He was to edit the next attempt at a complete edition of Johnson's works, but before he could do so, supplementary volumes were added to Hawkins's edition. In fact, just two days after its appearance, John Stockdale announced the publication of Johnson's *Debates in Parliament*. These actually appeared within six weeks, and, as Fleeman points out, Stockdale must have known that Hawkins had omitted these works from his edition. Stockdale was from 1784 to 1790 engaged in publishing many parliamentary debates, so he was well aware of Johnson's contributions in that kind.[27] Stockdale advertised Johnson's *Debates* as volumes 12 and 13 of Hawkins's *Works* and sold them along with the other volumes, despite the complaints of Hawkins's publishers. In an act of shocking appropriation, Stockdale's title page reads, "The |Works |Of Samuel Johnson, LL.D. | In Thirteen Volumes." His second title page is more accurate: "Debates|In|Parliament.|By Samuel Johnson, LL.D.|In Two Volumes." In his preface, Stockdale interprets his inclusion of a double title page. He says that these "Parliamentary Orations . . . are

"The editors fail to report:

"1 The presence of titles for the *Idler* papers in the index to the *U. Chron.*

"2 The existence of a MS (SJ auto) entitled 'Hints for an Idler' at Yale.

"3 The existence of various states of the 1761 ed. (there are variants at least in the head ornaments in the Contents leaf in v. 1).

"4 They fail to use typographical evidence to show that the same printer was responsible for both *U. Chron*, and *Idler* 1761.

"5 They have overlooked the nature of the texts of the Dublin reprint . . .

"6 They ascribe some authority to the 1767 2nd ed. . ."

27. Among Stockdale's many such publications was *A Full and Accurate Account of the Debates on the East-India Bill, in the House of Lords* (London, 1784).

given to the world in a form so convenient, that they may either be considered as a proper Supplement to the Works of Dr. Samuel Johnson, at the same time published by the London Booksellers, or regarded merely as the Parliamentary Debates of that celebrated Orator."[28]

Stockdale's major editorial failing is that he translates the Lilliputian code names that Johnson used in his "Debates in the Senate of Magna Lilliputia" to throw a thin veneer of artistry over the obvious breach of parliamentary privilege. Johnson's "Walelop" in Stockdale is "Walpole," and "Sprugs" are "Pounds Sterling." Stockdale says he "thought it a duty he owed to the Author and the Reader, to lay aside the barbarous terms, which had been contrived as much by the vanity as the caution of Cave" (*Works*, 12:vi). A modern editor would not do this, and there were people in 1787 who did not like the idea. Stockdale subjoins a note to his preface:

> Some gentlemen, for whose taste and discernment the Editor has a high respect, having observed, that the barbarous jargon, which had been employed by the vanity or caution of the Editor of the Gentleman's Magazine, was mentioned too generally in the foregoing Preface, and that the Lilliputian terms, which once obstructed the reader's progress, would now gratify his curiosity, the Editor has subjoined the fictious [*sic*] names of persons and places with the real ones, as they occur in the Debates of that miscellany." (*Works*, 12:x)

These lists of "fictious" names must have been added late, however, for they are not in the second volume of the uncut copy in the Hyde Collection or in the British Library copy. Whether or not this late addition makes amends for the editorial indiscretion, Stockdale's remained the standard text of Johnson's *Debates*, copied by all future editions of Johnson's works, until the *Yale Edition*.[29]

There were two more supplementary volumes of Hawkins's edition to come. Volume 14 was published in the same year that Hawkins published his eleven-volume edition (1787), though the title page, foreseeing some delay, reads "1788." According to Fleeman, the editor of this volume was Isaac Reed, although his name never appears.[30] The publishers were Stockdale and a group of four booksellers named Robinson, including George Sr., who had been involved in publishing a twelve-volume edition of Henry Fielding's *Works* in 1783. Reed was a Shakespearean editor, notorious for keeping his identity secret in all publications, but famous for his learning and his helpfulness to other scholars. In addition to having recently revised Johnson's edition of

28. John Stockdale, preface to *Works*, 12:ix. Text citations are to this edition.

29. *Debates in Parliament*, vols. 11–13 of *The Yale Edition of the Works of Samuel Johnson* (hereafter cited as *YE*), ed. Thomas Kaminski and Benjamin Beard Hoover, text edited by O M Brack Jr. (New Haven, Conn., 2012).

30. Fleeman, "A Critical Study," 293. Fleeman notes (293n3) that Allen T. Hazen made the same discovery (*Samuel Johnson's Prefaces & Dedications* [New Haven, Conn., 1937], 201n2). For more information on Reed's editorial work, see Arthur Sherbo, *Isaac Reed, Editorial Factotum* (Victoria, Canada, 1989).

Shakespeare, Reed had edited some of Johnson's fugitive writings in *An Impartial Account of the Life and Writings of the Late Reverend William Dodd, LL.D.* (London, 1777). In a couple of notes to this work, he had suggested that Johnson was the author of the "Petition of William Dodd to the King" (1777) and, at least, the reviser of "Dodd's Last Solemn Declaration" (1777). Several of Johnson's writings for Dodd first appear in Johnson's *Works* in volume 14. This points to Reed as the editor of the volume, as does his "association" with "two MS lists of [Johnson's] minor works," many of which appear in volume 14.[31]

Reed was a more careful editor than Hawkins or Stockdale. He chose copy-texts with some care, preferring first printings in most instances. His great achievement, however, was bringing so many of the miscellaneous writings into the collected *Works*. Some of the pieces he added had been in Davies's *Fugitive Pieces*, but Reed gave them new authority by including them in Johnson's *Works*. More importantly, he added many prefaces, dedications, and advertisements that Johnson did for others and which were most likely to be lost or overlooked. New attributions have been established since Reed's volume, and some missing works have been found. More may surface, and some Johnsonian writing may be disentangled from the work of others. However, with Reed's volume, collecting the writings of Johnson was substantially complete.

The contribution of volume 15 (1789), the last of the supplementary volumes to Hawkins, was not insignificant, but most of its contents were already attributed to Johnson. His translation of Father Lobo's *Voyage to Abyssinia* (1735) occupies almost four-fifths of the volume. In fact, the title page of the volume reads *A Voyage to Abyssinia . . . Translated from the French by Samuel Johnson, LL.D. to which are added various other tracts by the same author, not published by Sir John Hawkins or Mr. Stockdale. The Works . . . Vol. XV* appears as a half title.[32] The bulk of the remaining pages are devoted to six reviews from the *Literary Magazine*. In addition, there are only two dedications, the "Account of the Cock Lane Ghost," two letters, and a slight poem ("Nugae Anapaesticae," 1782). The unlikely editor was George Gleig, a minister in the Scottish Episcopal Church and a friend of Bishop Berkeley. His duties in Stirling left him some time for writing, however, and he contributed to journals in London such as the *Gentleman's Magazine*.[33] He once visited London. Fleeman suggests that Gleig's connection to the booksellers Elliot and Kay, who signed him on as an editor of Johnson, derived from his work on the third edition of the *Encyclopedia Britannica* (1797), which was in progress after the completion of the second edition in 1784. Gleig wrote a life of Johnson for the third edition, but he may well have done his editorial work on Johnson first.[34]

Gleig dedicated his volume to Arthur Murphy, expressing the wish that Murphy had been Johnson's biographer, instead of Hawkins. In his general preface he condemns

31. See Fleeman, *Bibliography*, 2:1639n1.
32. See Fleeman, *Bibliography*, 1:9, 2:1639–40.
33. See *ODNB*, s.v. "George Gleig," by Nigel Aston.
34. See Fleeman, "A Critical Study," 375–76 and n3.

Hawkins as a biographer, an editor, a critic, a writer, and even as a magistrate: "[H]is mistakes are numerous . . . his taste is deplorable . . . his style is tedious . . . and . . . his vanity and egotism are in a high degree disgusting" (*Works,* 15:1). Gleig supports these assertions by quoting liberally from Murphy's lengthy and highly critical review of Hawkins's *Life* in the *Monthly Review*.[35] Gleig is grateful to Stockdale for restoring much that Hawkins had excluded from his edition by publishing volumes 12–14 of the *Works*, but he takes issue with some of his attributions, particularly the "Memoirs of the Late Dr. Berkeley," his friend (*Works*, 14:421–26). A lengthy footnote recounts the meeting between Johnson and the philosopher's son, which results in George Jr. rejecting a later request from Mr. Allen, then vice-principal of Magdalen Hall, Oxford, for materials to help Johnson write a life of Berkeley.[36] Gleig adds a few pieces to the canon; he hesitantly and mistakenly adds "Cebes" from the *Preceptor*; but, aside from his condemnation of Hawkins, his main concern is the addition of Father Lobo's *Voyage*. Gleig concludes his general preface with four lines from Horace, *Epistles* 2.1 (128–31), describing the ideal poet. He says these lines apply to Johnson "in the character of a *moralist*, a *biographer*, a *critic*, and a *poet*":

> *—Pectus praeceptis format amicis*
> *Asperitatis et invidiae corrector et irae:*
> *Recté facta refert; orientia tempora notis*
> *Instruit exemplis; inopem solatur et aegrum.*[37]
> (*Works*, 15:10)

Arthur Murphy

On January 15, 1790, William Seward wrote to Samuel Parr on behalf of Thomas Cadell, one of the partners who had published Hawkins's edition of the *Works*. He asked if Parr would "undertake an Edition of Dr Johnson's Works, with his life, & a Critique on his writings?"[38] The notoriously irritable schoolmaster, the contentious composer of Johnson's epitaph on his statue in St. Paul's, either failed to respond or responded in the negative. This was lucky for Johnsonians because Parr's record of completing what he started was not strong; he had a tendency to get bogged down in details, which would have made editing Johnson impossible, and his one attempt at a life is a heap of undigested notes and reflections.[39]

35. *Monthly Review* 76 (April and May 1787): 273–92, 369–84.

36. *Works*, 15:4–6n. Allen is possibly Hollyer Allen (ca. 1730); for his connection to Johnson, see *The Letters of Samuel Johnson*, ed. Bruce Redford, 5 vols. (Princeton, N.J., 1992–94), 1:163n5; Boswell, *Life*, 1:334; and *Johnsonian Miscellanies*, 2:125n.

37. "The poet . . . moulds the heart by kindly precepts, correcting roughness and envy and anger. He tells of noble deeds, equips the rising age with famous examples, and to the helpless and sick at heart brings comfort" (Horace, *Satires, Epistles and Ars Poetica*, trans. H. Rushton Fairclough [Cambridge, Mass., 1978], 407).

38. Beinecke Library, MS Osborn C 505.

39. Samuel Parr, *Characters of the Late Charles James Fox, selected and in part written by Philopatris Varvicensis*, 2 vols. (London, 1809).

Having been turned down by Parr, or never having heard from him, Cadell approached Arthur Murphy, who accepted the job on June 21, 1790. Murphy's long, highly critical review of Hawkins's edition in the *Monthly* had prepared him for the task. He agreed to replace Hawkins's long life of Johnson with his own preliminary "Essay on the Life and Genius of Samuel Johnson, LL.D." He declared that "the works must have a new arrangement, as near as may be in chronological order."[40] He said that the works not by Johnson had to be thrown out, and he asked if the publishers would consider adding Johnson's *Debates in Parliament* and some letters. However, everything Murphy "added" had already appeared in one of the four volumes supplementary to Hawkins's original, eleven-volume edition of the *Works*.

Like his predecessors, Murphy did little real editing. He made some use of Piozzi's *Letters to and from the Late Samuel Johnson, LL.D.* for some of Johnson's poems;[41] but most of the textual differences between Murphy's edition and Hawkins's can be described as corrections. Fleeman concludes, "In the main therefore this edition of 1792 is a reprint of the 1787 edition of *Works*, with no textual evidence to suggest the consultation or use of the supplementary volumes of 1788–89" ("A Critical Study," 396). Nevertheless, it was published in London in 1792 with the subtitle *A New Edition, in Twelve Volumes*. In all of Murphy's work, Fleeman finds only a few changes to Johnson's Latin poems, and these, he speculates, were made by Bennet Langton. Murphy's edition was frequently reprinted, and his introductory "Essay on the Life and Genius of Johnson" was reprinted three times on its own (*Bibliography*, 2:1641–58). Evidently, Murphy's "Essay" was successful, despite the earlier presence on the market of Boswell's *Life* (1791).

Alexander Chalmers, Anonymous

Murphy died in 1805, and Alexander Chalmers took over as editor of Murphy's *New Edition* in 1806. Under Chalmers's direction, the canon was only slightly altered, and Murphy's "Essay" continued to introduce Johnson's works.[42] Chalmers contributed to the editorial improvement, however, through his concern with Johnson's periodical writing. For his *British Essayists* series (1802–3), he had revised the text of the *Rambler* greatly and those of the *Idler* and *Adventurer* lightly. Chalmers collated the folio edition of the *Rambler* with the revised edition of 1756. Although he often preferred the 1756 edition, without trying to distinguish authorial from compositorial revision, his editorial work on the text was unprecedented in the history of editions of Johnson's works. Chalmers also enlarged the canon with five *Adventurers* omitted by Murphy, along with the original *Idler* 22. He added some dedications, including the one to Parliament in *The Evangelical History of Our Lord Jesus Christ* (1757), despite the fact that, as he says, "Mr. Boswell cannot allow that Dr. Johnson wrote this, because 'he was no croaker, no declaimer against the times.'"[43] This dedication, however, had been printed

40. Houghton Library, MS Hyde 75: 3.353.1.

41. Piozzi, *Letters to and from the Late Samuel Johnson, LL.D.*, 2 vols. (London, 1788).

42. For an assessment of Chalmers's contributions, see Bonnie Ferrero, "Alexander Chalmers and the Canon of Samuel Johnson," *Journal for Eighteenth-Century Studies* 22 (1999): 173–86.

43. *The Works of Samuel Johnson, LL.D*, [ed. Chalmers], 12 vols. (London, 1806), 1:iv.

by Gleig in volume 15 of the *Works* (1789). Almost all of Chalmers's other additions to Murphy's *Works* had been printed before in volume 14 of the *Works* (1788).

Two editions of Chalmers appeared in London in 1806, one in octavo and one in duodecimo, the latter very faultily printed by E. Blackader. An 1809–12 Boston edition followed Blackader's, as did an 1816 pocket edition in eighteenmo. The octavo was reprinted in 1816 and 1823, the latter with a revised advertisement by Chalmers describing it as the "seventh" edition. This then became the basis for the infamous 1825 Oxford edition, the last attempt at a version of Johnson's complete works before the *Yale Edition*'s, which was begun 130 years later.

Two Scottish editions appeared amid the Hawkins, Murphy, and Chalmers lines of Johnson's *Works*. The 1806 Edinburgh edition (published for Bell and Bradfute, James M'Cliesh, and William Blackwood) replaces Murphy's introductory "Essay" with an epitome of Boswell's *Life*. The anonymous editor displays his Scottish nationalism by breaking into the biographical narrative to bristle at some of Johnson's comments in his *Journey to the Western Islands* (1775). For example, when Johnson suggests that the Scots should "drop a seed into the ground" and grow trees, the editor complains, "Alas! Johnson was totally ignorant of the nature of the operation of which he talks thus easily, and of the expence and difficulties attending it."[44] In the following paragraph, the editor claims that the Scots are now superior in agriculture to the English, although they were behind when Johnson wrote. He admits that the Scots have overreacted to Johnson's criticism because they were jealous of their southern neighbors, but he nonetheless faults Johnson for being blind to Scotland's beauties.

The anonymous editor also criticizes Johnson's "abundantly absurd" argument in *Taxation No Tyranny* (1775). However, he concludes with Sir William Jones's judgment that "his Dictionary, his moral essays, and his productions in polite literature, will convey useful instruction and elegant entertainment, as long as the language in which they are written shall be understood."[45] One of the Scottish publishers of this edition, Bell and Bradfute, abandoning their Scottish editor, joined forces with the English publishers in 1823 to produce the last important edition of Chalmers's version of the *Works*.

Also published in the midst of the Hawkins, Murphy, Chalmers line of *Works* was an edition printed in 1816 by and for J. Graham at Alnwick, a town in Northumberland about halfway between Newcastle and Edinburgh. Like the Scottish edition of 1806, the Alnwick edition used Boswell for its life of Johnson, but in fact printed the whole of it, rather than the epitome that appeared in 1806. Fleeman notes that "some additions were made to the canon on the basis of attributions by Boswell but mainly deriving" from the supplementary volume 14 of Hawkins's *Works* (1788). The text, Fleeman finds, comes mostly from Murphy's edition of 1801, but there is "evidence of some independent editorial activity."[46]

44. *The Works of Samuel Johnson, LL.D.*, 15 vols. (Edinburgh, 1806), 1:4.

45. *The Works of Samuel Johnson, LL.D.* (Edinburgh, 1806), 1:lv, cviii.

46. Fleeman, *Bibliography*, 2:1679. I find evidence of "independent editorial activity" in the Alnwick version of Johnson's dedication to John Hoole's translation of Tasso (*Works*, 1816, 10:209).

Reverend Robert Lynam

In 1824, the last year before the Oxford edition, there were three editions of Johnson's *Works* by three different publishers. One of these was produced by Thomas Tegg, who found his niche in the industry as a republisher of important works. As he said himself, "My line is to watch the expiration of copyright."[47] He then jumped in and produced the works for a cheaper price than those on the market. Tegg published cheap editions of Johnson's *Dictionary* (1813), Blackstone's *Commentaries* (1830), Smith's *Wealth of Nations* (1822), and Hooker's *Ecclesiastical Polity* (1839). His edition of Johnson's *Works* (1824) is merely a reprint of the Murphy edition of 1820, though presumably Tegg argued he was printing the Hawkins edition (1787), which was then beyond the maximum of twenty-eight years allowed by the Statute of Anne (1709), a limitation not refuted in the famous case of Donaldson v. Beckett (1774) and not extended until 1842.

When Tegg published his edition of Johnson's *Works*, he had to compete with another edition produced in 1824 by George Cowie in London. The editor, Reverend Robert Lynam, was a Roman historian who had also edited the works of the fifteenth-century poet John Skelton (1824) and those of the moralist William Paley (1823). He also supplied in 1824 an introduction to the works of William Robertson, the author of the *History of Charles V* and other important historical works. However, Lynam, who was very busy in 1824, found something special about Johnson, for his introduction praises Johnson for qualities of mind worthy of the best classical authors:

> His depth of reflection satisfies the most acute and penetrating reader; and at the same time the pomp and harmony of his language give pleasure to the most critical ear, and the most refined taste. The panegyric which Pliny bestowed upon one of his contemporaries, conveys no exaggerated flattery when applied to Dr. Johnson. Nihil est illo gravius, sanctius, doctius; ut mihi non unus homo, sed literae ipsae omnesque bonae artes in uno homine summum periculum adire videantur—Quantum rerum, quantum exemplorum tenet? Nihil est quod discere velis, quod ille docere non possit.[48]

Lynam's claims for his edition are equally grand. He says that, though "[t]he present impression is comprised in Six Volumes . . . it contains all the productions of the Author that have been ever inserted in the largest and most complete editions." With revised and augmented notes, it is "as complete as the exactest care can make it, nothing being omitted that can gratify the admirers of the great and incomparable Johnson."[49]

47. Thomas Tegg, *Extension of Copyright* (London, 1840), quoted in *ODNB*, s.v. "Thomas Tegg," by James J. Barnes and Patience P. Barnes.

48. *The Works of Samuel Johnson, LL.D.*, ed. Robert Lynam, 6 vols. (London, 1824), 1:3–4. Lynam quotes Pliny's *Epistles* 1.22.1–2, with some parts omitted: "He has no equal in moral influence and wisdom, so that I feel that it is no mere individual in danger, but that literature itself and all the liberal arts are endangered in his person. . . . his knowledge of human affairs . . . are such that there is nothing you might wish to learn which he could not teach" (Pliny, *Letters and Panegyricus*, trans. Betty Radice, 2 vols. [Cambridge, Mass., 1969], 1:69).

49. *Works*, ed. Lynam, 1:3–4.

Finally, in 1824 Baynes and Sons published a duodecimo edition of Johnson's *Works* in twelve volumes largely based on the 1823 Chalmers, but with a few minor changes. This 1824 edition omits misattributed verses on Sir John Lade along with genuine epitaphs and sermons that appeared in 1823. It adds the preface to volume 3 of the Harleian Catalogue. This is a fresh attribution for which the anonymous editor deserves credit. However, he concludes his introductory advertisement with claims for his edition that are belied by the title page. He says, "In presenting, therefore, this complete and long-called-for portable edition of Dr. Johnson's Works—an edition in which the utmost care has been taken to ensure correctness of text, and neatness of typographical execution—an essential benefit is conferred upon society." Unfortunately, the "correctness of the text" does not get off to a good start with the spelling "Cambbidge" on the title page.

Francis Pearson Walesby

Fleeman concludes his treatment of the 1824 Baynes edition with the important statement that "This edition appears to have formed the working copy-text for Walesby's Oxford edn. 1825" (*Bibliography*, 2:1690).[50] The Oxford edition, the original object of Fleeman's research, reflects a long line of editions that are largely dependent on each other. For this reason it is, as Fleeman says, "no better than its predecessors, and in general is worse, simply because it stands further away from the earlier editions, and the frequent intervening reprints have done little more than accumulate textual corruptions" ("A Critical Study," 406). This edition had nothing to do with Oxford University Press. The books were printed in Oxford by the firm of Talboys and Wheeler, not by the university, but they bear an Oxford University device on their title pages. The principal publisher was William Pickering of London, who produced the *Works* as part of a series called "Oxford English Classics." The series included Hume's *History of England*, with Smollett's continuation (1827), the works of the historian William Robertson (1825), Gibbon's *Decline and Fall* (1827), and Boswell's *Life* (1826). The whole series amounted to forty-four volumes. Johnson's eleven-volume *Works* was bound in red cloth (a signature Pickering innovation) and sold for 8 shillings per volume.[51]

Fleeman's anger about Pickering's edition and its unwarranted reputation issues in a rather nasty biographical note on the editor, Francis Pearson Walesby, the Rawlinson Professor of Anglo-Saxon at Oxford. Fleeman says that Walesby "was really a lawyer and . . . died Recorder of Woodstock" ("A Critical Study," 405). Fleeman concedes that the cloth binding of the edition has historical importance,[52] but he will not praise the edition's typography, despite the approval of Geoffrey Keynes, the bibliographer of Pickering, who distinguished the edition with an asterisk. Fleeman says, "Tal-

50. Fleeman's conclusion that this edition was the copy-text for the Oxford edition slightly detracts from his statement in his dissertation that the Oxford edition "followed Chalmers's edition of 1823 in the main" ("A Critical Study," 405).

51. See Geoffrey Keynes, *William Pickering, Publisher: A Memoir & a Hand-List of His Editions* (London, 1924; rev. ed., London, 1969), 16, 74.

52. In fact, Pickering had been using cloth since 1820. See Keynes, *William Pickering, Publisher*, 14.

boys and Wheeler used a 'Modern' typeface with hair serifs which serve only to make heavier the vertical shadings of the letters: the result is irritating to the eye, like endless ranks of upright fence posts" ("A Critical Study," 407). Gothic typefaces have often been described as resembling a picket fence, but Pickering's font is not excessively angular. To my eye, I admit, the thickness of the vertical strokes is oppressive, partly because it is unrelieved by the paper-thinness of the serifs, but this is not the source of Fleeman's disgust with the edition. He is angered by the undeserved place of honor it held for over 150 years as the standard edition of Johnson's works.[53]

Despite Fleeman's dislike of Walesby, he concedes that he did "some independent work," adding bits that Chalmers did not include in 1824. These works are the preface to volume 3 of the Harleian Catalogue and Johnson's sermons, all of which had appeared in print before. His only true contributions to establishing the canon are the inclusions of an epigram on Colley Cibber and a Greek epitaph on Goldsmith. Still, this is more than later editors attempted, before the *Yale Edition*.

Non-Editors, 1825–1955

Most of the editions between the Oxford edition and the *Yale Edition* concentrated on making the existing texts more readily available in handier and less expensive collections than their predecessors. Jones's University Edition (1825), for example, boasted that it made available Murphy's texts "verbatim . . . in 2 beautiful volumes, boards, with fine engravings, £1. 8s" (*Bibliography*, 2:1699). This version of the *Works* was part of Jones's University Edition of British Classic Authors. It was stereotyped, and the plates were bought before 1850 by H. G. Bohn, a prolific publisher of university texts, who produced four more impressions of the text. The plates later passed to William P. Nimmo, who produced several impressions, including one under the rubric of the "Standard Library" (ca. 1881).

Meanwhile, in America in 1825, a version following the first Chalmers edition (1806) appeared, advertising itself as the "second American edition." Another product, in two volumes, set in double columns, called the "First Complete American Edition," was stereotyped and produced by various publishers, mostly in New York. One of these was Harper & Brothers, which produced the works in two octavo volumes through most of the nineteenth century. In 1903 the Literary Club issued its sixteen-volume edition, lacking a life, an introduction, or even an advertisement. Its only paratext is a note at the beginning stating the number of sets produced "on Special Water Marked Paper" and indicating whether they are part of the "Literary Club" or "Extra Illustrated" edition. The Club edition has a half-leather binding with blue cloth. The plates are sepia-toned engravings of eighteenth-century figures, some of whom are not mentioned in Johnson's works. The margins are wide, the type large, and the paper

53. Even the *Oxford Encyclopedia of British Literature* recommends the Oxford edition for any works not yet covered by the *Yale Edition*. See *Oxford Encyclopedia of British Literature*, ed. David Scott Kastan, 5 vols. (Oxford, 2006), s.v. "Samuel Johnson" (by Robert Folkenflik). This has been the standard scholarly advice because the Oxford edition is accessible, and in most cases there have been no better choices, except for relatively inaccessible first editions.

creamy and soft, but there is no reason to believe the text has any value. A check of a Greek quotation in the *Rambler* found several errors in a few lines.

Between 1903 and 1955, publications of some of Johnson's works appeared in every year except five—the war years 1918, 1919, 1938, 1939, and 1944.[54] Among these publications were some selections from the works and some distinguished editions, such as George Birkbeck Hill's edition of the *Lives* (1905), but there were no complete editions of the *Works*. The absence of new *Works* during this fifty-year period set the stage for the arrival of the *Yale Edition of the Works of Samuel Johnson*.

Allen T. Hazen, John H. Middendorf, et al.

On December 10, 1951, Allen T. Hazen circulated a "Proposal for a New Edition of Johnson's Works." Some of the highlights were these:

> The edition is planned . . . in 12 volumes; the Letters and Debates probably to be omitted. . . . the apparatus is to be minimal. The text printed is to be sound, as the first requisite, with enough apparatus to enable users to follow the textual problems. Non-technical bibliographical notes should identify clearly the textual problems involved. Explanatory annotation is to be helpful and adequate, but never discursive or all-inclusive. Critical introductions to each piece should serve as new but general studies of the work, short essays that would deserve reprinting. . . . the edition ought to be ready to print within about two years.[55]

By June 20, 1952, Hazen had approached Columbia University Press with the proposal and been turned down. At some point after that, the University of Illinois was approached, but it, too, was unwilling to make the commitment. Thanks mainly to Herman W. Liebert, who would later become the librarian of the Beinecke Rare Book and Manuscript Library at Yale, the project was adopted by Yale University Press some four years after its first proposal. On February 24, 1955, Hazen, the Hydes, and perhaps a few others met in New York to discuss editorial board membership. Not long afterward, on May 31, the first meeting of the Editorial Committee of the Yale Johnson was held at the Knickerbocker Club in New York. The first roster of the proposed committee included Frederick W. Hilles, Herman W. Liebert, Robert Metzdorf, E. L. McAdam Jr., Allen T. Hazen, James Clifford, Bertrand H. Bronson, Arthur A. Houghton, Donald F. Hyde, and Mrs. Donald F. (Mary) Hyde. The committee obtained grants from the Aaron E. Norman Fund of New York and from "four private individuals."[56]

After some negotiations, President Alfred Griswold of Yale University officially appointed the first members of the editorial committee: Liebert (chairman), Hazen

54. In fact, Fleeman's *Bibliography* documents the publication of work by Johnson in every year from 1733 to 1984, except for those five and 1957, 1961, and 1980 (2:1809–71).

55. Houghton Library, MS Hyde 98 (827).

56. Presumably, they were the Hydes, Liebert, and Houghton, though I cannot confirm this. The information presented here on the first formation of the committee comes from *Johnsonian News Letter* 15, no. 2 (1955): 1–2 and from Houghton Library, MS Hyde 98 (859, 953).

(general editor), Bronson, Walter Jackson Bate, R. W. Chapman, Clifford, Robert Halsband, Houghton, Hilles, Donald and Mary Hyde, William R. Keast, McAdam, Metzdorf, L. F. Powell, S. C. Roberts, and D. Nichol Smith. The committee's avowed purpose, as stated in the original Style Guide (1956; rev. 1957), was "to present a sound and readable text of Johnson, for use by graduate students, literary critics, literary scholars, and informed literate readers." The founders of the edition added, "It will not be planned primarily as a text book for use in secondary schools, or as an exercise in ingenuity of bibliographical annotation." The *Johnsonian News Letter* enthusiastically reported: "Now at last we are to have a new set of volumes, produced in the best tradition of modern textual scholarship and including everything which can definitely be ascribed to Johnson except the *Dictionary*. We throw our collective hats in the air and shout 'Hurrah!'"[57]

Precisely how the edition would live up to the "best tradition of modern textual scholarship" and how it would best serve its intended audience has continued to be debated for some time. Over the very long run of publication, which is still not complete, various editors have interpreted the aims of the edition in various ways. This was inevitable from the start, since the assembled group of editors came with preestablished and differing views about scholarly editing. Nonetheless, there was general agreement on some editorial principles. For example, the committee agreed that "the copy-text will for most pieces be the first edition, into which authorial revisions and editorial emendation are to be inserted, with textual notes." The idea was not to recover what Johnson wrote in the manuscripts he submitted to his printers "but to present what he approved in normalized proof from his printer" (Style Guide, 4). Although this general resolve left many questions about specific texts unanswered, and though it was a principle not strictly observed by some editors, it was still an immense advance over all earlier editions of the *Works*, which really had no editorial principles concerning the texts.

There was also agreement that annotation would include textual and explanatory notes. Yet, here again, there were differences of opinion and some widely divergent practices. There was a plan, but it left a good deal of room for interpretation. The committee's resolution on "Explanatory Annotation," incorporating discussions in May and September 1955 and March and September 1956, began with these somewhat whimsical instructions: "Before writing footnotes, try to imagine a user who starts to read SJ, perhaps in Australia, fifty years hence. Then plan the notes" (Style Guide, 3). The intention of the further instructions was clearly to limit the amount of annotation because most of the instructions are negative: "Notes will not summarize all modern scholarship on each work"; "Notes should not become merely exclamatory, laudatory, or discursive; no monographs on matters mentioned incidentally in the text"; that is, don't be like George Birkbeck Hill, who is explicitly mentioned; biographical notes should be "Not encyclopaedic, as in Yale Walpole" (Style Guide, 3–4). The instructions attempted to establish a somewhat breezy style for the edition and to steer it away from

57. *Johnsonian News Letter* 15, no. 2 (1955): 1.

the perceived turgidity of scholarship like that in the Yale Walpole and the Victorian clutter in scholarship like that of Hill's *Lives*. Even cross-references within the Johnsonian canon were to be limited. If cross-references are included, said the Style Guide, it must be remembered that "references to any other edition will seem peculiar once the present edition is complete." Therefore, editors should "try to make references to a work, not a page of an edition. Within the edited work such as *Lives of Poets*, they can be to pages of the Yale edition, with p. 00 to be corrected in proof" (Style Guide, 4). The Yale *Lives* would appear fifty-four years after this was decided, so editors of other volumes would, for once, have had plenty of time to correct proof, had they heeded this suggestion.

The first volume of the edition to be published was *Diaries, Prayers, and Annals* (1958), edited by E. L. McAdam Jr. with Donald and Mary Hyde, whose manuscript collections supplied some of the necessary materials. Since this work was already underway, the volume was invited into the edition after the fact and so is anomalous in several ways. It relies much more on manuscripts than the other volumes do, and the layout of the text is different from that of all other volumes. Numbers rather than letters are used to cue textual notes, for example, and, instead of explanatory notes, there is a running narrative at the foot of the page that serves to fill in the gaps in the text's autobiographical material. The contents of this volume are also anomalous in relation not only to the rest of the *Yale Edition* but also to all earlier versions of Johnson's works. Except for a few prayers, which had appeared in Hawkins's and later editions, none of the material printed in volume 1 had before been part of a collection of Johnson's works. The prayers had been published in their own separate volume, and much of the rest of the material had appeared in biographical works about Johnson, but none of this material had earlier been considered part of Johnson's complete works.

Many reviewers, notably Joseph Wood Krutch in *The American Scholar*, welcomed volume 1, but some had qualms about the desirability of including such personal documents in an edition of collected works. Furthermore, the *TLS* reviewer found many errors, including some particularly embarrassing ones in the interpretation of Johnson's Latin and Greek notes.[58] Fredson T. Bowers, then the doyen of American textual scholarship, issued a scathing condemnation of the volume's editorial practice. Even allowing for the edition's intended appeal to general readers rather than specialists, Bowers found numerous failures both in the way the manuscripts were represented in type and in the accuracy with which they were transcribed. He concluded that "the editors' transcriptions and their notes on the formation of the completed text are insufficiently trustworthy for scholarly use . . . [and] we have no definitive editions of the texts that appear here."[59] Disheartening as this judgment might have been, there is no doubt that the Yale text is a great improvement over previous versions of this material, and it added much to the Johnsonian canon. However, a new test of the edition would come in the later volumes, those based on previously printed works.

58. Krutch, review in *The American Scholar* 28, no. 1 (1958–59): 114–16; "Solitudes of the Great Bear," *TLS* (March 6, 1959): 121–22.

59. Bowers, *Journal of English and Germanic Philology* 57 (1959): 132–37 at 137.

When the *Idler* (1758–60) and Johnson's contributions to the *Adventurer* (1753–54) were published in volume 2 of the edition (1963), reviewers noticed that the Yale editors had decided not to present Johnson's works chronologically.[60] Not even the presentation of the works in this one volume is chronological, with the *Idler*, begun in 1758, coming before the *Adventurer*, to which Johnson made his first contribution in 1753. Without chronology or any other discernible reason for its sequence, the *Yale Edition* must be confessed to be no better in this regard, but no worse, than earlier editions. Issues of sequence apart, many reviewers of the "informed literate reader" class expressed admiration and gratitude for the work, but professional editors were dismayed. Although they approved of the editorial principles applied to the *Adventurer* by the renowned L. F. Powell, many roundly criticized the textual scholarship in the *Idler*. Powell, following the Greg-Bowers method, used the first edition as his copy-text, while inserting authorial revisions and corrections from later editions. J. M. Bullitt and W. J. Bate, however, unaccountably took their copy-text of the *Idler* from the revised second edition, while inserting revisions from the first and third editions. This choice drew the ire of Bowers, who also criticized the editorial committee for deciding to modernize capitalization and italicization. Bowers sagaciously discovered erroneous transcriptions and unskillful emendations, even in Powell's editorial work.[61]

Meanwhile there was dissension in the editorial ranks. W. J. Bate's letters to Donald and Mary Hyde are full of frustration about the deliberateness of other editors. "I wonder what they do with their time," he complains. He wants to "forget Yale and the whole whacky contingent there" and move the project to Harvard. When he is going to England, he writes to Mary Hyde, "I'll not see Powell or even let him know I'm coming, or I'd pick up a book & crown him; he took a year to change my notes to the Adventurer by simply making them wordier . . . he then took another 3 years to write his 3-page textual note. He now wants me to make some changes in the form of my Idler notes."[62] Bate had more cause to complain of delays as time went by. In fact, looked back at in a few decades, the pace in the early days of the edition would seem brisk.

Volume 6, *Poems*, appeared in 1964, edited by McAdam with George Milne, and volumes 3–5, the *Rambler*, in 1969, edited by W. J. Bate and Albrecht B. Strauss. *Poems* was compared somewhat unfavorably to the Oxford edition, a fate that would later befall the Yale editions of *Journey to the Western Islands* and *Lives of the Poets*, texts that were produced with richer annotation by David Fleeman (Oxford, 1985) and Roger Lonsdale (Oxford, 2006), respectively. Like the *Idler*, the *Rambler* was severely criticized for its selection of copy-text, its limited textual apparatus, and its avowed "leanness" of annotation. Many scholars are sympathetic to these criticisms, but in these early volumes the Yale editors sought, perhaps unsuccessfully, to join the principles of the best scholarship with the ideals espoused by their major literary contemporaries—

60. See, for example, Clarence Tracy, review in *Queen's Quarterly* 70 (1963): 140.

61. Bowers, "The Text of Johnson," *Modern Philology* 61 (1964): 298–309.

62. W. J. Bate to Donald and Mary Hyde, March 17, 22, and July 24, 1964, Houghton Library, MS Hyde 98 (514).

critics like Edmund Wilson and Lionel Trilling. These men of letters were not scholarly editors, and their ideas about editions are embodied in projects like The Library of America: volumes with simple editorial plans, no textual apparatus, and very few explanatory notes. Moreover, there were several members of the committee who did not much care about scholarly niceties. Donald Hyde, for example, wrote to Bate on February 21, 1958: "We had a good meeting of the Johnson's Works Committee last Saturday though I do feel they spend a lot of time on rather trivial editorial details. It is difficult for my mind to find them particularly inspiring."[63] To their credit, however, it must be said, as far as the extensive correspondence shows, neither Mary nor Donald Hyde involved themselves in the board members' squabbles. The Hydes insisted on the inclusion of the diaries, prayers, and annals, which some scholars—such as Mary's beloved R. W. Chapman—regretted, but not even Mary Hyde, despite her own scholarly credentials, tried to influence choices of copy-text or decisions concerning annotation.

Gradually, the orientation and conception of the edition changed as the first generation of editors passed away and were in most cases replaced by scholars with stronger editorial and bibliographical inclinations. Allen T. Hazen, a superb bibliographer, was supported when he became ill by the appointment as associate editor in 1962 of John H. Middendorf, who became general editor in 1966; Donald Greene was added in 1964. Sometime between 1971 and 1975, Gwin J. Kolb, and a little later, O M Brack Jr., also joined the editorial committee. Those chosen to edit volumes, but not invited to serve on the editorial committee, tended also to be editors, rather than critics, by trade and inclination.

Arthur Sherbo's two-volume edition of *Johnson on Shakespeare* (volumes 7–8) appeared in 1968. Its textual strategy, unlike that of earlier volumes, impressed scholars, one of whom suggested that not even Fredson Bowers could complain.[64] The notes and textual apparatus in these volumes are richer than those for the periodical essays. Nevertheless, some critics lamented the omission of material printed by Johnson—"factual glosses" and notes by other editors that contribute to the "variorum" quality of Johnson's edition.[65]

Three more volumes of the edition appeared in the 1970s: Mary Lascelles's *Journey to the Western Islands of Scotland* (vol. 9, 1971); Donald J. Greene's *Political Writings* (vol. 10, 1977), and Jean Hagstrum and James Gray's *Sermons* (vol. 14, 1978). As a group, these volumes exhibit a stronger adherence to the Greg-Bowers theory of the copy-text, and a greater willingness to provide scholarly commentary. Both the *Sermons* and the *Political Writings* are notable for bringing new material into the body of Johnson's works. The *Political Writings* volume in particular represents an editorial advance over the earliest volumes in the edition, especially as it grapples with the thorniest part of the Johnsonian canon, the periodical and pamphlet publications.

63. Houghton Library, MS Hyde 98 (514).

64. Shirley White Johnston, review in *Eighteenth-Century Studies* 3 (1970): 404.

65. See, for example, John Hardy, "Johnson on Shakespeare," *Review of English Studies*, n.s., 21, no. 81 (1970): 86–88 at 86.

Unfortunately, the *Yale Edition* was slowing down at the same time that it was finding its editorial balance. Only one volume was published in the 1980s—Joel J. Gold's *A Voyage to Abyssinia* (vol. 15, 1985)—and only one in the 1990s—Gwin J. Kolb's *Rasselas* (vol. 16, 1990). The later embodies more fully than any previous volume the traditional theory of the copy-text, and, with the possible exception of Greene's *Political Writings*, it is richer in annotation than any previous volume. *Rasselas* departs in obvious ways from the earliest volumes, and it set a high scholarly standard for succeeding volumes. As Claude Rawson said in the *London Review of Books*, "The new edition of *Rasselas* is the fullest to-date, long-awaited and worth waiting for."[66]

By 1990 only three of the original editors of the *Yale Edition* were still living, and none would see the publication of another volume. Happily, a burst of energy for the edition began in the new century. Volume 17, *A Commentary on Mr. Pope's Principles of Morality*, a work of translation, edited by O M Brack Jr., was produced in 2004 and included Johnson's brilliant review of Soame Jenyns's *Free Inquiry into the Nature and Origin of Evil* (1757). Volume 18, *Johnson on the English Language*, edited by Gwin J. Kolb and Robert DeMaria Jr., followed swiftly in 2005. Kolb lived just long enough to see his second volume of the edition in print, but, sadly, John H. Middendorf died in 2006, four years before the publication of his life's work, *The Lives of the Poets*. Volumes 11–13, *Debates in Parliament*, begun many years ago by Benjamin B. Hoover but finished by Thomas Kaminski with help on the text from O M Brack Jr., were published in 2012. Only two volumes remain: the early biographical and miscellaneous prose writings, edited by Brack. These volumes involved the editor in the bibliographical briar patches of Johnson's periodical writings, but they are nearing completion. The first (volume 19) is in press, and the other (volume 20) well underway.

When these are finished in the next two or three years, the *Yale Edition* will be complete in twenty-three volumes. It will be by far the best edition of Johnson's works ever published, but it will not be a complete edition of Johnson's works. That desideratum, established on the eve of Johnson's death, will still be unachieved. The most obvious reason is that the *Yale Edition* does not include the body and bulk of the *Dictionary* (1755). An edition of that work has long been in progress at Birmingham University, and it once seemed on the verge of publication, "but what are the hopes of man?" Furthermore, there are many works not in the *Yale Edition* to which Johnson undoubtedly contributed. A volume of these, edited by O M Brack Jr. and Robert DeMaria Jr., will be published in due course by Bucknell University Press. Even then, there will be much Johnsonian work outstanding. The most pressing problem is that we shall never know precisely all that Johnson wrote. Some is lost, like his contributions to the *Birmingham Journal* in the early 1730s and some sermons that he wrote for others. Some is buried within the work of writers whom he edited at the *Gentleman's Magazine*, and some is for various reasons unidentifiable.

In the end, as Fleeman himself concluded, there will never be a complete edition of Johnson's works because there will never be a complete bibliography of his writings.

66. Claude Rawson, "Samuel Johnson Goes Abroad," *London Review of Books* 13, no. 16 (August 29, 1991): 15–17.

The *Yale Edition* is likely to be the best we can hope for, at least from a print edition. A digital edition, like the current editions of the *OED* and the *ODNB*, could be continually revised. Thanks to the generosity of the National Endowment for the Humanities, the digitization of the *Yale Edition* is now a prospect. When it is completed in spring 2014, it will be possible, gradually, to revise earlier volumes; to add works, if they are accepted into the canon; and to link up with an edition of the *Dictionary*, as well as related works, such as Boswell's *Life*. From the digital version of the *Yale Edition* we may get a fuller view of Johnson's works, and we will surely get an open-ended view—one that can change as our knowledge of Johnson changes. However, this digital database will also never be a complete edition of Johnson's works, and it will never pretend to be. This is only fitting because we can be sure that our knowledge of Johnson will keep changing, and, like our knowledge of all that is good and great, it will never be complete.

Index